GOLD Breeds GREED!

by

Jeff w. Bulgin

SEMI-AUTOBIOGRAPHY

Trapped in a dodgy Partnership
Mining for Gold in the Rhodesia Bush ;
Scouts, Be Prepared, Adventure in Africa

First edition 2017

ISBN 978-0-620-78137-4
eISBN 978-0-620-78138-1

Published by the Author using Reach Publishers' services,
P O Box 1384, Wandsbeck, South Africa, 3631

Edited by Vanessa Finaughty for Reach Publishers
Website: www.reachpublishers.co.za
E-mail: reach@webstorm.co.za

Reach
PUBLISHERS

Cover designed by the Author
Website: www.JeffwBulginAuthor.com
E-mail: JeffwBulgin.Author@gmail.com

jwbfc
self-Pub

Book genre:

Autobiography – Adventure – Africa

A semi-Autobiographical Book covers a particular period / certain events in the life of the Author, with poetic licence to embellish the Story and to enrich it with Historical and Wildlife anecdotes. Names can be changed to protect the identity of certain Characters.

Jeffrey was UK-born in Oxford;

Raised in Harrow;

Educated in Hull;

Immigrated to South Africa;

Continues to roam around the wild, intriguing African Continent;

Occasionally visits London for a civilised Pint.

Thanks

<u>Those who helped Review/Sponsor this self-Publication;</u>

<u>who wish to preserve</u> a piece of Bulgin Family History;

Jan, Rich, Marianne, Marie-Louise, Jeff, Mark / Martin

<u>Old Rugby Mates;</u> SNOBs London UK / Pirates Jo'burg SA;

Bob Berger, Piet Hendrik, Jack Maynard, Paul du Plessis,

Dave Thursfield, Henk Steyn, Ed Smith, Kobus v.d. Merwe

<u>Together with;</u>

Gordon Whyatt-John. . Hotelier, Johannesburg, S. Africa

Margaret Wakeling. . .Book Club, London, UK

Susan Shearer . . . . . . Book Club, Johannesburg, S. Africa

Dave Finbow . . . I/Net Manager, Amsterdam, Netherland

<u>Artistic and Literary Consultancy;</u>

Annleah. Director, KKK Ltd, Nairobi, Kenya, East Africa
(Kiende Kommunications Kenya Ltd)

<u>Original</u> Maps Sketches Photos Book Covers <u>by the Author</u>

"I love you Africa . . ." PJ. Powers

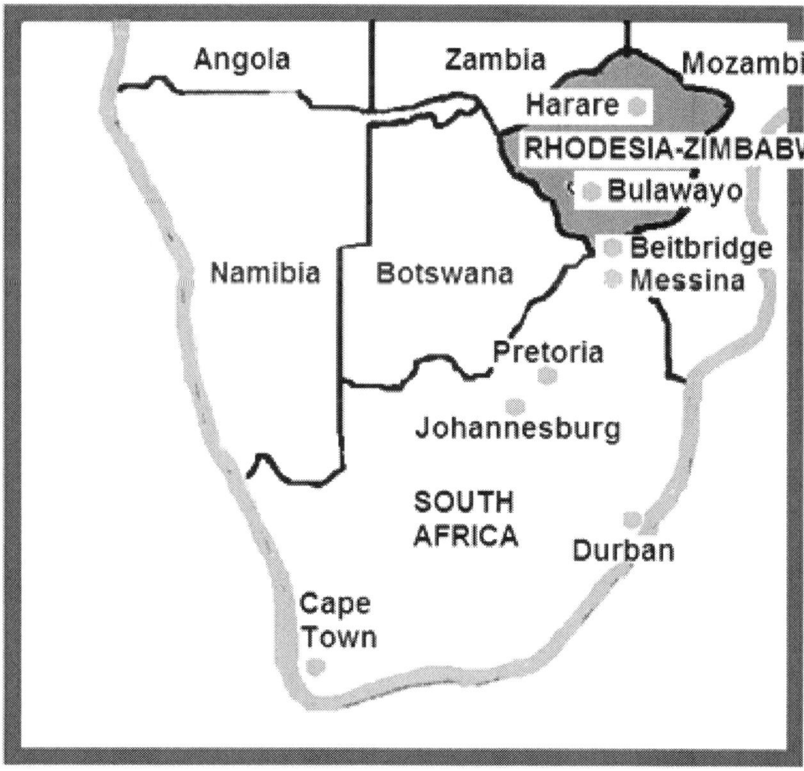

Preface / Introduction

My aim is to bring to life the two main, antagonistic characters – *Joseph (the son) and myself (the author) – embroiled in an increasingly untenable relationship as they battled to get an old disused Goldmine up and running – a compelling Story, that reveals a way of life and human characteristics that haven't really changed over the centuries: greed, mistrust, lust for Gold… replicated in our violent confrontations with hostile Humans, and our daily struggle to survive against the elements in the wild African Bush – déjà vu; the Gold Rush of the* ***1890s****; Colonel Baden-Powell (Boy Scouts Founder)* ***1896****.*

As I describe characters, people, scenery and events, *I strive to make the words conjure up the pictures in my mind, and by 'painting' a backdrop tapestry of this vast land, and embellishing my Novel with Historical and Wildlife anecdotes, I endeavour to add richness and colour for those Readers who have yet to experience the exhilarating freedom and excitement of the Southern African Continent.*

Note:

The body of my Adventure Story – based on a personal Gold Mining experience *– has the skeleton (synopsis), where the bones are my recollections, to which I've added the flesh, sometimes blatantly exaggerated like an overflowing voluptuous bosom, but more often in a humorous vein.*

With memory fading, and not having a mining/ mechanical background, some of the technical aspects and descriptions might unintentionally cause mild annoyance to the Small Worker Gold Mining Purist.

Delve in, and Good Digging!

PART I - The Trip

Part II - The Trek

Part III - The Rains

Part IV - The Golden Days

Part V - The Letter

PART I - The Trip

Train Ride to Amsterdam – Time to Dream

Have you ever had that feeling, when you're just so tired that you can hardly keep your eyes open…? You battle, half-closing eyelids getting heavier, flickering open, blinking, your head slowly nodding… then gone, drifting into a hazy cosmos… dreaming of events, mainly from the past….

The sound of heavy rain rattling on the roof awoke me; the noise was growing more and more intense. My eyes slowly became used to the darkness, when suddenly an explosion of light and the racket stopped abruptly!

I had to chuckle to myself – I was sitting in the carriage of a train that had just gone through an automatic 'train wash'.

As the train slowly moved along the tracks into the vast parking areas of a railway shunting yard, I realised that I had fallen asleep upstairs in one of those double-decker Dutch InterCity trains. There was no one else to be seen.

I quickly ran through the carriages; not a soul in sight!

When I reached the driver's compartment and tapped on the window, his surprised wide-eyed look was something to behold.

He laughed loudly and unlocked the door, and we joked about the incident as we walked through the parked trains towards a small office. One of the staff very kindly drove me back to the passenger station, where I caught the next train and proceeded on my journey to the City of Amsterdam….

This incident took my mind back into the past, to our tin-roofed shack on a small gold mine near Fort Rixon in Rhodesia.

Sometimes the torrential rains would hammer down relentlessly all night long at a rapid tempo, with that noisy, yet somehow soothing, sleep-inducing 'rrrata tata tata, rrrata tata tata, rrrata tata tata…' as the driving sheets of rain would race across the metal roof, drumming out an eerie staccato beat.

Other memories came flooding in of those times as a 'small worker' gold miner living in a remote, sparsely populated area of the African bush, teaming with wildlife, including leopards and venomous snakes.

There were no African villages in this part of the country; our closest rancher 'neighbour' lived eight miles 'down the road', and the police post was even farther away. A trip to the nearest town was a rough, bumpy two-hour drive on hard dirt tracks (murram roads).

You rarely saw anyone, so a special, very welcome event was an old miner or a rancher calling in for a chat, often bringing a loaf of bread, a bottle of milk and a newspaper – such treasured items from the outside world!

Dozing away again…

I began recalling the events and how I was 'lured' into the bush mining for gold, blinded as many others over the years by 'the fever' – gold fever – a powerful aphrodisiac, which I was to experience and hear countless stories of the victims of this rare, incurable 'disease'….

Transported back in time to the offices of International Computers Ltd in the City of Johannesburg, South Africa, where the 'spark' had been ignited….

The five years since we had left Europe had passed by very quickly.

Marianne and I, as newlyweds, had immigrated to South Africa on the Windsor Castle Ocean Liner, sailing in search of a 'new life', as hundreds of thousands of migrants had done over the last three centuries – although, of course, the big difference was that our voyage was an enjoyable two-week holiday cruise, compared to the misery and hardships that some had endured a century earlier on an exhausting three-month passage, many never surviving to see their 'Promised Land'.

My job as a computer programmer might sound a bit boring, but it had led to frequent travel to work with companies all over South Africa, allowing us to spend our free time enjoying that immense 'world in one country'.

The wonderful outdoor way of life, frequently visiting the vast game reserves like the Kruger National Park (larger in size than the country of Holland!), where we would spend days enjoying the scenery, 'tracking' down and viewing various species of animals, like the mighty ancient elephant and the 'armoured tank' rhinoceros.

Most of the people working in this new fledgling computer industry were under 30 years of age, and prone to enjoy an odd party or three – frequently overindulging, like on that particular evening…

The 'Spark'

… Last night's party ended very, very late and now I'm in the office suffering from a bad hangover and lack of sleep, battling to keep awake as I peer at rows and rows of figures on a computer screen, wavering, blurring, bouncing up and down, having a very hypnotic effect…. The eyelids are just too heavy; all the will in the world can't stop them from wanting to shut out the light, or at least cut down the glare a bit by blinking very, very slowly…. Now, almost in a sort of trance, I can hear voices murmuring faintly in the background…. Then, through this

vague, peaceful 'twilight zone' comes a rasping, snorting, thundering noise!

"How the bloody hell can you tell me that now! We're supposed to leave early tomorrow to drive up to my brother's gold mine in the north of Rhodesia!"

"I w-w-wanted to go, but the M-M-Mrs (wife) wouldn't let me," the other voice lamely muttered, partly stuttering. "She told me, 'No! Three days' drive up there, two days at the mine and another three days back – that's over a week! And who would take the kids to school? Who would help with the week's shopping? Who would entertain Mother-in-law over the weekend? No! No! No! You cannot go!' she insisted."

Seconds of awkward silence were broken by a further explosion of sound.

*"But you promised! I've got all this mining equipment in the back of my pick-up ready to deliver to my brother, and **now** you're telling me that you're not going to help me with the driving! Jesus, how can I bloody well drive for three days on my own – becoming drowsy from the heat and the glare of the sun could cause me to fall asleep at the wheel and crash! You'll get me killed, you rat! And I wouldn't be able to stop and pull over by the side of the road for a nap because of the terrorist situation. Hell, you're a waste of space! You bastard!" he shrieked.*

Instantly, my eyes opened wide, and, breaking the pregnant silence that followed, I heard this calm, quiet, yet assertive voice – surprisingly coming from my own mouth:

"Joseph, I'm your other driver; what time do we leave in the morning?"

Truck Ride to a Gold Mine in the African Bush

Our manager was very surprised to hear of our imminent journey to visit a gold mine in Rhodesia, and, although it was very short notice, he found that it was a once in a lifetime opportunity that we shouldn't pass up, and happily arranged the 10 days' leave that we had asked for.

Joseph gave me directions to his place in the West Rand suburb of Johannesburg; we agreed that I would come over at 8 o'clock in the morning, so that we could make an early start to our three-day drive up to Rhodesia.

Although we were colleagues in the same computer company, I didn't really know Joseph that well. However, his stories about his youth and growing up on a family gold mine always intrigued me – 'the last of the small workers, an endangered species', he used to joke to us – so what luck to be able to go and actually visit one.

I'd also heard that Rhodesia was far less developed than South Africa and with an abundance of wild animals, not just confined to the game reserves, but roaming free. It would be such an added bonus for me to be able to observe them close up and take some photos, especially when we were driving through the more remote areas of the bush.

Well, when I got home and told the family that I had taken time off work to go up to Rhodesia to visit a gold mine, they were so excited; they all wanted to come with me! My daughter, Marie-Louise, said we should make some sandwiches for the journey, and that she would like to take her favourite doll, Neville. Little Jeffrey was just pleased we were going on holiday again! Disappointment filled their little faces when I told them I would be going without them, because I had agreed to help a man with the driving on a long, long trip up north to Rhodesia.

Marianne lifted them onto her lap and gave them a cuddle, and promised that next time we'd all go on holiday together.

After putting the kids to bed, we had a few neighbours over, and talked about my trip the following day to the gold mine, and about Rhodesia itself.

One couple had actually been on an organised tourist visit down a big gold mine in the Orange Free State Province. It was huge, they said, employing thousands of miners, more than a kilometre deep, and there were these endless tunnels with railway engines pulling wagons, and even stations! It was like the London Underground Transport system – but cleaner! Quite a contrast to the small mine that I was about to visit, judging by the stories that Joseph often related about when he was a kid on his father's gold mine in the bush.

It was always relaxing to spend an evening with a few friends having a drink outside on the terrace, and we chatted away for hours.

My good friend, Hugh, himself a Rhodesian, said he wished he could come with me; he really missed the place, and the warm, friendly people.

"You can feel a different atmosphere as soon as you cross the border from South Africa," he said, "there being no 'apartheid' laws of racial segregation in Rhodesia."

"But if all the races get on so well with each other, why are there the black extremists who are killing ordinary civilians?" queried Cecelia, another neighbour.

"Well, the problem arose when the Rhodesian colonial government of Ian Smith declared UDI – Unilateral Declaration of Independence – from Britain in 1965 after talks had broken down over the proposed new 'one man, one vote' constitution. Britain officially stated that 'the colonies with large numbers of white settlers would not receive independence, except under the conditions of majority rule'.

"The colonialists, on the other hand, had favoured a more gradual form of evolution and accommodation between all the different races. Britain called for immediate UN sanctions on imports and exports to try to squeeze the country into submission and put an end to the 'illegal white regime'. The black militant extremists, led by Nkomo and Mugabe, then in their early fifties, grabbed the opportunity to fight a bush war to gain power, as had recently happened in other former European colonies.

"For the last few years, as well as their everyday working life and jobs, white Rhodesians have to do six-week spells as reservists in the police or the army; they help to patrol the borders in order to prevent the insurgent guerrilla fighters coming into the country to carry out their cowardly 'hit and run' tactics – these are the acts that you frequently read about in the newspapers: intimidation, killing, torturing, raping and brutalising the 'soft targets' of missionaries and their own fellow black Rhodesians in the remoter bush areas. It's déjà vu – in the late 1890s, Cecil Rhodes, leader of the new independent British Colony Southern Rhodesia, called in the troops of the British Army to fight the same rebelling native Matabele and Shona tribes, when national heroes like Frederick Selous and Colonel Baden-Powell, founder of the Scouting Movement, became household names."

Hugh began to go into more detail, but it was now becoming late; eyes were getting bleary, heads were beginning to nod, and we decided to call it a day. They wished me a safe drive to the gold mine in Rhodesia and looked forward to hearing all the stories when I returned home, when we'd get together for a few beers and a braai (BBQ).

So, with the words '*be alert and very careful, especially when driving in the remoter bush areas*' still ringing in my ears, Hugh and our other friends finally left.

The Road North

Early the next morning, I drove to Joseph's place in the West Rand.

Over a cup of coffee, he told me, sheepishly, that he hadn't yet actually loaded his pick-up with the equipment to take to his brother's mine – he just hadn't had the time!

We would still have to collect it from an old mine called East Geduld, which meant driving right across Johannesburg and out to the East Rand, an hour and a half away. There, we'd see the storeman who had conducted the auction the previous week, when Joseph had successfully bid for various bits of mining equipment that his brother, Cain, wanted.

"Come on, quickly, finish your coffee!" Joseph exclaimed a bit nervously, and rushed outside to the pick-up, beckoning me to follow. "Hurry up now, and let's be on our way!"

"Okay Joseph, I'm right behind you; let's go," I replied, thinking that the mine was seemingly aptly named 'Geduld', meaning 'patience' in the Afrikaans language – which I had the feeling I was going to need plenty of on the coming drive up to Rhodesia!

However, this was Joseph's trip; to deliver some equipment to his brother's mine. I'd just go with the flow as a second driver along for the ride, through a country teeming with wildlife, which I was eagerly looking forward to seeing, together, of course, with visiting a real working gold mine!

When we arrived at the East Geduld Mine, the storeman's wife told us that he'd gone into town to pick up some supplies and would be back for his lunch.

"But don't you have the key for the store? We want to get our stuff now," said Joseph eagerly. "Look, here's the receipt; let's load it up and go, because we've got a long three-day drive up to a mine in the north of Rhodesia, and we can't just sit around here wasting time until your husband gets back."

"Aach no, sorry man, I don't have a key; that's my husband's business, eh! He's always very punctual, though; are you sure he knew you were coming here this morning?"

"Er… well, we didn't actually make a definite appointment; I thought he would be here all the time."

She gave Joseph a quizzical look, shrugged and went back into her house, leaving Joseph standing there, a bit wide-eyed and with his mouth gaping open!

"It's not my fault!" Joseph blurted. "I thought a storeman would be at the store throughout the day; I mean, it's his job, isn't it? Now we've got to hang around for a couple of hours until he comes home for his lunch! We won't be able to leave until this afternoon, and we've got such a long drive ahead of us!"

"Let's hope he doesn't meet any of his mates in town and have a few drinks before coming back," I remarked, ribbing him a bit!

"But his wife said he'd be back for lunch, didn't she? And that he's always very punctual!"

I smiled wryly and walked off towards a huge pylon-like structure jutting out from behind some old buildings with rusty red, corrugated-iron roofs.

"Joseph! Is this similar to your brother's mine? Is it as big as this?"

After a few moments sulking, he came rushing over and, like an excited school boy, started gushing out all the facts without even pausing for breath.

"Wow! This was a really large mine, much bigger than Cain's small workings; the sheer size of everything and that huge hill of mine waste testify to this having been a very big gold-producing mine for many years. That pylon-like structure is what they call the headgear and you can see the cables going down from it into the mine shaft. They're attached to a big metal skip container that is winched up from underground full of rocks – the gold-bearing ore – that are then tipped onto a conveyor belt and transported to the mill, where the ore is crushed before going through the processes of extracting the gold! Hey, but look over there in that fenced-off overgrown area; you see that tall wooden frame? Well, that's an old 5-stamp mill just like the one on Cain's mine; those five long metal poles sticking out of the top have heavy metal 'feet' attached to them, which are mechanically driven up and down stamping and crushing the ore to a fine grit – hence, the name stamp mill. They were the original ore-crushing machines in the old mining days of the gold rush a century ago! But there are still plenty in operation in Rhodesia, especially on the smaller mines."

The next hour or so was really captivating as Joseph enthusiastically told me everything about mines and explained each bit of equipment that we saw as we wandered around the old mine site.

It was such a warm day; I sat down to rest for a few minutes on a stack of old railway sleepers and lit a cigarette.

As I puffed out some smoke rings, one of them made an apt frame for the scene – the rusty red headgear starkly contrasted against the golden backdrop of the 'mine dump' hill, which was glowing yellow in the midday sun.

Quite beautiful, what a lovely sight, and, as I looked into the distance, I could see many other golden mine dumps rising out of the flat highveld landscape.

I instantly recalled that, when we first arrived in South Africa, I had sent my parents a postcard of an aerial view of Johannesburg City, with dozens of these huge man-made golden hills stretching into the distance – the City of Gold (eGoli), built on the flat highveld land mass. ('Veld', meaning flat arable ground, on a 'plateau' some 5,000 feet above sea level.)

This land had originally been a farming area, sparsely settled by the boers – the early white Afrikaner settlers – until the gold rush of the 1860s changed all that – forever!

Joseph joined me and instantly continued his verbal guide to the gold mining history of this area.

"Those 'dumps' have been built up over many, many years, you know, probably since the late 1800s. In fact, they were created by the waste sludge pumped out from the final gold extraction process – they are rectangular shaped, with fluted, rutted sides as one layer of sludge solidified and capped the previous layer – like a multi-layered cake – as the dumps rose steadily in height, year after year. There is still some gold in those dumps, but too small to be extracted by the then-known processes. However, there's talk now that in the coming years those huge golden hills will vanish forever, as the giant mining companies, like Anglo American and de Beers, have discovered a way of extracting even the tiniest of gold particles.

Water will be piped into the dumps to liquefy them before pumping the resultant sludge to another location for further gold extraction processes, finally being run off into one of the old disused mines."

That prophecy proved to be oh so true!

Some years later, I revisited Johannesburg and went to that same East Rand mining area again; most of those huge golden dump hills that had dominated the horizon in the past had completely vanished, leaving only old mining buildings and rusty metal structures poking out of the flat highveld landscape.

Sadly, a beautiful, visible 'golden' part of Johannesburg's past development had gone forever – a piece of history that had helped create and shape the bustling city of today from the hundreds of small mining camps that had mushroomed in numbers in the gold rush days, when men from all walks of life had flocked to the area, gripped by gold fever and the thought of making a fortune from this precious yellow metal.

At 1pm on the dot, a large man eased himself out of his pick-up and belched a couple of times as he approached us – an 'inebriated glow' exuding from his eyes.

He came to a stop, swaying gently, and shook hands with Joseph. "Name's Jaap Engelbrecht…. Oh, it's you! Aach man, so you've come to collect your goods at last, eh?" he mumbled.

"Yes! And can we load them straight away?" retorted Joseph impatiently.

The man grinned and patted his bulky midriff. "No man, first I need my lunch!" he stated and swung around, wobbling like a spinning top, and plodded off.

"But we want to…" Joseph began to snarl, but my quick thump on his back knocked the wind out of him, causing him to gasp for breath instead of mouthing off a stream of unpleasant words – words that would not only have upset the storeman, but, more importantly, would have caused even more delay to our already five-hour-late 'early morning' departure for Rhodesia.

It wasn't long, though, before he emerged from his house and signalled us to back the pick-up into the huge warehouse, and we quickly loaded everything onto our pick-up, getting a little 'high' from the alcoholic fumes and deafened by the regular ear-shattering belches erupting from deep down below in the large frame of this heavy-breathing overweight storeman.

After thanking him for his help, Joseph couldn't get out of there fast enough; he revved the engine, full throttle, slammed it into gear and, with the tyres squealing, we roared off… then total silence!

Joseph had switched off and gone into a quiet, reflective mode, which I found perfect, just perfect!

. . .

We headed back towards Johannesburg before swinging north, passing through the suburb of Orange Grove, which was about six kilometres from the old Jo'burg city centre. A colleague of mine once told me that his grandfather, as a teenager, had shot a lion when he trekked on a hunting expedition to this then-'wild bush' area – hard to imagine as we whisked through this now-built-up city district in just a matter of minutes!

On northwards across open farmland punctuated with farmhouses, and passing through a small place called Halfway House.

In the old days, the horse-drawn stage coaches would take a whole day from Johannesburg plodding through the bush to reach this stopover, where both the weary passengers and the exhausted horses would rest overnight before proceeding on again the next day to Pretoria – a full two-day journey!

How times have changed; only 30 minutes later, we were approaching the City of Pretoria and could see the massive, stark building of the Voortrekker Monument/Museum, built **in honour of the Voortrekkers (pioneers) who, back in the 1830s, had left the Cape Colony to escape British rule.**

Leaders like Louis Trichardt had started the 'Great Treks' to break free from British control – which they found was undermining both their Dutch language and their religious freedom – and they trekked vast distances to many areas, stretching right up to the present borders of Rhodesia and Mozambique. These deeply religious Calvinist Christians had endured great hardships as they literally battled and fought various local African tribes before reaching their 'utopia', the promised Biblical land of milk and honey.

Pretoria – one of the three 'seats' of the South African Government – with roads lined on either side with the blue-purple, blossom-bedecked jacaranda trees; what a wonderful sight. Everywhere you looked was ablaze with the colour of these magnificent trees; hardly surprising that Pretoria was known as Jacaranda City!

Individually, these trees were also striking. In many homesteads, they had been planted next to the houses for shade as well as colour, making a mauve blotch on the landscape, especially noticeable in the more remote dry browny-green bush of the mining and farming areas.

Despite all the hanging around since we left Joseph's house, we had already clocked up 200 kilometres, so we pulled into a garage on the main road near a place called Warmbaths to fill up with diesel, to make sure we had enough fuel to get us up to Rhodesia.

We were fascinated watching a yellow-billed kite bird perched on the roof of the garage holding a small half-eaten rodent in its claws whilst it ripped off more flesh from the dead body with its vicious-looking yellow beak.

We drove on through vast, open expanses of indigenous bush/shrub land – the savannah – sparsely covered with thorn trees and bushes.

Long, straight stretches of road disappeared into the distant shimmering haze; my eyes became strained by continually squinting through the dusty windscreen and it was really difficult to stop nodding off!

The occasional small 'thin' whirlwind would break both the monotony and the view down the road as it swirled around, causing a lot of dust to be kicked up. One whisked across the road right in front of us – actually 'hitting' us – causing the pick-up to shake and rock quite violently for a few seconds.

In the distance, I could see many more kites dotted high in the sky.

It was quite stunning to watch their graceful, soaring flight as they slowly circled, gliding effortlessly, drifting upwards in the blue, blue sky by using the thermals – updrafts caused by the heat.

Mile after mile, one is compelled to watch as they keep circling in the skies – Joseph told me they are continually searching and scanning the ground with their apparent 'zoom'-sharp eyesight, ready to swoop down on anything appetising, then they suddenly 'drop' at great speed and hit the target animal below and sweep back up into the sky again, looking for a suitable thorn tree to perch on to devour their catch – absolutely breathtaking to watch.

'Mother Nature' put on some of these wonderful natural shows, which certainly helped keep one alert.

Occasionally, a ferret or a mongoose would scuttle across the road, some successfully and others not as lucky; we frequently saw kites ripping bits from these flattened dead creatures before flying away as our vehicle approached.

Occasionally, there were the remains of a flattened kite; probably just like people, some of them have got slower reactions or worse judgment than others. I saw one of these yellow-billed kites on the road ahead of us noshing on some animal remains, and, as we drove nearer, the kite quickly took off towards us, but a loud thump on the top of the windscreen told us not quickly enough! Yucky! This squashed 'kite hamburger' bulleted into the air, probably landing on the road behind us to be completely flattened by the next vehicle that came along.

What a shock; this once-beautiful bird was now just a gruesome mix of mincemeat, blood and feathers splattered all over our windscreen.

We pulled over to the side of the road to clean and scrub these grizzly remains from the glass before we could continue with our journey.

To drive across these vast, open spaces was unexpectedly relaxing and enjoyable; there were very few vehicles on these roads compared to the city 'rush-hour jams' around this time of the evening.

Proceeding northwards, we passed through Potgietersrus, an area of huge baobab trees, some reputably being thousands of years old and steeped in the myth and legend of the local Venda tribes.

These mysterious trees can grow to more than 25 metres in height, with massive trunks nine metres in diameter! They have short, thick, stubby branches sticking out like arms, and thinner, twisty branches protruding from the top of the trunks rather like hair; they look so weird, and it is easy to imagine them coming to life with big eyes in their trunks, lumbering towards you – like in a kid's fairy story; very spooky!

On to Louis Trichardt, a small, sleepy town in Northern Transvaal nestling in the foothills of the densely forested Soutpansberg Mountain range.

The town was named after the famous Voortrekker who was one of the first Afrikaner 'boers' (farmers) to settle here back in the 1830s; this fertile agricultural area is now renowned for fruits such as litchis, bananas, mangoes and nuts.

As we neared the town, the light began to fade very quickly, as if someone was using a 'dimmer switch'. Barely a word had been spoken since we left Johannesburg, as Joseph had been concentrating hard as he drove flat-out to try to make up lost time, but the sudden, virtually instant darkness caused us both to utter/grunt simultaneously, "I'm knackered; let's stop here for the night!" Which we did!

We checked into a small residential hotel.

The owner, a guy called Hendrik, took one look at our sweat-stained shirts and told us that we still had time for a refreshing beer or two before they finished serving supper.

At the bar whilst we were chatting to him, I asked if he would book me a 'with costs' phone call to England.

"No! No!" he said irritably. "I'm not going to have my guests and residents woken up when the exchange calls back at ***3am*** in the morning!"

I politely informed him that it should take less than half an hour to be put through, but if we weren't connected by the time we finished our supper he could cancel the call – to which he agreed.

We had only just started on the soup when an excited Hendrik came rushing in shouting, "You're through to England; quickly, quickly, take it behind the bar!"

As I walked into the barroom, several of the 'locals' were enthusiastically saying to each other in the Afrikaans language how amazing it was that, within 15 minutes, this 'redneck' was speaking on the phone to England, all those thousands of miles away.

I bantered with these local Afrikaners in Dutch – which was the original language base for the Afrikaans language – and told them that this redneck was talking to his redneck brother in London.

(Redneck is a term originating from the Englishmen who came to South Africa, many never wearing hats in the strong sun and, thus, ending up with red, sunburnt necks!)

They understood my comments in Dutch and, although slightly embarrassed, they smiled spontaneously and we all chuckled heartily together; what nice, genuine country people.

I was phoning my brother, Rich, to tell him that I was going up to Rhodesia to check on a small gold mine, whereupon he mused, "Got the gold fever already?"

This started me smiling and some of the local Afrikaners found it most amusing when I told them what my brother had said; infectious laughter spread through the bar, with everyone making such a noise that Rich and I could hardly hear what each other was saying.

The local phone communications in these outlying areas were limited and not very reliable, with everyone having to share the 'joint party' lines, and, when another person started speaking on our 'line' in Afrikaans, this totally confused my brother, who hung up!

I then realised why Hendrik thought it would take hours to get through to England; with these joint party lines, it could take that long to get through to talk to someone locally, maybe only 15 km away – just down the road!

When I got back to the dining room, Joseph had already finished his supper and gone to bed.

I gulped down the now-cold soup followed by a monster T-bone steak, and, after one quick beer in the bar with Hendrik, I bounded up the stairs to my room; within microseconds, I must have flaked out into a deep, deep sleep, after the really interesting and unusual first day of our journey to Rhodesia.

A Stitch in Time…

In total contrast to the blackness of the night, bright sunlight was streaming through the windows, urging us to spring to life to make an early start for the border crossing into Rhodesia.

The clear blue sky, with the backdrop of the mountains behind Louis Trichardt, together with the greener vegetation and trees in this part of the

Transvaal, made such a beautiful picture; I clicked my small Kodak Instamatic camera to record what looked like the start of a perfect day.

Nice and early, at 6am sharp, we took a quick shower, followed by a sumptuous breakfast – we were in good spirits and keen to be on our way. All was looking good, but, as we approached the pick-up: "Shit! We've got a flat tyre!"

After changing the wheel, we went back into the hotel and asked Hendrik where the nearest garage was. He told us it was situated in the road behind his hotel, but it only opened at 7am, whereupon Joseph impatiently strode out towards the vehicle shouting, "Come on; come on! We have to get going; we need to start off early. We'll just have to stop at the next town and get a garage there to fix the puncture. We can't waste a whole hour sitting around here doing nothing!"

An hour waiting here, or an hour there; what's the difference, I thought, but, with both of us still in a good mood, we drove off through the winding picturesque mountain roads; it really was quite stunning scenery, the vastness of it all, and an eerie quietness reigned; very relaxing… when, suddenly: "BANG!"

The pick-up suddenly lurched violently to the left. Joseph fought hard, using all his driving skills to keep us from going over the edge and plunging into the valley below…. finally, we skidded to a halt!

"Shit! We've got another puncture!"

"God, that's unbelievable; two flat tyres in the space of a few hours! But at least we're safe, Joseph! That was great driving! Otherwise, we would have been 'flat', flat as bloody pancakes if you hadn't prevented us from flying off the road and crashing onto the rocks down there!"

"But now we're stuck out here with two flat tyres!" Joseph moaned. "We're never going to get to my brother's mine today."

"What!" I retorted. "Are you crazy? I thought you'd said that it was a three-day drive, with two overnight stops to make sure that we would get there safely, in one piece?"

"No, no, we could have made it in two days if we hadn't been held up for hours by that drunken storeman at the mine yesterday! And now this! Why does everything go wrong? Why does everything happen to me? It's not fair; it's just not fair!"

After Joseph had calmed down, I took the wheel off and waited for a 'lift' to take me and the two wheels back to the garage in Louis Trichardt – it ***would*** be open by now, for bloody sure!

It wasn't long before a large truck came past going the other way back to Louis Trichardt, and the driver smiled knowingly as he looked at the two wheels, both with flat tyres.

"Hey, bit silly, man; you must learn never to drive on these roads out here without at least one spare, pumped up ready for action! You must be city boys, from Johannesburg, right?"

I nodded in agreement, and he roared with laughter, showing a great cavern of broken and missing teeth – and, as I looked into his 'gaping chasm', I went cold for a second as I thought that's how we could have ended up, or far worse, with smashed bodies and even death if the pick-up had skidded over the edge.

He dropped me off at the garage in Louis Trichardt, and, when I thanked him for helping, he just smiled and, as he drove off leaving me standing there with the two punctured wheels, he said, "You city boys had better take three spare wheels, to be sure, eh!"

Raucous laughter behind me made me turn around to see none other than a grinning Hendrik!

"Aach man! I won't take the piss out of you, eh, but you got to laugh at situations like this, 'Van de Merwe's Law'!"

"Yeah." I chuckled. "A bit like 'Murphy's Law' for the Irish, or as 'Sod's Law' would have it, Hendrik, when things go wrong, often a second even more disastrous event would happen! 'Superstitious laws' about people and their (bad) luck seem to be the same worldwide!"

"And some people just bloody well ask for it, eh!" mocked Hendrik.

"You're dead right, mate; we were stupid to drive off without a good spare just to save sitting around here for an hour! Now, some four hours later, Joseph is sitting back there in the mountains in a pick-up with only three wheels! He'll be moody as hell and working himself up into a right old state!"

"Let's hope he keeps his eyes open, though, and stays inside the pick-up, as there are wild caracals (lynx) in those rocky hills – hungry as hell!" he teased, with a wicked grin.

By the time the punctures were fixed and I got a lift back to the disabled pick-up, it was already around midday; I gave a forlorn-looking Joseph a cooldrink and a sandwich, which I'd bought in the town.

"Cheer up, Joseph; shit happens – that's life, mate!"

"Yes, but," he started grumbling, "I wanted to get an early start; we should have been through the Rhodesian border at Beitbridge yesterday and well on our way to the mine. If we get more problems we might not get up to Cain's place until Saturday! And I promised him and my father that they would have the equipment on Friday, at the latest. If we don't get there by tomorrow night, they will both be so mad at me!"

The wheel was bolted back on and I took my turn to drive.

A disconsolate, depressed-looking Joseph slumped back into the seat next to me and started nibbling his nails – *Silence is Golden*, a popular song by *The Tremeloes* group, seemed perfectly appropriate, and I started humming it to myself as we drove on further north towards the border.

Since we'd left Johannesburg (Jo'burg), we'd driven through several South African towns on the way, including Pretoria, Potgietersrus and Louis Trichardt, and I was really pleased as we passed Messina (Musina) to see the road sign 'Beitbridge 15 km'.

I put my foot down and, in no time at all, we were there, at the border.

As I pulled up in front of the South African Passport/Customs building, a bleary-eyed Joseph awoke, rubbing his eyes and blinking in the strong sunlight.

He smiled as he recognised that we were actually at the border crossing into Rhodesia – at last.

We checked through the SA control quite quickly, filling in all the forms, including an export licence for the mining equipment that was on the back of the pick-up.

It was well known that South Africans turned a blind eye and had no problems allowing the much-needed equipment across the border; anything to help the hard-pressed economy of Rhodesia, which was struggling not only to find ways around the stranglehold of world sanctions, but also to fund and equip the military offensive against the terrorists.

We climbed back into the pick-up and slowly drove over the bridge across the Limpopo, a wide, muddy river that wound its way on through Mozambique, flowing into the Indian Ocean several hundred kilometres away at a place called XaiXai.

Passport control on the Rhodesian side was also no problem, but, at Customs, they thoroughly checked the mining equipment and supplies, listing all the items methodically.

"Good afternoon, sir," one of the officials said to Joseph. "Where's your import licence for these goods? We need to cross-check them and then you can be on your way."

I thought Joseph had fallen asleep again – but no, only his brain had some two weeks earlier in Johannesburg when he was planning this trip!

He never had a lot of colour in his cheeks, but what there was had drained from his face – perhaps out of his gaping mouth!

"But... but, err, this is mining equipment much needed in your country and we're bringing it to my brother's gold mine near Hartley. He told me just to load it all on the pick-up and to drive it up from South Africa; if a licence was required, he would have told me, wouldn't he? Why can't we continue on our way; why are you causing these problems?" he yelled angrily.

"Fine, sir," the expressionless Customs officer blandly replied, "but you still need an import licence, which you should have arranged through the Rhodesian Trade Commission in South Africa before you left – it would have been so much simpler."

Waving aside a protesting Joseph, who was becoming quite rude and offensive, the Customs officer told us that, without the import licence, we couldn't take the pick-up into Rhodesia.

"What! You expect us to carry all that bloody equipment to Hartley on our backs!" screeched Joseph.

"No, sir, but you do need the import licence. I mean, it is common practice in every country worldwide."

I hastily intervened and asked the Customs man what options we had.

He advised us to drive with him to the Rhodesian Customs building, where the vehicle and the contents would be impounded and held overnight.

In the morning, we could complete all the necessary paperwork in the office.

"What!" exploded Joseph, the colour pouring back into his face through the huge pulsating veins on his long neck. "No, that's not fair! Why can't we do it now?"

"Problem is, sir, the Customs offices closed at 2pm and will only open again at 8am in the morning."

"But then we're going to be another day late and my father will be so angry; we should have been there *today*!" a sulking Joseph grunted, then climbed up and sat on top of the boxes in the back of the pick-up.

Brian, the Customs guy, got into the front and directed me where to drive.

He was a friendly middle-aged man, and, with a mischievous look in his eye, he turned to me. "Shall I tell your mate that I forgot it was Saturday tomorrow, when, of course, the offices are closed, so he'll just have to be patient and wait 'til Monday to clear your goods?" He chuckled.

I laughed too and said Joseph would probably have a heart attack, and we'd never get the equipment up to his brother's mine!

We parked in the Customs house compound, took our bags and walked for a few minutes to a cosy looking guest house, which was run by Brian's aunt.

Joseph, looking absolutely drained, said he'd had enough, it was a lousy day, and he slunk off to bed.

I had a 'sundowner' couple of beers with Brian, and, on listening to him, I began to realise how serious the situation was in Rhodesia.

"Worldwide sanctions are hitting us hard," Brian informed me. "South Africa is our main support and we rely heavily on them for goods and fuel flown in by air, or by rail via Plumtree, Botswana, and road traffic through Beitbridge. It is only this border with South Africa and the border with Botswana that don't need to be patrolled by the military to prevent the terrorist incursions into our country to carry out their hit and run tactics of sabotage, looting and killings. Residents of Beitbridge are lucky in that respect, although they still, as reservists, have to carry out six-week spells of duty on the other borders

"Most Rhodesians are very unhappy with Britain, who they feel had 'sold them out' by being coerced to take quick action by their ex-colony, the United States of America, which ironically still had its unresolved 'black/white' issues, which had been dragging on for many, many decades! In typical two-faced American diplomacy, some of their leaders were calling us 'white racists' and exerting pressure through the United Nations to apply worldwide sanctions against our new fledgling independent state."

We had a really long, engaging conversation, followed by a hearty supper complemented by a strong nightcap before we both decided to call it a day.

As we climbed the stairs, Brian said apologetically, "Sorry to delay you and put you to all this extra trouble, but it's your mate's attitude; who does he think he is, demanding that I do what he commands! With all his shouting and abuse, and in front of other travellers too, I had to take a stand; I had no alternative – if he'd been reasonable and discussed the situation calmly, I'm sure we could have found a way around the problem there and then, and you both could have been on your way already."

. . .

As soon as my head hit the pillow, I was out like a light.

But it seemed like only seconds later that I was blinking and squinting in the bright sunlight as Joseph was shaking me, telling me to get up so we could – wait for it... make an early start!

I splashed my face with cold water and stretched my eyelids to try to hasten my conscious awakening to a brand-new day.

As I slowly negotiated the stairs into the dining room, one of my other senses came to life on smelling the delicious aroma of coffee percolating on the stove; that musical, bubbling noise was quickly drowned by another noise — incessant 'verbal diarrhoea' gushing from the mouth of an over-excited Joseph! He couldn't stop 'rabbiting' on and on that we were in Rhodesia at last with the equipment for Cain; we made it despite that drunken storeman and this awkward Customs official!

"Let's go; let's go. We need to get cracking; we have to be in Hartley before dark! Come on, eat up; eat up!"

Well, I badly needed those two large mugs of the sweet, dark brown 'wake up' liquid before I was ready to devour the full English breakfast that was placed in front of me – absolutely delicious; what a start to the day!

With fully laden stomachs, we strode down to the Customs compound raring to sort out the paperwork and be on our way.

Brian was extremely helpful and even Joseph had a grin on his face as the necessary temporary import documents were quickly made ready; everything was listed and we were told that Cain would have to apply in Salisbury for a full import licence, when, most likely, the goods would be categorised as exempt from import duty.

"Well, that's great!" said Joseph, now beaming from ear to ear. "What a relief; thanks a lot, Brian, for all your help."

We set off, nice and early for a change, heading for his brother's mine at Hartley on the road to Salisbury. Joseph, in a much happier frame of mind, suggested that, if we took it in turns driving every couple of hours and only stopping to refuel, we should make it to the mine by early evening.

"I'll drive first, and here, take this note I've jotted down with the directions to Cain's place in case I fall asleep when you're driving!" He joked, "And I've put the local pronunciation/name in brackets; you never know, we might get lost and have to ask some of the local Africans the way!" He chuckled away to himself.

Well, this was a much happier and friendlier Joseph than the one I'd experienced over the first two days' driving, which should make the trip even more enjoyable from now on.

I scanned the list quickly:

Beitbridge, West Nicholson, Bulawayo, Shangani, Gwelo (Gweru), Que Que (Kwekwe), and then follow signs to Hartley (Chegutu), and ask!

He was bubbling with enthusiasm again and kept me entertained with numerous facts and stories about his childhood living on various small gold and chrome mines in the bush.

He had two younger brothers, both of whom now had their own gold mines – Cain, who we would be seeing this evening, and Matthew, who we'd visit at his Gwaza Mine near Gwelo on our way back down south.

By midmorning, it was getting very hot indeed, and we were dying to sit in some cool shade and have some cooldrinks.

Near West Nicholson, we turned off the main road and up a track towards a small hotel and garage.

Man, I had a thirst on me and I could have downed a couple of frosties (cold beers), but they would have to wait until the evening; they would only make our thirst even worse as well as making us more vulnerable to dozing off when we drove further in this heat.

Suddenly, we were surprised by two big giraffes escorting us, cantering alongside the fence with that peculiar rocking motion as both their back legs are swung simultaneously outside their front legs, causing their heads to move backwards and forwards on the ends of their long, long necks.

Joseph accelerated quickly. "Let's see how fast they can run!" But they were still galloping alongside us even as we reached a speed of almost 50 km per hour – before he had to brake hard, screeching to a halt as we pulled up in front of the hotel, covering everything with a huge cloud of dust!

Inside the restaurant, it was nice and cool.

A slight welcome draft was being generated by an ingenious sort of 'air conditioning' contraption, consisting of three doors hanging from the ceiling joined together by a rope.

The waiter who brought over the cooldrinks could see we were hot and dusty, and asked if we would like it to be even cooler in the room. A nod from us sent him over to the far wall, where the rope went through a hole; he banged hard on the wall and told a young boy sitting outside to start pulling the rope up and down – instant cooler air started blowing across our sweaty bodies as the doors swung backwards and forwards; it was really 'cool' – in both senses of the word.

I was sitting with my back to the window, when all of a sudden I heard this strange scraping, rasping noise behind me and the room became a little darker. Joseph was sitting opposite me and, as his eyes opened wide with a disbelieving look, I quickly turned around and got a shock to see the huge head of a giraffe with a long, dark mauve tongue licking the glass windowpane behind me!

What an unexpected sight, and to have this magnificent animal's face only a few inches away from my own – luckily behind the glass!

Then it stuck its tongue out and licked the window again – the tongue was about 12 inches long, like a large pork fillet that was past its 'sell by' date!

After that relaxing, cooling, refreshing short break, we left to go outside to the pick-up and, as we opened the door of the 'cool' restaurant, a sudden blast of heat hit us; it was like when you open the door of a hot oven!

But, when we actually got into the pick-up, we realised just what it would actually be like to climb into a very hot oven! Instant sweat started pouring off our faces and bodies; we quickly wound down the windows and drove off, to continue on our way up north.

Now it was my turn behind the wheel, and it wasn't long before I began to feel the hypnotic effect of the 'mirages' that danced around in the distance on the hot tarmac roads we were driving on.

I'd heard of people lost in the desert dying of thirst, who would see such a 'stretch of water' in the distance; a mirage. I'd always thought that was a hallucination, someone just dreaming of drinking some refreshing water, but it is, in fact, a natural effect, and, as the road stretched out before me, the heat haze, together with these mirages, made me feel very dozy.

Joseph had told me, in fact, warned me, that driving long distances on your own in this heat was dangerous. There were frequent accidents and deaths along these roads because a driver dozed off and veered from the road into the bush! But, with two drivers, chatting away, that really helped keep people awake and alert – and boy, could he chat!

After an hour or so, even with Joseph's incessant talking, drowsiness was gradually taking over; my eyes were getting very tired with continually squinting through the windscreen – all that dust and the heat; I wasn't used to it. Blinking frequently, forcing my eyes wide open and 'stretching' my face, desperately trying to stay awake, but I could feel my eyes slowly beginning to close… half opening… then closing again…

"Hey!" shouted Joseph.

Immediately, I forced them wide open and looked at him.

"Shit! Was I asleep, or maybe I had just one long blink?' I asked, worried and very concerned.

He assured me that it was only for a split second; he'd been watching me closely, because, if you weren't used to driving on these long, straight tarmac roads in this heat with virtually no traffic around, it was so easy to be lulled into this situation. If I felt sleepy again, the best was to stop, get out and walk around the vehicle a couple of times to clear the head – a really useful tip that I later used many times whilst driving on my own, even in colder climates.

Then, only moments later, man, I thought I was hallucinating!

I saw this cheetah padding across the road straight ahead of me, stopping and looking at us approaching. I slowed down as it moved into the bush; what a beautiful sight. I'd never seen a cheetah before.

I stopped, waited, peering into the bush for a better view. I took out my camera, but the cheetah was so wonderfully camouflaged I could hardly make out the shape, and, with a swift movement, it was gone.

We reached Bulawayo, the second largest city in Rhodesia, and decided to stop for a break and have something to eat at Greys Inn – apparently a very popular hotel, frequented by both ranchers and miners when they came into town. An apt name as well I thought, especially to cattle ranchers, who surely knew what 'grazing' is all about!

Over lunch, Joseph enlightened me about some early Rhodesian history and Bulawayo in particular.

"I used to love history at school," he began, "learning all about some of the founders of Rhodesia, who wielded great influence in those times of early British Colonial Africa; Cecil Rhodes, Frederick Selous, the American scout Burnham, and Baden-Powell – all of whom became very firm friends. Everyone knows that Rhodesia was named in honour of the pioneer **Cecil Rhodes** by Queen Victoria when she granted it the status of A Protectorate of the British Empire in 1889, but the other three men also made a huge impact on Southern African history.

"**Frederick Courteney Selous** was only 19 when he sailed to Africa, where he hunted and explored the little-known regions north of the Transvaal and the Limpopo River shooting elephants and collecting specimens of all kinds for museums and private collections. His travels over some 20 years added greatly to the knowledge of the country.

"**Selous** took part in the first Matabele uprising of 1893 and was wounded by native rebels during the advance on Bulawayo. It was during this advance that he met fellow scout **Burnham**, who, although he had only just arrived in Africa from America, took charge over the small scouting party to Bulawayo.

"**Burnham** was an American scout and world travelling adventurer. He joined the British South Africa Company and the British Army in Colonial Africa. Rhodes had appointed Burnham to scout for the project – his dream – 'The Cape to Cairo' railway. Burnham distinguished himself in several battles in Rhodesia and became Chief of Scouts of the British Army.

"When the second Matabele rebellions broke out in 1896, **Selous** took a prominent part in the fighting which followed, serving as a leader in the Bulawayo Field Force. It was during this time that they both met and fought alongside **Robert Baden-Powell**, who was then a major and newly appointed to the British Army headquarters staff in Matabeleland.

"**Burnham** became instant friends with **Baden-Powell.** On many sorties into Matabele rebel territory, Burnham taught him outdoor skills and scouting, which **inspired Baden-Powell,** planting the seed that would later lead to the founding of the **International Scouting Movement**.

"And to bring you right up to date, the **Selous Scouts** is our Special Forces Regiment of today's modern Rhodesian Army – named, as I'm sure you've guessed, after the British explorer Selous, and… oh, I probably shouldn't tell you this really, but the Selous Scouts' sole mission is the clandestine elimination of terrorists/terrorism both within Rhodesia and into, where necessary, the hostile neighbouring countries…. It's hush-hush, but a cousin of mine is a member of these Special Forces… but we can't sit around all day talking; we must hurry. We've still got a long drive ahead to my brother's gold mine."

Duly refreshed – and educated – we pushed on towards Shangani on the road to Gwelo, where another brother of Joseph's was mining.

The increasingly stifling heat made the pick-up feel like a sauna, sweat continually dripping off my face and running down my back – my shirt and shorts were soaking wet – I'd certainly lose a few pounds on this trip!

Joseph pointed to a wreck in the bush off to the side of the road; it was a large mangled heap of rusty metal, which was obviously a caravan in its former days. On such a straight road, I wondered if the driver had just fallen asleep and crashed. Joseph said that it could have been so, but, probably, the guy was driving at night and some kudu were crossing the road. He'd heard stories of how kudus get scared of the headlights of an approaching vehicle and they try to jump over the 'lights', but their legs and bodies hit the caravan/trailer behind, and… end of the road! Dead driver, dead kudu and plenty of scrap metal; another reason not to drive at night, unless it's unavoidable – because, if it's unavoidable, even missing a kudu could be unavoidable – the Irish would say!

I'd seen kudus in the game reserves in South Africa; wonderful creatures – a large antelope about the size of a cow, but slimmer and more gracefully built, with two long, twisted horns, almost regal in appearance.

When disturbed, they can scamper up rocky slopes with majestic ease, springing, almost 'gliding', across the rock-strewn terrain.

The vastness of the open country around us was captivating, with nature providing occasional welcome distractions.

We saw a small group of some 25 to 30 impala (a medium-sized antelope – the name coming from the Zulu language, meaning '*gazelle*') running towards the road in front of us; only a few had crossed and the rest had stopped. So I also stopped, slowly reversed and turned the engine off, then quietness, not a sound – strange, but exciting! They stood bunched together, nervously twitching, looking at us, nudging each other as if debating if it was safe to go and cross. Suddenly, one ran and the rest quickly followed, bounding across the road, one or two springing high in the air, as if the tarmac was too hot, scorching their tiny hooves. (Impala are capable of leaping 10 feet into the air and also jumping a distance of 30 feet — Olympic Gold medals in both events!)

It was enchanting to see these attractive light brown bucks with white underbellies and tails, gracefully prancing across the road in a flash, joining the rest of the herd in the bush on the other side.

No need to get out of the pick-up for a break; this sight had completely enthralled us and, now wide awake, we continued our journey on to Shangani, past a rail depot where we could see stacks of timber, tractors and machines brought in by train; these goods would be collected by the local ranchers and miners.

On to Gwelo, not stopping though, and driving straight through the town.

On the outskirts of Que Que, we pulled into a petrol station for fuel – for both the pick-up and our bodies! A refreshing cooldrink was quickly consumed before continuing on further, munching the sandwiches we'd bought.

Little more was said, as we were both getting very, very tired.

As the light began to fade, we saw the signpost to Hartley; our journey was nearly at an end.

Joseph excitedly waved the handwritten map-diagram of how to get to Cain's mine in my face. After a few kilometres of bumping along a dirt road, Joseph suddenly exploded and shouted, "There it is! There it is! There it is! There's my brother's gold mine; see the lights on the headgear sticking out above those trees! We got here with the equipment as I said we would! Cain will be so pleased, and my father won't be able to moan at me this time!"

As we approached the mine buildings, our headlights lit up a man waving to us. Cain was shouting. "You're a bloody day late as usual," he teased Joseph. "Dad will be really unhappy with you!"

"But it's not my fault!" Joseph blabbered away. "That bloody drunken storeman in Johannesburg… two flat tyres on the way, and…" He was cut short by Cain's laughter.

"No Joseph, no problem at all." He grinned. "Pleased you both got here safely with the chemical supplies and that equipment I need; some of these small spares don't cost much, but you just can't get them in Rhodesia; even the Mines Department has difficulties."

I had met Cain once before when he came down to Johannesburg earlier in the year to purchase an expensive Jaguar E-type sports car from the money he'd made on his gold mine.

He'd taken Joseph and a few of us out for the evening, and told us what it was like living in the bush and being the boss of his own gold mine.

Perhaps that evening in Johannesburg listening to Cain's mining exploits had kindled an unknown flame inside me, which had caused me to spontaneously utter those 'words' back in the office a few days earlier: *Joseph, I'm your other driver; what time do we leave in the morning?*

He led us to his house, typical of the ones found in the bush with long covered verandas running along two sides of the building.

It was great to sit in a comfortable chair again, on solid ground so to speak, stationary, no movement, no vibration at all! Not like in the pick-up over the last three days – yes, it had actually taken us the originally planned three days! Now it was easy to relax and unwind with a few frosties and some home-made biltong (dried strips of game meat), chatting away for an hour or two – what a delicious and delightful way to end a really absorbing day.

Fire in the Hole!

A loud clanging sound awoke me, and a few minutes later there was a knock on the door. As I struggled to wake up, the door opened and I saw this tray of tea 'floating' towards my bed. Hallucinating?

No, because, as I squinted, I could see that it was being carried by a small boy – but when the tea was placed between the beds I realised that the tea tray carrier was, in fact, a very small white-haired old man.

He greeted us with a smile and stood staring at me.... "Mdevu, Mdevu!" he exclaimed.

Joseph told me his name was Zikweleka, and he was admiring my large moustache; we shook hands, yet he looked a little sad and kept tugging away at the one or two curly hairs of his 'beard'.

But, with an even bigger smile, he left the room shouting, "Up, up, up! Breakfast and work, work, work!"

The 'gong' sounded again, resonating loudly through the compound calling the miners to work at 5:30am! This was a lot earlier than I was used to, but, a few minutes later, I was wide awake drinking strong black coffee on the veranda. Joseph had gone with Cain to set the daily tasks for the mine workers and would be back for breakfast at about eight.

I found this so relaxing, just watching the sun slowly coming up above the trees and hearing muffled voices and murmuring in the distance as the mine boys set about their work.

This early morning tranquillity was suddenly ended by the sounds from a big alternator motor kicking into life, followed by shovelling noises and banging noises, which, soon, were all drowned by the loud thump, thump, thumping noise of the 5-stamp crushing mill, which I could see sticking out above the trees about 100 metres away from where I sat.

The time slipped by slowly, with the houseboy (Zikweleka) appearing occasionally and topping up my coffee cup – he was always grinning and tugging at his 'whiskers', as if urging and encouraging them to grow longer!

At 8 o'clock, Cain and Joseph joined me on the veranda.

Zikweleka gave us all coffee, followed by eggs and bacon and plenty of toast. Quick, silent munching soon devoured this early morning spread – truly scrumptious and I was amazed how hungry I was.

"You work up an appetite here," Cain said. "Lots of walking around in the fresh air making sure everything, and importantly everyone is working properly. I'll take you underground, but if the hoist is being used for bringing rocks to the surface you'll have to use the safety ladders – a 200-foot climb that makes your legs ache, your throat dry and well ready for a cooldrink and a 'Zikke special' morning feast!"

After breakfast, Cain told me that he would give me a tour of his gold mine whilst Joseph would be busy with checking the spare parts and logging in the chemical stores we'd brought up from South Africa.

Cain explained to me that these have to be locked away in a special hut for safety and to prevent theft; only he and the head boss boy had keys.

"And the explosives and detonators used for blasting have to be kept in an underground metal safe. Both the Mines Department and the explosives (AE and CI) company storage depots carefully monitor this, more especially now with the problem of the terrorists. You also have to be very careful when taking on new mine workers, thoroughly checking their ID and a reference letter from their last place of work, which you then verify by phoning that mine. If it doesn't all tally, you don't employ them – this helps cut down possible terrorist infiltration and future problems."

Dressed in white baggy overalls and wearing a bright red safety hat, I went off with Cain.

First, we would go underground to see where it all started with the blasting of the rock faces. We would follow the whole 'process' through to the crushing of the gold-bearing rocks in the 5-stamp mill, finally seeing how the gold was extracted using a James Table – I was really looking forward to that!

After a short walk along a sandy track, we emerged from the bush and into an 'oasis of action and noise'!

I stopped for a minute to take it all in; it was like a panoramic photo stretching from the tall headgear structure on the one side through to the massive wooden frame of the 5-stamp mill on the other.

I slowly scanned the whole scenario:

- The tall wooden headgear with cables attached to a large metal skip bucket

on wheels, which poked out of the mine shaft entrance.
- Dozens of African workers to-ing and fro-ing like ants across this industrious 'stage'.
- A green-helmeted African orchestrating this scene with his flaying arms and barking rasping commands.
- Two other workers struggling to push a cocopan wagon piled high with rocks along rail tracks leading to the towering 5-stamp mill, which was very similar to the one I saw on that disused mine back in Johannesburg at the start of our journey a couple of days earlier. This 5-stamp mill dominated the skyline; a roaring 'beast' drowning all the other noises as it thumped and stamped the rocks into powder.

"Wow!" I gasped as I absorbed this busy setting – my first glimpse of an operating 'small worker' gold mine.

"Yeah, it grabs you, doesn't it?" remarked Cain. "Wait 'til you see the rest!"

We walked across the hard, dry surface towards the mine entrance, the shaft next to the headgear and the hoist (winching machine).

"In this shed is the alternator, the all-important 'heart', powering everything on the mine and in my house too," Cain continued, "and this is the main entrance to the underground mine, the inclined shaft with the rail tracks and the safety ladders leading down into that dark, black hole."

I could see a big metal container attached by a cable to the hoist machine – this metal 'bucket on wheels' would be winched up and down on the rails in the shaft, bringing the rocks to the surface for milling.

Cain pointed to it and said, "Jump in the skip, then; its empty, and you can ride to the second level. I'll take the ladders and work off some of that Zikke-breakfast and meet you down below."

I squeezed myself into this metal 'cocoon', which came up to my chest.

BANG!

It shuddered and shook as we lurched forward and started rattling downwards on the inclined rails into the darkness – pitch-black! I switched on my hat-lamp and could see how the shaft was completely timbered on all sides with gum-poles – that's a lot of timber, I thought, maybe a forest or two!

I rumbled past Cain, who was about halfway down the ladders, and descended further into clouds of dust, which swirled around eerily in the light from my hat-lamp.

The atmosphere was filled with mustiness; you could even taste the thick dust hanging in the stagnant air – there was no ventilation in these tunnels!

Another loud clanking sound as the skip bashed to a halt!

A huge African helped me out of my 'luxurious' vehicle, and, with a toothy grin, pointed at Boss Cain, who had just reached the last rung of the ladders – and believe it or not he wasn't even breathing heavily.

"Nice ride?" enquired Cain. "Now follow me and we can see the start of the whole mining process – the drilling of the holes for the dynamite sticks, ready for blasting the rock face."

We trudged down a drive tunnel off to the side, splashing through wet areas, sometimes stumbling, causing the lights on the helmets to make 'criss-crossing' beams on the walls and the roof; they reminded me of the searchlights in a Second World War film scanning the skies at night searching for an enemy plane that could be shot down!

The further we went along the tunnel, the thicker 'the fog' became and the noise level was intense; we stopped a few metres away from a group of Africans who were busy drilling into the rock face. Cain signalled to them to stop and he explained to me what they were doing. These men were wielding heavy 'drilling machines' called jackhammers, which worked on compressed air; they were connected by long rubber hoses that went all the way back up to the surface to a compressed air machine – a bright yellow Atlas-Copco compressor that I'd seen near the mine shaft entrance.

These jackhammers don't actually drill like a domestic drill with a revolving bit, but had a long pointed solid metal bar that hammered and smashed up and down, making a hole in the rock face; just like a man with a hammer and chisel, except obviously much quicker and more effective.

The clouds of choking dust generated by this drilling were swirling around and already aggravating my eyes and parching my throat, making it hard to swallow. Cain got them to continue working, and started laughing as he pointed at the huge African who had helped me get out of the skip.

He explained that most jackhammer boys use their machines by holding it at waist or chest height as they lean, pushing hard, battling to hold it firmly against the rock face in order to drill the hole.

But this African called Dick was so big and strong, and loved to show off to a visitor, Cain told me, by holding it at crutch height; the other workers howled with laughter as his pelvis thrust and gyrated like a rock star, shouting loudly, "Big Dick, big Dick!"

After a minute or so, the heavily breathing African stopped, with sweat pouring from his huge frame – but still laughing!

We went back to the mine shaft.

"This time it's your turn to use the ladders to climb up to the surface; it's about 200 feet, so we'll see how fit you are!" Cain joked as he clambered into the 'Rolls Royce', which rumbled upwards towards the small spec of light above us – the shaft entrance opening.

Well, I made it to the top without too much difficulty. Cain was quite surprised, as he was expecting me to collapse in a heap gasping for breath when I emerged from the big hole in the ground. I told him that I used to run up and down six flights of stairs at the office as part of training for rugby; however, I must say that my legs were already feeling heavy and began to ache as we walked towards the 5-stamp mill towering above the mining sheds.

Cain continued telling me that the jackhammer boys drilled the holes to a fixed depth keeping to a regular pattern set by the 'explosives' boss boy.

Each hole would have a stick of gelignite pushed deep inside with a detonator attached to it; these were all linked up by a long wire connected to a control box on the surface.

When all the underground workers had finished their shifts for the day, the mine was cleared for safety reasons. The explosives boss boy checked the connections to the 'loaded' holes to make sure that the explosion would be localised at the selected rock face in the drive tunnel.

This was to ensure that, when the control box plunger was pushed down, the explosion would only bring down a few tons of gold-bearing rocks – not like in the silent Charlie Chaplin movies where the whole mine would explode and collapse, much to the delight of the audiences, leaving Charlie Chaplin with a quizzical look on his face, scratching his head.

After the blasting, the mine was left overnight for all the dust and bits to settle. The next morning, another group of workers, 'the lashers', would go in with pickaxes and sledgehammers to break up the rocks, which were shovelled into wheelbarrows, pushed along the rough uneven floor of the tunnel and finally loaded into the skip – with a capacity of one ton of ore, to be winched up to the surface.

From there, the gold-bearing rocks were tipped into a cocopan and pushed along the rail tracks that we were walking along, to be emptied into a large hopper container, which 'fed' the 5-stamp crushing mill.

Man, when you stand next to the 5-stamp mill, you realise what a monster it is, both in size and the roaring noise that it makes!

The ginormous timber frame some five metres high housed five huge 'stamps' (heavy metal feet) that are lifted and dropped mechanically by a rotating camshaft. These five '750-pound feet' lift and fall about 30 times a minute, pounding away and pulverising the rocks to yield a finely crushed sand that mixes with the pumped-in water to form a fine sandy slurry, which washes over a concentrating table with raised, diagonal metal ridges that slow the heavier material – mainly gold particles – to a stop, whilst letting the rest of the lighter 'sands' flow on further to be pumped away into dams. There, the finer non-visible particles of gold are later extracted through a cyanide treatment process.

As this James Table concentrator vibrated from side to side, the heavier sands containing mostly visible gold slowly travelled to the left-hand side of the table, where it formed a thin yellow line.

Watching this 'golden snake' slowly sliding its way down the gulley into a 'recovery pot' was captivating, even intoxicating – instant money!

"And to think," said Cain, "that most of the small worker mines around here closed down in the 1960s because at the fixed gold price of $43 per ounce it had become uneconomical to continue mining. But now that the free market price is around $100 per ounce even the re-milling of the old waste dumps is profitable for a small unit of some 50-odd workers like my set-up here.

"And because of the UN sanctions on Rhodesia, the government is crying out for foreign exchange to buy fuel to keep the industries going and to finance the bush war against the terrorist insurgents of Nkomo and Mugabe. So we actually benefit from this situation as we get an immediate payment when we take the gold to the Bank Assay office for weighing – just like in the old Wild West gold rush days!"

"Sounds like a good system; instant reward!" I exclaimed. "And I bet the old miners went straight to the bars and blew it all!"

"Talking about that, it's after 1 o'clock and Joseph is still busy, so let's go into town and collect the food rations for the mine workers; we can have a break, go to the pub for lunch and meet a few of the locals – you'll enjoy listening and chatting to them, I know."

No second invitation necessary!

I climbed into his pick-up; a couple of the mine boys leapt into the back and we zoomed off to Hartley Town, a few kilometres away.

He parked right in front of the hotel and we walked across the road to a general store/butchers where Cain ordered 50 rations of meat and four sacks of mealie meal (65 kilos each) to be collected after lunch.

"I always buy on credit," Cain told me. "It gives me 30 to 45 days' grace to pay; it all helps a bit. You don't have to carry cash around either, and once a month I drop off a cheque to them. I deal with this store for my own food as well. There's the Mines Department for hiring essential equipment, and the builders' suppliers for everything else – a monthly payment to them too; easy to keep track of. I keep life as simple as I can, thus less hassle!"

On entering the hotel pub, we were warmly greeted by Henk, a robust barman with bright red cheeks which colour co-ordinated quite nicely with his dark crimson nose and his bloodshot eyes – a sight one frequently came across in these small mining/farming communities, Cain told me in response to the quizzical raising of my eyebrows.

WHAM!

A pint of beer with a good head was plopped down in front of me. I looked at it, feeling my thirst buds and my dry, parched throat urging me to swallow some of this delicious-looking light brown liquid.

"Well, are you going to drink it? Or have you so fallen in love with this virgin pint that you just want to hold it and caress it!" Henk hollered, much to the amusement of a few regulars who were sitting at the bar.

THUD!

My empty glass answered his question, and I uttered those immortal pub words: "Another pint, barman, please!"

"No, no, Henk, give these two young lads a beer from me," said an old man who was sitting next to us.

"Thanks George," replied Cain. "Meet a friend of mine from down south, Johannesburg, visiting for a few days."

"Oh, a city boy, come to join the new gold rush have we, son, now that the price of gold has virtually tripled? Just like in my father's day in the '80s last century; some came in suits, some came in rags, some educated, some illiterate, but most of them went home in rags!" He chuckled.

"Gold was like a magnet; it attracted all sorts – from the aristocracy and adventurers, down to rogues, vagabonds and thieves – but only one or two ever made it rich. Most of us have spent the whole of our lives prospecting, working on this gold reef, then that reef, always dreaming and believing that after the next blasting, when the dust had cleared, it would reveal a rich seam with visible gold staring you in the face!"

"Dream on, George," teased one of the regulars. "You drink too much, and the only thing staring you in the face is your bright red bloodshot eyes in the morning when you look in the mirror!"

"I don't drink too much – just enough!"

"I noticed that we passed several other mines on the way into town today; are they all gold mines?" I asked.

"Yes," said Henk. "In fact, the town is named after Henry Hartley, a big game hunter and adventurer who discovered gold in this area way back in 1865, and the lure of gold brought all sorts of people to this area when mining first commenced here. Legend has it that this is the location of the famous 'King Solomon's Mines' and whether it's true or not, it is a fact that millions of ounces of gold were mined around this area by 'the ancients'.

"In reality, though, Henry Hartley only 'rediscovered' gold when he accidently stumbled across some old mine workings of the ancients whilst he was hunting elephants. Gold became one of the main reasons for the subsequent British occupation of Rhodesia and the founding of the old Hartley Town.

"By 1894, over 60,000 claims had been recorded with Cecil Rhode's British South Africa Company and over 200 syndicate companies were registered for mining purposes. When I was a kid, we frequently saw really scruffy men with their meagre possessions, spades and picks, stacked high on an overloaded donkey; these men had been travelling throughout this whole region searching, digging and panning for gold. It was really exciting to watch their faces as they tied their donkeys to the post outside the Assay office, and, clutching their leather pouches containing the precious 'gold dust', they would rush inside to get it weighed – they were great times!"

The mine boys loaded the meat and mealie meal rations onto the pick-up. Cain bought some cigarettes and tobacco for the mine store and we drove off back to the mine.

Cain went to check on the various gangs and to see if the underground tunnels had been cleared ready for the day's blasting.

As I sat down on the veranda in the warm afternoon sunshine, Zikke appeared and thrust a mug of steaming-hot tea in front of me.

I had enjoyed the day immensely and what a captivating one it was too.

A short while later, Cain beckoned me to come and join him; he was standing next to the 'detonator control box' – with the plunger in the 'up' position!

"Do you wanna do the honours?" he asked laughingly. "The workers are all clear now; we're ready to blast!"

"Yes, I sure would!" As I pushed the plunger downwards, I couldn't help shouting, "Fire in the hole!"

"You watch too many movies…" Cain started to say as I felt the tremor of the blast in the ground beneath my feet.

Shortly afterwards, smoke and dust began pouring out from the mine shaft, billowing upwards, temporarily blocking out the late afternoon sun.

The Spark Ignites

"That's a good day's work done," remarked Cain as we walked back towards the house.

He told Zikke to go and find Boss Joseph and tell him to join us for a beer on the veranda before supper.

Shortly, Zikke reappeared with a message from Joseph that he'd be about half an hour, as he was busy 'panning' some samples he'd taken from the river. (Scooping up some river bed sand with a prospecting pan – a bit like a shallow wok cooking pan – swirling this around and around whilst holding it at an angle, gradually swilling the lighter sands out of the pan until, hopefully, a small tail of the heavier visible gold could be seen.)

"Okay, not to worry. Our Joseph really has been obsessed with panning gold samples since we were kids on our father's gold mine. Joseph would always go off with a hand pick and chip away here, chip away there, occasionally rushing back to the house excitedly showing us a 'gold tail' in his prospecting pan. When Dad would ask him where he took the sample from, Joseph would go quiet, stutter a bit – err, err, err, over there somewhere behind those trees. He's always been a dreamer!"

Joseph joined us on the veranda a little later as the sun started its daily disappearing act of sinking below the horizon. Watching another glorious sunset with a cold beer in one hand, some home-dried biltong in the other, munching away and occasionally swilling it down with a few gulps of beer, I thought, *well, this must be like heaven!*

"This is the best part of the day, especially when I read how many ounces of gold we extracted from my very own private 'bank'; the only difference being that my 'underground vaults' don't contain cash or notes!" Cain joked.

"Yes!" exclaimed Joseph. "And I can't wait to get started on those 'high expectancy' claims that were pegged two months ago. When we meet Dad tomorrow, he'll have the results of the samples we took and the geological survey, which will show where we can drill for water. Then I'll be well on the way to having my very own gold mine."

"Fingers crossed, Joseph, because, even if the samples indicate good gold values, without the 'clear liquid gold', you have nothing! Water is essential to the whole mining operation, and of course you and your African miners cannot exist without it either!" remarked Cain.

Supper was served by Zikke; a mouth-watering stew made from various game meat, onions and potatoes – very, very tasty. I was amazed how hungry I was again and dished up a second, even larger helping.

There was no time for talking at the dinner table, as the 'talking machines' were housed in our mouths, which were far too busy processing the delicious helpings that were being fed into our own 'stamp mills'!

"Well, I'm off to bed," mumbled Joseph. "It´s been a long day, and we have to make an early start in the morning to go and meet Dad."

I joked that at least this time there'd be no drunken storeman to keep us from leaving at the crack of dawn!

Joseph raised two fingers as he left the room for bed.

"Fancy another beer?" Cain grinned. "There's always lots to talk about at the end of the day; helps one to relax before hitting the pillow."

Cain could see that I was getting really interested in this whole gold mining scene – perhaps already the 'gold bug' had bitten!

"It's a great life out here living in the bush, being your own boss; there's some manual work too – and running up and down ladders would certainly knock a few kilos off your beer belly! You'd be fit and healthy, and also earning a good whack if you started working on some gold claims like mine."

"Yeah, sounds pretty good; I'd certainly enjoy living and working in the bush, but I'm not mechanically or technically minded at all! Like with cars, I get in and drive; if something goes wrong or the car stops, I get out and call the AA Breakdown service man to come and fix it!"

"Sure, and that's exactly what you do when you're running a mine like this – you employ a good mechanic!" Cain chimed in. "As you've seen today you also need a senior boss boy with a blasting licence who controls the jackhammer boys, the setting of the explosives, and the blasting, and a competent electrician/ welder for fixing things that go wrong or break – there will be plenty of those, daily and a hoist driver.

"But the 'extraction process' you have to control yourself, in a fenced-off, locked area, to stop the theft of gold – otherwise, you'd be doing all this hard work for nothing! If the extraction tables are in the open, any worker walking past can scrape his fingernails across the extraction tables, and hoard little bits of unrefined gold for later sale on the black market.

"I am constantly being offered small quantities of gold by Africans calling in on the pretence of looking for casual work – but if I bought some from them and took it to the Bank Assay office for refining to gold bullion, their chemists would know straight away that it was not from my mine. You see, each gold seam has its own percentages 'mix' of gold, silver, lead and other impurities.

"So to run a successful gold mine, just make sure you get recommended, experienced boss boys and artisans – if it breaks, they fix it; it's that simple. Well, in theory, in any case. But of course plenty goes wrong every day, and that's what keeps you on your toes! You have to figure out ways of sorting the problems, of improvising, fixing things with 'chewing gum, elastic bands and wire', because spares in this country are as rare as hens' teeth! Or to 'Rhodesianise' that expression, 'as rare as the bird of Zimbabwe's teeth'!

"The life is challenging, sometimes exasperating, but it's very enjoyable and fun working with the Africans; they're good people. And to help keep yourself sane, remind yourself constantly that, although this outdoor mining life is hard, working from dawn 'til dusk, it can provide you not only with a very healthy body, but also an extremely healthy bank balance too! But starting up a gold mine takes a lot of money and dedicated time. The first three to four months are critical; every cent you pour into the mine and every minute you work on site will determine whether you survive or not!

"And, of course, 'Lady Luck' has to be on your side as well! Oh, and another important thing if you do go mining, stick to drinking only beer; otherwise, you'll go down the slippery slope of the hard liquor-drinking miners and end up looking just like Henk from the pub! Well, good night; think about what we discussed. See you for breakfast."

With those words and thoughts buzzing around in my head, I downed my beer and sort of 'half sleepwalked' to my bed….

. . .

As a kid, I was fascinated by the tuning fork and enjoyed banging it on my father's piano, listening to the sound resonating outwards and feeling it vibrating in my hand as well.

On the mine, their early morning 'gong' was, in fact, a monstrous version of that; a huge metal bar hanging from a tree, which, when struck by another bar, produced the same effect, but magnified many, many times:

"Clang-yang-yang…. Clang-yang-yang…. Clang-yang-yang…."

You just couldn't block it out of your ears or your mind, no matter how hard you tried. You became instantly awake, like it or not!

Today, though, it didn't 'shock me awake' as it did when I heard that alarm noise for the first time, and, as this loud, reverberating sound gradually lessened, another most welcome early morning sound took over: "Up, up, up! Coffee! Work, work, work!"

And there stood the diminutive figure of Zikke beaming an early morning smile at us from behind a huge pot of coffee.

"Breakfast will be early this morning," he politely informed us, "but first Boss Cain wants you to drive the pick-up around to the storeroom and load up some machines that Boss Matthew needs in Gwelo."

Welding equipment, a 2 hp water pump and three large empty plastic drums were duly secured on the back of the pick-up, and we joined Cain on the veranda.

"Thanks, Cain, for your wonderful hospitality, and taking so much time to show me and explain the workings of a producing gold mine, from A to Z."

A flash from the past as I recalled the letter symbols of the metals in the 'scientific periodic table' from my university chemistry studies, and quoted, "Well, actually, from Au (gold) to Zi (zinc), which you showed me you used in the extraction process."

"Great you remembered so much." Cain laughed. "And you could put some of your chemical knowledge to good use on a gold mine – if the gold bug has hit you already!"

We both smiled and he winked at me as we drove away.

The two-hour drive to Gwelo passed by very quickly as we chatted continually about the fabulous time we had spent at Cain's mine.

"Fascinating – perhaps intoxicating is an even better word," I remarked. "And you can see that he thoroughly enjoys his life out there in the bush working on that gold mine."

"Yeah, and so does my other brother, Matthew, on his mining set-up; in fact, I'm the only one in the family who's not mining for gold in Rhodesia, but I want to change that soon, real soon! When we meet my father for lunch, he'll have already been to the Mines Department and collected the 'test assay results' of the samples we took on my registered gold claims. Hopefully they will be rich enough to make it worthwhile to set up my own gold mine at last – I just can't wait! Hey, take this turning here off to the right."

After bumping along a dirt road for a few kilometres, we pulled into Matthew's mine. This was noticeably smaller than Cain's set-up; it was very open with only one or two trees, and, apart from the 5-stamp mill set-up, the only other buildings on it were a couple of tin-roofed shacks.

His brother came over to greet us, and, as we shook hands, I said to him, "Good to meet yet another gold-mining brother, Matthew."

"Call me Matt, please, not Matthew! Our parents had a preoccupation with Biblical names; they didn't think of the teasing and the taunts we would have to suffer at school when we were kids. 'Did you kill your brother today, Cain?' And poor old Joseph – he used to sweat profusely and his shirts under the armpits had that yellowy-brown crustiness – the kids used to taunt him constantly: 'Here comes Joseph in his shirt of many colours!'"

Matt was very similar looking to Cain – dark hair, medium build and very suntanned; a complete contrast to Joseph, who was taller, slimmer and very pale in complexion, with curly orangey-red hair, almost 'albino' looking.

Over coffee, Matt told us how he had re-pegged the claims of this old abandoned mine about three months previously, and even now the recycling of the waste dumps through the mill to extract any remaining gold was proving quite profitable.

Meanwhile, his underground 'team' was busy pumping out a flooded drive tunnel, clearing up and assessing which sections of the mine would be the best for starting full-scale operations in the next two to three weeks.

He was pleased we'd brought the equipment from Cain's mine, especially the extra pump, which would really help to speed up the de-flooding process.

"Dad said he would meet us for lunch at the Midland Hotel at 12 o'clock. We'd better get a move on; store this stuff quickly and be on our way. You know how he hates to be kept waiting," remarked Matt. "Let's all go in your pick-up, Joseph; my driver needs mine to collect rations and stores from town. I can also direct you to the Midland Hotel in case you've forgotten where it is! We don't want you to get lost now, do we!" he jibed.

Joseph was not amused by this innuendo; he revved up the engine to full throttle and slammed it into first gear. We hurtled forward, the pick-up shuddering as if expressing Joseph's annoyance and anger, and we roared off in a cloud of dust!

"Joseph! If you ever get us there in one piece, Dad wants the two of you to drive with him in his pick-up to check progress on those claims!" Matt shouted, in order to be heard above the engine noise. "I'll take your vehicle and we can meet back at my house later for supper."

"So you don't live on the mine like Cain does?" I asked.

"Unfortunately not. Cain is very lucky to have such a great set-up, his spacious house on site and his own Master Chef Zikke, who's been with the family a long, long, time... and always cooking delicious food. When we were kids, he made us eat everything – otherwise, we'd end up as small as he was, he used to tell us!"

The streets of Gwelo were very wide, allowing vehicles to park 'nose first' in front of the stores and small shops; Joseph 'pointed' the pick-up into such a parking space right outside the Midland Hotel.

Their father was sitting outside on the terrace, and he beckoned us to come and join him.

"Hi Dad, pleased to see you; how's Mum? Meet a colleague from the office down in Johannesburg."

As he rose to shake hands with me, I could see where the two sons, Cain and Matt, got their facial characteristics from – an uncanny likeness; all three of them looked so similar.

Their father, Ray, although probably approaching 60, was still quite a handsome man. He had a thin pencil moustache and his pale blue eyes twinkled from his brown weather-beaten face as he introduced himself to me; he thanked me for sharing the long drive up with Joseph to bring the equipment that Cain needed for the mine.

I told him it had been a real pleasure; I had enjoyed the trip immensely, especially the time Cain spent with me on his mine – quite an experience.

"Now Joseph," Ray began, "you know I want to help you get started with your own mine, but your mother is not keen at all and as you know very well, what she says goes! She feels that starting on these new virgin claims – especially without sound money backing – would turn out to be a time consuming and costly disaster."

"But. . ." Joseph was cut short, as his father forcefully continued, telling Joseph just to listen and not to interrupt him again; he told him twice – once in words, then followed by a glaring look that would have stopped a bull elephant in full charge!

A quiet subservient utterance of 'okay Dad' and Ray continued to outline not only the plan for today, but also his mother's ideas for Joseph's mining future.

"After we've eaten lunch," he continued, "we'll drive out to the claims and review not only the initial assay sample results from the Mines Department, but also their geologist's report on potential on-site sources of water; this would give us all the facts and figures about these claims, which we can discuss later in the evening back at Matthew's house.

"The Africans we left working on the claims should have finished the trenching (surface digging) by now, so further samples can be taken to be assayed for their gold content. We will also look at other alternatives, including your mother's idea of raising money through you selling shares down in Johannesburg; start with all your workmates at the office, like your colleague here for example – perhaps he can help by telling people what he's witnessed here in Rhodesia."

"Yes, that's a great idea, Dad!" shouted Joseph excitedly. "Also, several of them have met Cain as well, when he came down to Johannesburg and took us out for an evening meal; they were all very impressed with his gold mining stories, and several were quite envious of him owning an E-type Jaguar sports car. Yes! Yes!" he enthused.

Water Divining

Joseph and I climbed into Ray's pick-up and we set off to check on Joseph's claims, which were about an hour's drive away.

We left the main tarmac road and followed some cart tracks for a few hundred metres through a very green area covered with young trees until we came to a gate with a notice on it, which read 'Kattle K Ranch'.

As we approached, a tall African ran towards us and opened the gate; about 50 metres away, I could see two tents and a small camp that had been set up by Ray's workers.

They were very pleased to see us, especially when they saw the sacks of mealie meal, the meat rations and the drums full of water in the back of the pick-up; their faces lit up completely when Ray gave them each a pouch of tobacco.

Ray explained to me that, although he didn't own this land – it belonged to the Kattle K Ranch – his mine boys were legally entitled to be working here; these 'claim block' areas had been measured, 'pegged' (with official notices nailed on marker poles) and registered with the Mines Department under the name High Expectancy 1-5 for the 'purpose of mining precious metals and minerals'.

Most ranchers had no problems with other people legally setting up mining operations on their property, as they knew it was for the production of gold so necessary for foreign exchange currency, and for the good of their beloved country, Rhodesia.

"Okay Dad, what values did we get from the samples?" Joseph bubbled expectantly. "I'm sure they were good!"

"They were quite patchy as one would expect, as we are only in the initial stages of determining the potential of this area; today, we'll show the workers where to dig deeper, with some 'cross' trenches to set up a grid from which more sampling must be done."

Ray grabbed the map of the claims and walked over to an old African (*mdala*) sitting under a tree; he had a few words with him, whereupon the *mdala* jumped up, grinned, pointed towards me and drew out a hunting knife as he approached me – the slightly puzzled and concerned look on my face caused Ray to erupt into laughter. "Don't worry! He's not coming to attack you! He's just seen and selected a branch to cut off from that tree behind you!"

It was a young supple tree, and the *mdala* had quickly cut off a forked branch and was busy trimming it.

He then put the backs of his hands together as he took the forked ends, holding one in each hand with the remaining stick of the branch pointing upwards – he looked most uncomfortable. Ray told me he was a 'water diviner' and hopefully he would locate a good source of water on the claims.

We watched as he slowly, with outstretched arms, traversed over one claim after the other.... Suddenly, the branch vibrated violently in the *mdala's* hands and bent towards the ground, as if being pulled by an invisible source!

"That's good!" exalted Ray as he hurried over to the old African.

"Yes, that makes good sense! Look on this map; the geologist has highlighted three different places on the claims to test bore for water. But the water diviner, however, has pinpointed only this one, which coincides with a geologist-marked location. Great! So we've got a good potential water supply and we'll get the borehole drillers up here next week to test how deep the source is."

He turned to me, his eyes bright and twinkling. "You see, quite often the old methods practiced for hundreds of years give better results than modern technology can deliver; now we only have to drill one borehole instead of perhaps the three, if we had followed the geologist's recommendations – his locations are based on the rock formations and strata, and highlight any potential 'cavity' that could house water, whereas the water diviner only picks a place where there is definitely water. It is an old practiced art; few people have 'the calling' – hey, why don't you have a go?"

After the forked branch was placed 'correctly' in my hands – forcing my shoulders to become contorted and hunched – I walked up and down, feeling very uncomfortable and awkward, zigzagging over the same area that had delivered such 'success' a few minutes earlier – nothing, not even a twitch!

"Ooh, by the look on your face, you're not at all convinced; you seem very sceptical that a water diviner possesses such a 'gift'. Okay, hold the forked branch in your hands again; the *mdala* will stand close behind you, wrapping his arms around you so that his hands can be placed on top of yours, gripping them tightly – now start walking together over the same area again."

Well, I felt a bit like a clown in a circus as the two of us, 'bound together', shuffled in unison across the grass, both holding onto a forked piece of wood sticking up in the air! If my mates could see me now, they'd piss themselves with laughter! We proceeded very slowly; well, with the awkward positioning of our bodies, snail pace was the only speed possible!

I know I must have had a silly grin on my face as we moved over the area, thinking to myself perhaps this is a joke, with Ray and the *mdala* having agreed on the 'spot' beforehand where they would put on the 'show' of the shaking fork, tipping it to point downwards to the ground. I mean, if they drill a borehole later in that same spot – or somewhere else on the claims – I would never know, would I?

Suddenly… *SWISH!*

The forked branch started shaking vigorously, vibrating and actually bending and twisting in my hands; was the *mdala* behind me causing this?

I was determined not to be fooled and started resisting the twisting pressure on my wrists; I really battled, but couldn't stop the forked branch from bending downwards to the ground, almost tearing itself out my grasp! Shit! Scary!

What an unnerving occurrence! I began rubbing my very sore wrists, much to the amusement of Ray, Joseph and the *mdala* – but they really did hurt!

I gave a 'defeated' grin and shrugged, and we all had a good laugh about it.

A truly unforgettable, incredible incident that still, today, totally amazes me when I think back to what happened.

After giving instructions to his workers about further trenching and sampling, Ray joined us in the pick-up and we headed back to Gwelo to meet Matthew at his home for supper.

Over these last few days, things were getting more and more alluring, and were opening up a whole new world to me; a 'world and a way of life' that had, in fact, been practiced in these areas of Rhodesia, virtually 'as is', for over a century – remarkable!

Dusk was gently blanketing the remnants of the sunny day as we pulled up outside the entrance to Matt's small bungalow.

His African houseboy came to the gate and opened it for us; we drove in, through an ornate portal made from differently coloured rocks.

"You see we rebuilt it, Joseph, since that time when you crashed into it, knocking the top off and smashing the cupboards you were bringing to us on the back of your pick-up truck!" Matt announced.

"It wasn't my fault!" Joseph burst out irritably. "It was late at night and there were no lights on it either!"

"That's why I chose a luminous paint this time so that even you, in one of your dreamy moods, couldn't fail to see it!"

Joseph whispered in my ear, "Just ignore him and those silly comments of his; both of my brothers have been pestering and making fun of me ever since we were youngsters."

"Dad, come and sit over here; a large whisky and plenty of ice – just the way you like it. Can I get you two a cold beer each?" enquired Matt.

A nod with a 'yes please' smile were all that was needed and, instantly, a cold beer was thrust into my hand; that cool, refreshing 'hop juice' seemed to evaporate as it met the hot, dry insides of my mouth, and in one long 'slok' – it was gone!

"Anyone for seconds?" asked Matt with a wry smile as he handed me another – how could I refuse!

"On such a warm, balmy evening, let's have a braai out on the patio; there's heaps of boerewors (sausage) and steak, some salads and baked potatoes. We can continue discussing things together whilst I look after the meat," Matt suggested.

Joseph was fidgeting around uneasily, as he had been all day, still anxious to know why his parents were not keen on him opening up the new gold claims on his own.

Ray started explaining to Joseph that working from scratch on virgin claims would not only be very costly, but very time consuming too; his lack of experience and know-how would mean that Ray would have to make constant trips to help sort out problems as they arose – a 'six-hour round trip' from his mine in Belingwe!

"Worse still, Joseph," interjected Matt, "those claims are far, far too close to me! I'd be running back and forth every time you made a cock-up! It wouldn't be – ouch!"

A swift kick from Ray halted Matt's 'point of view'!

"Stop this bickering and listen!" Ray continued as Matt ruefully rubbed his shin, probably wishing too that he'd been standing further behind the 'safety barrier' of the hot braai fire.

"Joseph. Like it or not, the 'High Expectancy' claims are out; they would be far too costly."

"Then I'll just have to sell more shares in Johannesburg!" he wisecracked.

"Grow up, Joseph! This isn't a game!" Ray snorted. "You need to show potential buyers that not only will they get their money back, but with a handsome profit as well. A much better idea is to open up an old mine like Cain did, where the shafts have already been sunk and timbered, where there's borehole water available or the water table level inside the mine can be continually pumped for your water supply. From the Mines Department records, we can see the potential of a mine, any known ore reserves and the monthly gold output before it closed down. By sampling the old dumps, we can get an estimate of the money that will come into the business during the first few months, whilst the underground development is being set up ready for full-scale gold production."

"But," Joseph blurted, "all the old mines have already been 'pegged' over the last year; I've told you so many times that I should have started mining up here months ago, but you never listen to me! I've told you so many, many times! Now you've ruined everything; you won't let me mine my own virgin gold claims and there are no old gold mines left to be pegged! Why do you always do this to me; it's just not fair!" he whinged.

The twinkle in Ray's eyes immediately switched off, being replaced by a cold, laser-type stare that reduced Joseph to a whimpering heap.

"I'm going to get Mum to back me; you'll see, you'll all see!!"

The awkward silence was broken by his brother, Matt. "Joseph. Just listen!"

"Yes, Joseph," continued Ray, "you're actually quite right; all the good 'old gold mines' have been pegged – but a few crafty older miners have registered some of these mine claims, although they have no intention of mining them themselves; they are only interested in 'tributing' them out, for a fee of five percent of the total yearly gold output!"

Joseph beamed a huge smile, which stretched from ear to ear – almost splitting his face in two!

"So Dad, you have one lined up for me, then? Why didn't you let me know! This is fabulous news! I'm going to be a gold miner at last, just like my brothers, Matt and Cain! Fantastic! I'm so excited; where is it? When do I start?" He bubbled, on and on….

"First of all, we'll visit an old miner friend tomorrow at his ranch to discuss tributing some registered claims from him; after that, we'll go to the mines themselves and see what we think about the whole set-up."

"That's such good news, absolutely wonderful! I just can't wait!" Joseph enthused. "I'm off to bed now; we have to make an early start in the morning!"

Now where had I heard that before!

He left the veranda, skipping with excitement, mumbling, "Mum will be so proud of me!" He whistled away to himself, oblivious of the chuckling amongst the three of us.

Ray, Matt and I chatted on into the night; a nightcap seems to be conducive to promoting stimulating conversation.

"So where are these mines, Dad?" asked Matt.

"Well, tomorrow we'll go first to Que Que to see an old mate, Pat, to discuss the possibilities, and afterwards we can visit the actual mines in the Insiza area, past Fort Rixon."

"What, near the Claremont mine?" enquired Matt.

"Actually, there are several blocks he's pegged, including the Claremont and the Nelly mines. He tells me that both are mainly 'banded iron stone'; good, steady five to six 'dwts' (penny weights, about ¼ ounce of gold to the ton of ore rock), but with some patchy 'quartz reefs' with lenses of visible gold."

"Sounds like a good set-up, and maybe Joseph could employ an experienced miner to help him, if he raised enough money through selling shares down south?" remarked Matt. He then turned to face me with eyebrows raised expectantly, and uttered, "Perhaps you'd be interested in putting money into this venture?"

"Well yes, maybe, but I just wouldn't put money in and leave it to Joseph to run the operation on his own!"

"Don't blame you!" Matt laughed, quickly shoving his chair backwards to avoid the flaying boot of his father that narrowly missed his other shin.

"Okay Matt! Okay!" Ray snapped. "We all agree that Joseph should ideally have someone to help keep him 'on track'; he does sometimes act like a dreamer and not a 'doer', but remember he's your brother; don't keep running him down and…"

He paused in mid-sentence, and a smile began to stretch his thin moustache as his whole mood changed; his eyes were twinkling again now, and he was in full 'sales mode' flow. "Yes, how about it?" he said to me. "Around the age of 30 is an ideal time to start small worker gold mining; you seem to have an affinity for this rough life in the bush and you'd soon learn the mining side. I also sense that you're a bit more organised than Joseph, so you could help him sell shares when you both get back to Johannesburg."

"Mmm, that's possible, but would there be enough gold to live on and to support the two families?" I retorted. "I see the rest of your 'family' gold mines are all 'one-man' shows!"

"There would be enough once you get into full production – you'd be living very well indeed. However, you'll need to raise some capital to cover the costs incurred in the first few months when you'll be busy preparing and setting up for the full running of the mine. But it's a great life; you're free, you're your own boss, nobody to order you around or tell you what to do, eh Matthew?"

Matt grinned sarcastically, rubbing his sore shin as he winked at me.

"Well youngsters, that's all; time we went and slept. Got a busy day tomorrow!" remarked Ray, terminating the evening's events abruptly!

Lying in bed later, reflecting on everything that had happened on this trip so far, I began to think that small worker gold mining was a good proposition.

Once you got the gold out of the ground, you had a guaranteed 'cash buyer' – the government. There wasn't the usual business headaches and costs of marketing and selling your product, no people to chase for money owed, and, when the final product is 'sold', you receive instant cash from the Central Bank of Rhodesia – what could be safer than that!

Yeah, it seemed worth the gamble of getting it up and running within three to four months – even having to deal with Joseph's absent-mindedness and his wishy-washy ways!

I decided there and then. "*Yes!*"

I would put money in, but only on the condition that I would also work on the mine in a 50/50 partnership; no way would I leave that dreamer, Joseph, on his own at the helm! The ship would almost certainly go around and around in circles, until it finally disappeared up its own… 'til it sank!

Five Percent

Morning came around quickly, but there was no tea in bed here, no Zikke happily calling out 'breakfast! Up, up, up!' – only a loud knocking on the door, followed by: "You want some coffee or not? We're leaving in ten minutes!"

As we were 'marched' towards the pick-ups, Ray informed Joseph that we had a long, busy day ahead of us, and he was not in the mood to go into any details about anything that was discussed last night.

He just said, "We looked at various options after you went to bed, Joseph, including starting a partnership with your friend here from Johannesburg both working together on the mine. But let's not get ahead of ourselves; first thing's first; we're off now to Que Que. After we've visited Pat and agreed to tribute his pegged gold claims, the three of us can sit down and work out some more details as to how we are going to set things up between the two of you, okay?"

Tacit nods from both Joseph and me seemed to satisfy his old man, and the quietness of the morning was only broken by the sudden gurgling sounds of the diesel engines of the pick-ups as they warmed up before springing to life.

Joseph drove off with his father and I followed in the other pick-up.

We turned off the main tarmac road and onto a dirt road, which we followed for several kilometres before we reached a gate with a sign:

The Lord says Forgive Trespassers –
Not me, I shoot the Bastards!
HOOT and WAIT!

Wow, this guy sounds like a weird one, I thought.

Ray hooted twice loudly, and Joseph got out and walked over to open the gate to allow us to drive through.

Two big black rottweilers suddenly appeared from out of the trees, growling and snarling menacingly. Joseph cried loudly, "Shit!" Then he ran hell for leather back to the pick-up and jumped in!

A dishevelled 'hillbilly'-looking man wearing a dirty blue chequered shirt and well-worn army camouflage trousers emerged from the undergrowth – and he was carrying a shotgun!

Ray called out to greet him. The man grinned, showing a set of yellow teeth. His dense black beard covered virtually his whole face and neck. With thick black eyebrows and a mop of unruly black hair, there was hardly any actual face to be seen, but what there was, was dark mahogany brown – it would be hard to determine which part of the world his family originally came from.

He walked off with Ray, chatting away like long-lost mates do. Joseph and I followed in the two pick-ups.

After a couple of hundred metres, we stopped in front of a dilapidated building that poked out from the trees surrounding it.

The roof was patched up with odd bits of corrugated iron and it sagged quite dramatically where the chimney stuck out – or perhaps better described as 'lent out at an angle'! One of the windows was boarded up, and, as we started climbing the steps of the wooden veranda, the whole building appeared to creak! And, did I see the chimney wobble?

What a decrepit looking hovel!

He invited us in.

Well, if I thought the outside was bad, you should have seen the inside – ***it was squalid***! A dark musty room, which smelt of smoke, old cheese and various other stale odours, none of which were in my memory bank!

But they are now, *vividly*!

And flies! I had never seen so many flies in my life!

They were everywhere, buzzing around your ears, continually getting on your eyelids and crawling on your arms; you just couldn't shake them off! Absolutely disgusting!

And it looked like Pat had a never-ending task to get rid of them.

Hanging from the ceiling and walls were brown sticky strips with dozens of flies stuck to them; dotted around the room were old tin lids full of a dark red paste, which seemed to attract fly after fly to meet a sticky end – forming a black crust of their corpses!

Pat asked us to sit down, pointing to some large well-worn leather furniture.

I plonked my backside down in one of the armchairs, which promptly gave way in the middle; my legs shot up in the air, knocking a 'fly-catching' tin lid off the arm and sending it skittering and clattering across the floor.

Immediately, a very large African woman appeared and picked it up; she beamed a huge warm, friendly smile and asked, "Tea?"

Our 'nods' encouraged her to return with four large mugs of tea, which she distributed amongst us, and then wobbled her way out again.

"Yes Ray, as you can see, times are hard. I won't bore you with all the details, only to say I had real bad luck on my last mine. We were sure that we were so close to the 'mother lode'! But it was not to be. We had worked for over a year on the B2 mine, putting everything we had into it; occasionally, we hit a small pocket of visible gold, which spurred us on, hoping to strike it rich! But we ran out of money completely, not even a cent left to pay the mine boys. After nearly 40 years mining for gold, my dreams were shattered and finally over. I was left penniless, stony broke."

"Sounds like Shakespeare," Joseph derided. "2B mine, or not to be mine! Ouch!" A swift slap on the back of the head from his father instantly quelled his laughter.

"Have some respect, Joseph!" He snorted. "Be quiet and listen!"

"Luckily for me," Pat continued, "my late father had bequeathed this small farm and a few head of cattle to me. I eke out a pretty miserable existence here, so I thought I'd go back to small working for gold – one last 'shit or bust' time; that's why I pegged the Claremont and Nelly mines in Fort Rixon.

"I'd known the old manager, a chap called Bester who had worked on those mines until they closed down in the '60s; he told me there was still plenty of gold to be mined, and at today's prices it could prove to be a winner for me. The main reefs were five-foot wide, of low grade banded ironstone, yielding six dwts (approximately ¼ ounce) of gold per ton.

"Some small lenses/pockets of visible gold occurred in narrow quartz seams running through the granite rock, along the same seven-mile long 'strike'. I pegged all the 'claim blocks' and registered them with the Mines Department. They are good mines, Ray, which have produced tens of thousands of ounces of gold this century.

"The shafts are well timbered; there's plenty of water – some of the underground drives are flooded at present, being below the water table. But I just couldn't take on the backbreaking work on my own; that's when I thought of tributing them out – are you interested, for five percent of monthly gold output?"

"Well Pat, it's not for me; I've got far too much on the go already! But these two young guys are very interested – this one is Joseph, my son, and a mate of his up from South Africa."

"Okay, that's fine with me! Let's go through some of the information that I have acquired – the reports and maps of the mines and gold reefs in that area."

Ray poured over the maps and the information for half an hour or so, asking Pat a pertinent question every now and then.

"Okay Pat, you've got a deal! I recommend that these lads tribute the mines from you for five percent of gold output."

We all shook hands on this 'gentleman's agreement' – apparently a common gesture in Rhodesia, where a man's word is his bond – and agreed to meet again to finalise and sign the 'tribute agreement' when Joseph and I returned to Rhodesia in a month's time.

"Ray, I can read on the young miners' faces that they would prefer to have a signed, albeit temporary piece of paper, which they can take home with them;

you remember how it felt, that warm feeling, clutching the documents of ***your first very own gold mine***!"

Whereupon he took out a pen and scrawled a few relevant lines on one of the maps, which we all then signed!

Wow, it had happened! Just like that!

I was now going to work in the Rhodesian bush as part owner of a gold mine!

We thanked Pat, climbed into the pick-ups and drove off; I would follow Ray and Joseph to a place near Shangani where we could have lunch, and conclude what we were going to do with our newly acquired gold mines.

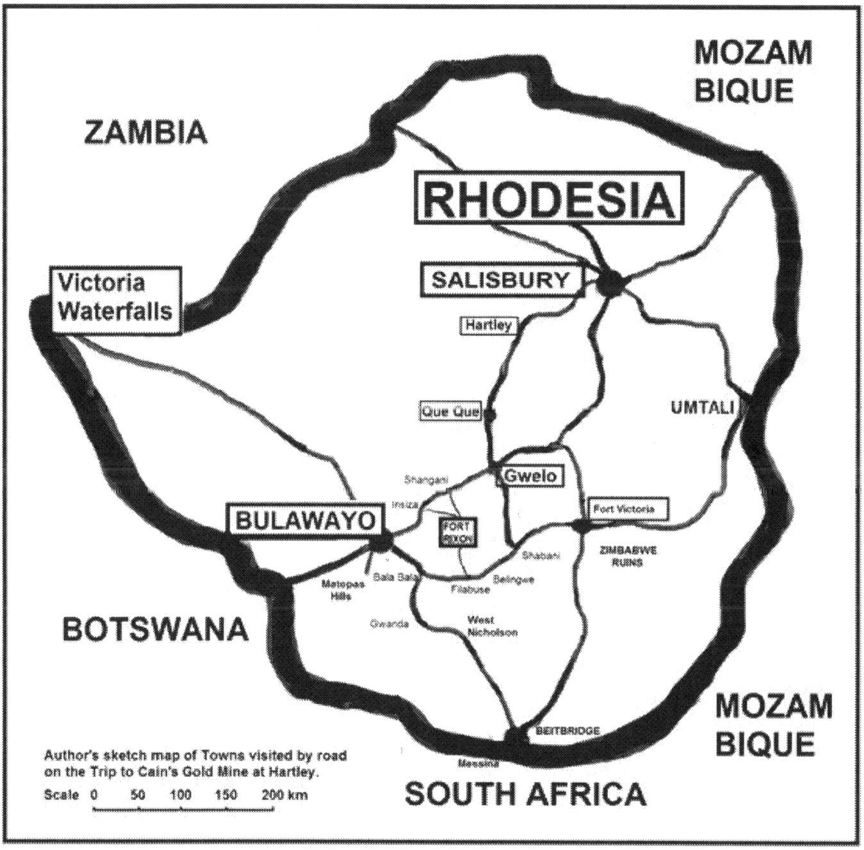

Author's sketch map of Towns visited by road on the Trip to Cain's Gold Mine at Hartley.

Man, the old brain whizzed around, constantly jumping from one thing to another – there had been so many events and happenings over the last few days! As one image flashed into my mind, it was hurriedly chased out by other images, all scrambling for my attention, a sort of involuntary 'brain-storming session'…

then, suddenly, we were there, outside the café in Shangani; time for putting some of those images and figures into an agreed format.

Moving from the heat of the driver's cab to the cooler veranda was very, very welcome… and the cold lemonade even more so.

The dark, sodden stains on the backs of our shirts and around the armpits were witness to the hot and sweaty ride we'd just completed in our 'metal boxes on wheels'!

Joseph was first to speak, seemingly very determined to get his point across before he would be 'gunned down' by a cold, penetrating stare, or a swift, vicious kick in the shins from his father!

"I will only work the mines on my own!" he virtually spat out. "People can put money in, but I want to be the boss of my own gold mine! Dad, you promised me!" he rattled on, repeating the same theme over and over again.

He suddenly stopped, surprisingly aware that Ray had not interrupted, and he had been able to get his demands across.

"You agree, Dad?" he asked, with a look that was a mixture of total amazement and relief.

A blunt: "No!"

Coupled with his father's expressionless look, this started a staccato tirade of jumbled-up whinging remarks spewing from his mouth, against a background of an ever-darkening blood-red face and wild staring eyes almost popping out of their sockets!

"It's not fair! Why are you always against me! Why do you always favour my brothers! Just what do I have to do?"

BANG!

His father's fist thumped down on the table, the bottles and glasses jumping in unison and the 'whinging machine' came to an abrupt halt.

"Joseph," his father began quietly, "working on the mine is hard, sometimes soul-destroying work and you need a partner, end of the story; I suggest the two of you split the work between you."

"Okay, okay, I want underground mining operations!" came the rapier response from Joseph's lips.

A smile spread across his face as his father nodded in agreement.

Ray turned to me. "Surface operations, milling, extraction and the general running of the mine would be your baby."

"Yeah, that'll be fine," I replied, "and, of course, as we spoke about briefly last night, I'd be willing to put up my half of the money, Joseph and I becoming full 50/50 partners."

There was slight pause before Ray continued. "Problem is, Joseph doesn't have any money, which means he'd need to sell shares to raise the other half; that is not easy or guaranteed and worse still it could take months, giving long delays, which you both can ill afford!"

"What about another way to raise some extra money?" I interjected. "Cain was telling me there's such a shortage of vehicles and certain mining equipment in Rhodesia that even second-hand ones command very good money. So instead of putting all of my capital into the mine, I could use some of it to buy second-hand items down south, which we could then sell up here, for maybe double the price?"

"That's a sound idea; it would certainly help raise more capital, and much quicker too. There'd be difficulties, of course, with the Customs department when you sold them, but there's always a way!" responded Ray with a wry smile – and that twinkle was back in his eyes again; a look that I would get used to seeing whenever there was something unconventional, dodgy or even downright underhand in the offing!

"Right, let's settle it this way then; I will donate 'my experience' on Joseph's behalf, which should balance things out between the two of you. I would use my contacts at the Mines Department to try to arrange money through mine development loans. That, together with help to find good mine workers and my advice on running the mine. Are you both happy with that?"

"If we all agree!" exclaimed Joseph excitedly. "Well, we can start immediately; isn't that right, Dad? Wonderful!"

Smiles all around; gentleman handshakes once again.

And the set-up of a 50/50 partnership was born between Joseph and me.

We toasted each other with our now lukewarm drinks and left the café.

Ray told me to follow them to Fort Rixon, where, with the help of Pat's maps, we'd spend a couple of hours reconnoitring the mines that we would be tributing and living on shortly.

The Claims

As we swung off the tarmac onto a dirt murram road, Ray's pick-up instantly kicked up clouds of dust into the air, most of which blew in through my open window. This was my first taste of real Rhodesian bush, or perhaps I should say my first taste of real Rhodesian dust!

Then I remembered they'd told me to keep my windows closed when driving on dirt roads and the air blower off; otherwise, the whole cab of my pick-up would be thick with dust – and they were right!

I quickly wound up the window only to feel the temperature in the cab soar.

It was now midday. The hot sun blazed down on the metal roof; the heat was stifling. My hands were becoming clammy and sticking to the steering wheel. Inside my mouth, my tongue and throat were parched dry, yet the outside of my face was a stream of sweat, the salty liquid even running into my eyes.

I began to get more drowsy, the sweat pouring off my rather overweight 'straight from the city' body, and I found that constantly peering through the windscreen at the swirling clouds of red dust had a hypnotic effect, rather like driving in a snowstorm – except that the temperatures were at different ends of the thermometer scale!

It was so hot and humid, the sweat trickling into my eye sockets impairing my vision; my eyelids felt heavier and heavier, flickering, touching, almost sticking together, fighting to keep them open.... Have to stay awake....

"SHIT!"

Suddenly, a big truck appeared right in front of me looming out of the swirling dust clouds!

I was jolted into wide-awake mode!

I steered hard to the left and my pick-up lurched over, just missing this truck, which hurtled past, showering me with even more dust and small stones, reducing visibility to virtually nil.

In a flash, my wheels had ploughed into the thick drifts of sand on the edge of the dirt track, causing my pick-up to skid violently to the right, then slither from one side to the other as I battled to regain control, finally getting it pointing in the right direction again.

After this narrow miss, I decided to follow Joseph and his father at a much greater distance, and soon realised that not only was it much more pleasant actually seeing the bush I was driving through, but, as I was not being constantly submerged in clouds of dust, it allowed me to open the window a fraction to let in some welcome fresh air.

There was no danger either of taking the wrong track, as I could easily follow which way they went when the road split, because, although the thick red clouds of dust they kicked up would quickly settle and clear, a 'wispy, white-grey' cloud still hung in the air, 'pointing' the way for me.

Well, I thought, *I've got a lot to learn now that I'm going to live in the bush – but I get the feeling that I'm really going to enjoy it!*

We stopped at Fort Rixon, which was just a very small collection of buildings, including a police station, a post office and a small store with a phone booth outside and a petrol/diesel pump station.

Ray started filling up his pick-up with diesel, whilst Joseph and I stretched our legs and washed the dust out of our mouths with a warm lemonade – wet, but not really nice at all!

The road forked here and it wasn't really clear from Pat's directions which way we should go.

Being brought up in England, we were always taught 'if you don't know the time, if you don't know the way, ask a policeman'.

So we walked over to the police post and were met by a tall, thin man bearing the telltale signs of having recently been exposed to the hostile African sun – pink and bright red blotches, with various layers of skin peeling and flaking off his face.

He greeted us warmly, introducing himself as Peter; he was a young guy in his early twenties and had a very broad Yorkshire English accent.

His response to our request for clear directions to the Claremont mine was: "Right, you go here, up top, then turn left, right?"

"What!" exclaimed Joseph.

Having lived in Hull, Yorkshire, England as a student, I interpreted for Joseph, pointing out that, when Peter says 'right', he could mean 'okay' or he could mean 'right'- okay?

"Now I'm even more confused than ever!" Joseph blurted out – and that was saying something!

When we told him we were coming back up to Rhodesia in a month to mine at the Claremont, Peter was really pleased.

"Hey, be good to have another couple of young guys around here; there are too many old and rather boring ranchers in my area. Make sure you call in to see me as soon as you get back up this way. I'll introduce you to another Peter, my boss; he's about your age, I think. We'll have a few 'jugs of ale' and a BBQ together – be good fun."

Beep. Beeeeeep. Beeeep! Ray was hooting, beckoning to us to come back to the vehicles, and shouting at us, "Hurry up, you two; we haven't got all day. We must get on!"

Joseph was already climbing into Ray's pick-up as I bade my farewells to Peter, who winked at me and said, "Good luck with those two; I think you're going to need it!"

"See you." I smiled wryly. "For a beer or two, next month!"

We drove off, making sure we took the fork to the 'right', right! Okay!

The road was much firmer here, not so much dust, but a lot bumpier.

In fact, on some rutted corners, the whole vehicle vibrated violently, real bone-shaking stuff as it 'crabbed', bouncing and drifting sideways.

Man, you always have to be so alert when driving on these bush roads!

After about 10 minutes, I saw a Jeep approaching us from the other direction; it slowed down and the driver waved, but Ray just kept his foot flat down as he sped past – which I found rather rude.

I pulled up alongside the Jeep, greeted the driver and asked if this was the right way to the old Claremont mine.

"Sure is, there is only one way – you can't get lost," he joked. "Drive straight on for about six kilometres to where the road takes a sharp bend to the right, just before it descends quite steeply from the ridge. Are you coming to mine at the Claremont? We'd heard someone had been registering the claims!"

"All being well, in a month or so," I replied. "There will be two of us coming up from South Africa with our families."

"Good, we need some youngsters around here to liven the place up a bit. My name's Des, by the way; I have a ranch north of Fort Rixon. You'll be mining on Jackson's land, then, so you'd better be prepared; he's a prickly character and he hates miners with a passion!

"But we're not all like that; all over the country, you'll find the Rhodesians very friendly, especially out here in the bush. Any excuse for us to get together, and everybody has time for each other, as you'll find out when you're at the Claremont mine – there'll always be passers-by popping in for a cup of tea and a chat. So I hope it all goes well; call in and see us when you start mining. I'll be able to give you the 'lay of the land' around here."

As we parted ways, Des commented, "And don't forget to bring the family to meet my wife, Irene – she can never have enough visitors to chat to!"

I drove on, through a landscape of mainly thorn trees (acacias) and tall, light, yellowy-brown grasses; everything looked extremely dry!

Our mine claims were located in this part of Matabeleland, which had been suffering from extreme drought conditions for several years; everyone was praying for good rains, especially the farmers and the ranchers.

As I came around one corner, I had to brake hard on seeing a vast dry river bed about 10 metres wide immediately in front of me.

I slowly transversed it by going down the slope of the bank, across the bottom – not a drop of water to be seen – and drove up the other side.

Suddenly, right in front of me – 'boi-ing, boi-ing, boi-ing' – a buck, about the height of a big dog, bounded across the road and disappeared into the long grass; wow, such a beautiful, gracious, delicately built creature.

It wasn't long before I came across Ray's pick-up parked under a tree on the side of the road. As I pulled up, Joseph excitedly called out to me that he'd found the old Claremont mine shaft, and that his father was looking for the other mines that were indicated on Pat's map of the area.

"We have only found the old mine shaft entrances!" Joseph shouted. "Obviously when they closed down this mine they dismantled and took all the mining equipment away: they must have stripped the headgear, the stamp mills and the main buildings; in fact, everything of value on the surface."

Moments later, Ray appeared from the bushes, sweat 'bubbling' on his dark brown face (reminded me of a chocolate pudding cooking in the oven) – but at least he wore a bush hat to cut down the glare and shade the face, unlike Joseph and me, who were really suffering in this blazing sun. That's definitely one thing that will be at the top of my shopping list – a bush hat!

"The shafts look in excellent condition; good timber and well looked after," Ray said. "We don't really have to spend much time here now; there's not a lot to see and Pat tells me the company that last mined here about 10 years ago were a very professional lot, so there shouldn't be any nasty surprises underground safety-wise.

"Over the next few weeks, I'll get all the information and discuss the claims with the Mines Department engineers; they can advise which of the old mines on the claims would be the best one to open up for full mining operations – all the pros and the cons.

"I'll check the waste dumps and sands, which will be 'sampled' as well to confirm gold values; this will give a good indication of the gold they could yield, which will help with the start-up running costs. But let's go now to the Nelly 404 mine site – after a quick 'reccy' we can all go home; it's been a long, tiring day, especially in this heat."

We got back into the vehicles and drove, much slower this time, all our necks straining to see… what, if anything, we could see!

We passed several old ruined house sites set back off the road, but easily picked out by the purple-mauve flowering jacaranda trees contrasting vividly against the yellowy-brown bush. There were quite a few patches of these beautiful trees dotted along the road.

On reaching the sharp bend to the right, as Des had directed, we drove straight ahead along a track leading towards the remnants of a ruined building, indicating where the Nelly mine was situated.

Hundreds of concrete blocks, bits of old rusted machines and equipment were lying around all over the place.

We got out the vehicles, and walked over to the mine shaft of the Nelly 404.

Ray explained to us that the timbers of the inclined mine shaft were in good condition, as were the wooden ladders that led downwards, next to the rails into the darkness below.

"Well, we have accomplished a hell of a lot in the last couple of days," Ray stated. "Now, I don't know about you two, but I'm driving home to my mine and your beloved mother! Let's keep in touch by phone. Any second-hand equipment that you identify at the mining auctions, I can check if there's a demand for it in Rhodesia – that would certainly raise some extra capital when you bring the equipment up here to be sold.

"When you two get back to Rhodesia after you have sorted out things with your computer company and completed all the immigration procedures with the Rhodesian Embassy, we will make plans for setting up your new company, prior to beginning the mining."

Ray made a quick dash, climbed into his pick-up and gunned it back onto the dirt 'main road' in a huge cloud of dust!

It reminded me of a magician disappearing in a puff of smoke!

Joseph stood there for a while, bemused, puzzled looking, and then suddenly started to dance around wildly – it looked like an Irish jig – happily singing over and over again, "I've got my own mine at last, my very own gold mine. I'm so happy, so happy, oh, so happy! Hey partner, what a great few days! I can't wait to get back up here again next month to start mining for gold, yippee, yippee!"

I agreed with him – the start of a very intriguing adventure, for sure!

I took one last look from the ridge across to the distant hills some 30 kilometres away; a vast expanse of nothing but bush, except for the occasional homestead – wonderful! I felt completely at ease here.

Strip Roads

I drove off with Joseph smiling and humming to himself; he said he felt dead beat, and soon fell asleep.

At one stage, the road narrowed to nothing more than a cart track, a bit overgrown with grass growing between the two wheel-tracks. This obviously saw very little traffic, but it was easy, relaxed driving and I could enjoy the scenery we were driving through, being pleasantly surprised by an occasional reedbuck or a small duiker that swiftly crossed the track as we approached.

At Filabusi, we turned onto yet another kind of 'strip road'; this time, it was a graded dirt murram road, but with two parallel narrow strips of tarmac an axle width apart.

You drove with your four wheels on the strips until you met a vehicle coming in the opposite direction; both vehicles would then move over to their left so that only the 'driver's side' wheels were on one strip until you'd passed each other, when it was back onto 'your very own' two tarmac strips of road again!

These strips were a great idea, which really worked and was obviously far cheaper and easier to maintain than a full tarmac road surface.

Of course, from a driving point of view, progress was slower than on a full tarmac road, and our journey took longer; however, it was certainly much, much faster and less dusty than being on an ordinary dirt murram road.

After overtaking a slow-moving truck, we bumped violently back onto both strips again – the edges had broken away in places, so it felt like hitting a curb, causing Joseph to suddenly wake up, and, blinking in the bright sunlight, he exclaimed, "Oh great, we're on the strips! Oh, I enjoy driving on these roads so much! Let's stop for a quick break, and let me take over. As youngsters, Dad would let us take the wheel; it was great fun and that's how we all learnt to drive by the time we were 13 years old. And the most important thing Dad taught to us was to always slow down, and move over to the left as we approached a blind rise of a hill."

Joseph, tapping into his 'encyclopaedia mind' once again, went on to explain that these strip roads were the brainchild of a man called Stuart Chandler.

During the 'depression' years of the 1930s, to prevent people from starving, the government had organised work for them laying the strip roads all over the country. By 1938, strip roads covered a total distance of nearly 3,000 kilometres, including an unbroken stretch from the capital, Salisbury, all the way to the Beitbridge border with South Africa.

"A good thing we're living in the 1970s and not the 1930s," I interjected. "We would never have made Beitbridge to Cain's mine in *one day* on such a strip road! And *you* would have been late again, Joseph, and in big trouble!"

Joseph laughed and laughed; he was so much more relaxed and of good humour ever since the 'sealing of the deal' for tributing the Claremont and the Nelly mines earlier in the day.

These 'two-strip' roads were apparently unique to Rhodesia, and anyone who's ever lived there or visited the country will have unforgettable memories of driving on them – whether in this hot, dry, dusty weather, or probably even more vividly in heavy rains and at night!

As they stretched out before you into the distance, they were like thin grey strips of carpet on a light brown floor laid over the gently rolling hills.

Joseph told me that these undulations of the road were due to the fact that it crosses the southern end of the Great Dyke, the reef of valuable metals, which stretched for more than 500 kilometres across Rhodesia; not only gold, but especially in this area, asbestos, chromite and emerald mines – he had actually been brought up around here on his parents' mines (both gold and chrome) near the town of Shabani, and he started to relate in great detail 'chunks' of his childhood.... I must have dozed off, because Joseph had to really shake me hard to wake me up when he parked in front of the Fort Victoria Hotel as dusk was beginning to fall.

After checking in, although it was still only about seven in the evening, we went straight to our room and 'crashed out' on the beds; we were neither interested in food nor even a cold beer, surprisingly!

Only sleep, sleep and more sleep!

. . .

The next day, we really did make that 'early morning start'!

Up at 6am on the dot!

The 'wake up' call, a loud knocking on the door, caused us both to spring into action! And still wearing the clothes we'd slept in, we downed a swift cup of coffee, 'checked out' of the hotel, jumped into the pick-up and sped off on the road to the Beitbridge border.

The scenery in this part of the country was vastly different to the dry yellows and browns of drought-stricken Matabeleland; we drove now through tribal trust lands with countless picturesque African villages set in green tracks of land alongside the tarmac road.

No impala or reedbuck racing and prancing across in front of us as we approached; here, we saw only goats and more goats, and the odd stubborn donkey standing in the middle of the road staring at us, with that disinterested look of 'so, I'm not moving; just go around me'!

Near Bubye, we pulled into the Lion and Elephant Motel for a midmorning coffee break. As we strolled around the grounds munching a very tasty egg and bacon sandwich, we came across a large fenced enclosure behind the motel in which we saw, to our surprise, a family of leopards, including two small cubs – gorgeous; what a beautiful sight!

Our energy levels topped up, we proceeded in complete silence to Beitbridge, some 50 km away; tiredness had even quelled Joseph's virtually non-stop 'encyclopaedia disclosures'.

We seemed to be there in a flash, and in no time at all we had cleared the border and were back on the road leading straight down to Johannesburg.

This stretch of the journey also sped by, with us taking it in turns to drive and only stopping for petrol and cooldrinks.

After seven long, gruelling days, we just wanted to get home now!

Our last 'port of call' was a garage at Warmbaths, when the 'trip meter' of our pick-up clocked up 2,500 kilometres -- reaffirming the vast distance we had actually covered, travelling on all types of surfaces: tarmac, gravel, graded, dirt, murram, strip roads and cart tracks though the bush – but what an exciting and enjoyable journey it had been.

From the garage workshop, loud music was blaring out a very popular tune – *I'm on the top of the World* by *The Carpenters*, which put a huge smile on Joseph's face, and he started singing along at the top of his voice with his own words:

"Yes, I'm on the top of the world, lookin' down on my own mine,
And the only explanation I can find,
Is the gold that I've found, very deep underground,
Will make me rich, and happy in my mind…"

As our tank was being filled with diesel for the last time, another pick-up crept past us, pulling up at the pump opposite. I watched its wheels slowly rotating, around and around, and wondered just how many times each wheel of our own pick-up had gone around on this trip – more than a million times each, for sure!

Jesus, it makes you think how much faith we put in those little bits of rubber, wrapped around the wheels of the metal boxes we drive in!

There was little talking as we drove on. Both of us were deep in thought about the eventful last few days in the bush; the characters we had met; visiting the gold mines; tributing our own gold claims – it was like after having watched a really good, exciting movie, you would think about and dwell on the various scenes that had captured your imagination.

However, this had been no film – but pure reality, real life!

Shortly, I would be telling my family and friends about leaving the bustling South African city life that we had enjoyed so much, and moving to live on a small gold mine in the middle of nowhere.

The trek to the unknown in the bush didn't faze me at all – in fact, recalling that **Baden-Powell, the founder of the Boy Scout Movement**, was about my age when he had **made such a journey up to Rhodesia from South Africa at the end of the last century** gave me a warm, comfortable feeling, and I was prepared, come what may.

Like thousands of youngsters, I had joined the Scouts for fun, outdoor camping, getting the badges and being with my mates.

However, as I became older, I realised what an effect those 'B-P' years had on 'honing' my character – self-confidence, interaction and awareness of others, respect, self-reliance, and, above all, to '**be prepared**' for anything that life can throw at you – personal strengths and awareness that I knew I could rely on completely.

Although B-P was a military man, a colonel in the British Army in the 1890s, the **spirit of adventure into the unknown was as exciting now as it was in those times** – and I couldn't wait to get cracking!

My thoughts turned back to the present and to what was discussed the previous day in that roadside cafe at Shangani, and all that had to be done before we could embark on our new mining venture.

Over a warm Coke – yes that's right, not a cold beer! – the three of us had 'toasted' to the success of the mines that Joseph and I would be working on together as 50/50 partners. We had all shaken hands on the set-up – a gentleman's agreement – which we would formalise as soon as we returned to Rhodesia to start our mining operations.

My side of that deal would also include the purchase of two extra second-hand Peugeot pick-ups, certain mining equipment, and the loan of some capital money, which we would 'legalise' in the set-up of our new company.

From Joseph's side, his father would 'advise' us; he would use his knowledge of small worker gold mining; his help to get experienced mine workers; good equipment; and deal with the Mines Department in obtaining a development loan, which would be a welcome aid, helping us with the initial costs of starting up our mining operations.

Whatever the future held, or whatever would transpire, we had agreed on working together to run the gold mines that we had tributed from Pat.

. . .

The Start of a 'Golden Partnership'!

Sounded great and exciting, but who would have expected what was to evolve over the coming months…?

The problems caused by ranchers; fiercely opposed to us mining for gold on 'their land':

- Firing shots in the air to chase off our workers from our 'registered mine sites' when we were away picking up supplies in town!
- Constant clashes between us brought to mind the 'message' of that old musical song… why can't the cowboys and the miners be friends!

A deluge of torrential rains for six weeks, ending a three-year drought, caused severe flooding in the mine and made the dirt roads impassable for heavy trucks to make equipment and fuel deliveries.

The escalating threats of terrorism; the need to be extra vigilant, we being especially vulnerable:

- When transporting and storing explosives for the mine.
- When recruiting new mine workers from different parts of Rhodesia and the neighbouring countries.

Tragic deaths; a murder on our mine added to our burgeoning problems.

Trapped in a dodgy partnership with a crafty old miner and his unreliable, irresponsible son, who would rather get workers up from underground to paint the roof of a store – to make it look smart for his father's visit, instead of keeping those same workers down below, working flat-out to help stop the mine from flooding and collapsing!

His father, Ray, cunning as a fox, using his contacts and friends to help fast track the development of our mine. Shrewd, manipulating, but secretive, and was he genuinely on our side? Or was there a devious, ulterior motive behind his zealousness and his increasingly meddlesome involvement…?

Looking back, I can see now that I had suddenly been transformed overnight from a city boy into an adventurer – perhaps already blinded by 'gold fever', and **'the lure of gold'**…

……………………………………………………………………………………

Part II - The Trek

Disbelief; Upheaval…

As we headed towards the bright lights of the City of Johannesburg nearing the end of our week-long, thoroughly enjoyable and unforgettable trip, we both got our second wind, transforming us from 'limp dolls' into excited 'wound-up' animated machines!

Talking rapidly about everything: the gold mines, the characters we'd met – Hendrik, Cain, Zikke, George and Pat – the bush, the animals, jumping from one topic to another, just not able to get it all out quickly enough in one go!

Time flew by… only breaking out of our reminiscing when we passed a signpost to Windsor Park, where I lived.

"Hey Joseph, if you could drop me off at home now, I'll come and see you over the weekend to collect my car – save me the extra driving to your place and back this evening."

"Yeah, good idea, partner, and you lucky bugger, you'll be in bed fast asleep before I get halfway home!" retorted Joseph with a grin – or was it a grimace?

We turned off into Windsor Park, a brand-new suburb with unfinished dirt roads and no street lighting at all; instant darkness took over, with only our headlights showing the way, and for a moment it was like driving in the Rhodesian bush again.

This newly created, expansive residential area was only sparsely settled, the odd few completed buildings being dotted around in between mainly empty areas of natural bush veld that were designated 'building plots'.

It was hard to read the newly erected street name signs lit up by our headlights and we had to pull over for me to get my bearings.

"Hey Joseph! Look over there; those are the duplex houses where I live. See, there's my wife sitting outside on our terrace; that one there, the one that's lit up!"

He pulled over, shouted a quick 'hello, can't stop', followed by 'see you Sunday', before roaring off into the darkness, eager, I'm sure, to get home as quickly as he could.

"So how was the trip to Rhodesia?" my wife asked excitedly.

I downed the beer in one go, so cool and refreshing, and replied, "Great! And you'll be seeing more of Rhodesia in the coming months!"

"What! What do you mean? What have you been up to?" She laughed.

"Well, we're going to live up there next month – working in the bush, on our very own gold mine!"

"Oh yeah?" She laughed again. "That's a good one! No, be serious for a minute; have you got a computer job there?"

"I'll tell you all about it in the morning, Marianne, but no computers; we're going gold mining! So start packing! But now I've just got to go and crash in bed; I'm 'Christmas crackered' (totally knackered)! Oh, and let me sleep in; we've got the whole weekend to talk about it," I mumbled as I climbed the staircase. "And please, don't let the kids wake me up too early, okay! Night…."

. . .

I gradually began to sense that feeling – you know, when you're moving into semi-consciousness, when your eyelids are clamped shut, sending you back into that wonderful world of deep, deep sleep… but for how long, I don't know….

Marianne shook me gently, whispering in my ear, "You must get up now and tell us all about your holiday."

It was fun recalling some of that trip up north, but the kids were really only interested in hearing about the animals, especially that giraffe licking the window behind me at the West Nicholson Hotel.

"Were you scared?"

"And how long did you say its tongue was?"

"And what colour?"

Their insatiable young minds quizzically lapping up every detail, but still insisting 'why, how, what'….

To give us a break from being grilled by the two young detectives, we decided it would be a good idea to serve them some cooldrinks on the terrace. Once the kids were outside in the warm sunshine and their little friends had asked them to come and play, a certain calm descended on the afternoon – and, thankfully, an end to my 'ear bashing'!

This gave Marianne and me a chance to grab a cold beer and find a quiet place in the shade where we would be able to talk to each other – uninterrupted!

"From the excitement in your voice, the trip to the gold mine in Rhodesia was obviously a very enjoyable experience," Marianne began, "and I can tell from that look in your eyes that something 'big' is about to happen! I've seen that look twice before. The first time was five years ago when you said 'let's get married and go to South Africa next month'! And then again just last month when you told me you were expecting to hear from a computer company in South America with a job offer in Rio de Janeiro, Brazil! And now Rhodesia; gold mining! What next?"

"Marianne, it is definitely Rhodesia! And opening up an old gold mine! Our lives are going to be changed overnight, upside down, you could say. And it will be very different from starting work for another company, who would pay relocation costs, a hotel for two months to help with settling in to a new country, and, of course, very importantly, a salary from day one! It will be totally the opposite with this gold mining adventure – yes, it will be an adventure for all of us, you, me and the kids!

"Simply put, we have to pile all our possessions and furniture into a truck and drive it to the gold mine in the Rhodesian bush, where an African hut will be our 'hotel' for the first few months, *and*, there'll be no guaranteed income/salary either! On the contrary, I have agreed to put money into the mine, and it will be three to four months if things work out well for us – before the gold we extract will start giving us an income; hopefully a big fat income - *for life!*

"The set-up will be a 50/50 partnership with Joseph, the guy from work who just dropped me off. I'll put up most of the capital and his father, an experienced 'small worker' gold miner, will 'donate' his expertise, giving advice on buying the necessary mining equipment and employing experienced African mine workers, together with dealing with the government Mines Department for assistance and possible loans/grants. It's a gamble, but so is life! It's not going to be easy, but I know we are going to enjoy it. On Monday, I'll give one month's notice to the company, and next month we'll pack up, and start on the long and winding road to our gold mine in the Rhodesian bush!"

"So that's it, then!" Marianne sighed. "I can see that excited, all-consuming look in your eyes I guess 'a man must do what a man must do'! And I'll start sorting out 'what I must do, what a woman has to do'!"

We raised and clinked our beer cans together, toasting each other. "To a golden future, with a capital 'G'."

It wasn't long before the kids returned, and, of course, I knew it was only a matter of time before their 'machine guns' would be reloaded with many more questions that they would rattle off nonstop into the evening….

Before they would eventually fall asleep!

. . .

The weekend was very busy, just one long 'festival'; eating and drinking with our friends and neighbours, while I recalled the events of the journey to the gold mine.

They all seemed very interested – some quite amazed, to hear of our future 'trek to the goldfields of Rhodesia'.

One of the more conservative neighbours just could not understand us leaving the comfortable, 'fun in the sun' life, living and working in South Africa, to go and trek into the unknown, living in the remote bush in terrorist war-torn Rhodesia.

"You are both totally, truly, truly crazy!" he commented, shaking his head in pure disbelief!

Well maybe, but one thing that I'll definitely miss would be the 'lazy Sundays' relaxing in the large communal garden area of our housing complex – especially around midday, when all the blokes, who were mainly young Brits, Germans and South Africans, would play darts in a thatched rondavel/hut near the swimming pool, whilst the women and children would sit around chatting and swimming.

This particular Sunday morning, I was feeling decidedly rough, undoubtedly punishment for the late, late Saturday night enjoyment.

I plopped myself down beside Hugh and grabbed a beer from the 'swimming pool fridge' – a few beer crates submerged under the water to keep the beers *lekker* cool on a hot, sunny day.

This combination of a cold beer and cool feet dangling in the pool was the best proven cure for a hangover that I'd come across!

We started chatting about what I'd seen on my trip to the gold mine, and Hugh became completely fascinated, as, in spite of having been brought up in Rhodesia, he had never experienced anything like this.

He was 'wowed' by my new venture, working our very own gold mines.

It seemed almost unreal to him, in this day and age.

Hugh's wife, who came and sat next to us, used to work as a tourist guide for Air Rhodesia and Flame Lily Holidays, and she urged me to make sure that I visited some of Rhodesia's major and historic attractions – giving me her well-rehearsed sales patter:

"When you get the chance, you must get to see such places as the **Victoria Waterfalls**, regarded as one of the 'seven natural wonders of the world'. Here, the Zambezi River pours over the waterfalls, some 100 m high and 1.7 km wide! It's mind-boggling! Another great mass of water, also on the border with Zambia, is the recently man-made **Lake Kariba**; the dam wall – 600 m wide – holding back a lake of more than 5,000 sq. km!

"Then the **Zimbabwe ruins**, simply astonishing; an ancient city with towering walls built of rocks without mortar, the eerie, silent remains of a society that disappeared into Rhodesia's unwritten past. A city that was once the capital of the 'Kingdom of Zimbabwe' in the 11th to 14th centuries, and became a centre of an international trading route for mainly ivory and gold. Some estimates indicate that more than 20 million ounces of gold were extracted from this area, many historians regarding the country as being the place of the biblical King

Solomon's mines.

"And you must visit the **Matopas Hills**, south of Bulawayo, an area of some amazing 'abstract sculptures' of huge granite rocks, some as big as houses, delicately balanced on top of each other, jutting out high into the sky above the trees. On the summit of one of the massive, bare granite hills is **the grave of Cecil Rhodes**, the colony founder – 'Rhodesia' named after this pioneer.

"He had sailed to this continent as a poor, sickly immigrant, but, through exploiting the vast 'diamond and gold fields of Southern Africa', had become an extremely powerful leader, and wealthier, they say, than Queen Victoria, who signed the Royal Charter in 1889, making Rhodesia a protectorate and part of her vast British Empire.

"Another prominent Englishman of those times, and a close friend of Rhodes, was Colonel **Baden-Powell** (founder of the Boy Scouts movement), who had commanded the 13th Hussars Mounted Troops during the native rebellions in 1896, when Rhodes had one of his greatest personal triumphs. Unarmed and alone, he met the rebelling native Ndebele chiefs in the Matopas Hills and persuaded them to return to the 'ways of peace'."

"Its history repeating itself all over again," remarked Hugh with concern. "Rhodesia is such a beautiful country too, but now there's the terrorist problems and a bush war against the black insurgents. Difficult times ahead for all the people living there, black and white; all have to bear the brunt of this new 'native rebellion', and this time with the United Nations Sanction Oil Embargo adding further to the disruption of their everyday life.

"It's a terribly ironic situation we're in, because the reason for Ian Smith declaring UDI was to give more time to try to find a better, more gradual form of evolution, not revolution; and certainly not condone the mad rush by the British Government 'to get it off our hands' as quickly as possible by imposing the British 'one man – one vote' democracy.

"It just wouldn't work here; it would mean that overnight a mass of poorly educated black people would have to run the whole country under the leader of the largest tribe – nepotism, corruption, you name it; that's how the 'pyramid' tribal system works in Africa! Prime Minister Ian Smith and others felt that this would be a disastrous development for Rhodesia, having observed the consequences and rapid deterioration caused by the despotic new rulers of several other recently 'liberated' former colonies, including their neighbour, Zambia (formally Northern Rhodesia).

"Rhodesians call it equivalent to a 'one man – who has the only vote' system! Tribal dictatorship! Perhaps we should have a new word for it, '**despotcracy**', or even '**despotcrazy**'! So, since UDI, it's been a war against the terrorist insurgents of the Nkomo and Mugabe factions based in the neighbouring recently independent countries of Zambia and Mozambique – which is now in chaos itself, internal 'civil wars' of blacks against blacks, as the tribes fight each other to gain power, supremacy and control of their newly 'liberated' country!

"And it's just this type of situation that Rhodesians envisage would happen in their own country, between the Ndebele tribe of Nkomo, and the Shona tribe of Mugabe; the two largest tribes, with their long histories over the centuries of hatred, fighting and wars. But unfortunately it looks like this situation is going to continue for years, so, my mate, always err on the careful side when you're up there. Just make sure you keep a wary eye open – we don't want to read about you in the newspapers down here!"

Well, with that sobering thought, I grabbed another beer and went to play darts, knowing that this Sunday would undoubtedly be rounded off by a relaxing braai with friends and family late into the evening.

Yebo, I would certainly miss these Sundays!

. . .

My next-door neighbour, Terry, drove me into town and dropped me off at the office, where I met Joseph entering the reception area.

"Thought you'd probably be too busy to pop over to pick up your car at the weekend, but you can come home with me after work, not a problem! Hey, and another thing, let's ask our workmates out at lunchtime for a beer and a pie at the pub next door; that way, we could tell them all in one go that we'll be leaving the computer world, and going to start up our own gold mining company in Rhodesia next month."

Needless to say, the 'lunch hour' proved far too short; everyone was so interested to hear all the stories of our trip, and even more so that we would be living and mining for gold in a remote area of the Rhodesian bush. It was well into the afternoon when our manager, Dave, decided we should call it a day, but insisted on buying a 'one for the road' round of drinks – twice!

. . .

Over the next few days, we met at work very early each morning so that we had time to plot and plan what had to be done during the coming month.

It was proving to be an extremely busy, rush-around time, what with handing over customer projects to other colleagues, as well as all the mine-related stuff: immigration formalities, purchasing vehicles, attending mining auctions, export/

import permits – the list went on and on…

Having clients in Pretoria proved to be very handy for me, as it allowed me to visit the Rhodesian Embassy to go through the normal immigration process; Joseph, being a Rhodesian, was spared this ordeal.

The staff at the embassy were very helpful and friendly; however, as anyone who has immigrated to another country will know, officialdom works at its own pace… what could have been sorted out in one meeting invariably takes several trips.

I was handed a brochure titled 'Rhodesia, land of opportunity'.

The official, however, told me that, although the facts and figures were current, the main heading 'land of opportunity' might seem a little optimistic under the present circumstances.

The brochure was full of information on climate, housing, health services, education and transport; very useful for immigrant families settling in the towns and cities.

But for me, the only topics of interest that stood out were:

People:
European: 267,000, mainly from Britain and the Commonwealth.
African: 5,449,000, predominately from the two main tribes; the Mashona and the Matabele.
Harmonious race relations, based on mutual trust and respect, which had been the hallmark of the country and its peoples in the past and the present, ***ensure the continued peace and tranquillity of Rhodesia into the future.***
I thought, *obviously the terrorist tribal leaders,* ***Mugabe and Nkomo, have not read this!***

Customs Rebates & Concessions for Immigrants… included two vehicles per family – which meant that, between us, we could bring in the planned four Peugeot 404 diesel pick-ups duty-free.

On our third visit to the embassy, our passports, duly stamped with the immigration details, were handed back to us by the ambassador, who wished us God's speed and good luck – you'll need both!

Rather thought-provoking for our future life in the bush that lay ahead!

. . .

As far as the mining side was concerned, Ray phoned us regularly at the office, giving long lists of items that we should be on the lookout for at a mining auction – Joseph and I took a day off work to visit the 'viewing day' of one such mining auction sale, armed with the said shopping lists, highlighting the essentials items:

Hoist, double drum, air hoist; with details of rope strain, high speed brakes;
Welding machines (2);
Block & tackle (3 ton, 5 ton);
Spanner sets, stocks & dyes sets, pipe vice, underground bells;
Compressor;
Various other items, like two dozen paraffin lamps and 50 carbide lamps.

But, Ray's request for 'long-john underwear' from Woolworths was ignored!

. . .

We arrived at the East Geduld mine, and, as we approached the huge warehouse auction room, a familiar shape came into view; none other than Jaap Engelbrecht.

When he recognised Joseph, he slapped his hand against his forehead, his eyes rolled heavenwards and he uttered, "Aach man, not you again! You've come to torment me, eh! I thought you'd left us and gone up to Rhodesia for good!"

"Well, sir, we did, and we are now living in Rhodesia and mining on our own gold claims in Matabeleland," bragged Joseph, waving Ray's list in front of Jaap's face. "We've only come down here to South Africa to check out some of the essential equipment we need to buy at these auctions and ship it back up to Rhodesia!"

"Hey man, great for you; aach you know what?" He laughed. "I'm getting a soft spot for you two greenhorns! Come on, give me that list and we'll walk around the warehouse to see what's available, eh!"

"Fantastic, sir. We've raised capital to get our mine up and running, and we'll pay good prices for the best that's available!"

"Well actually," I quickly intervened, "we greenhorns have a limited amount of cash, which we need to use wisely; can you give us any advice in identifying good second-hand equipment to bid for at the auctions – and at reasonable prices! We are not technical people and don't want to bid on equipment that's duff or unfixable; we understand that it's '*foets-toets*', take it 'as is', and we can´t afford to end up with any 'white elephants'."

"Tell you what, you give me two hundred as a fee and I'll sort out the equipment you want; some machines that I recommend might not look very nice, may be a bit bashed in here and there, but then people at the auction won't bid very high prices for them, you see! But I'll identify only mechanically sound and easily fixable items for you, okay? You come back the day before the auction starts and I'll show you what I've got lined up for you. What's your total cash limit for bidding, eh?"

"Two thousand for a compressor, hoist, block and tackle, welding machines and a Peugeot pick-up in reasonable condition; they are the main ones."

"You think I'm a bloody magician, eh? Well, actually, you're right, man; I am! I'll do you proud, maties. *Moenie* worry *nie*; all will be *baaie lekker, dankie* – really good."

As we drove off, Joseph asked, "Do you think we can trust that drunken storeman? I mean, you've just given him cash money; he might decide to go into town to get plastered with his mates in a pub and forget all about us!"

"It's a chance we have to take, Joseph, but I feel he's genuine, and strangely enough he wants to help you and me – and if he gets us half of what we want for that price, I'll be doubly happy!"

So things were beginning to happen quickly now.

The Rhodesian immigration formalities had been finalised and the mining equipment we needed was being identified by our old friend, 'Jaap the Belcher', who would assist Joseph at the auction next week.

Vehicle-wise, I still had to buy a new Peugeot 404 diesel pick-up for my own use, and hopefully with a bit of luck we would get two second-hand pick-ups, either next week or at the following auction in a month's time.

That was the plan, and later we would sell the second-hand ones in Rhodesia at double the price – that would swell the coffers a bit!

On the personal side, there was packing, packing and more packing!

And sorting out our paperwork mountains that we'd accumulated in various boxes over the last few years!

In that respect, Joseph had it quite easy; apart from a six-month mountain of his own – his pregnant wife! But, staying in a furnished rental apartment, they could just lock the door and go, so to speak. We, on the other hand, had lived in a two-bedroom house full of our own furniture, most of which we would be taking with us – especially the really beautiful robust Kiaat hardwood items, like the beds, settees, armchairs, coffee tables and our pride and joy, a stand-alone bar with three bar stools.

Many pictures and statues that we had collected over the last five years would also add to the burgeoning loads that would 'migrate' with us!

We decided not to use a removals company, although it would be easier, but one hears so many stories of damaged goods 'on arrival' – that's one extra worry we definitely didn't need.

As both Joseph and I would be making several 'round' trips to Rhodesia in the coming weeks, we could easily take all of the household effects and goods with us, safely and soundly… or so we thought!

. . .

Suddenly, the month was up!

We were no longer working for a computer business in Johannesburg, South Africa; now we were preparing to move everything up to Rhodesia, to start working on our own gold mining business full time.

As a farewell to South Africa, we held one last party at our place, 8 Letaba.

So many of our friends and neighbours filling up an almost-empty house – most of the furniture and larger goods had already been stored in the garage of a neighbour, Jacques, who lived across the road in the Marakesh Duplex apartment complex.

He had kindly given us a key; we could call by any time to collect our stuff over the coming month or so, 'no hurry, no worry' – a frequently used African expression.

Much eating, drinking, dancing, talking, saying goodbye to so many people we'd known for five years – a very enjoyable night, for sure, but also tinged with a touch of sadness.

By 3am, we had hugged, kissed and shaken hands with the last of our guests. Now it was time to wearily climb up the stairs for the last time – which seemed so much steeper than usual – and just flop down onto the mattresses on the floor without even taking off our shoes!

Out for the count!

. . .

Surfacing around midday, we gradually got back into the land of the living with the help of mug after mug of strong black coffee.

The reality then began to dawn on us that we still had to pack all of our personal effects and goodies into and on top of our Volvo 122S car.

After filling the suitcases to bursting point and strapping them on the roof rack, there was still so much left over; we carried it all outside and spread everything on the grass verge next to the car – we stepped back in utter amazement; it resembled a village 'bring and buy' sale!

"How is all that, plus the four of us going to squeeze into our car?" Marianne exclaimed with a loud sigh!

Well, we pushed and squeezed things into every corner, under the seats, in the boot, into any gap we could find, but we were only halfway through our packing marathon when the light of the day began to fade.

That brought another problem, as there were no street lights in Windsor, so we had to rely on two neighbours to focus the headlights of their cars to light up our packing marathon as we carried on….

At last, at 9:30pm, three hours after darkness had fallen, we crawled off in our totally overloaded car to spend the night at the home of our friends, Malcolm and Eve.

That was a 15-kilometre drive away, near the airport, and we would have to use the main roads to get there, so we just hoped that we didn't come across any police.

With our car packed solid and all the suitcases and boxes piled high on the roof rack looking like an upcountry African bus, *and* with the kids sitting on Marianne's lap in the front seat, that would have spelt instant happiness to a ticketing traffic cop! And end of the road, even before we started!

We finally reached their house, luckily without incident.

Malcolm welcomed us and escorted us to a large table on the terrace, where there was a welcome sight – cold beers and braaied boerewors; fabulous! After the second beer, though, that was it; I was finished, totally stuffed, and I was shown to one of the spare bedrooms.

. . .

Apparently whilst I slept on through the next morning, Marianne and Eve had emptied the Volvo completely and repacked everything again – one by one, shoe by shoe, toy by toy, filling every little nook and cranny they could find.

Quite ingenuously, they had left a small 'tunnel-like' gap in the back, so that Marie-Louise and Jeffrey could climb between the front seats and then crawl backwards into that gap, squeezing themselves into what was, in effect, a 'giant sleeping bag'.

I awoke around 1pm to a delicious smell wafting through the open window, and I could hear the crackling noise of the boerewors and chops roasting on the braai.

Squinting in the bright sunlight, I had to use my automatic aromatic pilot nose to guide me to the source! There, I was met by a mob of excited kids, all pulling and pushing me in different directions.

"Hello Uncle!" screeched Sarah in my ear. "Why do you get up so late? We've been out here in the pool for ages!"

Over lunch, we discussed not only our imminent trip, but also arranged that, when I came back later in the month, Eve would drive one of the other pick-ups loaded with furniture up to Rhodesia in convoy with me, then spend a few days with us in Gwelo before flying back to Jo'burg.

A Christmas visit to Rhodesia by their whole family was also pencilled in, which would be great fun for all of us over the festive season.

Out at the car, Malcolm and I secured the roof rack and the cases – doubly roped! – just to be sure to be sure, as the Irish would say, to make certain nothing could fall off on the long trek north.

At 3pm, we hugged and bade farewell to our good friends and set off on the long 'road to Rhodesia' – the beginning of an exciting new life!

Truck Ride to Our Own Gold Claims

So just one month since Joseph and I made that journey up to Cain's mine, I left Johannesburg and started following the same route, although with totally different objectives and with a very precious sleeping human cargo – instead of boxes of mining supplies.

Strangely enough, there was also the same quietness in the vehicle as on the first leg of the previous journey when Joseph had gone into a sulky mood following the 'storeman fiasco'; the kids were fast asleep and we didn't talk, as we were both concentrating hard on keeping awake and alert, the heat being so oppressive.

Numerous yellow-billed kites were circling in the blue sky, but this time I couldn't watch and enjoy their graceful flight, because I was the driver.

The heat and the haze on the road predictably caused me to feel a bit drowsy, so I took Joseph's advice of stopping the vehicle, getting out and walking around – that really cleared the head and eased the sore eyes considerably.

Almost a replica of the last journey, dusk was falling and it began to get dark as we approached 'good old' Louis Trichardt Town – and boy was I pleased to see that same hotel where Joseph and I had lodged a month previously.

Even nicer was to be greeted by a smiling Hendrik, who, on recognising me, rushed to the car and almost ripped off my hand with his enthusiastic, prolonged hand shaking.

"Just take out what you need for the night, eh, and you can park your car over there in my garage. It'll be quite safe, man, but lock it for now. You and your good lady must first come and have a drink with me and tell me all your news, eh?"

"And what about my children?" Marianne retorted indignantly.

"You kidding me, eh? There's no room in your car amongst all that luggage."

"Ice cream!" I called.

And out crawled Marie-Louise and Jeffrey, shouting excitedly, "Strawberry! Strawberry!"

"Well, it'll be a baboon's arse!" mused Hendrik, smiling as he whisked them up, carrying one under each arm.

As we entered the hotel lounge, a buzz started spreading around the room as a few of the locals recognised me. One of them called out to me in Afrikaans, "How's it, redneck; have you come here to phone your brother in London again, eh?"

But, before I could answer, there was a long, shrill warbling ringing tone of an old-fashioned phone, and they all started laughing and pointing at me – until it turned out to be the wife of one of the locals.

He was a huge 'boer' farmer, well over six foot and weighing maybe 20 stone, with hands the size of a bunch of bananas – the phone looked so small in his hand as he grabbed it from Hendrik.

This was probably a regular occurrence, because he held the phone well away from his ear and we could all hear the frantic demanding voice of his wife. "Come home for supper immediately! Or do I have to come and get you!"

He grimaced, raised his eyebrows, shrugged his broad shoulders, and, with a resigned look and his head held down, he quickly left the pub.

After a relaxing evening meal and a few drinks, the family went up to their room whilst I went and gave the car keys to Hendrik so that our packed Volvo could also be put safely to bed for the night.

When I entered our bedroom, there was quietness, only punctuated by the gentle 'purring' of the peacefully sleeping family.

. . .

Morning came, the sun rose in the sky, but the 'zzzzzz-ing' noise from our sleeping family continued.

It was around 10:30am when a gentle knock on the door finally awoke us all from our slumbers.

"Breakfast is ready, if you would come down in the next 10 minutes please?"

Well, instant action!

Bodies springing out of bed, fast, blurred movements as clothes were whisked on, and then, rather like in the comic books as the figures rushed from one scene to another – 'whooooosh', and in literally seconds we were all sitting around the dining table.

The little ones were thankfully on their best behaviour; no noise, just politely asking for some fruit juice and cornflakes.

Marianne raised her eyebrows and shrugged in answer to my quizzical 'asking a question' look; it all seemed too good to be true.

"Oh what sweet, well-behaved children," said one old lady at the table next to us. "It's such a refreshing change to see youngsters being so polite and eating nicely."

When... *Crash!*

Marie-Louise's chair tipped backwards, crashing to the floor as she jumped up, and, screaming at the top of her voice, she marched towards the highchair where her favourite doll was seated for breakfast!

"Christ Neville! Stop picking your nose! How many times do I have to tell you! Why don't you listen?" she shouted as she whisked Neville out of the high chair and proceeded to give him a few hefty whacks on his bottom.

I sort of half-smiled an apologetic glance at the old lady, whose eyes had almost literally popped out of their sockets!

But you can't say anything, really; it would only make matters worse, so you must just sit there quietly – but actually rather enjoying this amusing incident.

After the late breakfast 'entertainment', we collected our things from the room and we came out of the hotel to see our car – clean and sparkling in the sun; even the tyres were being polished with black shoe polish!

Approaching midday, we bade farewell to Hendrik, thanking him for such a comfortable overnight stay.

This was just the slow relaxing beginning to our day that we needed, certainly not one of those famed 'early morning start' fiascos of the last trip to Rhodesia with Joseph!

We made more room in the back for the kids so that they could actually sit on top of bags close to and almost in between the front seats. Here, they could easily see out of the windows, and the miles just ticked by as we played various games like I spy, and counting different-coloured cars.

Excitement grew as we arrived at the South African passport control at Beitbridge, and, with the formalities completed, we drove slowly across the bridge over the Limpopo River.

"Oh look, down there, that's a nice dirty brown river!" exclaimed Jeffrey. "Wish we could go down there and get all mucky playing in it."

"Not me," said Marie-Louise. "The crocodiles will bite your legs off!"

On the Rhodesian side, the paperwork for the temporary import permits was quickly formalised. I enquired if Brian was around, only to be told that he was on his six-week border duty.

We drove off, and this time I took the right fork to Fort Victoria, a more direct way to get to Salisbury where my cousin, Michael, lived.

"Can we go now and see the giraffe with the long tongue?" shouted Jeffrey, jumping up and down, causing small boxes and clothes to tumble over us into the front seats.

"Not this time, kids; we are travelling on a different road."

It was hot in the car and, within minutes, the littl'uns were snoozing away.

As we were nearing Fort Victoria, we saw a sign to 'Zimbabwe Ruins' and agreed that, the next time we came this way, we would definitely visit this world-famous historical site.

These tarmac roads were in good condition, and nice and straight too.

The Volvo 122S is a driver's car, which can eat up the kilometres very quickly when you're in the 'speed mood'! We sped northwards!

We chatted about meeting up with my cousin, Michael, whom I hadn't seen for maybe 15 years or more. He had very kindly said that Marianne and the kids could stay with him, his wife and their three slightly older children until I could find a place to live; even if it takes a month, that wouldn't be a problem. Family can be good… and sometimes you can be really lucky!

We drove through the capital city of Salisbury, following Michael's very precise directions and taking the Borrowdale Road.

As the sun was beginning to go down, we passed the Borrowdale Racecourse, and a few kilometres later pulled up in front of the gate to his large plot, 'Five Acres'.

A friendly hoot, our kids waking up, his kids running to open the gate, and one, two, three… in a flash, we were all sitting on his terrace having a welcome sundowner drink – to wash away the dust!

We chatted for a while about what we'd both been doing over the years since we last met. It wasn't much longer, however, before tiredness started sweeping through our bodies; excuses not needed, we all went and hit the sack!

. . .

The next morning, we awoke with the warm sunshine lighting up our room and the aroma of fresh percolating coffee enticing us, luring us out on to the veranda; it tasted just as good as it smelt, cup after cup… cup after cup!

They told us how Jeffrey and Marie-Louise had kept them chatting and telling stories until after midnight! Little 'wide awake, tape playing machines', Mike called them, but eventually he had managed to find their 'stop button' – a promise of a ride on his daughter's pony in the morning; that had instantly done the trick!

Well, what a wonderful weekend it was too, just mooching around, nothing particular to do, no place to have to go to – utopia!

And we really needed this break after those hectic, chaotic last few weeks in Johannesburg when, from dawn to dusk, endless meetings, appointments, immigration sessions, auctions, packing and farewell parties! There never seemed to have been a spare minute in any of those packed-solid 16-hour-plus days!

And now here we were in Rhodesia, relaxing, chatting with my cousin and occasionally even cat napping!

We looked at some old photos of when we were kids growing up together in NW London, which triggered many memories of family relatives.

Once you start recounting these stories of your youth, other old times come flooding back into your mind from the human 'computer brain storage' – not only initiated by seeing an old photo; sometimes even a smell or a favourite song would cause instant recall of an event – truly amazing!

Time had flown by.

One last braai together followed by a nightcap signalled the end of this unwinding weekend for me, as I had to be up at 5am – yes, that's right, 5am, 'to make an early start'!

The Tribute

The next morning, I headed down to Gwelo Town for the signing of the 'tribute agreement' with Pat Burke.

This would give us the rights to mine for gold on the 'registered claims' of the Claremont and Nelly mines.

The tribute agreement would be signed by all of us at the meeting, and later ratified by the Rhodesian Government Mines Department.

The Midland Hotel in Gwelo would be the venue for the 'ceremonial breakfast' signing, being the centre of 'the compass'; me from Salisbury (N), Pat from Que Que (W), Ray from Belingwe (E) and Joseph, who was driving back for this meeting from South Africa (S).

It would be good to hear from Joseph how the bidding went at the mining auction in East Geduld. Hopefully our special consultant, Jaap Engelbrecht, had identified some bargains of good second-hand pick-ups and various items of equipment that were on the list – items that could be resold at a profit.

Driving down to Gwelo in the quiet of the early morning, I had plenty of time to reflect on what still had to done before we could even think about pulling gold out of the ground….

Once the tribute agreement was signed, we would liaise with the **Mines Department, which would supply us with all the information** we needed – detailed underground maps, sketches of the shafts and drives, valuations and development reports, as well as the actual gold production figures from the Claremont and Nelly mines – going back to the 1890s if we wanted!

They would also **help locate any mining equipment** we needed from some of the old gold mines that had closed down, as well as machines in their own storage yards across the country.

Any bulky equipment we bought at the auctions in South Africa would be railed to Rhodesia, except for the **second-hand Peugeot diesel pick-ups**, which we planned to drive up ourselves loaded with smaller items/machinery and all of our furniture/personal effects.

We also needed to **take on mine workers**; they would have to be carefully vetted, because of possible terrorist risks, and we would have to **build a village for these workers** and their families, since we would be mining in a sparsely populated area in the bush.

The construction of **various mine buildings and two houses** – one for Joseph and one for myself – added to the seemingly never-ending list!

Numerous **new business accounts** would need to be opened too, with suppliers, timber yards, diesel depots, and general mining and provision stores **for food and meat rations for the 60-odd workers** we planned to employ….

The 'to do' list flashing through my mind was getting longer and longer… when thankfully the sight of the Midland Hotel shot me straight back to the very beginning of that list – the '**tribute agreement**'!

I pulled up in front of the hotel terrace where there was a row of pick-ups parked 'nose-in', most undoubtedly belonging to ranchers or miners.

I squeezed my Volvo into a small gap, and, as I opened my door, accidently nudging the pick-up next to me, I heard a long, low growl and the huge black and tan square head of a rottweiler poked out from an open window, its glaring eyes firmly fixed on this 'human' who had dared to wake him up.

As I moved cautiously between the two vehicles, another monster growled and stood up in the back of the pick-up; he towered above me, staring at me with that intimidating, penetrating glare that only the huge, powerful animals have.

I smiled. Two rottweilers; yes, two huge rottweilers – well, at least Pat was here on time for the meeting, I thought.

"Good morning, youngster miner," came the greeting from the dog's owner. "You're the first here; come and join me for coffee."

As we shook hands, a loud honking noise accompanied by a squeal of brakes alerted us to the arrival of two more pick-ups – those of Ray and Joseph!

Ray quickly mounted the terrace steps, announcing, "This will have to be a short meeting, as Joseph will be driving back to South Africa tonight! His pregnant wife, Jane, is having complications carrying my first grandson! That's assuming Joseph has done something right at last; I don't want another giggly granddaughter! So let´s get on and finalise this tribute now!"

Pat immediately pulled out the tribute papers and started explaining the content of the paragraphs of the eight-page document, most of which he had already filled in:

The Memorandum of a Tribute Agreement*, made and entered into by and between the Grantor (Pat) and the Tributor (Ridge Top Mine), represented by Joseph and Myself, for a 3 year Period, paying a Royalty of 5% of the Total Gross value of the Gold won by Tributor at the said Mining Locations, - listing all the Claims' Names and their Registered Numbers with the Mines Department of Bulawayo….*

The tribute agreement, in duplicate, was duly signed and witnessed, and I was asked to deliver it to the Mines Department in Bulawayo on Thursday for verification and registration.

This meant we'd be one hundred percent 'kosher' and could commence setting up our mining operations near Fort Rixon in the Insiza district of Matabeleland.

"It was a long way to drive from South Africa just for my signature," Joseph mused, "but it was worth it; they're all ours now! Fabulous, flipping fabulous! At last, my very own gold mine, and working with my partner here, fabulous!"

His eyes beamed with joy and pride and his mouth boasted a 'new moon' smile; happiness personified! Perhaps this might be just the tonic he needed to overcome his complexes with his father and his brothers… perhaps?

"Well, let's make sure you drive back on a full stomach," Pat said, ordering the full English breakfast for the four of us.

"Thanks, Pat; that's just what I need," Joseph replied wearily. "In fact, I haven't eaten. . ."

The curt bark of his father cut him short, Ray declining the offer for both of them, saying that they had to get straight back to his mine in Belingwe so that Joseph could see his mother before he had to drive back down to South Africa again.

I felt a bit guilty for already enjoying this meal 'in my mind' as I walked with Joseph to his pick-up, knowing that he would have to suffer another long drive in the heat on an empty stomach.

Joseph updated me on the situation, saying that Jane had not been well at all and was feeling very uncomfortable. She was nervous about having to undergo some more tests with the gynaecologist, so he just had to be back there for her as quickly as possible.

He would stay overnight at his mother's home and get up at 'sparrow fart' – to get an early morning start!

"Good news, though, from the East Geduld auctions," he enthused. "We successfully bid for a mobile compressor and a white Peugeot 404 diesel pick-up in good working order, and both at a reasonable price, as you can see from these receipts I've brought back."

He handed me a bunch of auctioneer's receipts and ownership documents, together with a scrawled handwritten note from our old mate, Jaap Engelbrecht – written just like he talks, eh!

"Hey Greenhorn, moenie worry nie, I give that white bakkie a good service to make sure it is very roadworthy eh, we don't want any major bits dropping off on the road to Rhodesia. Come and see me when you get back down here again, man. Engelbrecht."

Ray hooted impatiently, revved up angrily and drove off furiously!

And Joseph hurriedly – like father, like son – bade farewell and said he'd see me in a week or so, jumped into his vehicle and quickly chased after Ray – who was already out of sight!

Pat grinned. "They don't know what they're missing, and Ray will probably stop on their long drive for a cooldrink and a tasteless sandwich at some hot, dusty garage. I've known that man for over 40 years; he's always rushing around, jumping from one thing to another, rush, rush, rush, but he will probably get far less done today than we will, despite our extended 'business' breakfast session! I call him 'Mr Worry in a Hurry'!" He laughed.

During breakfast, I listened to Pat telling me all about our newly tributed gold claims – it was really thought-provoking, factual and very educational, giving me a good insight into gold mining in that Fort Rixon area….

It was well into the afternoon before we called it a day, agreeing to meet the following Monday at the Claremont and Nelly mines.

He drove off, with his two bodyguards standing motionless in the back of his pick-up – huge, magnificent, powerful animals that looked as if they were carved out of solid ebony!

I went off to locate the Outspan Caravan Park, to meet a Mrs Lezure and get the keys to my new home.

She was a short, dark woman, probably of Indian origin, with long jet black hair. Her heavy horn-rimmed glasses magnified her eyes virtually to the size of the frame completely dominating her small face.

And boy could she talk – even quicker than Joseph; she rattled off all the rules for hiring a furnished caravan, hardly pausing for breath and with virtually no lip movement at all – just like a seasoned, professional ventriloquist!

She gave me the keys, took my cheque and, with a friendlier expression, pointed out a children's playground. Fabulous, and, with shops and the Midland Hotel just down the road, this would be the ideal temporary home for us until I could build our own house on the gold mine.

Gone 5 o'clock already; time to take that short stroll to the Midland Hotel terrace and have a few quiet beers whilst perusing the tribute agreement and all the paperwork of our newly acquired mobile compressor and the second-hand Peugeot diesel pick-up.

On my next visit down to South Africa, I would arrange the clearance and export documentation for the compressor, which would need to be railed up to Bulawayo, Rhodesia.

The white diesel pick-up, however, would be driven up to Rhodesia loaded 'to the hilt' with some of our larger furniture, like the heavy king-size Kiaat wooden bed – I'd just have to find a place to store the stuff temporarily; perhaps at Michael's smallholding near Salisbury, or even at Cain's mine; we'd see.

Believe it or not, I was beginning to feel quite peckish again.

The food was served – Guinea fowl in red wine – my favourite!

I devoured with relish this extremely tasty, but potent wild game casserole, followed by an Irish coffee… and then took the short, and probably 'zigzag' walk back to the caravan!

. . .

For the next couple of days, I hung around with Matt on a sort of familiarisation tour, accompanying him on his rounds to the various stores and suppliers of goods that I would soon be buying from for regular provisions and food for our own mine workers.

I even made my first purchase – as I had promised myself I would a month previously when sweltering in the hot sun reconnoitring the Claremont mine with Ray and Joseph. A wide-brimmed bush hat, so necessary to keep the sun from blistering your face – and scorching your brain!

Matt introduced me to the Gwelo Mines Department engineer – a very influential and essential ally to the small worker gold miners.

He explained how each gold mine was located in a particular mining district, and all mining activities from prospecting to gold output returns had to be registered and administered through that local Mines Department.

Our mines would fall under the Mines Department of Bulawayo, the same town we would also be using for delivering and processing our gold at the Barclays Bank Assay office there.

I was beginning to understand 'the lay of the land' now, and also the amount of driving that I would be doing regularly in the coming months.

The Towns of Bulawayo and Gwelo, situated on the main tarmac road to Salisbury, were roughly two hours from each other, and also equidistant from our mines; a neat 'triangle', which I pencilled in on my road map.

A 12-kilometre drive on dirt roads from our Claremont and Nelly mines would take us into Fort Rixon, a small outpost consisting of a handful of buildings – the local administration centre (for anything to do with roads and rivers, phones and post), the district BSAP police compound (where we had met Peter on the way back to South Africa from our visit to Cain's mine), and the local shop/garage 'complex' – a wooden shed that also housed a small public phone booth and a lone petrol/diesel pump.

A further 35 kilometres on the dirt roads would lead on to Shangani, where the railhead depot and storage yards were situated – our collection point for any mining timbers and gum poles railed in from the upcountry forests.

Author's sketch of locations in Fort Rixon-Insiza area;
- our Gold Mines - Nelly 404 & Claremont.
- Towns visited regularly to pick up supplies, Mines Dept., Bank Assay Office.
- lessor known 'small zimbabwes': Dhlo Dhlo ruins, Regina ruins.

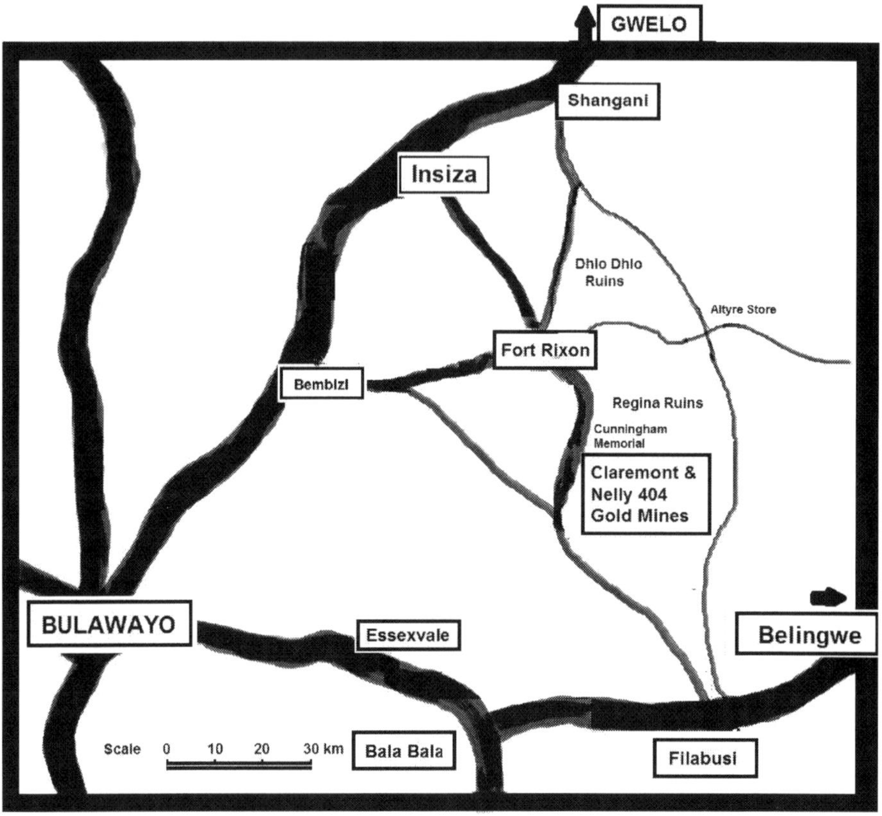

Prospecting and Pegging

The next day, I drove down to Bulawayo, where Ray and I had an afternoon meeting with the mining commissioner to make his acquaintance and to register our tribute agreement – the handover took precisely 10 seconds, including the handshake!

Then, with a typical detached civil service air, weighted heavily with political overtones, he informed us stiffly that the honourable Mr Jackson, a very influential and respected rancher in these parts, had called in earlier to see him and to lodge an official complaint about us mining on his land – and I hadn't even set foot on it yet!

Jackson had complained that a prospecting notice put up on his land in the name of Ridge Top Mine was an old one for Ray's Belingwe district mine that had been altered, and, thus, was not valid.

(Apparently Ray had pegged this 'block' in a rush on his way home to Belingwe after our meeting the previous Monday at the Midland Hotel; Pat had told him that this Claremont parallel block needed to be pegged urgently, as it was an important source of water for us).

The rancher had also left a letter for us – with a copy to the mining commissioner, of course – stating that it was also illegal for us to cut timber on his land, as we didn't have a timber licence, but he was willing to supply us with cut 'cords' of wood.

When Ray read the proposed charge, he exploded and angrily shouted at the mining commissioner, "The man is a hustler, trying to extort money from us at four times the normal rate; we will apply for our own timber permit immediately – today, right here and now! Follow me!"

We went straight down to the mining engineers/acquisition section, where we met two friendlier gentlemen, Martin Curtis and Ronnie Cummins.

Whilst they were arranging a temporary timber licence for us, they warned us that Jackson had called in earlier and was in a foul mood, bitching about the gold mines on his land being reopened again; he had hoped the problems with miners were over for good when the mines closed down 10 years earlier.

He had also renewed his old prospecting licence, took some prospecting notices and left abruptly, saying he would screw those bloody new miners by correctly pegging the Claremont parallel mine block to prevent use of a critical source for pumping water for mining operations.

They told us that, several years ago when the mines had closed down, Jackson had tried mining for gold there himself on a small, part-time scale.

It was a total disaster and had left him with this embittered, anti-mining attitude and a jealous resentment of gold miners.

Martin processed a prospecting licence for me and advised me to go to Fort Rixon very early the next morning and re-peg the disputed prospect notice claim before Jackson could.

He also showed me on a map two other unclaimed blocks that I needed to peg to protect 'the integrity' of our mining area; this would stop Jackson and any other 'chancers' from causing disruption to our mining operations.

If there was any more help we needed, please call them, as they would always be on the miners' side against the occasional petty, selfish rancher like Jackson, who was only out to cause problems to try to prevent any mining operations on his land.

"We are here to assist in any way possible to get your mines up and running to produce the much-needed gold for the Rhodesian foreign exchange coffers!" Ronnie stated emphatically.

There was still time before Barclays Bank closed to visit their Assay office, where I was shown around and explained the procedures for weighing and purifying the gold from our mine once I had the necessary official 'Licence to sell' – sounds like a James Bond movie!

I watched with fascination when an old miner came in and had his pouch of gold weighed on the old-fashioned precision weighing scale; his smile grew as more weights were added, until the balance was struck and he was told '22.55 ounces of crude gold' – wow, that's more than $2,000 for that small blob, which looked like a dirty wet tennis ball!

. . .

The next morning, I was up at 4am and drove down to our mining claims to meet Ray, armed with the necessary prospecting notices and the official Mines Department stenographed maps that Ronnie had loaned me, showing the blocks we needed to peg to prevent Jackson playing his disruptive games.

As I passed through Fort Rixon, the first light of day was breaking, the darkness fading as the sun began to nudge its way above the horizon, causing that orange glow to spread slowly across the sky – what a beautiful sight.

I got out of the car and sat on the bonnet, gazing into the distant kaleidoscope of changing shades and colours.

I'd once read: "There are a thousand reasons to enjoy a sunset." I felt this would be one of many more to come, but I wouldn't linger longer; there was work to be done and I didn't want to rattle Ray's cage!

Everything looked so tranquil, almost unreal in the half-light as I drove off along the dirt road; a total contrast to the noisy early morning, packed city roads that I had been used to!

What a pleasure to see **a** wild reedbuck crossing ahead of me and disappearing into the browny-green grasses of the bush, instead of watching hordes of people hurrying across a painted zebra crossing on their way to work in those monstrous, concrete office tower blocks!

Ray was at the mine already with two of his workers sitting in the back of the pick-up. He handed me a welcome mug of hot coffee from his thermos flask, telling me that Joseph had left for South Africa early in the morning with the instructions (*orders!*) not to dilly dally around down there – poor Joseph; he was always getting it in the neck from his old man!

We spread the detailed Mines Department map out on the bonnet and made our 'pegging plans' for the morning.

Firstly, we located Ray's invalid prospect notice – which was also upside down! Strange that Jackson hadn't complained about that as well!

I replaced it with one of the Ridge Top Mine signed by me and witnessed by Ray, which I then, with great satisfaction, nailed to the post – my very first one, and probably the best, knowing that we had got there early enough before Jackson to prevent him from screwing us!

A strange shiver came over me as I hammered in the nails, the sensing of the miners a century ago, rushing, arguing and sometimes fighting to stake their gold claims by nailing up their prospecting notices. Not much had changed since those days, I guess – this was our 'mini' gold rush experience!

So the flooded Claremont parallel mine was now correctly pegged – by me! – ensuring our future secure source of water; essential for mining operations on our nearby mines and also importantly for personal use, both for the workers and ourselves.

Armed with the prospecting notices, a 30-metre tape measure, some nails and a hammer, and accompanied by his workers carrying metre-long gum poles and a sledge hammer, we trudged through the long grasses and the thorn bushes to locate the corner peg of our existing claims (pegged by Pat).

From here, we measured out the two blocks, which was not easy, sometimes having to hack our way through the overgrown bush – and it seemed that the spot where the peg had to be placed was always in the middle of thick thorn!

The sun was getting hot now; our bodies sweating profusely.

Two hours had just ticked by as we put up our 'discovery pegs' and signed (correctly!) the prospecting notices, but we had accomplished what we'd set out to do; namely, **to protect the integrity of our mining areas.**

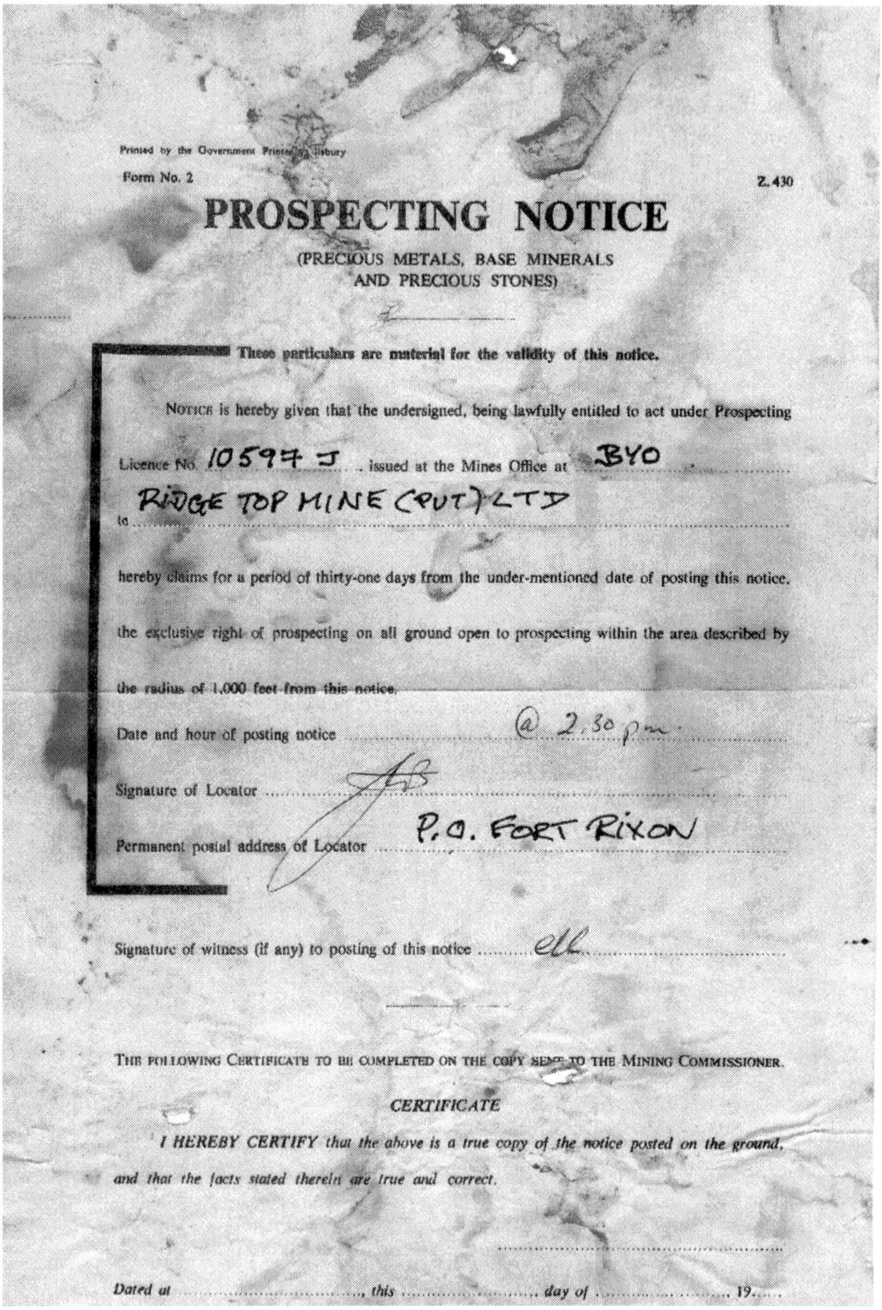

Printed by the Government Printer, Salisbury

Form No. 2 Z.430

PROSPECTING NOTICE

(PRECIOUS METALS, BASE MINERALS AND PRECIOUS STONES)

These particulars are material for the validity of this notice.

NOTICE is hereby given that the undersigned, being lawfully entitled to act under Prospecting

Licence No. 10597 J issued at the Mines Office at BYO

to RIDGE TOP MINE (PVT) LTD

hereby claims for a period of thirty-one days from the under-mentioned date of posting this notice, the exclusive right of prospecting on all ground open to prospecting within the area described by the radius of 1,000 feet from this notice.

Date and hour of posting notice .... @ 2.30 pm.

Signature of Locator ....

Permanent postial address of Locator .... P.O. FORT RIXON

Signature of witness (if any) to posting of this notice ....

THE FOLLOWING CERTIFICATE TO BE COMPLETED ON THE COPY SENT TO THE MINING COMMISSIONER.

CERTIFICATE

I HEREBY CERTIFY that the above is a true copy of the notice posted on the ground, and that the facts stated therein are true and correct.

....

Dated at ...., *this* ...., *day of* ...., 19....

Now it was time for Ray and me to leave the mining claims and carry on with our plans for the day.

A succession of various different noises followed:

The gulping down of half a mug of coffee.

The gurgling of a diesel motor as it sprang to life.

The roaring, over-revving as Ray shot off, covering me in a cloud of dust to go…? I've no idea where – he didn't say – but, as Pat had told me, he was always rushing around – 'Mr Worry in a Hurry'!

When the dust had cleared, I scanned the area where we would be mining; nothing but a few ruined mud houses, odd bits of rusty metal and hundreds of broken concrete blocks scattered around the dry parched ground – any minute now, I was expecting to hear the theme tune of an old cowboy film and watch the tumbleweed rolling towards me in a cloud of dust!

I set off on the road back to Fort Rixon in my Volvo, having to drive carefully because of the low road clearance of the car, especially on the excessively bumpy parts of these dirt roads.

It would be much easier in a couple of weeks when I would be driving in my new Peugeot pick-up built with a much higher suspension, very necessary for driving on these types of bush roads.

I arrived at the police compound houses. A quick knock on the door. Surprise!

Peter welcomed me inside, saying that I had great timing; he was having a late breakfast – I must have smelt the bacon frying!

"Well, I must say, there is something very special about bacon being fried. The aroma that wafts on the air, drifting, beckoning one to follow and track down the source, followed by the actual pure enjoyment of capturing the full flavour, munching away slowly, mouthful after mouthful!"

As we ate, I told him about my first few days as a 'learner' miner, and of Jackson's sneaky tricks to cause us grief.

"Oh yeah, that man – he's the most disliked of all the ranchers around here. Most of them you'll find are very friendly and they'll go out of their way to help you if they can. But him, be very careful; he is on virtually every district committee – and the chairman of most, and it seems that he's bent on stopping you mining here!

"It's so ridiculous. There's been mining in this area for a century, but that resentful old fart feels the miners are stealing *his gold*, from *his land!* Jackson is also anti-hunting, and very possessive about 'his' wild animals – although they roam freely across the whole district – so be very careful, because he'll charge you with poaching if he catches you shooting on his land.

"However, there are plenty of other ranches where you can get 'steak on legs' for supper! Next time you call in, we'll arrange to show you some good places down in the valleys where you can hunt for buck. And with regards to hunting,

I'll fix you up with the necessary hunting licences and permits, together with a firearms permit, and, if you don't already have a rifle, I'll sell you my spare one, right? Okay!"

I had taken an instant liking to Peter and could sense that we'd be sharing some fascinating times together in the future.

He showed me around the police post, remarking that the only time the cells were full was once each year after the 'police braai and party' – not with thieves or criminals, but locals who'd had far too much to drink and were quite happy to be 'locked up' for the remainder of the night!

I left Peter and headed back to Gwelo, with his words from a month ago still ringing in my ears: "At the junction, turn right, right! Okay!" I smiled – and did as instructed!

After a further bumpy, dusty, sweaty 40-minute drive, I really needed a break from the hot sun and the sweltering heat, and decided to pull up in front of a small hotel in Shangani.

I looked at my watch – 12 o'clock – and thought, *well this 'mad dog the Englishman' is getting out of the midday sun!*

And man, it was so relaxing to sit in the shade on the hotel veranda, sipping a refreshingly cold beer on a Friday afternoon.

I gazed across the great expanse of bush and koppies (small hills) stretching to the mountains in the distance, and thought, *what a great way to end my first week on the job!*

. . .

Early Saturday morning, I shopped in the town and filled up the fridge with enough food and drinks to last the weekend, because, after driving to Salisbury and picking up the family from my cousin's place in Borrowdale, I sure wasn't going to go anywhere – except maybe a leisurely stroll over to the Midland Hotel!

I jumped into my car – I was really in the mood to 'burn it up' on the nice, smooth tarmac road to Salisbury – and gunned the Volvo 122S, racing through the gears as I sped northwards.

In no time at all, it seemed, I pulled up in front of 'Five Acres' to be greeted by little, laughing, jumping up and down, naughty looking children!

They had been thoroughly spoilt by my cousin's family, whom we thanked for providing us with such an enjoyable stay, but now the littl'uns were so excited about seeing our new home and wanted to be on their way. "Now, now, pleeeease!"

A few hours later, we pulled into Gwelo Town, and, when Marie-Louise and Jeffrey saw the caravan park, they went bananas!

"So you kept your promise; we really are going to have a holiday together!" shouted Marie-Louise.

They couldn't get into the caravan fast enough, and went exploring, bouncing up and down on every bed they could find – laughing and giggling to each other the whole time.

Thankfully, they began to tire quickly; all the excitement and travelling had exhausted them and they soon flaked out, making it easy to scoop them up and dump their limp little bodies in bed.

Peace at last, sitting outside on a warm, balmy evening, enjoying a bottle of good cabernet sauvignon red wine, with some snacks – choice cheeses and crispy crackers.

Chatting, nattering and relaxing as the evening slowly slid past the midnight hour, signalled by the soothing, melodious chimes from a church clock tower in the distant darkness….

. . .

"Monday, Monday, so good to me…" A song by *The Mamas and The Papas* drifted into the room as I slowly struggled to wake up.

And the cup of tea that 'drifted' up to my bed carried by a small boy, Jeffrey, was certainly a good start to my Monday, and I was excited that I'd be meeting Pat again around mid-morning at our claims down in Fort Rixon.

After an uneventful two-hour drive, I neared the mining area and could see two huge jacaranda trees jutting proudly out of the bush about 100 metres off to the right of the dirt road.

I got out of the pick-up and walked along a track through the undergrowth, and was surprised to suddenly come across a large open area that was obviously a well-laid-out garden in days gone by.

There were ruins of two old houses, and next to each was the magnificent canopy of branches of a jacaranda tree in full bloom; around the base of the trees, the fallen blossoms made a beautiful purple-blue carpet.

These ruins had good, solid foundations and would be ideal sites to build our houses on; the faded red-coloured floors were a reminder of the daily hard work of wax polishing them in the past – and soon again, I thought!

I walked back to the road just in time to see an approaching pick-up, which gave the illusion that it was pulling a huge dust parachute behind it – Pat was here!

As we were shaking hands, his two rottweiler companions leapt out from the back of the pick-up and came over and nudged me forcibly with their massive heads – a sort of greeting, I guess.

An immediate chill went down my back as I thought of sharks, which, after the first 'sounding out' prod, would come back at you again with a ferocious biting attack! Luckily, these two had no such thoughts, being well-trained and fully aware of whom or what was a threat to their master.

"Meet Dempsey and Rocky Marciano, two of the best heavyweights in their class!" joked Pat as he thumped them both on their flanks with heavy, resounding claps. "Let's first check the various claim blocks and do any necessary pegging to link the blocks into one large consolidated mining area. We can go later up to the Fort Rixon Club for lunch by the dam, and I'll give you information on some of the essential things you need to do right away. Also, a bit of background on 'who's who' and 'where's where' in this area, which will probably save you some embarrassment in the future, and certainly save time when you drive on these little-used dirt roads with hardly a signpost or a marker to guide you."

We started at the Claremont parallel (which I had proudly re-pegged on the Friday) and located the shaft entrance to the Claremont mine.

This had been the biggest and deepest of the gold mines, Pat told me, going down some seven levels – 700 feet!

"Although the old 5-stamp mill concrete bases are in good condition, it would be better not use them," Pat suggested. "A future problem from milling on this site would be that any leakage of cyanide from the waste dams would slowly seep down there into that seasonal stream below. It's only a dry donga at the moment, but come the rains it will be flowing strongly and would spread any contaminated water to other ranching areas. If we resumed milling on this site, all responsibility for the conservation of this area would rest with our mine – and you know who the chairman of the conservation association for the Insiza District is! Yes, Jackson!

"And he would love to be constantly on your back if you started milling here, 'cos he's dying to find any excuse he can to prevent us from mining! So you either divert the flow of any new dams, or you mill from another site on the Nelly 404 mine, which I reckon is a better and a cheaper option. However, we'll peg this block of the 'Claremont sands' waste dump for later recycling to extract any residual gold there might be – I took some samples last time I was here, which look promising."

We crossed the dirt road to visit the old ruined houses that I'd seen earlier, with their wonderful jacaranda trees.

I could already see myself living there, and sitting under the shady spread of these trees, relaxing and drinking a refreshing… cup of tea!

Pat's advice was to register and split off these house sites to be separate from the mine blocks; this would establish them as our bona fide dwellings, and make them 'untouchable' by any mischief-makers, like the said right honourable Mr J!

After nearly three hours of tramping around in the heat, we drove off to the dam for a cool beer.

Over lunch, Pat told me all about the locals, a few weird characters whom I'd probably come across, where the various ranches were located, distances and which roads to take, etc. I hastily scribbled down everything in my other 'little black book' – phone numbers to be added later!

"You also need to see Ian Davidson at the Fort Rixon administration office to arrange a PO Box number, and apply for telephones – one for the mine and one for the house, both of which would be on the same joint party line, shared by, amongst others – our Mr Jackson!"

"Oh shit, I can't seem to get away from that man! I'll have to be really careful what I say about people when I use the phone; I would never be sure if I heard a 'click', was it a normal disturbance, or a ghost listener logging into my conversation for future scandal," I jested.

"Yes, you'd better watch what you say, because you can actually liken these joint party lines to be the equivalent of a local (gossip) newspaper. There are few secrets out here in the bush! And another thing I must tell you, that although surprisingly we didn't see any today when we were walking around in the bush, this area abounds with snakes: the extremely poisonous puff adder, the black mamba and the cobras, so make sure you always have a snakebite kit in the pick-up."

We drank one last cold beer, raising our glasses and toasting to: "The success of the Ridge Top Mine, the Nelly 404 and the Claremont,"

Then we parted ways, Pat calling out as he drove off, "Just phone me if you need to know anything more; my number's on the tribute agreement. Good luck – to both of us!"

Minutes later, after I'd travelled only a few kilometres, the engine started stuttering a bit and I noticed that the temperature gauge had gone into the red 'warning' section!

I immediately stopped the car, with steam belching out from under the bonnet! And oh dismay when I lifted it up to look inside; there was no fan belt. It must have broken and dropped off, causing the engine to overheat rapidly.

"Sod's law! I have no spare fan belt. Shit!" I cursed under my breath.

A hooting noise, accompanied by an enveloping cloud of dust, announced the arrival of a 'white knight'! None other than Policeman Peter!

From his toolbox, he produced a woman's stocking – not his, he assured me – and wound it around the fan pulleys and knotted it very tightly; that did the trick and the spinning fan began to cool the engine immediately.

"That's great!" I uttered as I drove off. "Thanks Pete; I'll buy you a new pair – what's your favourite colour?"

He laughed and waved goodbye, I think – well, I couldn't see all of his fingers!

And the stocking repair held out to get me back home – what a good improvisation.

. . .

Cornflakes and cold milk; blue sky and hot sun; woman and warm smile; proven combinations for a perfect beginning to a man's utopian day! However, reality soon struck.

Hot metal car; wet, sweaty shirt; dusty, dry throat! I was on the road again, this time to Filabusi to meet Ray; we would check on some equipment that was for sale at an old closed-down gold mine there.

The ongoing drought in Matabeleland was really bad, and, as I turned onto the dirt road, huge dust clouds billowed out behind my car and hung in the hot, dry air like the belching smoke from a steam train as it sped across the prairies in the old Wild West.

We met up in Filabusi; I climbed out of my hot 'dust bucket' - and into his!

We then bumped and bounced very slowly down a rough, rutted dirt track; my Volvo would not have made it, probably having the whole exhaust system ripped off!

A three-stamp mill indicated that this had been a low production gold mine – in comparison to the top gold-producing Claremont mine in the early 1900s, which had a 10-stamp, and later in its heyday, a monstrous 15-stamp mill.

Ray also checked out a James concentration extraction table, but found it to be in poor condition – so we left empty-handed.

However, the main reason for this trip was to take on my first three African workers, whom Ray had brought along from his own mine: Langton, a builder who had worked for him for many years, and Gwabuya and Nduna.

Ray also gave me a very important card – a general dealer's business account in his name that could be used at several suppliers and stores in Gwelo to purchase food, clothing and tools, etc.

The Africans loaded all their stuff, including machetes and some food rations, into the boot of the car and the four of us set off for Fort Rixon, driving carefully and slowly negotiating the bad stretches of the dirt roads.

But, due to the increased 'African load', occasionally the low clearance of the Volvo inevitably caused the noisy grounding of the bottom of the car!

Luckily, we made it to the mine without any serious problems.

I'd decided the workers' first task would be to start clearing the proposed mining site of thorn bushes, and collect all the cement blocks, old metal sheets and bits of rusty equipment that were strewn over an area of many thousands of square metres.

My first task, which proved to be anything but easy, was to get these instructions over to the workers.

Langton understood 'funny galore' (a South African mining language. 'Fanagalo'/Pidgin English), and, by using the odd English words, coupled with pointing, various other gesticulations and facial expressions, it all helped to get my message across, but oh, so very slowly – it was like playing charades with a deaf old auntie!

Well, I certainly would have to learn the local Ndebele native language quickly, and get a boss boy who spoke reasonable English; otherwise, the sun would begin to set each day *before* I'd been able to give the workers their daily tasks!

With further flaying arms – looking like a traffic policeman in rush hour – I 'told' them they could use anything lying around to build a rough shelter in one of the old ruined buildings. This would suffice for a night or two – there being no possibility of any rain with the severe drought – until they had built their own hut with a grass roof.

Before I left, I told Langton he must stay on the mine site while I was away and not to go 'walkies', except to look for water.

After many gesticulations, eventually, by using the old 'walking fingers' idea, I got through to him – when at last a big grin spread across his up-to-then-puzzled-looking face!

With the Jackson problem in mind, I wrote a note stating that Langton and the two helpers were officially working for our mine on our claims registered with the Bulawayo Mines Department, and 'told' Langton that he must show this note to any man who came and wanted to know why they were living here and clearing the site.

. . .

The next day, I made the Midland Hotel my 'office' so that I could phone several mines at various locations across the country regarding second-hand mining equipment: 5-stamp mills, James Tables, hoists and some other smaller items.

It proved extremely difficult to get through to anyone; most mines were in the remoter bush areas on joint party lines, which always seemed to be busy with other people and other conversations!

The only success from a whole day's phoning was the Horn Mine in Gwanda, where a 5-stamp mill was for sale.

So, after a frustrating day, I was pleased to see two smiling little faces peering through the window at me.

"Come and have your big beer with Mummy on the terrace!" Marie-Louise shouted – naturally, one has to obey such forceful commands!

And that was the start of a nice, relaxing evening…

. . .

On Thursday morning, I used the general dealer's card to get supplies and some food for Langton's gang, and drove down to Fort Rixon.

I was hoping to see them busily toiling away in the sun, but, when I arrived at the mine, there was not a soul to be seen anywhere.

Jesus, what now, I thought, as I started to look around the site….

Several minutes had passed by; nobody around… then, suddenly, Langton appeared warily from the bush and beckoned to the other two to come out.

"Shit! What have you all been doing? Nothing has been cleared at all; what's the problem?" I asked him testily.

Langton, looking around nervously, began to tell me in his broken English that they had started collecting and stacking the cement blocks when a Jeep pulled up, and a man with a gun told them to get off his land!

"Did you show him the letter I left with you?"

"No, no, we plenty scared! He told us go! Go! Shot the gun in the air! We ran into the bush. At night, we sleep here in that building, and in the morning we go back to the bush and wait for you!" Langton babbled on.

I was fast beginning to realise that another huge time consumer for me, besides the daily driving, would be 'communications':

Getting my instructions through to the African workers.

Getting through to speak to people on these joint party lines.

And trying to get through as well to Jackson, to defuse a rapidly escalating series of disputes!

"Okay Langton, carry on with clearing up; I'll go and see Jackson now."

When I arrived at his house, I was told that unfortunately Mr Jackson and his wife had gone to Salisbury for a few days. So I left a note for him, with a copy for the mining commissioner, whom I would be seeing on Friday.

Dear Mr Jackson, please do not intimidate my African workers by firing a gun to scare them away. They are legally on our mining location.

I have instructed them to cut poles and grass, enough to build 10 huts.

When I get back from South Africa to live permanently on the mine, we can meet up and discuss any issues regarding timber and water usage.

Ridge Top Mine, Manager.

cc: Mining Commissioner, Bulawayo.

At the mine, I told Langton that Jackson would not be coming back again, and added that they should cut poles and grass to build the huts, as well as finish clearing the mine site completely while I was away in South Africa.

We unloaded the food, mealie meal and other rations, and I gave him Ray's phone number, in case of an emergency – it would take a big problem to get them to walk the 12 kilometres to the Fort Rixon phone booth!

By the time I arrived back in Gwelo, it was already getting late – another day had just shot by. I could see that this 'driving to work' each day was going to eat up my time, until I could actually live on the mine as planned.

There was a message for me at the Midland Hotel from Joseph, saying that he would be back in Rhodesia on Friday in time for our meeting with the mining commissioner at 11am.

However, he would have to return to Jo'burg afterwards, because, unfortunately, Jane would have to stay there another two weeks to complete her treatment; when he would bring her and she would stay with his mother on the family Belingwe mine.

. . .

The following day started on a good note; Joseph and I pulled up in front of the Mines Department at the same time – and on time!

Amazingly enough, the mining commissioner was a little friendlier towards us too, especially after I gave him a copy of the Jackson 'shotgun' letter.

"Yes, it would be a good idea for us all to meet together with Jackson; we need to sort out these 'teething' disputes and problems, and also to get to know each other a little better."

"But he was going to shoot our workers!" Joseph burst out. "He should be locked up!"

A swift kick in the shins would have shut him up – if Ray had been present! But, miraculously, not another word came out of Joseph's mouth; it was as if he sensed that his father was present – there in spirit!

"Well, any further help we can give you," the mining commissioner continued, "just let Cummins or Curtis know, especially if it's to do with equipment. If you can locate any second-hand items you need for your mine, Cummins will visit to check the condition of the items. We would purchase any good equipment, lease it to you and you would pay us a monthly amount.

"This helps cut down on your initial capital costs – it's an expensive undertaking reopening an old mine, as you'll no doubt find out! And when you are permanently settled on the mine, I can explain another financial help that you can apply for, called a mine development loan. Note, I said '*apply for*' – it is not guaranteed!"

We thanked him for his time and advice, and went down to see Ronnie, to ask him to visit and check on the 5-stamp mill that I'd located at the Horn mine, Gwanda, and, if it was in good working order, would he set up the necessary lease/hire monthly agreement for us.

As we left the building, we both felt pleased that the meeting with the mining commissioner had gone well, and that he had realised that some of Jackson's complaints were rather malicious and unfounded.

We visited Barclays Bank to check on the procedures and which documents would be required for importing the mobile compressor from South Africa.

We were told that we'd have to pre-pay (in South African rand) the full rail freight charges to Rhodesia, including onward delivery to the Mines Department in Bulawayo, for inspection and clearance.

Once the goods arrive in Bulawayo, we should come back to the bank with the South African Railways freight papers, together with the SA export documentation, so that an application could be made to the Central Bank of Rhodesia for an import licence, which would enable us to clear the goods and pay the appropriate Customs duty.

Joseph sped off to spend the night at Matt's place, while I cruised back to Gwelo – yet another day gone, but, as with everything in life, one has to take things one day at a time – and one document at a time too, it would seem!

Always Expect the Unexpected…

Early the next morning, Joseph pulled up in front of our caravan at 5am sharp! And this time we really did make our first 'bona fide early morning-start' to drive down to South Africa.

We made very good time, and were both pleasantly surprised when we reached the Beitbridge border just after eleven.

We crossed over the Limpopo River, which looked even muddier than on the last trip, and took the road south heading for Jo'burg.

Joseph would stay with Jane until she was well enough to travel, when he would bring her and their belongings up to Rhodesia.

I would see Jaap Engelbrecht to collect the 'serviced' white Peugeot pick-up and drive it back up to Gwelo loaded with some of our furniture.

With the two of us alternating between driving and snoozing, it was the perfect recipe to get to Jane's place in time for supper.

After some tasteless spaghetti, I was feeling pretty knackered and left the two of them 'lovey doving'; I had politely turned down the invitation of instant black coffee, in flavour of – I mean 'in favour of' – instant black-out!

. . .

After an unappetising breakfast of burnt toast and coffee, Joseph drove me over to the East Geduld mine to see Jaap Engelbrecht.

The white pick-up from the auction looked like the workhorse we needed; not pretty – with a few dents and rusty patches – but, when Jaap started it up, it ran sweetly, albeit noisily.

"Purring like an angry leopard about to pounce!" he shouted above the noise. "That's a tough vehicle; it'll last you years, eh!"

We agreed to meet him again at the next auction, when hopefully we'd acquire some more bargains – with his help.

"*Tot ziens*, man!" Jaap shouted. "You look after that purring 'snow leopard', eh man!"

Joseph and I left and went our separate ways.

I drove off to see Malcolm and Eve, who lived a mere 20 minutes away.

We were so pleased to see each other again, and, although it was only a few weeks ago that we'd left to go up to Rhodesia, there was such a lot to tell – weeks packed full of exciting images and new experiences: places, partners, gold mines, the bush and some real old characters… and to tell them about all the troubles with Jackson, the cattle rancher bent on stopping us from mining for gold on his land – would it be constant confrontation and conflict, like in the musical, *Why Can't the Cowboys and the Miners be Friends?*

Or would there be an amicable way to coexist – on the same small 'dot' on Planet Earth?

They found all the stories quite amazing, and in this day and age too.

"It's like reading a novel about life in the last century!" Malcolm declared. "It's really mind-boggling!"

We talked on for many hours about the 'Rhodesian saga' update – sustained by ample food and drink – and we were only cut short by the sudden surprise of the sunrise!

Wearily, I levered myself into a bed, but with grave doubts that I'd be able to wake up before sunset!

. . .

But children have other ideas, and they soon found a way to prise their uncle out of his rest nest!

Three mugs of hot strong black coffee got enough caffeine into my system to allow me to climb back into my 'new' white pick-up – aptly named the Snow Leopard by Jaap – and drive over to Windsor Park to our old Letaba home, and visit my good friend and neighbour, Terry.

It was another long, enjoyable evening recounting recent events – a curtain call of the previous session with Malcolm and Eve – finishing late and dutifully 'nightcapped' as bed beckoned.

. . .

After a really refreshing sleep and an energy packed egg and bacon breakfast, Terry and I drove over to Jacques' garage and started loading some of my furniture; a very bulky Kiaat wood king-size bed, the kids' beds and boxes full of the basic things that we would need when we moved out of the caravan and into a house in Gwelo Town.

The packing boxes were stacked high, draped with a huge thick black plastic sheet over the lot, and firmly secured with ropes. The pick-up was transformed in shape, now resembling a small lorry!

I thanked Terry and said I'd be back down in Jo'burg within two weeks in the Volvo 122S – the car he wanted and had agreed to buy from me.

Tokoloshe

I left the northern suburbs of Johannesburg and headed for the border.

With such a heavily laden pick-up, the progress was slow, but steady, and I hoped that I'd be able to make it to the border before darkness descended.

About 10 km from Louis Trichardt, I saw an old Mercedes on the side of the road. A young, well-dressed African woman standing next to the crashed car waved me down.

She told me that she had been feeling sleepy on the long drive from Johannesburg, and must have dozed off; luckily, neither she nor her young son had been injured.

She said her father was a chief of a district near the border, and she would pay me to give her a lift there.

I refused to accept her money, but said I would take her, and the three of us drove off towards Beitbridge.

I pulled into the garage at Louis Trichardt to fill up the pick-up with diesel.

As I climbed out, a heavy thump on my shoulder almost knocked me over.

"Hey, how'sit man, you've come back up this way again, eh!" exclaimed none other than Hendrik.

"*Ja, baie dankie*, how'sit with you, man?" I replied. "Sorry I won't be able to stay tonight at your hotel, but I've got to make it to the border before dark."

Then he glanced into the cab of the pick-up, and, on seeing the black African woman and her coloured son, he exclaimed, "Ooh! Talking of darkness, even in my hotel you can't eat 'royal game', sorry man! But have a good trip!" He snorted as he turned and walked away.

A few kilometres from Messina, the African woman asked me to stop at a dirt road turn-off that led to her father's village – the young boy immediately jumped out and went running off down the track, skipping and springing into the air like an impala.

She turned to me smiling and said that she wanted to give me something for my kindness, then, leaning forward, she began to unbutton her white blouse, revealing her naked breasts. My gasp startled her, but she laughed as she carefully removed a leather necklace with a small wooden pendant that was nestling in the cleavage of her full bust, and rebuttoned her blouse.

"Wear this; it will always protect you and your manhood from the evil spirits of the 'Tokoloshe' – it has been blessed by my uncle, the witchdoctor," she explained in perfect English, and handed me the necklace. The pendant was a beautifully carved male phallic symbol.

We shook hands; she blessed me for helping her, a total stranger, and walked off, calling out to her son, who was now a mere speck in the distance.

I reckoned it was still about a 20-minute drive flat out to reach Beitbridge, so I put my foot down hard on the accelerator pedal and 'roared off' – although the sound was less 'lion-like' and actually more like the purr of a leopard, just as Jaap had said.

I got through the South African Customs with just minutes to spare before the barrier came down. It was almost closing time and the officials didn't show much interest in me or my fully loaded pick-up.

On the Rhodesian side, the paperwork was hastily completed before they also happily waved me on through, with that 'thank God it's the end of the day' look, and I drove over to the guesthouse run by Brian's auntie. She told me that he was still on border duty, so it turned out to be a quiet, restful break, and a very good night's sleep – which I badly needed!

. . .

Up simultaneously with the sun and on the road again even before the birds were looking for their early morning worms.

This white Peugeot 404 diesel pick-up of mine, masquerading as a small lorry, just chugged and chugged on steadily at 100 km per hour. I was pleasantly surprised at the 'pulling power' (torque) of the diesel engine, as it ate up kilometre after kilometre – both the hills as well as the flat stretches with unhurried ease: West Nicholson, Gwanda, Bulawayo, Shangani, Gwelo, Que Que and Gatooma all flashed by, quickly disappearing from my rear-view mirror, and now I was approaching the turn-off to Hartley, and then on to Cain's mine, where I would be storing this first load of my furniture.

Unfortunately, Cain was not at home, but Zikke, beaming from ear to ear and tugging at his 'moustache', was a wonderful, welcome sight. This small African was 'Mr Hospitality'. I was shown my room, given a bowl of hot water for washing, and later on the veranda he brought me a cold beer and a bowl of game stew to eat… followed by hot black coffee, 'with a top of whisky to help you sleep, boss'!

. . .

The resonating gong alarm at 5:30am – a sound that I would soon be getting used to on our own mine – announced to the workers exactly the same message as the Zikke early morning greeting of 'up, up, up – work, work'!

After breakfast, I drove the pick-up around to the veranda, and started unloading my furniture and packing boxes with the help of two other workers, Mobil and Philemon; everything was carefully unloaded and stacked in a small storeroom there.

One last cup of coffee before driving off to Gwelo – you could say that 'coffee' and 'driving off-ie' were already becoming 'synonymous' in my new driving/mining life!

At the caravan, I received a mixed welcome – Jeffrey was laughing his head off and cuddling me all the time; Marie-Louise just stood back, with a resentful look on her face.

"You upset Neville; you didn't say goodbye and you just drove off while we were sleeping!" she stated gruffly and stamped her feet. (God, girls seem to become women when they reach the tender age of four years old!)

To laze around for a couple of hours was great, playing with the kids, on the swings, kicking a football and hide and seek…

After looking all over the caravan park, Marie-Louise did not find it funny at all to be told by her mother that, if she wanted to find me, she should try the Midland Hotel terrace. Well, what better a place to hide on a hot day, with the added attraction of that cold 'magic potion' to cool me down being close at hand! When she finally found me, and saw a waiter bringing a cold strawberry milkshake over to her, well, her sad-looking mouth quickly turned from an 'n' into a 'u' – she was all smiles again!

An early evening braai of lamb chops and boerewors was enjoyed by us all – who stayed up the latest? I don't know… but it certainly wasn't me!

. . .

The following day, I spent most of the time in my Midland Hotel 'office' phoning and planning for the next week by setting up various appointments; in Fort Rixon (Ian Davidson), in Bulawayo (Curtis, Mines Department) and the Shell depot (L.T.R. de Ziel, sales manager). I also contacted three other mines about 5-stamp mills and James Tables – it was so much easier, and nicer for a change, covering hundreds of kilometres in a day 'on the phone', instead of sitting in a metal sauna box on wheels!

And, after the phone session, only having to walk a mere 200 metres back to the caravan park and enjoy a lovely, lazy, long weekend – nothing planned, nothing to do and nowhere to go!

. . .

Monday changed all that! I leapt into the white pick-up and headed for Fort Rixon to meet Joseph – if he remembered to come back from SA!

When I swung off the tarmac road and onto the dirt road – oh, what a difference! The higher suspension of the pick-up took the bumps and dips in its stride. I could look at the scenery now as I drove, instead of keeping my eyes fixed on the road ahead scanning for ruts and potholes as I had to do when I was driving in the Volvo, with its low road clearance.

First stop was the administration office in Fort Rixon to meet Ian Davidson; he looked to be a genial old fellow, sitting behind a wobbly looking desk piled high with folders and papers.

He lifted his head, pushed his small, round wire-framed glasses back further onto his nose, and politely enquired, rhetorically, "You must surely be one of the young fellows up from South Africa who are opening up the old Claremont mine; correct?"

Before I could answer, he just carried on talking to himself as he fumbled with one of the piles of folders. "Oh, here they are; fill in this form for a PO Box, and this one to apply for a telephone line – both essential means of keeping in touch with the wicked outside world, eh?"

He chuckled as he continued 'playing cards' with numerous papers, quite oblivious to the fact that I was still standing in front of him. After a couple of minutes watching this 'Pickwickian' type scene, I politely excused myself and went off to meet Joseph at our mine.

When I arrived, he was sitting in the shade of a big tree, drinking tea.

He bubbled with excitement, spurting out all the news and events of the last ten days – in five minutes flat! Joseph had brought Jane and their personal goods up to Belingwe, where she would stay with his mother until I could sort out a house in Gwelo for all of us together.

We spent some time fully discussing the plans for the coming two weeks.

He would go back down to SA, deposit the cheques that I gave him and draw some cash that we would need for the coming auction sale. He'd also go and see Jaap Engelbrecht and get a list from him of the chosen 'good condition' equipment that we should bid for.

I would drive down in my Volvo and meet him on Sunday at 12 midday in 'La Catina', opposite our old office in Johannesburg, so that we could prepare for the auction, and also make a list of outstanding things that would have to be completed before finally leaving South Africa for good and driving back up to Rhodesia for the very last time with the rest of my goods and any further items we bought at the next auction sale.

I wished Joseph a safe trip and went to speak with Langton, Gwabuya and Nduna to check on their progress. They had cleared the area of thorn bushes, concrete blocks were stacked neatly and all the metal was piled in a heap, but there were no cords of wood or grass bundles to build the huts, which I had instructed them to cut first! (Ray had told me, even warned me, that, if you are not around all the time, don't be surprised about anything; they will do things in the order they want – and at a snail's pace!)

I went and marked out an area of flat ground about 200 metres from the mine; this would be our new 'mine village'. My first official act as 'town planner' was to designate that the 'high street' went straight through the middle of the area, and I told Langton to build 10 huts (Phase One) on the left… or was it the right? Confusion! Well, we were facing each other, silly buggers, so it was back to Policeman Peter's sign language again – my finger pointing to the appropriate designated section of this new 'housing estate'.

We unloaded a sack of mealie meal and some other food rations. I told Langton that, whilst I was away in South Africa, Boss Ray would call by every couple of days to drop off their meat rations and to check on the progress of building the huts in our village.

I then hurried back to Gwelo for a late appointment with an estate agent, who had shown me a three-bedroom bungalow in Lundi Park. It was a good size, built on a quarter-acre plot with a garden front and back, big enough for both families to live in.

I signed the lease for six months. This would give Jane plenty of time to have her baby and spend the first few months bringing up the child in an urban house – with all the normal comforts of electricity, hot water, local shops, fresh milk and food, her doctor and the hospital nearby – before she and Joseph would move to the mine at Fort Rixon nearer to Easter time.

My family would only stay in this Gwelo house for a month or so, whilst our new home on the mine was being built, and then we'd move into the 'super-shack' before Christmas – with or without a roof. Apparently, there was a shortage of corrugated iron sheets in Rhodesia; they were as rare as 'the bird of Zimbabwe's teeth', Cain had told me.

. . .

The next morning, I met with Martin Curtis in Bulawayo, and he showed me around the Mines Department offices and storage yards and explained the procedures for leasing/hiring the equipment. Hopefully, he would soon locate the machines we required and transport them to our mine.

He gave me the names of two reliable transport companies to use, and the phone contacts of half a dozen timber companies that supply gum poles and cut timber.

When we ordered from these various forest locations, the timber would be railed down to Shangani Railhead Depot.

We would have to collect it in, or rather on our pick-ups and drive the 50-odd kilometres on dirt roads back to the mine – sometimes it could be two or even three trips for a big load of wood!

I made acquaintance with several other colleagues of his, including Bob Slabbert (chief surveyor) and Gerry Garland (mining engineer).

"Do you play snooker?" Gerry enquired. "'Cos if so, the four of us can go to the Post Office Club for a pub lunch and play a few frames of snooker – that gives us a nice break from the office, and is a good relaxing way to get to know each other, I always find."

After a very enjoyable and instructive lunch break, they went back to their office, and I drove to meet the sales manager of the Shell depot, Leo de Ziel.

We discussed the estimated monthly diesel usage that we would require when the mine was fully operational. He recommended that we take two storage drum units of 5,000 litres each. I should phone him when we had made a site ready for these storage tanks, which could then be delivered and erected by Shell, 'free of charge' – three words that were music to my ears! Once they were in place, our first delivery of ordered diesel fuel could be delivered by road. Shell had a weekly delivery route when a tanker lorry would visit ranches and mines in our area.

The week was disappearing fast and there was much to do before I left for South Africa at the weekend, so, early on Wednesday morning, Marianne and I drove up to Cain's mine in Hartley to collect our stored furniture. We would now be able to move it straight into our new Gwelo house when we got back later in the afternoon.

Green Mamba

This seemed such a short trip in comparison to some of my recent 'Rho-SA' journeys, and, in a flash, we pulled up at the house on Cain's gold mine. Zikke rushed and opened the door for Marianne.

"Welcome, welcome, welcome! Wife of British Mdevu!" He excitedly rattled off the words, beaming from ear to ear. "Come, come, come Madam, tea, tea, tea!"

We went through onto the large veranda, and Zikke served us with tea and biscuits. He produced from his pocket two old, well-worn postcards; one was of Queen Victoria of the British Empire, and the other a post card of Buckingham Palace. "That's in London, England!" he proudly stated, and went off and fetched the key to unlock the storeroom.

The light was not working, but I could see well enough; our furniture was near the open door. I pulled hard to slide the heavy Kiaat wood double bed into the doorway, and went to get the pick-up and drive it around to the veranda for loading. Zikke called two others, Mobil and Philemon, to help get our stuff out of the storeroom.

I had hardly reached the kitchen when an excited Zikke pushed past me, shouting, "Danger, danger, danger! A big snake! Bad snake!" Seconds later, he came rushing back the other way with a long wooden stick, and I followed him quickly out onto the veranda.

My eyes quickly soaked up the scene: two wide-eyed Africans staring at the bed, which was lying against the wall with a leg broken off; Marianne with a surprised look on her face; and a thin green slither of a snake protruding out from under the bed.

I was just about to shout out 'shit! You've broken my favourite bed because of this tidily little grass snake' when Zikke struck quickly with the big stick, smashing down hard – whoosh! Surprisingly, a thicker coil of the snake appeared. Zikke struck several times, harder and quicker, and, in seconds, there were only the smashed remains of a one-and-a-half metre-long green mamba – one of the deadliest poisonous snakes of Rhodesia!

Zikke scooped up the dead snake on the end of the stick and quickly, but nervously, ran back through to the kitchen, shouting, "Mdevu! Come, come – come outside!"

I followed him into the yard, where the hot water boiler was situated. He opened the furnace lid and threw the snake into the burning wood fire.

"You evil, evil snake! Burn, burn, burn!" He turned to me and said, "We burn bad snake; snake's wife doesn't know he was here; she won't come to bite us!"

We returned to the veranda, where the two Africans still stood, mouths gaping and staring at the broken bed, and Marianne explained to me exactly what had happened.

When I had slid the bed out of the storeroom, I must have awoken the green mamba, which was probably coiled up in the springs. Mobil had taken over from me, and, together with Philemon, they struggled to pull the heavy bed out of the store, lifted it up and awkwardly came onto the veranda.

It was then that Mobil felt something moving against his chest, which was pressed up against the bed. The snake had started slowly uncoiling itself, the coils now becoming visible, when at the same time both he and Marianne shouted, "Snake!" Whereupon Mobil, with that strength born from sudden fear, tossed the heavy bed in the air away from himself, and it fell against the wall, breaking off one of the legs!

"Jesus, Mobil had a close call there!" I exclaimed. "He could well have been a 'goner'! Zikke, let's have a break; let everyone calm down, and get these two some water to drink. Looking at their shocked faces, I think they need it!"

Suddenly, Mobil, looking very grey and frightened, fell to the floor, shaking violently, his eyes rolling back in their sockets, leaving two white 'marbles' staring at us! He started convulsing, his body twitching, jerking up and down as he slowly slid across the floor in a snake-like movement – then silence, and he lay there motionless. Zikke told us not to touch him…. After a few minutes, he began shouting and making weird noises, and suddenly jumped up and rushed off screaming wildly at the top of his voice.

Zikke translated for us. Mobil was convinced that someone had put a curse on him – or perhaps even on Mdevu himself – and the Tokoloshe had turned into a deadly snake, ready to kill to fulfil the curse. He would not work at this mine any longer; he was going back home to his parents' village!

After all the excitement had died down, we found a replacement for Mobil and carried on loading the rest of the furniture onto my pick-up – albeit in a more careful, quieter, restrained mood, with troubled looks on our faces. The green mamba could easily have bitten either Mobil or myself, with possible fatal results! That was an extremely close call.

We had just finished loading my pick-up when Cain arrived and came onto the veranda to greet us. On hearing what had happened, he explained to us how scared the Africans are of the Tokoloshe and the curse of the witchdoctors! Even amongst the well-educated Africans of Southern Africa, many have an instilled, inbuilt fear of the Tokoloshe.

I told him about the African woman I'd given a lift to on my way up from Jo'burg, and showed him my pendant.

"Ooooh, that's great… if the munts see that around your neck, they'll know you've been protected by a witchdoctor… and they will be very wary, even scared of you!"

Zikke, on seeing the pendant, immediately started shouting and laughing nervously. "Mdevu is protected from the Tokoloshe; that's why the snake didn't bite him!"

Over a late lunch, we learnt a lot more of the role and the power of the witchdoctor in the African society, and of his 'hit man', the Tokoloshe – no wonder the early missionaries in these parts had such a hard time in spreading the word about Christianity. How could a distant queen in England and Jesus up in the sky have more spiritual power in Africa than the local African witchdoctor and his Tokoloshe!

The excitement, and the intriguing stories at an end, Marianne and I bade our farewells and headed back to Gwelo. We drove slowly over the dirt roads, because not only were we heavily laden with all the furniture, but Cain had also strapped some extra equipment that Matt needed on top of everything in the back of our pick-up.

There had been no drought in this district of Hartley – not like the three-year drought in Matabeleland – and the tracks were very muddy and slippery. The overloaded pick-up slithered all over the place, and at one point finally slid off the edge of the track altogether, and we were stuck in the soft mud on the side.

A vehicle coming from the other direction saw our plight and pulled up. "Hello Ma'am, can I help? Oh, it's you, young man!" Henk uttered with a surprised expression. "Nice that you have come back to Rhodesia to start your gold mining. And I see you've still got a hell of a lot to learn about driving on these bush roads."

He hooked up a tow rope to our pick-up and slowly pulled us out of the ditch and back onto the centre of the dirt track.

"Now we'll let your tyres down a lot; that way, you've got more rubber on the road, which will give you a better grip on these muddy tracks. Go slowly; it's only another few kilometres to the main road, where there's a petrol station where you can pump some air back into those tyres, so you can drive safely and quicker on the Salisbury-Bulawayo tarmac road. Good luck with your mining venture – you're down in Fort Rixon, Cain told us. And make sure you call into the pub and see us next time you're around Hartley – there'll be a 'virgin pint' on the bar waiting for you!" He laughed.

That help and advice from Henk was really appreciated, and, with another 'trick' learnt, we set off to our new house in Gwelo.

. . .

Over the next few days, we were busy as hell, moving into the new house. First the stereo system had to be set up, so that we could have good music blaring out – to ease the pain of moving in! When you're listening to your favourite singers, like *John Denver*, *The Rolling Stones* and *Demis Rousseau*, time just flies by, and it makes moving much more fun….

After three hectic days of carrying, lifting, shifting, moving and shoving furniture around, the song *It's Been a Hard Day's Night, and I've been working like a dog* by *The Beatles* seemed very appropriate, and, with everything finally in place, we could relax on the settees and enjoy an evening of self-indulgence!

. . .

But oh, Saturday morning; what a struggle to get out of bed. But I had to, to start my long two-day drive down to South Africa to meet Joseph in Johannesburg at lunchtime on the Sunday.

I climbed into my Volvo for this last trip, as I had agreed to sell it to my mate, Terry, in Jo'burg. On the tarmac roads, I could cruise at higher speeds and much more comfortably than in the Peugeot pick-up, but that was temporarily short-lived. I had reached the Shangani turn-off and was back on the dirt roads again, heading for Fort Rixon – I had to drive more carefully here, keeping an eye out for bad pot-holed sections of the murram track, but still, it was enjoyable to travel slowly through the bush, so appealing to me.

Langton and the other workers were surprised to see me and leapt to their feet, trying to hide their cigarettes behind their backs, but soon realised that the tell-tale cigarette smoke wafting up from behind their heads had spoilt their ruse!

I brushed aside the 'we have tea break – we work hard' comments and told them that Boss Ray would be along shortly, and would come by regularly to check on their progress. I was beginning to learn that a little white lie often does the trick to keep them on their toes!

After repeating to them the jobs that had to be completed while I was away, it was back on the dirt road again, direction Filabusi. It was hot and sunny. I felt in a great mood and was whistling away to myself whilst keeping a wary eye on the dirt track ahead. But, as I came around one corner…

THUMP!

I wasn't quick enough to avoid a large pothole and the Volvo had 'bottomed out' with a loud thump, followed by an annoying clattering sound – like tin cans being dragged behind a newlyweds vehicle; the exhaust system was completely buggered!

On jacking up the vehicle, I took off what was left of the silencer box and wired the rest of the exhaust pipes to the chassis.

As I revved up, the Volvo engine now sounded more like a tractor, and I literally 'chugged' off – this was a noise I would soon be getting very used to when constantly driving in the diesel pick-ups.

From Filabusi, however, it would be smoother driving. I would be on tarmac roads again, all the way down to Johannesburg – some 900 km away.

. . .

I stayed the night at Beitbridge, and, after a good night's sleep, crossed over the border early and made my way quickly – but not quietly! – taking the road leading south, down to Johannesburg.

It was just as much pleasure as on my first trip to drive across these vast open spaces, and especially to watch the kite birds again, gliding effortlessly, floating in the clear blue sky.

I had become intrigued with these birds and had read some delightfully engrossing articles about them. A yellow-billed kite can see an object that appears 10 times closer than we humans can see it, and, coupled with their ability to magnify the centre of their visual field, the bird can concentrate completely on the targeted small animal in the middle of its sight. It is not distracted by any surrounding bush vegetation or other movements on the ground as it swoops down and grabs the prey in its claws, before sweeping back up into the sky again.

Just before noon, I pulled up right in front of La Cantina. I was amazed that there were so many empty parking spaces – but, of course, it was a Sunday!

Joseph was sitting on the terrace and called out to me. "It feels so strange to sit here and look at the old office across the road; so much has happened in the last few weeks, I can't even remember the difference between 'computer bits and computer bytes'!"

"I can!" I retorted. "But it's the 'food bites' that I need now, and more than a few 'bits' – I'm starving!" I immediately ordered a large pizza and a pint of cold lager.

After a short break whilst I devoured the food, we discussed our plans.

Joseph showed me a list of items that Jaap Engelbrecht had identified as potential 'good buys' for us at the auction the next day. Great, it included another second hand Peugeot 404, so, together with a new 404 that I would be buying, and Joseph's blue one, that would make three pick-ups that we had with us here in Johannesburg – enough to carry any mining equipment we bought at the auction and the rest of my furniture and goods back to Rhodesia. I was very pleased and relieved to realise now that I would not have to make yet another round – 'SA-Rho' trip solely to collect any remaining furniture – phew!

Joseph gave me a wad of bank notes that he'd drawn from the bank on cashing my cheque; hopefully, it would be enough to bid for all the items we wanted at the auction.

We parted ways, and I drove off towards Windsor to stay the night with Terry, when I would show him the 'modified' Volvo – the agreed sales price would have to be adjusted downwards to allow for a new replacement exhaust system, of course!

. . .

Monday morning, I drove the Volvo to East Geduld and met Joseph and Jaap in the yard of the auction warehouse.

"*Goeiemore!* Well maties, there's not so much buyers here today, eh, so you 'ookies' might well be in luck and get what you want for less money than normal, eh? But I have to leave you on your own now to do the bidding, as the auction is about to start. Remember what I told you – before you start bidding on an item, agree the highest price that you would pay for it, and stick to it! Don't get carried away with the excitement of auction bidding, eh!"

So Joseph and I noted down the 'wanted' items: the grey second-hand Peugeot pick-up, a hoist with full accessories, and a five-ton block and tackle; we also agreed on the maximum price we would bid for each of these items.

Well, it was indeed quite exciting bidding at an auction for the first time, and the grey diesel 404 pick-up and the hoist were successfully bid for – and at slightly less than our top limit, so we were pretty chuffed!

The block and tackle was next up. I looked around, but Joseph had wandered off somewhere and I couldn't see him – so I put in a low opening bid. Another man raised it. I bid again and waited. The auctioneer was saying, "Going for the last time…"

"I'll raise it another 50!" Someone at the back of the room shouted out a new bid – shit! That voice belonged to none other than bloody Joseph!

The auctioneer stated, "Going, going, gone!" Down came the hammer with a thump, and it was all ours – but 50 wasted notes!

Jaap bellowed across at Joseph, "*Stomme Lul!*" If you really want to know what that means, look it up in the Afrikaans dictionary… and you'll see how appropriate those two words were!

"Jesus, why the bloody hell did you outbid me? It was already ours!" I angrily demanded of Joseph.

"Well. I went to the toilet, and when I came back into the auction room I saw the auctioneer was about to bang his hammer down to end the bidding, and, as I couldn't see you, and as it was still below our 'ceiling', I raised it another 50!"

Speechless! Absolutely speechless; what more can you say to a man who believes in his own confused 'Irish' logic! Exasperating, and I thought, *hey, this Joseph has got to be watched day and night if we're going to make it through the critical first three months to get our gold mine operational.*

We settled the auction payments with cash, were given our receipts and told to come back the next day to collect our goods.

"Never mind, eh! I'll be at the warehouse *all day* tomorrow, especially for you, Joseph!" Jaap laughed as he clapped him on the shoulder.

"But it's not my fault, is it?" Joseph said to me. "I had to go to the toilet, *didn't I!*"

Sometimes, it's better when you're dumbstruck just to keep quiet, because, the more you challenge such 'logic' – if that's the right word – the more ridiculous the situation becomes.

. . .

The next day, Terry drove me in his 'newly acquired' Volvo 122S over to East Geduld so that I could collect our 'newly acquired' pick-up and goods from the auction warehouse.

Jaap was really looking after us; he had already loaded everything onto the grey Peugeot 404 diesel pick-up for me.

"And I've thrown in a dozen old hurricane lamps – they were on your list, but for some reason they were not auctioned yesterday," he said with a wink! "Good luck with your gold mining venture – with a partner like that, you're really going to need it, eh!" Jaap merrily exclaimed. "Come back and see me again eh – when you're a millionaire!"

My one remaining task was to buy a brand new Peugeot 404 diesel pick-up; both Joseph and I had driven around to various car dealers in different parts of the Johannesburg suburbs, but they all gave us delivery dates of two to three weeks – far too long to wait with our tight schedules.

We were contemplating the unpalatable alternative of having to make yet a further 'SA-Rho' round trip just to collect a pick-up, when Joseph heard of a hail-damaged Peugeot pick-up in Florida, West Rand, where he used to live.

I immediately drove over to see the dealer, who showed me the vehicle; there were a dozen or so small dents in both the bonnet and the cab roof. Florida lies in the 'hail belt', and sometimes the hail stones can be as big as chicken eggs, so garage owners normally make sure that the vehicles are either inside in the showrooms or outside under strong netting – obviously not the case with this beige pick-up that I was looking at!

To me, though, the damage was really only superficial, and, more importantly, the pick-up could be available in 24 hours; and, when the dealer offered me a 15% 'damage' discount, the deal was struck! Everything was falling into place – 'timeously'!

. . .

Joseph picked me up at Terry's place the next day, and we drove over to the SAR transport office (South African Railways) – which was under the main Johannesburg Railway Station – to fix up the paperwork for the mobile compressor that was bought at the first East Geduld mining auction.

This large green machine, weighing two and a half tons, would be collected by road transport from Jaap's warehouse and railed from Jo'burg Station up to Bulawayo, for onward shipment to the Mines Department Yard c/o R. Cummins.

We prepaid the full costs of road and rail transport from East Geduld, South Africa to Bulawayo, Rhodesia.

With that last main job out of the way, Joseph took me over to Florida to collect my brand-new, beige Peugeot 404 diesel pick-up – with the slight 'dimpled effect' body modifications!

We agreed to meet the following day at Windsor Park to collect the rest of my furniture and boxes from Jacques' garage, and get it all loaded onto the three available Peugeot pick-ups that we now had at our disposal, ready for the long haul back up to Rhodesia – the last long haul, thankfully.

. . .

After a 'black coffee' breakfast, Terry and I gingerly made our way over to Jacques' garage, unlocked the door and began to figure out how we could best 'spread' the furniture and boxes between the three vehicles – there was actually more than enough for four 'normal' loads!

Our ideas and 'solutions' were quickly confused by the sudden new arrivals, Malcolm and Eve, and a bright-eyed, bushy-tailed Joseph – and then confusion reigned!

A grumpy, clearly 'suffering' Terry stepped in and said – forcibly – that this bickering was not doing his hangover any good at all, and, as a neutral, he would allocate several bits of furniture to each of the three pick-ups, which could be topped up from the mountain of packing boxes.

Tacit agreement was followed by the 'beavering-away' five of us steadily whittling down the number of boxes in the garage.

It took a few hours, a few mishaps, a few laughs – and a good few cold beers to help cool us down on such a hot sunny day – before everything was finally loaded and firmly secured on the three Peugeot pick-ups.

Around midday, there was a mass exodus of people driving in different-coloured vehicles: Joseph (blue + Load 1), Eve (beige + Load 2), myself (grey + Load 3) and Malcolm in his Citroen station wagon (green + empty beer crates!).

Joseph would head off straight away for the Rhodesian border and stay overnight somewhere on the way up.

Eve and I would leave the next morning after a good night's rest and drive at a more leisurely pace, as she was not used to driving long distances – and certainly not in such a heavily laden pick-up.

She had decided to take her young daughter, Sarah, with her for company, and that little chatterbox would definitely help her to stay awake when the temperatures soared later in the day, when drivers became prone to 'SSS' – Spanish Siesta Syndrome! Symptoms are instant heavy eyes, followed by an uncontrollable urge to fall asleep!

We would play it by ear, driving in convoy and making our way at her pace; an overnight stay in Louis Trichardt – our 'halfway house' – being the planned aim.

We would continue on to Gwelo, arriving at the Hudson Road house a day later than Joseph – if we didn't come across him somewhere en route!

I had a horrible, nagging vision of Joseph sitting by the roadside with two punctured tyres, but surely we couldn't be in for yet another disaster! Lightning doesn't strike twice!

Smashed

Refreshed, and after one of the longest recent sleeps I can remember, I started up the diesel motor, and, on hearing the bubbling start of the diesel engine of Eve's pick-up, we drove off, on the road to the north.

Once we'd passed through Pretoria, there was only the one main road to follow to the Rhodesian border, so I decided that it would be easier if Eve lead our convoy. That way, she could drive at a speed she felt comfortable with, and I wouldn't have to continually look in my rear-view mirror to check if she was still behind me! It worked out so much better for both of us and we reached Louis Trichardt without any problems late in the afternoon.

Hendrik greeted us warmly, and treated the 'ladies' like royalty. He fussed over them, repeatedly checking that everything was all right with the evening meal, and was there anything, anything at all that he could do for them – this was a rather unusual side of Hendrik that I'd not seen before; not the gruff 'take it or leave it', 'don't wake up my residents!' Hendrik.

He kept chatting to them, asking where they were from, what they were doing driving up to Rhodesia… but he got short change out of Eve, who was clearly dead beat and just wanted to go and have a relaxing sleep!

For my little bit of relaxation, though, I chose the pub; a few beers would round off the day nicely.

Hendrik came behind the bar and continued in this unusual 'chatty vein', seemingly determined to have a long conversation with me; he even bought me a drink, and that was a first as well!

Then, suddenly, abruptly breaking the trend of our conversation, he enthusiastically exclaimed, "Heraah man! How's you do it, eh? We just can't work it out; every time you come to Louis Trichardt, you're in a different vehicle and with a different woman! My regulars reckon that you're some sort of polymous… er, poligywhatsit… you know, someone who has many wives – like the Africans! And that you're busy smuggling vehicles into Rhodesia!

"I mean, when we first met a few weeks ago, you were driving a blue pick-up, with that albino-looking guy – the silly impatient one, when you had those two punctures! The next time, you arrived in a white Volvo car with a white woman and two small children. Then you surprised us all when we saw you in a white pick-up with that well-dressed black woman and the coloured boy. Now today, it's a grey pick-up, and a beige pick-up, with a different white woman and another little white girl! You certainly seem to like different colours, eh? Both in your vehicles and your various women! What's your secret, man?" Hendrik enquired, forcefully.

"Mmmm – well, Hendrik, let me tell you. On my next trip up this way, I'll be in a black pick-up with a yellow Chinese woman and twins!" I replied, tongue in cheek, downed my beer and left Hendrik with a puzzled look on his face, his mouth contorted in a quizzical grin.

. . .

The rest of the trip was quite uneventful – fortunately – and, later the next afternoon, we arrived at No. 7 Hudson Road, Gwelo, to be greeted by Joseph, Jane, Marianne and the kids. Jeffrey and Marie-Louise were so pleased and excited to see their friend, Sarah, again. They rushed off together outside into the sunshine, laughing and giggling, while the rest of us sat down to late afternoon tea and sandwiches.

We chatted about this latest trip up from Johannesburg; Eve was chuffed with herself that she had driven such a long distance.

"I really did enjoy myself, and was pleased Sarah was with me too; she was so excited and kept pointing out things as we drove – like those monstrous baobab trees. We'd never seen anything like them! However, I must say that I was pleased when we arrived at the hotel in Louis Trichardt; I don't think I could have driven any further without having a full night's sleep!"

"Yes, I agree with you; it's so important to break a long journey, and it makes the rest of the trip more enjoyable – and not further punishment! By the way, Joseph, Hendrik was in such a friendly mood, most unusual for him, but he told me he hadn't seen you on this trip – did you manage to make it to Beitbridge and overnight there at Brian's auntie's guesthouse?"

"Oh, err, err... It was okay; all w-w-went well, no problems, no problems at all. I arrived here at the house yesterday; it took two days, just like y-y-you did!" he stutter-stated. "Didn't I, Jane?"

"Yes," concurred Jane. "He got here in the afternoon and unloaded the pick-up straight away, putting everything in the garage – he wouldn't let me help him, although I told him I could carry some of the smaller things to the garage; I'm not an invalid – I'm only eight months pregnant! But he insisted that I stay indoors – he's such a caring husband!"

"Thanks!" Joseph acknowledged, with a proud grin spreading across his face. "B-b-but there's no time to sit around and talk to you; I have to leave now and go to Hartley to collect a very important book from Cain – it's called *Small Working – Precious Metals and Minerals*, issued by the Mines Department of Rhodesia."

We walked out together to where the pick-ups were parked in the driveway. The two heavily laden ones that Eve and I had driven up looked like small lorries with the thick black plastic sheeting covering the furniture and stacked boxes. They made Joseph's pale blue pick-up, which he'd already offloaded, look quite small and lonely parked next to its two 'big brothers'!

He quickly leapt into his blue pick-up, revved the engine, and, with tyres squealing, he roared off!

Strange fellow, I thought, and went back into the house and joined the others – three ladies chatting away merrily, having cracked open a two and a half-litre jug of South African red wine!

When bed eventually beckoned, I drifted slowly into a well-earned relaxing sleep, knowing that we were all together now in Gwelo, and that I wouldn't have to make yet another two- to three-day journey down to South Africa and back.

At last, all of our personal goods, and the furniture too, were now safely up here in Rhodesia.

. . .

I awoke to the happy sounds of kids running around; the noises from their shoes clattering on the carpet-less floors mingled with their laughter echoing through the empty house.

I joined Eve and Marianne, who had already begun unloading the pick-ups.

We took the furniture straight into the house and were just about to start removing the boxes when Matt arrived.

"Hi! Pleased to see you managed to get these other two loaded pick-ups safely to the house. By the way, where's Joseph? Did he tell you about the crash he had the other night?"

"The crash! What crash?" I asked, in a surprised tone.

Matt went on to tell us what had happened. "About 1 o'clock in the morning, there was this loud 'BANG' followed by crashing and crunching noises in my garden! I leapt out of bed, grabbed my handgun and switched on the veranda lights, rushed outside, and… what did I see? Joseph's pick-up covered in concrete blocks from my portal gate entrance, and bits of wooden furniture scattered around on the ground!

"Déjà vu! He had done the same to me once before! I shouted at him, 'Jesus, what the hell are you doing; are you blind! You bloody well crashed into the portal entrance again! Don't you ever bloody well think of the height of the stuff loaded on the back of your pick-up before you drive in to someone's driveway?' But a dazed-looking Joseph jabbered on and on that he hadn't seen anything; he just heard a loud crash and the pick-up stopped abruptly, causing him to bang his head on the windscreen…. Whatever happened, he wasn't sure, but he was dead tired… and he brushed past me, and went inside and flopped down on the sofa, fast asleep.

"The next day, when he finally woke up – about 2pm – we cleared up all the mess in the driveway. I said to him, mockingly, 'Well done, Joseph, you've done it once more; you've destroyed my portal entrance yet again! Actually, you're bloody lucky that the gates were open; otherwise, you would have seriously bashed in the bonnet and front end of your pick-up, instead of just having a few dents and scratches from the falling bits of the portal! But you've really smashed up some of your partner's furniture; like the remains of the top half of that Welsh dresser on the back of your pick-up, behind the driver's cab – and take a look here, these look like wooden pieces from an armchair! Let's strap all the broken bits securely on your pick-up and then you'd better get over to Hudson Road now and explain to them what happened – they are not going to be happy with you – that's for sure!' And he drove off, without saying a word! But you are telling me that he hasn't said anything at all about the accident? And where is he now, then?"

On learning that Joseph had gone off to Hartley, he became very annoyed with his brother and rushed to the garage, calling out, "Come on, let's go and see how bad the damage is!"

Inside the garage, everything was neat and tidy – there was the Kiaat wooden bar, with the three bar stools nicely lined up in front; behind them were just packing boxes neatly stacked up almost to the roof – but not any broken wooden furniture to be seen.

"Jesus, I hope he didn't go and dump all the broken stuff and throw it away!"

Matt uttered in an embarrassed, yet concerned voice as he poked around and moved some of the boxes.

"Oh shit!" exclaimed Matt. "Here they are! Look, your broken stuff is here under the torn plastic sheeting, hidden behind the boxes!"

"The bloody arsehole!" I spat. "Why the hell didn't he tell us about the crash, instead of hiding all the broken stuff in here? Now he's sneaked off to Hartley, and leaves us to find out everything on our own – what an absolute tosser!"

We moved the bar and bar stools into one corner of the lounge, and arranged the other settees and tables; it began to look really cosy.

However, we decided to leave all the broken furniture in the hallway, so that when Joseph got back he'd see it... and have to spill the beans, and we would all listen, with our ears wide open!

Matt stayed for lunch and we had a braai together.

It made a real change just to sit quietly and chat after the recent two-day drive from Jo'burg, Jane's pregnancy update, and to catch up on Matt's news too, but Jane had insisted that the word 'Joseph' was taboo in any conversation – which nobody disagreed with!

By mid-afternoon, there was still no sign of Joseph, and Jane was getting worried. So I took all the kids in the back of my pick-up and drove to the Midland Hotel; they enjoyed strawberry milkshakes on the terrace while I made a phone call to Hartley. Cain told me that Joseph had stayed overnight, but he should be back in Gwelo by now.

We all returned to the house and were in the lounge busy unpacking boxes when we heard Joseph's pick-up come into the driveway, then a key was carefully inserted in the lock and he partly opened the front door, very slowly... and closed it again quickly, but quietly. We all listened in silence to the sound of his footsteps crunching on the gravel path as he went around the back to the kitchen door.

A few moments went by, and he came striding into the lounge, proudly announcing, "I got it! I collected that important book from Cain – it will really help us! It's full of tips on small worker mining, ways to get better gold extraction... lots of diagrams and photos!" Then it dawned on him that there was absolutely no response from any of us; just a wall of blank, silent faces staring at him!

Jane broke the silence. "Joseph, why did you lie to me and hide all the broken furniture in the garage?"

"But I didn't hide it!" Joseph rudely interrupted her. "I just put it in the garage. I was going to tell you later, because I knew you'd be angry with me! You see, I drove through the night to get to Gwelo to surprise you, but I couldn't remember the house number and drove up and down Hudson Road in the dark, getting more and more tired and annoyed with myself!

"So I drove over to Matt's place, but forgot about his portal gate entrance and crashed into it. But it's fine; the pick-up wasn't damaged at all, really… only a few things on the back were broken – but it wasn't my fault. I'd driven all the way from Jo'burg in one go, and I was totally knackered, and I just didn't see …"

"*The bloody brightly coloured luminous blocks* of Matt's entrance portal!" I interjected angrily.

"But don't you see, I wanted to bring all of your stuff safely up to Gwelo as quickly as possible – I thought you would be pleased! So when I crossed the border just before it closed, I decided to drive straight through to the house, saving the cost of a hotel too! You see… It's not fair; I tried… but when you're very tired, you don't always see everything… so…" His gradually getting-fainter voice trailed off completely… then silence.

"Better to keep your mouth shut and appear stupid than to open it and remove all doubt," I replied, shaking my head in disbelief as I paraphrased a quote from Mark Twain. "That's absolutely, painfully pathetic, Joseph! What a bloody great start to our partnership!"

Those were the only words that I could muster; how do you deal with such infantile behaviour and his 'Irish' logic, which he seems to believe!

Joseph went and slumped down on one of the 'not broken' (yet?) pieces of our furniture, his shoulders sagging, but his face portraying a strange expression – not one of apology, or even regret for his recklessness and stupidity, but more of an expectant air that he would receive at least an eight out of 10 score for his valiant attempt! The plonker!

"Enough is enough for one day." I sighed. "Let's get out and leave Jane alone with Joseph; perhaps she can pump some sense and normality into that strange mind of his!"

The kids rushed outside and jumped onto the back of my pick-up.

Eve insisted on driving again, and took us all into Gwelo for a refreshing playful afternoon in the park, followed by supper on the terrace of our 'second home', the Midland Hotel – far, far away from the maddening… *'whinging machine'*!

It took me a long, long time to get to sleep, as I was thinking about Joseph's constant catastrophes and his ridiculous, ranting and raving behaviour…

Our 'gentleman's handshake' partnership agreements…

The setting up of our new Ridge Top Mine company…

And our first board meeting next Friday at his parents' mine in Belingwe…

All these things, burning around and around in my mind…

And then, was I dreaming about the sound of the hoist bells that indicate the depth level of the hoist bucket?

Or had these thoughts already begun to set *real alarm bells ringing*!

Ten Percent

To wake up with the sun warming the room through the open windows, the chirping of the birds in the garden, and the clunking of cups and cutlery being set out on the terrace table ready for early morning bacon and eggs – how could one fail to be in a good frame of mind, ready for whatever the day has to offer; the sad fiasco of the smashed furniture already beginning to fade into the past.

And today, a special day; the formalisation of our 50/50 partnership and the creation of our new company, 'Ridge Top Mine (Pvt) Limited'.

We had planned to meet at the Belingwe mine, where Ray and his wife, a chartered secretary, would help us with the registration of the company and familiarise us with the administrative procedures, together with the necessary documents and reports that had to be regularly submitted to the Rhodesian Government Mines Department.

Around four in the afternoon, I turned off the Filabusi Shabani main road and followed a rutted track, then pulled up in front of an old mine house.

It looked very similar to Cain's, with those long covered verandas, where the cool shade provided a welcome respite from the sun and the heat for a tired, sweaty traveller – like me!

A small African man jogged over to me, a huge smile spread spontaneously across his face – the white teeth looking like a zip, joining the top half of his coal-black face to the lower half. He took my bag, beckoned for me to follow him and showed me into a large dining room.

There was a woman sitting by the window, her red hair ablaze with colour as the late afternoon sun lit up her rather chubby face.

"Well, pleased to see you got here on time!" she boomed as she struggled to prise herself out of the armchair, looming larger and larger as she heaved herself into a standing position.

The woman was enormous – or should I make up a new word, 'abnormous' – temporarily blocking out the sun as she moved in front of the window.

She was glaring at me constantly as she negotiated her way slowly around the large table in the middle of the room, whilst the wooden floorboards uttered their squeaky disdain for the burden they were having to support – some 300 pounds, at least!

Her voluptuous bosoms began to nudge each other, like two little fat boys pushing each other out of the way as they attempted to get to the front of the dinner queue!

She was a good six-foot-three, maybe six foot four inches tall, and her long arm craned down towards me, her extended hand resembling a bunch of ripe, plump bananas, but there was nothing soft in her vice-like grip, which literally brought tears to my eyes!

"So you are the one who is going to help my favourite son, Joseph. I'll be watching you closely as you work together, so don't go upsetting Joseph, as he can be a little oversensitive and forgetful at times."

There was no point in me commenting on that – 'silence' is often synonymous with 'prudence', I have learnt.

Then, on hearing loud hooting, she abruptly swung around, skittering one of the chairs across the floor as she wobbled out of the room at full steam, her massive buttocks beginning to gather momentum. Her baggy black tracksuit trousers looked like a dustbin bag full of porridge, which was sloshing around in all directions as she hurried outside.

I heard Ray's voice calling out, "Hello Popette!"

Popette! I had to smile to myself, and went to meet him.

"Good to see we all got here on time. Joseph's gone down to the mine to fill up with diesel. Phew, it's been a hot day! Let's sit down and relax on the cool veranda, and have a sundowner before we chat about the momentous pile of things both you and Joseph will have to assimilate over the weekend – and then put into practice on your own mine!"

It wasn't long before Joseph arrived and climbed up the veranda steps to join us, where he was enthusiastically greeted by his mother.

"That's enough, Mum!" Joseph gasped, somewhat embarrassed, struggling to get air as his mother gave him a 'bear hug' cuddle!

"Popette! Put him down and let him have a cooldrink while we go through and prepare for the meeting."

Only a few minutes had passed before Ray bellowed, "Come on you two; we haven't got time for you to sit around outside. Let's get started!"

Joseph and I joined Ray and his Popette, who were seated at the long table.

I hadn't noticed earlier, but her chair was massive, much wider than the other chairs and with broad, sturdy arms, a bit like the 'queen's royal throne'!

Stacked on the table in front of her was a pile of folders.

She handed out a small book and a pen to both Joseph and me, 'in which we *must* make notes'.

Ray explained that his wife was a chartered secretary, and she had already processed the necessary paperwork to set up our new company, Ridge Top Mine (Pvt) Limited.

She would stay on to take the minutes of the meeting, which would cover the main topics on the agenda, namely:

- The allocation of the shares;
- The appointment of the directors;
- The different job responsibilities and their official titles;
- The set-up of the directors' loan accounts.

We were handed a document showing the name of our registered company and its two directors – Managing Director Ray, and Joseph.

Ray immediately added that by invitation I was present, and hereby appointed a director… and, before the words that were forming in my mouth could be uttered, Ray explained that he had to be 'the managing director' in order to add credibility to the company when dealing with the Mines Department and the various suppliers.

This would enable him to use his experience and contacts to help get the mine up and running – as we had all agreed at the Shangani Café meeting on the way back to South Africa from the trip to Cain's gold mine.

He quickly continued, rattling the words off in a 'machinegun' flurry, that there were 100 shares in the company, and he would have to take 10 shares in order to 'legitimise' his official capacity as the experienced senior advisor in our company!

He smiled as he calmly continued, saying that I should not worry, because I would receive more than the agreed 50/50 split between Joseph and myself, and, as the major capital investor, I had been allocated 45 shares to Joseph's 40, with five shares remaining unallocated.

The angry look on my face as this first bombshell struck home caused a long, ominous silence… my mind whirring away to find the right words… and Ray's smarmy smile quickly vanished as his lips tightened and his eyes adopted that cold, penetrating stare that I had witnessed last month when he was talking, or rather issuing orders, to Joseph!

"But that is *not* the 50/50 partnership between Joseph and I that we all shook hands on in a 'gentleman's agreement'!" I stated angrily.

"You're right," Ray replied. "I didn't want to do this, but in order to give you the promised help, I have to have a 10% share and be managing director.

Otherwise, it would look like a token 'sleeping partner' involvement in your mine, which would jeopardise any government loans or grants that I pursued with the Mines Department for your Claremont and Nelly 404 mining claims.

"But we have compensated for that by allocating you more shares than Joseph, so you are now the major shareholder!" His smarmy smile spread across his relaxed lips once again, but both of us knowing that I was screwed, as I had burnt my bridges by already having sold up in South Africa and having purchased three vehicles, and…

"So much for a Rhodesian gentleman's handshake!" I spat.

"I don't see what your problem is!" interjected his wife. "You're already getting more shares than my Joseph…"

"Excuse me, Madam!" I cut her short. "You have no say in these affairs, and you are only here to take the minutes of the meeting!"

BANG! Ray's fist thumped down on the table. "There's no need to be rude to my wife!" Then, turning to her, he said, "Don't get upset, Popette; these youngsters get quickly irritated and have still got a lot to learn. Now let's have a break, take some coffee on the veranda and continue in half an hour or so – I have some very important phone calls to make!"

Joseph immediately started muttering, "I don't think that's fair at all! Why should he have more shares than me! That's not 50/50! That's just not fair!"

Ray completely ignored his comments, and went off to do his phoning in his office….

A few spoonfuls of sugar took away the bitterness of the coffee, but not the bitterness that I felt welling up inside me – this was not a good start, and certainly not the best position to be in… entrapped, snared and a few other synonyms erupted and kept bubbling away in my head…. Somehow, I've got to make a better deal….

"Well, let's get started again!" Ray called from the dining room. "We've still got a lot to cover this evening."

We all sat around the table again and proceeded to put on paper the other agreed functions and responsibilities.

"Joseph will be responsible for the underground mining operations," Ray continued, "and is hereby appointed underground supervisor…"

"No! No!" Joseph asserted. "I must be called underground manager!"

"Agreed?" Ray sighed, raising his eyes heavenwards. My nod confirmed, and he turned to me and continued. "It is resolved that you are responsible for the management and administration of the mine, for all surface operations, including buildings, machines and water, with the grand title of 'mine manager' – if that's okay with you, Joseph?" he added sarcastically with a snarl, his top lip creasing up into a very unfriendly disfiguration.

"Surface operations to include milling and the extraction of the gold, and it is hereby resolved that you will also be appointed as the accredited gold agent of the company, allowing you to carry, deliver and 'sell' gold to the Barclays Bank Assay office. You will also be responsible for opening the necessary company bank accounts – either in Bulawayo or Gwelo, your choice – and for finding a suitable accountant who would be prepared to keep the company books. Our accountancy work is handled by a man called Mr. Frost, who is very competent. All these items to be confirmed at the next board meeting.

"Both of you should submit up-to-date records of the moneys spent so far on the company's behalf, including capital loans – both cash and equipment. The company financial year would run from 1 April to 31 March each year," Ray concluded, pushing his chair backwards and standing up.

"I've duly noted all that in the minutes," his wife added, "and there being no other business on the agenda, we can close. . ."

"Whooh!" I interjected. "This 50/50 business is still sticking in my throat, leaving a bad taste in my mouth, and your calculated timing, Ray, was obviously pre-planned. I have no choice but to accept your 'grabbed' 10% shareholding, which, together with you being the managing director, would certainly provide the necessary clout when dealing with the Mines Department and the suppliers. However, in order for me to officially sanction that, and so that we can kick off in a more agreeable manner, I put forward that another director should be appointed to add balance to the decision-making and the running of the company – I nominate that my wife, Marianne, becomes the fourth director!"

"No!" shouted Joseph. "I'm dead against that; he's already got more shares than me. Let's out-vote him, Dad!"

"It's two to one, then!" stated Ray firmly. "You're out-voted… Joseph! Popette, please write down in the minutes that, on the agenda for the next board meeting, Marianne will be invited with the purpose of appointing her as the fourth director!"

"Kindly note down as well that it will be the *first* matter on the agenda!" I added forcefully.

A tacit nod from Ray signalled to the scribe to start scribbling a suitable sentence in the minutes of the meeting.

"Okay, that's it. All agreed? Let's wrap it up until tomorrow, when we'll discuss what has to be done on the mine – it is very important that you get cracking and get the mine up and running in the next three months, because it is critical that you start gold production as soon as possible to provide at least an operating income to cover running costs. Come, Popette, let's make it an early night!"

Her bulbous, podgy face lit up like a Halloween pumpkin, and she spun on the spot and sped out of the room, closely followed by an 'anticipating' Ray, with such a smirk on his face! Watching them leave, I just couldn't imagine a jackal and a hippo 'doing it'! I quickly blocked that unsavoury image from my mind and said goodnight to an 'also not looking at all happy' Joseph – the other so-called 50/50 partner – and I retired for the night.

. . .

The mine's alarm clock gong belted out an early wake-up call – for the mine workers, not for me!

I just turned over and went back to sleep, dreaming of a Zikke-type 'hello, hello, hello' cup of tea in bed… I wasn't disappointed either.

At 9 o'clock on the dot, a 'knock, knock, knock' on the door announced that the tea had arrived.

I slurped down two mugs of African tea, made with boiled milk – *lekker* for a change, and really good to get you going first thing in the morning – in both senses! And then for the other two *'Ss'* – a quick cold-water *shower* and a *shave* – before I headed out onto the veranda.

As I was making myself comfortable in a large wicker armchair, the houseboy appeared carrying a big pot of coffee and some toast and marmalade.

With that huge beaming smile on his face, he told me that Boss Joseph had left early for Gwelo, and Boss Ray was down at the mine.

Well, what an unexpected relaxing start to the day.

I really enjoyed the thick brown toast with butter, and the imported Old English marmalade with big chunks of orange peel – which really adds to the ginger colour and stiffness of my handlebar moustache!

An hour or so passed by before I saw a vehicle approaching the house and skidding to a halt, showering the whole compound with dust.

"Only got five minutes!" Ray snapped irritably. "Early this morning, we had a call that Jane was not feeling well, so Joseph left immediately for Gwelo to go and see her. I have problems too… with a few workers at the mine, and don't have any time for our meeting today!"

Between mouthfuls of gulped-down coffee, he informed me that I should sit down with his wife this morning to go through all the administrative tasks and paperwork for our mine.

"Oh, and another thing, I have seven mine workers whom I've just fired – you can take them to Fort Rixon when you leave!" he shouted out as he rushed down the steps of the veranda.

A loud revving of the engine, and he gunned the pick-up off to…

"*Way over yonder, to a place I belong…*" I started humming this very popular song by *Carole King*.

The creaking floorboards announced the arrival of plump, pompous Popette!

"Now where has that man gone?" she asked me irritably. "He's never here when I need to talk to him! Never mind, let's go through all the administration duties and requirements that you will have to deal with, including the records that must be kept for the Mines Department. Meet me in the dining room in five minutes, and don't keep me waiting!" she rasped, her voice grating away, causing her chubby cheeks to vibrate gently.

For the next two hours, she spoke almost non-stop – I could see from whom Joseph learnt and developed his ability to 'blast one's eardrums' incessantly with countless facts and figures.

She kicked off with **company administration and accounts**, a brief summary being:

- A register of employees was required by law:
  Full names/country of birth/district registered in/ID (*stupa*)/date joined/job/pay scale/the mine they were last employed at and a reference – their ID and reference letter must be held on file whilst they are employed by our mine.
- Time book. Days worked/shift/absences/character – if a troublemaker, useless, lazy?
  Notice to be given – one day, or for monthly paid it was one month.
- And the usual administration books:
  Creditors/debtors/loan accounts/wages/bank-books/vehicles, equipment and maintenance/cash and expenses/correspondence files.

We then discussed the records that had to be kept and the returns that had to be sent on time to **the Mines Department** – failure to do so could lead to heavy fines, or even the loss of the claims, and our gold mining business!

- Claims. Pegging and registration notices/development work done/inspection notices/gold production…
- Returns and payments to the Mines Department/workman's compensation/labour returns/pneumoconiosis/health certification…
- Prospecting: I should write a letter to the Rancher Jackson on our Ridge Top Mine-headed notepaper stating:

Dear Sirs,
In terms of section 34 (1) (b) of the Mines and Minerals Act chapter 203, I hereby advise you that we will be prospecting further for metals and minerals on your Farm.
Yours sincerely,
Signed: Mine Manager.

- Prospecting procedures:
- Correct pegging of the claim blocks, with prospecting notices and discovery poles.
- Registration notices completed within one month.
- Six metal beacons erected in concrete blocks within a further month, detailing registration details of the claims held by our company.
- Timber agreements:
  Under Mining Regulations Sections (3–10), detailing the types of timber that could be cut on the rancher's land for hut building and firewood.
  I already had the temporary timber permit, and we were busy cutting wood for hut building – I had sent Jackson a note before we went back to South Africa, saying we would confirm our wood usage and charges when we were back in Rhodesia working on our claims.
- Gold production:
  I was the accredited agent licensed to 'sell' gold, and, when we started producing gold, I would have to take the 'raw gold' (sponge) after extraction to the Assay office in Bulawayo, for weighing and crediting to our mine bank account – that *will be* a happy feeling!

She handed me a **letter from Barclays Bank** detailing the procedures and the payments we would receive for 'our gold':

…The Bank has negotiated with the Chamber of Mines and the Reserve Bank of Rhodesia to improve the system and speed up the payment to Customer Mines for the Gold lodged with them.

- *Initial Payment: on receipt of the 'raw Gold', $25.00 per fine ounce will be paid as soon as the bullion has been assayed; this payment would normally be paid within 24 hours.*
- *Interim Payment: Gold Bars weighing less than 100 troy ounces will have to be accumulated and composited into larger bars. These Gold bars will be dispatched to the Reserve Bank of Rhodesia to be sold on the free market. From the proceeds 70% of the value would be credited to the Customer Mine within two to three weeks.*
- *Final Payment: After the Gold has been refined and returned to the Reserve Bank,*

final accounts would be prepared and a final payment made of the balance of the 5% held, less charges and adjustments, normally with six weeks.

- *<u>Silver Payments</u>: For the small portion of Silver held in the raw Gold sponge, payments are irregular and will be paid when the Reserve Bank sells the bars of Silver.*

  Barclays Bank is pleased to announce these changes, which means Customers should now receive almost all of the proceeds of their Gold within three to four weeks.

  – ***(Amen to that, I say!)***

  Signed: <u>The Chief Assayer of Barclays Bank</u>

She also showed me her **gold production log**, which included details of:

The mine name/date/weight of the raw gold sponge, together with the dates and payments received for:

<u>Gold</u>: Initial/interim/final payments.

<u>Silver</u>: Ad hoc payments, as and when received.

"Now," she continued. "**The Toilets – Drainage/Sewerage** for both you and your workers are extremely important, not only for your health, but also to show the land owner that you are responsible and are treating both his land and his cattle with respect. He will come and check as soon as he sees more African workers on the mine," she informed me as she handed me some diagrams, with the measurements and materials to be used:

- A single toilet (with a seat) for us, and the digging instructions for the 'long drop' drains, down to approximately eight feet deep.
- <u>Compound latrine drains</u> for the mine workers, consisting of two reinforced concrete slabs, each with a 20-centimetre diameter hole in the middle, 'French-type squat toilets', to be dug to approximately 15 feet in depth.

  One double unit should be near the office, downwind, of course!

  A larger unit with three sections would be needed in the mine village.
- Both types of toilets would have screens made using poles and hessian walls painted with a concrete wash for sturdiness.

"Make sure you get these dug to the correct depths; otherwise, you'll soon know by the awful smell!" She laughed sarcastically – but at least it was a laugh! A laugh that broke the stern, bulldog-like face that always seemed to epitomise her bullying attitude.

So, after a really stimulating and informative session with her, I was looking forward to setting up the basic paperwork and records.

I would also need to employ a good experienced clerk to handle the daily tasks of:

- Time and attendance, and pay sheets for the workers.
- Stores. Ordering for both the mine and our shop, where we would keep essential basic items that the workers could buy 'on tick' until their next pay day.
- Keeping the mine workers' records up to date.

"Here, take this spare concertina folder; it has 31-day sections, which you'll find invaluable for keeping abreast and up to date with the various 'notices and returns' for the Mines Department, in order to be sure of timely reporting to them – otherwise, there could be disastrous consequences!"

And she proceeded to tell of such a 'disaster story' of a big gold-producing company mine near Bulawayo.

The administration manager was an alcoholic, and was very slapdash and careless with the administrative records. One of his clerks noticed that the claim on which the main shaft and hoist machinery were located had not been renewed.

The clerk was sharp enough to resign, and, after the necessary time period of seven days had lapsed and the claim had become forfeit, he re-pegged it under his own name.

The ex-clerk went and informed the company of the re-pegging situation, and that their workers were trespassing on his claim!

AND the mine shaft was to be closed!

This would mean effectively that gold production of hundreds of ounces of gold a month would be lost, as it would take many months to sink a new shaft and get the mine operational again.

After a speedy resolution by the company, the ex-clerk tributed 'his claim' back to the company for 5% of gold production, and was paid a large sum of money on top of that too!

"Today, that ex-clerk is a millionaire! That shows you how important keeping good records is in the gold mining sector!" she added. "Oh, one last thing. I've put together a 'truck emergency kit' in this bag for you – Joseph already has his. Always carry it in the pick-up wherever you go; it consists of:

- **"Pick and a shovel,** for digging you out if your pick-up gets stuck in the mud/blackven soft soil, and, of course,
- **"Tow rope,** so that someone can pull you out!" And she grinned, again!

- **"Tools:** Hammer, nails, wire and an axe/chopper.
- **"Prospecting licences,** pegging and registration notices.
- **"Sample bags** for soil/rocks, to be assayed by the Mines Department.
- **"A snakebite kit.**

"Where you are mining, there's an abundance of poisonous snakes; black mamba, green mamba, Egyptian spitting cobra and the worst of them all, the puff adder – it lies in the sun on the mud tracks where people walk in the bush, and does not slither away when humans approach, unlike most other snakes. It strikes very quickly and is deadly poisonous!

"We call this the **'be prepared' kit**, taking a leaf from **Lord Baden-Powell**, who, as a young colonel, fought against the local natives in the Matabele Rebellion wars in 1896, in the mining area where the Claremont mine is situated!"

I thanked her for giving me all the basics, as a 'starter' for me.

She replied gruffly that she was doing it for Joseph, so that I could be of help to him in getting the mines up and running to produce gold.

We parted on a slightly more cordial note than on the previous day's steamy, and sometimes explosive, confrontations between us.

The houseboy jumped on the back of my pick-up and pointed out the way to the mine, which was several miles way.

As we pulled up, Ray's head boss boy (of the family mines), called Staff, came over to greet me; he was a tall, good looking African in his fifties, with an amicable smile.

He informed me that Ray had had a big argument with some of the workers in the morning, when he informed them that they no longer had a job on his gold mine. But, before he could explain further, they started shouting and screaming abuse at him.

Ray just exploded, jumped in his truck and roared off.

"What was the problem?" I asked.

"Nothing really; they have been paid off and have been assured of a job on your new gold mine, but they don't want to leave this mine, where they live with their families! Ray says these seven workers are now yours, and you should take them back to your mine in Fort Rixon. Your new boss boy is this one, Tachibone; he speaks a bit of English, so you should deal with him."

He gave me the other workers' names and jobs:

- Ndabazabo – junior boss boy – underground;
- Tabari and Mucharaveni – underground jackhammer boys;
- Fana Petros – lasher;

- Dereery – builder;
- Situnda – general work/cook.

A Riddle?

How do you get seven workers, their equipment and belongings, a 60 kg sack of mealie meal, two wheelbarrows, some spades and other tools onto the back of a pick-up?

I'm not sure, really! But, with the vehicle being totally overloaded, with its springs bent almost straight instead of their normal arc shape, I got into my pick-up and crept away cautiously, bumping and bouncing along a rutted track – which seemed endless!

When we reached the tarmac road, I pulled up and called out to Tachibone, "Has anybody or anything fallen off?"

I heard him chuckling away as he translated for the new workers, who started laughing and shouting amongst themselves.

We cruised comfortably along the tar roads and the strip roads until we reached Filabusi – the rest of the journey on dirt roads was very slow and painful, but we reached the mine late in the afternoon, just before sunset.

Langton and George helped to unload the pick-up and look for places for the new workers to sleep in the few huts that had already been built.

I left them to sort it all out.

I was pleased to be on my way back to the Gwelo house, which I reached after dark – the end of a very long, eventful, but traumatic weekend!

I mean, I was hit out of the blue by Ray's drastic changes to our agreement.

It was obviously pre-planned, and cemented by his carefully orchestrated speech showing that he was invaluable to us.

Nevertheless, it was hard to swallow his Mafioso tactics: "I'll make you an offer you can't refuse!"

I was beginning to think that this 'golden partnership' was fast turning into **'golden partner-shit'**!

Part III - The Rains

Why Can't the Cowboys and the Miners be Friends?

It's hard to say 'goodbye'; saying 'goodbye' is the hardest thing – not only for lovers, but also for young children, and today three little friends will be crying, cuddling and laughing as they say their prolonged 'goodbyes'.

Sarah, Marie-Louise and Jeffrey were loaded onto the back of the pick-up with all the luggage. Eve grabbed the car keys, insisting on being the driver yet again, and proceeded to ferry us all to Bulawayo Airport, a two-hour drive away.

We sat down on the terrace outside the terminal building and had a farewell drink together.

Eve was so pleased that she had come to Rhodesia to see us, and said that she'd enjoyed the long drive up from Johannesburg immensely.

As we chatted away waiting for the flight to be called, Sarah and Marie-Louise were huddled together whispering to each other – Jeffrey had wandered away to watch the airplanes taking off and landing.

Then it was time to go…. We cuddled each other, and said how much we were looking forward to seeing each other again in a few weeks, together with Malcolm, Sebastian and Simon, when we would celebrate Christmas together on our mine in the Rhodesian bush.

The thought of something good like that always makes saying 'goodbye' easier… or, as the French would say, '*au revoir*', which I think sums it up better for good friends; not 'goodbye, gone forever', but 'bye, 'til we meet again, soon'.

We spent the rest of the day in Bulawayo, leisurely exploring and getting to know the city a bit better. Although I'd visited Bulawayo many times, it had always been limited time-wise to a few business hours, and limited building-wise to the Mines Department and the Greys Inn Hotel.

However, today I could spend time with the family window shopping, and visiting the beautifully laid out Bulawayo Park, with its colourful flower beds and exotic blossoming trees – and the swings, of course! Good fun and very relaxing after the recent eventful few days.

However, on the drive back to Gwelo, occasionally a thought flashed into my mind of the recent board meeting with the 'godfather' laying down the law, and amending the 'gentleman's agreement' into the new 'Constitution according to Ray'!

That was such a bloody annoying and disappointing start to the mining venture.

But, as my mother used to tell us, 'you've *made* your bed; now you've got to lie in it'!

In reality, I'd never been good at making beds, but I'd had some really enjoyable times in them! And I had always been pretty successful in getting out of them again!

. . .

The loud squeaking of the letter box opening and the thud of a bunch of letters hitting the wooden floor signalled the start of an administration day.

After downing a cup of coffee, followed by toast and marmalade, I decided that it was just too noisy in the house to be able to concentrate. So, with a wad of letters in my hand, I walked to my 'Midland Hotel' office and began slitting open the post:

+ Two letters from Immigration, requesting more information about our intended stay, and the full details of our employers – us!

+ Monica Trading, the clearing agents, enclosed copies of our 'entry into Rhodesia' forms, on which we had declared both 'household goods' and 'personal vehicles' under the exempt from duty section. We would have to wait for Customs/Immigration in Gwelo to officially stamp them as cleared goods, in order to release them as duty-free!

+ Pat Burke had replied to my letter, and listed all the claims that had been pegged and registered by him. He would be visiting us at the mine within the next two weeks to erect an official discovery peg on the last claim that he had pegged.

+ Shangani Telephone Department had sent an acknowledgement of our written request for two phone lines, one to the mine office and the other one to the house.

+ A Post Office Box number for Ridge Top Mine, Fort Rixon was confirmed by Insiza Rural Council.

Old Davidson had also enclosed an acknowledgement of our request to lay a pipe under the Fort Rixon-Filabusi main murram road, with a copy to the Insiza Roads Department Engineer.

This pipeline would allow us to pump water directly from the flooded Claremont parallel mine shaft to our house site – it would be an essential lifeline for the family.

+ Saving the best 'til last!

A plump brown A4 envelope from the Mines Department containing forms, together with a voluminous narrative of some 20 pages detailing the Workman's Compensation Act and our obligations as employers to comply with the labour laws of Rhodesia.

I completed the temporary returns.

A reminder would be sent to our mine in six months when I would be required to complete full returns for all of our workers.

My in-tray empty, I started to pen a few letters that I needed to send:

+ To Mr Curtis (Mines Department yard), informing him that we had railed a green portable compressor from South Africa, freight fully paid, to the Mines Department in Bulawayo.

Please advise me when it arrives, so I can collect the accompanying documents and visit the bank to apply for an import licence and Customs clearance.

+ To Mr Mullins of Deep Mine. Sorry to hear you are closing the mine, but thanks for recommending Willie, who we shall employ as our mine supervisor. We understand that you will no longer require him after next week, and we look forward to meeting you and Willie shortly.

+ To Fred Stewart of R. J. Stewart & Sons (the previous company working on our claims), kindly requesting any documentation or underground plans of the Claremont and Nelly 404 mines that were still in their possession.

Also, if it were possible, we would appreciate a visit from him to our mine – any time.

I bought some postage stamps, and, with a 'QLSF', those letters were on their way via the Rhodesian postal service.

(Quick-Lick-Stick-Flick into the post box!)

That completed the morning's work, and just in time too. The family invasion of noisy, thirsty and hungry souls could be heard as they clattered up the wooden steps of the hotel terrace.

We found a table in the dining room and sat down together for lunch.

Barely had my raised glass touched my lips when a waiter came over and told me that Joseph was on the line and wanted to speak to me urgently.

I responded urgently… in one minute flat – to slowly down that cool, refreshing pint of beer!

And quickly went to the reception area and took the phone.

"Jane and I are in Bulawayo," Joseph began. "My father wanted to meet us at the garage where he'd left his pick-up for a major service. We'll go back with him shortly to the family home in Belingwe, where we'll celebrate my mother's birthday. Cain and Matt are also coming down; it will be great to be all together again, when undoubtedly it will turn into an 'all-nighter'!

"Dad has given me 20 almost new carbide lamps to supplement the few we already have, and advises us to throw away the old nozzles and get new ones – good consistent bright light is essential when working underground. Check if you can buy 30 new nozzles and a sack of carbide in Gwelo."

(*A carbide lamp has carbide powder in the lower half, below a reservoir of water. The water drips onto the carbide, causing gas to be emitted, which, when lit, gives an immensely clear bright beam of light.*)

Joseph continued, "We called in at the mine on our way to Bulawayo, and delivered a pick-up full of equipment that we bought at Farm Aid, using my father's general suppliers card again: four wheelbarrows, 10 picks, 10 shovels, 240 metres of hessian, three saws, 10 kg of assorted nails, five hammers, nine mine hats – yellow ones. Tomorrow, Matt and Jane will take Dad to Bulawayo to collect his pick-up. Later, Matt will drop Jane back at the Gwelo house, which means I can bring our new clerk, Crispin, and three other workers from Belingwe to our mine tomorrow evening."

"Right then, Joseph, I'll go into Gwelo tomorrow, and it's important I sort out our own supplier account cards too; we can't keep using your father's. Well, enjoy your mother's party tonight, and don't forget to say hi to Cain; tell him we must meet up again soon."

We drove back to the house, and, while Marianne was bathing the children, I grabbed a beer and walked around our garden.

I had a nice surprise too; behind the garage, I was amazed to see our first gold!

No less than 20 sheets of the hard-to-get corrugated iron sheets.

Now that's just what we needed for the mine, so I decided to 'borrow' them – to be replaced when I could – and loaded them onto my pick-up straight away.

. . .

The next morning was another very busy one spent in Gwelo, applying for business accounts with various suppliers, looking for the best combination of discounted prices, and, more importantly, good credit facilities.

The owner of Farm Aid – a general supplier of everything from mealie meal to beans, to picks and shovels, right through to hats and clothes of all descriptions and uses – said he would give us 120 days' credit.

Sounds good, but I'm sure the old bugger had upped his prices a hell of a lot; they looked expensive.

But I suppose he looks at it this way:

"Some ain't gonna make it; some are – and those that do are sure gonna make up for the losses of those that don't!"

I was beginning to get writer's cramp after filling out all the application forms for credit facility accounts with the butcher, the baker and the candlestick maker… actually, a butcher, a milling company and a hardware store that sold hurricane lamps!

I needed a break, and it was now time to grab the chance and squeeze in a short liquid lunch at the Midland Hotel, where I could make some phone calls at the same time to upcountry timber suppliers to obtain information on costs and delivery times.

However, nearly an hour was spent in fruitless attempts; I only managed to speak to one timber supplier on a joint party line, but only very briefly, and confusingly too:

"When can you deliver 50 gum poles to Shangani?"

"No! You don't say; you didn't hear about Mrs Jones' daughter…"

"Four-inch thick gums…"

"No! She's pregnant…"

"So, expected delivery…"

"Six months…"

"That's far too long; I need the gum poles urgently! Who am I talking to?"

"Please get off the line; you're very rude. This is a private conversation…"

"Hello, is that you, Sue?"

Now there were three conversations on the go, raised voices shouting.

"Hello! Please get off this line…"

I'd had more than enough!

I swallowed my beer and left to collect the supplies that I had ordered earlier in the morning.

My pick-up was duly loaded with a 60 kg sack of mealie meal and 20 kg meat rations, placed on top of my newly acquired 20 corrugated iron sheets – which would be used for roofing the office and the storeroom.

Some food, meat and vegetables, and pots and pans for myself, together with two hurricane lamps, were placed on the front seat, and I set off on the road to Fort Rixon.

I reached the mine just as the rain started, but I was too knackered to unload the pick-up.

I just grabbed the stuff on the front seat and rushed for the shelter of my new home!

So here I am now, in the middle of the bush, spending my first night alone in a grass-thatched hut, with the thunder rumbling, the occasional jagged streaks of lightning flashing around the dark skies and the rain tipping down, incessantly!

Looking through the open 'hanging black plastic sheet' door, I can see my nearest neighbour in another hut – the 'cordon bleu' who is preparing my evening banquet.

As we didn't have a cook on the mine yet, I chose this one – pot luck, you might say!

His name is Situnda, and that's about all he does throughout the day – he loves to 'sit under' any shady tree he can find!

He is old too, and about the only thing that he does well is to smell.

Like in the *Beatles* song, 'Man, I can smell your feet a mile away' – and I'm sitting only 20 feet away!

Situnda speaks no English, and my Chilapalapa language is still pretty poor – no, that's the wrong adverb, 'ugly' poor!

I lit one of the hurricane lamps…. Aaah no!

The new wick was smoking like hell, choking clouds of eye-watering fumes were filling my hut, and I couldn't see a bloody thing!

Nothing for it but to take it outside, and stand in the pouring rain until the smoke in the hut cleared!

Luckily, the rain was not cold; it was like having a lukewarm shower – but it was wet!

And so this bedraggled figure stripped off and quickly sprang back into the hut to dry off and put on some fresh clothes.

I took four portions of ration meat, two onions and some rape vegetable and put them into one of the new large pots, and some potatoes into another one.

I pointed to Situnda's fire and shouted to him, "*Faga lapa!*" (Put it on the fire!) And awaited my fate.

I just thought, *I hope he adds water to the pots*… But thought again, they would be full of water from the torrential rain by the time he got back over to his hut!

The result: a pot of steaming stew was placed at my doorway, and I was amazed; it tasted quite good! And as I devoured each hot, steaming spoonful, faint chanting noises could be heard from the mine village compound some 200 yards away – well, it certainly was different to working in the computer industry in Johannesburg City.

. . .

Joseph arrived back just before 8am the following morning with several new workers on the back of his pick-up.

He told me the rains were so heavy last evening that he'd decided not to risk driving on the wet, slippery dirt roads at night.

Some of our more curious workers came over to the pick-up to see who the new arrivals were; maybe an old friend they'd worked with in the past?

One of them, Tachibona, was all smiles when he saw his *mafaz* (woman) on the back of the pick-up – the very first female resident in our village.

As the numbers of permanent workers increased in the future, many others would also bring their wives and small children to live in the mine village; they would hopefully have a calming influence on their sometimes raucous men!

Our new clerk/storekeeper, Crispin, introduced himself, and luckily for me he spoke very good English.

While Joseph went to our hut to have a relaxing cup of tea, I sat down with Crispin to discuss registering all of our workers – including the three who came with him from Belingwe.

I was surprised when he opened his bag and produced a hardcover A4 book with the label 'Mine Workers Register – Ridge Top Mine, Fort Rixon' and said, "Let's start!"

He got busy straight away checking the ID *stupas* and reference letters of these new workers, together with another six local African farm workers whom we were taking on, bringing the total now to 21:

Elliot – houseboy/cook. (A big welcome to you, Chef!)

Matshe and Samson– general lashers.

Together with the six local farm workers:

Walter, Fana Abias, Willias, Agrippa, Madina and one called Amos, who said he'd just been fired by Farmer Jackson.

One old *mdala* gave me his *stupa* and said that he'd left his last job 10 years ago.

I asked him, through my new translator/interpreter, Crispin, where he'd worked since.

His eyes lit up as he proudly produced another piece of crumpled, folded paper, and told me it was a reference from his last job.

It was written in beautiful, flowery, old-fashioned English long-hand, and read:

To whom it may concern. – Duplicate Reference.

This is to certify that the bearer, Matshe Ndeovu (RC.X 3737 Shabani) has been working for Belingwe Mine as a compound policeman for two (2) years. He has been a good worker in his job. His previous reference letter got burnt when his house got burnt when it caught fire.

I recommend him to anyone who can offer him job.

Yours faithfully, Daniel Joseph. Mine Clerk, dated June 1948.

I joined Joseph for a cup of tea, and we had our first actual 'tête-à-tête' on the mine.

He excitedly told me that Matt had spoken to him at their mother's birthday party and we could take over his 5-stamp mill, because it would be too big for his new scaled-down operation. The ore being currently crushed was of a much lower gold content than expected, and Matt would now concentrate on processing the old mine dumps again, using a small ball mill crusher and a mercury covered copper plate for gold collection.

He would dismantle the now-redundant 5-stamp mill and a James Table, which we could collect the following week and transport to our mine.

On top of that, there would be another 15 to 20 experienced mine workers who would be available, if we wanted to take them on.

Well, that was great news for us; a 5-stamp mill and a James Table in good condition – and available! Fabulous news!

Joseph was in a happy frame of mind and suggested that we go and make the rounds of the whole mining area to check on the progress so far.

We walked down to the mine compound on the track that had been completely cleared of thorn bushes, and a gang of mine boys was busy filling in all the potholes and ruts.

Once they had finished this, their next task would be to dig a large, deep trench, 12 feet by five feet, and 15 feet deep, for the village latrines – a hessian-screened unit with three sections of 'French-type squat toilets'.

There were also two houses that were being built of 'dagga' blocks (dried mud), which still needed a lot of work.

The one for our new coloured mine supervisor, Willie, had two rooms built up to roof height, using dagga blocks and dagga (mud) as cement.

Dereery, the builder, was busy fixing up another old dagga house, putting in two window frames, but still had plenty to do before the tin roof could be put on. This house was for our keenly awaited senior boss boy, Staff, who should be here on the coming Saturday, according to Joseph.

We decided to site the office and storerooms close to the mine shaft of the Nelly 404, where the headgear would be erected too – there was still plenty of building work to be done.

We were debating how to get hold of another builder quickly, when an old rattling truck rocked up. I think it is best described as an ox wagon with a motor!

Out jumped a large man, who exclaimed with gusto, "I am Samuel, master builder. I'm the greatest builder you ever did see in your life! You want a good builder, I'm the best! You want a fast builder, I'm the fastest! You want a. . ."

I cut him short and laughingly said, "If you can build as good as you can talk 'Cassius', we'll employ you!"

So Samuel, 'Cassius', was taken on trial – if he built the office to our satisfaction on an existing concrete foundation, we'd employ him.

"Why do you call him Cassius?" enquired Crispin.

"Well, Cassius Clay, the world champion heavyweight boxer, is the world's fastest-punching, fastest-talking. . ."

"Oh, I get it!" said a grinning Crispin.

We sited the workers' latrine some 50 yards away from the proposed office – downwind, of course – and a gang of workers would dig a large, deep trench for a double unit of the concrete slab 'French-type squat toilets', which would have screens for privacy, made using poles and hessian walls painted with a concrete wash for sturdiness.

Joseph started to instruct and show three workers how to build a dry-stone base out of rocks and some waste-schist for a large water tank, to be installed close to the Nelly 404 shaft.

I drove off to our house site with a couple of the surface workers and loaded some old concrete blocks onto our 'getting more useful everyday' Peugeot pick-ups.

As I reversed back along the bush track and pulled out onto the dirt road, a Jeep skidded to a halt in a cloud of dust with the horn honking continuously!

A young chap jumped out and exclaimed, "Al Swartz, telephone engineer from Shangani! And I must say, it's not often on these roads that one has to slam the brakes on hard to avoid another vehicle backing out of the bush!" He chuckled.

We shook hands and drove to the mine, where I showed him the office site.

"This phone is needed very urgently," I informed him. "At present, we have to drive all the way to Fort Rixon exchange phone booth each time we need to place or receive a call – it's bloody time wasting and so frustrating, especially with these rains!"

"Well, looking at the proposed site for the office phone, this would be connected to the nearest telephone pole, which is about 600 yards away. And where is the house phone required?"

When he saw the site, he exclaimed, "Oh, there will be no problem here at all. The joint party line to the Jackson ranch passes over there, a mere 20 yards away!"

"Great! So when can we expect this phone to be connected?"

"Oh… in about three weeks or so!"

F… F… Flabbergasted is the word I'm after! A phone is so essential out here in the bush.

"I'll confirm to you the exact date that I can connect you up!" Al said as he jumped into his Jeep and drove off.

And, as if to add insult to injury, Joseph and I also had to leave immediately to drive to the Fort Rixon telephone booth to do some essential phoning!

Driving behind the telephone engineer in the dust clouds kicked up by his Jeep was really 'rubbing our noses in the dirt'!

After several attempts, I eventually got through to the Shell depot, and was informed that someone would be sent to erect the two 5,000-litre diesel storage tanks within the next few days!

Umvuma Forest was next on the list, and, unbelievably, I was connected first time straight through, and the party line was crystal clear! I asked for quotes for gum poles for mining supports, and cut timber for mine ladders and for our houses.

Prices were reasonable, transport charges were excessive, and the delivery times were three weeks – it seems to be the magic number around this area!

And it's amazing how much time it takes to make just two phone calls.

We'd had enough – 'phone phrustration', I called it – so we drove over and called in to see Ian Davidson again, who, as Secretary of the Insiza Rural Council, was also responsible for beer licensing permits.

He told us that there were two types:

Firstly – amazingly enough – 'beer brewed by the employees'!

The rules and standards would be far too expensive for most groups of workers, and that's probably why most choose to have illegal 'Changaa' distilleries hidden away on the farms, and in the bush!

And secondly, 'beer purchased by employer'.

I completed the application forms, with copies to Chibuku Brewery, Bulawayo and the BSAP Police, Fort Rixon, which would allow us to order up to 80 gallons of beer a weekend from the Chibuku Brewery. Yes, 80 gallons! That should be sufficient for the mine workers to 'sail' through Saturday night and 'dive' deep into Sunday morning!

On the way back to the mine, we saw some very tall gum trees about 100 yards from the road, towering above the bush thicket and thorn trees.

It would be a godsend if we could buy the trees from the rancher, and cut them ourselves.

This would save us hours of wasted time driving to the Shangani Rail Depot to collect the poles.

There was a signpost – 'Macaveni Ranch – S & J Schur' – and we turned off the road and drove down a winding dirt track, kicking up more dust that settled on the already dust-laden bushes and thorn trees... on and over the brow of a small rise, when were surprised to see several bright purple flowering jacaranda trees that 'popped' up into view. On rounding another bend, we were treated to an amazing contrast to the dusty brown bush we'd been driving through – a vast, colourful panorama of lush green lawns, the reds, yellows and oranges of blooming flower beds, blossoming bushes of all shades, and the cool blue of a large swimming pool!

"Wooow!" exclaimed Joseph and I in unison. "What a beautiful oasis!"

Two large beige ridgeback dogs bounded towards us as we stepped out of our vehicle.

A woman waved and called out a friendly 'good morning, don't worry, they won't bother you whilst I'm around' as she descended the terrace steps of an old, but palatial abode and walked down the long green-grassed slopes towards our pick-up.

She was a pleasant-looking woman in her forties, with a warm smile and a whole mouthful of crooked teeth, which seemed to get in each other's way when she started speaking.

"Hello, I'm Jeanette, and you two must be the young men from South Africa who are reopening the Claremont mine. Come with me. You must be thirsty; we can have some tea while we chat."

The gum trees were not for sale, she explained. "It would be a crime to destroy them; they are the last remnants of what was a well-treed area before the miners, over a period of several decades, chopped down every tree they could find to use as timber in their mines."

She showed us around her house, which she informed us was built in the 1890s by one of Rhodesia's early pioneers, a man called White.

She and her husband had preserved it, and, where necessary, restored it to its original state, exactly as it was last century.

Very high ceilings and large 'sit-around' open-hearth fireplaces, adorned with magnificently carved wooden surroundings of figures, depicting some epic ox wagon treks into the hinterland of Rhodesia.

The polished wooden floors gave slightly, producing a strange echo that shadowed us as we toured the house.

All in all, a most beautiful mansion.

It made our makeshift beds and a table made of old concrete blocks all jammed into a small, cramped African hut look a bit sick. Still, if all goes well…

The main 'dirt highway' between Fort Rixon and Filabusi passes through the middle of our mine claims for a distance of about one kilometre.

On the other side of the road to the Nelly 404 mine is a huge stone water tank, which is owned by Rancher Jackson, an embittered old bastard, who, as previously mentioned, is going out of his way to make life as difficult as possible for us mining our claims on his ranch.

This tank is fed from borehole water pumped by a windmill, and it is always overflowing.

But, he had written a letter forbidding us to use the water from the tank for any purpose whatsoever, with copies sent not only to the mining commissioner, as usual, but also to the Insiza Conservation Authority and our local Insiza Rural Council – both of which, incidentally, he is the chairman!

Water was a huge problem for us.

Our water pumps had not yet been delivered, so we were unable to draw water from either the flooded Claremont parallel or the Nelly 404 mines on our claims.

When Joseph and I arrived back at the mine, Crispin told us that, shortly after we had left, a tractor and trailer had driven around the whole mining area. All the 'cut-down' metal drums, which Jackson's cattle drank from after heavy rains filled them, had been removed.

Mr Jackson had instructed the driver to load them onto the trailer, with anything else, rusted or not, that could be used for holding water.

Crispin had just finished telling us this story when two of our building boys came back with empty water cans, saying that Jackson had stopped them filling up at the water tank, and said if he caught them again he'd get the police to lock them up!

Well, that was all we needed, because, without water, everything grinds to a halt!

Not only for building, but for personal use for us and our miners – drinking water, washing, cooking and cleaning clothes.

We had been desperately looking for a temporary solution until we could find an alternative water supply, or, even better, get our water pumps pumping water from our underground mines – there's enough down there to fill the Fort Rixon dam!

When Joseph was back in Gwelo, he'd buy eight 25-gallon plastic drums to hold water, but he would not be returning to the mine until Saturday, so we still had the problem of getting enough containers that we could fill up at Jackson's tank at night – to give us enough water to last throughout the following day.

This would mean that none of our workers would be seen during the day visiting to collect water from Jackson's 'swimming pool' – Jesus, if he knew we actually went swimming there early every morning, he'd have a cadenza!

Our African workers were even more upset and angry than we were, because, in their culture, to deny someone access to water is as bad as killing them!

We started scratching our heads as to where we could get some containers when George, the first worker I had employed, came over and told us of an old *mdala* called 'Feet', who lived a few miles down the road from the ridge.

He was a local chief and he might be able to help us.

Now it turned out that Feet had been working for Jackson for many years, and, when we told him of the water tank problem, he exploded, uttering a stream of very abusive words in perfect English; 'words' that even I wouldn't dare to write down!

He immediately began shouting some instructions to his wife and daughters, who quickly rushed off carrying small cans.

Feet rolled a large old metal drum over to the fire and began to melt some tar to patch up a hole in it. He'd just finished when the women came back with several containers of water for us, which Feet and George loaded onto the back of the pick-up, and, laughing, Feet exclaimed, "This water comes straight from Jackson's house pump!"

That cracked me up, and tears of laughter ran down my cheeks as we all shuddered with utter merriment! But, before we could thank him, Feet had vanished, leaving us standing there alone.

A few moments later, he appeared wheeling an old bicycle and told us to follow him in the pick-up. We turned off the murram road and bounced, literally kangaroo jumping, along a track for about 300 metres into the bush.

He stopped, and, smiling a broad, broad smile, pointed to a small stream. "Look over there! That is natural running water, which is public, and Jackson has no say over it! This should solve your water problem until you can start pumping your own supply!"

We quickly filled up the big tar-patched drum, using the smaller containers to scoop up more of the clear, fresh water from the stream – to us, this was lifesaving 'liquid gold'.

He handed me a small brown paper bag, saying it was a welcoming present for us.

It contained four fresh eggs – Jesus! They couldn't have been any better, even if they were made of solid gold!

Back at the mine, and in a much more relaxed frame of mind, Joseph and I exchanged notes, and, armed with a long 'shopping/things to do' list, he set off for Gwelo, and would phone me at 6pm on Friday at the Fort Rixon phone booth.

This 'remote' phoning was a hell of a drag, driving, each time, a 30-kilometre round trip, and never being one hundred percent sure if you would actually speak to the person you wanted – you might not even be able to get through to them, or they might not be available, and quite often on these joint party lines it was pot luck if you could hold a one-on-one conversation without being interrupted by the 'gossip girls'! But it was our nearest and only form of contact with the 'outside world' – as Ian Davidson would say!

With half a dozen workers and all of the containers we could find – even an egg cup would have helped – I drove off into the darkness and parked the pick-up near to Jackson's large, still-overflowing water tank.

The workers formed a chain, laughing and chanting as the water-filled containers sped through the night air – they really enjoyed this; I couldn't have given them a better present.

We offloaded the drum and various containers at the chosen places where water was most needed, both for building and personal use.

Utterly exhausted, I went and sat in my hut.

Situnda brought me a pint mug of coffee, which I drained in no time at all, and immediately flaked out on my bed into a deep, deep sleep – it's so easy after working outside all day in the sun, from 5:30am!

. . .

That damn 'Japanese water torture' woke me up at about three in the morning, with the constant drip, drip, drip on my face.

Torrential rain was hammering away on my grass roof, water pouring through in several places!

In the darkness, I struggled to move my bed – a mattress on planks, on blocks – into such a position that the water only fell onto the bed in one place, at the foot end, which I covered with a plastic bag. It was fortunate that Joseph was not sleeping here tonight as well; otherwise, there would have been no room at all to make such a manoeuvre.

Luckily, the rain had stopped when I next awoke to the sound of our daily 'start gong' – a large piece of metal, vibrating after being struck by another metal bar.

This gong was hanging from the branch of a huge tree, the 'prison tree', which we had inherited; a leftover from the last time there was a working mine here – the 'prison' consisting of a metal bar-loop sticking out of the tree trunk, and any 'law breaker', invariably a worker who had injured another during a drunken fight, would be padlocked to it until the police came to take him away.

As I emerged from my wet, sodden 'bedroom', I was greeted by Crispin, who told me that most of the 10 huts in the village compound were also leaking.

"Crispin, the 55 spare bundles of cut grass that I'd bought from a native woman a few weeks ago can be put to good use today. Tell Langton, the builder, to thatch the roof of my hut properly with 10 more bundles, but first let's go with him to the workers' compound to find out how badly the roofs of other huts were leaking."

Langton soon identified the 'big leakers', like my hut, and Crispin arranged for the remaining bundles of cut grass to be used to fix these rain-related roofing problems.

Walking back from the compound, I noticed how quickly paths and tracks are worn in the grass veld. Although we had only been on the mine for a couple of weeks, the tyre tracks leading from the buildings to the dirt road were quite noticeable, and you could clearly see where the workers had trampled through the tall grasses, making new footpaths leading straight to Jackson's water tank – and, unfortunately, these were distinctly visible from the murram road too!

Since the water problem had grown more urgent, extra workers were needed to help prepare the large dry-stone base for the water tank at the Nelly 404, so I allocated those who were normally helping Cassius, the builder, who hadn't turned up for work. Cassius was not staying in the mine compound yet, and lived about 40 miles away in a native reserve township.

By the time I got back to my hut, it was already past 8 o'clock – Jesus, two hours had flashed by!

Situnda was preparing the 'potegai', which is mealie meal mixed into a stiff paste and flattened between two sheets of metal. When it's been on the open fire for 40 minutes, it becomes a thick biscuit, crispy on the outside, but a sticky, soggy porridge in the middle.

A picture of fried eggs immediately appeared in my mind, so I politely refused a piece of potegai that Situnda brought over to me, and watched him walk towards the mine with the tray (a rusty tin lid) full of potagai pieces for the workers' 'nine-sies'– a little extra that we give them on a five-minute break at 9am, which they seem to appreciate.

Just then, a lone figure on a bicycle approached, and, as the person drew nearer, puffing and panting louder and louder, I could see the sweaty being of none other than our builder, Cassius.

He virtually fell off the bicycle, and, amidst all the puffing and spluttering,

I gathered that the axle on his motorised ox wagon had broken, and he'd been riding this bike for two and a half hours to get here.

I watched Cassius as he walked, or rather meandered like a drunken man over to his 'office building' project, and was glad in a way that he was so knackered after his bicycle ride; otherwise, I would have had to listen to his 'I'm the greatest…' for the rest of the morning!

With the weekend coming up, I left for the Fort Rixon phone booth to phone and check if we could get beer on Saturday for the mine boys from the Chibuku Brewery in Bulawayo.

They told me that they had no record at all of the Ridge Top Mine, Fort Rixon having a licence to buy beer.

Bugger it, I thought, and drove straight down to see Ian Davidson, who informed me that the brewery would not sell beer to our mine until they had a copy of the Insiza Rural Council Beer permit.

"*And*, that copy is in the sack over there, and will not go out until the next mail run!"

"Sounds like the old Wild West!" I remarked. "Everything waiting for the stage coach to arrive!"

"Indeed, just like in the old Wild West!" he said, and began smiling as thoughts of the past conjured up pictures in his mind and he started recalling stories of how, as a young boy, when he first came up to Rhodesia from South Africa, he used to travel with his grandfather by ox wagon into areas where there were no roads at all, to go prospecting for gold in the bush – sometimes for two or three weeks at a time.

In those days, African runners delivered the mail to a settlement like Fort Rixon once a week!

Years later, they used horse-drawn stage coaches that would carry everyone and everything, including the mail.

It was enthralling to hear his vivid descriptions and stories about those bygone times, and I was becoming more engrossed listening to his exploits as a youngster… when, suddenly, he stopped.

And, as if I wasn't there at all, he got up and shuffled over to another desk and started to fill out a form that his African clerk had given him.

His clerk began calling out numbers and names… and the old man was in a different world to me.

I looked out the window and saw that the 'modern stage coach' van had arrived, and, realising that the mail would completely dominate him for a good while, I slipped out and drove back to the phone booth to make a few more calls.

Unfortunately, it was after 1 o'clock and the exchange had closed for lunch – I'd been listening to old Davidson reminiscing for a good hour, and would now have to wait in the pick-up until the exchange opened again at 2pm.

I must have dozed off…

Suddenly, I awoke to the sounds of heavy rain; it was belting down… then I heard a strange tap, tap, tapping noise on my window.

"There's a call for you!" shouted the exchange operator, and he rushed back out of the rain and into the store.

I maneuvered my pick-up closer to the small hut so that I could reach out through my window and pick up the black, heavy duty phone horn, which was housed under a small covering hood that protected it from the rain.

"Hello… Hello… buzzzzzz… click!"

The African operator called out to me, "The line is dead; it happens quite often with these heavy rains!"

I was hugely disappointed, and once again frustrated with the phone situation! Such a waste of time driving all that way to Fort Rixon just to get an annoying buzzing in my ear!

I went into the store and bought some different types of tobacco and snuff for Crispin to sell in our shop, and drove back slowly on the slippery roads, through yet another downpour.

The nearer I got to the mine, the lighter the rain became and it was hardly drizzling at all when I pulled up in front of the partially built office/store

Crispin told me that all the boys had been working through 'til the end of their shift at 2pm in the on-off light drizzle.

Most of them seemed to be performing okay, although I had my doubts and my beady eyes on a couple of them. Mind you, if they were not supervised the whole time by either yourself or a good boss boy, they would be lying down in the shade, sleeping – I suppose that's one good thing about these rains; the ground is far too wet for that!

The next hour or so was spent going through the equipment stores with Crispin.

He had made various books and sheets for booking stock in/out, and would be recording items issued to each worker, including overalls, raincoats, mine hats, carbide lamps and various other small items of equipment.

We also checked the 'time book' and updated the workers' 'tickets' to see who should be paid the following morning.

The mine workers are paid by a ticket system.

Each day that they work is recorded on a small pink ticket card.

When 30 days have been marked off, they are due to be paid.

Those who have not missed a single working day on that ticket will get an extra bonus, and their wage rate increases the longer they stay with us, and so does the bonus.

We checked all the tickets, and, on my very first pay-out day, I would have to pay just the one worker, George.

When I came out of the office, I was pleased to see that the rain had stopped completely, because I had to get back in my pick-up and drive again to Fort Rixon to receive the 6pm phone call from Joseph.

Some good news this time.

He had bought the 25-gallon plastic drums we needed for water storage, and he had also put in a $300 offer to buy one of the old prefabricated houses from the Bata Shoe Company, which was in the process of building new houses for its staff.

If we could get one of those, we would demolish it ourselves and transport everything to the mine. It would probably take six trips or more from Gwelo to the mine using the pick-ups, as there would be a mountain of stuff to take:

Prefabricated walls and ceilings, a bath, toilet, piping, wiring, window frames, doors, flooring and, most important for us at the moment, a whole roof full of corrugated iron sheets, which don't seem to be available anywhere in Matabeleland.

That was good 'keep your fingers crossed' news indeed!

As I began my return trip to the mine, dusk was drawing nearer and one of the pure delights of living in the bush occurs – you are treated to an impressive nature show.

A small, light brown, four-legged animal (like an English fox) scampered across the road; groups of grey and white speckled guinea fowl were running around chaotically in all directions on the road in front of me as my pick-up neared, before they flew off to the side at the last second, narrowly missing being struck by the bumper of my pick-up.

The occasional pair of fast ears and bushy tails streaking across too.

And some dainty buck with black and white tails springing off into the bush as I approached.

As I rounded a corner, to me, the most beautiful sight of all, five kudus gracefully swept across the track and bounded into the cover of the bush.

These large, gorgeous, regal-looking antelopes stood motionless amongst the camouflaging foliage and thorn trees – I could just make out the shape of one or two of their heads and the pink ears with white insides, which were lit up by the last rays of the flickering light of day.

Such enthralling sights make a journey in the bush so enjoyable.

I pulled up in front of my hut and saw that Situnda had put the pot of stew back on the fire again.

The thought of that re-reheated stew triggered off a terrible 'stomach ache' feeling – then I remembered that I hadn't been for two days!

Suffice it to say, I felt a lot better a few minutes and some fifty yards later!

And, believe it or not, that stew tasted really good – or had I been out here in the bush too long!

I simply gobbled it down.

As the thunder and lightning began their nightly performance and the rain pelted down, I climbed into a dry bed, blew out the hurricane lamp, and, with the comforting knowledge that my newly thatched hut was one hundred percent waterproof, I quickly fell asleep.

Forbidden Pool

After a long, 'dry' sleep, I woke up feeling good, and slipped up to Jackson's 'swimming pool'.

It was so refreshing floating in the cool water, watching the sky becoming redder and redder.

What a wonderful sight – very slowly, as if in a camera slide-by-slide show, first the distant hills became outlined with a pale pink line, followed by the trees becoming similarly highlighted… then the dark, shaded hills and trees transformed into the greens and browns as the light was slowly increased by Mother Nature's dimmer switch, until I could see everything in its natural glory at the start of a brand-new, and, for a change, bright sunny day!

From my hut, it's a mere 100-yard walk to the mine through the bush with its awaking, melodious sounds, instead of the 45-minute drive it used to take me when I worked in the city, battling through the traffic-jammed morning rush hour, with hooting, angry voices and gestures being exchanged between frustrated motorists, to arrive at, and be incarcerated in a cold grey concrete office block for the rest of the day – such completely contrasting scenarios!

I called all the mine boys together and told them that they would be working until 1 o'clock on Sunday, and unfortunately the Chibuku Brewery would not deliver beer this weekend to the mine – and waited for their reactions….

None! Not a single complaint, so Crispin had obviously done a very good job last night of reminding everyone that, as we were only just starting up the mine, some things take time to arrange, but we would soon put them right – like we did with the leaking huts!

I received a more favourable response – in fact, even some jubilant shouting and yelling – when they learnt that Crispin and George had made an arrangement to collect beer from the farm workers at Feet's place.

George was even happier than the rest of them.

He was paid the $9 ticket wage, 50 cents bonus and $5 for the 55 bundles of grass that his wife had cut.

I then spoke sternly to my workers. "We have a very serious problem, and you are not allowed to get water from Jackson's big water tank near the road!"

I explained further that water was now to be taken from another of Jackson's water tanks that was nearer to my house site. This tank was inaccessible from and could not be seen from the main murram road.

However, we would only collect the water at night, until Joseph brought the large 25-gallon drums, when we could get all the water we needed from our new source, 'Feet's stream'.

That heard and acknowledged by nodding heads, but probably to be broken many times each day, they all went about their work.

Cash-rich George asked for two days off.

Cassius also wanted to go home to try to fix his motorised ox wagon, and would only be back on the Monday or Tuesday.

I wandered over to the house site, lit a cigarette and sat on the edge of the old foundations, admiring the view across to the distant hills – captivating!

I crossed over the road to the old mine dumps of the Claremont, and could see that the recent heavy rains had washed more from the slimes dams, down the hill into the small river bed, which was now flowing.

It was a good thing that Pat had warned us not to mill at the Claremont site, because of this very problem. That's why we had chosen to set up a 5-stamp mill at the Nelly 404, and to build new slimes dams.

From the top of the dumps, I could see an overgrown track, which I followed and came across two more open mine shafts, almost certainly on the same gold reef.

Standing on the old concrete stamp mill block, I looked down and saw an army of Matabele ants, thousands of them, forming a long snaking black column several inches wide as they swarmed through the bush. These black ants are about an inch long and can give you quite a nasty bite.

I watched them for several minutes as they moved across the ground. They were going one way empty, and coming from the other direction carrying grubs, some larger than themselves.

They didn't seem to have any traffic rules about keeping to the right or to the left – they were crawling 'higgledy-piggledy' all over each other in their hurry to do their work.

Suddenly, a huge rock fell into the middle of the column. (Whoops!) Immediately, some of the ants went berserk, making loud, horrible angry hissing sounds as dozens of them started attacking the rock – Jesus! Was I glad that I was standing on top of the concrete block!

Meanwhile, the procession of food-carrying Matabele ants made a slight detour to go around the rock, leaving their soldier ant colleagues ferociously attacking the enemy rock!

Back at the mine, I told Crispin to get three munts to start clearing our proposed mill site.

One must chop the thorn trees, one must dig up the stumps and the third must fill in the holes, and not all three doing the same job; i.e. one does it while the other two bloody well watch!

I spoke to Dereery, the builder, and his assistant.

If they worked a double shift on Saturday, they would get an extra day on their tickets.

They had to put a corrugated iron roof on the dagga brick house destined for Staff, and it must be ready tonight – he should be coming to the mine with Joseph this evening.

Oh, tonight! As soon as Joseph arrived, I would leave straight away for the house in Gwelo.

To civilisation, to a hot bath and a Sunday morning lay-in, followed by a cup of tea that doesn't taste of dirty socks! Heaven!

Off to Fort Rixon yet again, to phone Willie to find out why he had not turned up this morning for work, and was told that his boss, Mr Mullins, had asked him to stay on for a few more days.

I bought some more sugar, soap powder, biscuits, bread, soap, aspirins, razorblades and some fresh rolls for Crispin's shop – they were more expensive than in town, but our workers appreciated that they could get 'the basics' from our shop when they needed them – and 'on tick'.

Hunger pains dictated that I should try one of these fresh rolls, which I ate dry as I drove, but, on my return to the mine, I fried myself some onions and soft scrambled eggs, which made the perfect succulent filling for a second roll.

I went to check how much of the clearing work at the main Nelly 404 shaft had been completed, which was sometimes difficult to judge when there were lots of workers rushing around – or, rather, ambling around, holding their pangas and carrying bits of bushes!

As I opened the gate to the Nelly 404, I noticed something brightly coloured on the side of the track. I looked more closely and saw a little ball of dung with two bright turquoise dung beetles remaining dead still and leaning against it – probably whistling nervously, trying to be inconspicuous!

I stood completely still, and, after a few seconds, they started fighting over the dung ball, until the 'victor' stood on its front legs and started rolling the ball of dung along using its back legs – quite a fascinating sight.

It then dawned on me that this was close to where I had relieved my aching stomach the previous evening. I checked the exact spot, and saw about 20 of these dung beetles making my excrement into balls about ten times their own size, ready to start the long roll home – free, 'roll away' bush sanitary services!

(*Sacred to Ancient Egyptians, the dung beetle is truly a fascinating beetle.*

Without these busy creatures, we could not live in the tropics, as we would be knee-high in dung and swamped by flies!

The dung beetles' importance to the ecosystem can be seen in a study of a one and a half kilogram pile of elephant dung on the African savannah. The elephant dung attracted thousands of dung beetles and the whole pile had been eaten, buried or rolled away by the dung beetles – in just two hours!)

At the shaft, there was such a commotion going on and work had stopped – the boys had come across two snakes while clearing the dense undergrowth, and they refused to carry on.

On assessing the situation, I could see that they had cleared the area from behind the office up to about 10 metres from the shaft, which left an isolated patch of thicket in a slight dip in the ground.

I told Crispin to get some diesel from the can on my truck, pour it over the undergrowth and set it on fire; there was no danger of it spreading and it would burn itself out.

Any snakes that survived would be slithering their way at top speed to safer snake country!

The crackle of the burning bush could still be heard as I walked down to see how Staff's house was progressing.

It turned out that the corrugated iron sheets that we had borrowed from our rented house in Gwelo were not enough to cover the complete roofing area. There was only one thing to do: 'patch that thatch' using bundles of grass and pray that it didn't rain on Staff's first night at our mine – otherwise, he would have to sleep with Joseph in our hut!

Dusk started to darken the mining area and the grey laurie (go away!) birds were quiet at last. These birds have a cry that sounds like 'go away, go away', and they act as a sort of early warning system to other wildlife.

The sky became blacker and blacker, being filled with ominous rain clouds. Thunder crashes and streaks of lightning were going berserk, and not too far away either. Well, I hoped Joseph didn't bring Staff back tonight, because he'll get soaked in his house with a patched-up roof!

I looked towards Fort Rixon and could see the light from headlights flashing and flickering up and down, reflecting off the wet foliage in the bush as a vehicle approached.

Joseph had arrived!

He looked very down and upset, and told me that he had experienced a long frustrating couple of days; he'd not slept at all. His wife, Jane, in her ninth month of pregnancy, had kept him awake the whole time.

"But everything is okay with Jane?" I asked.

"Yes, she's fine; she's not the problem. It's Matt! When I went to see him, the 5-stamp mill and the James Table had all been dismantled and were stacked ready for transporting to our mine, and..." His voice trailed off.

"And...?" I prompted.

"While I was there, he got a phone call from that bloody father of mine, who managed to persuade Matt to continue mining and milling for another few months, and only then decide if the mine was viable. So Matt will erect it all again and continue his underground mining operations!"

"Shit!" I exclaimed. "So that present for our mine of a 5-stamp mill in good working condition has been cancelled by your father – one begins to wonder sometimes whether he is really on our side or not!"

"And that's not all," Joseph continued in a subdued voice. "When I went to check on the old prefab houses at Bata, they had all been sold! Why do things go wrong all the time? Why does this always happen to me!"

"*To us*, you mean!" I retorted. "We'll just have to push Ronnie Cummins at the Mines Department to pull finger and get us one of the 5-stamp mills he's been telling us about, *won't we*!"

Silence... and the familiar blank, vacant stare could clearly be seen, even in the flickering light of the hurricane lamp, and I realised that there was no point in continuing a one-sided conversation.

I drove off to Gwelo in the pouring rain, thinking it was probably just as well that Staff had not come with him tonight; otherwise, Joseph would have had even more problems to clutter his troubled mind!

. . .

I woke up without any bugs crawling over me, and no bits of corn dropping on my head as the rats spat them out!

And instead of a strongly smelling Situnda bringing me a mug of tea and invariably spilling at least half of it as he fumbled to open the plastic-sheet door of my hut, today, a bright beaming wife brought in a pot of tea, placing the tray on the bed, together with the Sunday paper.

This was the first time I'd read a newspaper since coming to Rhodesia; I'd not had the time, being so busy creating my own news stories!

We drove the kids to the memorial park for the morning.

Petrol rationing hadn't started yet, thank God, but the hours that garages could stay open had been drastically curbed, 6am to 9am and 2pm to 6pm. However, it wouldn't be long before severe cuts would have to be introduced for both industrial and personal use, as the 'flow' of petrol into the country was being drastically curbed by the UN Oil Embargo Sanctions – only at the Port of Beira in Mozambique had some oil companies defied the UN and offloaded their precious cargo of oil – or 'black gold', as the Rhodesians named it!

And, of course, South Africa was doing it's very best to help Rhodesia survive, by also transporting oil by road and by rail!

It was so pleasant and relaxing to sit in the shade of the trees and watch the kids playing.

Jeffrey, trying to copy the bigger children, chasing after them until his little legs gave up and he tumbled over, his knees getting greener and greener as the morning wore on.

Matt popped around to see us and asked us out for a few 'pots' at the Midland Hotel.

We met some of his friends, and it was fabulous to have a few civilised pints on a Sunday lunchtime – it was like being back in England.

He called me aside and said he was sorry to offer us a 5-stamp mill on the one day and take it back on the following day – but he had been advised by his father not to give the mill to us; he must continue mining, but with reduced shifts restricted just to the daylight hours.

"I was in two minds whether to carry on or not, and we argued about what *he* wanted, and what *I* wanted! But when he said he would fund my whole operation for the next three months – *he won*! How could I refuse an offer like that; it would cost me nothing and will give me time to decide if the mine was really viable or not. Sorry mate, but that was that! However, if things don't work out for me and the mill becomes available in a few months, then it's all yours!"

"Thanks Matt, but if we are not milling and producing gold in three months we'll have gone under, end of the road!"

A thought struck me; there had been several times already where the old man had changed things at the last minute to benefit himself, and not honouring his original agreed commitment to us. Perhaps that was what the old man was plotting! Let us get everything in place ready to start gold production, and he would take it over when we were forced to pull out due to lack of further working capital!

Several miners who knew him in the past had warned me to keep a wary eye open.

"But I do have some good news for you," Matt continued. "There'll be another 18 workers available because of the reduced working shifts. Also, you can have some corrugated iron sheets to put back in the garden at Hudson Road to replace the ones you borrowed, okay! Come to the mine tomorrow morning and collect them."

That was a great Sunday, being back in 'civilisation' and enjoying for the first time in Rhodesia; reading the Sunday newspaper in bed; Sunday lunchtime beers with friends; a Sunday roast leg of lamb; and relaxing, watching a little Sunday television, albeit 'songs of praise'!

. . .

An annoying nudging in my ribs startled me, and I heard Marianne gasp, "Oh! It's your mum's birthday today; how could we forget!"

I slurped down some coffee as I dressed, and dashed down to the post office to send a greetings telegram.

HAPPY BIRTHDAY MUM [STOP] YOU ALWAYS TOLD US BETTER LATE THAN NEVER [STOP] YOUR SON IN THE SUN [STOP] HELLO GRAN AND LOVE FROM RHODESIA [STOP].

At the Midlands Milling Company, they had no ration beans in stock.

"Perhaps tomorrow," I was told.

However, luckily for me, Farm Aid had several 90 kg sacks.

Beep, beep!

It was Matt, who was busy loading bags of cement onto his pick-up.

He shouted out a greeting and told me to follow him to his mine.

When we arrived, I could see that 'our promised', but unfortunately 'still his' 5-stamp mill had already been reassembled, and a ramp had been built so that the loaded cocopans from the shaft-head could be pushed to the mill and the ore tipped into a large hopper, ready to be fed into the stamp mill by a lasher with a large shovel.

An old Peugeot truck drove into the compound, followed by a Datsun pick-up.

Two guys in their late forties came over to speak to Matt and asked for some water for the old Peugeot that was boiling and bubbling away like mad.

They chatted together about Matt's mine, and told him of some problems they were experiencing where they were mining, 20 km further down the track.

One of the drive tunnels had caved in, due to careless work by a new worker who had just obtained his first blasting licence.

"You have to supervise the munts the whole time," one of them said, shaking his head ruefully. "Otherwise, there's always problems!"

Matt introduced me, explaining that I was working with one his brothers, opening up an old mine along the Claremont/Nelly reef.

"Well, bugger me!" said one of them. "I was manager of the Claremont working for R. J. Stewart & Sons from 1959 up to 1962 when old man Stewart decided to close the mine down."

And he began to reminisce over those times.

His description of the mine and the various sites added to what I already knew.

They had been mining good gold in the blue quartz reef, but it was too patchy, the lenticular reef frequently petering out, making the extraction too costly.

Fred Stewart had decided to move out to another of their mines, which was richer and being worked closer to the surface.

But there was plenty of gold left in the Claremont, which had gone down to the seventh level (approximately 700 feet deep).

"I was just telling Matt about our cave-in problems underground, due to careless blasting work by a new worker. When you start working underground, you must always check and double-check with regard to using explosives. Once when I was on leave, my drunken assistant manager couldn't be bothered to go underground to supervise the drilling of the holes before blasting.

"When a drilled hole is still intact after blasting, for safety reasons, a piece of wood should be placed firmly in the hole just in case the explosive didn't go off, thus warning jackhammer boys not to drill there again. But one of them must have seen this hole and thought he'd save himself a bit of effort by just making it deeper, and 'BAMM'!"

He had suffered severe facial damage and three other workers were injured, with bits of rock embedded in their flesh – luckily, no one was killed, but it is a sharp reminder that you must be so careful with explosives underground.

"Well, mate, it was good to meet you," Ben said, as he wrote his phone number on an empty cigarette packet. "Remember, any information you need on the Claremont, just call me, okay! And also don't forget, if you hit the 'mother lode', we'd love to celebrate it with you – come and pick us up in your Rolls Royce!" he added with a twinkle in his eye, which could have been an inner reflection of the gold he was dreaming about!

So, with their truck's 'thirst' and their own quenched, Ben Bester and his friend drove off.

It's fabulous the way these old miners go out of their way to help you if they can – exactly the opposite to a certain awkward rancher neighbour of mine!

One of Matt's boss boys, Costa, came over and gave me a list of the workers who were being laid off. We went through it together to weed out any known trouble-makers, and the lazy ones, which left 14 available experienced mine workers. These would swell our numbers to 35 – plenty for now, but we would need to take on an extra 25 to 30 workers when we were fully operational underground, and milling around the clock with three shifts.

The corrugated iron sheets were loaded onto my pick-up, and I drove back to town to the Customs/Immigration department to check on the clearance of my two Peugeots and all my personal effects.

I had received a letter from a Mr Brook stating that there was a query over the declared values of the pick-ups and would I call in so that we could sort out the matter.

He was a friendly, helpful sort and showed me that one amount on the document seemed to have been altered by the clearing agent, but, apart from that, he assured me everything else was fine.

Suddenly, there was a loud knocking on the door, and in walked what can best be described as 'a human gorilla'.

His long, swinging arms arced around his fat body as he walked towards us, his podgy round face with shifty, beady eyes darting around the room looking for 'problems'.

There was a tremendously thick black growth of hair fighting its way out from under his collar.

I tell you, if you stripped him off, he could go to an animal fancy dress party as he stood, or, rather, stooped!

His name was Smit, and he announced to us in a commanding tone that he had just that very morning been transferred from Salisbury to take over the immigration/imports section – just my bloody luck!

I had brought all our goods, including the pick-ups, into Rhodesia as duty-free immigrants' allowances, which meant we didn't have to fork out any money unless we sold them within one year. We'd be able to use them on the mine as private vehicles, but the mine wouldn't officially buy them from me for that first year.

Smit quickly scanned the documents, and, with a sneering, pleasurable grin on his face, he informed me that he was not satisfied that the vehicles were for our private use, and demanded to see bank statements for the last three months as proof that I, and not the mine, had bought them in South Africa.

And, with regard to the second-hand pick-up, he disputed the value, and said he would only allow a 10% depreciation per year on the vehicle, and not 25%.

He slapped the forms down in front of me with a bang, and, glaring at me with that 'I'm going to make your life very difficult' look, he stated that they all had to be redone!

"Each vehicle has to be on a separate form, one for you and one for your wife, which she has to sign herself. And you must also get those South African bank statements before I will process anything further!"

I uttered under my breath something that rhymed with *Smit*!

He then left the room with a smug grin on his podgy face, leaving Mr Brook and me looking at each other in disbelief.

This meant more delays, with further letter writing to my bank in South Africa, and, until we were able to get the white second-hand pick-up cleared by Customs, and the depreciated value agreed for duty and tax purposes, we couldn't sell that vehicle to raise the extra capital as we had planned – and were counting on!

Matt badly needed a good, reliable runner to replace his ancient jalopy, and was prepared to pay the duty and the tax on top of our asking sale price, but now, with the Christmas/New Year holiday period only a few weeks away, this further delay could mean his crippled pick-up would have to survive another month or more – and our bank balance too!

Time for a strong black coffee at the Midland Hotel, where I could phone Curtis at the Bulawayo Mines Yard to chase him up, and also confirm Joseph's meeting with him for the following day. That was most urgent now that we were not going to get the 5-stamp mill from Matt!

Unbelievably, Curtis told me that the inspection of the 5-stamp mill, alternator and hoist had not yet been approved by a certain Mr Pope, the regional mining engineer, who wanted to meet us, first for a general chat and to discuss why we wanted this equipment!

Good God! More bloody wasted time. Parkinson was right; there are far too many government civil servants in this world – and most of them should be shot on sight!

There was, however, one good bit of news.

Ronnie Cummins had left a message for me that the mobile compressor railed up from South Africa had arrived at the Mines Yard, and I could collect the accompanying documents from his office when I was next in town.

One last visit, to Lewis Lumber to check if they could deliver the timber we required any quicker and cheaper than Umvuma Forest.

They took down the details and would work out a price quote for me, and phone the message through to the Fort Rixon exchange – a useful bush message board arrangement for us.

In the old gold rush days, such message boards could be found all over the country, at each supplies store, hotel or police post – they were the only way miners could keep in touch with each other.

Off to the Farm Aid supplier to collect a 90 kg sack of ration beans, 10 pockets of cement, plastic sheeting, cutters and pliers.

I decided to go on the hunt again for the illusive corrugated iron sheets that we needed so desperately, and checked first at the auctioneer's yards – no luck!

A drive through the back streets to check with various Indian general dealers was proving equally fruitless… until one of them told me that the old Phoenix Theatre was being demolished by the company MacDonald & Son.

In a flash, I was there, and saw this big man in a kilt.

He was standing there amongst the stacks of wood, doors and windows taken from the partially demolished theatre, but I smiled to myself when I saw that the whole roof was still complete, untouched; plenty of corrugated iron sheets – enough for our house and all the buildings on our mine, for sure

When I asked if I could buy the whole roof, the canny old Scot's bronzed face cracked into a broad grin, and he said, "I'll tell you, laddie, what I've told all the others; when I take it down in about two weeks, it will be 'first come, first served' – and laddie, you'll have to fight your way past a hundred Africans all clamouring for this iron sheeting!"

It was now getting late in the afternoon, so I decided not to drive to Fort Rixon, but rather have a meal at home with the family and an early night.

My alarm clock was set for 3:30am – in order, as Joseph regularly, but often monotonously would say, "To get an early start!"

. . .

I drove along the tarmac road towards Shangani in total darkness, my headlights occasionally picking out a tractor, but there was no other traffic at all on the road.

As I turned onto the dirt road towards Fort Rixon, I could see from the shining reflections of my headlights in the puddles on the muddy road that there had been a lot of rain during the night.

It was about 5 o'clock. Darkness was vanishing as it scurried to another part of our world; dawn was breaking, and the brightness of my headlights was paling as Mother Nature's 'big headlight' began to cause red and orange streaks to race across the early morning sky.

On rounding a corner, I saw this large black eagle in the middle of the road.

I slowed down, but was almost on top of the bird before it began to flap those powerful wings.... It was about bonnet height and going in the same direction as the pick-up, so I was treated to this fabulous view of the clawed feet hanging in front of the windscreen, with the wings beating up and down until they had achieved enough propulsion to lift this large bird up and above the truck, to soar away into the brightening skies.

Immediately, I noticed more eagles, some in the trees, but one or two on the edge of the road.

I pulled up, and, using my binoculars, I scanned both sides of the track, and could see other black eagles on a bare, wet, open patch of ground on the left.

And the reason?

Hundreds of frogs springing around on the waterlogged ground trying to evade vicious beaks and sharp claws...

I drove on, and every now and then witnessed the common sight of rabbits scampering along the road, darting this way and that, until they veered off into the bush to avoid being hit.

Then, suddenly, right ahead of me on the dirt road, I saw a tall grey bird with long, long legs.

It looked at my pick-up approaching, turned quickly around to face the other way and started running down the road.... As I drew nearer, it half turned its head and, on seeing how close I was, in desperation, it opened the huge span of its wings and ran on with a very comical, wobbly run as it began to slowly flap them until those extended wings lifted it from the ground, when, more impressively and very gracefully, it gained height and banked off to the right – nature's superior, original 'Concorde'!

I found out later that this very large bird was a secretary bird, having an eagle-like head and crane-like legs, giving it a height of more than four feet (1.3 m), and a wingspan up to seven and a half feet (2.2 m).

I pulled into the mine compound, and, on opening my door, was greeted by Joseph, all 'ponced' up in a light powder-blue safari suit.

After being treated by Mother Nature to such beauty and graceful power on my early morning drive, it was a complete contrast to behold my spindly, white pasty-faced partner!

Joseph was about to shoot off to Bulawayo to meet Curtis, until I told him of my phone conversation. I suggested that, as the matter was so critical to us, he and his old man should go together, since the old man lent some mining credibility to us 'greenhorns'!

Joseph went into a mad flap and ran to his vehicle, saying that he was leaving immediately for Belingwe to pick up his father, and go straight to Bulawayo to the Mines Department.

"Joseph!" I called out. "Do us both a favour; go the other way, over to Fort Rixon and phone your father first to check if he's available!"

I was pleased to see when he turned onto the murram road that the muddy water kicked up by his pick-up was 'pointing' in the direction of Fort Rixon, and thankfully not Belingwe.

About an hour later, he returned and told me that his father blew his top at this latest delay and the ineptitude of some people in the Mines Department, but he could not go to Bulawayo.

He suggested instead that he would phone an old partner of his called Mr Dillan, now Minister of Mines with the Rhodesian Government, and would get back to us when a new appointment with the mining commissioner in Bulawayo was confirmed.

After pacing up and down for a few minutes muttering to himself, Joseph came over and sat down with me under the branches of the prison tree – I thought of locking him to it until he calmed down, but that proved unnecessary; Situnda brought over a mug of hot tea, which seemed to do the trick.

I updated Joseph on my trip, carefully avoiding the other disappointing news of the delay in the Customs clearance of the vehicles. And, of course, not mentioning that the 5-stamp mill had already been rebuilt at the Gwelo Mine, *and,* that his father had offered to sponsor Matt's mining for the next three months – *three bloody months;* money that could have contributed towards our costs – his so-called partners – to help our cash-strapped company's situation!

But Joseph was pleased we would be getting another 14 mineworkers from Matt, and, when Staff came as our senior boss boy, we would have a hardcore, experienced team of workers on our mine.

After a while, Joseph was in a more cheerful mood and he related to me some more amazing developments in the Rancher Jackson saga.

On Monday, Joseph had left to go to Fort Rixon to make some phone calls, but he'd only driven a few kilometres when he realised he'd forgotten the shopping list for the mine shop, and he turned back.

For once, it would transpire that his absent-mindedness would prove most fortunate.

Apparently, as soon as he had left the mine, Jackson had appeared on the scene – it's very strange, because he never comes when we are there. He'd stomped around the whole mining area, shouting at the Africans, telling them that they were not allowed to use his blocks and dagga bricks for work on the buildings, and he would prosecute anyone who touched these blocks or any scrap metal on his land!

"I pulled up and went berserk!" Joseph said excitedly. "And told Jackson that we were going to mine here whether he liked it or not! We would not be intimidated by his bloody-mindedness or his threatening letters, and the sooner he got used to the idea the better! And when Jackson started complaining to me that we must not take water from his tank or he would prosecute us, I laughed and said we didn't need to use the water tank anymore, as we were now filling up from a local stream, to which Jackson replied that we must not use the road to the stream, which was on his land! I told him to bugger off our mining claims, as he was disrupting our legitimate mining business! At that point, Jackson cooled down a bit and told me that he had only written those letters about forbidding us to use water and timber in order to 'open negotiations' with us!"

Joseph carried on to tell me of Jackson's request for us to make a list of every old cement block, every dagga brick and any pieces of scrap metal that we had used, and how much we were prepared to pay him for those items. Otherwise, he would put his lawyers on the case, and all the buildings that we were erecting would be pulled down!

Wisely ignoring Jackson's baiting, Joseph had said he would have to consult with his partner and see if there was a possible arrangement we could come to.

"That was well said, Joseph; we can consult with each other – *indefinitely*! But now it's time for a water run to the stream on *his land*!"

The drums were loaded, and, with a few boys, I drove to the turn off that leads down to the stream. The track was very bumpy, with one huge crevasse/hole that was difficult to get around, even with an empty load….

But, on driving back with eight large 25-gallon drums full of water, the weight was too much.

I slowly steered the pick-up around the hole, but I didn't have enough torque power to get up the slope; it was virtually impossible! In fact, impassable!

The boys jumped off and I told them I'd have another go, but they must help by pushing the pick-up as soon as it started to slow down. I reversed and took a running start.

The pick-up reared and bucked, water sloshing everywhere, but I managed, with the boys' pushing power, to make it to the top of the slope and onto the murram road – but unfortunately having lost far too much water.

On the next water run, we'd have to take some picks and shovels to fill in that hole and to level the track.

Joseph had a good laugh when I told him about it, and we went for a walk around the claims to see how things were progressing.

He told me that he couldn't stand the strong smell of Situnda in our hut any longer, so he had promoted him to be a policeman, which pleased the old *mdala* no end – he even asked for a bloody policeman's helmet!

In his place was Elliot, a clean-looking young man who would cook and do the washing for us.

He also speaks reasonable English, a real blessing for me, my Chilapalapa being in the 'nappy' stage, in all senses of the word! Joseph, though, had no such problems, having grown up on the mines, and could speak their language fluently.

Cassius was still blaming Rancher Jackson for the lack of real progress on building the office.

"Cassius, the quickest? Even a tortoise moves quicker than you!" I ribbed him. "And you must finish all the block work of the walls, *today*!"

He said, "That would be no trouble!"

I replied, "You'd better be right; otherwise, they'll be plenty of trouble, *for you*!"

I thought I'd go over to the house site, to plan a few things in my head.

As I approached the murram road, I saw Elliot carrying a plastic container and walking on the well-worn path from the road to Jackson's water tank.

I reminded him that he was not allowed to take water from the tank, except under the cover of darkness – at night!

He replied that it was for us, for cooking.

"Oh well, all right, get it quickly," I replied. "But each time you get water, you must walk a different way to the tank, then you won't make such an obvious path that Jackson can see as he drives past on the road. Do you understand?"

"Yes Boss!" was the reply.

But I had learnt from bitter experience that they always say 'yes' just to please you! So, being a bit crafty, I asked him to repeat to me what I had just told him.

He replied virtually word for word!

Well, I was surprised and quite impressed; at last, a houseboy who listened and understood English – until I watched him walk straight along the same well-worn path again!

Jesus, you really can pull your hair out sometimes trying to get the message across!

The area around the house site was very spacious and should provide us with a huge garden someday. Although the grass was very wild and patchy, it would be fun for Marianne and the kids to gradually restore a large lawn, and add some other plants and flowers.

Besides the two large flowering jacaranda trees, there were a few other big trees that gave good shade, adding character too. But, behind this area of the 'old European garden', it was real thick African bush and acacia thorn trees.

Joseph and I had packed up our things and were ready to leave for Gwelo, so that we could each bring seven ex-Matt mineworkers and their belongings back to our mine the following day, when suddenly that 'oh crap! I've just remembered something' look came into Joseph's eyes!

"We can't go! The conservation officer is coming in the morning to see us, and discuss issues relating to the slimes and sand dumps."

We mulled it over and decided that it was best if only Joseph went to Gwelo in the evening, because Jane was 'due to drop' in the next few days.

I'd stay overnight, and see this conservation chap in the morning, and come up to Gwelo afterwards to collect the other seven workers from Matt's mine.

Joseph had just driven out of sight when the rain started to fall heavily again – I always seem to be the one who has to sleep in the hut when it rains!

Mind you, he'll have a tiring journey back to Gwelo in the heavy rain storms driving along these slippery dirt roads.

. . .

Elliot was calling out repeatedly 'coffee is ready!' for quite a few minutes before the message eventually got through to me.

I forced myself out of the haze of slumber and stepped into the stark, bright morning sunlight.

With the early morning mug of coffee, I was given a letter that one of Jackson's farm workers had dropped off earlier.

It was not only about the usual 'stop using my cement blocks to build a shed on my land' or 'stop taking water from my water tanks', but, this time, 'hot off the press' following on from the accidental unplanned meeting with Joseph yesterday:

"*...I understand that you are now getting water from the river on my land, and you are using a track which is a conservation problem, an environmental hazard!*"

Well, that's one problem that could be immediately solved, as it was time for the morning 'water run'— so I took five workers with picks and shovels, as well as the empty plastic barrels, and drove down the disputed track to the stream, which, with the heavy rain the previous night, was now deeper and flowing faster.

While the barrels were being filled, three of the boys set about hacking up mud and shovelling it into the crevasse. We collected some big stones from along the river bed and patched them into the track to give more 'grip' and prevent our work from being washed away the next time it rained.

The fully laden Peugeot pick-up glided, with the odd bump or two, up the slope without any problems, and we didn't spill *a drop*! Well, we had the lids on the barrels this time!

The barrels were unloaded at the compound and the building areas.

I didn't need any, because I prefer to drink that sparkling fresh water direct from Jackson's tank, and do you know, the more stroppy Jackson gets the sweeter the water tastes, especially like now when I swallow a mouthful or two whilst I'm swimming in it!

My morning swimming body exercises done, it was now time for my tea, and for my jaw exercises – to fight their way through a bowl of very thick, very chewy mealie meal porridge.

As my tongue was trying to remove the last traces of that sticky porridge from my teeth, a Mazda pick-up arrived, and out stepped a huge set of smiling teeth with an outstretched hand in front of them.

"Bedford, Robb Bedford's the name, land conservation officer for this area." He beamed as he proceeded to crush my hand with a crippling handshake – well, he certainly wasn't 'hand conservation'; that's for sure!

We chatted as we walked, and I explained to him what we were going to do, and where we would be siting the new locations of the slimes dams and the cyanide tanks.

He was happy with the positioning of them, and said he would write a letter to the mining commissioner, with a copy to Jackson, confirming that we had made more than adequate provisions in terms of conservation of the environment on our mining claims, especially so by siting new dams well away from the seasonal streams and dry river beds.

(*Most of these rivers are only 'storm rivers' normally remaining bone dry throughout most of the year, until the heavy rains come and bring them to life for a short period.*)

We climbed into his pick-up and headed for the stream, and drove down the rough track that Jackson was complaining about being a serious erosion problem.

Robb said that the lazy old bastard, Jackson, should have fixed it during his 20-odd years on the ranch, and not start belly-aching about it now.

He suggested an improvement, though, to the work we had completed in the morning.

All that was needed now were two or three 'dip in the road' type channels to run the rainwater away, off to the side of the road, instead of letting it run all the way down the road to the river, causing even more ruts.

"That will be easy enough to fix properly," I told him. "I'll get one of my gangs to work on it straight away this morning."

Back in our new 'reception area' – a thatched grass roof on poles, with a table and two seats made from Jackson's old cement blocks – we had a long chat together over a cup of tea.

And what a difference in the taste, to have milk in the tea again – a gift from Robb, together with a loaf of bread and a newspaper, the customary 'standard' for a visit to someone living in the bush.

He invited me to come to the Fort Rixon Country Club on a Wednesday, which is the men's boozing and darts night, and is a good time to meet some of the other ranchers and farmers.

The club is built on the banks of a man-made lake/dam, and we were welcome to come regularly as visitors until we got to know more of the local members.

Once a week, they put down nets and sell off all the fish they catch – mostly bream and mudfish. That awoke my taste buds! Fresh fried bream once a week, and for the workers a treat of mudfish to supplement their meat, mealie meal and beans rations.

There was an airstrip close to the dam, which meant that my good mate, Alan, could easily fly up from South African to stay with us when we were more established.

"Don't forget to come along to the club soon," Robb repeated as he climbed into his pick-up. "You'll enjoy the company, and meeting some real characters too!"

Birth of a Village

Besides water, the most important thing on my mind at the moment was wood; timber for house building and gum poles for underground in the mine. That meant driving to Fort Rixon again to make follow-up phone calls to the upcountry forest companies.

On the way, I spotted another small 'wood' of gum trees off to the right of the road, and I could see a signpost to 'Ashburner Ranch'.

I turned off the road and followed the track until I came to a large open area in front of a sprawling ranch house.

A tall figure was in the process of juggling with his long limbs, trying to place them in the cab of his pick-up. He looked like a puppet on strings!

On hearing my vehicle approaching, he stopped and proceeded to unfold himself slowly, levering himself out, and rose to his full height – six foot six inches of bony limbs, and his shirt was flapping in the wind against his washboard ribs, beating out the soft rhythmic sound of a skittle band.

After the 'Robb hand-crushing' incident, I decided this time I would 'attack' the handshake, but, for such a big man, it was surprisingly gentle.

He knew exactly who I was, the mines we were working on, and he'd heard that I was interested in buying gum poles – which he was prepared to sell to me.

All he wanted to know was the price!

But when I told him the Umvuma Forest prices, the dollar signs in his eyes immediately disappeared, as did his interest in selling the gum trees!

I tried pushing the point further, but he remained absolutely adamant.

I informed him that we had registered claims on his land, the Blighty and the Blighter mines, registered under a tribute agreement.

He told me that his father had worked these mines in the 1940s and they were completely worked out, so there was no need for us to waste our time tramping all over his land.

It's strange that several miners and the Mines Department tell us that the mines are viable, especially since the price of gold had recently trebled, yet the ranchers go out of their way to fob us off and run us out of town! *Why can't the cowboys and the miners be friends…?*

Though Ashburner's way of trying to stop us mining on his land was in complete contrast to Rancher Jackson's shotgun approach!

When I thanked Ashburner for his encouraging words and said that I would no doubt be bumping into him again, his smug, sarcastic reply was, "I'm not going anywhere; I'll still be here next year… but I don't know about *you*!"

Off down the road to Fort Rixon administrative office to post the letters to the South African banks, urgently requesting backdated statements for both Joseph's and my bank accounts.

Without these, we had come to a complete standstill in dealing with Smit, which meant we couldn't get official permission to sell the second-hand white Peugeot 404 pick-up to Matt, which would raise around 2,000 much-needed dollars.

I had to make some calls from my favourite phone booth, but, unfortunately, it was already 1:45pm and I'd have to wait another 15 minutes before the lunch break was over, but, in the meantime, I could stock up with more things for the mine shop.

The fastest-moving items appeared to be: tobacco, snuff, sugar, coffee and bread.

At 2 o'clock, amazingly enough, I was successfully connected to Umvuma Forest at the first attempt, and I was put through to their sales department.

"Hello. Hello… brrrrrr!"

They say that patience is rewarded – so I tried again, and again, and again – it was third time lucky; I was put through.

"Sales department, can I help? Click, click, click…" This voice became very faint; I could barely hear what was being said, only a voice asking me to speak louder as the person on the line was having difficulty hearing me too! 'F-f-frustrating' phones!

Needless to say, I was not in the best of moods when I reached the mine, and the scene that greeted me caused me to explode!

There was Dereery, the builder, sitting down in an unfinished house and smoking a cigarette whilst talking to Crispin.

And Elliot trying to stamp out his cigarette, but not quickly enough as a few wisps of smoke drifted upwards from under his shoe.

And Langton, who thought he'd be clever by holding it in his pocket, and starting to walk away.

"Langton! Come here!" I called out, and asked him how the building was going, deliberately talking very slowly to him until I could see on his face that the heat in his pocket was getting too much.

"Ooouch!" he shouted, and threw the cigarette away and started screaming; the hot, still-burning head of the cigarette had fallen off inside his pocket and was scorching his leg.

He flayed around, beating his leg as he tried to put it out!

The others howled with laughter at this shouting, dancing buffoon.

I angrily shouted at them, "Anyone caught smoking in future will lose their bonus!"

And I sent Elliot back to the house site, Crispin to the store, Langton to his hessian/cement 'communal' hut building, and told Dereery and his helpers to carry on with the roof and the 'dagga–ing' of the house walls!

Crispin in particular annoyed me the most, and I lectured him that he was in a senior position and should help keep workers working, and not smoking!

To which he replied, a really lame excuse of: "I didn't see them."

"Don't be so bloody stupid! You can see, hear and even smell smoke, using what God gave you! Now use your other God-given gifts – use your legs to walk quickly to the store, and get those fingers updating the stores books; otherwise, you'll get my God-given size 10 boot up your… another part of your God-given body! I'll be back shortly to check on all the updated stores lists!" Well, you've got to put your foot down occasionally… although maybe putting it somewhere else might prove more effective!

I stomped off in my size 10s to check on Langton.

He had finished only the walls of the communal hut, which was for the new munts to stay in whilst they built their own huts – but there was still no roof!

"Jesus wept! Why haven't you finished the bloody roof? The house was like this when I left you this morning!"

The pathetic reply of 'there were no poles, sir' really got my goat, and I shouted at him, "Well cut them!"

And, if he had replied 'with what shall I cut them', Harry Belafonte and I would probably have killed him!

But he continued with another trivial, moaning response of: "But the trees to cut are too far away, over that hill, and it is almost time to knock off!"

Which angered me even more, and I shouted at him, "*Then you'd better run quickly, Langton! Go!*"

When I checked back on the other errant workers, Dereery had finished plastering the walls with dagga.

Crispin showed me the stores book with all the 'ins and outs', which looked perfect, and, would you believe it, Elliot had made me a pot of tea, which was neatly laid out with the gifts that Robb had brought with him in the morning: fresh bread and a pint of milk, which was resting in cool water in my fridge – an old 2 lb jam tin!

I must shout at them more often; it seems to work!

Crispin informed me that, in the Lower Gwelo Native Reserve where his family live, he can buy gum trees of any size for just 25 cents – if you are an African!

But he could try to arrange something through his brother.

Considering we would pay anything from $2 to $3 for a large 30-foot tree from Umvuma Forest, that sounded incredibly cheap.

So Crispin and I decided that I would take him to Gwelo, and he could show me this native reserve forest just outside the town, and also meet his brother.

We stopped at the Fort Rixon exchange just after 6pm to await a phone call from Joseph.

We had started this new 'system' to avoid any misunderstanding and wasted time or unnecessary journeys.

I sat there for maybe 20 minutes waiting for the ringing sound of the phone – but nothing!

Suddenly, a loud screeching noise filled the air as Joseph's pick-up skidded to a halt!

He apologised for not phoning and for being late, but said he thought, instead of stopping and waiting to make the call from somewhere on the way, he'd drive straight through to see me in person at the exchange. His Irish logic was beginning to make sense! Very worrying!

He related to me the latest news.

He and his father had been to the Mines Department and they had met Pope and Curtis.

Minister Dillon had obviously shaken them up, because they were so very, very helpful.

Pope promised they would inspect and procure all the equipment we needed, from a mill to an alternator, from pipes to train rails! And they kept reiterating that it was their duty and pleasure to help miners, especially the younger ones, and they were always ready to help, anytime!

Well, well, this guy Dillon must have kicked their 'aces' very hard!

Joseph had brought with him seven more mine boys and their possessions from Matt's mine, and I was expected to go there the next morning to collect another four, not seven as arranged, since the three others wouldn't be available for another week.

I briefly updated him on the state of things and what work was being done.

He reckoned it was a sound idea to take Crispin to check out the local gum poles situation.

It was worth a try for this very cheap supply – if we could get away with it!

The skies were darkening quickly, ominous black clouds looking ready for action.

Suddenly, those large spots of rain began to splatter on the pick-ups with that 'pinging' sound.

"Well, Joseph, it looks like you're going to have a real christening at last – not for your expected baby, but a stormy, torrential rain-filled evening. Let's hope that the fragile grass roof holds out!"

The boys on the back of Joseph's pick-up started shouting and were getting soaked as the heavens opened up – luckily, I had some large black plastic sheeting in my pick-up, so we threw it over the noisy complaining munts to cover them. It 'ate' them up very quickly, leaving a writhing black mass under it, jostling for position in the back of the crowded pick-up.

Crispin and I left them and drove off towards Gwelo, laughing at the thought of Joseph moving his makeshift bed around inside the hut, desperately trying to find a position where the water wouldn't pour in from the grass roof, all over his slumbering body!

The thunder grew louder and louder; that whiplash, cracking 'BANG' was now directly overhead and made you jump every time, even though you were expecting those ear-splitting sounds!

It was raining so bloody hard now, it was like peering through a wall of shimmering water, and even the bolts of lightning were mere flickers, like someone trying to light a cigarette with a dud cigarette lighter!

The rain was literally coming down in sheets, the noise on the cab roof was deafening, and, at times, the visibility was so bad that we were reduced to a walking pace – although thank God we were inside the cab and weren't actually having to walk outside in this deluge!

The rains continued like this all the way back to Gwelo.

On the tarmac road, the driving was a little easier, although very tiring due to constantly staring through the windscreen, especially when it was splashed with muddy water caused by a vehicle passing from the other direction. You would see the faint hazy headlights, getting brighter as it neared, and, although you were ready for that sudden 'THUMP' of a bucketful of brown water hitting the windscreen, it still made you cringe, and your eyes had to strain even more to look through the blurred, reduced visibility for a few seconds as the windscreen wipers battled to give a clearer view!

We stopped at the house in Gwelo for a quick cup of strong black coffee, to sharpen the brain and rest the eyes for a few minutes.

Marianne looked fabulous, but Jane looked like death – not even warmed up!

Apparently she'd had some urine infection, and was also just getting over the flu, poor soul.

The rain was easing off as we climbed back into the pick-up and drove through the tarmac streets of Gwelo Town, turning onto a dirt road towards the Lower Gwelo Mission.

All the way, it was 'bump and slide' as we snaked our way along the slippery road.

After a few miles, I asked Crispin if we were getting near the mission.

Crispin then dropped a bombshell. Apparently 'just outside Gwelo' was, in fact, 18 miles!

Jesus, 18 bloody miles! Well, I might as well go on now; you can't drop off anybody in the middle of nowhere in weather like that.

We drove on, sliding and slithering around corners on the wet roads – very similar to driving on snow-covered roads – sometimes reduced to almost a standstill by flood water storming across the track. We forded a fast-flowing stream, ploughing through the swirling waters.

It was at this time that Crispin spoke for the first time since that '18 miles to go' bombshell.

"There's a store just up here on the left, Boss; you can drop me there."

When I enquired how far it was still to his place, he replied, "Only about a mile, but, judging from the fast storm water in that donga we just crossed, we could never make it to cross the main river, which could be as much as six feet deep of raging water! It would be impossible for you to get through! I can get across over the river, though, using a wire basket that holds two people, and slides along a cable hung between two trees on opposite banks of the river, so I'll be ok now. Thanks Boss!"

Enough said. I dropped him off, made a forced seven-point turn on the narrow track, and drove back to Gwelo the same way we had come, and in the same manner – 'bump and slide' as the pick-up snaked its way along the slippery dirt roads.

When I eventually reached home, I was knackered!

Marianne and Jane had given up waiting for me, and, luckily, had already gone to bed.

I thought I'd join them – well, only my wife, of course!

. . .

I drove Marianne and the kids into Gwelo early that morning.

My new Peugeot needed its 5,000 km service at the garage, which was quite close to where they were demolishing the old Phoenix Theatre, and we wandered around to see if the old Scot MacDonald was there.

Would you believe it, as we walked in, I saw an African standing on the roof pulling off a sheet of gold – well corrugated iron, actually, but harder to come by than gold.

I spoke to the coloured man in charge and asked him if he was taking the complete roof off today.

He replied, "Yes, and it should take about two hours."

I told him I would buy the lot, and, remembering what MacDonald had said to me last time, we all sat down by the gate – first in the queue – and waited!

It was just after 8am.

At 9:15am, MacDonald rolled up, and I went straight over to him.

"Good day. You remember the last time I saw you – you told me that I could only buy the corrugated iron sheets when they are actually being taken off the roof – and it is first come, first served! Well, they're pulling them off now, and

I've been here since 8am, first in the queue, and I want to buy the whole roof."

He 'ummed and ahed' and said, "It might not all be off today, laddie."

"Well, I was told that the corrugated iron sheets will be off in less than an hour!" I replied.

"There's also another man who wants to buy it all."

"You told me first come, first served and I've been here since 8am!"

"But there's a lot there, probably more than you need, laddie!"

"*Listen!* I have a house, on a mine, in the bush, *without a bloody roof!* And until I get one, my wife and kids can't come to live with me; they have to stay here in Gwelo! *And*, I'll pay you *cash now*!" I waved a bundle of notes in front of his tired-looking, bloodshot eyes.

"All right, laddie, you can have it all!" he responded irritably, snatching the notes.

Even better, after chatting with him further, he threw in, for the same price, roofing nails and the ridging for joining the two halves of the sloping roofs.

In the end, I got 96 of the eight-foot corrugated iron sheets for $132, and also two CBH windows frames, with glass for $10 – cheap, cheap!

(CBH were the ones with two opening windows and a central row of glass panes.)

Well, what a fantastic start to the day!

Now Marianne and I would be able to move into our own 'Bush Bungalow' for Christmas as planned. And the office and the other half of Willie's house could also be roofed! What a relief!

That called for a celebration cup of coffee at the 'Le Chat' restaurant.

While we were chatting away, Marie-Louise and Jeffrey had gone over to torment another little girl of Marie-Louise's age, and they played together happily for quite a while.

We finished our coffee with a delicious piece of black forest gateau, and stood up to leave when the mother of the girl called over to us, "I'm sorry, but you can't have them; I'm taking them home with me!"

The woman told us that she lived on a ranch near Shangani.

They had been there for more than a year now, since they had moved down from Zambia, and this was the first child of her daughter's age she'd met. And that little Jeffrey was as naughty as a little boy should be!

Gayle was her name, and we chatted away together over yet another cup of coffee.

She invited us to call in the next time we went to Fort Rixon; maybe we would like to stay the night as well. She seemed very nice, good fun too, and wrote down directions to the ranch, together with her phone number.

Gwelo Customs/Immigration department was next, and I thought, as things were going so well, I'd push my luck with Smit.

As I walked in, I saw the old gorilla, who grinned – or sneered; it's difficult to know which.

I handed him the duly signed forms he'd given us for each vehicle, together with the invoices and the receipt documents, and asked if that would be sufficient in order for him to clear all the vehicles.

He replied sternly, "No! Not without your bank statements."

"And on what authority do you have to demand to see my personal statements from my bank in South Africa?"

"I think a Rhodesian company bought these vehicles for you, so, under Section 9, Sub-Paragraph 3, Part (i)…"

I might have guessed that old Smit would trot out shi-omething like that!

"AND, you must also get a CVR form for each of the vehicles from the Gwelo Municipal Offices!" Smit added triumphantly with a sarcastic smile, slowly curling his top lip, showing his nicotine-stained teeth.

I left him and went to the municipal building, where I was given a form to register my beige Peugeot 404.

Back at the Customs department, I filled it in and had it stamped, showing I had legally brought the vehicle into the country.

Back to the municipal offices again, where an officious-looking woman gave me yet another form.

I filled in this one too, and both were stamped, but still the woman would not register my car until I showed her an insurance certificate with the new car number on it – the bloody number she had *just written down* on the form in front of me!

I told her that my insurance company in South Africa informed me that I must let them know the new car registration number, so that they can give me a new insurance cover note for Rhodesia, and I showed her the old one, covering my Peugeot with the temporary number.

"Not good enough! Next?"

What an old bitch.

I'd always been a member of the AA, the Automobile Association – not the other one! And so I thought I'd visit their offices and ask for some help – this all seemed so petty to me.

At the AA Mutual Insurance Company, I was told that the easiest and best way was to get a $5 special cover note for the period of my road tax, valid until the end of January.

That would give me plenty of time to sort it all out.

Armed with a new insurance certificate, I went back to see the old f-f-faggot, and the dear old s-s-soul stamped everything, and then asked me for $10!

Ten dollars! The money was flowing out fast; that left us now with only $1,250 cash, with about $10,000 tied up in the trucks and the mobile compressor that we couldn't sell until Customs cleared them!

And we were going to need more cash any day now for:

Monthly Mines Department hire purchase (already $500 each month).

Import permit costs for the compressor ($120).

And the workers' wages in a couple of weeks, and bulk diesel – (around $700).

So we desperately needed 'boodle', but fast, because these mounting costs couldn't be put on our store credit accounts!

Thank God though for Farm Aid and their 120 days credit, because, even if something was much more expensive there, it was worth it to us, and that is where, of course, they make their money!

Still, it was the only way that we could survive at the moment, so we were really very appreciative!

I collected my vehicle, fully serviced and all legal again, gathered the wife, kids and their shopping, and drove around to the Phoenix Theatre.

Half of the corrugated iron sheets were loaded onto the Peugeot, and we drove home.

It was hard work unloading the iron sheets, which took me about three quarters of an hour – not used to doing all this manual labour. Supervising that it gets done, yes, but doing it, no!

Time to visit Crispin to check on the gum pole situation.

Marie-Louise and Jeffrey pleaded with me to take them for the ride, so, with them on board, we headed for the Lower Gwelo Mission.

The road to the mission was really bumpy now, as the hot sun had dried it out from the night's heavy rains, leaving deep ruts in places, but it was much quicker progress than on the previous evening.

We passed by the store where I had dropped Crispin, and came to the river ford.

We ploughed through the water, and, as it was still pretty deep, we made huge, beautiful sprays going right over the top of the pick-up. The kids loved this and wanted me to do it again!

So I turned around and we enjoyed the sight of the sun flickering through the showering 'rains' we created – twice, before we continued on our way to meet Crispin and his brother.

They took me to a large sprawling fenced plantation forest, where there were thousands and thousands of gum trees stretching as far as the eye could see.

"Fabulous, but how am I going to get them, because they are in this fenced area with the forest ranger's office situated at the entrance over there?" I asked them. "Better you get the gum poles, take them to your home, strip them and cut them into six-foot and eight-foot lengths, and I'll come and collect them when ready – and we'll agree a fair price as well. Oh, and Crispin, make sure you are at the Hudson Road house by 12 o'clock tomorrow; we need to get the iron sheets loaded and back to the mine – we don't want the builders to have another excuse to sit around and smoke all day, do we!"

The comment embarrassed Crispin slightly.

We raced back to Gwelo – well, I've never known a speed trap on a dirt road yet! Marie-Louise and Jeffrey laughed and shrieked as they bounced around like ping pong balls!

After dropping them off at the house, my next call was at the Phoenix Theatre to collect the windows and the rest of the corrugated iron sheets, which seemed to take forever, as I had to wait for the last few sheets to be taken down from the roof.

I only just made it to Farm Aid before they closed for the day.

At our friendly, lifesaving '120 days credit' store, I purchased a few axes, 90 kg salt, muti (medicines) – cough muti/stomach muti/brain muti? – batteries, pots, shoe polish, soap and plenty of other things for the mine boys.

This was a great set-up, because we deducted the value of what they bought in our mine store from their wages, but got 120 days credit from the Farm Aid store, so it means, 'in theory', we had a small source of income now. In reality, just a delaying, saving of paying out cash!

Matt had left a message at the Farm Aid store, asking me to meet him at the Midland Hotel.

He was sitting on the terrace, staring at his pint of beer, looking rather dejected.

Matt told me that his old truck had finally given up the ghost, seizing up completely that morning.

"Is there no way I could use one of your second-hand pick-ups immediately?" he half-pleaded.

An idea struck me!

"Hey Matt, if I could get our old white pick-up insured and road licensed in the same way as I did with my new one this morning, then it would be legal road-wise. And if you sold your seized-up jalopy and gave us the money as a deposit, we'd have some instant cash, which we badly need! And you could borrow the white pick-up just for the one day – *every day* – until I could officially sell it to you!"

That put a smile back on his face!

Agreed, I would fix up all the paperwork in the morning, he would sell his truck, for which he'd been quoted a price of $900, and both of us would be getting something we badly needed.

"About those extra mine boys, though," Matt added. "Unfortunately, I had to keep three of them in order to help Staff finish off reassembling all the equipment, but I will bring them to your mine in about a week's time – hopefully in my 'new' second-hand white Peugeot pick-up! Thanks."

At 6pm, I called the Fort Rixon exchange as arranged with Joseph, and told him all the news about 'legalising' my own pick-up and getting cash for 'lending' Matt the second-hand white Peugeot.

"Great, be even better when we can get the full price from him when we legally sell it! Tonight I won't be coming back to Gwelo," Joseph said, "as I'm going to Que Que early in the morning with an engineer from the Mines Department who will inspect an alternator and evaluate it for us. So could you take Jane for her 10:30 morning check-up at the hospital tomorrow?"

"No problem, Joseph, and since you'll be in Que Que, bring Willie back with you; we'll be needing him and his blasting licence very soon."

"But what if his wife and children aren't ready to come with him? What about ..."

"Well, it's up to you, Joseph; if not, you'll just have to make another trip to Que Que to collect them another day, but we can discuss that later, not now; I've had a long day. Goodnight Joseph!"

. . .

First thing in the morning, I went back to the municipal offices again to collect more CVR forms – one for the white Peugeot 404, and two more to give to Joseph for the other vehicles.

And surprise, surprise! It only took half an hour to get the paperwork completed for 'Matt's' white Peugeot and have it registered, mainly because I now knew all the answers – and I was back at home already, sitting drinking coffee at 8:45am when Matt walked in.

"When do you think it will be ready?" he asked, and was amazed to hear that everything was fixed and he could 'borrow' it straight away!

He told me that the garage would tow his pick-up in today, and they would give him a firm price on Monday, so hopefully we would have some 'bread' by Tuesday.

He departed, and I sat around waiting for 10:30am so that I could take Jane for her check-up, before hurrying back to the mine loaded with the corrugated iron sheets and all the supplies.

After Jane's check-up, we went to the chemist to collect some prescriptions for her on the way home, and I drove straight back into town to make a couple of phone calls.

I spoke to Umvuma Forest again, and repeated the order that I was given on Wednesday, but once again there was nobody in the office who could give me a firm delivery date.

However, they promised that somebody would, without fail, confirm a definite delivery date, and would leave the message for me at Fort Rixon exchange message board in the afternoon.

Once again, I couldn't get through to Shell to check when the diesel tanks would be delivered and installed on our mine.

Marianne was waiting by the gate talking to Crispin when I arrived back at the house, and she informed me that Jane's contractions were regular and about every 10 minutes – but getting quicker, and would I stay around instead of going back to the mine just in case of an emergency, until either Joseph or somebody else with a car came along.

About 3:30pm, Jane said it was every five minutes and she wanted to go now!

Marianne helped me to 'load' her into the front seat of my pick-up and I set off to the nursing home, with Crispin balancing precariously on top of the corrugated iron sheets and supplies.

"Oh why isn't that stupid husband of mine here?" she kept saying, over and over again; tacit agreement from me!

Well, what a happy surprise for Jane! As I was parking my vehicle, Joseph pulled up next to us, leapt out and ran to open her door and help her get out.

He was bubbling with excitement, and told us he was so looking forward to the birth and that he would soon be a father!

He pointed to Willie and two others who were sitting in the back of his pick-up, and went rambling on about why he'd decided to bring Willie, but not…

"Joseph!" Jane spoke deliberately forcefully. "Do you want me to give birth in this car park! Stop blabbering on, and help me into the hospital! Please!"

As I drove off, I called out to Jane and wished her success with the birth, and said that we would come to see her and the baby later.

After an uneventful journey, Crispin and I reached the mine at dusk after a long day, mainly to-ing and fro-ing from one place to another, and sitting around waiting.

I told him to get some help and drive over to my house site to unload all the corrugated iron sheets.

I went straight to bed, despite a few Africans wanting to complain about something to me.

I told them I'd see them in the morning.

. . .

Dawning morning told me that Joseph had not returned to the mine, so I hope there were no problems with the birth!

Crispin had gathered all the latest news last night, and was busy relating it all to me, as usual.

Apparently Dereery had finished Willie's house on Wednesday night and had been sick since then and wanted to go to hospital. Joseph was going to take him yesterday, but didn't have the time. Dereery complained of stomach pains, headaches and nausea, so I gave him two aspirins, told him I would see him later, and asked Elliot to make some hot soup.

However, Dereery refused to eat the soup, saying it would only make him sicker.

So, up to date with Crispin's summarised news, I checked how the new munts were progressing with their hut-building *gwazas*.

When we take on new labour, we give them three days rations and tell them to build their own huts. Anybody who refuses, we don't employ. It's a good way of testing their will to work and also whether they obey instructions. It sorts out the very lazy immediately, although I find that laziness seems to be part of the male Africans' inbred character.

Two of the huts were coming on very nicely, and, in fact, the roofs were being grassed already.

But the other hut had only a few base poles erected and part of the roof poles, and there were three working on this hut! And, in fact, these were the same three munts who came complaining to me when I arrived at night. They wanted me to give them hessian to wrap around the poles and cover it with a cement wash – just like the one Langton built as temporary accommodation for any new workers.

I stressed to them that they must go and cut their own poles like everyone else did, and finish building their hut by tonight – otherwise, there was no job for them!

As it was such a nice dry, sunny day, I decided to walk over to my house site, and saw that the concrete foundations and base had all been cleared, showing the reddish-coloured, polished concrete floor underneath, and I could see the shape and size of the rooms by the remnants of the demolished walls.

All the bricks and blocks were stacked up and the rubble was in piles.

They had now started clearing the other old house site about 50 yards away, on which we would build Joseph's house.

Back up at the mine, I met a deliriously happy Joseph – Jane had given birth to a son.

He'd just popped in to give me the news and said there was a celebration party in Gwelo tonight at the Midland Hotel. And on Sunday both Jane and the baby could be visited in the hospital.

"Oh, and I brought Willie and the two other workers," he added hurriedly as he climbed into his pick-up and shot off! The happiest I'd ever seen him!

I called Crispin over and told him to look after Willie and help him settle into his new house over the weekend.

Dereery, the one who built this house, started moaning again to Crispin that he had worked much too hard getting it ready on time for Willie, and he was feeling very sick and had to go to the Belingwe hospital.

I gave him some more aspirins, and told him that if he still felt bad on Monday, Joseph could take him to the hospital in Belingwe.

"No! I will die by then!" he exclaimed.

"Actually, Tachibona could take you now. Go with him on his bicycle to Filabasu Hospital; that's nearer – only 35 km!" Crispin suggested.

"No! You give me an advance of $8 *now*; I have to go to the Belingwe hospital *today* – it's nearer my home!"

"He's pulling the weight!" Crispin interjected.

I laughed and told him, "You mean he's swinging the lead!"

Whereupon he started grinning – another 'Crispinism version' of a proverb.

"But you're right; I'm also convinced it's just a scam to go home with a pocket full of money after only having worked here for a few weeks – probably never to be seen again! Both Joseph and I will be back on Monday… so, it will either be Belingwe hospital… or Shangani Morgue for Master Builder Dereery!"

I left a dejected, defeated Dereery wandering back to continue his work, while I headed off to Gwelo… and **party time**!

Which was to be followed by a lazy Sunday at home, and time to take Marianne and the kids, and Neville, of course, to see Jane and her new baby son in the Gwelo nursing home.

. . .

Early Monday morning, I drove into Gwelo to the African bus parking area.

A group of miners with the sun reflecting off their bright yellow mine helmets was the 'beacon' that I headed for.

One of the miners was about a foot taller than the others, or was he standing on a box?

It took quite a time before the extra four mine workers from Matt's mine were loaded and squeezed into the back of my pick-up with their belongings, especially the giant of a man who had several saws and other building tools, metal boxes and a ladder. And he hadn't been standing on any of those; he was just very, very tall!

With the ladder jutting out from above the driver's cab, we looked like a fire engine as we set off for Fort Rixon.

Back at our mine, Crispin got busy with registering and checking the IDs and references of these new workers.

Including the miners whom Joseph had brought last week, we had employed an additional 11 Africans to our growing workforce:

Goliath – this 'mystery' giant builder;

Tauchira and Alexander – mill lashers;

Banzi, Paniche, Bamoso and Misheck – underground lashers;

Cleorphus, Saul, Enoch and Jonas – general workers.

I asked Crispin to put them straightway on their first task of building their own huts, stressing that they had to be ready within the 'three-day limit'.

A refreshing cup of coffee and a cigarette, and then I was on the road again, this time to Bulawayo for meetings with both the mining commissioner and the Mines Yard engineers.

I stopped at the Fort Rixon exchange and placed a call to Umvuma Forest.

Great news. The gum poles I'd ordered would be delivered on Tuesday by rail to the Shangani depot; these poles were required for building my first real house in the bush – a tin-roofed shack, with hessian walls painted with a concrete-wash to make them stiffer, stronger and hopefully waterproof!

On arrival in Bulawayo, I called into the Mines Yard office to collect the documents that had been delivered with the green compressor railed up from South Africa, and, armed with these, I went to Barclays Bank to apply for the import licence.

A very distinguished-looking gentleman called Mr Emerson met me, shook my hand warmly, and, 'after you, young man', politely showed me into his wood-panelled office.

He sat back in a comfortable maroon leather chair and relit his pipe, puffing away as he listened to my request.

When I handed him the SA Railways documentation, the SA export licence and the Rhodesian Customs papers, he pulled out a glass monocle, and, after juggling it into place by means of a few facial twitches, he carefully perused the paperwork.

"That all looks honky-dory to me, what, what! I'll follow this through for you, and when we get Central Bank approval I'll post it to you. What is the address of your mine?"

I explained to him that we didn't have a PO Box for the mine yet, so it would be best to post it to me, c/o R. Cummins, Mines Yard, Bulawayo.

"Ah Ronnie! He's a jolly good fellow; I play snooker against him quite often and he's a damn good potter of the balls, eh what!"

We shook hands and he escorted me out of the building.

Back to the Mines Department, where I spent the next few hours – there is such a lot to learn about all the rules and regulations in order to be able to talk to the right people who could assist us on a whole range of issues:

Explosives: The mining commissioner gave me a copy of the Act and the regulations concerning the collection of boxes of gelignite and igniters from the AE & CI dynamite depot (African Explosives and Chemical Industries).

But first, we had to have an underground, lockable explosives safe, which I could collect from the Mines Yard in two days. It must be buried six foot deep with steps leading down to the safe door, and, until we had this magazine installed, we could not apply for **our explosives permit**.

Blasting licences: I told him that our senior boss boy, Staff, had a current one that needed to be transferred to our mine, and Willie, our new mine supervisor, had an out-of-date licence.

The mining commissioner explained to me that Willie would have to pass an exam before his licence could be reissued, and, if I brought him with me to Bulawayo when I came to collect the explosives magazine, he could read the rules and take the simple exam.

I spent some more time with Ronnie Cummins, who was extremely helpful with information on:

Mine claims – Protection rules/dates of inspection/… and the mandatory notices.

Labour regulations – Pneumoconiosis and labour returns, etc.

This session with him added greatly to my knowledge that I had gained from the 'crash course' with Joseph's mother, after that ill-fated meeting in Belingwe with the 'Godfather'!

And he gave me several Mines Department booklets concerning our obligations when we stared mining operations – so Willie was not the only one who had to study!

Each day would bring new challenges, mostly requiring the study of these books covering the various regulations in the provisions of the Mines and Minerals Act, and the Mining Regulations of Southern Rhodesia – a full 250-page manual of rules that were written in that 'not easy to understand' civil servant language, where a sentence that could be written in simple English is invariably padded out to fill one and a half pages, and refers to dozens of other rules too – paragraph this, sub-section that, clause (i)…

With a head buzzing with information, I headed back to Gwelo, where I bought two window frames (C2H; C4H) for our shortly to be built 'shack' on the mine, before enjoying a relaxing evening at the Hudson Road house.

It would be fantastic when our new dwelling on the mine was ready to live in.

The countless hours that are wasted in this 'driving to work' each day – a full 170 km round trip, 'Gwelo-Fort Rixon-Nelly 404 mine-Fort Rixon-Gwelo' – mostly leaving at the crack of dawn, and only returning after the sun had set.

And, of course, also being able to live a normal home life, seeing the family for breakfast each morning, spending evenings together, visiting some of the rancher neighbours, and the odd Sunday spent at the Fort Rixon club and fishing in the dam.

. . .

My morning started by visiting the four suppliers in Gwelo that we were doing regular business with, and had applied for an account with business credit facilities.

After negotiating and agreeing the final terms, the necessary documents were signed and I was issued with a business account card by each supplier, which allowed us unlimited purchases for the Ridge Top Mine. Wow! That would certainly be a great help – together with some favourable credit terms:

Midlands Flour Mills: Bakery, meal (30 days credit), and a 2½% discount for 'cash and carry' – well, there's absolutely no chance we'll ever try to get that discount!

Miekles Stores: Clothing, etc. (30 days, with books closing on 15th of the following month, and accounts sent on the 25th – which is really giving us up to 60 days credit!).

Paramout Butchery: Meat rations (30 days credit).

Farm Aid: For everything else! (120 days credit – possibly our saviour!).

I would need to set up some more journals, which Crispin would keep up to date for:

Purchases:

Cash purchases (e.g. timber, special ad hoc);

Credit purchases (with the four Gwelo suppliers);

Mine purchases (Shell, Chibuku beer and AE & CI);

Together with monthly repayment records for:

The Mines Department – hire/lease agreement monthly payments.

Mine Development Loans? I hope this one doesn't remain blank for too much longer!

I put the pick-up on 'automatic pilot' – well, that's what it seemed like, as I had made this Gwelo-Shangani-Fort Rixon-mine trip dozens of times already and was beginning to give names to the ostriches that would often run in the open veld for several kilometres keeping abreast of my pick-up – and they can run almost as fast as giraffes, about 40 to 45 kilometres per hour!

It's strange too that, when you make such long journeys regularly, you have more time to enjoy the surrounding bush and game, and the actual trip seems shorter every time!

I soon reached the Shangani railhead depot to collect the gum poles I had ordered from Umvuma Forest that would be used for building the main structure of our mine house.

Unfortunately, I didn't have any of my workers with me, as I had come directly from Gwelo, so I had to load the 40 gum poles myself, each eight foot in length, onto the back of my pick-up and secure them firmly with ropes.

Sweating like a pig in the hot noonday sun, I had worked up one hell of a thirst!

The best solution to that was to put my pick-up on 'automatic' pilot again, this time in the direction of the Shangani Hotel.

Needless to say, it was the old one-two-three trick that did the necessary; one hour's rest, two cold pints of beer and three cheddar cheese and pickle rolls, and, feeling satisfied, I drove off to the mine carrying the heavy wooden cargo on board.

Although I drove slower than usual, and carefully avoided most of the holes and bumps in the road, occasionally I hit a bad one, causing the gum poles to bounce up and down and rattle against each other – what an 'ear-shattering' noise; it sounded like a building collapsing!

I was pleased when I reached the mine with all the gum poles still on the back of the pick-up.

This part of the trip on the bumpy dirt roads from Shangani seemed to have taken as long as one of those epic 'South Africa-Rhodesia' journeys, but, in reality, it was only two hours.

At the house site, Langton, Nduna and Mashua unloaded the gum poles and window frames.

I showed Langton a rough diagram of the planned building, and we proceeded to measure out a 20-foot by 20-foot square on the red-painted floor of the old house foundations; this would form the base on which our new house would be built.

We would use 18-inch by six-inch hollow cement blocks to build a 'three-cement-block-high' wall forming the perimeter of our square house. Gum poles would be cemented into the wall at regular intervals, and rolls of six-foot-wide hessian sacking material would be unwound and stretched from pole to pole and nailed in place forming the outside walls, which would be painted with a cement-wash to add stiffness and thickness.

Other timbers would form an A-shaped frame onto which the corrugated iron sheets from the demolished theatre in Gwelo would be nailed to form a sloping tin roof.

Once the house 'shell' was completed – and it had to be done before Christmas – we would cut out rectangular shapes in the hessian, and fix the necessary timber supports to house the three window frames. And until I could find a wooden door, we'd have a thick black plastic sheet hanging in the opening of the doorway.

Believe it or not, dusk was already beginning to darken the skies – another day had shot by!

Elliot, my new houseboy – although I didn't actually have a house yet, of course – was busy preparing a stew on an open wood fire outside my second, recently built 'grass-roofed' home.

Now that the mine was becoming busier, with workers continually walking past my old hut as they went back and forth between the mine and the village, I had decided to have another one built next to my house site.

And once the house was ready for us to live in, Elliot would take over this hut, which was handily situated 20 metres or so from where the house would soon be erected – perfectly placed for performing his household duties.

With spoon in hand, I was ready for the first evening meal, which would be a good indicator of his cooking abilities – and, in fact, the stew turned out to be damn good; I virtually vacuumed it up to satisfy my huge hunger, before I flopped into bed.

. . .

The 5:30am gong was struck, the loud reverberating sound echoing through the still, early morning air. Shortly afterwards, there was a gentle tapping on the entrance to my hut.

My new protégé, 'a la Zikke', quietly and politely asked if I wanted a cup of tea – nice, really nice!

I sent Elliot to the mining village to tell Willie to be ready to go to Bulawayo at 6am, and to bring his expired blasting licence with him.

From Fort Rixon to Bulawayo was the best stretch of dirt murram road in the district, being regularly 'graded' (smoothed and de-potholed) by large machines with a 'snow plough' type contraption on the front.

We made good time and, by 8am, we were having a cuppa coffee in the Mines Department waiting for our appointment with the mining commissioner.

He greeted us curtly and got straight down to business, placing the documents for a monthly contract for the explosives safe in front of me to sign.

He told me it was in the Mines Yard ready for me to take away today.

"Now two other things," he added. "You'll have to write a letter to the Mines Department, Salisbury stating that you have installed an explosives safe underground on your mine. They will send you an authorisation to allow you to collect explosives from the AE & CI depot, transport them and store them at your mining location. You should receive this letter within a week."

"That sounds good, but please make a note to use our house address in Gwelo for all correspondence, because we haven't yet been allocated a post box at Fort Rixon in the name of Ridge Top Mine."

I handed him Willie's expired blasting licence.

"Hmm… Right, Willie can do the exam today. I'll give him some 'extracts' from the Mining Requirements and Explosives Act, which he can read this morning, and we'll examine him after lunch. He'll need two photos as well –

there's a chemist shop down the road where he can have them taken. So, if all goes well, which I'm sure it will, **Will**!" And he roared with laughter before continuing. "You can come back in about three hours to collect Willie and his new blasting licence for the Ridge Top Mine."

I gave Willie some money for lunch and the photos, and drove the pick-up into the Mines Yard so that the explosives magazine could be 'block and tackled' onto my vehicle and firmly secured – I wouldn't want it breaking loose and bashing around in the back of the pick-up on the trip home to the mine – that would be a whole new, unwelcome panel-beating catastrophe!

As I was walking towards Greys Inn, I heard a familiar voice call out to me – well, well, well, it was Rancher Des.

"How's it going?" he asked as we shook hands. "Tell me all about it over a beer and a ploughman's lunch. I'll buy this time, but we'll eat somewhere more expensive on you next time – when you strike it rich!" He laughed heartily, and we entered the pub together.

Over the next couple of hours, I told him about our progress so far.

We had employed some 40-odd Africans – *some very odd!* – and they had built a village compound that consisted of 20 huts so far.

The whole area around the Nelly 404 shaft had been cleared, and we had built an office, a store and a few other dagga buildings.

We were busy making a huge dry-stone base for a large water tank, water being our biggest problem… actually, the second biggest problem; Jackson was definitely our number one problem!

"As you know, Des, it's essential to have a water supply for running the whole mining process, and for our daily personal usage too. Ironically, the first-level drive tunnel underground is knee-deep in water, but we can't start pumping yet, because we are still waiting for the pumps and an alternator to be delivered, and Shell to bring and install two 5,000-litre tanks and deliver the diesel fuel we so badly need."

I then proceeded to tell him more about our number one problem, Jackson.

The shotgun affair!

And we were **banned from using water** from his overflowing water tanks to drink and to wash with, and, even more ridiculous, he was now even hassling us about **collecting water from his river**!

"Well, I did warn you about his festering hatred of people mining on his land.

But I am sorry that he's really got it in for you; wish there was something I could do about it – if you were on my land, you'd be having full English breakfast with us every morning! Hey, but you must make sure you keep going; once you're pumping your own water, there'll be little else he can do – it's just while you're starting up that you are at your most vulnerable, and he's doing his damned-ness to try and chase you off *his land*!"

"I guess that's true, Des. But look at the time, its 3 o'clock! I have to collect the explosives safe and one of my workers, Willie, who hopefully has a brand new blasting licence."

"I must dash too, and get back to my better half, Irene. Don't forget to pop in next time you go through Fort Rixon – if I'm not there, Irene would love to make you lunch and have a good natter, especially if your wife and kids are with you! Good luck."

When I walked into the Mines Yard, Willie was slouched against the bonnet of my pick-up, looking really annoyed.

He told me that he'd failed the test because he didn't understand all the new words and measurements, and showed me the test papers – indeed, everything was in metres and centimetres, not feet and inches, and this had totally confused poor Willie.

He climbed on the back of the truck, still looking quite bewildered, and we headed for the mine.

. . .

The next morning kicked off in a busy fashion.

Matt arrived early in the white Peugeot pick-up with the extra mine workers and Staff, who would now be the official senior boss boy on the mine.

He was pleased to join us permanently and to stay in our village with his wife, instead of alternating and spending a few days at Matt's mine, then to Ray's, backwards and forwards….

The other five workers sat outside the office whilst Crispin checked their IDs and registered them into our mine employee register. Matt gave me a bunch of their previous reference letters, and said that his mother would post to me their new references for working on his mine.

With Staff on our books as well, we now had two miners with blasting licences, albeit one out of date, which could only be renewed if Willie passed the test at the second go, and Staff's that needed to be transferred to our mine.

In addition to Staff, the new workers were:

Phillemon, Robson and Samuel – the timber boys who had been helping to re-erect the 5-stamp mill and other outstanding tasks at Matt's mine;

Juta – a mechanic/electrician, who inevitably was nicknamed 'Sparky';

And Naison, an experienced builder who knew what had to be done and how to do it – instead of the so-called builders like Langton who, apart from hut building, the only other thing he knew was how to wield a hammer and a saw – an African version of the Russian flag?

A quick chat over a cup of tea when Matt told me some great news – he'd got $900 for his old clapped-out pick-up, which he'd deposited in our mine bank account as part-payment for the white Peugeot pick-up, and, when we could officially sell it to him, he would pay us a further $1,000.

He then drove off in his – 'ex-ours' – old white Peugeot Diesel 404 pick-up.

The dust had hardly settled when another vehicle pulled up and hooted. It was Al Swartz from the Shangani Telephone Exchange Depot.

"Hello! Since you don't seem to have a PO Box yet, I thought I'd pop by and drop this letter off," he began, "although I'm afraid that the date of connecting your phones won't please you; it's three weeks – *three weeks from today*!"

"Jesus!" I remarked. "This bloody three weeks; it's always three weeks… what's with this three weeks every time!"

"Well, my fault really," Al added apologetically. "I didn't submit diagrams with the distances between the existing joint party lines to both of your required phone locations, sorry! But I'm here now, so let's do it straight away!"

"Okay mate, at least you're honest; let's begin here with the office phone, which will be housed in that office/store building over there with the tin roof."

Al made a quick sketch and measured the distance to the nearest pole on the Ashburner-Jackson joint party line.

"Six hundred and twenty-three yards," he remarked. "That'll allow me to work out the number of 20-foot wooden gum poles we will need to erect."

(*Note: a hundred years earlier, Cecil Rhodes stipulated the use of 20-foot, two-piece* ***metal telegraph poles****, for protection against the wood-eating white ants.*)

"Al, tell me something, why do some government departments use yards, and others like the Mine Department use metres?" I asked.

"Realistically, it takes time and money to switch from the imperial system to the decimal system, but we will all standardise on decimalisation eventually. But now let's go and check the siting of your house phone."

We walked down the track to the house site, and, when he saw that the red-painted floor of our new house still had no walls and no roof…

"Oh no!" he exclaimed. "I have to confirm on the diagram that the phone is housed in a dry room under a tin roof – this will delay things even more, until the house is built. Sorry!"

"But how about a compromise; let's look at my outside kitchen that's built with dagga blocks – it has no roof over it yet, but it only needs two corrugated iron sheets to form the roof; wouldn't that do as our phone booth?"

"Okay." He chuckled. "If you promise to nail or cement the iron roof on top of the walls, I'll submit it as an outside, tinned-roof phone booth, and then the date given in that letter will be honoured. Fine, good thinking. I'll be back with the poles, wires and phones – *in three weeks*!" He laughed.

As he drove off, he was still smiling, and shouted out through the window, "Everything takes three weeks in Rhodesia! Get used to it!"

The next vehicle that pulled up, screeching to a halt, covering both Crispin and me in dust… was none other than 'the son of Mr Worry in a Hurry'!

Joseph leapt out of the pick-up and ran towards me shouting excitedly that the mine must be fenced immediately, or we would be forced to close down the mine.

He ranted on and on, waving his arms in the air… until he realised that only Crispin was standing in front of him – I had gone to the pick-up to open the door and welcome the three VIP passengers, Marianne, Marie-Louise and Jeffrey.

They were so excited, and pleased to be able to stay at the mine, and I called Elliot and told him to take them over to my new hut and make them something to drink and eat.

I would be back later, after this 'fencing problem' had been sorted out.

Joseph, visibly shaking and sweating, handed me a letter that was from the mining commissioner (cc Jackson).

"You see, Jackson has stated that we must fence our mining locations for the safety of his cattle, in terms of Section 172 of the Mining and Minerals Act, and that it must be completed by the 31 December! That would cost us hundreds and hundreds of dollars! We have to get cracking and start fencing now… but where do we get the money from? That's more than our total credit at the Farm Aid store! And if we don't do it, our mines will be closed down for good!" His agitated voice continued.

"Look Joseph, that bastard is determined to close us down; this is his latest trick to cause us more financial problems whilst we are trying to set up a working mine – he knows that the cost of wire fencing the claims would be exorbitant," I replied. "So what we'll do is this. I'll write Jackson a letter, with a copy to the mining commissioner, of course, asking him to provide us with an aerial map, showing exactly where his cattle water tanks are situated in the vicinity of our mines. Hmm… and, as it's near Christmas/New Year, we'd like a month extension until the 31 January – I'm sure he'll agree. That'll also give us time to… ah, we'll think of something, okay?

"Now Joseph, let's get back to the task at hand. Bearing in mind that from next week, if all goes to plan, we're going to be inundated with deliveries of diesel tanks, diesel fuel, all kinds of equipment, alternators, rails, pumps and pipes etc., which will allow us, at last, to start to set up the infrastructure of our mine. We are going to be very busy, and we will need all of the workers to be available full time, which means that all the hut building and clearing the drive tunnels underground has to be completed this weekend – the workers will have to **work double shifts** on both Saturday and Sunday."

"Good idea; it just has to be done! I'll get Staff to tell the underground boys about working the whole weekend, so that we'll have a full complement of our mine workers ready for action on Monday. That'll be great; I'm so pleased that things are beginning to roll!"

"Well Joseph, I will only be pleased when I hear the sound of the wheels as the **cocopans roll,** roll on the rails taking the ore to the **mill with its loud stamping roar**!" I replied. "And other real mine-working noises; from **the hoist** winching up the ore from underground, the **engine room**, **pumps thumping away**! These are the noises of **full gold production** – and **sweet music to our ears**."

"Oh, I agree with you, but this Rancher Jackson is trying to spoil all that! You are going to talk to him, aren't you?"

"Of course, but for starters we'll send a letter, and we'll procrastinate with as many meetings and proposed fencing diagrams/options as we can, until either he gives up or we find the money for the fencing, okay! *Moenie* worry *nie*! (Don't worry!) And thanks for bringing my family down to the mine – I must go and have some lunch with them now. Why don't you go home to Gwelo, Joseph, and spend a long weekend with Jane and your son. We'll be back on Sunday, when we can plan what has to be done during the coming week."

He drove off and I went to check on the progress of the hut building, and could clearly see that we needed more workers to help; otherwise, they would never be finished, even with double shifts on Saturday and Sunday.

Back at the mine shaft, I climbed down the ladders to the first level, where I met Staff, who was busy checking the condition of all the timbers and ladders, marking the sections that needed to be replaced. He agreed to release five or six of his underground workers to go 'topside' and help with the hut building over the weekend.

I finished off writing the letter to Jackson regarding the fencing issue, and dropped it off at the Jackson Ranch as we drove past on our way to see Mdala Feet, to discuss the growing of vegetables and supplying them to the mine.

The old chief warmly greeted Marianne and lifted our little ones out of the pick-up, telling them to go and play with his children.

We sat down in the shade and worked out a plan for growing vegetables for our mine workers.

I gave him packets of seeds for cabbage and rape, which he would cultivate and sell the vegetables back to me: four cents a large cabbage; three cents for rape.

He'd also deliver six fresh eggs twice a week – lekker – and could possibly get milk for our kids, once they were living permanently on the mine.

This would be a good local source of fresh vegetables for us and the workers.

Either Feet would deliver the produce to the mine or I could pick it up, a quick 10-minute drive – not the usual five-hour return journey to get food supplies in Gwelo!

Slowly, more and more things were beginning to revolve around the mine, and, when the house was ready in two weeks, much less driving, thank God – the 'monumental mileage' and the 'killing kilometres' would be drastically cut!

I had already experienced, over the last couple of days, how much easier and more relaxed life would be with Marianne and the kids on the mine – especially enjoying a meal of fresh game meat sitting around the open wood fire, before calling it a day.

. . .

It was an eerie morning; an unusual mist hung over the bush.

The three builders working on the house appeared as dark silhouettes against the grey, misty background, flitting backwards and forwards as they performed their *gwaza* of cementing the blocks onto the floor base to form the lower wall of our new 20-foot square abode.

About midday, I went to see Staff and Crispin at the office to update them on the progress so far, and what needed to be done over the coming weeks.

We had now taken on enough workers for setting up the basic working of our mine – when the gold production started and we were running three shifts over a 24-hour day, we would need to raise the number to at least 60 workers.

I reiterated to them that from Monday next week we were awaiting deliveries of equipment from Fox & Bookless, and fuel tanks from Shell, and all the workers had to be available.

I stressed again that the mine boys would have to work a double shift today, Saturday, and again on Sunday, to make sure that all the huts were completed for the 15 new workers we'd recently taken on, and that, underground, the drive tunnels had to be completely clear of rubble and old rusty equipment.

"When the morning session ends shortly," I continued, "I will tell all the workers to come back to work in the afternoon, and both of you can explain to them in Ndebele or Chilapalapa why they have to work these extra shifts this weekend."

At 1 o'clock, the knock-off gong sounded; the hut-building workers began emerging from the bush and ambling towards the office where Crispin would normally 'tick' them off for the day – but today he had to inform them that they must be back at 2pm to work another shift.

One by one, they nodded, some grunting as they slouched off slowly… then one of the workers, Gwabuye, stopped. "But it's Saturday afternoon; why should I work!"

Then another worker turned back and shouted, "I don't work today; I go to see girlfriend! Not work!"

Others began mouthing off… their numbers swelling by the arrival of the underground workers, until suddenly there was a crowd of 30 to 40 African workers in front of me, all shouting '**No! No! No!**' and waving their arms wildly.

I told Staff to explain to them that, over the weekend, all the huts had to be finished and the underground drives completely cleared, as all workers would be needed on Monday to unload the heavy transporters bringing in equipment, fuel drums and fuel.

This meant everybody having to work double shifts today and on Sunday.

"No! No!" shouted Samson, a huge muscle-bound Zambian.

"I'm not working either! No beer! No work!" exclaimed Phillemon, a six-foot giant built like a brick shithouse… and the shouting of objections continued despite the efforts of Staff and Crispin to calm them down.

The noise level grew louder and louder and I could see on the faces of some of the workers that it had reached fever-pitch and we could be heading for a riot.

In those uneasy few seconds, the start of the *Indian Uprising* film flashed before my eyes.

That had begun with one or two Indians refusing to move, then more and more, working each other into an angry frenzy… the mob finally getting out of control, and started fighting and wrecking everything in sight – total disaster!

And here I was, in a similar situation, as the pumped-up African workers began to stamp and chant, getting nearer and nearer to where I stood next to the pick-up, the swirling dust rising up, partially enveloping them – it was like being in front of a herd of charging, angry buffalo!

I found myself subconsciously fondling the carved wooden pendant hanging from my neck, which then started to vibrate violently, and, spontaneously, my other arm lunged through the open pick-up window and pressed the hooter continuously…. Immediately, 40 roaring African voices went silent, and 80 bulbous white eyes stared out at me from their dark faces….

"*No work! No job!*" I shouted back at them, and instructed Staff and Crispin to tell them that anyone who didn't come back to work at 2pm, and again on Sunday, would be fired and paid off!

I calmly turned away, climbed into my pick-up and slowly drove off at a leisurely pace, keeping my eyes firmly fixed on the developing scene in my rear-view mirror… preparing for a fight, or would it be war?

I reached the house site and told Marianne of the gathering 'storm'!

"Will they come back to work?" Marianne questioned uneasily.

"Fingers crossed, maybe yes, maybe no, but we will soon know which way the wind doth blow!"

I related to her the story of a Mr Maddocks, a previous mine manager of the Nelly 404 mine during the Matabele rebellion of 1896, when the local Ndebele tribes were working up a head of steam and marauding around in the bush! "Two natives calmly came up to him, on the very claims we are standing on now, and suddenly exploded into a frenzied attack, smashing his head in with knobkerries, and also leaving his assistant half-dead on the ground…"

"Oh, great!" exclaimed Marianne irritably. "You can really put someone's mind at rest!"

Two o'clock came and went… and our three house builders had not yet returned to work.

"Another cup of tea? Something stronger?" mused Marianne.

"Yeah, one more, then I'll go and see what's happening on the mine."

As I drove towards the mine, I fully expected to see the three builders ambling towards the house site – those three had been with me the longest, but, apart from a small duiker buck that scampered across in front of me, the road was deserted.

I pulled up in front of the office; not a soul to be seen anywhere; it was very quiet.

Not looking too bright, I thought as I opened the door.

"Good afternoon, sir!" Crispin said snappily.

"Where is everyone?" I asked.

"All back at work, either in the village finishing the huts or underground clearing up."

"And what about my three builders! They didn't come back to the house site this afternoon?"

"Aah, well, sir, in any barrel of apples, there's always one or two bad ones; as the proverb says, too many bad apples spoil the feast!"

I smiled – yet another Crispinism proverb!

"Thanks, but it seems like we have three bad apples who are spoiling my new house!" I replied. "Go to the village and bring them here right away!"

Shortly later, Crispin appeared from the bush on the track that lead from the village with three slouching shapes dawdling behind him.

"Ah Langton, you've been with me for a long time; why are you not back at work this afternoon?"

He continued to hang his head, staring at the floor in silence… then he jerked up his head and blurted out, "I'm not working today!"

"Okay Langton, you have no job here; you are fired! Crispin, you can pay him off!"

"And Mashua, are you going to work today?"

"No!"

"And Nduna?"

"No!"

"Okay! You can all collect your belongings from the village, and Crispin will pay you off! None of you will get a reference letter from this mine!"

"Oh, no!" gasped Langton. "I want to stay! Work! Please! I like it here!"

"Then Langton, get back to the house site; I'll send Naison, the new builder, and one of the timber boys to join you there, and you can continue building this afternoon, and, of course, work the two shifts tomorrow, Sunday! Crispin, I'll leave you to pay these two off, and our new policeman, Situnda, can see they pick up their belongings from the village and escort them off the mining claims. I'm leaving for Gwelo shortly. See you on Monday morning."

"Hi! *You* look very relieved!" Marianne greeted me as I pulled up.

"For bloody sure; we didn't want any more Matabele rebellions on these claims! Now they're all back at work again, bar the two I fired, so let's get our stuff together and hit Gwelo for a late Saturday sundowner and some supper at the Midland Hotel."

"Good idea!" echoed three voices simultaneously.

I walked over to the house foundations, where Langton, Naison and Matshe were all busy working, laying and cementing the blocks to build the low outside wall of our new house.

"Happy you took me back, *mzee*," Langton said with a slightly nervous grin.

"Okay Langton, and make sure you do a good job on the house!" I replied.

We left them working and drove off towards Fort Rixon.

On the way, we passed two lone figures carrying their belongings, and sweating in the heat of the full afternoon sun as they trundled along the hot, dusty road….

Illicit Brew, Liquid Trouble

I sat bolt upright in bed, coughing and gasping for breath, my actions jolting Marianne into instant consciousness.

"What's happening?" she exclaimed worriedly.

"Phew!" I replied, my heavy breathing slowly subsiding and returning to normal….

That was a weird, scary dream. I'm still shaking about what I saw and experienced; it was so real.

I was standing in an open stretch in the bush, when, suddenly, a herd of buffalo came crashing through the undergrowth towards me; the thundering noise of hundreds of hooves beating down on the ground was frightening!

As the wild-eyed beasts got closer, the heads of the leading two raging bulls transfigured as if a skilful cartoonist had modified their appearance so that their heads took on the characteristic resemblances of Staff and Crispin.

Then, in a cloud of dust, these two bulls skidded to a halt right in front of me, and the rest of the herd continued rumbling past on either side of me!"

A short silence was followed by chuckling… which grew into raucous laughter, and the two of us, with tears in our eyes shook with merriment, as the uncontrollable laughter filled the room.

. . .

During breakfast, we still had the odd giggle or two about last night's dream.

"I guess it was symbolic, but in reality those two, Crispin and Staff, really did help to stop the ranting and raging herd of our mine workers from causing a real disaster. But what I find very strange is what happened when I subconsciously fondled that wooden pendant necklace. I had never touched it before; it just hung round my neck. But when the angry African workers became threateningly close to me it started vibrating wildly and one hand uncontrollably lunged through the open pick-up window, hitting the hooter, which continuously blasted out 'my angry sound', overpowering the noise of the rioting mob, causing instant silence – and the workers standing quietly, meekly staring at me with bulbous white marble-like eyes! When that African woman gave the pendant to me, she said that it had been blessed by her witchdoctor uncle, and 'it will protect you and keep you from harm'! And it bloody well did!

"This is the second time now. Remember at Cain's mine as I lifted up that bed and was pulling it out of the storeroom, when a deadly poisonous green mamba snake hidden in the springs of the bed slowly started uncoiling itself next to my chest! Cain himself said something was protecting me from death, either God, or, as the Africans firmly believe, my pendant blessed by the witchdoctor!

"And now yesterday on the mine, I had no gun with me to fire into the air to scare the wild rioting Africans to calm them down, but uncontrollably my left arm thrust through the open window and I pressed the horn continuously, immediately causing the rioting workers to stop in their tracks! Weird; was it just a coincidence? Or was it witchdoctor protection? I don't know, but I'm just pleased the situation is under control again… but under whose control?"

And we laughed loudly, but with a slight nervousness.

"I've also been thinking about the slogans that the rebellious workers were chanting. 'No beer!' 'No work!', and I really must phone the Chibuku Brewery tomorrow to make sure that our first order of 60 gallons of beer will be delivered this coming Saturday. We don't want a repeat of yesterday's revolt, do we? But now, let's forget all about that and enjoy a normal relaxing Sunday with the little ones! Why don't we take them down to the park for the afternoon, let them burn off some energy, to ensure that we get a good sleep tonight!" I said, with tongue in cheek.

. . .

"Rainy days and Mondays always get me down…" A song playing on the radio by *The Carpenters* was drifting into the room; such a morbid ballad to start the week off – and today is Monday, and it's pouring with the rain! It's tipping down, unbelievable; where does all this rain keep coming from?

One thing is certain, though; that song will be sung with gusto by the ranchers and farmers in Matabeleland, as, at last, the three-year drought has been truly ended, with a vengeance!

But, rain or no rain, today Joseph and I were going to open our official company bank account, and push hard to get an overdraft facility.

As I made the short dash from the house to my pick-up, I got absolutely soaked, and must have looked quite bedraggled as I entered the bank, water still dripping from my nose and moustache.

Joseph, who had spent the weekend at Cain's mine with Jane to celebrate the new addition to the family, was waiting in the reception hall.

"Had a good shower this morning?" he joked as he saw me. "At Cain's place, it was hot and sunny the whole weekend; totally the opposite of sodden, soggy Gwelo Town."

The meeting was with the bank manager, a Mr Crow, who showed us into his office.

He sat down behind his desk, leant forward and asked, "So what can I do for you, young man?"

There followed an embarrassing silence, due to the fact that Mr Crow had RES – remote eye syndrome; some people refer to it as 'one eye is on holiday' – and one eye was looking directly at me, and the other looking at Joseph!

After what seemed like an eternity, we both suddenly blurted out at the same time, "Me? Fine!"

The meeting was brief, but proceeded smoothly.

We gave him copies of the articles of association of the company, the company registration certificate, and copies of the references from both our individual private banks in South Africa.

Numerous forms were filled in and signed, together with a specimen signature card for Joseph and me – we had all agreed that Ray would have no dealings directly with the mine bank account, and would not be a signatory – a suggestion that I had put forward!

The manger grilled us for quarter of an hour or so before granting us a $500 overdraft, which was equivalent to the current month's wage bill, and he told us that we could increase it when we employed the further anticipated 20 workers – not a bad start to a rainy Monday.

I handed him a copy of the letter that I written to Mr Smit, (cc the Reserve Bank), and asked him if there was anything he could do in order to speed up the clearance process.

Customs & Immigration,
Customs Dept. Gwelo,
Attention Mr. Smit.

7, Hudson Road,
Lundi Park,
Gwelo.

Dear Sirs, *Ref; 21534 – Peugeot 404D pickup, Engine No.695255*

I wish to apply for the immediate clearance of this vehicle so that I can sell same, as I am in desperate need of extra capital for a Gold mining venture in Rhodesia.

Yours faithfully…

cc Reserve Bank

He smiled, wished us well and said he would follow it up and contact me if he received any response from the Reserve Bank.

We shook hands and walked outside into the pouring rain – but with smiles on our faces.

At the Midland Hotel, we sat down together to discuss the ever-increasing amount of equipment and supplies that we needed at the mine before the Christmas shutdown.

Transport was very expensive, so we decided we would ferry as much as we could with our pick-ups, but the large equipment and fuel, etc. would have to be delivered by transport companies.

During this coming week, Joseph would make daily 'freight runs' to the mine before going to his parents in Belingwe for the weekend with Jane to present the baby boy to Grandfather Ray and his beloved Popette.

Joseph's tasks included:

Drive to a native reserve north of Que Que to pick up Willie's wife and kids, and take them and their belongings down to our mine.

Buy four more large plastic drums (25 gallons each), which we would keep in the store, only to be used for the weekend beer from Chibuku.

The first delivery was for the coming Saturday, which I would confirm when I phoned the brewery.

Collect supplies from the Farm Aid store.

A long list: plastic sheeting, heavy axes for chopping down trees, 10 bags of cement, and hopefully they'd supply us with 10 more sheets of corrugated iron, new ones, without nail holes in them – existing nail holes on the second-hand sheets can cause a lot of problems and leakage if they're not fitted carefully – as I was soon to find out!

Cut timber from The Plate Glass Company had to be transported to the mine; namely 3"x2" timbers cut to sizes, 12 12-foot pieces, nine 10-foot pieces, four 20-foot pieces and seven 14-foot pieces.

As regards the food for the mine workers, 60 kg sacks of mealie meal, beans and the meat rations would be collected every two days by whoever was in Gwelo at the time.

My responsibilities for the week would be:

A visit to the mining commissioner to discuss the Jackson fencing problem.

Make various Bulawayo 'collection runs'.
Stay in the Fort Rixon area for Pat Burke's visit on Friday.
And, most importantly, oversee the introduction of the Chibuku beer deliveries and the ensuing Saturday night festivities as the workers consumed 60 gallons of beer and enjoyed themselves – that's 480 pints!
And, on Saturday evening, I would personally check in the mine village compound to make sure that everything 'flowed' smoothly – we didn't want any problems.
A phone call to Chibuku Brewery would confirm that our first beer delivery would be on Saturday morning.

With the coming week sorted out, I left Joseph and went to the Zambezi Metals Company with a long list that Staff and our mechanic/electrician, Sparky, had compiled for me.

The names and uses of these items, apart from 'sets of nuts and bolts', were completely foreign to me – dog spikes? Fish plates? But, as Cain had said to me a few months previously: "Get good, experienced boss boys and a mechanic/ electrician to fix what breaks, and to order any necessary parts!"

With all the items duly boxed up for me and loaded on the back of my pick-up, I drove the short distance to No. 7 Hudson Road, looking forward to another evening meal and a hot bath.

. . .

When you are sleeping and have become used to a certain background noise that suddenly stops, it's the 'missing noise' or the 'new quietness' that actually wakes you up – I checked the clock, 5:30am, and peeped through the curtains. The noise had stopped; it had stopped raining!

Within minutes, the sun, which hadn't been seen for days, was taking this opportunity to appear, showing off its brightest and hottest start to the day.

After spending a few quiet hours whilst the others slept making notes and recording expenses from a wallet full of receipt slips from the previous week, I told Marianne to get the kids ready, as we'd be going to stay at the mine for a few days, but first I'd phone and check with Gayle to see if we could also stay one night at her ranch – so off to my other private 'phone booth' in the reception of the Midland Hotel.

Gayle told me that the rains had not been so heavy for the last few days where she was, but I could not use their main track from the Fort Rixon road to their ranch house, as the swollen river was still flowing too strongly.

She gave me an alternative route, turning off the Bulawayo tarmac road 10 km past Shangani.

The roads from there were not too bad apart from a few dongas that we'd have to plough through. And we were most welcome to come over for dinner and stay the night, but on one condition – we had to bring the small naughty ones with us!

At Midlands Butchery, I was told that they had been suffering from lack of meat deliveries due to the abnormal heavy rains making it difficult for cattle ranchers to get to the abattoir slaughterhouses – sorry, but they could not supply me with the boys' meat rations today.

Actually, not to worry; it worked out quite well, as we wouldn't have to fill up Gayle's fridge with packets of ration meat, which I'd be able to get the next day when I was in Bulawayo.

What a welcome we received.

Gayle and her husband, Trevor, were great hosts, wining and dining us 'til well into the night, while their daughter and the house girl entertained Marie-Louise and Jeffrey in another part of their home – a rare occasion for us; out of sight, out of mind. A real, refreshing change.

Their stories and experiences of their first year of cattle ranching in drought-stricken Matabeleland were not only interesting and informative, but we also learnt that everybody has problems when starting up a new venture, especially in the bush, but the secret is, as Trevor put it to us: "Grit your teeth, ignore the whingers, and above all don't let the buggers get you down; enjoy the time together, giving it your best shot – that upsets them the most!"

We talked on for hours and hours… until it was time for one last nightcap.

"Here's to you both; we wish you success. May the mine be full of *gold!*"

. . .

Trevor kindly let me use fuel from his diesel storage tank to register 'full' on my pick-up dashboard instruments, and, with Gayle's huge breakfast similarly accomplishing the same for my body, I set off on a full stomach for the mine to pick up Staff.

Marianne and the kids would spend the rest of the day on Gayle's ranch – I would pick them up later in the afternoon on my return from Bulawayo.

When I reached the mine, I found Staff sitting outside the office waiting.

He showed me his blasting licence, which we would reassign to our mine when we saw the mining commissioner later in the morning.

Staff had another long list of items we needed to buy from K.B. Davies – a supplier of mining equipment and accessories.

As we drove off, Elliot ran over, flagged me down and jumped on the back of the pick-up, and we headed off for Bulawayo.

First stop was to visit the mining commissioner, who gave me a bit of a roasting about the fencing complaint from Jackson. He'd seen my letter requesting an extension past 31 December, but said that, under the Mining Regulations of Rhodesia, it was quite specific and he could not authorise or amend the date.

I told him that Jackson's constant harassment and unreasonableness was premeditated and designed to add to our costs, in an attempt to stop our gold mining operations on *his land*!

If Jackson persisted, we would appeal to the Minister of Mines himself – potential gold production was a much-needed foreign exchange tool and must surely take preference over a petty-minded rancher's blatant disruptive attempts to close us down – he was even being ridiculed by some of his fellow rancher neighbours.

The commissioner leant forward, and, speaking in a quieter tone, he advised me, 'off the record', to speak to Jackson personally and find a way to delay, defer or extend the deadline! God, he is a bit human, after all.

I showed him Staff's blasting licence, which he took, then wrote the name of our mine in the extension section, signed it, and rolled a rubber stamp slowly and deliberately on an inkpad before raising it like a weapon and thumping it down on the licence document next to his signature!

And that was that, short and sweet – unbelievable!

With two things already going my way with this gentleman, I took the opportunity to raise the subject of Willie failing his blasting licence test.

"The reason he failed was because of the new rule to examine mine workers using the metric system measurements instead of the old imperial ones."

And I reminded the commissioner: "When Willie came in to do the test, you actually said to him 'don't worry, a man of your long mining experience will pass the test; I'm sure you will, *Will*', and you roared with laughter! Was that an 'imperial' laugh? How do you expect a simple, but experienced miner-blaster to learn in an hour these metric words and measurements, which to him might as well be in Chinese! Can we not arrange a practical test for him, so that he can prove that he is competent and have his licence renewed?"

With raised eyebrows looking over the top of his glasses, and with a totally disinterested expression on his face, he cleared his throat and replied, "No! Rules are rules!"

"But Mr Commissioner," I interjected forcefully, "if you want to see how confusing the situation is with both the imperial and the metric systems now being used, just look at this list of items that we are about to purchase for our mine. They are in **feet and inches**; **centimetres and millimetres**, **pounds and kilograms** – both **imperial and metric**, and often mixed terms on the same document. It's ludicrous to expect a semi-literate miner to have a grasp of these so quickly! Why can't the blasting licence be examined in both?"

The blank look persisted, as did the non-response.

I suppose two favourable results in one day is a lot to ask of a 'by the book' civil servant; if he granted me the third, he would feel that he was losing some of his almighty power!

The silence that persisted indicated the end of the conversation!

"And some (seed) fell on stony ground, as the Bible says! Come Staff, let's go; at least we've got one blasting licence for the mine – you'll just have to work double shifts, won't you!" I joked as we left the office.

We popped downstairs to see Ronnie Cummins; he had not received the Rhodesian import licence for the South African compressor yet; pity.

However, there was better news when I called into the bank to see 'What, What' Emerson.

"I've had no response so far; damned annoying what! But let me get on the jolly old blower, and see if I can hasten things along for you, what." He listened carefully, then smiled as he replaced the receiver. "Good news, old man! The import licence has been granted and will be in the post today! Now, good day to you, sir!" And he patted me on the back as he shepherded me out of his office.

We still had to do a lot of errands in Bulawayo before returning to pick up Marianne and the kids from Gayle's ranch on our way back to the mine.

Staff was dropped off at K.B. Davies, armed with his list of items we needed to purchase for the mine – on credit, of course, as these would be charged to our new company mine account card, which Joseph had arranged the previous week.

The list included a variety of items; a mix of both metric and imperial measurements, as I had pointed out and shown to the mining commissioner – all to no avail!

Stocks and dyes;

20 8 x 1½" bolts and nuts (" is short for inches);

1 auger for width 6" nails;

5 kilograms (kg) 5" – 6" nails;

100 feet of ½" steel wire for the windless hoist;

Windless and bucket;

2 kg of ½" washers;

2 kg of 1 mm nuts (mm is short for millimetres)

A guide – *If you don't want to be as confused as Willie:*
Imperial v. (metric):
Measurements - approximate:
1 inch = 2.5 centimetres (cm), or 25 millimetres (mm);
1 foot = 12 inches (30 cm);
1 yard = 3 feet = bit less than 1 metre.
Weights:
1 pound (less than ½ kilo, kg);
Liquids:
1 pint (more than ½ litre);
1 gallon (4½ litres).
- Hardly surprising that Willie had problems with his blasted blasting licence exam!

The sales manager of Shell was out of town. His assistant could not give me any definite dates for the delivery of the diesel storage tanks, but said, "However, if you pay $150 today, I'll try to plan for a delivery of the diesel tanks early next week, but I can't promise and must warn you that all of our schedules are stretched to the limit because of the constant bad weather. Many rivers are in flood, and our drivers are having great difficulty delivering fuel to the outlying farms and mines, some of which have been cut off for several days. Even with overtime, working from dawn till dusk, our staff are having problems delivering to our existing customers, and they come first, sorry! But I will try; I understand how critical the diesel fuel problem is for you."

I came out of the building to find that it wasn't actually raining or thundering; thus, I reckoned the rumbling noise was being emitted from my stomach, and not from gathering storm clouds!

Time to pop into Greys Inn for a quick pint and a pie, while Elliot went to buy something to eat for himself and Staff and take it to him at K.B. Davies.

After my lunch break, I'd have to collect them and the ordered items, not forgetting the meat rations either – otherwise, there would be thunderous rumblings from our 40 mine workers!

Then the usual 'load and go' routine – loading everything onto the pick-up and leaving Bulawayo to collect Marianne and the kids from Gayle's ranch on our way back to the mine.

Jeffrey and Marie-Louise were happy to climb into the back of the pick-up with Elliot and Staff, who held them tightly, acting as human seat belts as we drove along some bumpy dirt tracks.

Gayle had informed me that the river was still too swollen for us to cross, so we had to drive the long way around – back onto the tarmac road towards Shangani, taking the murrum road to Fort Rixon and arriving at the mine after dark, about 8 o'clock in the evening.

All that was left to do after a very long day was the 'unload and go' routine – unload the truck and go to bed!

. . .

Our mining village was constantly growing in size as more new mine workers built their own huts, so much so that I had to allocate them 'plots' on the other side of 'the High Street' in order to accommodate them.

The numbers had now swelled to 41 African workers, the majority of whom were working well and were no trouble; however, the 14 workers from Matt's mine were a different story.

Matt's boss boy, Costa, had supposedly screened them for us in order to root out the lazy ones and any trouble-makers – well, all I can say is, the 'screen' must have had great big holes in it!

Two of those workers refused to build their own huts, saying they were underground mine workers, not hut builders – so they were sent packing!

Another five of them had formed a gang, trying their bullying tactics on some of the other workers. However, these five were the most skilled underground workers Matt had identified for me, so it was a case of wait, constantly watching, and see!

These five had also complained that our mine was the only mine they had ever worked on where there was no weekend beer, and they had to travel to Shangani for a 'Sunday session'!

I think at the Matt's mine they were used to going into Gwelo in the evenings after work – only two to three kilometres away – and drinking regularly in the shanty bars 'til late!

Out here in the bush, the nearest bar was 40 kilometres away; no chance for a quick few beers after work for them!

Beer seems to be an important and necessary catalyst for the Africans getting together on the weekend to relax and enjoy themselves.

That's why I was so pleased – relieved, even – to have confirmation at last from the Chibuku Brewery that they would do a beer run to our mine this coming weekend.

Crispin and I were busy discussing how we should sell the beer to our mine boys when one of Rancher Jackson's workers appeared at the office and handed me a note:

To the Mine Manager.
This is a final warning!
Any of your African mine workers that are found on my land, drinking the local Changaa brew with my farm workers and worrying their women, will be forcibly held until the police arrive!
We will prosecute them to the full, and report to the Mining Commissioner that action must be taken by you as their Employer to stop this trespassing or face the consequences!
Jackson.
cc: Mining Commissioner, Bulawayo.
cc: BSAP Fort Rixon (British South Africa Police).

"Jesus! That's all we need!" I exclaimed, and instructed Crispin and Staff to tell and stress to all our workers that anyone caught trespassing and drinking on Jackson's land would be fired and paid off immediately!

"And I don't have to guess who those workers were, Crispin; it smells just like the 'gang of five' to me! Also remind the boys that from this Saturday there will be no need for them to go drinking on Jackson's land, as 60 gallons of Chibuku beer will be delivered to the mine. That's 480 pints of beer between 42 workers, which should be enough to lubricate their throats over the weekend!"

After spending the next few hours on administration with Crispin, I was about to go back to our 'hut home' for a relaxing evening with the family when a police Jeep drove into the mine compound.

A smiling Policeman Pete climbed out and warmly shook my hand.

"Hello. Good morning to you. But before we go any further, I must first address police business, as we have received a letter of complaint from Jackson warning your mine boys to keep off his land and not to drink the local brew there with his farm workers. So please, make sure it doesn't happen again. We also have a copy from Davidson, Fort Rixon Administration that you now have a valid permit to sell beer to your mine workers over the weekend, starting with a delivery of 60 gallons from Chibuku Brewery this Saturday.

"That's good timing, and should solve your latest problem with Jackson! I'll make a follow-up, and note that the matter is in hand and he should not experience the problem again. And for good police-public relations, I'll drive down there now before it gets dark and deliver this note to him personally; he's always easier to talk to over a sundowner! By the way, Christmas is fast approaching and traditionally the police hold a children's party.

"It helps show the youngsters that the police are their friends, and we let them see how the handcuffs work and give them a tour of the cold, damp-looking prison cells – a reminder to them that it's best to keep the peace when they get older; a double-edged sword, so to speak. And for the big kids like you, there will be the New Year's Eve 'bash' at the Fort Rixon club, an evening to remember – and certainly not hard to forget when you are suffering from a mighty hangover on New Year's Day! Look forward to seeing you there!"

. . .

I awoke on hearing the noise of a truck arriving.

As I sleepily pulled back the black plastic sheet door of our hut, milk and fresh bread were thrust into my hands– it was Pat Burke visiting us as promised, but I didn't expect him to be here at 5:30am! Our mine start gong was only just being sounded.

"Bloody hell, Pat, you must have got up at 2 o'clock this morning to be here and be waking me up at this time!"

"No, actually at 5am; I was staying down the road with the Ashburners. I hadn't seen them for a while, and his father and I were good friends, and had worked together a long time ago on the Blighty and the Blighter mines on his property."

"Elliot!" I shouted through the open doorway. "Make some coffee for all of us and give the kids some of this milk and bread when they wake up. Sorry Pat, you were saying something about the Ashburners?"

"Yes, that was a crazy mine to work on; there were no real shafts sunk like on the Claremont and the Nelly. We just burrowed our way into the side of the hill, where Ashburner's father had found signs of ancient gold workings. We were youngsters and a bit green – just like you and your partner. We should have taken it slowly, planned the tunnels with proper timber supports, but we were so excited by the richness of the ore that we literally chiselled away and shovelled the gold ore out along the narrow tunnels. In places, we had to crawl to get through from one tunnel to the next, just like the ancients did, I suppose, and we opened up a vast labyrinth of honeycombed tunnels.

"One day, I was going along the narrow tunnels with two munts following closely behind me, to get to the place where we'd been working the previous week, when I heard a low growl… I turned quickly, shining the lantern into a large dug-out cavern on the side of the tunnel, when I saw these eyes looking at me from out of the darkness. Instantly, there was a loud, terrifying roar, which echoed through the tunnels, and I saw it was a leopard! I panicked and dropped my hurricane lamp, which crashed down on the floor, bursting into flames!

"Christ! That was our saviour! With flames and smoke billowing out from that small cavern entrance, the munts and I scrambled and fought our way along the tunnel in our mad rush to get out and away from that wild cat! We ran like scared rabbits to my truck, jumped in, slammed the doors and, with hearts pounding and gasping for breath, we sat, watched and waited for a ferocious leopard to come charging out of the tunnel.

"But it didn't! When I got back to the ranch house and told Ashburner about this incident, he just laughed and said there were so many entrances to those tunnels, the leopard would be long gone! Leopards were quite common in those days, and the thought that there might be one lurking in the darkness of the tunnels made us wary each time we entered the mine. One day, the inevitable happened; there was a cave-in and we were lucky to get out alive. It had become far too unsafe to risk continuing to mine there any longer. So Ashburner decided he'd stick to cattle ranching instead!"

Burke and I spent the next few hours walking around our claims, while he told me about the various mines, their history and, more relevantly, their past gold production and the potential output possible.

"The old mines like the Siruis and the Hlatin were rich, around one to two ounces of gold to the ton of rock, mainly in the white and blue quartz reefs. The ancients had started the mining there over 2,000 years ago, when gold was sent to Israel in the times of King Solomon and the Queen of Sheba. The way the ancients mined was simple and effective; the only way of identifying a prospective gold mining site was to actually see 'visible gold' in the granite rocks. However, the process was similar in principal to the way that gold is mined today."

Burke continued, "They obviously had no dynamite to blast the rocks in those times, but they created a similar way of doing it by building large fires next to and under the protruding rocks, and when the granite rocks were extremely hot they would pour water over them, which would crack, split and explode the rock into fragments, sometimes the flying pieces badly wounding the miners.

"They had no crushing mills, but they placed these pieces of gold-bearing rock into groves or indentations on a large granite boulder and pounded them with hammer-like tools until the rock fragments became powder, when the pieces of visible gold could easily be picked out – and yielding many ounces of gold to the ton."

Pat could see that I found his stories fascinating, and he suggested that I would enjoy reading up about the ancient miners and their gold trade routes through Africa, generally recognised as using a series of fort-like settlements, such as the Regina ruins and the Dhlo Dhlo ruins in the Fort Rixon area, and their world-famous big brother, the Great Zimbabwe ruins, near the Town of

Fort Victoria.

After an interesting morning with him, we had the lunch together with Marianne – and the 'kids behaving badly' provided real entertainment for Bachelor Pat! He found them most amusing, and, still with a smile on his face, he thanked us and went on his way.

I walked over to the office for an afternoon administrative session with Crispin, who was busy getting all the books up to date – and we went through them together; a habit we had agreed to do once a week, normally on a Saturday.

Come 5 o'clock, I had a pleasant surprise.

Unbeknown to me, Pat had also brought four bottles of Castle Lager and a newspaper with him, which he and Marianne had hidden out of my sight.

And now, miraculously, two unexpected happenings:

Sitting outside, and having a sundowner – made possible by a rare appearance of the sun, and the welcome appearance of the 'Castles' from Pat. There is a God, after all!

. . .

It was my first lay-in while actually living and staying on the mine.

A cup of tea in bed and a chance to read a newspaper, which was an airmail edition of the UK *Daily Telegraph*. Glancing at the headlines, one realises that nothing really changes over the years; they could have been from the 1950s, or even the 1930s – dock strikes, prime minister attacked by opposition, Aussies thrash England in the cricket 'Ashes' series, and the humorous cartoons that not only make you laugh, but generally get their 'message' across much better than a half-page report.

Van Gogh was right in saying that . . . *a caricaturist had always been an expressionist, playing with the likeness of the victim, and distorting it to express just what he feels about his fellow man . . . and the situation.*

A leisurely breakfast with the family and a chance to chat and play with Marie-Louise and Jeffrey for a couple of hours, before I strolled up to the mine to see Crispin.

He had selected three workers who deserved the chance to be the 'mine publican' and 'sell' the beer this weekend.

The chosen one, though, was Saul, who would be in charge of the barrels of beer and can sell pints to the other workers. Whatever money he collected, he gave me half, retaining the other half for himself – that could be a sizable amount of money too; more than a month's wages!

To be chosen as the 'beer seller of the month' would serve as an additional inducement for the mine boys to work hard and to keep out of trouble – in drinking terms, 'a double' incentive!

The knock-off gong sounded and we paid 13 of our African workers – our first big pay day, and those 13 workers were excited to have some money in their pockets, most of them anticipating the imminent arrival of the Chibuku lorry, with its precious cargo of weekend beer.

Then came a real surprise for me – I was amazed.

Crispin came over and told me that eight mine boys wanted to do something else with their money, rather than just drinking it!

They wanted me to buy them men's suits, using part of today's wages as a deposit, and paying the balance off at the end of January.

"It's in our tradition to look smart to go home for Christmas," Crispin informed me, "and next week when the mine closes down, they want to have their new suits to take with them."

Crispin and I huddled together, and agreed that we would buy suits for only six of them, but not for Paniche or Banzi, who were part of this trouble-making 'gang of five' that had been drinking on Jackson's land with his farm workers the previous week.

The scribe pulled out his pen and made the entries into the back of the pay book for: Robson, Crispin, Tachibona, Alexander, Staff and Elliot, with the sizes of the suits they wanted, and, when I next went into Gwelo, Crispin would go with me to buy their suits.

The workers were milling around the office area when suddenly all pandemonium broke loose! One of them shouted, "I can hear the faint noise of an approaching lorry!"

There was shouting and the women started screaming and dancing; the noise was deafening. Then another louder noise began to take over, the loud chugging noise of a diesel lorry – the approaching Chibuku beer lorry!

Hastily, three of the clean Bata barrels that we'd reserved for beer were rolled out of the store and across to where the Chibuku lorry had parked.

The following scenes were something to behold!

This Chibuku lorry was the shape of a small petrol tanker.

The driver climbed out, attached a long, flexible tube about four inches in diameter and pulled a lever when Chibuku beer started squirting into the first barrel.

Small tin mugs suddenly appeared from the tops of the women's dresses and were quickly filled by dipping them into the foaming brew in the barrel – and just as quickly drained by those women! Then the men took over and immediately followed suit, and it became quite a noisy, but friendly sampling party.

This beer was not like the traditional clear light golden brown of a pint of English beer or a German lager, but a creamy beige foaming brew!

But I just had to taste it!

It was my first and only drink of this Chibuku beer – it was a thick, porridge-like liquid, which left a sticky, creamy taste in my mouth, rather like after eating cold spinach! Yuck, never again!

I left this carnival atmosphere and went to the hut house for an afternoon of playing with the kids and teaching them some more nursery rhymes.

As the day faded, the noise from the mine village became louder and more raucous – 'the boys were partying'!

About 8 o'clock, I thought I'd better drive up there to have a look see.

I pulled up outside Staff's house and we walked around together.

Everybody seemed to be having a good time and, in fact, Phillemon, who had started the chorus 'no work, no beer' during the strike the previous week, called out to me, "Thanks for the beer, Boss."

I asked Staff to keep an ear open. Hopefully there wouldn't be any trouble, but if there was he should send someone to my hut, as we would be sleeping over on the mine.

He agreed, noting the concern on my face, us both knowing that our policeman, Situnda, would be like a feather in a hurricane when it came to attempting to discipline any worker who had blown a fuse.

The partying continued well into the night; however, we didn't have to worry about any neighbours complaining – our nearest one was eight miles away!

. . .

During the night, the sound of the rain on the thatched roof had muffled, to a certain extent, the raucous laughter and shouting from the Saturday night revellers in our village pub – but now, nothing stirred.

I called out for Elliot; it was past 10 o'clock and we wanted some tea before we left for the Gwelo house, but there was no one around.

A few minutes later, a tired-looking Elliot came running down the drive and shouted, "Good morning, Boss." He apologised that he hadn't lit the fire yet. "Tea is on its way, Boss!" he called out as he began to rattle through the pots and pans.

"No, Elliot! We are on our way! Forget the tea; we must leave now!"

Luckily, the rain had stopped, although the road was still a bit slippery – especially when we drove up the bank on the other side after fording a flowing donga, but at least I had a clear view through the windscreen, and I didn't have to put up with the recent constant clonk-clonk, clonk-clonk, clonk-clonk of the windscreen wipers as they fought to remove the muddy smearing caused by splashing when an oncoming vehicle past us by.

"Let's hope that Joseph doesn't have too many problems with the weather as he drives from his parents' mine near Belingwe on Monday to a native reserve near Que Que to collect Willie's wife and five children! With all their belongings piled in the back of the pick-up, the last thing he needs is a deluge like the one I had to drive through when I took Crispin to the Lower Gwelo Mission – those sodden, slippery tracks tested my reactions and driving skills to the full, and luckily for me the pick-up didn't slide and do a nosedive into the gullies created by the fast-flowing storm water rushing along the softer sides of the dirt tracks!"

"True," said Marianne, "but Gayle was telling me that these abnormal rains were a godsend to the farmers and ranchers who have had to experience and survive the three-year drought in Matabeleland. She said it always seems to be either too much or not enough; it's such a hard life for the farmers!"

"It's a bloody hard life for us too at the moment," I replied. "We've got too much water in the flooded mine, but not enough water above ground for our own use, and absolutely *no* diesel to get the pumps pumping! And this excessive rain is making the roads impassable for heavy tankers, and Shell has refused to bring the storage tanks and diesel fuel we urgently need!"

. . .

I spent the whole of the next day at the Midland Hotel on the phone, trying to chase up several companies to give us firm delivery dates, but I had little joy and there was little enthusiasm in the voices of the people I spoke to.

Phones are such impersonal objects. You can never be sure whether someone is telling you the true facts; you just can't see the expressions on their face to be able to judge.

I'd quite often seen a colleague in the office who is talking on the phone and he puts his hand over the mouthpiece and says 'got a right annoying one here; he's pushing, pushing for a completion date', followed by a bare-faced lie to the customer: "Sorry, but I'll have to phone you back tomorrow, as I must leave now for a dentist's appointment!"

And with Christmas just around the corner, people's thoughts are filled with the preparations, mince pies and Christmas pudding, and taking time off to pop out of the office to buy presents! Nobody seems interested at all in good customer service at this time of the year!

But in the case of our fuel delivery, the whole cycle – 'order, dispatch, delivery' – in the end depends on the driver, the weather and the condition of the dirt roads.

There is only so much that we can collect with our pick-ups, but, as regards fuel and large equipment, we are at the mercy of the transport companies with their 30-ton transporter trucks and trailers.

However, one such company, Fox & Bookless, seemed keen and gave me a quote for collecting a large alternator (already approved by the Mines Department) and four 30-foot gum poles from a mine near Hartley, and travelling down to Bulawayo to pick up further equipment at the Mines Yard, including the large green compressor, all to be delivered to our mine on Thursday – and at a reasonable $250 inclusive of all charges. I was well pleased.

I contacted Ronnie at the Mines Department straight away to check that everything we needed was in their yard, ready for collection on Thursday, and asked him if he had received the import licence for the South African compressor yet.

He confirmed that it had come with a letter from Barclays Bank, and all we had to do was to pay $105 Customs duty to clear the compressor.

I next phoned K.B. Davies, who were also very helpful and would get one of their vans to deliver our order to the Mines Yard on Thursday morning – 50 pockets of cement and a large pestle and mortar, which would be added to the Fox & Bookless transporter load.

That's great; things were beginning to come together. However, phone calls to the suppliers of our two most urgent pressing problems, Shell Diesel and the Shangani Telephone Department, proved frustratingly fruitless!

. . .

On my next journey to the mine, I had to drive slower and a bit more carefully on the dirt roads, as, besides a full load – the rest of the corrugated iron sheets from the Phoenix Theatre that I'd stored at the Gwelo house – I was carrying 10 sheets of glass for the various windows in the office and our partly finished palatial abode.

I also had putty, tar and, very importantly, a toilet seat for our yet-to-be-dug long drop toilet!

All these items would hopefully contribute to our new house being ready to move into before Christmas.

Boxes containing 10 assorted overalls, leggings and goggles were piled high in the cab of my pick-up, making visibility rather limited as I negotiated the tricky dirt roads.

Mission successful; not a pane of glass broken or even cracked, and everything was successfully offloaded and put in the storeroom.

More good news too; Crispin told me that all the workers enjoyed the Chibuku weekend, and there were no incidents on either the Saturday or the Sunday – very pleasing to hear.

Crispin locked the storeroom and climbed into the front of the pick-up with me.

Alexander leapt onto the back and we left, heading for Gwelo, where they would spend the next day buying the Christmas suits and other extra things to put in the store for the workers who weren't taking Christmas home leave.

I dropped them at the bus terminal and told them to make sure they were there at 10am on Thursday, when Joseph would meet them and take them back to the mine.

The Law Must be Obeyed!

Up very early and away before dawn, as there was much to arrange on the mine site to accommodate and store the ordered equipment. Gangs of boys would have to 'strengthen' the dirt tracks with rocks and schist, to allow the heavy transporter lorry and trailer to drive close to the 'chosen sites' where the heavy equipment could be unloaded, namely:

The alternator (55KVA, 6 LW Gardner 85 HP) with a fuel tank and switchboard, etc., and the green compressor (ex-South Africa) would be unloaded from the transporter near the main shaft, together with the four thick gum poles, each 30 foot in length that would be used in the construction of the headgear.

Thirty-eight lengths of 20-pound rails that would be used to build a short rail link between the headgear situated at the mine shaft and the 5-stamp mill. When the mine was operational, ore brought to the surface by a hoist skip/ bucket would be tipped into a hopper, to be fed into cocopans, which would transport the ore to the 5-stamp mill along this rail track.

Fifty pockets of cement and 155 metres of 2" black water-piping would be unloaded straight into the storeroom.

It was 5am when I turned off the Gwelo-Bulawayo road at Shangani and headed for the mine. At this time of the day, if it's not raining, of course, the air is very still and the quietness gradually gives way to the soft noises of the bush as the wildlife and the birds commence their daily routines for survival….

Suddenly, loud noises and a blaze of headlights as an ambulance was racing towards me clanging its warning bells! I pulled over immediately to let it through, thinking as one does and trying to imagine what catastrophe could have happened out here in the bush at such an early hour – certainly not a car pile-up! Perhaps a heart attack and an elderly person being transported to hospital, or worse still, the dead body of an elderly person who had already been transported to Heaven!

I mused over the possibilities as I drove on, only to be surprised to see a native police constable standing in the middle of the road, waving me down – a common sight in the city, but out here in the bush? As I slowed, I scanned the surroundings for a clue, but saw nothing; no crashed car, and no dead animal on the road!

"Excuse me, sir, its urgent!" He babbled away, "You must take me *now* to the police post!"

"But it's only 200 yards down that track?" I queried.

'Yes, sir!" he replied nervously. "I mean, will you come with me to the police post? It's very urgent! Bad things have happened on your mine, and the officer on duty wants to talk to you!"

A few minutes later, I was sitting in his office, listening intently as a story of bloodshed and mayhem began to unfold…

The Night of the Long Knives! The Street Walkers of Soho! Who Killed Cock Robin? In fact, a tragic mixture of them all!

Apparently, around three in the morning, one of our mine workers arrived at the police post shouting out and asking for help. He had ridden from the mine by bicycle, and it took a while, amid his puffing and panting, for him to blurt out what had happened – a huge fight and many badly injured!

The police had phoned for an ambulance to go straight away to Ridge Top Mine, loaded the exhausted messenger and his bike into the back of the police Land Rover and driven off immediately for the mine.

When they had arrived, Staff explained to them what had happened.

Some of the mine boys had bought bottles of Changaa from a farm worker's illegal 'still', and, on returning to the mine, they started drinking heavily. One had brought a prostitute to the mine village, and, as the boys became more and more drunk, they started fighting over who should have the prostitute next!

Tachibona's wife had tried to rescue the girl from this drunken orgy, but Banzi had knocked her down, whereupon Tachibona had hit Banzi!

Then Banzi's drunken friends attacked Tachibona with a knobkerrie, hitting him across the face, splitting his mouth and knocking out his front teeth!

Phillemon had taken the prostitute to his hut, and, when Paniche and Bamoso had tried to enter, he had drawn a knife, hacking off three fingers from Bamoso's hand. Paniche had intervened and was slashed across the face, blood pouring from his eye and forehead.

Paniche had gone berserk and fought Phillemon for the knife, wrestling him to the ground and stabbing him in the chest, causing him to bleed profusely!

By the time the ambulance had arrived, Phillemon had bled to death.

His body had been loaded into the ambulance, together with the badly injured Paniche, Tachibona and Bamoso, to be rushed to Shangani Hospital.

"Shit!" I exclaimed. "And that was the one that raced past me a few miles back!"

"Yes, they took away the dead body and the badly injured. We have three more in the cells; the prostitute, Enoch, our witness who saw it all, but is so scared of Banzi who started the fighting that we've had to put them each in separate cells. Your senior boss boy, Staff, told us that Banzi, Paniche, Bamoso and the dead worker, Phillemon, are known trouble-makers and part of a 'gang of five'!"

"That's right, and they have caused nothing but problems and the bullying of the other workers ever since I took them on from another mine near Gwelo."

There was a loud knock on the door and in walked Peter.

"I've heard what happened; this is terrible news, and just the sort of ammunition that Jackson needs to close you down! What happened to your *askari*/policeman?"

"Situnda is his name. We took him on as a general worker/cook, and later made him an *askari*, more of a watchman than a policeman; we never expected any trouble like this! He's probably either fast asleep still or he took off when the fighting started and is still running through the bush in panic!" I replied.

"Look," Peter continued, "the magistrate will be here on Monday for the hearing, when the details of this event will be brought before him, and undoubtedly your workers will all get jail sentences or worse, especially Paniche! But we also need to assure the magistrate that you have things in hand now, which, when included in his judgment, will help us nullify the 'ammunition' that Jackson could use against you from this major tragic disturbance on his land!

"So my advice to you is, firstly employ a strong, fearsome *askari*/policeman who is experienced and has worked on the mines and knows the problems. Most importantly, he must not be from a Rhodesian tribe; best is either a Zambian or even a Portuguese East African – local workers fear them! When you employ him, and do it in the next few days if you can before the judgment, because then we can interview him, check on his background references and register him with the Fort Rixon Police Station. This will be a big plus for you, and it will be included in the magistrate's ruling. Secondly, buy him some handcuffs and build a jail house where any trouble-makers and the drunks can be locked up overnight – you can phone us in the morning to collect them!"

"Now Peter, you have highlighted another major problem we have – we still don't have a bloody phone yet, and have been told that it'll be another three weeks before it's installed! So we have to come to the Fort Rixon exchange phone booth every time we need to make a call!"

"Well then, instead of phoning us from that phone booth, just bring the trouble makers straight to us; save us a journey!" remarked Peter drolly, causing us all to laugh, and breaking the uncomfortable atmosphere. "Come and have some breakfast at the house; you look as if you need it!"

"And some strong black coffee, preferably with a shot in it!" I joked.

"Not whilst I'm on duty, sir!" ribbed Peter.

A bit more relaxed and fully fed, I drove off to the mine. My 'Joseph early morning start' had not materialised, and there was still so much work to do preparing for the arrival of the big transporter truck the next day, loaded with our essential mining equipment.

"Oh God, no!" I said to myself. Jackson would be coming to the mine this afternoon for our meeting to discuss the fencing problem.

Last time I spoke to him to arrange this get-together, he was in a reasonable mood and told me that, when my wife and kids were living permanently on the mine, we could take water from the tank for our personal use. Even better, he would get Feet to bring us fresh cow's milk regularly, maybe even tethering a cow on our house site – the kids would love that, and watching Marianne milking it too! One of his farm workers could collect the excess milk each day. Unfortunately, he undoubtedly would have heard about the fighting and the death on the mine last night… joint party lines news.

But fingers crossed; let's see how the cards fall this afternoon….

The mine was abuzz with stories of the fighting and the death of Phillemon, but Staff had firmly controlled the situation, and soon had everyone working to prepare the sites for the heavy transporter to unload. Wheelbarrow after wheelbarrow full of rock waste was being tipped out on any soft spots of the track to the mine shaft, to make a firmer road for the huge vehicle.

At 2 o'clock on the dot, an old Land Rover pulled up – it was Rancher Jackson and his wife.

"We're not stopping, so we won't be getting out of the vehicles!" she proclaimed loudly. "I don't know all the things you discussed with my husband, but after the death last night you can forget about using *water* from our tank, and the *cow* is remaining at home on the ranch!"

I wish you were, I thought!

"And furthermore, we will do everything we can to get you and your bunch of ruffians off our land! You must not be allowed to mine on *our land*!"

"Madam, may I remind you that we have government approval to mine these claims, from the centre of the earth right up to the surface! And *you*, in fact, are herding your cattle on top of *our land*!" I said testily!

"Well, the utter check of the man! Come on, drive off; we are going!"

And that was the end of the meeting!

A fortune teller would have said that we had been dealt the Queen of Spades card, known as 'The Lady of Death'!

Jesus, what a day; surely things can't get worse!

. . .

Oh yes they can, I said to myself the next day on hearing more bad news when I arrived at the Shell depot in Bulawayo.

"I'm sorry, sir, but we are even further behind schedule due to more heavy rainfall. We definitely cannot deliver and erect the fuel tank on your mine before Christmas. The earliest date would be in the first week of the New Year."

"Oh Sh-Sh-Shell!" I blurted out. "No fuel, no power, no pumping water… three big fat 'nos'; definitely not a good start to the day!"

This meant that no useful work could be done on the mine, so it was good that we had already decided to close down the mine from Saturday until the New Year.

Water would still have to be collected from the river each day as usual in the large plastic drums, but, apart from that and the Chibuku beer lorry deliveries, there would be little going on.

"Get even worse? Oh, yes they bloody well can!" The words exploded out of my mouth on being told that the South African compressor could not be loaded on the Fox & Bookless transporter today, because Customs wouldn't clear it without the Commerce and Industry endorsement stamp on the import licence!

"What? God, you make a grown man cry!" I shouted. Yes, I shouted at Cummins. "You told me yesterday that all we had to do was to pay $105 Customs duty today!"

"That's what we thought too; the letter from the bank granting the import licence didn't mention anything else, but when we took the documents to Customs this morning that's what we were told."

"Shit! We must phone Commerce and Industry straight away," I demanded. "This is getting bloody ridiculous!"

On speaking to their administrator, he said that they were waiting approval from their head office in Salisbury, and should hear back within a week.

"Jesus! Within a week! Listen, I've hired a huge transporter truck, which is standing here in the Mines Yard waiting to be loaded; it's costing me time and money!"

"Well, it wasn't marked urgent. Look, let me phone Salisbury and I'll get back to you after lunch; I promise I will call you," he replied.

"Lunch, why not? No point sitting around here; come Ronnie, let's go over to Greys Inn and have a pub lunch while we wait!

"Do you know, Ronnie, for the first time in my life, I'm not really enjoying a pint of beer! Fights, death, Jackson's wife, Commerce and Industry… they're all leaving a bad taste in my mouth," I whinged. Yes, I whinged! Me, not Joseph. God, I hope it's not contagious!

"Aach man, you're okay; come on, the second pint and a steak and kidney pie will soon bring you back to normal," Ronnie consoled me.

And he was right.

At 2pm, the administrator from Commerce and Industry phoned me back at the Mines Department and said he had now officially applied the stamp to the documents. "Which means you can pick them up now, and, if you hurry – they close at 3pm – you can pay the Customs duty and be on your way!"

With the custom clearance documents in my pocket, I went back to the Mines Yard.

The portable green compressor had been loaded onto the transporter trailer – all the other equipment and cement bags were already on the back of the main truck.

A powerful roar was heard as the engine started, black fumes belching out from the tall vertical exhaust pipe, then the soft crunching noise of the large wheels slowly rotating on the shingle driveway as the driver cautiously maneuvered this modern-day beast of burden through the narrow gates of the Mines Yard and set off for the mine.

The F & B driver reckoned it would take about three hours to reach the mine, depending on the condition of the dirt roads.

I was much quicker, of course, and, as it was not raining, I went to see Peter.

Luckily, he was off duty, and we sat on his terrace chatting about the day's events as we downed a few early sundowners. In no time at all, we were recalling recent amusing incidents, and the day's problems were quickly forgotten….

The jet-black F & B transporter and trailer suddenly loomed into view, towering above the thorn trees, looking completely out of place driving on the narrow dirt road through the browny-green bush. The massive motor sent out roaring noises like an elephant on heat as the driver changed the gears to negotiate the sharp right turn-off to the mine.

Hundreds of startled birds flew into the skies to escape from this new beast that was thundering through the bush disturbing all the wildlife.

Then, just the same as a passing thunderstorm, the noise gradually lessened, sounding further and further away until the quietness of the bush returned to normal.

It was time to leave.

"I'll call by tomorrow, Peter, and complete the necessary documents and statements concerning the death and the fighting. Let me go now and catch my transporter up!"

We arrived at the mine together just as dusk was falling.

The thunderous sounds of the transporter had carried for miles in the still evening air and had alerted everyone of our imminent arrival.

Joseph was standing there in the road waving excitedly.

Crispin, Staff and a crowd of workers were also eager to see the new arrival.

"I see you've brought my Christmas presents," he joked, "even the one from South Africa! Wonderful! Now we just need a 5-stamp mill, hopefully the one Ronnie and I are going to inspect tomorrow near Que Que… and we can start producing gold, and become rich!"

We decided that the heavy transporter should be parked on the bend of the solid murram road, as it was becoming dark and we couldn't risk it sinking and getting stuck in some of the softer tracks leading to the mine.

With the side lights on, there was no danger for the odd vehicle that might pass in the night, and we would move the transporter at first light the following morning and start the unloading.

The driver and his mate would sleep in the cab, and I asked Crispin to organise some food and drink for them.

Elliot had already made a stew, which Joseph and I shared with the F&B transporter men.

Then it was time for us to talk seriously.

We drank countless cups of coffee as we mulled over the tragic events of the Tuesday night Changaa binge that resulted in the death of Phillemon.

I related to Joseph my conversations with Peter, who had advised us to get an experienced police/*askari* urgently, so that his registration with the police could be completed before the magistrate's hearing on the Monday.

This would go in our favour and be included in the magistrate's summing up and judgment – and, very importantly, take some of the sting out of any Jackson protest.

"And Jackson is not the only one to be feared!" I exclaimed. "Yesterday, I had that arranged meeting with him to discuss an amicable solution to the water and timber situation. As Sod's Law would have it, the news of the fighting on the mine and Phillemon's death had spread like wildfire – maybe not an appropriate saying in rain-ravaged Matabeleland – but, suffice it to say, the joint party lines must have overheated!

"And when Jackson's old Land Rover pulled up, an angry looking wife started spitting fire, demanding that we get off their land. She was viciously vocal! She didn't even get out, and Jackson just sat there next to her and didn't say a word – until she commanded him to drive off, when he uttered two words: 'Yes dear'."

We laughed, but it was nervous laughter. This drastic situation was far from funny; we were in danger of having the mine closed.

"I have already spoken to several people at the Mines Department this morning to help us get a first-class police/*askari* and to contact any mines that they know of that are closing down and possibly could have a redundant *askari*."

"Yes. My father told me that he'd heard about the incident on our mine, and would spread the word – there are one or two chrome mines closing in the Shabani area. Let's pray we get lucky!"

. . .

I don't think I even had time to close both eyes before I was jolted into action by the pulsating sound of the start gong.

I sleepily walked over to the office just as a bleary-eyed Joseph emerged, and we wandered together towards the small side lights of the F&B transporter.

"I think it's best that we unhook the trailer and leave it on the road for now. The load won't be so heavy and the transporter can creep slowly along the track and park near the mine shaft, where we can unload the alternator and the rails," Joseph suggested. "I'll get Staff to make ready the large block and tackle and shear legs for lifting the equipment off the lorry."

"Agreed, and Crispin can round up all the workers, and have wheelbarrows-full of rocks and stones ready in case the unthinkable happens and the transporter gets stuck! Hopefully all the extra loads of stones and shingle we covered the tracks with will suffice."

Brrrmmm! Brrrmmm! Roaring noises that put the birds to flight as the mechanical monster revved.

And, very slowly, the transporter crawled forward, crunching the stony surface, but already leaving deep ruts, which was very concerning.

In the action of changing gear – just that split-second pause, caused the heavy download weight to win the battle over the forward momentum – the vehicle was stuck!

"Battle stations!" Joseph shouted, and 40 African workers converged on the stricken transporter.

Crispin got busy organising shovels to dig out soil in front of all the wheels and push rocks into the resulting holes. Joseph and I drove our pick-ups and parked five metres in front on the sunken beast and connected tow ropes to the front tow-hitches of the driver's cab.

With an extra 40 BP power – boys' pushing power – at the ready, engines were started up, and, at Staff's signal, the two pick-ups, the transporter and 40 straining African workers began their joint efforts to free the monster truck.

A lot of noise, a lot of shouting, but absolutely no forward movement of the transporter at all!

A rethink was necessary.

This time, about a metre of ground was removed in front on each of the driving wheels.

Planks of wood were laid in these newly dug shallow troughs, and large rocks were jammed in the ground behind each driving wheel. We were all busy for another hour or more putting everything in place, before Plan B was put into operation.

The driver would engage reverse gear, Staff and Crispin would push the planks of wood under the wheels as the truck fractionally rocked backwards, then the driver would hoot as he engaged second gear, and the two pick-ups would start pulling and the 40 Africans would start pushing… and, slowly, the transporter edged forward and continued at a slow, steady pace until it reached the firmer ground in front of the office.

Wild cheering and shouting, accompanied by the triumphant blasting of the transporter's booming hooters, celebrated the success and the release of the trapped transporter.

After a gruelling three hours' work, we needed a break to allow everyone a welcome respite.

The main hurdle overcome, the resulting unloading of the alternator, rails, piping and pockets of cement went smoothly.

The driver was so pleased; he said he'd envisaged having to spend Christmas on the mine!

I'm sure with this in mind that he made very sure that he had enough momentum at a walking pace speed to sail over those bad soft patches, and he hooted like hell in celebration as he drove back onto the murram road.

A newly formed 'gang of five' surveyed the scene – the driver, Staff, Crispin, Joseph and myself – and agreed on the best way to unload the green compressor from the trailer; namely Plan C.

Using the two pick-ups with tow ropes, and not forgetting the 40 BP African pulling power, we edged the trailer slowly forward along the dirt track until it was 50 metres clear of the murram road.

Then workers were rushing this way and that, with shovels and wheelbarrows-full of rocks and schist – it reminded me of the column of Matabele worker ants that I had seen in the bush!

With wielding shovels flashing in the sun – yes, the sun had appeared temporarily to help us celebrate – an area of ground was prepared and made firm to accommodate the compressor, which was slowly lowered down the ramp of the trailer by ropes attached to 80 straining muscly arms!

The big green South African compressor stood proudly in the brown Rhodesian bush with the golden sun reflecting off the chrome instrument panels.

The trailer was pushed back to the murram road, where a waiting driver was ready to hook it up again to his transporter. Delivery documents were signed, and the F&B transporter was ready to return to Bulawayo, where the driver and his mate would be able to spend Christmas after all!

Joseph was going to leave for Gwelo, and would go with Ronnie Cummins on Saturday to Que Que to view a 5-stamp mill – that would make a fantastic Christmas present for us!

Joseph quickly jumped into his pick-up, revved like crazy, banged it into first gear and shot off like a bat out of hell, to make sure he didn't have to drive all the way to Fort Rixon following behind the slow transporter and trailer.

As the two vehicles disappeared into the distance, gentle rain began to fall.

Well, at least we had enjoyed a few dry hours; we would never have accomplished the unloading operations if the heavens had opened up – the rain would surely have tipped the scales against all our heroic, strenuous efforts!

20th Century Bethlehem

The loud clanging of the start gong shattered the quiet of the early morning as I pulled up in front of the mine office.

"Good morning, sir," Crispin greeted me. "I'm busy preparing a list of the workers that will be paid today, and there are a few others who have asked for an advance, because they want to travel home for the Christmas period."

"Okay Crispin, we'll go through that shortly, but first get Elliot to make me a cup of tea; I am so thirsty."

I started going through the books with Crispin, although I wasn't really in the mood to concentrate on them after the excitement of the previous day, and soon decided I'd walk over to the house instead to check on the building progress.

"I'll leave the pick-up outside the office, Crispin, as it is a visible reminder to the workers that I'm still around, somewhere!"

"Yes, a good idea, sir, because you are the cat!"

"The cat?" I queried, with raised eyebrows.

"When the cat is away, the mice play all day!" He laughed.

"When the cat is away, *you* and Staff better make sure the mice *work* all day, I say! Otherwise, no pay!" I stated firmly, but with tongue in cheek!

I ambled along the murram road and turned down my 'driveway' – a gently meandering 100-yard-long dirt track through the bush, with the acacia trees leading into a two-acre clearing and the house site.

The noisy boys could be heard working on the house as they prepared the last stages for the completion of my 'palace' – a square building, with two windows set in the rather wet concrete-washed hessian walls and an open doorway through which I entered and looked up at the timber-framed supports for the roof. Today, the corrugated iron sheets would be nailed on to provide us with a 20 square foot area of covered living space, protected from the wind and the rain… and surprise, surprise, the drizzle had started again, normally the prelude to a deluge!

Saul was busy putting the glass in one of the two windows, and I checked with Builder Naison that he had everything he needed to get the roof on today; corrugated iron sheets, five kilos of four-inch roofing nails, roof ridging and tar for sealing the joints.

Langton was heating up a large tin of tar on the fire, but I got the feeling that we'd need to buy a few extra tins of the black sticky stuff, as the rains seemed to be set in for many more days to come and a leaky roof would be disastrous once the house was filled with our possessions and the furniture that we would bring down from Gwelo.

I went outside and followed a narrow track for about 50 yards to the edge of the ridge where the ground dropped away sharply down into the valley.

There stood my new, smaller construction – at last, I could use my own long drop instead of frequenting the rather nauseous public workers' latrines near the office.

And it was good to see that Langton had finished the surrounding screen of the concrete-washed hessian wall, fixed on an iron roof and cemented a one and a half-foot-high brick 'box' with a wooden toilet seat; this extra luxury item covering the eight-inch diameter hole in the concrete slab of the long drop.

What a pleasure to sit here, high and dry, whilst the rain tinkled down on the iron roof – which caused some human tinkling too!

Yes, this toilet was a comfortable success, and, to test that the depth was correct, I unleashed a couple of bombs, and counted… one, two, thud! Yebo, a good eight-foot deep!

Now for the '*coup de grâce*', the icing on the cake!

Using a Stanley knife, I carefully cut out a two-foot square flap in the hessian wall, and voila! Fabulous, my 'loo with a view' was complete!

I now just had to wait for a dry day when the storms and heavy rains had ceased, in order to be able to enjoy a peaceful, pleasurable early morning sunrise sanitary session, looking through the 'window gap' at the panoramic view across the valley to the distant hills… with a chance of an occasional rumble of thunder to be heard – my own?

The only disappointment with the house so far was the concrete-washed hessian walls.

With the recent weather mix of guti (a wet 'hanging' mist early in the mornings) and the intermittent, but incessant heavy rains being blown by the strong winds, these walls had become soaked and inside the house there was a musty dampness.

I told Elliot that, once the roof was finished, he should build a big fire in the middle of the house. That would counter the dampness in the walls by drying them out, and also help to remove that dank odour that perpetrated the air.

As I walked back to the mine, the rain moved up a gear in intensity, and I hurried to get into the office for shelter.

A sudden loud hooting noise made me look around to see an approaching small, rusty looking Ford that was very heavily laden, especially on the passenger side, which was much lower – it was as if the springs were broken.

It pulled up and out jumped a large beige Labrador, closely followed by a very good friend of ours from South Africa.

"Graham, how'sit?" I exclaimed as we greeted each other enthusiastically with a bear hug.

"Jesus, you have lost weight!" he replied, rather amazed.

"True mate. In fact, in the last three months, I have gone from a fit rugby playing weight of 102 kilograms, down to a super-fit, ladder-climbing, 'pick-up-sauna'd' trim 80 kg! Unbelievable, and I had to get new shorts; 'two for the price of one', they say in the adverts, but for me it was 'two made out of one' of my old shorts!" I joked. "So where are Malcolm, Eve and the kids? They are still coming?"

"Of course they're coming; they are dying to see what life on a small gold mine is like. I left a day before them, but they should be here tomorrow, probably later in the afternoon."

"That's fabulous! Marianne and the kids can't wait to see them. We had such an enjoyable Christmas at their place last year, didn't we?"

Suddenly, we heard loud creaking noises, and saw Graham's car rocking from side to side – the door flew open and a giant of a man squeezed his way out and came over towards us.

"I gave this man a lift," Graham said. "He was walking on the dirt road near Filabusi carrying several bags, so I stopped, and he said something to me that I didn't really understand, but when he uttered 'Ridge Top Mine' I signalled to him 'me too', and he climbed, with difficulty, into the back of my small car."

The large African stepped forward and spoke to Crispin, and handed him a letter.

Crispin's face lit up as he read the note. "This is Amon, our new *askari*/ policeman!" he proudly announced as he introduced this 'six-foot-plus' hunk of muscle, resembling those body builders whose necks seem to be an extension of their shoulders.

And a 'six-foot-plus' smile beamed from this massive chunk of dark black ebony, and luckily for me, instead of offering his hand for a bone-crushing handshake, he just raised his hand and said 'Boss! Boss!' as he nodded several times.

"He is from Zambia. He doesn't speak much, and he understands very little English," Crispin continued, "but I knew him on a mine near Belingwe several years ago, where he was feared by the workers and there was never any trouble when he was around!"

"He doesn't have to speak at all!" I exclaimed. "One angry glance from him, even the gang of five would have started quivering in their boots – if Amon had been our policeman from the very start!"

I extended my hand to him, which he shook, firmly but gently, whereupon a kind of acknowledgement grin crossed the lips of Amon, my new policemen, and I knew we had an instant understanding.

"I'll take Amon with me to Fort Rixon when I leave to register him with the police; he couldn't have joined us at a better time with the magistrate's hearing due next week Monday. Crispin, when he gets back, you can allocate a hut for him to share; forget about the usual 'three day, build a hut' rule. And make out a ticket for him, because he will be starting immediately, today – and let all the workforce know that. *Spread the word!*

"Well Graham, you got here just in time, as I was about to leave for Gwelo where we rent a house. Five minutes later and you would have had to spend the night in my grass hut instead of sleeping overnight in a real bed. And tomorrow you can help with the last 'trek' of our SA furniture and possessions from Gwelo to our new mine house – and please don't call it a shack when you see it! It's got hessian walls, and the roof is being fixed on today, so hopefully by tomorrow we'll have a dry place to store all our gear and at last sleep in our own beds in the Rhodesian bush."

I left instructions with Crispin that more friends from South Africa would be arriving by car the following afternoon, and he should greet Malcolm, Eve, Sebastian, Simon and Sarah, and help them find an area of firm ground on which to put up their tents.

"Tell Elliot to build them a fire and look after them coffee and hot-food wise until Graham and I get back from Gwelo tomorrow."

Crispin paid out 15 more workers who had completed their 30-day ticket plus bonus, and three were paid an advance. An air of excitement spread quickly as they gathered around and collected their money; most of them would be leaving for home to spend the Christmas week with their families.

There were only two roads to travel on from the mine.

South to Filabasu, Belingwe and Shabani, or north via Fort Rixon to Bulawayo, or on to Shangani and Gwelo.

Those heading to the towns and villages in the south had started walking already.

Those heading to the north had climbed into the back of my pick-up with all their luggage – squeezed up tightly like sardines in a tin!

Amon swaggered slowly towards the pick-up, put one hand on the side rail and looked at the two mine boys who were sitting with their backs to the driver's cab. They instantly stood up and clambered out hurriedly with their bags to make way for the massive frame of Amon, who would, from now on, be affectionately known as my 'pet gorilla'!

And what a sight too – sitting there amongst the other mine workers, he looked like a pigeon chick that had been hatched in a nest of tiny sparrows!

As we drove off, the heavens opened; it was like driving through a waterfall!

I stopped and told Graham to drive in front of me and I'd follow in case he got stuck or had an accident on these slippery roads, which was a real possibility driving a car that had such small wheels.

It was fun too watching Graham negotiating the dongas, with his car slip-sliding and zigzagging up the other side! So similar to my experiences in the Volvo two months previously.

We made it to Fort Rixon without any unfortunate incidents – or so I thought!

However, Graham told me that he'd been shit-scared crossing the fast-flowing donga river fords in his little car.

I watched him as he carefully lifted himself out of his seat, and then very slowly, and very deliberately, walked with an uncomfortable-looking gait, with his thighs tightly pressed against each other, as he snail-paced his way towards the police station's ablutions…

Peter was really pleased that I'd brought along our new worker, Amon – he checked his ID and reference letters as he registered him as our mine *askari*/ policeman.

Peter said that he would make a recommendation to the magistrate that we had taken concrete action to prevent any further fighting like the incident that had led to the tragic death on our mine. This would be duly documented, and he would make sure that Jackson received a copy as well, which should dampen the explosive incident that Jackson would love to use as ammunition against us to close down our mine.

We thanked Peter and arranged to have a Christmas drink together in the next couple of days, and left Amon to find his own way back to the mine – he'd need to use all his strength and muscled leg power to cross the increasingly faster-flowing storm rivers we had just crossed!

At one stage on our journey, Graham got stuck on the exit slope of a donga, half in and half out of the water, with his car engine spluttering and coughing until it finally gave up and stalled!

The workers jumped out of my pick-up, waded through the raging waters and pulled and pushed the car to higher ground.

Luckily for Graham, Sparky, my mechanic, was travelling with us and, after about 20 minutes of removing plugs, ignition bits and pieces, drying them and spraying everything with anti-damp muti, the old jalopy coughed once and sprang to life again, much to the relief of a very concerned-looking Graham, and we proceeded on our way to Gwelo.

There, eight happy, in fact, slightly merry Africans climbed off the pick-up, and one of them, Gwabuya, holding a half-empty bottle of Changaa, offered me a Christmas drink – one sip and that was enough to put Changaa on the same list as Chibuku beer; i.e. once tried, never, never ever to be repeated!

I took Graham into the Midland Hotel, where we had a relaxing pint or two while I waited for the 6 o'clock phone call from Joseph.

We reminisced about our Windsor Castle ship voyage to South Africa, recounting many amusing incidents we'd had on that journey…

But back to the present, we were in Rhodesia and experiencing the terrible weather conditions that were causing real problems across the country.

Graham told me that he'd left South Africa in hot, sunny weather, but, after crossing the border at Beitbridge, he'd seen nothing but rain, constant rain.

"Yes, we've been rained on for the last couple of weeks; there had been a three-year drought in Matabeleland, which is now well and truly broken – or better said, washed away! But let me go and check if Joseph's call has come through yet."

I picked up the phone at the reception, but almost dropped it again from shock as this raging voice blasted away.

"A total disaster and a complete waste of time!" Joseph shouted down the phone, which I had to hold several inches away from my head to prevent severe 'ear burn'!

"Ronnie and I went to inspect the 5-stamp mill, which I had seen a week previous when I picked up Willie's wife and kids, and it seemed to me to be in good working order. But today, when we saw the dismantled stamp mill in parts lying on the ground, we were shocked. Useless, absolutely useless! The top of the massive 20-foot-long, square wooden king posts were rotten, which I obviously couldn't have seen when I was standing in front of them looking up, could I, so it's not my fault, is it! And so yet again, there'll be no 5-stamp mill for us before the Christmas break! We're so annoyed to come all this way for nothing – and are now having a beer and a meal in a hotel near Que Que, where we'll stay overnight."

"Okay Joseph, yet another bloody disappointing quest for a 5-stamp mill, but stress to Ronnie that he must keep on searching for us; it's critical! By the way, the first of my South African visitors, Graham, has arrived and will help us to ferry all my stuff from the Gwelo house to the mine using the two pick-ups. We need to be living on the mine by Christmas Eve when another family from South Africa arrives for the week.

"And I'm really looking forward to the week off too, as there is nothing else we can do until early January in the New Year! Oh yeah, one good thing; I've taken on a brute of an *askari*/policeman, who is now registered with the Fort Rixon Police – that should help us when the magistrate reviews the murder case.

"So Joseph, have a Merry Christmas week in Belingwe with the family. Let's meet at the Gwelo house after the Christmas break on Monday 31 January, when we can rethink how we are going to survive and overcome the lack of fuel, phones and water! And unfortunately the weather forecasters say it could still go on for weeks! But let's hope they're wrong; we need some luck. So, see you in 10 days' time, Joseph; I'll be up at the Gwelo house by 11 or so that morning, okay?"

"Yes, that's fine, any time on Monday morning. No rush, we'll be in all day. With a young baby, Jane and I won't be going out to celebrate the New Year; we'll just have a quiet weekend. Best wishes for Christmas, and we'll see you Monday week then."

. . .

The kids were so happy to see Uncle Graham again, and while they were playing with him and his dog, Mushla, and telling him all about living in the bush with the wild baboons, it allowed Marianne and I the chance to slip out onto the veranda for a chat.

She was very pleased that our new mine policeman, Amon, had been registered with the Fort Rixon Police, and, on listening to my description of my pet gorilla, she exclaimed, "A man mountain! He should be able to keep the trouble-makers under control and stop the drunken fighting for good. And is the house finished? Can we move in for Christmas?"

"Yes, we will. I left the builders working on the roof. Poor buggers; it's difficult and dangerous work, because it's so windy and the rain keeps pouring down most of the time, but it'll be on by tomorrow, I'm sure. And it better be, because Graham and I will take most of our furniture and the heavy stuff in the pick-ups tomorrow morning. And on Christmas Eve we will take the rest, and all of us will move into our 'little shack on the ridge' for good!"

"It's sounding exciting! And with Malcolm, Eve and their children, we're going to have a fabulous Christmas, one to remember, I'm sure." Prophetic words! "By the way, this letter from Barclays Bank came for you; perhaps more good news?"

I opened it eagerly; it was from Crow, the Gwelo manager, but just more time-wasting waffle.

It said that Exchange Control wanted to know the proposed selling price to enable them to consider our application to sell the white second-hand Peugeot pick-up… but why, I thought? Well, probably best to call in to see him after Christmas to find out more.

"F-f-food's ready, "Graham stuttered. "It's my s-s-specialty you all like so much, chicken f-f-fu-kurry!"

As the evening wore on, we were constantly chatting, with laughter filling the air – until the two and a half-litre flagon of South African red plonk (cheap wine) was finished, and the last flickering candle was snuffed out!

. . .

It was a strange feeling, déjà vu, to be loading the furniture onto the pick-ups again.

Luckily, it was not raining, although the clouds were all shades of grey, and, ominously for us, the nasty black ones were on the horizon in the direction that we would soon be heading – the road to Fort Rixon.

With black plastic sheeting wrapped around our cargo and securely strapped down, the two fully loaded pick-ups left from the Gwelo house, Graham in the beige one and me driving the second-hand grey 404 pick-up.

As we turned off the tarmac road at Shangani and onto the murram road, the rain started again.

I stopped and told Graham that, with such a full load, we'd let the tyres down a little in order to give better traction on these slippery dirt roads, and it's better not to use the brakes; the gears can slow the vehicle without that sudden stabbing on the brake pedal, which could cause the pick-up to slide and skid out of control.

Another tip. "When we come to a donga, slow right down, put it in second gear and then slowly descend into the flowing waters, keeping a constant slow speed as you exit up the other bank. That way, you're unlikely to get stuck, but if you have any problems, just hoot!"

But luckily he didn't have to hoot until we approached the house, whereupon three builder boys wearing bright yellow raincoats leapt out through the door opening.

"Sorry Boss!" Naison called out. "Too much rain; we couldn't work up on the roof!"

I looked up and could see that only a few corrugated iron sheets had been nailed on so far. The rest of the roof was open to the heavens – and when the heavens had opened, the rains had poured in. There was water everywhere. The only dry place was in a small corner where the builders had been sitting around a roaring fire under the cover of those few nailed-on iron sheets.

"You have a problem, Naison, because that roof has to be fixed on by tonight! Tomorrow, we are moving in – my wife, kids and all our furniture! You just have to get back up there, rain or no rain, and nail those iron sheets on! Get it done and I'll give you all an extra bonus on your ticket – because it's Christmas!"

The trucks were quickly offloaded and the furniture safely stored in the house under some black plastic sheeting.

I told Elliot to sleep in the house and keep the fire going all night. We would be coming back in the morning with the rest of our possessions, to live here in our new home!

The roof *had* to be fixed on properly, so that it would be dry inside!

As we left, I looked back at the house; a sombre picture in the rain, a dark grey shape with two yellow blobs on top – Naison and Langton were back up on the job again!

I let Graham drive ahead and followed about 100 yards behind to avoid all the mud and spray being kicked up by his vehicle on the slippery muddy roads, but, when we turned onto the tarmac road at Shangani, it was a lot easier driving.

The rain had eased considerably by the time we reached the Midland Hotel in Gwelo, where I had a date with Barman Tex.

This visit had nothing to do with mines or equipment, but to collect Christmas presents for Jeffrey and Marie-Louise.

Tex pulled three pints of beer and toasted us. "To a very Merry Christmas and hope to see you before the New Year." And he called out to one of the waiters, "Bring in those dangerous dogs!"

The waiter returned, amongst much laughter, with a large cardboard box in which there were two small black puppies.

"They are cross-breeds between my black female labrador called Chocolate, and my neighbour's randy black and white collie that we call Jumper – he jumps over my fence and then jumps on top of my labrador! These will be great presents for your kids; it's good for them to grow up with young animals."

"Let's have one more for the road!" Graham ordered enthusiastically. "Because it's Christmas. Happy Christmas to us all!"

We were welcomed warmly on our return, when volley after volley of questions were fired at us.

"Are we getting any presents this Christmas?" Marie-Louise asked anxiously.

"Does Santa know we're in Rhodesia now?"

"How will he find his way through the bush to the mine?"

"Unfortunately, because of the heavy rains and the floods, Santa can't get to the mine, so he left a present for each of you at the Midland Hotel; that's why Graham and I went there to meet him. Now go outside to my pick-up; there's a big box on the front seat."

Wh-o-o-sh – they shot out of the house…. then we heard the pick-up door open.

"Oh, they are so sweet!" called out Marie-Louise, and two excited young kids carrying two puzzled-looking puppies came rushing into the brightly lit room.

"I want this one with the white patch on his cheek. Just look at the way he stares at me with those big begging eyes. I'm going to call him Oliver, after the poor boy in that story book that you read to us."

"And I'm going to call this one 'Nose'; just look at his sad face. I think it's because his nose is a funny shape!" Jeffrey shouted.

Well, those early Christmas presents kept the kids busy the whole evening; they loved them, which allowed us to pack all our belongings back into the boxes again, ready for the last stage of our great trek from South Africa to Rhodesia. Our belongings would have travelled from Johannesburg via Hartley/Gwelo/ Fort Rixon… and, finally, to our little house on the mine.

Black Tar

Christmas Eve always seems to be a mad rush around, buying presents and tasty goodies, dashing in and out of packed shops….

We had all of that too, but how many people move house on Christmas Eve?

However, we were just so pleased that we would be in the mine house for Christmas and even the rain didn't get us down as we loaded the two pick-ups with box after box, after box….

It was well into the afternoon before we had everything ready, and then the fully loaded 'trek wagons' left.

Marianne drove with Marie-Louise and Oliver in the beige 404, Graham and Mushla in his rust-coloured Ford, and accompanying me in the grey diesel pick-up were Jeffrey and Nose.

First to the Midland Butchery to pick up ration meat for the mine boys and two large boxes of meat for our Christmas meals that I had ordered the previous week – just to be sure.

Enough T-bone steaks, lamb chops, boerewors, pork chops and chipolata sausages for 10 people to last five days! More than 100 pieces of meat of different tastes and different shapes!

I hoped it would all fit into the paraffin fridge that we would pick up at the

Fort Rixon Police Station on our way back to the mine.

. . .

The rains continued unabatedly, and, after two hours of watching the windscreen wipers constantly wiping away the water, together with a used handkerchief performing a similar job of cleaning the 'fogged-up' glass on the inside to allow some visibility through the windscreen, we arrived at the Fort Rixon Police Post.

Peter welcomed us enthusiastically and straight away arranged with the house girl to make mugs of hot chocolate for the kids, whilst we would take coffee in the charge room.

"Let me tell you first about the magistrate's visit. He was here this morning and said it was very sad for him to preside over yet another 'death by stabbing' case caused by a drunken brawl on a small, remote mine in the bush. He had listened to the evidence from the two witnesses, Enoch and the prostitute called 'Precious', but Banzi was sent back to the cells for continued interruptions, shouting and abuse – contempt of the court! His decision was that Banzi should be transferred to Bulawayo prison, where he would stay until Paniche and Bamoso were transferred there from the Shangani hospital, when he would hand over this murder case to the Bulawayo Judiciary Court.

"As far as you're concerned, the magistrate made a notation for the record on the judgment proceedings confirming that you, the mine manager, were not present at the time of the fighting, but, since that incident, have employed an experienced *askari*/policeman who will prevent such a tragic occurrence happening again. I'll circulate a copy of this to the Insiza District Council, the Mines Department, and, of course, to your good friendly neighbour, Jackson!"

"Jesus!" exclaimed Graham. "You've had a murder on your mine already! And several workers seriously injured in drunken brawling! Aren't you worried for your own safety?"

Peter interrupted, and said that out here in the bush you're actually safer than in the towns and the cities. "It was unfortunate that the gang of five worked at Ridge Top Mine – they would have caused problems anywhere! But, now that the mine has employed a tough *askari*/ policeman, there should be no more such incidents. But hey, but you'd better get going now with your loaded vehicles; it'll be dark soon. Oh by the way, the paraffin fridge that I promised you was delivered to your mine store this morning – a good thing too, as I can see that there is absolutely no room on your vehicles."

"That's really great, Peter," I replied. "Otherwise, we'd be stuck with a mountain of rotting meat – we've bought enough meat for 10 people, to last us over the Christmas period! That fridge of yours will be a life saver! And if the rain ever stops over the next day or two, pop in and join us for a Christmas braai."

We exchanged Christmas greetings, and our convoy moved off slowly in the pouring rain.

The light of day was fading fast as we pulled up in front of the house.

I could see the flames of a fire flickering through the open doorway and thought, *At least Elliot has had a fire burning, so the place should be dry and not so damp.*

These thoughts were quickly dispelled as I walked through the doorway.

"Jesus Christ! What's been going on here?" I exclaimed. "It's like a huge bloody sieve!"

I looked up and could see water pouring through the holes in the roof on one side of the room, but the other side where Elliot was sitting next to the fire was completely dry.

"Elliot! Go down to the mine and get Crispin and the two builders, Naison and Langton, back here immediately! This is bloody ridiculous!"

So there we were, Graham, Marianne, the kids and me, standing in the dry side of the room gazing in disbelief at the water sieving through the roof on the other side – it was like being in a large shower room after a rugby match!

Then suddenly we all burst out laughing together; we just couldn't stop. What a crazy situation to be in on Christmas Eve! Three vehicles full of household furniture and packing boxes parked outside in the rain, with our new home looking like a gigantic sieve as the rain continued pouring through the holes in the roof and flooding the floor.

All of a sudden, another vehicle arrived and out stepped Malcolm, Eve, Sebastian, Simon and Sarah, who ran through the rain into the house.

"Bloody hell!" Malcolm exclaimed. "It's raining harder inside here than it is outside in the bush! I've heard in the building trade that when they get the roof on they celebrate with a 'roof wetting' party, but this is crazy!"

Nevertheless, here we all were, and it was time for hugging and greeting each other, and laughter filled the air as the 10 of us and the three dogs stood on the dry side.

"It's like looking at Victoria Waterfalls!" Simon shouted.

"Is it never going to stop raining up here?" asked Eve. "We've seen nothing but rain since we crossed the South African border yesterday morning! This is totally opposite to the hot, dry, dusty Rhodesia we experienced when Sarah and I drove up from SA last month with your furniture!"

"You got here yesterday?" I queried.

Malcolm went on to explain that they'd arrived yesterday late in the afternoon.

Crispin had been very helpful and showed them a place to pitch their tents.

But, halfway through the night, water had begun seeping into the tent from under the groundsheets as heavy rain pounded away on their tents!

"We had no option but to leave the tents and go and sleep in the car. Luckily, we came in the large Citroën Estate vehicle – if we'd been in your tiny car, Graham, we would have been sleeping 'double decker' on top of each other!"

The merriment quickly abated as three drenched figures appeared in the open doorway looking very apprehensive.

"Well, well, well, Naison and Langton! What the hell have you done to the roof? Look at it! It's leaking like a 95-year-old's nappy pants! How did you manage to do this?" I remonstrated with them. "When I left to go to Gwelo, the few sheets that had been put on the roof made a dry area where you had built the fire; what's the problem?"

"The dry side is the half of the roof that I put on!" stated Naison proudly. "The other side was done by Langton!" He pointed to a dejected figure – the one who had committed the crime!

Crispin went on to explain to us in English what had happened. "You instructed them to each do their own half of the roof when you left. Naison had already nailed on five or six of the second-hand corrugated iron sheets that you purchased from the Phoenix Theatre in Gwelo. The problem with these old, used iron sheets is that they have the nail holes in them from when they were first fixed onto the theatre roof.

"Naison, being an experienced builder, had banged the new nails through the old holes at the top of the 'hill' of the 'hills and valleys' corrugated iron sheets, and put hot tar over them to seal the holes. Langton, on the other hand, had started his half of the roof, but with the first sheet upside down, banging the nails into the virgin 'hill tops', with the old holes now in the 'valley troughs'.

"Once the first one was in place, the following sheet slotted in next to the other, but, of course, also with the old nail holes in the 'valley troughs'! Until all the iron sheets were in place and the roof was completed. But unfortunately with all the sheets upside down, and the rain water just pouring through these holes."

"Unfortunately! Rubbish! Right, there's no way we can put plastic sheeting over the roof tonight; the wind is too strong and it would be ripped off. So you two must get back up on the roof now, and put nails in all the old leaking holes in the troughs of the iron sheets, and use lots of hot tar to seal them so that the rain doesn't pour through anymore – and we can sleep here tonight in the dry!"

I instructed them to get on with it immediately!

"But," began Langton, "we've used up all the. . ."

I cut him short! "I've brought some more large tins of tar, Langton, and Elliot will keep the fire burning so that you can melt all the tar you need. Now get on with it! Crispin, fetch another four boys to help preparing the tar and handing it up to Naison and Langton on the roof. It has to be completed this evening; we want to spend Christmas Day in a rain-proof house! Get on to it straight away; otherwise, there will be no Christmas Day beers for them. By the way, did Chibuku deliver the special Christmas 80 gallons of beer today?"

"Yes sir! And I have locked the four barrels of Chibuku in the storeroom – 'out of sight, but not out of the mine'!"

We cried with laughter at yet another Crispin version of a proverb.

"Crispin, we'll leave you now and drive over to the dry storeroom to have a Christmas Eve drink together while you make sure they fix the roof properly, so that it doesn't leak anymore!"

Crammed together in the storeroom, we began our Christmas celebrations.

What a wet start, which we added to as a crate of beer was brought in from Malcolm's car, and the traditional Christmas 'downing' began in earnest!

"In this heavy rain and with the strong winds, I'm not sure if putting nails in the old holes with a big blob of tar on top will be fully successful, but it should at least reduce the water flowing through the holes to just a drip or two – we can cope with that, even if it means sitting around wearing the workers' bright yellow raincoats with hoods!"

"Yeah, we'll survive, don't worry," said Malcolm. "It can't be worse than sleeping in our tents in this atrocious weather!"

Time slid by as we happily and noisily celebrated being together again….

A sudden 'clang-yang-yang, clang-yang-yang' noise startled our guests, but they smiled when Crispin entered and said, "I banged the gong to announce that it was midnight on Christmas Eve! And to tell you that the builders have finished tarring the roof – it's not leaking anymore!"

"Or probably any less!" Malcolm chirped in. "We might still have to sleep in the cars again tonight if we want to be dry!"

We rushed out through the rain to the vehicles, and the four-car convoy headed back to the hopefully warm and dry house.

There were still one or two holes leaking badly and a few dripping, but luckily they were all in the one corner, probably due to the builders rushing the last bits to finish it off and go home!

Elliot had removed the fire and cleaned the floor of the house, and had thoughtfully prepared some soup for us.

We slurped down the hot soup and began beavering away as we dashed in and out of the rain, quickly unloading everything from all four vehicles.

I shot back to the mine store with Graham to collect the paraffin fridge.

On our return, we primed and pumped the paraffin fridge and hallelujah! We could feel that the side of the freezer box was getting cold!

"That's a relief," I said. "Come on, let's stuff all the meat inside as quickly as possible; we can sort it all out in the morning – or, rather, the women can, while we men try to get a fire going outside in our telephone booth. Tomorrow we've got a Christmas dinner to cook, and the women can relax and take it easy."

Christmas in a Barn with the Animals

It took the best part of an hour to arrange the house.

Packing cases were stacked up in one corner and buckets were placed on top, strategically under the few bad leaks.

The beds were pushed up next to each other in a dry corner – half the house was already full! Dead beat kids went out like a light and were distributed amongst the beds.

We arranged the other half of the room with all the kiaat-wood furniture, placing the two long settees, an armchair, coffee tables, the bar and three bar stools in a 'square' – the flickering light from two hurricane lamps adding to the convivial atmosphere; it began to look really cosy.

Malcolm asked me to come outside to his car to get the Christmas tree – in all the excitement and rushing around in the dark and the rain, I hadn't even noticed the large tree strapped to his roof rack!

The seven-foot tree was erected in the middle of the house and Marianne and Eve took on the task of decorating it, which was a bit tricky in the shimmering light and, occasionally, we heard the 'pop' of a Christmas ball exploding as it hit the ground, closely followed by us singing 'and another one bites the dust'!

Meanwhile, Graham was preparing a gourmet dinner for us – he opened a few tins of baked beans and started warming them up on a small camping gas cooker plate that he'd wisely brought with him.

The three dogs sneakily sidled up to him, to be near the warmth – and probably nearer the food as well!

Malcolm and I hooked up the stereo set to a car battery.

The LP we put on the turntable was by *Credence Clearwater Revival* – an apt name – and we all felt at home as the first track blared out into the night – '… *I wanna know, have you ever seen the rain, I wanna know, have you ever seen the rain, coming down…'* – accompanied by adult voices straining with gusto, providing a somewhat out of tune backing group.

And that bloody rain 'coming down' now started to be driven by strong winds into the house through the doorway! But, with more black magic plastic sheeting, we managed to plug that leak – a monster one too, eight foot by three foot!

Now we could all relax at last. It was a fine feeling.

After gobbling down our supper of baked beans with bread, we were ready for Christmas Eve! Sitting around, chatting and laughing about the situation, we really were enjoying ourselves; good old friends can always make the most of a chaotic situation!

Graham cracked open a bottle of Nederberg Cabernet Sauvignon and we toasted each other.

"To the most unusual Christmas Eve we've ever spent!"

The room was a wonderful sight.

The tall decorated Christmas tree held prime position in the middle of the house – the light being reflected off the Christmas balls hanging from its branches, and the flickering light from the hurricane lamps dancing around the room, combined with the constant clinking of glasses and the boom-boom-booming of the stereo bass, made this our own, very special disco club atmosphere.

Malcolm remarked, "I was thinking, with the 10 of us and our three animals all squeezed together and sleeping in this small hut, it's a bit like a 20th century version of the Bethlehem Bible story!"

"And *you* are one of the three wise men? Yeah!" Eve chipped in, laughing her head off.

"But I suppose we're luckier than they were 2,000 years ago, because we are in both 'the stable' and 'the inn' – with enough red wine in here to make a Catholic priest jealous!" Graham added.

The conversations and the laughter carried on and on… until around 4am, when we adults faded completely.

Marianne and Eve squeezed into bed with Marie-Louise and Sarah.

For us three men, the two long settees would provide two very comfortable beds to sleep on, but the armchair would be just a place to 'sit-sleep' – for Graham! He lost the toss!

. . .

I half awoke, my tongue feeling around the inside of my mouth – *yuk!*

I certainly didn't clean my teeth after our Christmas Eve celebrations, and the persistent throbbing in my head indicated that they had been very heavy celebrations indeed!

A strange rustling noise forced me to open one eye, and, squinting in the dim early morning light, I could see the shapes of the three small boys dwarfed by the large Christmas tree looking at the wrapped presents and shaking them – I thought it prudent to close the eye again and let events take their own course….

Through a background of loud music, noisy boys and giggling girls, I could hear Crispin's voice – yes. Crispin's voice? Calling out, repeatedly, "Morning sir! Happy Christmas everyone!"

And another voice joined in; that of Elliot. "Coffee! Strong coffee!"

You can't fight against it forever, so I forced myself to get up – and what a wonderful sight too! The kids sitting around the tall, colourfully decorated Christmas tree, excitedly opening their presents. Kids always have amazing powers of recovery and they looked healthy and happy. Marianne and Eve were joining in the celebrations, laughing happily, but looking decidedly jaded. Malcolm and Graham were still sleeping peacefully, until…

Sebastian, Simon and Jeffrey did the 'dripping cold water on their faces' trick – it worked instantly! And, although they were looking the worse for wear and decidedly hungover, they soon joined in the Christmas spirit – the strong black coffee with a little added whisky spirit playing a major part in their Christmas Day resurrection!

"Morning everyone," my voice croaked out. "Happy Christmas! And Crispin, good morning to you too! What do you want so early?"

"Early, sir? The early bird has already eaten the fat worm!" he replied, and laughed loudly.

"Yes, it's nearly 11 o'clock, Daddy!" Marie-Louise called out happily, adding her voice to the majority who were trying to get the three 'not so wise' men up and running!

"Crispin, do you have a present for me, or what?"

"No, sir! But as you can hear, it is still pouring down with rain, so I think it's better to hold the Ridge Top games tomorrow, when hopefully it will be a drier day. I also want to suggest that I open the mine bar at 12 o'clock today for the mine workers, but I will keep two of the 25-gallon drums of Chibuku beer in reserve for tomorrow's athletic games festerings."

We couldn't stop laughing, and I had to correct him. "You mean 'festivities'!"

Crispin was a diamond; he had everything under control.

I agreed with what he suggested, and he went on his way out into the heavy rain with a large piece of black plastic sheeting draped over him that went down to the ground.

His head poked through a small hole in it, and, as he moved off, this black pepper-pot-shaped object seemed to glide effortlessly across the flooded garden, as if he was walking on water!

Malcolm, who was watching Crispin intently, suddenly began sniggering to himself and said he had a little joke to tell us:

"Jesus came back to Earth and appeared in a London pub wearing a long white robe. He could not believe all the drinking, swearing and rowdiness that was going on, so he went to the bar and started calling out loudly, 'I am Jesus, the Son of God, and have been sent back to Earth to try to save you all from this immoral decadence!'

"'If you are Jesus,' someone called out, 'show us a miracle!'

"Jesus took them outside to the River Thames, and the crowd gasped as he began to walk barefoot across the water… but then, he began to sink slowly as he walked, and, puzzled by this, he called out to St. Peter, 'Why am I sinking? This didn't happen the first time I walked on water?'

"The reply boomed down from the heavens. 'You didn't have holes in your feet the first time you tried that'!"

Hungry mouths had to be fed, and a braai was the best solution. Graham and Malcolm set about trying to light a fire in the metal braai stand they'd brought with them.

Marianne and I went to the fridge to check the meat, but, disappointingly, the only part of the fridge that felt 'cool-ish' was on the one side of the freezer box that we had touched in the evening.

"Bummer!" I uttered. "There's a hell of a lot of meat in there; perhaps it's too much and the fridge can't cope! In any case, take some T-bones, lamb chops and boerewors out for the braai, and we'll check the back of the fridge."

I put in a new wick, filled up the paraffin container completely and lit it again.

Hopefully, with less meat and more 'power', that would do the trick!

Outside, Malcolm and Graham were battling to light the braai; the wood was so damp and we had little charcoal – the strong wind and the rain weren't helping us either!

Probably your best friend in the bush is diesel – for your pick-ups, pumps, power alternator and, as we learnt today, also for lighting a braai! I poured some diesel from a reserve container over the wood and charcoal and lit it! There was no 'whummmph' like with methylated spirits; the flames crept slowly across the charcoal until it was all burning nicely.

It was now around 1 o'clock and small mouths were asking:

"When's the braai going to be ready?"

"My tummy is rumbling!"

"We're so hungry!"

"Can't we eat now, pleeeeease?"

However, the wind and the rains were proving too much, as the men battled continually to get the braai going, but to no avail.

We decided to move the braai into my telephone booth and threw on some more wood, dousing it with extra diesel… and it began to smoke like hell!

"Bad idea!" we uttered in unison, and took the braai outside, leaving it to re-establish itself.

Graham, who was shielding it successfully from the rain with an umbrella, wasn't so lucky with the strong, gusting winds, and we frequently heard him coughing and swearing as he disappeared in clouds of thick grey smoke!

Malcolm and I took a hammer and a screwdriver and proceeded to knock and lever out some of the blocks of the phone booth, making two large window openings.

Once most of the smoke had cleared, the braai was put back and there was enough room for someone to stand inside by the braai and supervise the roasting of the meat – Malcolm volunteered.

Eager young helpers brought out two large plates stacked high with the meat; T-bone steaks, lamb chops and boerewors.

Unfortunately, one little boy slipped on the wet, muddy ground, scattering all his 'wares' everywhere, much to the delight of Graham's dog, Mushla, who grabbed a big T-bone steak and ran off. The two puppies were too slow and we managed to rescue the rest, washed off the mud and delivered the 'bush-marinated' meat to the chef!

Rain, mud and diesel all added to the flavour, and the 10 of us tucked into the food with relish, eating until we were ready to pop!

A few wines to finish off a royal Christmas dinner – and the three wise men were on their journey again to a distant land – the land of nod….

A couple of hours did the trick and we were ready to continue celebrating again.

The evening was spent listening to music, nice and relaxing, and playing games with the kids; cards, I spy, throwing the dice, and that most popular miming game, Charades – enjoyed by all, both big and small.

. . .

Boxing Day breakfast consisted of cornflakes and cream crackers; no one was brave enough to venture outside in the rain to attempt to light the braai fire to fry some eggs and bacon.

It was then that we began to notice a strange odour in the house – the culprit? That bloody paraffin fridge! And opening the fridge door caused cries of:

"Oh God! It stinks!"

"Close it quickly!"

"Oh, my stomach is turning!"

"Shut it, please!"

The fridge was kaput, not working at all; nothing inside was cold and the meat had reached 'Stage 1' on the rotting cycle.

All the meat was quickly washed and salted and peppered to prevent it reaching 'Stage 2'.

The three men, feeling better and a little wiser today, braved the weather and squeezed into the braai booth and began roasting all the meat – plateful after plateful were taken inside and consumed, whilst the three of us snacked and enjoyed a few beers over the next couple of hours. Boring? Not at all; anyone who has enjoyed roasting meat in the open air with some good friends and a crate of beer will testify to that – and to the delicious aroma of 'braaing' steaks, pork and lamb chops, complemented by the smell of the beer 'steam', rising each time a little beer was thrown over the braai coals to douse any overzealous flames to prevent them from scorching the meat!

The rain gradually eased off, and, at last, stopped. The Ridge Top 'Olympics' could begin!

Everyone piled onto the back of my pick-up and we drove to the store, where about 20 of the African workers had gathered.

They were each given a pint of Chibuku to relax these super athletes, while we looked around for some suitable equipment for the various throwing events, like the shot-put and the javelin.

I told them that the winner of each event would get three bonus days on his ticket – loud cheering broke out, and all the 'athletes', suitably warmed up and encouraged by the power of a pint of Chibuku, lined up for the sprint.

The 100 Metres

"Go!"

Langton's little legs pumping away raced him clear of all the other runners. He won easily.

Old George pulled up holding his knee, several others stopping as well to help him – a smart move; a good excuse to stop!

The javelin was next, throwing a 3”×2”, two-metre-long timber. This event was chaotic, with two competitors smacking themselves around the head as they attempted to hurl the unbalanced javelin. But it was hilarious to watch and the mine boys seemed to be enjoying this get-together.

The shotput.

I demonstrated how to throw-put a lump of metal, weighing about five kilograms. Amon, the easy winner.

The Long Jump

Quite a few workers entered, many of them slipping and skidding on the wet muddy ground, but again Langton was the easy winner.

Hammer Throwing

The builders not surprisingly dominated this event, as they wouldn’t lend anyone their hammers!

Suddenly, there was a loud ‘CRACK’.

In seconds, the skies turned black and the thunderstorms struck; strong, blustery winds and rain pelting down on my athletes, who sprinted towards the village to get out of the rain – they all could have easily beaten Langton in the 100 metres!

Back at the house, the ‘black plastic door’ had been ripped off by the fierce winds and already there was a lot of water inside on the floor that needed to be mopped up.

We built a makeshift dam wall in front of the opening to prevent further water flowing inside and soaking the two large Axminster carpets on the floor.

A new longer, wider and heavier door flap was made from hessian, covered with the black plastic sheeting and hung up, which not only stopped the rain being blown into the house, but also made it much easier to get in and out.

By the time we had finished fixing our new door, the wind had dropped.

And, more importantly, the rain had stopped.

I suggested that it would be good for us to light a big bonfire outside – sitting around a roaring fire would warm us all up and bring more Christmas cheer.

Malcolm and I drove to the office, collected a cord of wood and, in no time at all, thanks to Elliot and a large dose of diesel, the flames of the fire were dancing upwards into the ever-darkening evening skies.

We sat in a circle, and began chatting and laughing together, when, suddenly…

“Dib dib dib!” shouted Graham loudly.

“Dob dob dob!” answered Malcolm and I automatically, and the three of us began to laugh.

“What’s so funny?” Eve asked. “And how do you all know that chant?”

"I learnt it when I was in the Cub Scout movement, back home in Merthyr Tydfil, in Wales," Graham replied, "and it is a chant that Baden-Powell initiated when he founded the Scouting Movement many years ago. It's actually '**dYb dYb dYb**' and means 'do your best; do your best, do your best'. To which the others around the campfire reply 'dob dob dob' – 'we'll do our best; do our best, do our best'! So we were all in the Cub Scouts in our youth; what troop were you in, Malcolm?"

"I was brought up in Toronto, Canada."

"And I in West London, England," I added, "which just goes to show what a worldwide organisation Baden-Powell founded. There are millions of youngsters in virtually every country in the world, and everybody knows the famous words '**be prepared**' – the motto associated with **B-P**. However, maybe you don't know that, as a colonel in the British Army, Baden-Powell fought in Rhodesia in the 1890s during the Matabele rebellions, and in the same area we are living in now – Insiza District, Matabeleland!"

For the next hour or so, the three of us recounted countless stories of the outdoor adventures and camping trips we went on, some of the amusing incidents we remembered, and, above all, the badges we'd achieved for activities ranging from first aid to athletics – which were sewn onto the sleeves of our jumpers and worn with pride, a visible reminder of our achievements.

There is no doubt that Lord Baden-Powell gave millions of youngsters the encouragement to try things, **do the best you can**, and to be adventurous.

That, coupled with self-assurance and having respect for other people, put so many youngsters on the right 'track', and in an enjoyable, fun manner too.

Then, just as suddenly as the rain had stopped earlier, it began now to tip down again and we all rushed inside to the noise of the hissing and spitting sounds as the rain tried to douse our campfire, but it couldn't douse our spirits. Be prepared; oh yes, we certainly were!

I tuned in to a local station on a small battery operated radio, a Christmas present, which crackled away... and we heard the latest weather forecast; widespread rain, and more rain....

This was of real concern to Malcolm, Eve and Graham, who would be leaving early in the morning to drive up to the Victoria Waterfalls on the Rhodesian-Zambian border.

"I am so looking forward to staying in the Victoria Falls Hotel – and a room with a bathroom, **and a toilet**! Even if they don't have your 'loo with a view'!" Eve exclaimed sarcastically as she pushed aside the hanging black plastic door and made the 50-yard dash to the long drop!

On her return, just as she was entering the room, another song by the group

Credence Clearwater Revival was belting out from the stereo set, and we all merrily sang along with the very appropriate, topical words:

"… Long as I remember, the rain keeps coming down… and I wonder, still I wonder, who'll stop the rain!"

The Rains

At first light, I drove up to the mine office to meet with Staff and Crispin to discuss what should be done over the next few days whilst the mine was closed. There would still be more than 20 workers staying there, and we wanted to make sure that there would be no trouble!

Amon was given strict instructions to check that there was no illegal Changaa alcohol being drunk in the mine village. We had issued him with a knobkerrie and a rhino whip (made from rhinoceros hide) together with some handcuffs, which he would use to padlock anyone causing problems to the prison tree.

He was an experienced mine policeman and well used to handling potential trouble-makers, and came highly recommended from the Big Bonanza Mine, which had just closed down.

He was known as a loner, a Zambian who didn't mix with Rhodesians – we had already noticed the effect his presence had made.

Staff would be in charge of the Chibuku beer delivery and he, together with Amon, would police the weekend drinking sessions; at least the 'gang of five' were no longer a problem – Phillemon was dead, and Paniche and Bamoso were both in hospital until they recovered from their serious stab wounds, when they would join Banzi in prison to await trial.

That drunken brawling episode had reduced the numbers of our workers down to 37, 15 of whom had gone home for the Christmas break.

In addition to his regular patrols, Amon would make a fire for us in the morning, and again in the evening until Elliot returned from leave.

Staff would call at the house each day to update me, as Crispin was also taking a few days off, but should be returning before the mine reopened – weather permitting, of course!

"You should expect that a few of the workers won't come back after Christmas," Crispin informed me as we got into the pick-up. "Out of sight, out of the mine!"

"Very appropriate, Crispin!" I laughed heartily; his version was spot on!

The Citroen Estate was parked close to the house and our visitors' bags were being quickly loaded in the drizzling rain.

Crispin gingerly added his bag to the load.

"But your car is so low to the ground," Crispin said with concern in his voice. "You won't be able to cross the flooded fords!"

"Although we are heavily laden, Crispin, have no worries; this car has hydraulic suspension – watch this!"

He started the engine, and Crispin looked in disbelief as the body of the car slowly rose from the ground.

"And Crispin, if we come to a flooded donga, I can raise the car body again, but much higher using this other lever, making the ground clearance just as high as that of a pick-up."

Crispin's eyes almost popped out of his head as the car rose even higher off the ground.

Our visitors waved goodbye and their vehicle moved off slowly, splashing through the flooded garden, and turned onto the road towards Fort Rixon.

When they reached Bulawayo, they would drop Crispin at the bus station, where he could catch a bus home, and the Citroen would then head for the Zambian border en route to one of the seven natural wonders of the world, the Victoria Waterfalls, discovered by – or, rather, first seen by a European, the famous missionary and explorer – 'Doctor Livingstone, I presume'.

With our friends gone, our house immediately seemed so much larger and more comfortable too, especially when eating – being able to cut the meat on your plate without elbowing the person next to you!

What a marvellous Christmas that was, a most enjoyable break; the first one, really, since the visit to Cain's mine by Joseph and myself all those months ago.

In the hectic times that followed, we had been constantly on the go; completing immigration formalities, packing, the countless South Africa-Rhodesia treks in the pick-ups carrying equipment, furniture and household goods; then the frequent daily drives Gwelo-Fort Rixon-Bulawayo, ferrying equipment, supplies, African workers, food and gum poles to the mine – *unbelievably*, our four pick-ups had already clocked *more than 30,000 kms* between them!

And now, four lazy days when we could spend time together in our little house in the African bush – four days before the mine would reopen in the New Year.

All in all, that would total a wonderful week away from:

The constant catastrophes of my problematic partner, Joseph;

The regular written ravings of Rancher Jackson; and

The non-deliveries and maddening delays caused by the Mines Department and sundry other suppliers.

With the continuous torrential rains keeping us cocooned in our castle, we had nowhere to go and nothing to do except entertaining the kids – and completing some very necessary house and roof repairs.

. . .

Naison and Langton worked hard in the constant drizzling rain over the next few days 'sealing' our house.

Their first task was to get up on the roof and find the nail holes that still leaked, and plug them with tar. This turned out to be a fun game for Marie-Louise and Jeffrey.

Naison would let the water from the rain build up at each tar-sealed nail hole in turn, and the kids would scream out 'that one; that one' every time water trickled through a hole.

It took most of the day before I was satisfied that the roof was leak proof, and it was fully tested in practice by a sudden downpour just after Naison and Langton had finished – hopefully they made it back to the village without getting soaked, but thankfully we were dry at last, only one small leak by the door opening.

I decided to close that opening the following morning and sited the new door entrance on the opposite, sheltered side of the house. We would certainly be more protected and have less rain and water being driven in by the strong winds – another lesson learnt;

First check who knows… which way the wind blows!

Naison sealed up the old opening by building a three-block-high wall with an extra hessian panel, whilst Langton and I made a new opening in the hessian wall on the leeward side of the house. There, we added a small porch three corrugated iron sheets wide, supported by gum poles cemented into a new low block-wall. This gave us added protection from the wind and the rain, and the house was decidedly warmer too.

I was so pleased with the building work that Langton and Naison had completed for me that I put two extra bonus days on their tickets.

We were beginning to get used to the quietness of the bush again.

Apart from the sounds of the birds early in the morning and the occasional barking of baboons as they passed through the undergrowth nearby, there was no noise at all – the normal background noise of the working mine was strangely missing.

It was as if time had stood still, although we were reminded of the passage of time by the hourly chiming of our clock and its constant staccato 'tick tock, tick tock, tick tock…'

. . .

The 'clang-yang-yang, clang-yang-yang' of the start-work gong reverberating loudly through the still morning air brought our holiday to an end.

"Tea is ready, sir. Good morning!"

Elliot was back and had put two mugs of tea on a box under the new porch. What a difference for us to be sitting outside sipping an early morning cuppa, even though it was still raining.

Elliot told us that the rains were very heavy at his home, and, on his way to the mine yesterday, he was very scared when he had to wade through a fast-flowing river ford crossing that was almost waist deep!

I turned on the radio only to hear more repeated warnings of severe flooding and blocked roads, and advising people not to travel in this severe weather.

There was also an alert that the Gwaai River was flowing strongly, a **metre** over the road bridge; the bridge that Malcolm would have to drive across on his way back to Bulawayo from Victoria Falls.

I assured Marianne that even crazy Malcolm would not attempt to cross it, even with his hydraulic jacking system at full clearance height; he'd get swept away!

"So they probably won't be back here for a day or two, but don't worry, I'm sure they'll find somewhere to stay until the river subsides. But now go and wake the kids up, get them dressed and we'll all go to Gwelo. I have arranged to meet Joseph at the house today to discuss our urgent pressing mining situation."

Although it was raining, Jeffrey insisted on being in the back of the pick-up with Elliot, who unbuttoned his bright yellow hooded raincoat so that Jeffrey could sit on his lap.

When Elliot rebuttoned it so that only Jeffrey's head poked through, we had to laugh; they looked like a mother kangaroo with a baby in its pouch!

Very slippery roads all the way to Fort Rixon confirmed that the rain storms were widespread.

I called into the police post to check with Peter on the state of the roads to Shangani, and, more importantly, which rivers and dongas were hazardous.

Although we'd been suffering for more than a week with torrential rainfall, upcountry the rains had been less heavy, so the storm rivers were flowing, but crossable with care at the main fords.

"But be careful, sir!" cautioned Peter. "On your return to the mine, you might find that they have been recharged!" Police terminology!

What a pleasure to drive on a tarmac road again, so smooth and so much easier.

The time passed quickly as we listened to Marie-Louise trying to teach Neville a song – needless to say, the dumb doll didn't learn a damn note!

We pulled up at No. 7 Hudson Road.

"Oh no!" I exclaimed. "Joseph's pick-up is not here! Let's check if there's anyone home!"

Knocking on the front door brought no response, so I went around to the back, but the kitchen door was also locked and the garage ominously empty!

"Best we go to the Midland Hotel to make a few phone calls to try to locate Joseph. Let's hope there are no problems with Jane and the baby."

My first call provided the answer.

"Joseph told me to tell you if you phoned," said Matt," that he'd gone to Belingwe for a few days and he wouldn't be able to meet you in Gwelo on Monday…. Oh dear, that's today, isn't it! But you're not phoning from the Midland Hotel, are you…? Oh, you are? Sorry mate, but that brother of mine is a right tit!"

And in my mind I could see Matt holding the phone as he uttered those words, with a resigned grimace and slowly shaking his head.

"I know it doesn't help," he continued after a brief pause, "but you're only in your third month of experiencing Joseph the Wanderer, or the Scarlet Pimpernel, as my father used to call him – we seek him here; we seek him there! But we have had a lifetime of such frustrating, annoying incidents. The only predictable thing about him is his unpredictability!"

And we both laughed simultaneously.

"Yeah, it doesn't really help to get mad at him; I'll just have to treat him as another problematic child in my growing family of some 40 African workers and their families!"

"Well good luck; I hope you think of a system to be able to work with him besides padlocking him to the prison tree! Pity I can't join you for lunch at the Midland today; I'm very busy, but next time you come to town, okay!"

"You look as if you need a pint!" Marianne remarked as I rejoined them on the covered terrace. "Joseph has disappeared again, has he?"

"Ah, forget that WOS – waste of space – let's have lunch, then I'll pop in quickly to see Crow, the manager at Barclays, about the sale of the white Peugeot, and we'll collect the meat and mealie meal rations before we head back home – home to some sanity!"

The lunch was lazily long, but the meeting with Mr Crow, surprisingly short.

I gave him a proposed sale price for the second-hand Peugeot in the range of $1,500 to $2,000, and Crow's only words were: "I will expedite the matter and get back to you ASAP!"

That's *bank-eese*, very similar to *civil servant-eese,* where they are actually saying nothing relevant at all, but they want to give the impression that *they are doing something* to help!

. . .

Life can be funny – as we pulled up at the mine office, there was Joseph's elusive blue Peugeot pick-up and, unsurprisingly, there was quite a commotion going on.

Joseph was shouting at the top of his voice, his face getting redder and redder by the second, as he waved his arms around like an out of control windmill!

Crispin and Staff were trying to calm him and keep him away from Godfrey, one of the mine workers, who was looking unusually smart in a blazer and slacks.

I hooted, jumped out of the pick-up and called out, "What's up; what's the problem?"

Crispin told me that Boss Joseph wanted to fire Godfrey because he'd come back from Christmas leave wearing a school blazer from Joseph's old school.

"And he must take off the blazer immediately!" ranted Joseph. "It's from the expensive private school my father sent me to – and it's got prefect stripes and merit badges on it too!"

'My God,' I muttered under my breath. *'This is pathetic and embarrassing.'*

Then out loud I stated emphatically, "Joseph, just calm down! Godfrey can wear what he likes when he's travelling on leave. But, Godfrey, please take off the blazer and don't wear it when you're on the mine."

"Yes Boss!" He took off the blazer and folded it neatly over his arm.

"And if I see him wearing that blazer again, I'll fire him on the spot!" Joseph blurted.

"Joseph, just let it go; you're only embarrassing yourself in front of the workers."

"But it's so annoying . . ."

"Joseph!" I cut in. "I'll tell you what really is *bloody annoying*; me travelling two hours to Gwelo this morning for our scheduled Monday morning meeting at the house, only to find it locked and nobody at home!"

"But I left a message with Matt to tell you that I couldn't be there for the meeting on Monday, today!" he stated forcefully.

"And how was Matt supposed to let me know, by bloody pigeon post!"

"But it's not my fault, is it? It's the telephone company's fault for not installing our phone on the mine yet! If there was a phone, I could have called you myself, instead of phoning Matt and leaving a message, couldn't I!"

I really had to reign myself in, straining to prevent an uncontrollable reflex punch from silencing all his waffle!

"Well, unfortunately, we can't have the meeting now, can we," he continued in a calmer tone, "because I've got to leave to get back to Jane and my son in Belingwe. I only called in at the mine to drop off three of our workers who stay in the Belingwe area. But we could meet tomorrow, later at the Gwelo house; is that all right?"

"No, Joseph, listen, I'm expecting my South African friends back from Victoria Falls tomorrow, for a farewell evening before they head back down South again. However, we have an appointment on Thursday, 9am sharp with the mining commissioner in Bulawayo concerning the fencing of our mine locations and the possible start-up grants that are available. Afterwards, we can go and discuss our plans to get things moving again – as we were supposed to have done in Gwelo this morning, okay?"

"But I . . ."

"Joseph! Thursday 9am, mining commissioner, Bulawayo office; will you be there?"

"Yes, but I . . ."

"Fine, 9am Thursday! Now I'm going to take Marianne and the kids home for some supper."

"But I . . ."

A loud hooting came to my rescue, preventing more Irish idiotic logic spewing from his lips!

A dirty, muddy Citroen Estate pulled up next to us, full of laughing, normal people.

"How'sit? We had such a fabulous time up at the Victoria Falls, and on the Zambezi River too. What a beautiful country!" The words exploded from Malcolm's smiling face.

"Hi everybody!" Joseph greeted them sheepishly. "Okay, I'll go back now to Belingwe, and we'll meet at 9am in the mining commissioner's office in Bulawayo on Thursday. Bye everybody!"

And the pale man in the pale blue 404 drove off. Phew, that was hard work!

Dusk was falling, as was the heavy drizzle again, and we drove and parked the cars on the side of the house.

Graham jumped out of the car with his bag and rushed towards the 'old' doorway, almost smacking into the 'new' hessian wall!

"Wow! You've blocked it; how do we get in now?"

"Well, they haven't got a bloody chimney Santa, have they?" quipped Malcolm. "Guess there's an opening on the other side now."

"Hey, I like the covered porch, a great improvement; so you've been busy whilst we were at the falls," remarked Graham as we entered the room lit by two hurricane lamps that Elliot was busy setting on the bar and the coffee table.

"What a warm, cosy room you've created, Marianne, and it looks leak-proof, not like our Christmas 'singing in the rain'!" Eve added.

"Thanks Eve! Yes, that was something else, something to remember, a wonderful one-off!

But now let's hear all about your trek through the storms to the Victoria Falls."

Over the next few hours, we were enthralled by the stories of their trip as they related some of the best moments they had experienced.

Absolute astonishment, gazing through the spray caused by the momentous millions of litres of water per second gushing over the one and a half kilometre wide Victoria Falls – one of the most unusual waterfalls in the world.

It is created by the Zambezi River that suddenly plummets into a narrow 100 metre deep chasm crashing down into the river below – the sheer size of it and the raw power of Mother Nature was breathtaking!

Eve explained to us how they got their name, and she read out from the tourist pamphlet, which also had many photos of the falls:

"David Livingstone, the Scottish missionary and explorer, is believed to have been the first European to view Victoria Falls on 16 November 1855. Livingstone named his discovery in honour of Queen Victoria, but the indigenous name, Mosi-oa-Tunya – 'the smoke that thunders' – continues in common usage locally as well."

Many other magnificent moments as well when they took a boat safari along the Zambezi River – the game and the wildlife were fantastic!

Some huge African elephants on the river banks were the highlight – being a mere 10 metres away from the boat, the elephants look colossal!

But they didn't dare get that close to a huge hippopotamus, which opened its enormous mouth, revealing large vicious-looking pointed front teeth that stood like sentries in front of a huge yawning pink cavernous mouth.

The boat captain had abruptly turned away heading back towards the falls, shouting to them, "He's too dangerous! That one is what we call a 'rogue' hippo!

He's been known to suddenly submerge under the water, and, as you wait, anxiously straining to try to see his whereabouts, he'll suddenly explode out of the water next to the boat and, with his massive jaws, crush a small boat in half, occasionally dragging a badly injured tourist down into the murky waters to his death."

"We all got the cold shivers as he described the scene in gory detail, and we were pleased when the driver docked at a small island for a lunch and drinks – we needed them! All in all, a wonderful few days spent at the falls and on the Zambezi River!" Eve exclaimed.

The not-so-pleasant journey back was sometimes harrowing, and they had a near mishap crossing a fast-flowing donga.

Later, when they came to the Gwaai River, the water was flowing strongly several feet over the bridge, carrying branches and sometimes even whole trees that had been uprooted by the devastating floods upriver.

They spent an uncomfortable night with the six of them having to sleep in the car waiting for the water level to go down, and were only able to cross the bridge around midday.

Before we all flaked out, we toasted each other several times.

"To an unbelievable two weeks!"

"To the best, the most unusual Christmas ever!"

"To have had the opportunity to witness probably the best of the seven wonders of the world; we'll never forget that constant roaring noise – the 'smoke that thunders' – as the Zambezi River gushes over the mile-wide Victoria Falls and crashes into the river below!"

. . .

It was midmorning when bodies began stirring, tossing and turning, accompanied by gentle sounds – mostly snoring!

Marianne was already up, sitting on the porch, and I joined her for some tea.

That first cuppa tasted sweet as it surged down my throat, defurring my teeth on the way.

The second was even better as we chatted away, gazing through the light falling drizzle across to the bush.

A duiker, the size of a whippet dog, skipped across the grass, stopped, peered at us and then continued on its way, disappearing back into the bush.

"Wonderful," Marianne whispered, "to be able to be so close and watch the animals in our own back garden; we're very fortunate."

"Too true. But now unfortunately I'll have to leave this serene scene and drive to Bulawayo again to chase up our diesel delivery from Shell, which I paid for before Christmas! This lack of fuel is worrying. And since we don't drink spirits, I'll take any unopened bottles with me to Greys Inn – old Dave said he was always on the lookout for the hard-to-get-world-branded-makes of spirits. Get Elliot to take those two boxes and load them in the front of the pick-up.

I'll be back later in the afternoon, when our guests will probably be up – but let them sleep on."

A strange noise startled us; it was a cross between a husky 'good morning' and a long, rumbling belch – Graham had joined us!

"I overheard that you're off to town; can I join you?"

"Of course, Graham; I'll enjoy the company, but we'll have to leave now as we need to be back in time for Malcolm and Eve's last night with us on the mine."

"Smashing, boy-o!" he uttered in a pronounced Welsh accent. "And no need to worry, Marianne; I'll keep him on the straight and narrow. We'll be back before dark!"

On arrival in Bulawayo, I drove straight to the Shell depot.

Unfortunately, the news was not good. Leo de Ziel had taken the day off, and the Ridge Top Mine was not on their dispatch and delivery schedule for the coming week.

And I was told to expect even longer delays, as they were still trying to work off the backlog.

Mr de Ziel was the only one who could give me more information.

At Greys Inn, Dave was all smiles as we gave him the two boxes of whisky, other spirits and several bottles of liqueurs, Drambuie and Tia Maria. He paid us cash immediately and insisted we join him in the bar for a New Year's drink – how could we refuse!

But there was a whiff of danger in the air as we entered the bar…

"Happy New Year!" rang out several times, and the drinks began to be served in machine gun manner.

Everyone was in a good mood. Des and some other ranchers were having lunch together; Arthur and another colleague from the post office who I'd met playing snooker in the civil service club a month earlier; and several others from the Mines Department – the conversations were buzzing frantically, giving that low, deep-murmuring busy sound of a full, packed-out pub.

The drinks flowed, and the raucous laughter grew louder and louder….

The grandfather clock in the hotel foyer chimed, 'one, two, three, and four'!

Time for us to leave.

The rain was tipping down as we came outside and it was difficult to see what was pavement and what was road, as the water flowed like a wide river between the buildings lining each side of the road.

In Bulawayo, between the pavement and the tarmac road, there are storm gullies about three-foot wide and two-foot deep, which act as a fast-flowing drainage system to limit the amount of water building up on the main road – and they help a lot, normally.

Every 30 metres or so, there are concrete slabs bridging the gaps to allow people to cross or to get to their vehicles.

However, if you are not aware of or used to this, they can be difficult to see and also awkward to negotiate. Needless to say, 'boy-o' put one foot in the wrong place, lunged forward and went arse-over-tit, splashing around as he tried to stand up! Much to the amusement of onlookers, and to Dave as well, who had come out with us to say goodbye.

Graham's utterance of 'B** F** it' was drowned by a massive thunderclap overhead!

Although soaking wet, Graham was still in a good mood and we set off, on time to make it back to the mine by 6 o'clock.

However, the going was very slow due to poor visibility as the rains lashed relentlessly across the windscreen, and sometimes we were reduced to a speed of only 10–15 km an hour.

It's that type of fierce weather that you don't really benefit from having your headlights on.

Graham had been reading some tourist pamphlets and looking at a map of the area, when suddenly he exclaimed, "Hey, pull over and stop! Look at this. In a kilometre or so, there is a small road off to the right, which comes out about five kilometres south of your mine. It's got a name too, Trolley Road, so it should be better than just a cart track, and if we take it instead of going the longer route via Fort Rixon we'll make up lost time and be back before six."

The road turned out to be rather narrow in some places and very slippery and, at times, I battled to keep the pick-up going in a straight line.

But thankfully the rain had eased off considerably and we made good progress.

At one point, the road turned sharply to the right, and we slowed down as we went past several native huts. Small kids came running out, shouting and waving their arms at us, seemingly in welcoming gestures.

From one of the huts, a man in blue overalls and a yellow mine hat rushed out and stood on the track in front of us, frantically waving us down!

As we skidded to a halt, we could see a vast expanse of swiftly flowing water only 10 metres away in front of us!

It was George. He shouted to us, "Go back, Boss, go back! This river is in full flood and you can't get across here!"

We looked at the bubbling, foaming waters as they rushed by, wavelets crashing against the bank, causing clouds of spray that were illuminated by the beams of our headlights – our very own New Year's celebration display of shimmering lights.

George pointed to a metal cage hanging by cables stretched across the river, rather like the one near the Lower Gwelo Mission where I dropped off Crispin last month.

The cage was being bashed around by the swirling waters, with odd branches of trees being caught up in it and sticking out in all directions, making it look like a festive Christmas tree!

He told us that the cage was about 10 feet above the river bed – 10 feet! Throughout most of the year, the river was normally a narrow slow-flowing, zigzagging river, only one or two feet deep, and could easily be crossed by foot or in a pick-up.

"It's hard to imagine when you see such an angry mass of water roaring past you," remarked Graham. "Where does it all go?"

"Well, the huge volume of water raging down these rivers snaking between the hills and the high ground, on reaching the lower plains, would flood out to form large temporary lakes, which would soon disappear… the grateful parched ground literally sucking the water into its bosom!

"The three-year drought has been bountifully broken and the farmers and the ranchers are rejoicing! The last few weeks of continuous rains have answered their prayers; they are deliriously happy – unlike us, though!"

"Yebo, I guess it's one man's medicine is another man's *prison!*" Graham 'Crispinised' the saying with tongue in cheek! And indeed, the rains had *straight-jacketed* our mining operations, and our prayers had yet to be answered!

We were extremely annoyed that our shortcut turned out to be blocked – but George wasn't; he'd been wondering how he was going to cross the river to get back to work on the mine, yet another person's prayers had been answered; surely our turn must come soon!

We turned around and headed back the way we had come until we met the Bulawayo-Fort Rixon road again.

Despite our good intentions, it looked as though we would arrive home very late.

As we neared the police post, the pick-up suddenly became violently wobbly, slipping from side to side on the muddy road.

"Graham! Shit! That's all we need; a bloody puncture!"

I got the big torch out of my 'B-P' kitbag, and, under the light of the powerful beam, we proceeded to take off the wheel. It seemed that with each nut we removed the rains came down harder, and with the swirling winds driving sheets of rain into our faces it was almost impossible to see what we were doing.

However, eventually, with the spare wheel safely bolted on, we proceeded further on our mishap-ridden journey.

When we, two soaking wet, bedraggled figures eventually got home to the mine at 8:30pm,

Eve did not want to listen to our excuses or problems.

"Ah! You two just got jugged up in Bulawayo on the money from selling the bottles of spirits, selfishly enjoying yourselves and not giving a damn that we've been sitting here waiting. It's our last evening, but you two don't give a toss!" Eve ranted. "I've had enough; I'm going to bed. Goodnight!"

. . .

At breakfast, Eve apologised for her rude outburst the previous evening.

"But I was so upset that our last evening together was ruined; a taint on an absolutely fantastic holiday with you all."

Malcolm chipped in, "It was very unfortunate; you two must have been gutted after trying that disastrous shortcut to get back here on time, and having to fix a puncture at night in the pouring rain, but that's all water under the bridge."

"If there was a bloody bridge," Graham cut in, "then we would have been back on time!"

Laughter filled the room and broke the slightly awkward atmosphere, and we all continued to chat away merrily again as we drank a farewell coffee together.

With a huge sigh and in a sad voice, Eve concluded, "But let's forget last night; nothing could ruin our best Christmas ever. The kids have had a ball, but unfortunately we have to leave here now to drive back home to South Africa."

"Hey, why don't all the kids jump in the back of the pick-up? I've got to go to Fort Rixon to collect some fresh fish rations," I suggested. "We can drive up there together with you, until we get to the turn-off to Bulawayo."

"Yes, yes!" screamed five excited children and they scrambled and helped each other into the back of the pick-up.

At the turn off, we juggled the kids between the vehicles – Malcolm and Eve took their three children and set off in the direction of Bulawayo; the rest of us headed for the dam.

Luckily, it was a dry day, as the club had organised a New Year's lunch for the locals on the lawns leading down to the lakeside – 'locals' referring to the scattered dwellers across the Inzisa-Fort Rixon area, anyone within a 30 km radius!

There were braais, pots of guinea fowl stew (my favourite – the second helping tasted even better!), curries, salads and plenty of wine, which always loosens the tongues a little, getting the adults mingling and chatting to each other.

For the youngsters, a clown – no, Joseph wasn't there! A man who kept them entertained with clown's antics and acrobatics; the children's spontaneous laughter was a delight to hear.

It was good to see our rancher neighbours, Des and Irene, Stan and Jeanette, the Ashburners, and even Jackson and his wife made the effort to have a few words with Marianne and myself.

Jackson, in fact, called me aside and said he had no problems with me; it was the old fellow Ray whom he heard all about from other rancher friends of his.

"He has a poor record over the years in miner-rancher relations," Jackson continued, "always cutting corners; in fact, you can see that quite clearly here on my land, with his blatant illegal pegging of the Claremont parallel. And not to mention his . . ."

Policeman Peter interrupted what looked like the beginning of a tirade of moans and complaints that Jackson wanted to get off his chest. "Come on over and join the younger generation!" he joked. "Don't talk business; let's enjoy the start of a new year while we can. Even the weather has been kind to us today."

It made a real change to be with a large group of people. Over the last two months, I had been dealing mainly with individuals – in between countless hours of solitary driving and 'frequent futile' hours at the phone booth.

For Marianne, it was even more welcome, as, apart from Eve, she'd barely spoken to another soul out here in the bush, whereas today she could chat with other women to her heart's content.

The hours slid slowly by, and, in no time at all, it was beginning to get dark and last orders were being called – not for the drinks, but for those wanting to buy fresh fish!

Loaded up with bream for us and plenty of dogfish rations for the mine boys, we headed for the mine.

The kids stood up in the back of the pick-up with Graham and laughed and shouted as they played the 'rabbit counting' game, as rabbits dashed this way and that, trying to move out of the beams of my headlights.

Thump!

I stopped to pick up the dead rabbit and put it in the back – extra meat rations for the boys!

If Jackson wasn't so dogmatic about his 'no poaching' stance, the mine boys could catch and eat fresh rabbit frequently. It's not Australia, but the bush is crawling with them so to speak and I could easily put two boys permanently on the job as rabbit meat catchers.

The fresh fish and three fresh dead rabbits – there were two more loud *thumps* on the journey – were distributed by Crispin amongst the eager workers, who rushed off to the village compound to cook their supper.

As we retired after a full and very varied day, we could hear the contented murmurings from the village and see the odd glow of the African fires, so noticeable against the dark night skies again; another reminder that it was not raining; in fact, our first rain-free day.

I fell asleep, dreaming again of driving on those wonderful hot, dusty roads.

. . .

Early in the morning, I set off for Bulawayo with Graham following me.

He'd decided to return to South Africa, because there was not much more he could do or see in Rhodesia. These incessant rains and the flooded dongas were causing havoc to the roads, making driving no fun at all.

We stopped at Greys Inn for a coffee and spent a short time there recounting some of the unbelievable and enjoyable events of the past two weeks before he left. "To trek through the Rhodesian *rain*, back to the South African *sun!*"

I hastened over to the Mines Department and was pleased to see the pale blue Peugeot pick-up parked in the Mines Yard – that didn't mean, of course, that Joseph was actually inside for our meeting, but it did indicate that he was definitely somewhere in Bulawayo!

The mining commissioner was in a foul mood; you could see that he was still suffering from a 'New Year's cold', as he called it, and was determined to keep the meeting short.

"The deadline for fencing your mining locations has been extended to the 6 February, when Mr Jackson will provide the aerial map you requested and the four of us can come to an amicable fencing agreement, right? With regard to potential loans and grants from the Mines Department, I have summarised them in this letter and attached all the necessary application forms and the relevant requirements for the different loan types." Which he then proceeded to rattle off with indecent haste:

"**Establishment loans**, **a speculative loan, plant loans, exploration loans** and **development loans.** I suggest you study all this information and bring the application forms with you when we meet again on 14 January. Now if you'll excuse me, I have a lot of work to clear. Good day to you!"

And, in three minutes flat, we were standing in the corridor.

"Let's hope that one of these is destined for our future." I commented. "We really could use a loan to help 'kick-start' us after the disastrous delays due to these bloody continuous rains!"

"Rains! These rains!" repeated Joseph. "So much rain after the long drought, and it is still forecasted that the rains could go on for at least another two weeks! So what are we going to do? We're stuffed!"

"We're not stuffed; we just have to get on and do everything possible with regard to preparing the mine for when the rain stops, for when we can expect deliveries of diesel and equipment.

Now, assuming most of the workers have returned to the mine by the weekend, we should have 40 munts that we can put into groups of four to six, and set them various jobs to do. (*Gwazas.*) On the surface, there's plenty to do, clearing sites for the slimes dams and the cyanide tanks, there's wood cutting and hut building, making concrete blocks and building more storerooms, housing for the alternator and the hoist room, and… I'm sure to think of many more as well!"

"Yes, and underground too!" Joseph began to enthuse. "Matt is prepared to let us have a pump, which will allow us to start pumping out the flooded first level once we get the diesel fuel delivery from Shell. I'll collect it from him over the weekend when I'm in Gwelo. I'm also checking with our suppliers to see where we can buy a large 5,000-litre water tank to go on that base we built, so when we actually can start pumping we'll have our own water storage supply – at last! No more driving every day with empty barrels to be filled up from the river. No more relying on Rancher Jackson's 'generosity' – the water tank swimming pool!"

"Good. Well, if we at least get our own water supply, that'll save us so much time and hassle!

Now what about the 5-stamp mill? With the Christmas/New Year holidays over, the mine yard men must pull finger and get cracking! We don't want to have everything else in place and find ourselves still without a mill to crush the bloody gold ore!"

"I'll keep chasing Ronnie to locate, visit and approve both a 5-stamp mill and a James Table for us to lease from them."

"Joseph, you know what, perhaps it would be a good idea if, instead of buying meat rations in Gwelo, you drive to Bulawayo for them instead; that way, you can see the blokes in the Mines Department face-to-face. And why not even call in unannounced to see the mining commissioner to stress how important the situation is. That'll be much more effective than trying to speak to them on the phone. I'll keep pursuing Shell for a definite delivery date for the fuel tank and the diesel itself, but the atrocious weather has put them so far behind schedule, it'll be several more weeks, I reckon! A diesel delivery, together with the phone being installed on the mine, would be a godsend!"

We spoke for an hour or more, calmly and rationally planning our next week's priorities, and agreed to meet again in Bulawayo after the weekend, on Monday, 9am at the Mines Yard.

But no matter how good our planning was the one thing we couldn't plan for, the one thing above all that was crippling our whole operation – we needed the rains to stop!

It was ironic really; so much water was falling from the skies flooding the mine, which we could not pump out due to the lack of diesel fuel deliveries, and these same bloody rains were causing havoc to the dirt murram roads, preventing diesel from being delivered!

It was a catch 22 situation – I would be so over the moon when I could wake up one morning without involuntarily humming that bloody song, *'and I wonder, still I wonder, who'll stop the rain'!*

Beer for Free!

What a cold wet weekend – this guti mist was bone-chilling.

Inside our tin-roofed house, we just could not get warm.

During the day, the kids were okay – the playing and rushing around generated some heat in their bodies – but at night it was bitterly cold and the hessian walls added to the dampness, because the concrete wash remained wet the whole time.

Jeffrey was beginning to get chesty again, with a wheezing cough. This was not good at all, as he had suffered with severe bronchitis when he was a baby. We'd have to take him to see a doctor on Monday. But for now, in an effort to help keep him warm, the two heavy, thick woollen-based Axminister carpets were laid over the double bed and we all slept together – movement was restricted; once you were in, you were pinned down for the night!

. . .

Fortunately, on Sunday morning, the rain had stopped again.

The kids were still sleeping and we told Elliot and his wife, Judith, the new nanny, to look after them and feed them when they woke up; we'd be back in an hour.

This was an ideal time for Marianne to practice her driving skills.

She'd had a few driving lessons years ago in Europe, but she was pretty rusty.

On Christmas Eve, after a crash course – an unfortunate term – she was thrust into driving one of the pick-ups full of furniture from Gwelo back to the mine, and, although she drove reasonably well, she had stalled the vehicle several times when attempting to cross the fast-flowing dongas.

We were there to help her then, but she wanted to be confident driving on her own in these conditions, running errands to Fort Rixon and Shangani as well as the general conveyance jobs in and around the mine.

Clutch control is the most important part of driving, I think.

Once you've mastered this, pulling off and changing gears holds no fears – even on hill starts! You are in control and can concentrate on keeping the vehicle going in the right direction!

So I parked the pick-up at the bottom of a long, fairly steep incline leading up from the valley.

We swapped places and, for the next hour, Marianne laboriously practiced hill starts, over and over again holding it on the clutch, then driving slowly forward again.

Gradually, the kangaroo jumps were replaced by bunny hops until smooth, no over-revving hill starts became the norm, and a contented smile told me she was ready for action on Monday, when we needed to drive both of the pick-ups to the garage in Gwelo – the first and second gears on the grey Peugeot 404 were difficult to engage and had to be fixed.

Whilst we were away, the pools of water near the house had proved too enticing for the kids, and, on our return, we saw two little black/brown children splashing happily around in the muddy water, much to the amusement of Elliot and Judith.

"Jesus! Get them out of there!" I called. "And boil up lots of hot water."

The muddy, soaking wet clothes were stripped off, and Marianne and Judith washed the kids thoroughly with hot water in the tin bath.

Elliot brought over some hot soup, which warmed them up, but, even in fresh woolly clothes, they were still shivering a little.

"Elliot, bring some hot embers from your fire in one of those small metal drums with the holes in the sides and put it on the porch."

A combination of sitting close to that 'drum of fire', the hot soup, singing and clapping their hands did the trick – the shivers ceased and the smiles returned.

However, at night, Jeffrey began to sound like a ship's foghorn, as he frequently cough-barked, and occasionally was gasping for breath. He was getting worse.

. . .

After a sleepless night for of us all, at first light, we put Jeffrey in the beige pick-up, which Marianne drove, followed by Marie-Louise and me in the grey 404, and we headed for the Gwelo house.

By the time we arrived, Joseph had already left for Bulawayo as planned for our meeting at the Mines Yard – another unavoidable problem arising from not having a phone at the mine yet.

And this morning, in fact, really highlighted a potentially dangerous case; that of not being able to call an ambulance if Jeffrey's condition had become critical in the night!

Jane was pleased to see us all, and was happy to look after Marie-Louise whilst we took Jeffrey to see the doctor.

"Good thing you brought him in, and just in time too!" the doctor told us. "His symptoms are not yet critical, but he needs to be in hospital so that he can receive some intensive care 24 hours a day until he can breathe normally again; I suggest you don't take him back to the mine for at least a week. Do you have somewhere to stay here in Gwelo, because I would need to see him regularly as well, when he's released from hospital?"

I dropped them off at the hospital and went to the Midland Hotel to phone the Mines Yard and hopefully be able to speak to Joseph.

He was already there with Ronnie, and would spend the rest of the day checking on available equipment – they had earmarked several mines to contact, three of which had stamp mills for sale, and one a James Table.

Another fruitless call to the Shell depot, who were still way behind schedule with their deliveries – and oh, the frustration and time wasted due to the lack of a phone on the mine!

When I met Marianne at the hospital, she told me that Jeffrey was under sedation, but we could visit him again in the morning.

Oh, what a luxury to sleep in a warm, dry house.

After supper, I walked into the bathroom – not ran through the rain to the long drop!

And switched on a light – instead of trying to light a hurricane lamp with damp matches!

Oh what a pleasure it would be, living in our house on the mine when we had diesel, power, electricity and hot running water!

. . .

By morning, Joseph hadn't returned and Jane was getting worried, so I told her that I'd pop into the Midland Hotel to check for messages on our way back from the hospital.

We were pleased to see that Jeffrey was looking calmer and more relaxed – his naughty grin spread across his face as he saw his mother and sister.

The nurse informed us that he had responded well and could go home in a day or two, and it would be best if the family stayed in Gwelo until the rains stopped for good, which was forecast for the coming weekend – so, fingers crossed.

Light drizzle accompanied us as we drove to the Midland Hotel and we were pleased to sit inside a nice warm, dry place.

I called over a waiter. "Two cappuccinos, one strawberry milkshake, and are there any messages for me?"

He returned and served us our three drinks, and a five-word message from Joseph: "Gone to Belingwe. Tell Jane." Well, that's five words more than usual!

I collected some boys' rations and we went back to see Jane.

She gave a despairing sigh when I told her the message that Joseph had left at the Midland Hotel.

"At least I know he's okay, I suppose," she said. "I should be used to it by now!"

"Well, you've got Marie-Louise and me for company for the next few days," Marianne consoled her, "and hopefully Jeffrey will be out of hospital tomorrow, so that'll be a houseful until Saturday when we'll be returning to the mine."

After a coffee and a sandwich, I left them and headed for Fort Rixon.

We couldn't leave the mine boys alone for two days without one of us being there to supervise.

The very presence of one of us, in fact, even one of our pick-ups, actually helped; it indicated that we were around on the claims!

And, when Marianne was using the grey pick-up, there'd be a good chance that there would be at least one of the three pick-ups parked outside the office most of the time – a visible, silent sentry!

. . .

I drove into Bulawayo the next day to see Mr de Ziel, the Shell manager.

"No good news for you yet, I'm afraid; we are still catching up the backlog for existing clients, who come first, as I'm sure you understand. However, the weather forecast indicates that the rains should come to an end in the next few days, so why not call in on Friday? I'll be as happy as you when I can give you a firm delivery date."

At the Mines Yard, Martin Curtis had some better news.

Joseph had told Ronnie that he'd heard there was a mine near Filabusi with a good condition stamp mill and a James Table for sale. They'd tried phoning the mine, but the lines were down, but Joseph pushed Ronnie into going there to do an inspection for a possible purchase – he was unusually aggressive!

I had a list of things to purchase from K.B. Davies. Sparky, our electrician/ mechanic, had indicated various sundry items that he needed. He was working on the alternator, checking out and replacing certain parts on the main switchboard.

While I was chatting away to the owner, Doug French, an old man entered the warehouse.

He came over and greeted Doug, and excitably told him that he had found a company that could make the truncheons for his ball mill.

Doug introduced me to Mr Newmarch, who had been gold mining since he was a teenager.

He was also a very experienced mechanic and had designed a new ball mill, of equivalent tonnage throughput to a 5-stamp mill.

The K.B. Davies Company was working on a prototype that would go into production soon.

"A modern replacement of the dying dinosaur 5-stamp mills!" he joked. "Why don't you bring your partners in to have a preview on Friday? We are having an open day. You never know, if you can't obtain a working 5-stamp, this could be a possible alternative."

I went back to the Mines Department to leave a message for Joseph to please call in at the mine on his way back to Gwelo; we had lots of things to discuss.

As I drove towards the gates, I had to brake hard to avoid a head-on collision with another pick-up coming from the other direction which swung across right in front of me and swept into the yard – yes, a pale blue Peugeot 404!

A rather glum-looking Joseph sheepishly smiled as he stepped out the vehicle.

An extremely annoyed-looking Ronnie grunted '*Hello*' and walked off.

"Oh, oh, Joseph," I remarked. "What's happened?"

"Well, it wasn't my fault, was it?" he blurted. "I mean, if their phone was working, we could have spoken to the man at the mine, couldn't we!"

"And?" I queried.

"And we wouldn't have gone all the way to Filabusi for nothing!"

"So?"

"So it was a waste of time. There was a three-stamp mill and a James Table in very poor condition."

"Hang on, Joseph, was that the X-mine, a few kilometres on very bad dirt tracts from the Filabusi petrol station turn-off?"

"Yes, that's the one! And don't start blaming me. Yes, the man told us that my father and another young man had visited the mine . . ."

"Joseph, that other young man was me, way back in November!" I responded.

"Well, I guessed as much that it was you! And I know you're going to tell me that I should have checked if the mine had already been visited or contacted by us!"

"If you had, you'd have seen a bloody big red X crossed through the name!" I added.

We went inside and had a cup of coffee with a rather pissed-off-looking Ronnie.

Just then, the phone rang. Ronnie answered and listened quietly, and a smile began to crease his lips.

"Good condition, dismantled and in storage?" he iterated. "When can I come and view? And the asking price? Oh… okay, I'll be up there tomorrow, late in the afternoon. Fine, and thanks for phoning."

Ronnie prolonged the silence after the phone call. We could see him thinking as he mulled over the information he had just heard. Smiling, he said enthusiastically, "Well Joseph, perhaps your luck has turned. That was a call from an old colleague, who assures me that they are in first-class condition and available for transporting – two, yes two 5-stamp mills! I'm going to drive up to Salisbury tomorrow."

"Ronnie, Ronnie, can I come as well? It will save you all that driving on your own! Better still, I'll pick you up tomorrow morning and I'll drive us to Salisbury. We can view the 5-stamp together and stay overnight at my brother, Cain's, mine and I 'll bring you back to Bulawayo on Friday!" Joseph rattled off, almost pleading. His eyes opened wider and an exited look spread across his face anticipating a positive response from Ronnie.

"Okay, but *you will* do all the driving, Joseph!"

"Yes! Yes, I'll willingly be your driver for those two days, thanks. Thanks!"

. . .

After a rain-free night on the mine, it felt so much warmer.

The puddles on the grass had disappeared and the track to the mine looked decidedly drier.

The sun came out amongst the clouds, which had lost their black, ominous, threatening character of the last six weeks – yes, all those long weeks of waterlogged Matabeleland, and our bloody waterlogged mine!

Hopefully, the murram roads would dry out completely soon, and we could expect a delivery of diesel fuel in the near future.

The African workers were also in a good mood as they went about their work – that sun definitely not only gives us warmth and vitamin C, but seems to penetrate the brain, triggering the happier side of our characters.

Crispin and Staff formed a good team, and knew how to keep the mine boys working hard on their daily *gwazas* – and both of them could not tolerate lazy shirkers!

I was pleased as well with Elliot, who turned out to be a good cook, and, now that his wife, Judith, and their young baby had joined him, she would do the washing and ironing, together with babysitting when we wanted. However, this would only be occasionally, as Marianne always preferred to have the kids with her, whether on the mine, in a truck or visiting once the roads and tracks were hard again.

. . .

My meeting on Friday with Shell turned out to be a damp squid.

Although the rains had 'officially' ended today, Mr de Ziel didn't hold out much hope for a delivery to us for at least another week, maybe even longer!

"What's the problem? Is there a shortage of fuel? I've heard there might even be fuel rationing soon as the UN oil embargo bites harder."

"Well, that obviously will have an effect, but ranches and mines should be on the exempt list; it'll be mainly private usage that the government wants to curb. But your delivery problem is something different. We have a policy. It is up to the delivery driver, who knows not only the murram roads, but also the tracks leading to the fuel storage tanks on a ranch or on a mine. It is his decision! He checks, and if he thinks it's not 100% safe, he does not deliver. We can't afford to have a diesel tanker full of fuel stuck somewhere out in the bush!"

"But the murram road to our mine is fine; we get delivery of Chibuku beer each week delivered in a small tanker."

"Yes, I know the ones. But our tankers are much heavier, and don't forget they are carrying flammable fuel, which, if they get stuck in the remoter bush areas, could be an enticing target for Mugabe's terrorists – either syphoning the fuel off for their own use, or worse still blowing up the tanker! And that would be a well-publicised advert for their terror campaign! No sorry, but your delivery is totally dependent on the Shell driver's judgement."

More disappointing news at the Mines Department.

Ronnie and Joseph had viewed the two disassembled 5-stamp mills at a warehouse near Salisbury, and they were indeed in first class condition, no rot at all on the huge timber frames.

But the price the seller wanted was exorbitant and almost double the amount that the Mines Department would be prepared to pay to purchase it, and offer it on their standard monthly lease agreement to us.

Ronnie and Joseph were on their way back to Bulawayo, but would definitely be attending the open day for the Newmarch Ball Mill at K.B. Davies at 2:30pm.

That gave me one and half hours to entertain and sustain myself.

I tossed a coin. Heads the Greys Inn; tails the Lloyds Tea House.

As the coin spun heavenwards… *whoosh!* A hand plucked it out of the air before I could catch it. It was Des!

"Well, the gods have decided! Des, come and have a drink with me at the Greys Inn."

He was very upset to hear about young Jeffrey and his bronchitis problems.

"Yes, he's over the worst, thank God. In fact, I'm going up to Gwelo on Saturday morning to collect him, and bring the family back to the mine again now that the rains have finally stopped.

Before I leave for Gwelo, I'll get a few 'fire drums' and place them in the house – that should dry the hessian concrete-washed walls out completely so that the house will be warm and dry when we get back there on Saturday night."

"I think you are making a bad mistake; bronchitis is very serious! My advice to you would be to wait one more day, to be 100% sure! Come and stay the Saturday night with Irene and me!"

He laughed; a hearty laugh.

"Good one, Des; you're a right comedian! Okay, that's a deal; I'll bring the family during the afternoon – if it doesn't start raining again!"

"No chance of that. Look at the sky outside; not a cloud to be seen. The rains are definitely over!"

At the K.B. Davies open day for the Newmarch ball mill, there was a good crowd.

Joseph and Ronnie had also returned in time.

"It was a most disappointing trip," Ronne said to me. "After travelling all the way to Salisbury to view those 5-stamp mills, which were in mint condition, only to be told a price that was way above the Mines Department limit! But now that we are here, let's see what this chap Newmarch has to say about his new design ball mill for small workers – you never know what you're going to hear from an inventor."

After the presentation, there were a lot of technical and mechanical questions, which seemed to be answered satisfactory by Mr Newmarch, in a quiet, unassuming manner.

Ronnie and Martin were quite impressed, Ronnie, in fact, saying to us, "Look, we've been searching for a good condition 5-stamp mill since November, which has proved a fruitless mission. If this company can produce the Newmarch ball mill in four to five weeks from order as they say, you two should discuss it seriously with them and get a quote."

And we did indeed approach Mr French, and made an arrangement to meet with him and Mr Newmarch on Tuesday for a serious session.

We would also bring our partner, Ray, with us, so we could all decide there and then, either a 5-stamp pulverising stamp mill or the ball mill – a rotating drum containing heavy metal balls crashing around amongst the ore rocks and reducing them down to a fine sand.

That agreed, it was time for Joseph and I to head for home, and for once it was in the same direction, Gwelo, and to the same house in Hudson Road, to be with the same wives and children.

. . .

It was nice to be woken up in the morning with a smiling little face grinning away at me, even though he was tugging my moustache! Jeffrey was looking decidedly better.

During breakfast, I opened the mail, mainly bills and a very disappointing letter from Mr Crow of Barclays Bank.

"Oh no, it's about the sale of the white Peugeot."

...The Exchange Control regret that they are unable to approve the application and have directed that it be refused! – signed by Crow, Manager, Barclays Bank, Gwelo.

"Shit! Not half as much as I bloody well regret it, the sods."

"So you can't sell the pick-up to Matt yet?"

"Not yet, but I'll get approval in the end. Next option is to write to the Secretary of Mines, a real heartbreaking, desperate tear-jerker letter, pleading for the sale to be approved; otherwise, our mine will go under, and my family will be distraught, and we'll be left penniless, begging in the streets of Bulawayo… And perhaps I should add… and the only time my kids will taste fresh meat is when they *accidentally bite their tongues*! *Yebo, that* should do it." I chuckled, and we laughed away the disappointment.

After the appointment with the doctor, who cleared Jeffrey completely, the four of us left in the beige pick-up to visit Des and Irene. We would have to come back up to Gwelo in a week or so when the gears of the grey pick-up had been fixed, and Marianne could drive it back to the mine on her own.

Saturday at Des and Irene's made us forget all our woes and worries.

Well, have you ever been treated like royalty, waited on hand and foot, your every request being granted… meet King Jeffrey! He was being spoilt rotten by Irene and enjoying every minute.

Marianne and I had a wonderful time too, really enjoyable, humorous conversations, lekker snacks, and, later, we braaied well into the evening….

About 1am, Jeffrey was still trying to put off the inevitable. "But it's far too early to go to bed!"

Until Irene finally coaxed him, by a whispered promise in his ear: "Tomorrow we'll have a picnic lunch by the dam!"

. . .

Oh, to be woken up with bright sunshine streaming through the open windows once again – unbelievably nice. Hot sun, so you could sit outside on the terrace in just a pair of shorts, drinking a wake-up cup of coffee.

They had a wonderful ranch house, something like the one we would build on the mine – later!

Jeffrey sat on Des' lap as he drove the tractor around his ranch, towing the ladies and myself in an old wooden cart, an ox wagon – the one that his father had trekked up from South Africa in the early part of this century.

Irene had brought a picnic lunch, which she laid out on a blanket under some huge trees close to one of their small dams; an ideal setting.

Lucky too that we had brought our own waiter with us, Jeffrey, who merrily went from person to person, flipping the caps off their beers and chuckling away to himself.

It was difficult to imagine that this healthy, happy, rushing-around child was, just one week ago, a wheezing, coughing, gasping for breath, pale, pasty little boy – kids can recuperate so quickly! The doctor had, in fact, told me that if a feverish child had a temperature of 105, he was not unduly concerned; it would be back to normal the following day, but, if his wife had a temperature of 100, he would panic!

Dusk was beginning to descend, so we headed back to the ranch house – we had to leave for the mine, unfortunately.

We'd had a fabulous weekend with them and had invited them over to our mine for a meal in the near future. Des and I would fix a date the next time we met up in Bulawayo.

It wasn't long after leaving their ranch that I had to switch on my headlights full beam; it was getting very dark very quickly.

We drove past Fort Rixon on the road to the mine.

We were in a good mood, singing nursery rhymes to help keep us awake; it had been an energy sapping weekend.

"Let's play the rabbit counting game, shall we… Shit!"

Suddenly, in my headlights, a huge truck loomed, coming straight for us!

As I started braking like hell, I realised that this truck was not even moving – it was stuck in the road without any lights on, leaning at an angle!

I got out of the pick-up and went and looked up at the driver's cab; there was no one inside!

In the shadowy darkness, I could see that there was another vehicle behind, also leaning at an angle, sunk in the main Fort Rixon-Fibabusi murram road!

And from this lorry there were sounds of raucous laughter!

I walked towards it and read the advert on the side of the lorry – 'Castle Beer'!

I climbed upon the step of the cab and banged on the window – the laughter immediately stopped and the window was wound down.

"Sorry Boss, we're stuck in the road! Have a beer!"

The driver climbed down and explained to me what had happened.

The Castle lorry was on a delivery run when it had a puncture and slid into the softer mud on the edge of the murram road, and sank up to the axles.

He had radioed for help, and the horse (a towing lorry consisting of only the cab with a powerful engine) had come out to their rescue.

After several attempts to free the stricken Castle lorry, the horse itself got bogged down in the murram road. He radioed again and was told that yet another horse would be out with a crew to help them in the morning – so they decided to party!

I checked the road, but there was no space to drive past these two stricken lorries.

The driver then told me that a Jeep had passed by half an hour earlier, and gone around them by driving up on the side of the bank.

I checked this out too and the ground felt quite firm, so I decided to give it a go.

We slowly drove along the bank at an angle, passing the stricken horse.... It was going well when the right front wheel nudged forcibly against a rock, causing my pick-up to slide down the wet bank into the road, whereupon it sank in the soft, sandy edge! Shit!

So what do you do? Your vehicle is sunk in the road, with the wife and two small children squeezed into the cab, and it's pitch-black dark – no street lights out here, and it's getting late, past 8 o'clock at night now! Not much chance of a passing vehicle coming to our rescue before the next day dawned!

The hours passed by, and then, just before midnight, I saw some headlights approaching from the Fort Rixon direction, and a vehicle pulled up behind us.

And who was the knight in shining armour? None other than Policeman Pete!

"Wooh! Hey you unlucky ones, what are you doing out here in the middle of the night! Got nothing else better to do?"

He went on to explain that the African driver had radioed their Castle Brewery office and told them about this young family stranded in a pick-up, which had also become stuck in the road.

The office had phoned the Fort Rixon Police Post, and Peter, in his pyjamas – only joking! – had come to the rescue.

I went up to the cab of the Castle lorry; it was so quiet.

I opened the door and saw four drunken Africans out for the count, sprawled over each other on the seat, their limbs like spaghetti on a plate!

I shook one of them, but he didn't even stir.

Nevertheless, I thanked them all, and took three bottles of beer from a crate.

Back in the police Land Rover, where the kids and Marianne were nicely cuddled up on the rear seat, I produced the three bottles of Castle.

That lovely 'phuts' sound rang through the still night air – three times, as the caps popped off the bottles, and Peter, Marianne and I toasted each other to even better days, and slowly drank the refreshing liquid as we drove on towards Des and Irene's place.

As we pulled up in front of the ranch house, the lights immediately came on, illuminating the police Land Rover and the whole area in front of the terrace.

Des came out of the darkness down the steps, his shotgun by his side.

When we all climbed out of the police Land Rover, he gasped, "What's happened? Did you have an accident? Are you all okay… you don't look injured?"

"Des, we're fine; our pick-up got stuck in the muddy road and Peter came to our rescue. But it's a long story, and can we stay another night?"

"Of course; come inside!" he exclaimed.

Irene put the kids to bed, while Des insisted that the knight in shining armour and his rescued princess had a drink – and we all relaxed, musing over this quite bizarre incident!

"Well, that's certainly another 'first' for you!" Peter exclaimed as he got up to leave. "What next?"

We all laughed. Peter left and the rest of us went wearily to our beds.

. . .

The next morning, we all piled into his Jeep and Des drove us to the accident spot, where we were treated to an amazing sight.

Another, even bigger and more powerful-looking horse with a lifting crane had been busy.

The stranded horse and the Castle beer lorry had been extracted from their muddy grave, and were lined up neatly in a row behind each other, on solid murram ground.

And the horse with the crane was plucking my pick-up out of the mud and setting it down just past the churned-up part of the road, giving us a clear run home to the mine.

I thanked everybody, and said I'd be coming back shortly with a pick-up full of rocks and stones. The road had to be patched up; it was dangerous left as it was….

I returned with some mine workers with picks and shovels, and they started helping the drivers and the other Africans to repair the badly churned-up murram road, which was beginning to dry out quickly, leaving deep ruts that were already hardening in the hot sun.

Hopefully, the whole road would be fit for heavy traffic again soon – like a Shell lorry!

However, that thought was quickly dashed.

One of the drivers made a demonstration for me.

He took a wheel-changing brace, put it on a firm part of the murram surface and hit it several times with a mallet – the brace sank in, breaking the surface, and black mud oozed from the resulting hole.

"Jesus!" I cried out. "No wonder the Shell lorry driver won't deliver diesel fuel to our mine with the road in this condition!"

I was amazed, flabbergasted!

The road looked dry and hard, but obviously in places where it crosses some soft black-ven ground, once the crust is broken, you just sink up to your axles, whether you are in a heavy truck or driving a small pick-up like us! Unbelievable!

Well, I guess we are going to have to be patient with regard to the diesel delivery, I thought. A further setback, a week, two weeks? And there was nothing we could do but wait!

When the Castle lorry and the two rescue towing trucks started up their roaring engines, we hooted and honked as we waved farewell to each other, and headed off in different directions.

I arrived back at the house and was feeling pretty knackered, but, as I got out, Marianne exclaimed in a bubbly voice as she approached the vehicle, "Hey, that's really nice of them, so they gave you a present. Look!"

And there, in the back of my pick-up, was a whole crate of Castle beer.

People never cease to amaze me, and we *'Castled' and 'Castled'*... until we couldn't keep our eyes – or mouths – open any longer!

Part IV - The Golden Days

That was a most unusual, and a very tiring long weekend.

You could call it a 'that's life' sandwich! A rather harrowing uncomfortable six hours spent in the dark at night in the bush, stranded in our pick-up sunk in the dirt road, which turned out to be the filling between two wonderful enjoyable nights of hospitality provided by our new friends, Des and Irene, at their ranch!

After a quick cuppa tea, I left for an early morning meeting in Bulawayo, taking the Fort Rixon road. When I came across our accident spot, I thrust my foot down on the accelerator pedal – a diesel pick-up doesn't accelerate like a petrol vehicle, not like a sprinter. It slowly builds up latent power and then rumbles on like a huge second-row rugby player – unstoppable!

The pick-up bounced around, but powered on over the patched-up road, which was still extremely rough. I don't think any vehicles had been on this stretch of the road since the Castle beer lorry episode the previous night.

The journey passed by quickly, my thoughts pondering the justifications section of our establishment loan application.

Eagerly, I climbed the stairs to the mining commissioner's office for our arranged meeting.

"Good morning, I'm afraid he's not in this morning," his secretary said. "He apologises for the inconvenience, but he had to go to Salisbury at the last minute and will only be back at the weekend. Can we make another appointment?"

"Is he free next Monday?" I enquired as she opened a large maroon leather diary that revealed that he was indeed free, and she pencilled in 'Ridge Top Mine' in the vacant 10am slot.

Well, that was a disappointing start to the day; I wanted to go through the application with him in detail – there's no point just handing it in! This loan document had to be 100% correct, and I needed to gauge from his reactions as he read the justifying circumstances whether they were convincing enough for us to get the loan.

With all the delays we'd suffered over the last six weeks, what was a few more days to ensure we had the best chance of securing the cash!

At K.B. Davies, I joined Ray and Joseph in Mr French's office, and we were treated to a full presentation by Mr Newmarch, who referred to technical diagrams when answering our questions.

Ray was very satisfied, and said he had worked with ball mills in the past on a large mine and Newmarch's scaled-down version for small workers looked a good option, having a throughput of 30 to 40 tons of ore per day.

When Mr French assured us that the first production model could be ready and installed on our mine within five weeks from the order, the three of us agreed that this was the milling answer – we couldn't go on week after disappointing week chasing 'dubious-condition' 5-stamp mills all over the country!

We shook hands on the deal and agreed that Newmarch would come out to our mine on Thursday with a fully detailed official K.B. Davies quote.

He'd spend the whole day with us, checking on the best site for the ball mill and what we needed to prepare prior to the delivery and installation in five weeks' time.

It would then take a further week connecting up and testing at the ball mill site to ensure the harmonious integration of the ancillary items in the ore-to-gold production line – namely the hopper, auto-conveyor systems to feed the mill and the gold extraction room.

"By the end of February, we'll be ready to rock 'n roll!" Joseph shouted excitedly.

"Hopefully 'spin 'n crush' would be more desirable!" I added, smiling. "We wouldn't want to watch the mill rocking from side to side and rolling away down the hill, and far, far away!"

. . .

"That sounds really good news!" Marianne exclaimed. "So by the end of February you'll be able to make me a very large gold ring!"

"And golden earrings for me?" Marie-Louise chirped.

Elliot brought over a pot of tea and we sat outside in the warm sunshine of the late afternoon.

Suddenly, there was a loud crashing noise, and Crispin appeared out of the bush behind us.

"I hope I didn't startle you! But it's quicker through the bush than using the road. We have a serious problem, sir; Tachibona's wife is about to kick against the bucket!" he stated anxiously, and looked really shocked when Marianne and I burst out laughing!

"Sorry for laughing, Crispin, but the saying is 'she's kicked the bucket' when someone dies!"

He carried on earnestly and told us she had severe stomach pains and was coughing up blood!

"God, Crispin! We'd better move fast. Let's drive over to the village straight away, collect her and rush her to the Shangani Hospital. Marianne, we'll leave the kids here with Elliot and Judith and you can drive the pick-up – I'll be your navigator when we get to that bad 'Castle beer' bumpy patch on the road!"

We pulled up outside the hut and the woman was carefully loaded into the back of the pick-up. Naturally, Tachibona wanted to come with her, when he could also check with a doctor why he was still having pain with his jaw and one of his broken teeth – from being attacked and hit across the face with a knobkerrie in that fateful 'gang of five' fight, which had resulted in the stabbing to death of Phillemon!

Two other munts also wanted to go over to the hospital – if there's room and no supplies to collect, we take them, no problems.

Marianne's clutch control practising proved perfect! We crossed a flowing donga stream and gently climbed up the rise of the opposite bank – our patient didn't feel a thing.

And that bad patch on the road had been filled in and flattened, probably by the nearby Rancher Ashburner, so even driving over that fateful spot was silky smooth for our patient in the back!

It was dark by the time we were ready to leave the hospital.

Tachibona's wife had been admitted and he was going to stay the night as well.

After filling in the hospital paperwork, I came out to find that the pick-up had been moved from its nose-in parking spot and a triumphant-looking Marianne was sitting in the driver's seat ready to drive us home.

"That's fantastic!" I exclaimed. "And no bunny-hopping as you reversed out from the parking?"

"Well…" She laughed. "Do you know, actually I'd never used the reverse gear before. I didn't know how to work it, so I called over to an ambulance driver and asked if he could come and check, because I thought the reverse gear was broken. He got in, revved up and reversed it, and said 'I think it was jammed, madam, but it's okay now'."

We were still chuckling over this incident as a grinning Marianne put it in first gear and we set off smoothly, heading for the mine, for home.

. . .

Newmarch pulled up in an old well-used Peugeot 403, which had more dents and rust spots than original paint work.

He was wearing old faded 'round' trousers – ones that had been worn for many years without an ironed-crease in them – a jacket with pockets bulging with metal items that jangled as he walked, and a dusty brown Trilby hat – 'a la' Frank Sinatra!

Joseph joined us and we sat in the reception hut going through the K.B.

Davies ball mill quote.

We could choose between several options, but we settled on:

The five-foot diameter drum, 30HP ball mill, working with two thirds of a ton of metal balls, and having a throughput of 30 to 40 tons of ore per 24-hour working day.

We would place a firm order with Mr French at K.B. Davies the following day.

Newmarch asked us to show him around the claims so that he could make suggestions on the layout for the working area of the mine.

We walked down the slope leading from the mine shaft and surveyed the ground – an area of about 100 square metres, which still needed to be totally cleared of everything, from thorn bushes to rocks and large stones.

"You need to lay a railway track from the headgear next to the shaft for a distance of approximately 60 metres, down to this spot where we are now standing. It is quite a slope too. An embankment will have to be built in order to have a level rail track so that the cocopans, with a capacity of one ton of ore, can be pushed easily by the boys along the rails from the mine to the mill site, where the ore would be tipped into a hopper, to be auto-fed by an eight-foot conveyor belt system into the mouth of the ball mill crusher. The mill, conveyor systems and an extraction table room will stand on a 20 foot by 20 foot square concrete slab – a raised reinforced four-inch pad, with a one-inch slope for drainage and washing purposes."

"That's the size of the inside of my house!" I exclaimed, "Lucky we don't have to scour the country again for enough corrugated iron sheeting to cover this whole area."

"True, only the extraction room will need a roof," Newmarch continued, "but that concrete slab *must* be laid in one go – it'll take a gang of boys and two builders from dawn 'til dusk to complete, but the strength-spread of the reinforced slab depends on it being constructed in one day – not with sections being added on later. Electric cabling will be laid to a separate switchboard for powering the mill, conveyor, pumps and James Table.

"Water will be pumped from the water tanks near the office through plastic piping into the mill.

"And after the crushing process, water will flow, carrying all the fine sands and washing them over the James Table in the gold extraction room, and then running off the waste into the slimes dams. Gangs of lasher boys should start this mammoth task of building the railway embankment now; it will take hundreds and hundreds of wheelbarrows-full of soil and rocks, and you'll be busy for several weeks to complete it.

"Don't forget we're talking about an embankment that will be 60 metres long and three metres wide at the base, starting from ground level at the headgear and increasing in height to well over two and a half metres at the ball mill site – that's one hell of a lot of soil! And you'll need a Mines Department surveyor to come with a theodolite to carefully measure and certify your work for safety reasons."

After a full day's work, we sat down together in the reception hut.

Elliot had prepared some sandwiches and milky tea, making use of the traditional call-in gifts that Newmarch had kindly brought with him.

He was pleased with the proposed layout of the mining area, and would prepare some sketches and plans of:

The hopper size, the auto-conveyer system, the ball mill and the extraction table room.

We could collect these at K.B. Davies the next day when we were there to finalise the official sales contract agreement.

"Just being out here in the bush again rekindles some wonderful memories for me," he stated, and began to reminisce about the time he spent around Fort Rixon as a teenager, working for his father prospecting and mining for gold, initially near Shangani.

But, when his father became crippled with arthritis and could no longer continue with his passion for gold mining, Newmarch went to work on some of the larger established mines in this area.

"There were a whole string of maybe 50 gold mines stretching from Shangani to Filabusi. At night, as you drove along the road to Fort Rixon, there were odd patches of lights illuminating the mines and lighting up the stamp mills, whose thunderous noises filled the air as the small workers mined for gold throughout the night. It was an exciting time, vibrant, plenty of life, plenty of liquor and plenty of…"

He paused, then continued, smiling to himself. "Plenty of you know what! Gold and money attracted both men and women, but for different reasons! The Claremont mine from 1910 to 1915 was one of the hubs of this gold mining area, employing 30 white Europeans. It was a village far bigger than Fort Rixon is today, with houses for the families dotted on both sides of the dirt track – no luxurious graded murram road in those days, and when the heavy rains came – like we've experienced over the last few weeks – the ox wagons would struggle to get supplies through to the mines.

"Some of the small workers lived in tents, or shacks with tin roofs like yours; only the bosses had large brick-built houses. There was a nine-hole golf course; they held Gymkhanas and other social events; when occasionally a small worker miner would buy drinks for everyone to celebrate 'striking it rich/hitting the mother lode' – invariably from opening up a rich quartz vein showing visible gold, with values of up to 10 ounces to the ton of ore-bearing rocks! That was real money!

"Since the 1890s, hundreds of shafts have been sunk, most obscured today by the all-enveloping bush, as I'm sure you'll discover when you walk around here – and every shaft could tell a fascinating gold rush story. But, for every 10 you find, nine of them could tell of heartbreaking incidents, while only one of them made a man rich! And out of those rich men, most of them probably died in drunken poverty, and only a few enjoyed the full rewards of their labour!

"The lure of gold didn't bring much happiness to the majority of small workers; their obsession with gold gradually ate away at them, until they knew of nothing else. Well, young men, I wish you success, and hope you turn out to be two of the lucky few! After over 50 years of gold mining, my obsession for this precious metal has left me with literally only the clothes on my back, and my trusty old Peugeot 403. Although I am a mechanic by trade and an inventor, which I still enjoy, I actually have nothing, no family, and I live in a Red Cross shelter!"

And on that rather depressing note, Newmarch left… and drove down the road that he had probably travelled thousands of times over the last 50 years.

A sobering thought!

Joseph agreed to stay the night on the mine.

"We both have to be on time for that important meeting we have tomorrow; we can follow each other in our pick-ups to Bulawayo, to make sure!" Joseph stated emphatically.

Yes, Joseph, thankfully! I was about to suggest to him the very same idea, using the very same words.

I went back to the house, and, over several cups of coffee late into the night, I penned my very important letter to Mr Christie, Secretary of Mines.

It was well after midnight when I was finally satisfied that the letter had enough 'pulling' power, enough to get some action to hurry along this pick-up sale – we needed the money, now!

The Secretary of Mines,
Private Bag 7790,
Causeway, Salisbury.

Attention Mr Christie.

Dear Sir,

I immigrated to Rhodesia in November with the aim of starting Goldmining in the Fort Rixon, Matabeleland area, and as a means of bringing extra "Capital" with me, I purchased a second-hand Peugeot 404 Diesel pickup.

I obtained an Import licence, but with a two-year restriction on its sale.

I wrote to the Reserve Bank asking for this restriction to be lifted so that it could be sold, releasing badly needed cash for our Gold Mining operation.
Following 6 weeks of torrential rains, we have suffered severe flooding in our area which has damaged the local roads and tracks, preventing Mining equipment and Diesel fuel from being delivered to our Mine – we are bogged down and stuck in all senses of the words!

The Exchange Control replied, regretting that they are unable to approve my application and have directed that it should be refused!

I am now asking your help in lifting this restriction so that the Capital, lying dormant in my garage, can be put to work urgently to allow us to survive at this critical start-up time and helping us to become a Gold producer for the Rhodesian Government.

Yours faithfully, etc.
Ridge Top Mine.
cc Mining Commissioner, Bulawayo.

. . .

The next morning at K.B. Davies, Joseph and I sat apprehensively in Mr French's office.

When Newmarch arrived, French, Joseph and I all penned our signatures on the sale agreement, and chatted away whilst we waited for Ray to arrive.

We were already on our second cup of coffee before there was a phone call for Mr French, who relayed to us: "Ray has just told me that he has been delayed due to an unexpected urgent problem, but we should carry on without him.

He said if the sale agreement was signed by two directors of Ridge Top Mine, Joseph and you, that was sufficient; just 'pp' by his name on the documents!"

French was looking at me with a quizzical raising of his eyebrows, to which I replied with an embarrassed grin, hunching of the shoulders and a slow shaking of the head.

But the deal was done; Newmarch was ecstatic! Joseph could not stop smiling!

"We're on our way at last, partner!" he uttered triumphantly, and we went over to the Mines Department to tell them our good news.

Ronnie was very pleased to hear that we had ordered the Newmarch ball mill, to be delivered and installed by 28 February when we would be able to start producing the coveted gold metal.

He assured us that we could always count on back-up from the Mines Department in our future venture, and hoped it would turn out to be a winner. But, he cautioned us…

"However, mining is a gamble; very few become rich, but you can make a very good living from it these days as a small worker, now that the gold price stands at $100 to the ounce. A lot of the mines operated in this area when it was only $42 an ounce, but many had to close down because the costs became too high to keep on mining viably. But last year it shot up to two and a half times that value on the free market, so, with a small outfit of 50 to 60 workers like you're going to have, the odds are on your side.

"And if you read through this book, *The Geology of the Country around Fort Rixon and Shangani*, you'll get some valuable, accurate information from the Mines Department's official gold returns from over 100 mines, which have operated in the area, dating from the 1890s! You'll also notice from some of the names of the mines that many prospectors were adventurers who began their mining activities with hope and a prayer, and some were actually big game hunters like Henry Hartley, who, the story goes, came across ancient gold mine workings when an elephant that he was tracking through the bush and finally shot fell on top of an old mine shaft!

"Names like the Ivory Mine, the Adventurers' Mine, Dick's Luck Mine, the Cakewalk Mine, the Grand Slam Mine, the Great Hope Mine and many more. You can read it in my office, but unfortunately you can't take the book with you, but feel free to make notes, or even photocopies. And I'll get my secretary to bring you a large pot of black coffee!"

The book was most enlightening, and I noted down a few appropriate sections:

History of Gold mining* in the *Fort Rixon and Shangani areas

Mining for Gold has been carried out in these areas from ancient times, ***from 1000 BC****!*
Almost all the gold mines have been located on, or near the sites of ancient workings, some of which go down unusually deep. In the ***Nelly Extra Mine,*** *ancient fillings were found down to a depth of 150 feet on the incline …*

1894*. The first known pegging of claims in the area by Europeans, when the Nelly and Pioneer Reefs Gold Mining Company registered claims now known as the* ***Claremont Mine****.*

During the Native Matabele Rebellions in ***1896****, operations on that mine, and on the* ***Nelly 404*** *were suspended for two years, following the massacres of White Settlers and Miners.*

There was a steady increase in the ***1900s*** *of new mines opening in the* ***Fort Rixon area****, due to the extension of The Railway from South Africa, which provided an easy access for prospectors, and a quick way of transporting heavy mining machinery into the country – a stark contrast to the 1890s, when it took months of trekking with ox-wagons!*

After the boom times in the 1920s and early 1930s, the opening of new mines began to slow, but there was renewed activity again in ***1931*** *when Great Britain came off the gold standard, and the price of gold increased from £4.29 to £5.78. As a result of this 40% rise in the value of gold, within a few years, by* ***1936,*** *there were* ***32 mines working*** *simultaneously along the strikes in the* ***Fort Rixon and Shangani areas.***

However at the end of the Second World War in ***1945****, only 6 mines were operational, but The ex-Serviceman's Rehabilitation Scheme initiated by the Government, led to further reopening of some old mines, which however was short lived due to inefficient machinery and the lack of Electricity Supply Commission power to this region.*

The Gold Mining (Financial Assistance) Act of ***1963****, encouraged the reopening of some mines. Although* ***over 100 mines have declared gold outputs,*** *many of those that were no longer working were inaccessible, frequently the position of the workings could not be found.* *********

PRODUCTION of Gold *has been mainly from larger mines, among them being* ***The Claremont Mine*** *and* ***Nelly mines*** *– over 100,000 ounces of Gold were produced from these Mines.*
The book gave the mining history of gold production from ***three of the Mines on our Claims;***

The Claremont Mine, *first pegged in 1894, had shafts sunk down to the seventh level (700 feet). In 1910 a* ***15-stamp mill*** *was installed, capable of* ***crushing 3,000 tons*** *of ore per month!*

The Nelly 404, *also pegged in 1894, was established on ancient workings, and the mine is accessed from an inclined shaft down to the fourth level (400 feet).*

The Sirius Mine, *was reopened in* ***1931*** *with four shafts, and the main inclined shaft was sunk to 210 feet after the war. (Note, but we had only found one collapsed shaft though, whilst walking through the bush prospecting and trying to locate old workings on our claim area stretching over 2 miles.)* *********
The reef was lenticular, with narrow lenses of three to four feet in length, yielding values of gold from two, to an unbelievable ***ten ounces per ton****!*

"***Ten ounces of gold to the ton*** of ore! – *that's* what most prospectors searching for gold over the centuries have ***fantisised over!"*** Joseph commented excitedly. "However, a drive tunnel is two metres wide by two metres high, so the total amount of rocks that had to be blasted, mined and brought to the surface by a hoist to be crushed by the stamp mill could mean that the actual gold extracted would average out to be only four dwt – less than a quarter of an ounce per ton. Whereas the ancient miners used to burrow along small tunnels like rabbits, following these quartz lenses wherever they meandered to, and only took out ore that had visible gold in it."

"Do you know, Joseph," I remarked, "scanning through this book, there are a lot of similarities to our situation:

- Reopening some of the old mines, and mining on some of the same claims in the book too; the Claremont and the Nelly 404;
- When Great Britain came off the gold standard, and gold prices rose;
- The lack of electricity supply commission power to this region;
- The Gold Mining (Financial Assistance) Act of 1963.

"Several very uncanny similarities, Joseph; gold price suddenly increasing; no electricity!"

"You're right, and we are also applying for those financial assistance loans as well to help us get these old mines up and running – *if* we can get through all the numerous advisory boards and the red tape!" he exclaimed. "Which Mr Newmarch said was more difficult than getting gold out of the ground!"

With a lot more knowledge of our mines and a contract for the installation of the Newmarch ball mill by the end of February, Joseph and I felt much happier.

Having a phone on the mine and fuel being delivered to provide power would make us *ecstatic!*

. . .

Saturday morning administration with Crispin, and our usual end of the week duties.

I checked the attendance/wage book, and found that only two workers, Tabari and Fana Petros, both from Belingwe area, had still not returned from the Christmas break.

That wasn't too bad; I had feared far worse. I'd been told that some mines lose up to 25% of their regular workforce after the New Year break!

I went back to the house and sat in the shade under a big jacaranda tree.

Marianne and the kids had left already, with Elliot accompanying them; the kids loved to sit in the back of the pick-up and Elliot enjoyed the break from work to look after them.

They had taken my pick-up to go to Shangani to collect Tachibona, and hopefully his wife if she could be discharged – one could never be sure how seriously ill she was.

In the unusual peace and quietness, I took the opportunity to reply to a good friend of mine in South Africa called Dirk, who'd sent a Christmas card to the Hudson Road, Gwelo house address.

Ridge Top Mine (Pvt) Ltd

P.O. Fort Rixon. Rhodesia

Dear Dirk, *20th Jan*

Thanks, and I hope you and your family had an enjoyable Christmas too! Up here it was chaotic, but great fun with some Friends of ours from South Africa. We drove with all our furniture and belongings from Gwelo Town during heavy rainstorms, and moved into our big shed (as my wife calls it!) - on Christmas Eve, can you believe! There was no door, the roof leaked badly, we don't have power yet, only two hurricane lamps for light, no running water, and a 50 yard dash through the pouring rain to the long drop – an apt name for a toilet, don't you think!

Now that the rainy season is over, we hope things will start to improve for us. Flooding has caused havoc to the dirt roads and several Lorries had got bogged down - Shell still has not been able to deliver any diesel fuel to us – the life blood giving power and light to everything on the Mine. It's six bloody weeks since we placed the order for diesel!

Another huge problem has been getting a 5-stamp crushing mill in good working order. So we have signed up to be guinea pigs for a new Mill, called a 'Ball Crusher' – sounds rather painful, doesn't it! This will be delivered and installed on the Mine by the 28th February – we keep our fingers crossed!

You asked about snakes, perhaps to add to your live collection in your garden shed! I'll reply to you to let you know the ones that are more common in our area – An old Miner that called by the other day, told me there were more snakes than gold around here! Doubly disturbing news, eh!

Keep well

Directors: Ray Buffune (Managing) J.W. Bulgin Joseph Buffune

Rationing Robbery/Diesel Dilemmas

It was not only the rains and the flooded roads that were causing us 'diesel problems' – I had just received a letter that posed a threat to us running the crushing mill continuously for 24 hours a day.

Our original application for a diesel fuel allotment quota was based on:

A Gardner 6LW 85 HP alternator, with a consumption of four gallons per hour, 24 hours a day, which, converted from the old imperial to the metric system, was 3,300 litres per week.

However, this letter from a Mr Lightfoot, fuel rationing officer, Colway House, head office, advised us that, under the new diesel regulations to be imposed due to the UN oil embargo restrictions, our allotment had been cut by 33% to only 2,200 litres per week!

This was a maximum diesel allotment to be imposed, and, obviously, until we had the ball mill running, this new theoretical maximum limit would not affect us – if and when we actually, eventually, *ever* got a bloody diesel delivery!

But it would be a crippling blow when we were fully operational, limiting us to only two shifts per day instead of our planned three eight-hour shifts per day around-the-clock! Our mine could become borderline, maybe even non-profitable – a veritable calamity in the making!

Thus, I penned an urgent reply to Mr Lightfoot outlining these problems and requesting the full weekly diesel quota that we had applied for!

I was due to meet Lionel de Ziel at Shell on Monday, so I thought it would be a good idea to discuss the situation with him first, before posting my letter to Mr Lightfoot.

I was pondering this new unwelcome potential hiccup when the sound of a gently purring diesel engine alerted me to Marianne's return as she drove slowly through the acacia trees and bush along our 100-metre-long driveway from the main murram road.

I noticed that only Elliot and the other two munts were in the back of the pick-up, and, as Marianne, Marie-Louise and Jeffrey climbed out the cab, I called out, "What's happened; didn't you pick up Tachibona and his wife?"

Marie-Louise started crying and blurted, "We couldn't, could we! She was dead!"

And both she and Marianne started sobbing.

"Jesus! She passed away! Where's Tachibona?"

"He stayed at the hospital and said he wouldn't come back to work until he had sorted out the burial arrangements," Marianne added in a subdued voice – a sombre end to the day.

. . .

Joseph had told me at the meeting that the first and second gear selection problem on the grey pick-up had been fixed and he'd parked it in our garage at Hudson Road, so on Sunday we decided to drive to Gwelo to collect it and have lunch on the terrace of the Midland Hotel.

Having that extra pick-up running properly was good news.

Now that the rainy season had ended, we would be needing both 404s, as Marianne would have more daily errands to run – but hopefully not another tragic 'Tachibona-type' trip!

. . .

It was not 'rainy days and Mondays always get me down'… but sunshine, simply streaming through the open windows – yebo, those wet, damp nights were a thing of the past; we could sleep with the windows wide open again.

And it seemed that it was not only humans who were appreciating the new weather order.

We were quietly chatting over a cup of tea on the porch when we heard something moving through the bush at the far side of our garden, about 80 metres away.

We gazed intently in that direction, when, to our surprise, a large male baboon suddenly stepped out and onto the edge of the grass.

He gazed at us for a few seconds and then retreated, and we could hear the sounds of many baboons passing through the bush, just out of our sight.

"Well," Marianne whispered cheekily, "when we write to people in the future, we cannot say that our nearest neighbours are eight miles away!"

I decided to use the grey 404 to test out the gears fully, and left my beige one for Marianne to use.

The road to Bulawayo had dried out fast, and I had to get used to being covered in waves of dust again when a vehicle passed by from the opposite direction.

And I'd forgotten how quickly it warmed up in the driver's cab too, and sweat patches began to appear around my neck and armpits.

By the time I reached Bulawayo, the back of my shirt was soaking wet – a different kind of wet to the recent rain-drenched shirts I had become used to when dashing from the pick-up to a building for a meeting.

Mr de Ziel asked me to sit down; he had some news for me and said the shock might be too much! *Interesting*, I thought.

He had received a copy of the letter to us from the fuel rationing officer, and informed me that all new applications for diesel fuel had been similarly slashed by a third.

When I showed him the reply that I was intending to send to Mr Lightfoot, he made several suggestions, saying that we were in a chicken and egg situation.

"If you dispute the allocations," he told me, "it will just go backwards and forwards – it could be Easter before it's finalised, and in the meantime your mine will become high and dry!"

"It's already high and dry!" I quipped. "Not a drop of diesel to be seen!"

He laughed before continuing. "And I wouldn't be able to deliver any diesel to you until you accept this new quota allocation. So we'll make amendments to your letter stating that you agree to the cut down allocation, but ONLY TEMPORARILY – AND you stand by your original application for the full weekly amount and want this REVIEWED again with URGENCY. That way, even if they refuse it, you can still go to the appeals court to challenge them, but, of course, in the meantime Shell can deliver fuel to your mine."

"And do we have a firm date yet for our first diesel fuel delivery, something that I can plan to?"

"Yes. Now that the rains have ended, we should be able to clear our backlog by early next week, as well as fulfilling the normal deliveries. I'll get one 500 gallon (2,200 litres) fuel tank delivered next Friday and set up for you; it has enough capacity for your allocated weekly delivery, which I'll schedule for 4 February!"

"Allocated *temporary* delivery!" I remarked, with a contented grin.

"True, and we can install a second fuel tank on the mine when your *full* allocation is approved. So two weeks today you will get your first weekly delivery of Shell diesel fuel, and we can plan from there. Leave the letter with me; I'll add a note backing your claim and post it for you."

I thanked him for his help and ideas, did a hop and a skip, and went over to the Mines Department.

The mining commissioner showed me into his office and apologised for not being available the previous week, but he had been summoned to Salisbury unexpectedly to discuss the growing problem of the unavailability of trained staff due to army and police reservists' border duty commitments.

While he was there, however, he had spoken with head office about our potential application for an establishment loan, and was advised that confirmation of our mine's ore reserves would be necessary by taking fresh sampling surveys, as the ones on record were from the 1960s when R.J. Stewart ceased mining the claims.

Although we could argue that nothing had changed since then and no further mining had taken place, it would be mandatory to enclose fresh survey results to back up such an application.

Jesus, Joseph and Mary, I sighed as I gave the mining commissioner my filled-in establishment loan application forms, together with my back-up justifications for the loan.

He scanned the information quickly, and said, "I still would strongly advise you not to send this establishment loan application; it has very little chance of success and could take several months, time you can ill afford. Instead, it would be better to apply for a speculative loan. This is based on work done to develop the mine, work that you would be doing in any case, and it will range from 50% to 100% of the requested amount, to be repaid monthly on a similar arrangement to your equipment leasing agreements with the Mines Department. If you bring the speculative loan application forms in early next week, we can go through them, and I'll discuss it with my engineers and have it submitted by 4 February."

I met Ronnie downstairs in the Mines Yard.

"Do you need a wood stove?" he enquired.

"Yebo! That would be great! At present, the houseboy, Elliot, does most of the cooking on an open fire, but a wood stove would allow Marianne to cook oven dishes, and even make cakes and pies for the kids."

"Okay, well there is one available. Do you know where the RMS road delivery services 'drop off' point is? It's at the Altyre Trading Store, taking the fork going east at the Fort Rixon petrol station. Speak to the owner, Chris, and say I sent you. He was asking around in the pub on Saturday, saying that he had an old used wood stove that he traded in recently – it's up for grabs, and I thought of you. And it's free too!"

As I approached Fort Rixon on my way back home, there was still a couple of hours before it got dark, so I swung onto the road to the Altyre store.

What a nice change to drive along a different road, and I started whistling a tune that had been buzzing around in my head since I had heard it a few days earlier: *Take me Home, Country Roads* by that American country singer, *John Denver* – and I was really starting to feel completely at home in this Insiza-Fort Rixon part of the country.

I began singing at the top of my voice. "Take me home, country roads, to the place I belong…"

Then… *Bang!* Bummer! A bloody puncture!

I got the jack and the wheel brace out, and was busy cranking the brace to lift the pick-up higher off the ground so I could change the wheel when…

"Coo-ie, coo-ie! Help! Help!"

On turning around, I could tell that the words were emulating from a large pink 'blob' that appeared to be floating towards me down a track leading from a small farmhouse some 100 metres away.

The 'coo-ie, coo-ie' became louder and louder as a large European woman in a flowing bright pink nightie approached at full steam!

"Please come with me to the house; my husband is dead!" she shouted at me, panting away, gasping for air. "Please come, now!" And she turned and started running back along the track she'd just come down.

For such a large woman, she moved smoothly and quickly, and I had to jog fast to catch up with the lady in pink.

"In here, in here!" her panicky voice kept repeating as she opened the door and we entered.

In those split seconds, the sights and the smells of Pat's Hovel came back to me – *vividly*!

But, instead of the countless flies, the room was littered with empty bottles – not beer bottles, but bottles of 'Mother's Ruin' – gin!

"Over here quickly, look!" She pointed to a dishevelled-looking man slouched over the arm of a large leather chair with his head dangling!

'See! Oh my poor George, why did you die? Why did you leave me?" She sobbed hysterically. "Do something, please! Please!" she pleaded.

I felt his pulse – phew, he was still alive.

As I gently tried to lift his shoulders into a sitting position, he belched! A foul, gin-ridden belch!

"George is not dead!" I shouted at her. "He's only *dead* drunk!"

"Oh thank God, Doctor!" she gasped, emitting an intoxicating cloud, her breath also being laden with gin. "Is there a prescription that he needs to take regularly? And please, Doctor, stay for an afternoon cup of tea and my special fairy cakes."

I continued with her drunken charade, and replied, "I'd love to, but unfortunately I've got other sick patients to visit – a doctor's work is never done!"

And with her words, 'see you next visit then, Doctor', wafting on her inebriated breath, I made my escape and hurried down the track to look after my sick Peugeot patient!

The spare wheel was bolted on, and I continued on my way to the Altyre store.

There, with Chris' help, we loaded the amazingly heavy-for-its-size wood stove onto the back of my pick-up, and I headed home to the mine.

Marianne was so pleased with the free gift of a wood stove, and said it would certainly add to our range of meals, which at present was limited to stews and braais.

And she thought it would be a good idea to extend the porch and build an outdoor kitchen area where we could use this wood stove and also sit.

That idea of having the kitchen outside seemed a good one, because Chris had told me that, if we used soft wood, it could smoke like hell – advising me to use only hardwood to fuel the stove.

This solid-looking stove was made of cast iron and had two round hot plates on top for cooking, and a boat-shaped one for heating up a heavy 'cast iron' iron, which he'd also pointed out could be filled with red-hot charcoals – for remote-use ironing!

The oven part could hold a good size Pyrex dish, and I could already imagine the door opening, revealing a steaming hot shepherd's pie, which, as it was taken out, would release those wonderful appetising odours, which undoubtedly would be a nasal aperitif before a delicious nosh!

. . .

Joseph arrived at the mine around 11am transporting a huge water tank, which had been delicately balanced on the back of his pick-up, protruding out on both sides and from the back.

Many ropes criss-crossed over the water tank and were securely tied to the handrails on the sides of the pick-up to hold it in place.

"Morning," Joseph cheerily called out. "That was a trip and a half! It's taken me almost twice as long as normal to get here from Gwelo. I'm parched; I need a drink. Could you call Elliot to make me a pot of tea?"

He drove over to the large dry-stone base that had been built for the water tank and set about organising some workers to unload it.

I joined him later in the reception hut and updated him on the previous day's meetings in Bulawayo at the Shell depot and the Mines Department.

"Well, at least we've got a firm date for the installation of a fuel tank, and for our first delivery of diesel!" he said with enthusiasm. "And I guess a third cut in our approved diesel quota won't affect us in the short term, and that's good advice from Shell to pursue the matter further, right up to the appeals court if necessary. I'm sure they wouldn't turn us down once we are running a working, producing gold mine 24 hours a day. And the mining commissioner knows how the mine loan/grants system works, so if he advises us to go for the speculative loan instead of the establishment loan, let's go ahead with that."

"Okay Joseph, but there's quite a lot of information they require for the speculative loan, and we need to submit some development plans as well. I think you should drive down to Belingwe and discuss it with our MD this evening – this is exactly the mining/technical help that he promised us – first of all for free as part of your 'financial contribution' to our partnership, and then for the 10% of our mine that he grabbed from us!"

"Yes, I wasn't happy with that either; he always wants to control everything, and everybody! Let me leave for Belingwe now, and I'll meet you back here at the mine early tomorrow morning with his suggestions."

He jumped into his pick-up and raced off!

Suddenly, there was a loud squeal of brakes and the brake lights glowed 'hot' red as his vehicle slid to a halt.

He reversed quickly to where I was standing, stopped, thrust some letters into my hand, and, as he drove off again, he called out, "Sorry, forgot. Post from Hudson Road!"

Marianne had taken the kids to visit Jeanette Schur in that big, historical house set in a beautiful oasis – I still remember that place distinctly; that garden patch of wonderful colours contrasting spectacularly with the surrounding dry brown bush.

I asked Elliot to make me coffee and sat outside on the porch, placing the letters on my office desk – an emptied packing case.

I stared at one of them, a letter from Post & Telephones, Shangani – *at last, a definite date for the phone installations*, I thought. Wrong, oh so wrong!

They wished to inform me that the file for Ridge Top Mine had been misplaced, and would I make a fresh application on the enclosed forms!

Ph-Ph-Phones were driving me mad!

"*Jesus!* First it was phree weeks, then a phurther phree weeks! And now the f-f-file cannot be f-f-found!" I called out in despair, looking to the heavens! "Is there anyone up there!"

But, only one phing to do!

I revved up my Peugeot, banged it into first gear and almost did a wheelie down the track, just avoiding hitting a small duiker buck that shot across in front of me!

Our two dogs, Oliver and Nose, raced behind the pick-up along the murram road – two black streaks with dust swirling around them made a great picture, framed in the rear-view mirror.

The puppies were growing fast, but they weren't big enough or strong enough yet to sustain the pace for very long and soon dropped out of sight.

When I reached Shangani, I was sweating profusely; both my shirt and shorts were uncomfortably sticky and wet, and, as I pulled up outside the Shangani Telephone building and saw the closed doors, it dawned on me – it was lunchtime!

Nothing for it but to wait; this phone business had to be sorted out, here and now, *today!*

As luck would have it, their building was across the road from the Shangani Hotel.

Well, no point in sitting in the hot driver's cab of the 404 when I could be sitting in the cool shade on the terrace, admiring the view across the bush to the distant hills – and also admiring the light golden brown liquid that was rapidly emptying before my eyes from the pint glass as I tipped the beer down my open, parched throat… and, seconds later, I was looking through the thick glass bottom of the pint glass, which magnified the head and shoulders of a waiter standing in front of me!

"Was that good timing or what! Bring me another pint please."

I had more control over the second cold pint, which lasted about 20 minutes – slow, satisfying, savouring mouthfuls washing down some crunched-up cheese and onion crisps.

Ray, the barman, came over to chat with me, and I related my telephone problem to him.

"Oh yeah, were you dealing with Al, Al Swartz?" he enquired. "He went on six weeks border duty several days ago, and, like most companies and government departments, they are stretched pretty thin sometimes due to these call-ups, and we just have to bear with the delays and hold-ups. Come, I'll go with you and see Al's boss, Fred; perhaps he can help you."

Fred was sitting at his desk when we walked in.

He was in his 60s and had a bulbous body and a small head with a protruding nose and chin, and, as he craned his head forward, his long neck stretched out, showing old weathered hanging creases – which reminded me of a giant tortoise.

I smiled.

He smiled, although I'm sure it wasn't the same thing that I was smiling about!

He explained the position 'off the record' – obviously, he couldn't have put such reasons in a letter.

"I'm sorry, but we are so short of staff and Al's file on your mine has been misplaced. Do you have any copies of his diagrams, any details?"

"I've only got these scribbled notes, but it gives the distances from the main joint party line."

"Good!" he replied as he read them. "Now could you make do with only one phone for the time being? I see from your notes that the house phone is only 20 yards from the Jackson-Fort Rixon line. That would be far quicker to install than the office one at a distance of 620 yards, which would require erecting many telegraph poles and also permission to cross the Filabusi-Fort Rixon main road."

"I'll take that offer; a phone in our house will be a godsend! But, please don't tell me it's going to be *three weeks!*"

"No! I'll get onto it straight away, and, as I said, it'll be much simpler and, thus, a quicker installation than the proposed office phone. Let me check… I can schedule it for the end of next week; how does that sound? In fact, I'll come out there myself on the Saturday morning, 2 February."

"That would be great; we'll really be pleased to see you on Saturday. Thanks a lot, Fred, and your promise of a phone on the second is sweet *ringing* music to my ears!"

I was smiling to myself as I drove back to the mine.

On the open stretch of the murram road, my old friend 'Elliot the ostrich' kept me company for a few kilometres – it was wonderful to watch his long, strutting stride as he gracefully glided over the ground of the flat grassland savannah stretches.

His little eyes, in that rather small head of his on such a long neck, seemed to smile at me as he came to a halt, but he continued to watch me drive on further down the road.

Smiling? For sure, and I had reason to smile as well; the last few days had changed the landscape of our problems; prettier pictures were being painted, and the '**F**' word was changing from its rather unpleasant recent meaning into '**F**' for '**fantastic February**'!

Already on the new canvas, **f**irm dates were being etched in – new '**F**' dates:

1 February – **F**uel tank, delivered and installed by Shell.

2 February – '**F**one' installed at the house.

4 February – **F**irst delivery of diesel **F**uel!

As Joseph would say, '**flipping fabulous**'!

With these three **deliveries**, a whole multitude of awaiting tasks could at last be started and implemented on the mine; it was a real boost for us, which we badly needed after so many recent disappointments and delays.

And three letters, '**EWT**', representing the amenities and comforts that we take for granted when living in a city, would now highlight three welcome facilities that would greatly enhance our way of life out here in the bush, namely: **e**lectricity, **w**ater, **t**elephone!

On passing through Fort Rixon, I noticed the post 'stage coach' van was parked in front of the administration building, so I popped in to see Ian Davidson to check if there was any post, and to ask him when our PO Box could be available.

Unbelievably, he gave me the keys. I gave him the cash. He gave me a receipt. I shook his hand. We now had a **local post box address** as well – what an end to a truly wondrous day!

And, as I pushed on towards the mine, the sun was setting – and it seemed more glorious than ever.

"So tell me, how was your day?" Marianne asked.

"My mixed day?" I countered. "Well, it started off with a cruel letter from Shangani Telephone Department stating that they'd lost the file application for our phones on the mine, and we'd have to reapply all over again!"

"Oh no! That's unbelievable!" Marianne uttered, swallowing hard.

"But that bad news was too much to take, so I jumped in the pick-up straight away and drove to Shangani and spoke with the manager of the telephone engineers. Al Swartz is on border duty, and they had misplaced our file. Luckily, when this man, Fred, realised that our house was only 20 yards away from the Jackson party line, he promised that he would come himself on Saturday next week to install the phone in our house!"

"Then we can speak to Grandma and Granddad in England!" shrieked Marie-Louise excitedly. "We could ask them if . . ."

I continued, despite the interruptions. "And, you won't believe it, but on my way back I popped in to see Davidson at Fort Rixon, and he gave me these…. the keys to our post box! So Marianne, the phone will be installed at the house, which is actually better, because I'll be the only one using it most of the time, and it would only get misused at the mine office. And of course it's good news for you too. In future, if I'm going to be late or stay overnight at Gwelo or Belingwe, I'll be able to let you know, won't I?"

"Much better!" retorted Marianne. "And in an emergency, like if Jeffrey's bronchitis had become critical, I can always phone the hospital, or Peter at Fort Rixon Police, or Irene, or Jeanette; oh yes, so much better!" And she began smiling to herself.

"And to get our post box as well," I continued. "We're really going to be linked to the wicked outside world, as Ian Davidson always jokes. We can pick up the post daily; you can drive up there with the kids. It will make a break and you can arrange to pop in and see Peter, also his boss, Peter Ruck and his wife, who've got two small children the same ages as ours. Amazingly, Marianne, these last few days have seen a big easing in the main problems that have been hampering us, and, within a week, we should be celebrating.

“**Diesel fuel tanks** on the mine. So important to fuel the alternator to provide us with electricity for pumping water, powering the hoist and providing lighting for the mine buildings and our own house. **Water** – we will have our own water supply shortly, as soon as we are able to start pumping the water from the flooded mine into the huge water tank that Joseph brought to the mine this morning. This one is being installed near the office initially; later, we'll have a smaller one for the houses. Thus, **no more daily water runs** to Jackson's stream with 25-gallon drums on the back of our pick-ups!

“And **communications** we have the keys to the **post box**, so we won't have to rely on the sometimes-forgetful Postman Joseph – when he remembers to deliver the letters we get at the Hudson Road house in Gwelo! Plus the **phone**! That is definitely the item that's going to save me so much wasted time in driving to Fort Rixon and back just to phone or wait for a call. Not to mention the odd fruitless trip to Bulawayo for a meeting that a person has called off, but has no means of letting me know! And lastly, the best news of all!

“After chasing all over the country looking for that elusive second-hand 5-stamp mill in good working condition, we have now placed an order and signed an agreement for the delivery of a **brand-new ball mill**, which the K.B. Davies Company ensures us will be fully operational in six weeks; i.e. by the end of, wait for it – **F-F-February**! All in all, that means we're on our way at last, far less 'things to be done' whizzing around in my head at night – sleep will come so much easier!”

And it did.

. . .

Marianne told me during breakfast that they'd had a very enjoyable day with Jeanette, who had really spoilt the kids.

“Marie-Louise can already swim a few strokes, and she loved the swimming pool – a lot cleaner than the pools of muddy water that she'd been used to on the mine, but Jeffrey didn't like the water at all – it was too clean! He preferred playing, if that's the right word, with the two large Rhodesian ridgeback dogs – he only came up to their backs, but enjoyed stroking the raised furry mane that ran counter to the rest of the hair down their backs (from which the dogs get their name, ridgeback). But in the excitement of your news and all the happenings going on yesterday, I forgot to tell you that Jeanette invited us to come for a Sunday lunch at her house, and we should arrange a date with her next time we pass by.”

"Well, you'll be able to phone her soon to let her know!" I quipped. "And did she show you around her palace yesterday?"

"Yes, she did; it was quite breathtaking. Such wonderful high ceilings and so cool in there too.

"And the beautiful wooden panelling and the huge open-hearth fireplaces that you could actually sit in – it's given me a few ideas for our new block-built house that you're designing, like an open-hearth fireplace in the wall between the sunken lounge and the dining room. We'd be able to keep nice and warm next winter, even with the guti/misty weather. And we could also have a removable metal dividing plate for when only one room needed to be heated."

. . .

In front of the office, Crispin was talking to a stranger, a very tall, thin African who was waving a piece of paper in front of him.

"Sir, come over here, please; it's about Fana Petros, one of the workers who didn't return to the mine after the Christmas break. We'd heard he was in jail, remember? Best you read this letter from the court of Chief Maranda."

Chief Maranda sub office
P.O. Box 10, Nuanetsi.

Dear Sir,

To whom it may concern.

There is Nyamanza who is seeking FANA who ran away with someone's wife. And I admit him to search for FANA or PITROS and the Wife ANA NDLOVU.

Ndini Chief Maranda.

The handwritten letter had an official stamp of Chief Maranda's court, signed and dated 20 January – and on the back of the page was the same message, but written in Ndebele.

"Tell the messenger that Fana Petros did not return to work here, and we don't know where he is," I remarked.

"Sir, this is an official native court order; we must allow this man, Nyamanza, to search our village, and I'll escort him there to check in all the village huts, so that he can perform his duty, and report back to the chief that Fana Petros is no longer working for Ridge Top Mine."

Fana Petros was not the only one who didn't return on time – by midday, Joseph still hadn't turned up, so I thought I'd better drive to Fort Rixon and phone the mine in Belingwe to check if he was on his way.

"Boss Joseph has gone to Fort Victoria," the houseboy told me.

"Do you mean Fort Rixon?"

"No, Boss, Fort Victoria, past Shabane; the whole family went there yesterday!"

"Did they say when they'd be back?"

"Madam told me to have the lunch ready for 1 o'clock today."

"God, that elusive Scarlet Pimpernel!"

"Sorry, Boss, what?"

"Never mind, just leave a message for Joseph that I called. Thanks."

Time for a break.

I drove over to the Fort Rixon club, and, although it was closed, I managed to persuade the *askari*/barman to sell me a bottle of cold beer, and I ambled across the lawn down to the dam.

What a peaceful, tranquil setting, and I took off my boots and felt the water lapping over my toes as I meandered along the water's edge – birds were chirping away, and that grumpy cough-like burp of a bull frog, but not a human soul to be seen.

"What's this?" I said to myself as I looked down at a huge footprint, then another and another, the tracks leading to a very bushy thicket area about 50 yards away.

Woooh, hold your horses! My subconscious clicked in. *Get out of here quickly; those are footprints of a hippopotamus. Walk calmly, but quickly back the way you came to the pick-up.*

I was standing next to it sipping my beer and looking towards those bushes when a Jeep pulled up, and Trevor, Gayle's husband, got out.

"Hey, good to see you again; what are you doing here, apart from drinking that beer? I've just come to stock up the drinks in the club; perhaps you can help me. We take it in turns and this week I'm in the chair."

After unloading the crates of beer and boxes of spirits, Trevor took two cold ones and we sat down on the terrace.

"This is a nice job, and so relaxing when you've finished and can gaze across the dam, let your thoughts run wild and empty your mind! Cheers!"

"Cheers!" I replied. "I saw some hippopotamus tracks by the water's edge over there."

"Yeah, that's our old Henry the hippo; he's never caused any problems here, though – yet! But they are massive animals, up to 12 feet in length (4 m), and can weigh over three tons, the third largest animal after the elephant and the rhinoceros, and they are highly unpredictable too. You must steer clear of them; you never know with their temperament. They are even more volatile than the buffalo!

"You have to be very careful near lakes and dams, because the hippo comes out of the water to graze on the grass, especially after dark, and you must never, never ever get between a hippopotamus and the nearest water, because it triggers something off and they'll charge towards you, and… that could be your last view, staring into its cave of a mouth as its powerful jaws with four sword-like teeth perform precise amputation, or worse still, death! Their four canine teeth can be up to 45 cm in length, unbelievably almost half a metre each! Terrifying to think about, especially when compared to other dangerous wild predatory animals like the male lion, whose fangs are *only 5 cm long*! You're probably also not aware, but hippos kill *more* people in Africa, than any of the other wild animals!

"Last year, in fact, over on the other side of the lake where the river enters the dam, some Boy Scouts were camping, and in the night one of the Scouts came out of his tent and was walking away from the brightness of the campfire to relieve himself. Suddenly, he heard a thunderous noise and felt the ground trembling, and spun round to see a hippo in full flight charging towards him. The Scout sprinted off and ran for dear life, with the hippo gaining on him, but the Scout just made it to some large felled tree trunks, which he scampered up on top of. The hippo slowed, veered off and trotted towards the water and submerged.

"The Scout was very lucky that those tree trunks were so close by, as a hippo can easily outrun a human. Despite its stocky shape and short legs, it can run at a constant 30 km/hour compared to the likes of us, who at best can only sprint flat out for 100 metres or so! I reckon the Scouts learnt a valuable lesson that day. Hippos can be aggressive, not only in the rivers, but also when they are on land, and they will run for the water if startled or alarmed, and anything that gets in their way will be mowed down, humans included! Next time those Scouts will make sure they are not only well prepared, but also practise 'B-A' – '*be aware' of your surroundings*!" Trevor added, "And practise *very* hard for the athletics *sprint* badge!"

"Otherwise," I commented wryly, "it'll be 'B-P' – '*be prepared' to die!*"

We laughed, but it was a very serious matter! When you were in a wild animal's territory, whether of a buffalo, a leopard or a hippo, you have to be aware of their behaviour patterns and take all precautions to avoid confrontation, and have a back-up plan – preferably a weapon!

Back at the mine, there was still no sign of Joseph; he hadn't pitched up yet – how I looked forward to that phone in the house!

"Joseph hasn't come and we're out of boys' rations for tomorrow," Crispin informed me.

"Well, in case he doesn't appear on time, I'll send Marianne and the kids to Gwelo now to collect ration meat and beans, and they can also collect any post from the Gwelo house. I need to stay around here all day; I must see and speak to Joseph urgently."

After Marianne had left for Gwelo, there was nothing else urgent to do at the mine, so I thought I'd try to locate him by phoning Belingwe, and, if necessary, Matt.

I told Crispin that, if Joseph came this afternoon, he must wait at the mine until I got back from Fort Rixon, because we had to discuss and fully prepare our critical speculative loan application for the Monday morning meeting with the mining commissioner.

At the phone booth, a rare occurrence happened – I was put straight through to Belingwe, but, for all my troubles, I got just one short, sharp sentence.

"Joseph left after he'd had lunch with us; he should be there by now!" his mother curtly informed me, a conversation that lasted about five seconds flat!

I got into my vehicle and headed back to the mine yet again – for the second time today!

Jesus, all this wasted time trying to track down Joseph!

A few kilometres later, a vehicle approached me with lights flashing – it was Joseph!

"Crispin gave me your message, but I thought I'd save time if I drove to Fort Rixon to meet you; there's only one road, after all, isn't there!" he stated confidently.

"Let's go to the police station," I replied indignantly. "They'll let me use the interrogation room."

"Interrogation room! What do you think I've done wrong now! I only thought rather than wait at the mine I'd drive to Fort Rixon and maybe meet you on the way," he said agitatedly.

"No interrogation, Joseph; just a room where we can discuss and complete the speculative loan application – we can't do it here on the side of the road, can we?"

"Oh, I see; okay, I'll follow you," he replied meekly.

I introduced Joseph to Peter, who remarked, "Yes, I remember now; I met you very briefly several months ago when the two of you asked me for directions to the Claremont mine. Come in. You can use IR 2; it's got a large desk, but only one comfortable chair, of course – the rest are wooden benches for the prisoners!" he remarked with a grin, looking straight at Joseph.

Joseph started explaining why he hadn't come to our mine this morning as agreed.

He'd had to drive his mother and father to Fort Victoria to see an aunt who was not well.

"If there was a phone on the mine, I could have . . ."

I cut him short. "The phone is being installed at the house on Saturday next week. I was in Shangani on Tuesday and got a firm date from the engineering manager, who incidentally is coming out to the mine to supervise it himself. So in future you'll always be able to get hold of me at the mine, or at least leave a message! There'll be no more bloody lame excuses from you *anymore*!"

"Wonderful. Our own phone; that will stop a lot of misunderstandings, won't it!"

Somehow, Joseph manages to turn his unreliability into a sensible statement; I'm beginning to find that he plays the role of a scatty character in order to get away with his inconsistency and unpredictability.

I really must work out a way to monitor his movements; otherwise, when we were running three shifts, 24 hours a day, he wouldn't just be *'the Scarlet Pimpernel'* – he'd also be *'the bloody Invisible Man'!*

We went over the rough notes that Ray had made indicating the main developments of our mine and the terminology required for our application, but the whole application form, including the justification section, was still completely blank.

When I pointed this out to Joseph, he told me, "My father said it was better for you as mine manager to fill in the forms, including the diagrams and justifications, and sign them, because his handwriting is very bad and he always makes lots of mistakes!"

"So when did you actually sit down together and make these sketchy notes?"

"He was very busy and kept saying he'd do it later, and in the end he scribbled down these notes while we were waiting at the hospital to see my Aunt Agatha during visiting hours."

"Jesus! That's great; he really is pulling his weight and earning his 10%!" I said testily.

The interrogation over, Joseph left for Gwelo and I sat outside with Peter on the veranda.

"I remember saying to you when we first met and his old man was shouting at him and hooting the horn impatiently . . ."

"When you said good luck! And with those two, I'm sure you are going to need plenty of it!"

Finishing off Peter's sentence for him caused us both to laugh!

In the distance, we could see a vehicle approaching Fort Rixon, leaving the inevitable trail of swirling dust behind it.

"Isn't that Marianne driving that pick-up?" he enquired. He then added in a stern police voice, "Does she have a driving licence?"

A short silence and my smile gave the inquisitive policeman the answer.

"Ah, okay. What I suggest is that she takes a driving test tomorrow at our police station here in Fort Rixon. I've see her driving up and down these murram roads, and she looks quite confident.

There's no real problem on these local roads, but if she gets stopped in town, Gwelo or Bulawayo, she'll be in big trouble! Why not come at about 3 to 3:30 tomorrow afternoon for her driving exam, and afterwards we can have a braai and a few sundowners to celebrate!"

With the appointment made, my trusty stead carried me back to the mine.

"But I'll be too nervous!" Marianne said. "You know my English is not that good, and I find it so difficult to understand Peter's funny accent – if he spoke Dutch, there would be no problem."

"Aach man, don't worry; it's probably just a formality," I replied, trying to allay her fears.

We chatted away into the evening, with Marianne trying to answer the highway code questions, and some of her answers were sending me into fits of laughter – I could feel that Peter was going to have all his work and patience tested, tested to the full, as these two 'foreigners' battled to understand each other!

. . .

In the morning, I sorted through the post that Marianne had collected from Gwelo. One of the letters was a reply from Christie, Secretary of Mines:

Dear Sir, *ref; Sale of second-hand Peugeot Diesel Pickup.*

With reference to your letter, I sincerely regret that it is not competent for me to act unilaterally in this matter which you have already represented appropriately through your bank manager for consideration by the Reserve Bank.

In matters such as this the sole avenue available to you is to request your bank manager to re-present your application, reinforcing your need and the circumstances that the diesel truck, while being redundant to your own needs, is being denied to other interests while your mining operations continue to be inhibited by lack of finance.

It is hoped that your problems will be satisfactorily resolved in order that your contribution to the Gold mining economy need not be inhibited.

Yours faithfully,
R. Christie.
SECRETARY OF MINES.
cc; Mining Commissioner, Mines Department, Bulawayo.

What a well-constructed, informative reply, but not the answer that I was hoping for.

However, I would do as Christie suggested, and reapply through Crow, Barclays Bank, and I'd include a copy of Christie's letter – the content of which must surely carry some weight.

I immediately put pen to paper and crafted a suitable pushy letter to Crow.

I was not going to express my disappointment in such flowery, almost poetic language, and did not hide the fact that, after **eight letters** going backwards and forwards over the last two months like a series of unclear love letters, this lover was in no mood to take **no** for an answer – the matter **had to be laid**!

The next pressing matter, as also suggested by Christie, was to complete the speculative loan application, which took me the rest of the morning, but it had to be done thoroughly with convincing justifications – both clear and concise.

I would also enclose a copy of Christie's letter; every little bit helps!

Thoroughly drained of words and arguments, I needed a good break, so I was raring to go to Fort Rixon to enjoy a braai! A celebration, after Marianne had passed her driving test of course!

"Can I drive us there?" Marianne asked. "I think I need all the practise I can get, and if I have to sit next to you while you drive me there I'll be a sweaty bag of nerves!"

So the kids and I climbed on the back of the pick-up and Marianne drove off – smoothly.

We went via the post office so I could send the letter to Mr Crow of Barclays Bank – a crossbreed between demanding and begging – reapplying for clearance to sell the white Peugeot 404 pick-up.

I found it quite funny, Marianne driving the vehicle on her own into the police compound for the driving test – which would allow her to drive on her own if she passed!

We left her in the hot driver's seat, in both senses of the word, and went to sit in the cool shade on the veranda.

Policeman Pete went down to greet Marianne and climbed into the passenger seat.

The pick-up revved, not too loudly, and pulled off smoothly – that was a great start!

And we watched them disappear down the Altyre road.

Some 20 minutes later, a hooting, tooting Peugeot pick-up drove into the police compound and skidded to a halt!

"I passed!" shouted Marianne triumphantly as she ran towards the veranda. "The drinks are on me! Big ones too; am I thirsty!"

As we toasted to her success, Peter said that he was impressed – she had driven very well.

"It was only on the highway code section when I thought of not passing her…. It went like this:

"*'I'm going to ask you three simple questions. What do you do if you see a sign with a big arrow pointing to the left?'*

"*'Go left, of course!' Marianne stated.*

"*'And if a sign says STOP?'*

"*'You stop!' she answered cockily.*

"*'And on what side of the road do you drive on in Rhodesia?'*

"*'On the right!' answered Marianne promptly and emphatically.*

"*'On the right!' I exclaimed, surprised.*

"*'Er… yes,' Marianne continued. 'On the right side, which is the left side of the road, of course!' she added, laughing away to herself.*

"Well, I just couldn't keep a straight face and told her, '**You've passed**'!"

We laughed and chatted about the new driver of Fort Rixon as we walked over to Peter Ruck's house, where he was busy lighting a braai.

His wife called the nanny and told her to take all the children to the playroom, where she could entertain them and fill them up with milkshakes, cakes, chocolates and ice creams!

Marianne had such a large grin and we toasted to her – '**the only driver in Rhodesia who could drive both on the right side and the left side of the road at the same time**'!

I noticed some Scout regalia hanging on the wall and asked Peter if he was involved locally with the Scouting movement.

"Yes, we have over a dozen young teenagers from outlying farms and ranches in the Insiza District who meet every two weeks at the Fort Rixon club. Being in the bush, they love to go camping and my colleague teaches them how to track animals and enjoy learning about their habitat, together with detailed knowledge of firearms and their safe usage, and how to live off the land – all very necessary skills to learn in these troubled times! Their favourite place to camp is by the river where it enters the dam. There, they can swim and also catch fish, which they cook skewered on sticks over an open fire; makes quite a welcome change to game meat."

"Were they the Scouts involved in the dangerous incident with a hippo?" I asked him.

"Yes! And that was a close call too! But they all learnt an important lesson, and they certainly won't go out of the tents at night again. We were camping in big army tents around a campfire and there was a bucket in each tent for emergencies in the night. However, the youngster, Robin, was probably sleepy and just wandered outside for a pee – but, after a 50-yard sprint to the safety of some fallen tree trunks with a hippo breathing down his neck, he was wide awake! And still shaking too, even when we got him back to the tents. He had a very lucky escape that night!"

What an enjoyable evening with the two Policemen Peters, and we agreed to do the same again soon, and at our place.

Ruins

That was **the week** – it really was! Certainly the best week so far for our mining operations, and I fought against the automatic reaction to get up on hearing the 5:30am start gong, and just lay there for a while thinking about all the things that were finally happening; some even had agreed and confirmed dates!

As I thought of those words – ball mill, water tank, fuel tank, diesel delivery, telephone and PO Box – a smile spread across my face instead of the usual frustrated frown, and those words now had a beautiful-sounding ring to them.

Suffice it to say, I decided that enough was enough, and, after that busy rush-around week, a weekend off was called for – and well deserved too!

Elliot called out, "Good morning; tea is on the porch."

And, in no time at all, Marianne and I were sitting there discussing where we should go.

"The Zimbabwe ruins is the obvious choice!" Marianne said excitedly. "And it's a World Heritage site too, as famous as the Victoria Falls! When we drove close by on our way from Beitbridge up to your cousin, Michael's, place in

Salisbury, we said we would visit those famous ruins at the first opportunity."

"Good idea; it'll make a fabulous break for us, two days away from the mine! Let's wake up the kids straight away, get Elliot to pack some game meat and bread, etc. for braais, and go, go, go – it's a good three-hour drive from here!"

Our quickest way to get to the ruins was to bump our way down the road to Filabusi, turn onto the strip roads for a short distance and head for Fort Victoria.

From there, it was about 15 km to Lake Kyle, where we drove across the wall of the huge dam.

We called in at Lake Kyle Lodges, and booked a self-catering rondavel for the weekend.

The rooms looked very rustic, but comfortable, and we sat down for a bit of a rest, and some coffee and sandwiches.

The beds were draped with colourful Batik-style blankets, and several paintings adorned the walls, including a large panorama picture of the Zimbabwe ruins, with this text underneath:

"*The age old mystery riddle that had intrigued both archaeologists and visitors alike, a vanished civilisation which abruptly disappeared and left no record of a written language behind, which makes Great Zimbabwe one of the* ***truly lost civilizations of the world****, inspiring wild and romantic speculations linking it with the Queen of Sheba and King Solomon's Goldmines.*"

Well, that certainly inspired me to hurry us all up, and we eagerly made our way further south to the great Zimbabwe ruins.

I stepped out of the pick-up and scanned the vast area of stone buildings in front of me.

Absolutely astonishing! The only words I can think of to describe what we saw looking across a valley strewn with broken ruins, but dominated by a high-walled city, and we walked and walked until we were outside those high stone-built walls. But we still had to walk on further alongside those massive walls for about 100 metres before we found an opening.... It was then even more breathtaking when we were inside and walked between the outer wall and an inner wall along a narrow passage just wide enough for one person. I gazed up at the sheer stone walls that were maybe five to six times taller than myself!

I just had to take a photo of the kids – they looked like ants standing between two bricks! And with a huge tower rising even higher above those tall walls – a sight I'll never forget.

All this walking in the hot sun was very tiring, thirsty work and the two children with their short legs found it tough going, so we decided to call it a day and drove back to the lodge at Lake Kyle.

The kids had flaked out and we had to carry them from the pick-up and drop them in their beds.

That gave us time to sit outside and have a well-deserved drink and a braai – what a perfect end to a wonderful visit to one of the world's great historical sites, the mysterious Zimbabwe ruins.

As the sun went down, we sipped another sundowner as I flipped through the tourist booklet, noting one or two interesting facts:

Since UDI, the Unilateral Declaration of Independence from Britain in 1965, The Bird of Zimbabwe has featured on the new Flag of Rhodesia, replacing the British Union Jack…

In the valley below sits the Great Enclosure with almost a million hand trimmed granite blocks in its outer walls. The stonework is entirely without mortar, and the walls extend for over 800 metres.

A second wall, a metre inside the enclosure, forms a long, forbidding passage leading to the Conical Tower, which stands 11 metres high and with a base circumference of 17 metres – an outstanding and compelling feature, associated with fertility rituals…

. . .

We didn't wake up until almost midday; we were completely exhausted from all the walking in the hot sun exploring the Zimbabwe ruins, but what a day to remember!

I had planned to walk up the steep Ancient Ascent to 'The Acropolis' perched on top of massive granite rock hills; a guide had told me it had an even more breathtaking view of the Great Enclosure, but it would be too much on this short trip, and we decided to head for home.

After that wonderful break spent at the great Zimbabwe ruins, we thought it would be a good idea in a few weeks' time to visit the local, smaller Regina ruins and Dhlo Dhlo ruins, which were in close proximity to Fort Rixon, and to our mines.

Reading from the tourist guide, these formed part of a chain of dry stone-built fortified ruins, smaller 'zimbabwes', which stretched from the north-west of Rhodesia, hundreds of kilometres to the Mozambique coast.

Supposedly, they were forts built to protect the trade routes for gold and ivory in the 11th to 15th centuries, as they were always close to gold mining areas; areas that had been producing gold since the ancient workings in the time of the Phoenicians, circa 1000 BC.

What was really amazing was that these were the *only stone buildings* discovered by the early white pioneers and missionaries in the late 1800s – there were no other stone structures found at all! The only dwellings were the common mud huts and grass-roofed wooden huts that the African natives lived in.

So one can assume that they were built by an occupying civilisation of Rhodesia hundreds of years before, for the sole purpose of mining for gold. These established fortified stone-built settlements were for the occupying people to live in, and worship, whilst giving them protection and guarding their trade routes for handling gold, ivory and exotic animals.

Most archaeologists agree that the hundreds of African natives who worked in these gold mines must have lived outside of these 'zimbabwes', in huts in their villages; no evidence/remains of them were discovered inside the walled cities.

. . .

'Back to the grind' is an awful expression, but, following those glorious two days away from the mine, that's exactly what it felt like.

In Bulawayo, I met Joseph at the Lloyds Coffee House, where we went through the application and justification forms that I'd completed for the speculative loan, and we discussed what we should and should not say to the mining commissioner when we met him at 10 o'clock. He was such an unpredictable man and could be very annoying and frustrating at times, but hopefully it would be a quick few minutes' meeting like last time, which resulted in his approval to further our loan request.

Well, Lady Luck was on our side; not only did he commend our well-thought-out application, but he also made other suggestive arguments that we should use.

Then he flicked the friendly switch back into the normal civil servant position, and proceeded to bore us with another string of dates that our new speculative loan application would have to journey through!

"You must get the amended loan forms back to me by 4 February in order that they can be typed out and forwarded to the DAB advisory board by the 28th, and from there on to the MAB advisory board meeting in Salisbury at the end of March, for final approval…" He hesitated, and completely spoilt our enthusiastic mood by adding two little words, "*…or rejection!*"

The meeting only took a mere few minutes, but we would have to wait until April at the earliest to actually receive any money from that loan – i.e. *another three months* before it affected our cash flow, and money was getting tight!

Our monthly costs, including our Mines Department leasing agreements for equipment, were steadily rising, whereas a big fat zero still dominated the 'cash in' column in our books!

And that wasn't going to change drastically until we received some income from gold production – the earliest date for that was still at least six weeks away, assuming the Newmarch ball mill was successfully installed on our mine at the end of February, as promised.

Our other two irons in the fire were:

- Selling the compressor that was railed up from South Africa, for which we had applied to a finance company to do a lease-back agreement that would release the tied-up capital, and;

- Getting the approval to officially sell the white Peugeot 404 pick-up to Matt. He had already paid us a deposit for our 'special use' arrangement, but, when we had the go-ahead to sell, he could get a bank loan and settle fully with us – that would feed some welcome extra cash into our mine bank account.

Joseph headed back to Gwelo; he said Jane was not feeling well again and he'd have to take her back to the doctor.

Just one more thing to be done before I left Bulawayo – visit the plastic shop.

Martin Curtis had told me that their sample bags were much cheaper than buying them from the Mines Department.

I bought 600 Assay sample bags, costing $14 – that should keep us going for a few weeks.

I would set two sample boys on a *gwaza* straight away to sample the old dump by the Sirius mine shaft, and a further two to work on the Schist dump near the Nelly 404 shaft.

Curtis told me it would take two to three weeks to get the results back, giving us a very rough guide showing the dwts (penny weights) per ton of recoverable gold, and whether or not it would be worth it to process these waste dumps.

Both Cain and Matt had kept their mines running initially on the proceeds of the gold recovered from re-milling the old waste dumps, whilst they further developed their mines underground.

But the huge advantages they had were: a 5-stamp mill on-site, and diesel fuel to power their crushing mills – *from day one*!

We, on the other hand, were on about ***Day 101***, and still had no bloody diesel fuel or a crushing mill on our claims!

I arrived back at the house late in the afternoon and found Marianne and the kids sitting under our extended porch area drinking tea. Langton had built on an extra two metres; plenty of room to be used as the open kitchen/veranda, and it looked good too.

"By the way, Marianne, what's that unusual bird call I hear? It seems to be coming from that jacaranda tree over there."

"Ah, that's a surprise gift from the old Chief Mzee Feet. He brought two doves for us, and Langton made a wooden cage for them in the branches of that jacaranda tree. Feet said if we keep them locked in the cage and feed them for a couple of days, we can then leave the cage door open and they can come and go as they wish, and they won't fly away! They have such a soothing 'coo coo' calling sound; I really like it, and the kids do too. Well, I hope everyone is hungry; I've prepared a stew using our new wood stove in our new open kitchen! It makes such a change from cooking on an open fire, and it's going to be so handy here under cover when it's raining."

. . .

For the next two days, I based myself at the mine; there were so many manual jobs that needed to be started, and, of course, that meant closely supervised as well!

It was such a pleasant change not to have to drive each day, but to use Shanks's pony (London slang for walking); you certainly see and notice so much more when you're on foot.

Since Newmarch's visit to us the previous week, a gang of boys had been clearing every single solitary item that was lying around on the proposed site that we would use for our surface operations.

An area of some 10,000 square metres – 100 metres across in front of the office by 100 metres going down the sloping ground – had been stripped clean of rusted mining relics, natural bush and acacia trees. It had become transformed into a huge park, although there was little green grass, only patches dotted around on the predominately red-brown earth.

Armed with Newmarch's sketches and diagrams, Naison, Langton and I made use of the 30-metre tape measure to peg out the proposed 'gold-processing chain' of constructions, from the headgear at the Nelly 404 shaft entrance to the Gold extraction area, and through to the final stage, the cyanide extraction tanks.

Once we had completed that, I went and stood by the mine shaft entrance and, squinting at the scene of our day's labour, I could clearly picture how it would look when we were fully operational.

But looking is not enough, of course; we only had about five weeks to transform this empty area and make all the necessary sites and equipment ready, prior to the installation of the ball mill at the end of February.

The actual links in the surface operation processing chain were:

The alternator (house) to provide electricity through the main switchboard to drive the hoist (in its own building), cable-connected to a large bucket container on wheels, the skip, which, when full of rocks, would be winched up from underground by means of a cable passing around a large wheel at the top of the headgear construction. The rocks (ore) would be tipped into a huge hopper and used to fill the waiting cocopan.

The embankment, 60 metres of piled-up earth supporting a level rail track to enable the cocopan to be pushed to the ball mill site and emptied into another hopper, which would load the ore onto a conveyer belt system to be fed automatically into the mouth of the ball mill crusher.

Water would be pumped through piping down to the mill, which would operate from a separate switchboard linked by 80 metres (260 feet) of cabling to the alternator powering the whole ball mill complex, gold extraction tables, and pumps to pipe the watery waste to the two slimes dams, each approximately five metres in diameter.

The main initial task would be earth moving.

Digging out ground to make the slimes dams and using that earth to start building up the railway embankment – the major task – to which I assigned three gangs of four lasher boys each, and splitting this mammoth undertaking into three parts: digging and filling the wheelbarrows, wheeling and emptying the soil at the embankment area, and shovelling the earth to form the base of the embankment.

Two days flashed by. The workers beavered away under my supervision, swarming like ants across the site, shifting wheelbarrow after wheelbarrow full of soil and dumping this mass of earth and spreading it across the 60-metre by three-metre embankment area – but it hardly showed; it looked like a thin layer of chocolate icing on a cake!

It would certainly take them at least three weeks before we could begin the final stage of levelling the embankment and laying the rail tracks.

There was a lot of building work to be completed too; the alternator house, the hoist house, the gold extraction rooms and a bigger storeroom – these would need to be built from strong concrete blocks – not dagga bricks!

I would buy a block/brick former when I next went into town so we could make our own concrete blocks, 18" × 6" × 6" (inches), using a mixture of mine dump rubble, sand and cement.

Green Saviour

Thursday morning came and there was still no sign of Joseph. I had expected him to bring the meat and beans rations.

Nothing for it but to kill *three* birds with one stone – by going to Gwelo; see Joseph, collect the rations and check the post at the house.

Although we now had a post box at Fort Rixon, most of our letters-in-progress from the Mines Department, Customs, Immigration, banks and suppliers were sent to the No. 7 Hudson Road, Gwelo address still.

And of great importance to us at this moment was the anticipated letter from the leasing company with the agreements we needed to sign for the lease-back on our own green South African compressor. We had decided this was a much quicker way of raising capital than the difficult and time-consuming slog of trying to sell it.

This lease-back would immediately raise $3,000, so much needed to boost our ailing company bank account.

I arrived at No. 7 just as Joseph was reversing out of the driveway.

A stressed-looking Joseph and an ill-looking Jane told the story; their son in the carrycot on the front seat was the only healthy looking one of the three of them.

Jane had been suffering severe pains over the last few days, and he was about to take her to see the doctor again.

We agreed that after the doctor's appointment he would take her home and join me later at the Midland Hotel.

I let myself into the kitchen, made myself a strong black coffee and went through a pile of post.

Most of the letters in brown envelopes were from the Mine's Department, mainly administrative; protection notices concerning two of our eight claims that had to be renewed and paid for again and reissued as temporarily notices – we were not in a position yet to do any mine development work, and certainly *not being* able to protect these claims *with gold output production*!

That all still seemed so far away.

But there was one envelope that got my pulse racing. A stiff good-quality envelope embossed with a company logo – yebo, it was from the leasing company!

Dear Sirs,

Reference the C.O. Suisse Mobile Underground Fast Development Compressor

We have pleasure in confirming the attached Lease-back agreement with the Ridge Top Mine for the amount of $3,000.00.
Note; All three Directors must sign both original copies and return them to us, when we will Issue an Acceptance Advice and a cheque for $3,000.00 within 30 days.

Yours faithfully
FINCO
Branch Manager

It was so nice to have a warm, excited feeling after opening a letter – over the last few months, they had brought nothing but cold disappointment and more headaches!

I thought I'd better check all of the brown normally boring demand letters just in case there was something important; you can never know.

Well, bugger me, what a surprise; a letter from Crow of Barclays Bank.

We refer to your application for the sale of the Peugeot 404 Truck, and advise you that the Exchange Control have approved the sale very exceptionally.

Wow, the sob story had worked, after all, and lucky that I carried the documents for the white truck around with me. Now I could go straight to Matt; he would buy it officially and pay us TODAY – money going into the account; magic!

I ran to the pick-up, eager to get to the Midland Hotel and share the good news with Joseph.

A very concerned-looking Joseph came quietly and sat down next to me on the terrace.

"They still don't know what's causing Jane's problems. The birth went so easily, we both were so happy, but recently she has had excruciating pains in her lower regions; it's very worrying! I'm going to have to stay around here in Gwelo for the next few days until they find out what's wrong with her."

"Sure thing Joseph; you must be there for her. Health is the most important."

"And money is too!" Joseph blurted. "I know we are running out of money and desperately need to get the cash deals on either the second-hand white Peugeot 404 or the green South African compressor. All that capital we've got tied up in them still, and its four months now; it's so depressing!"

"*Well, perhaps this will cheer you up!*" I said with a smile as I pushed the FINCO lease-back agreement forms in front of him.

"But this says 'on condition that all three directors sign', and you know my father won't do that – yet again, he's screwing up one of our last chances of staying afloat!"

"Look Joseph, I've come to know your father's dodges well enough to have an alternative. See here, I also have agreed with the leasing company that our two signatures will be accepted if we use the grey 404 Peugeot as surety!" Then I said to him emphatically, **"Sign!"**

"Hallelujah!" he shouted. "Money; money; money! It feels like winning the jackpot! But that money will only be available in 30 days' time, so we're back to square one again – *no money*!"

"Another even better surprise for you, Joseph; read this other letter from Barclays Bank."

We refer to your application for the sale of the Peugeot 404 Truck, and advise you that the Exchange Control have approved the sale very exceptionally.

"*Hallelujah!*" he shouted again, this time even louder. "*Money; money; money!* Let me buy you a drink to celebrate our good news!"

So we happily clinked our glasses of beer. "Cheers Joseph!"

"Let me propose a toast. Cheers to you, the mine, and to us producing gold!" he enthused.

We downed the beers and I told Joseph that I'd pick up the boys' rations today, and if all was well with Jane he should come to the mine on Monday – the day of our very first diesel fuel delivery from Shell!

"And Joseph, what with the fuel tank coming on Friday and the telephone being installed on Saturday, this has the makings of a great weekend! Lots more celebration 'cheers' to come!"

He looked more buoyant now, and I felt that the proverbial ball had begun to roll!

I went to the reception desk and phoned Matt to tell him the good news.

"Stay right where you are; have a pint on me. I'll be there in 15 minutes." And he was!

We went through the documents – just to be sure, to be sure, as the Irish would say!

"Great, let's go to my bank right away. I'll sign the purchase forms and be able to give you a cheque there and then for the balance I owe on that white beauty 404!"

He came out of the manager's office with a smile on his face **and** a cheque in his hand, which I immediately took and went to stand in the cashier's queue.

The $1,000 cheque for the balance owed by Matt was safely deposited.

I walked jauntily over to the post office with our next source of income held tightly in my hand – the letter that would release another $3,000 of our tied-up capital.

The woman in the post office looked at me strangely when I kissed the envelope to the finance company, stuck on the stamps, and, smiling, pushed it back through the grill bars of the post office counter and said, "Fly like an angel into the bosom of our saviour!"

"Oh, is that a religious donation to our Lord and Saviour?" she asked deftly.

"No, not at all, Madam; it's a signed guarantee for a large donation coming my way from my saviour – the finance company!" I joked, and left her looking a little bewildered.

Time to load the rations, buy some fresh bread and milk and head for home, but with a very good feeling now that some capital money was *finally* being released from the equipment that we had brought up into Rhodesia.

. . .

I was at the office first thing to check on the progress of the earth-moving *gwazas*.

The slimes dams had been dug to a depth of one metre and the earth ferried to the embankment site, but it had not made any impression at all – only 'marking out' the 60-metre by three-metre base. There would be hundreds more wheelbarrows-full of soil needed to build it up to the required height and the earth would have to come from another site; we couldn't strip off the surface of our mining site in case the rains came back!

I told Staff to find an area that was not too heavily populated with thorn bushes, where earth could be dug easily and as close to the embankment site as possible.

I started walking back to the house for breakfast when I saw a vehicle approaching – it was a Shell lorry delivering the diesel fuel tank – at last!

"Staff," I called out, "get them to set up the tank at the place we marked out, and bring the delivery note to me at the house when they have finished erecting it."

I was only part-way through my breakfast when Crispin came walking down the driveway with the Shell driver.

"Here sir," he said. "Sign these; it's been erected at the correct place, so they can go."

That was that! Shit, it was two months late - I paid for it back in December!

But oh, what an important piece of the jigsaw puzzle too, which would open the floodgates and allow everything else to begin in earnest – diesel delivery on Monday, power, electricity and water; what rich, wonderful-sounding words.

Crispin joined us for coffee and was keen to hear that I wanted him to give me Ndebele language lessons each morning around this time.

He could use chalk on the kids' blackboard and easel to help instruct me and I would make notes.

Although I could get my message across to the workers with my limited vocabulary and a dozen or so phrases, I wanted to get a real grip on the language so I wouldn't have to get either Crispin or Staff involved so often when it came to the more complex situations.

And it would be nice to add another language to my CV – English, Dutch, German and Afrikaans. I'd become Quin-lingual (five languages) – sounds like swearing!

"Well Marianne, that was one important delivery and successful installation; now I am looking forward to the phone being connected tomorrow, then we can really celebrate!"

"And I'll try making a rice pudding for the kids using the wood stove oven for the first time."

Whilst they were busy with that, I decided to go to the mine, walking through the bush for a change to get a bit of fresh air.

Suddenly, something caught my eye, something white, poking out just above the acacia trees.

I stopped, picked my way carefully through the thorn bushes and could see a concrete memorial surrounded by a stone wall.

The memorial was about 10-foot tall, like a fat white pencil pointing to the heavens, and there was an inscription to the members of the Cunningham family and others who were killed in the Matabele rebellion in March 1896.

Ben Bester had mentioned that some miners and settlers were massacred last century in the Fort Rixon area, but I was surprised to find this memorial barely 300 metres from our house, and on our mining claims too!

A shudder and a cold chill ran down my spine as I read the plaque, which listed the names of the whole Cunningham family, ranging in ages from the father and mother, their grown-up children, down to three grandchildren, all bludgeoned to death.

I began to think about the tough times and hardships those early white pioneer settlers and miners went through in the 1890s.

Today, we have things so much easier, but we still bitch about this delivery being delayed, that murram road being too bumpy… but **they** lived where there were no roads, just bush, and they faced imminent danger daily from wild lions, leopards and elephants, together with the marauding armed and rebelling natives who were roaming in this area from their main Ndebele kraals at a place called Matopas, south of Bulawayo.

Déjà vu! Today, we had to be aware too of the current threat of the black Mugabe terrorists, especially the white ranchers and farmers and their families who lived in the remoter areas closer to the border. They bore the brunt and faced daily threats from Mugabe's insurgent guerrilla fighters who were based in neighbouring Mozambique.

I stood quietly for a moment with my eyes closed, and could picture the images (or ghosts!) of those hardy settlers as they were battered and smashed to death, no mercy shown!

It was then that I got this strange feeling that I was being watched and opened my eyes wide to be sure that I was actually awake and not daydreaming.

All of a sudden, I saw this black African face peering at me over the stone wall.

His head bobbed down out of sight immediately and my imagination began to run wild; was he alone? Was the African dangerous, and armed with an assegai or a knobkerrie?

I heard a sharp snapping noise and imagined a fully armed Matabele Zulu warrior crouching behind the wall, ready to pounce and attack me with flaying weapons!

The African head appeared again, but this time with a broad white-toothed grin spread across the coal-black face of my potential attacker.

"Good afternoon, sir!" shouted Feet, and the diminutive figure, all five feet of him, awkwardly clambered over the wall, unaware of the thoughts that had been racing through my mind! "I was coming over to the house to talk about the vegetables when I saw you cross the road and walk into the bush, so I followed you and watched you staring at the white tombstone. The remains of that poor family have been resting there in peace for so many years, but now the old black and white tribes are killing each other again! But around here we all get on well together, and we don't want any trouble."

"True, except for us and Jackson!" I jibed. "Now what about the vegetables? Are you able to start delivering them twice a week as we agreed?"

"No! I still have no vegetables for the mine. The cabbage and the rape that we planted became waterlogged and rotten, and I've run out of seeds for new planting; we need more!"

We discussed the vegetable-growing plans as we walked towards the mine, where he left me and disappeared into the bush.

Crispin showed me the prodigal diesel fuel tank, which lay in its large cradle, glistening in the sun – *a rather beautiful sight*, I thought, which would become even more appealing on Monday when diesel fuel was gushing into its empty belly!

At the house, I was greeted by a rather sad-looking trio.

"Problem?" I enquired.

"Yes! Mummy put the rice pudding in the oven when you left and now it stinks, just like that fridge full of meat did at Christmas." Marie-Louise sighed.

"Yes, it really did!" Marianne declared. "Most of the oven is hot-hot, but this part near the door is only slightly warm; see, there's a bit broken off, leaving a gap! When I opened the oven, there was that smell of sour gone-off milk; part of the rice pudding was cooking nicely, but the other part near the door had curdled! Do you think your mechanic can fix it?"

"Doubt it; it's made of cast iron. We'd have to check. In fact, when our phone is installed tomorrow, I'll phone French at K.B. Davies and ask him if it could be welded. So no rice pudding tonight… but we've got rabbit! As I walked past Elliot's hut just now, a very appetising odour filled my nostrils, sending an urgent message to my stomach to prepare and get ready to receive a fresh delivery of Elliot's healthy rabbit stew!"

Wired

There was an excited buzz in our house; we were all so keen to have the telephone installed – our isolation would be a thing of the past.

We could receive calls and make calls whilst sitting in the house – phone calls to whoever, wherever and whenever we wanted to, as simple as that!

Although getting through on our joint party line would still be frustrating at times, at least the hectic rush and an hour-long return journey to the Fort Rixon phone booth would be replaced by a relaxing cup of coffee, possibly with my feet up reading a newspaper!

Yes, a newspaper!

My mother was sending us the airmail edition of the *London Daily Telegraph* each Thursday, and I enjoy reading mainly the sport and the cartoons – but it has another benefit too; it's very thin airmail paper and ideal for rolling your own cigarettes!

Phone; newspapers; our connections to the outside world were growing – a reassuring feeling, to be sure.

"I can hear a Jeep!" shouted Jeffrey, and he and Marie-Louise ran off down our driveway to see who was approaching on the main murram road.

The faint bauble of a diesel motor became louder and louder, and suddenly stopped.

A few seconds passed before a revving noise started again and became louder and we could see a Land Rover intermittently through the thicket and acacia trees as it approached us along our driveway, emerging from the bush with two happy kids standing in the back of the vehicle.

The telephone team had arrived!

And with a surprise helper; Roy from the Shangani Hotel had come too.

We greeted each other, and Fred's workers began to unload the poles and phone equipment.

I sent Elliot to tell Crispin to send two lasher boys with pickaxes and shovels;

they could help to dig ***deep holes for the poles!***

Fred had his own ***large pliers for the wires,***

And, it wasn't long before the telegraph poles were ***erected and connected!***

And the final test:

Our wall phone was hung inside by the door and connected to our only source of electricity at the moment – a car battery!

Fred whirled the phone's handle around and around, creating that ring-a-dingle-ding sound of those sturdy black phones… and we all waited.

"Hello! Hello! Is that Fort Rixon exchange? It is! Good! This is Fred from Shangani Exchange Depot and we are testing this new line for the Ridge Top Mine, on the Jackson joint party line…. So, that's okay. I'll call in at Fort Rixon on our way back home later this afternoon to give you the paperwork and details for this connection to the Ridge Top Mine. Thanks. We'll see you shortly."

"Do you mean we can use *our own phone* at last?" Marianne exclaimed. "And we can phone our family in Europe?"

"Yes, and, as Ian Davidson would say," Fred replied, "you are now connected to the wicked outside world!"

"Fred, you don't know how pleased we are to have a phone, and we're very grateful for you coming out here on a Saturday. Next time I'm in Shangani, I'll take you both out for a celebration lunch – at your place, Roy!"

"We can do one better than that!" Roy smugly chuckled, and went over to the Land Rover and took out a large cool box. "We can celebrate here and now!"

When he opened it, it was like Aladdin's Cave – not full of glittering gold and diamond trinkets, but good, honest brown glass bottles of beer!

An hour or so went by with happy, harmonious and humorous banter as we celebrated with cold Castle beers and biltong.

"Actually, it's very appropriate that we're drinking Castle beer out here on your gold mine, because when Castle Lager was first brewed in Johannesburg at the end of last century it became very popular among the prospectors of the gold rush in South Africa. In the Castle Brewery office in Bulawayo, there's a picture on the wall showing the front page of the *Diggers News 1896*, which declared that Castle was a phenomenal success and had spread to over 200 bottle stores in the sprawling tented camps of tens of thousands of prospectors and gold miners. So here's to your next big celebration – *gold*!" Roy shouted as he removed half a dozen cold beers from his cool box and put them in the shade of our porch.

They drove away, leaving us to finish off the rest – beer and game biltong, what a tasty combination to celebrate *our double-delivery day!*

"We are '*phone-able*' at last, and Joseph can no longer use the lack of a phone on the mine as a lame excuse for his ineptitude!" This was my last whispered comment of the day as I turned over and went to sleep.

. . .

First it was breakfast time with the family… and afterwards, it was **phone time!**

I picked up the heavy black phone handpiece and whirled the handle around and around and around – what a nice friendly ringing sound – only to be shouted at in an extremely unfriendly manner, which made me hold the phone well away from my ear.

"Get off the line! We are talking!"

I put the phone back immediately, and Marianne and I looked at each other and grinned.

"I think I'll have to try a different approach; probably best would be to pick up, listen, and, if no conversations are on the go, I'll whirl the handle around and wait for the operator's friendly voice."

"Or what I would do – pick up, listen, and if no *interesting* conversations, whirl the handle!" Marianne quipped.

After a short coffee break in the house – so much better than having to sit on my own in the pick-up outside the Fort Rixon phone booth – I tried it again.

"Good morning, Fort Rixon exchange; what number do you want?"

"Ah, I don't actually know the number, but I want to speak with Des and Irene."

"Just a minute…"

I know it sounds silly, but I'd frequently phoned people all over the world on business, doing it out of habit, yet here we were, isolated in the bush, waiting for someone's words to come along those wires that we had hung from the telegraph poles the previous day – the anticipation was quite exciting!

"Sorry, no reply," the operator calmly informed me. "Put the phone down and I'll ring you back later once I get through to them."

"Thank you."

And so started my love affair with our joint party phone line.

The stark, shrill ringing of the phone startled us all; it was so out of place in our tranquil surroundings where we were used to the melodic birdsong sounds and our cooing doves.

"You're through."

"Hello?"

"Des speaking."

"Des, you are the first person I've spoken to on our newly installed phone; it's Ridge Top Mine calling!"

"Hey that's great news; you can't be without a phone in these troubled times. Put Marianne on the line; Irene is tugging the phone out of my hand and wants to speak to her!"

"Hello Irene, I'm so excited! We've got a phone now, so we can chat whenever we want to, but we'll keep it short and sweet today, how about…?"

Sweet, but decidedly not short – maybe 30 minutes?

. . .

"Good morning! And what presents do we get today?" Marianne asked me. "It's been like Christmas recently – the water tank; the fuel tank; the PO Box; the phone!"

"Not forgetting the new improved long drop toilet, and the shower that I have asked Langton to build for us this week," I added.

"And, of course, the wood stove."

"Oh shit, the broken wood stove! Let me phone K.B. Davies." I instinctively pulled out the pick-up keys from my pocket, making for the door, ready to drive up to Fort Rixon, but paused on seeing the wall-phone… "Oh yebo! Let me phone French right here and now! No return trip to Fort Rixon necessary anymore! This is great! Elliot, bring me a coffee, please!"

And we laughed.

More good news from French; the cast-iron wood stove could be mended by welding, and I could bring it into town anytime.

And to get our building plans on the go, I ordered a block former, which we would use to make our concrete blocks on the mine – who knows, we might even be able to sell some to Jackson!

My first Ndebele language lesson was strange.

Sitting outside under the shade of a tree, with the teacher, Crispin, scribbling words and sentences in chalk on the small blackboard whilst I made notes about some of the basics of the language.

We decided I should try to learn 10 new words and two related sentences each lesson, and practise on him whenever we were together in the office.

Learning this language would prove to be another form of time-saving. Communications and instructions would be clearer to the workers, resulting in the job being done correctly! *First time!*

Another New Year present rumbled past our house, the Shell lorry, bringing the proverbial 'gift of life'! This was the lifeblood that would *flow* through the alternator, generating electricity that would *run* through the connecting *'veins'*, bringing life to all – to our house, to the pumps, the hoist, the crushing mill and the extraction room equipment, where the gold would be collected – giving us a 'gift of a more comfortable life'!

I jumped into my pick-up and shot off to the mine – Joseph style!

"Good morning to you," Leo said as we shook hands. "I always come on the first delivery to a new customer, to oversee that all the fuel is pumped into your storage tank and, most importantly, that the valves function properly so that you can get diesel out when you need it!" he exclaimed, laughing and slapping me on the back.

As the tank was being filled with diesel by a long, fat hose, it reminded me of the first time the Chibuku lorry delivered the beer – that creamy looking runny porridge that the mine boys enjoy so much. Diesel was a decidedly better colour than Chibuku, but just as bloody awful taste-wise.

My next appointment on this busy Monday morning was with the mining commissioner in Bulawayo to hand in the speculative loan application.

At the Mines Department, speed seemed to be the essence of the day.

He quickly scanned the amended application and called out to his secretary, "Get this typed immediately, let me sign it and put it in the document delivery pouch for Salisbury head office! And good day to you, sir!"

Let's hope this initial 'sprint start' for our loan application led to a short explosive 100 metres, and not a bloody marathon like most of the things that the Mine Department dealt with!

The wood stove was unloaded at K.B. Davies and Mr French called over his welder to look at our broken door problem.

A couple of minutes' deliberation whilst feeling the edges around the broken section before the welder gave his thumbs up – it would be ready by the end of the week.

Three out of three, not bad; things seemed to be progressing well... until French enlightened me on the current status of our ball mill.

Apparently, they couldn't get the steel required as per Newmarch's specifications, due to the UN shipping embargo blockade of the Port at Beira in Mozambique.

"Newmarch is now in South Africa visiting a steel-producing company, and hopefully will be back by the end of the week with some good news," French explained.

"*Hopefully!* Hopefully with some good news! Hopefully with a truck carrying the bloody stuff with him from South Africa!" I remarked testily. "By the end of this week, you'll have *less than three weeks* to have everything up and running on our mine!"

We both looked at each other; no words were coming forth, but both our brains could be heard whirring away trying to pick the correct words; words that wouldn't cause a maybe regretted explosion.

French broke the ice. "Come and see me on Friday; I'm sure the problem will be fixed by then!"

"Are we referring to the broken wood stove? Or the potential ball mill broken promise?" I iterated sarcastically.

French quietly excused himself. I could see and feel his embarrassment, and he was a man who did not like to let people down once there was an agreement, a man of his word – no Rhodesian handshake necessary; *more like Scout's honour!*

He returned a few minutes later with the block former that I had ordered via our new phone.

"Please accept this block former as a gift; I feel really bad about this situation!" French added as he put the former in the back of my pick-up.

I popped into Greys Inn.

Ronnie was in the pub and was also disappointed to hear about the problems with the ball mill. He wanted to know more details; he might be able to help.

"Ronnie, I only know that the ball mill is round, what it costs and when the delivery and installation dates should be – the rest is technical mumbo jumbo to me! But please go and talk to French and obtain more blueprint details; the more heads working on this problem, the better!"

"I'll do that shortly – one for the road?"

"Not today, Ronnie; I must get back to the mine."

"The long and winding road… will never disappear. I've seen that road before. It always leads me here …" *The Beatles'* song was being constantly repeated in my mind. The journey seemed to be taking forever; it was as if everything was in slow motion, whereas I was praying that somehow Newmarch could transcend time and bring his finished ball mill into the future – a date that was *only three weeks away!* That news from French and the thought of another string of delays outside our control caused a worrying, nauseating feeling in the pit of my stomach – like after eating a strong Indian Vindaloo curry, you had the feeling deep down that something was about to go wrong and cause real problems!

But one just has to push on; there will always be another problem to be overcome… I began to chuckle to myself as I thought of a bit of graffiti that I'd seen on a toilet door in the Midland Hotel: *The English translation of the Indian 'Goan Vindaloo' dish was appropriately 'go and find a loo'! Problem solved!*

• • •

Marianne had taken the kids to Fort Rixon for the day to visit Peter Ruck and his family.

This gave me the ideal opportunity to catch up on informing everyone we knew or were dealing with of our new address – Ridge Top Mine, PO Box Fort Rixon, Insiza District – together with our phone number.

After making a list of them – a very long list – I wrote a short general note that I would photocopy later at Fort Rixon administration, and I started filling in the addresses on the envelopes…. I was beginning to get writer's cramp as the pile of addressed envelopes mounted, when thankfully I heard: "Good morning, sir!"

And there was Mzee Feet poking his head through the doorway.

"How are my vegetables?" I asked him.

"Very fine, but still very small; you'll be able to eat in two weeks! But I haven't come to tell you that. I think you should know that I've been watching one of yours workers, Amos, who used to work for Mr Jackson. I've seen him several times on the ranch talking to Mr Jackson – he's been spying on you! He is still working for Jackson!"

"Now that makes sense," I replied, "because Crispin has noted down several times that he mysteriously disappears for a couple of hours, normally on a Monday morning when things are very busy. Thanks Feet; I'll get rid of him!"

"Does your wife like chicken?" Feet enquired, producing a plucked chicken from his bag. "Boil it for a few hours; it makes good eating."

And the little old *mzee* went happily on his way.

Minutes later, Crispin knocked on my doorpost.

"Mzee Feet has just told me about how Mr Jackson always knows what we're doing – it's Amos! I've always been conspicuous of him."

I chuckled away to myself, and told Crispin the word was *'suspicious'* of him.

"He's a lazy worker too; are you going to dismiss him, sir?"

"Yes. Do it today; pay him off… but wait a minute; I have an idea." I picked up the phone and asked to be put through to Jackson. "Good morning to you. It's Ridge Top Mine; shall we have that meeting about the fencing issue this morning? Yes, in 30 minutes at the mine office would be perfect."

Crispin smiled, a knowing smile, as I told him, "Prepare Amos' pay, and when Jackson has been in the office with me for about 10 minutes, bring Amos with you and knock on the door and come inside. Ask me to sign Amos off with pay, because he has been absent from work too many times. We'll see if Jackson shows any embarrassment."

It was good to meet Jackson alone, without Joseph, as Jackson had a disliking for both him and his father; he didn't trust them.

I spread out the aerial map that Jackson had sent to me, with my markings in red showing my proposed fencing plans of our mine workings.

"But you can't do that!" Jackson exploded. "You can't fence off the cattle watering troughs and tanks; how will my cattle get to them? That's ridiculous! You must only fence off your mining buildings and the shafts, so my cattle can't fall down them!"

"I agree with you; we don't want any of your cattle getting injured, and that's why I've made the fenced-off area larger to accommodate our planned new trenching/sampling areas and two future shafts – see here, these red crosses, and I've left a corridor for your cattle to get to the water troughs."

"But that's no good; they'd have to go right around your fences, walk down the road for about 100 metres and then cut back. That's ridiculous!"

"And so is your insistence that the whole area be fenced off! There's probably less danger of your cattle falling down a mineshaft now, due to our mining activity, than there has been for the last 10 years that you have left the mineshafts open and unprotected! It's all a big farce to make us spend unnecessary money; another futile attempt of yours to prevent us from mining here. That's our proposed plans, which I'll send a copy of to you, and to the mining commissioner."

Jackson didn't reply instantly; he pondered the consequences of the fencing plan, grinding his teeth and pulling a few peculiar faces as he battled to digest this unpalatable plan that I'd laid out before him.

There was a knock at the door.

"Come in, Crispin!" I called out, and he entered, with Amos following him.

Jackson didn't even bat an eye at their sudden appearance, but Amos, looking very nervous, couldn't stand still and fidgeted around whilst Crispin asked me, slowly and deliberately, "Please check the pay packet, and sign Amos off, because of frequent absence from work during a shift."

However, Jackson did use this hopefully embarrassing intrusion to end the meeting with the old familiar line: "I'll be writing to the mining commissioner to reject your fencing plans, with a copy to my lawyer, of course!"

"Of course!' I reiterated, and went and opened the door to show him out. "Goodbye, Mr Jackson."

"Hmm, goodbye to you!"

Hopefully **plan 'J'** – J for Jackson – had stalemated the fencing problem and we wouldn't have to spend any more time on it – or money! Or worry!

Jackson had just driven out of sight on the Fibabusi road to go back to his ranch when another 'J' problem came speeding into the mining area and slammed on brakes, skidding sideways in a stock car racing spin manner, much to the amusement of half a dozen or so munts who clung on in the back of his pick-up laughing and cheering – Joseph had arrived, in style!

"I've brought the meat rations, I've brought two sacks of mealie meal and I've also brought six new mine workers from Matt's mine!" Joseph announced proudly, on his return to the mine after an absence of almost two weeks.

"And is Jane better now?" I enquired.

"She is back at home, but the doctor says she must rest and do nothing strenuous for two weeks; he doesn't want the stitches to tear – you see, the doctor explained to me in great detail what exactly she . . ."

I cut him short. "Okay Joseph, I don't need to know all the details, but I'm pleased she is on the mend."

We shared a pot of tea while I updated Joseph on the good things: phone, PO Box, fuel tank and delivery of fuel; and the bad things: Newmarch being in South Africa trying to locate and purchase the correct steel for some parts of his ball mill, Jackson's fencing and Jackson's spy, Amos.

"So it was Amos! I always wondered how Jackson only turned up to cause trouble at the mine when neither of us were there! Now for the next two weeks I'll bring the mine boys' rations every two days and the post to save you coming to Gwelo; that way, I can be around for Jane when she needs me. But let me get back home to her and my baby son; I'll be back in two to three days' time," he called out as he walked to his vehicle.

"Hang on, Joseph! Not so fast. We need to have a meeting with Staff right now to make plans for your underground miners; there's so much to do and prepare before the ball mill is installed and we get into full gold production."

"But Staff knows what he's doing!" replied Joseph with a petulant expression.

"Joseph, Staff is very capable, but you, I, Staff and Crispin have to lay out what jobs are to be done and when – *they call it making a plan*!" I added sarcastically, "*We are trying to run a gold mine!*"

That look, of a boy who had just been caught with his hand in the biscuit tin, spread across his face and he went and sat in the office.

Staff, Crispin and I joined him and we discussed what had to be done on a daily basis, with groups of mine boys and their *gwazas*.

"You see, Joseph, this is what I have done with my surface workers. Crispin has it pinned onto the office door so the boss boys and Crispin know what has to be done even if I'm not around, and I've got them to sign off on the *gwaza* task list each day."

"You want me to sign off every day!" he shouted. "You think I'm a school kid! You just want me to make a mistake so you can tell my father! Well, I'm not going to do it! That's that! I'm not going to sign. Staff, you must sign for me! I'm going home now to Gwelo, to look after my wife!"

He stormed out of the office and slammed the door.

A few seconds later, we heard another slammed door, the engine revving and the squeal of tyres as his vehicle shot off – leaving us three men, each with raised eyebrows and a bemused smile, staring at each other quietly.

I went back to the house, finished off addressing the envelopes and drove to Fort Rixon to see Ian Davidson.

He was quite happy to let me make photocopies of the new address letter, whilst he counted the number of addressed envelopes.

"There's 28 stamps, young man; you'll have to stick them on yourself and drop them in that sack over there for tomorrow's collection." And he continued shuffling papers on his desk and muttering – I think he was trying to remember what he was doing before I came in and disturbed him.

Have you ever licked 28 stamps? Very thirsty work, and, as I walked over to my pick-up, my imagination was conjuring a huge pint of cold beer – and would you believe it, who do I see approaching? Yebo, Policeman Peter.

He slowed and called to me through the open window, "My round; see you in the club at the dam." Then he drove on – closely followed by me!

When we got there – surprise! Peter Ruck's wife and Marianne were sitting on the terrace, watching the children playing on the lawn.

"How did you know we were here?" Marianne asked.

"A combination of licking stamps, a terrible thirst and talking to a policeman!"

As dusk settled and our thirsts were quenched, it was the end of a day out for the family, and we drove home to the mine.

We pulled up and saw Elliot standing by the wood stove, stirring a large pot.

"Ooo! That smells nice; what is it?" Marie-Louise exclaimed.

"It's chicken stew. I used the chicken Mzee Feet brought here this morning," Elliot replied, and began to dish it out onto four plates.

The rapid movement of stew via spoons to mouths quickly emptied the plates, which a smiling Elliot happily refilled.

The second helpings were just as tasty, and the four contented and full human beings retired for the night.

. . .

I wandered up to the mine as the sun was rising; a beautiful sight, which I never seem to tire of admiring, spending a few minutes in thought as the changing and brightening colours always seemed to lift one's spirits.

I met Crispin in the office and we had a cup of coffee as we went through the books.

He had already recorded the six new mine boys' details in the wage book and checked their *stupas* and reference letters.

Except for Joe Maduna, an ex-farm worker, the others were more skilled mine workers.

* George (II) – jackhammer/spanner boy * Juta – spanner boy * Joseph – timber boy * Bonfice – welder; most useful and needed * Masouso – underground boss boy *

These would add greatly to our underground team – and it still surprises me that yesterday Joseph showed no interest at all, not in them or the underground mining operations, until we really had to force him to participate! Let's hope that it's because he is worried about his wife – I'm beginning to doubt that too, but only time, and her getting better, will tell!

I shuffled in my seat; something felt uncomfortable and I removed a folded letter from my back pocket – it was from Dirk in South Africa. In all the commotion yesterday, I'd forgotten that Joseph had given it to me, and I hastily opened it.

Thanks a million for your informative letter - it was really great hearing from you.

It sounds like you had one whopping great New Year / Christmas - looks like you saw the new year in!, in the right way so it should be a good & PROSPEROUS new year - especially the way the Gold price is going up! Hope your 'Guinea Pig' Mill attempt pays off!

When I get a chance I'll definitely fly up with Alan in his new plane – a Christmas present from a rich Aunt, lucky Guy!

But in the meantime, tell me, how are the SNAKES up there in the bush? – Hell! There must be plenty.

If you ever come across any, or hear of anybody who catches snakes please ask them to send them snakes to me & I will pay them well.

I have over 20 different species of snakes behind glass in an old converted shed at the bottom of the garden, and am always on the lookout for more.

Give my best wishes to your wife

& Good digging!!

Dirk

Talking about good digging reminded me to check on the progress of my three groups of lasher boys who had the *gwaza* tasks of digging and transporting soil by the wheelbarrow-full to build the railway embankment – a mammoth task whenever I think about it, 60 metres long and more than two and a half metres high at the milling site end – but they were working well and the layers of soil were gradually increasing in height.

I prepared a letter to the mining commissioner (cc Jackson) with a copy of my fencing plans;

Mining Commissioner, *Fencing our Mine location*

Jackson had not agreed to my new plan to fence our location even though he had requested it, he called it ridiculous. I remarked that I also felt that the whole idea was 'Ridiculous' and suggested that it should be scrapped - grown men had more important things to do rather than play childish games.

Manager, Ridge Top Mine.

Let's see what reactions that brings, I thought. I would leave for Bulawayo straight away and personally drop the letter at the mining commissioner's office – be nice to get my oar in the water first!

A visit to K.B. Davies brought little cheer. Newmarch was still in South Africa, but he had at last found a steel supplier, MacSteel – now he was searching for a company that could use the steel to manufacture the specified parts for his ball mill.

I bought four large tarpaulins that would make ideal coverings for goods in the back of our three pick-ups and Matt's white one. The black plastic sheeting we used was too thin, getting torn too quickly, and had to be replaced after virtually every trip when a pick-up was fully loaded. On checking the tarpaulin sizes, I also found one size that would be ideal as a door for our palatial abode; it was very heavy and would not be blown inside the house, even in strong winds.

Another important purchase was 50 kg of chloride lime – for use in the long drops, both for hygiene and to prevent potent pongs!

We'd also learnt that, by pouring old cooking oil down the loo, it breaks the surface tension of the liquids so that the mosquitoes can't breed. Marie-Louise and Jeffrey were always having to put Dettol on those aggravating itching bites on their bums!

The Night has a Thousand Eyes

After a relaxing Sunday morning doing everything and nothing, dabbling here and there as a Sunday morning should be, we headed over to Des and Irene's for the afternoon.

They were such nice people, and they welcomed us with their characteristic warm friendliness.

The women drank 'spritzers', half white wine and half cold lemonade, a very refreshing drink, while Des grabbed a couple of cold cans and some biltong, and we ambled over to one of his storage warehouses.

He showed me his illegal brewery, well, actually, 'cidery'.

He said to me that he had been so impressed when on holiday in Devon in the UK by what the locals called Scrumpy – a very potent apple cider – that he had been experimenting and making his own brew.

A few mouthfuls of that wicked-looking cloudy drink caused him to cough and cough, almost gasping for breath!

"That is strong! Try some!"

I took one mouthful, gulped and spat out the rest – it was horrible!

And even finishing off the can of beer couldn't remove the muddy taste.

Proof time over, we headed back to the terrace as an army Land Rover pulled up.

"Uncle Des!" shouted a solidly built man in his early thirties as he sprang out of the vehicle.

"Auntie Irene, it's so good to see you, and I'm looking forward to one of your 'Big Five' specials. After six weeks with a tracking unit near the border, eating berries, roots and emergency packs, I could eat a horse!"

"Sorry Brendon, but horse is not one of the Big Five specials; T-bone steaks, lamb chops, chicken, pork chops and boerewors, but definitely not horse! Now Brendon, meet our newfound friends and their children; they've come up from South Africa and are reopening the old Claremont and Nelly mines."

The braai was lit and Des got some boerewors on the go – lekker tasters, aperitifs!

Anyone who enjoys a braai, or a BBQ, knows what a wonderful relaxing atmosphere there is, standing around the fire in the late afternoon sun, a cold frostie in one hand and some hot boerewors in the other, chatting away about whatever comes into your head, laughing together over a corny joke or two – yes, it's the best way to socialise and experience outdoor entertaining.

Once the braai was over and we had all eaten to the full, the women and children remained on the veranda entertaining each other, while Brendon and I joined Des and sat around a big bonfire.

The backdrop of the rapidly darkening skies was an apt scene setter for our conversations, which were becoming sombre and very disturbing.

Brendon was a senior officer in charge of Special Units, and their mission had been to root out certain terrorist groups operating inside Rhodesia and to continue tracking the insurgent groups as they hurried back across the border to their bases in Mozambique.

"These terrorists were 'big and brave' when they were threatening and shooting innocent, unarmed men, women and children – mainly black Rhodesians – but when they met the well-trained Rhodesian forces they fled in panic, like headless chickens, often dropping supplies that they had stolen from the villages they'd plundered, leaving a trail that even a one-eyed man could follow. You didn't even have to look at the ground for clues to track them; they were talking so loudly and laughing in what they thought was their safe haven village base back in Mozambique – until we opened fire on them! On entering their base camp, we counted 15 dead terrorists, and estimated that at least another 40 had fled, many of them injured! Inside the largest central hut, we found two dead Chinese instructors, and a veritable arsenal of weapons and boxes of ammunition."

"Chinese instructors?" I asked. "Chinese!"

"Yes, the Chinese are backing Mugabe's ZANU faction of mainly Shona tribesmen, arming them heavily and training them in their Mozambique bases. While the other major terrorist threat comes from Nkomo's ZAPU Ndebele tribal faction based in Zambia and trained by its Russian backers. The naive Western world, especially America, are pushing for independence for the blacks against the white regime diplomatically through the UN, hoping they will have some influence over a new all-inclusive black government of the country, and a 'preferred status access' to future trade of metals, minerals and even oil.

"The Russians and the Chinese have the same ambitions, but expect 'direct access' by arming and training the terrorists and being on friendly terms with the new 'potential president' after independence, either Nkomo or Mugabe – both of whom have been trained, and 'wined and dined' by the governments in those countries. That's politics; dress up your ambitions with whatever the current fashion is until you achieve your goals – of benefitting from a 'friendly to you' future black government.

"Nobody actually cares about the killings, torture and intimidation of countless black Africans as the two leaders jostle for supremacy, and for them, the higher the death toll, the more publicity they get promoting their ambitions – so-called 'black democracy'. And all these atrocities have been condoned by the United Nations and various governments that constantly provide funds and armed support for the 'freedom fighters' – they say it's the black Rhodesians against the racist white regime.

"Conveniently overlooked is the inter-faction fighting between the two main black races/tribes, the ZAPU and ZANU terrorist groups, which support one or other of the power-hungry national leaders, Nkomo or Mugabe, leaders who put up a 'United Black African Front' to the world in the name of democracy and 'one man – one vote'. *But each leader knows full well* he has to subjugate the black Rhodesians through whatever means necessary; by intimidation, raping, abductions and killing, in order to ensure that he triumphs – *failure to take complete power and control will mean his own bloody elimination.*"

"Man, that's a mind-blowing eye-opener!" I remarked. "The whole world, the major powers against little Rhodesia, and in the supposed name of democracy!"

"Very true, and the black leaders are manipulating the 'one man, one vote' system by stepping up intimidation of the black Rhodesians as they realise that a new independent Rhodesia will be *decided by the number of paper votes of the black Rhodesians at an election* – a 'democratic' system totally foreign to their traditional ways of tribalism. I've just given you a small insight into one incident somewhere on the borders, but believe you me, it's a growing cancer in the body of Rhodesia, a fast-developing incurable *revolutionary disease* – instead of *a peaceful, planned, treatable evolution!*"

We joined the others on the veranda for coffee and liqueurs to round off the evening, which, for me, was very informative, but extremely disquieting.

"Come over to our place next time," I called out as we drove off. "We can arrange it by telephone now; don't forget!"

It was a dark, starless night.

When there's no moon or stars, it is unbelievably black in the bush; there's no light to be seen anywhere. You literally cannot see your hand in front of your face.

If it wasn't for the pick-up's powerful headlights, we just couldn't drive; we'd be completely unable to see where we were going.

I told Marianne about some of the horrific stories Brendon had recounted to us of the atrocities Mugabe's insurgents were committing in the border areas, and the senseless slaughter of Africans in the villages opposed to Mugabe.

Brendon had warned me to always be on our guard even though we weren't near the border, as the terrorists might have other infiltration plans in mind to spring on any unsuspecting ranchers or miners in the bush areas.

"Do you think the terrorists will track down our way?" Marianne began with concern in her voice. "How does one recognise them? I mean, at night anyone can roam through the hundreds of square miles of virtually uninhabited bush. And you know, Irene told me. . ."

BANG!

The pick-up shook violently. I braked hard and the vehicle skidded to a halt.

I jumped out and saw we had hit a reedbuck about the size of a large dog, which lay twitching on the road in its death throes.

I took the hammer-axe from under my seat and went to put the animal out of its misery by whacking it on its head, whereupon its eyes rolled backwards and the body stopped quivering.

I lifted the warm body, a strange sensation, and struggled to heave it into the back of the pick-up.

"That was quite a shock!" I gasped. "With all that talk of terrorists, I should really keep my eyes firmly on the road; I only saw that reedbuck just as the pick-up struck it!"

We drove on. Luckily, the kids were still asleep, even though Jeffrey had slid off the seat, but was quietly snoozing away lying on the floor.

That crash had really woken me up, though, and I concentrated hard on the road ahead – well, the section that was lit up by my headlights; the rest of the bush was very dark.

We came across an area that was quite heavily treed, where the road narrowed and snaked through the thick undergrowth before crossing a dry river bed.

"This would be a good place for an ambush!" Marianne joked as we bumped across the donga and up the other side. "You can even imagine the armed terrorists staring at you from the cover of the bush!"

"Yeah, and you probably won't believe me, but I feel as if we are being watched right now," I replied worriedly. "*Shit! What's that?*" My heart jumped into my mouth.

In my rear-view mirror, two eyes were staring at me!

Then I roared with nervous laughter! "*Jesus, it's that bloody reedbuck!* Somehow, it must have staggered to its feet. I couldn't have hit it hard enough on the head; it's still alive, and it's standing up and staring at me through the glass window! Look!"

I jumped out again, climbed into the back of the pick-up and, as the reedbuck stood wobbling in front of me, I smashed it on the back of the head with the hammer – it dropped like a stone; this time, I had killed it for sure.

"That phrase 'the night has a thousand eyes' is becoming too realistic – terrorists, reedbuck, and now look at Marie-Louise with her large round eyes staring at us!"

We were still feeling uncomfortable about the incident as we pulled up outside our tin-roofed shack, and I went to Elliot's hut to see him about what I should do now with the dead reedbuck whilst Marianne put the kids to bed.

"Elliot is not there; he's probably down at the mine village," I told Marianne, "but here, help me lift this buck out of the pick-up and lay it there on the table by the wood stove."

"So what do we do now?" she asked.

"Let's go inside and get a large knife. I've heard that you have to bleed the animal; otherwise, the flesh bruised by the collision has a bad taste and goes rotten."

Our puppies started making weird noises, low growls even, and I told Marianne to make sure they were locked inside and to bring me a hurricane lamp.

I quickly went out onto the veranda with the knife – just in time too – to hear the snarling of a jackal, which was suddenly lit up by Marianne's hurricane lamp as it was sneaking towards the house, eyeing its reedbuck supper!

I threw the knife at it as I yelled out, and the startled jackal slunk off.

What happened over the next 10 minutes would have made a good scene in a Laurel and Hardy silent movie.

There we both were, staring at each other with that lost expression of 'what now?' on our faces – I even felt myself scratching the top of my head as I puzzled over what had to be done.

"I think firstly we should hang it up from the top of the roof so the jackals can't reach it."

We got out the bar stools and I stood balancing on two of them, and could just reach the wooden beam of the roof joint that poked out.

As I stretched up to get the rope over this beam, the bar stools began to wobble, but Marianne was quick to react and sat on one of them, holding my legs until the pyramid situation stabilised!

I finished passing the rope around the beam, and jumped down.

We tied the rope tightly around the hooves of the back legs and hoisted the beast upwards.

Marianne held the buck's head still, with its large eyes looking very sad, as I tried to slit its throat with the kitchen knife…. I used a sawing action, but the knife was too blunt to cut into the thick-haired hide.

The more I sawed, the more ludicrous the scene became as its head wobbled around, with its eyes almost winking at us, and we were reduced to tears, hysterical laughter taking over!

Suddenly, we heard more laughter – behind us!

"Let me help, Boss!" And Elliot rushed off to his hut and returned with a sharp panga.

One slash, 'whoosh' and blood squirted out everywhere, and we hauled the reedbuck even higher right up to the pinnacle of the roof.

We put a bowl on top of the bar stools to collect the blood dripping from the slashed neck, thanked Elliot for his help and went inside to bed.

Dink, dink, dink, dink, dink! The constant sound of the blood dripping from the buck's neck into the metal bowl was eerie, and we couldn't get to sleep.

I had to get up, grab the cloth from the table and go outside to lay it in the metal bowl. That reduced the noise considerably.

I called Marianne to come outside.

We looked on in silence at a truly amazing sight – the reedbuck hanging from the roof silhouetted against the moon that had come out. The body looked so long as it hung, stretched from its back hooves to the front hooves.

Back in bed, we could hear a muffled dripping sound, but nothing to keep us awake now; our long day had made sure that sleep would immediately take over all body functions!

Be Prepared

The start gong rang out and I battled to open my eyes. The eyelids were truly stuck; the eyelashes cemented together – the 'Sandman' had done a really good job.

Fingers rubbed and scraped to remove the 'sand', and, although I could partially see, I was still 80% asleep. Nothing for it but to 'feel' my way through the bush, climb up onto the concrete wall and dive into Jackson's water tank!

Instant awakedness!

Oh, it was a joy to float in it again; I'd forgotten how beautiful the ever-changing colours of the sky were at this time of the morning.

As I climbed out, I realised that I was still fully clothed; I hadn't even taken off my shoes in the sleep-hurry to get into the cool water, and I squeaked and sloshed my way back towards the house.

Elliot must have heard the splash as I dived into the pool, because he was standing in front of the house with a big grin as he handed me a mug of tea – a most welcome back-up awakener!

"Elliot, where is the reedbuck?"

"I cut it down; it's in the back of your pick-up. If we take it to the office, Crispin can have it cut into pieces."

"Come on then, Elliot; jump in the back and let's go. We can also check if there's anything that Crispin wants me to get in Bulawayo – you can come with me and Judith can take care of my family for the day."

We left with instructions to collect the mine boys' rations and a long list of items for the store – most importantly, 20 packets of tobacco and 10 small tins of snuff.

Snuff seemed to be the in thing; I noticed both Des and Brendon tipping a bit onto the back of their hands between the base of the thumb and forefinger before sniffing it up – perhaps this was a forerunner to the more potent forms of 'tobacco sniffing mixes' that youngsters use to become spaced out.

I checked for post at Fort Rixon – just the usual 'brown ones', which I would read later – and drove on further.

Elliot was cheering and banging on the cab roof as we sped along the murram road racing his namesake, 'Elliot the ostrich'.

The ostrich strutted along so gracefully and at great speed too with those long strides, and a proud 'smile' as he frequently glanced over in our direction.

For several kilometres, we enjoyed the sight of this male ostrich running at full stretch, its small head balanced on top of its long, pale neck, contrasting with the black plumage… until a group of two female ostriches with the lighter grey plumage came into view, and then our 'Elliot' decided that he could have much more fun than racing us!

At the Mines Department yard, Curtis informed me that he had allocated to our mine an Atlas Copco compressor, with two jackhammer drills, both air models, which could be delivered early next week. I signed the necessary lease document, $2,860 @ $103 per month – another nail in our coffin if we didn't get the Newmarch ball mill up and running in three weeks' time, as French had promised!

That caused me to swallow hard; that was just around the corner as it were and the last news I had was not good – Newmarch was in South Africa searching for steel parts!

Time for another visit to K.B. Davies.

French was not there, but an exuberant Newmarch was; he informed me that the parts he'd ordered while in South Africa were already being made according to his specifications and would be railed up to Bulawayo in five to six days' time.

He was jubilant, although, to me, five to six days meant yet another week would have passed on our fast-ticking clock!

However, not to dampen his enthusiasm, I joined in the spirit of things and said I was pleased it was all coming together.

We discussed matters thoroughly, including the need for the conveyer system to be included as part of the ball mill project… and the next dates for the various actions.

I left him, and, while everything was still fresh in my mind, I thought I'd write a letter to Mr French confirming the recent events since the signing of the order for the ball mill, and drop it off at K.B. Davies before I left Bulawayo.

What better place for letter-writing inspiration than the library – but that was for others, not for me, and, halfway through a pint at Greys Inn, my thoughts, and the ink, were beginning to flow:

K.B. Davies
Bulawayo

Ridge Top Mine
Fort Rixon
15th February

Attention Mr French

Dear Sirs,

We acknowledge receipt of your letter of 20th January confirming our valued order;
***One 5-foot Newmarch Ball Mill - ref: NBM/5/1 – detailed specifications**, and we thank you for recording so precisely the essential points which arose during our several discussions with your good selves.*

However I must inform you that it was the quoted 6-weeks delivery and installation which lead our Company to place the firm order on the 18th January, in preference to erecting a 5-stamp Mill at our Mining location.

I therefore cannot stress too much that the delivery of the Newmarch Mill and it being fully operational at the end of February is of critical importance to Ridge Top Mine.

We look forward to meeting you and Mr Newmarch on the 19th February to finalise planning, so that the Newmarch Ball Mill can be operating before sunset on the 1st March!

We are pleased to accept the services of Mr. Newmarch to supervise the installation and initial running of the Mill, until it is mutually agreed that the Mill is performing according to specifications, with a trouble-free running period of one month.

At today's meeting Mr.Newmarch stated that an automatic feed / conveyer belt system would have to feature as an essential part of the 5-foot Newmarch Ball Mill, and we would be pleased that this feature be included in the Test Ball Mill to be erected on our site.

The terms of purchase, subject to our acceptance of the Newmarch Ball Mill after one month of trouble-free running, are in order.

Yours faithfully
Ridge Top Mine,
Manager

I had a swift half with Dave, and dropped off the letter with Newmarch at K.B. Davies, where I also collected 10 more bags of cement – tomorrow, I would start making our own concrete blocks.

We had a growing need to produce building blocks on site; all the dagga bricks in the office and stores buildings needed to be replaced, not only for the strength, but also, as Crispin pointed out: "You can't make a hole through concrete blocks to steal from the store! But with dagga blocks it's easy… and quiet!"

. . .

During breakfast with Marianne, I told her about seeing Newmarch, and that both he and French would meet with us next week, when they would have some definite dates for the delivery of the ball mill.

"Newmarch is optimistic?" she asked.

"Newmarch is always optimistic, and, in reality, he could be family of Joseph's, as he dreams that everything will be all right – but without French and myself continuously asking and pushing him, he would be living in a trance and be like a ballroom dancer – 'quick, quick, slooow'!"

"You mean like Okie-Kokie Joseph – a dash dash here, and a rush rush there, in out in out, shake that gold pan about!" she joked.

At the mine, I first checked on the progress of the embankment *gwaza* boys and was pleasantly surprised; the level of the embankment was starting to rise in height, but there was still a long, long way to go.

"Today is block-making day, Crispin; I'll be experimenting on the mix of stone, sand and cement using different proportions, and tomorrow when they've dried and are set hard, we'll test which is the cheapest-strongest mix. Tell George and Joseph's good friend, Godfrey, to get a wheelbarrow and two shovels and meet me here in 10 minutes. Oh, and get the block former and also give them a drum that they can fill with water."

I opened the cubbyhole in the pick-up and took out my notebook, in which I'd jotted down some figures for block making that Des had given me.

The mix he recommended for mine buildings was: 15/1/1 – i.e. 15 parts of small and loose stones to one of sand and one of cement; we would use stones and chippings from the mine waste dumps.

For the house: 15 /7/1½, which would bond stronger.

With three workers, I should be able to make at least 100 blocks in a day….

And that's how the block making for our own usage started, which would give a supply of more than 2,000 blocks a month – enough to build my three-bedroomed bungalow.

In the beginning, it was pretty chaotic, but, by lunchtime, I had sorted out an easy way to get the block production line functioning well.

Langton had helped by showing the other two how to mix the ingredients with water to the right consistency and filling the block former, stamping it down firmly before releasing a block, which was laid out neatly in rows to dry and harden.

So I set the three of them a *gwaza* for the afternoon of 50 blocks, explaining to Langton the way to reckon it all out, so that it was easy to see and to manage:

To make five blocks required 15 shovels of stones (which filled a wheelbarrow) and one shovel of cement (10 shovels to the bag).

The afternoon *gwaza* would be 50 blocks:

Godfrey would collect 10 wheelbarrows of stones from the waste dump near the mine shaft and tip them out next to the pile of sand, ready for the block makers to use.

Langton and George would mix the stones, sand and cement to produce the blocks.

I gave them one bag of cement.

We broke for lunch and I told them I'd be back at 5pm, by which time they should have finished their *gwazas*.

The *gwaza* system is good when you set the workers a realistic task with easy to see results that can be controlled and checked.

If they completed the task early and either Crispin or I had ticked it off, they could finish for the day.

The rule is simple, but if they don't finish the task, often due to laziness when you are not around, they have to keep working – even if it means working into the night using underground carbide headlamps!

Back at the house, I found Jeffrey playing outside on his own – unusual!

On entering, I found Marie-Louise still in bed – very unusual! She had a temperature and had been confined to the house.

"It's so hot in here; can't I go outside?"

"Best you stay inside today," Marianne told her. "You'll feel better tomorrow."

We went outside and Marianne added, "You know, I've noticed over the last few days it is getting a lot hotter inside the house during the day. When the sun blazes down on the corrugated iron roof all day long, it heats up considerably. I even stood on a barstool yesterday so that I could touch the inside of the roof, and it felt really hot! Even with all the windows and the door open, it can become quite unbearable at times; that's why we live and play outside most of the time."

"Maybe we should put in some sort of false ceiling; I'll ask around. I'll also get Langton to fix us a shower room next to the long drop – I'll give him a sketch of what I want, but, until we have our own pumped water supply on tap, it will be very basic; a small hessian-walled cubical with a five-gallon drum with holes in it suspended above the cubical. When the kids are standing inside, Elliot can tip cold or warm water into the drum and water will pour through the holes, causing a shower spray – it'll help cool them down and I'm sure they will love it! You and I can still use Jackson's swimming pool, of course!"

When I returned to the office later in the afternoon, I saw the block-making *gwaza* group were doing very well.

Four neat rows of 10 blocks had already been made, and they were happily carrying on to finish their task early.

"Perhaps a *gwaza* of 120 blocks would be a better quota?" Crispin suggested, and I agreed that it would be a 120-blocks-per-day *gwaza* in future.

"Now, sir, please come into the office; Alex and Robson want you to help sort out their problems. They are very worried that they might be fined or even go to jail if you don't help them quickly."

First, Alex showed me his dog licence, which had expired the previous week, and Robson's radio licence renewal was due the next day.

I was amazed that they were so concerned being out here in the bush – in the town, I could understand it. However, I agreed to advance them the money and take Robson into Bulawayo on my next trip so he could organise both licences.

"Actually, I feel a bit guilty now," I told Crispin. "We have two dogs and three radios, and the thought of getting a licence for them had never occurred to me! But tomorrow I'll take Robson so that he and Alex can feel like law-abiding citizens and not worry every time a police Jeep came onto the mine!"

"We've finished our *gwaza*," Langton announced triumphantly. "Look, five rows of 10 blocks!"

"Great! Now Langton, I will need you for another job tomorrow to fix up our shower room next to the long drop – here's the sketch of what I want, so I'll put someone else on the block-making *gwaza*. Do you think George can make the mix correctly to the right thickness to pour into the block former?"

Langton's nod confirmed, and I left for the house asking Crispin to keep an eye on the block making when I was in Bulawayo the following day.

. . .

I shook Marianne to wake her up. "That's it; I've had enough! They have to go!" I whispered to her. "Listen to them; it's about 4:30am and all that bloody noise, waking us up every morning with that 'dum-dum-dum-dum-dum' as they run across the roof!"

"But the kids like them so much; what are you going to do?"

"Dum, dum-dum, dum, dum! They are going to die! I'll tell Elliot to make a stew from them; should be quite tasty too using those two plump doves."

"And what will you tell the kids? That they flew away!"

"Yebo, that's exactly what we'll tell them, and we'll eat the dove stew after they've gone to bed, just in case Marie-Louise smells a rat – perhaps that's not an appropriate choice of words."

I collected Robson from outside the office and we drove off to Bulawayo, picking up the post at Fort Rixon on our way – one letter from the Forestry Commission.

As we drove into the Mines Yard, I saw a pick-up go past with four red flags, one at each corner of the vehicle, driving slowly at about 20 km per hour.

"Hey Ronnie, what was that vehicle carrying?" I enquired.

"Dynamite! Every vehicle carrying explosives has to have those red flags to warn people that it has a dangerous cargo, and the speed restriction in the towns is also for safety reasons. Those are the rules at present for anyone ferrying dangerous material from the AE & CI depot to their mines, countrywide. However, you won't have to use the red flags, because the rules are changing at the end of this month. And before you ask me, I'm going to tell you why – it's a terrorism precaution! From next month, the new regulations kick in:

"No red flags; this only identifies to the terrorists that the vehicle is carrying explosives, and is very visible from miles away, allowing a group of terrorists to easily ambush the vehicle and steal the explosives. No thoroughfare through towns and cities: on 1st March, you will receive a route map from the AE & CI explosives dump site, highlighting the alternative routes to bypass the urban areas. How you travel for the rest of your journey is up to you, but it is suggested that you don't stick to a regular route – again for obvious reasons, and most importantly we don't want a potential time bomb driving through the centres of our towns and cities."

"Good morning," the mining commissioner called out from an upstairs window. "I want to see you about Mr Jackson's fencing complaint! Come on up, please."

"Oh, you're in for a hot session; we heard Jackson bitterly complaining about Ridge Top Mine yesterday when he was here. Good luck!"

The mining commissioner began in a haughty, disinterred tone and said that he had received my letter following Mr Jackson's visit to Ridge Top Mine.

"Mr Jackson was here yesterday, and said that the fencing plans were ridiculous! I agreed with him!"

"You agreed with him? But he's only out to cause us problems and to try to stop us mining there!"

"I know; that's why I agreed with him that the fencing plans were not only ridiculous, but unnecessary, and the deadline for the agreement was postponed – indefinitely!"

"Well, thank you! That's great news for us!"

"But the timber usage still has to be documented and paid to the land owner, Mr Jackson. You must meet him next week and produce a wood usage book. He's agreed to come to your mine on Monday the 18th. Once the book for recording and the payment terms have been agreed between you, this will remove his last objection to you mining on his ranch."

"We do have the full timber permit now, although there was a huge error in it. I sent it back and have just received the corrected version; take a look at this." I passed the letter to him.

Rhodesia Forestry Commission
P.O. Box 8111
Causeway
Salisbury
Ref: 835 12 February

To
The Manager
Ridge Top Mine
P.O. Box, Fort Rixon

Dear Sir,
Mining Timber Permit E4 / 74C

With reference to the Mining Timber Permit E4/74 issued to you on 7th February, (copy enclosed), there is an error in the size of the huts stated on the permit.

Please amend your copy to read;

12 huts of 3 m x 3 m, instead of 12 huts of 30 m x 30 m.

Yours faithfully

Secretary
Mining Timber Permit Board.

He read it, and then roared with laughter. "If you had gone ahead with that timber usage, there wouldn't have been a tree or a bush left on Mr Jackson's entire ranch! Let me know what you and Jackson agree. Good day to you!"

I popped down to see Ronnie again and told him of the fate of the fencing fiasco!

"Good for you; it was indeed ridiculous, pathetic – and a waste of so many people's time! But watch out; keep your eyes open and your claim/registrations up to date. Jackson must be really mad with you now. Don't give him, or rather his wife, who seems to call the shots, any excuse to complain further. He copies each complaint to the Mining Affairs Board – which could jeopardise your loan application."

With Robson and some rations in the back of the pick-up, and the dog licence and the radio licence on the front seat beside me, I turned on my (unlicensed) radio, held down the diesel starter warmer button and started the motor. The engine coughed, almost barked, as it sprang to life!

I dropped off the supplies at the store and drove straight to the house.

I was hot and sweaty, and pleased to see that both Elliot and Langton were waiting for me as we had arranged.

Those two triumphantly led the way to the new shower cubicle.

It looked pretty solidly built, and I took off my shirt and shoes and stood under the gigantic shower rose. It would probably get into the *Guinness Book of Records*!

On the signal, Elliot poured the water, which came spurting out. I screamed, and Marianne and Jeffrey laughed as I rushed out of the cubical shouting, "That was bloody cold water, Elliot!"

They all found this so amusing.

We went back to the house, where Marie-Louise called out in a weak voice, "What was all the laughter?"

I told her about the cold water shower I'd just had, to which she replied, "Can't I have one? I'm so hot in this house – it's like an oven!"

Indeed it was, so we moved her and the fold-up cot/playpen outside into their small playhouse, a thatched roof on four poles.

That should be a bit cooler, and she seemed more comfortable.

Marianne kept swabbing her down with cold water, but she had a fever that was burning her up and she was tossing and turning the whole time.

When evening came, we moved her cot under the sprawling jacaranda tree – our makeshift hospital – and, by midnight, although it was cooler outside, the fever burnt on.

I sent Elliot to fetch Amon, and, throughout the night, Marianne and Judith took it in shifts to keep Marie-Louise cool, under the watchful eye of Amon.

You can never be sure of which animals might be roaming in the bush in the vicinity of our house – there are many that hunt by night, including leopard and hyena, which are prevalent in Matabeleland.

. . .

At first light, we put Marie-Louise on the front seat between Marianne and me and we left for Gwelo to see the doctor.

The surgery wasn't open when we arrived, but luckily the doctor arrived early at 7:30am.

"A quick examination shows that she has scarlet fever, but she's over the worst now. How long has she been unwell?"

"Really, over the last few days, she hasn't been eating well, a bit moody, and the last two nights she's run a fever, which was so bad last night that she slept outside under a jacaranda tree whilst we tried to keep her cool through the night, swabbing her down with cold water."

"You did the right thing too, but she'll have to take some medication over the next few days."

Before heading back to the mine, we called at No. 7 Hudson Road.

There was no one home.

Off to the Midland Hotel where we could get coffee and some breakfast.

Marie-Louise perked up more and asked for a cold strawberry milkshake – good sign!

There were no messages for me at the reception. It seemed that Joseph had gone 'walkies' again, but I was in no mood to go chasing him telephonically across the country, even though he hadn't called in at the mine or phoned me the whole week.

. . .

Come Sunday, Marie-Louise was as right as rain again, so we took up Jeanette on her offer to come over in the afternoon and stay for a Sunday evening roast.

Turning off the murram road, we wound along the dusty brown track before emerging into the oasis – it was even more colourful and beautiful than the first time I saw it.

Jeanette came down the lawns to greet us, with her two bodyguards following closely behind her – the magnificent beige/brown Rhodesian ridgebacks.

We followed her back to the veranda of the house.

Jeffrey was so small compared to the dogs, but he stood boldly in front of one of them patting it on the nose, grinning and staring the dog in the eyes. He wasn't scared of them at all – and Rhodesian ridgebacks are used when hunting lions!

The other ridgeback walked closely behind me, playing his game of nudging me every few steps, his head poking me in my bottom, making me stagger slightly forward each time, letting me know who the boss was. And, when a 100-pound solid-muscled Rhodesian ridgeback keeps nudging you… you know!

(*Simba inja* in Ndebele – African lion hound – because of their fearless unintimidated ability to keep a 500-pound ferocious lion at bay while waiting for its master to arrive and get into position for a shot!)

Sitting on the veranda was her husband, Stan, who I'd heard had one of the finest herds of beef cattle in Matabeleland.

Next to him, an old man raised himself out of his chair and we shook hands; a very firm grip and you could sense that he was a strapping lad in his youth.

"Meet my uncle, and today we are celebrating his 95th birthday; he was a teenager in the 1890s and had first-hand eye witness experience of the gold rush from South Africa, together with some of the harrowing events of the 1896 Matabele massacres."

"Pleased to meet you," he said. "I hear you are working on the old Claremont and Nelly mines. After supper, I'll tell you an interesting story or two about them, and about the rebellion of '96 too. I was privileged to live through those times and to meet some of the great men and leaders of that era; Cecil Rhodes, Lord Grey of the BSA Company, Colonel Baden-Powell, Capt. Frederick Courteney Selous, and other military legends."

The evening proceeded nicely; sundowner drinks on the veranda, followed in the dining room by soup and wonderful helpings of Sunday roast beef, but I was eagerly awaiting the main course – his stories of the early gold mining days and the Matabele massacres at the end of last century on our mines.

After we had dined, the men retired to the study for coffee and brandy.

The old uncle kept licking and smacking his lips as if enjoying the lingering taste of the beef on them, and then he started to tell me his tales.

Although he was 95 years old, he was sharp and his recollections were delivered smoothly, often causing his eyes to light up with joy on recalling a character, or tearfully sad as he recounted some of the horrific, brutal killings he'd witnessed first-hand.

He had travelled up from Johannesburg with his father and older brother in the gold rush of the 1890s – not to dig for gold, his father told him, but to make their own 'gold' by selling supplies to all the mines.

He was only 14 at the time, but he drove one of his father's three ox wagons laden with mining supplies and sacks of food on what turned out to be a slow, arduous one-month journey.

He remembered vividly his first impressions of Bulawayo, an area of more than two miles long and half a mile wide of bare red earth, laid out and sectioned by ditches into blocks and streets – which reminded me of my 'laying out' plan for our mining village!

The centre of the town had a cluster of single-storey buildings made of brick, tin or wire-weave hessian mesh, and they were either bottle stores, public houses, dry good stores, mining supplies or mine syndicate offices.

Everywhere was bustling with excitement and enterprise. The people ranged from the well-to-do to the rough types and scoundrels, all there to search for gold!

"Can you imagine that scene when you drive into the City of Bulawayo today!" he quizzically exclaimed… and paused. His expression gradually changed from the excitement of his arrival in Bulawayo all those years ago to a more remorseful, saddened look, and he gulped down a glass of brandy before continuing.

"It was on 21 March 1896 when I left Bulawayo with my brother in an ox wagon loaded with food and supplies and headed for the Insiza Hills, some fifty miles from Bulawayo, to deliver the goods to Cummins Store – a full two-day trek! Dusk began to fall as we unloaded the wagon, when two figures staggered towards us from out of the bush. They were two badly injured miners from the nearby Nelly 404 mine, which had been attacked by Matabele warriors. Mr Maddocks, the manager of the mine, had been shot dead, and, although badly wounded, they had escaped by creeping through the long grass to get to Cummins Store.

"Shortly later, two men on horseback came galloping up. One was Mr Fynn, the Native Commissioner for the Insiza district. He had harrowing news. He had rushed to the Kildare farm to warn the families to flee, because the Matabele were uprising. But he was too late; everybody there had been brutally murdered. The whole Cunningham family had been bashed to death with knobkerries and battleaxes, and the mangled bodies of the small children had been thrown into a heap in a corner, like discarded ragdolls!

"On hearing this tragic news, Mr Cummins and another man immediately rode off to Bulawayo for assistance, warning several mines and homesteads on the way of the Matabele uprising, and telling them to rush to Cummins Store with all the weapons they possessed. At Bulawayo, Captain Gifford immediately set off for Cummins Store with a patrol of 40 mounted police, and they reached the store without incidence in the evening.

"However, at dawn, a large impi of some hundred Matabele, armed with rifles as well as the traditional knobkerries and battleaxes, launched themselves at the store. The attack was ferocious and lasted several hours; the Matabele were very determined to wipe us out, but eventually they were repelled and fled, quickly melting into the surrounding bush. Dozens of Matabele were killed, but thankfully only one policeman, with six others wounded. Captain Gifford made plans for the immediate evacuation of everybody, and, by midday, a procession of ox wagons and mounted police headed for Bulawayo."

Stan poured another brandy for his elderly uncle, who gulped it down.

He was silent for several minutes, then he uttered, "And that's the Cunningham Memorial on your Nelly 404 mine, dedicated to the Cunningham family and other miners and settlers who were massacred by the rebelling Matabele on that fateful day."

Without further words, but looking very sad and distressed, he left the room.

That signalled the end of the evening, and we drove back to the mine in silence – vivid and provoking thoughts flashed into my mind as we passed the site of the Cunningham Memorial, erected in memory of those hardy early white pioneer settlers.

. . .

Staff came to the house as I was eating breakfast, and asked if Boss Joseph was coming today, because we needed to discuss the next step to making the mine safer and workable now that they had pumped the first-level drive tunnel dry, and the water level in the main shaft was going down steadily.

"I haven't heard from him today, but grab a coffee from Elliot while I make some phone calls to try to locate him!"

I phoned both the Midland Hotel and the mine at Belingwe – no messages from Joseph!

I, however, left a rather rude, sarcastic message for him: "Joseph, your cup of tea is stone cold and your chair is still empty, but the Monday morning meeting with Staff was progressing well, despite no input from the underground supervisor. Call me; we have a phone, remember!"

Staff gave me a list of the sizes of the gum poles he required for some re-timbering of the main shaft, which I phoned through to Umvuma Forest straight away:

60 x 10 ft – 2 butts

100 x 8 ft – 4/5 butts

8 x 17 ft – 10 butts

Which they confirmed would be railed to Shangani Depot as soon as they received the cheque.

I walked back up to the mine with Staff, who enquired whether Boss Joseph was unwell, as he hadn't come to the mine very often these last few weeks.

That type of question is very difficult to respond to, and is best left unanswered.

Ring, ring! The sound of a bicycle bell broke my awkward silence – Feet peddling his bicycle towards us towing a small cart laden with vegetables.

Ring, ring!

"Your first delivery of our home-grown rape and cabbage. From today, I'll be delivering each week; the vegetables are growing well," he stated.

He unloaded the goods and Crispin paid him cash; also giving him more packets of seeds.

This was very good news!

With the normal ration meat, beans and mealie meal, and fish on Wednesdays, the mine workers would now get vegetables each week too! And, of course, extra meat occasionally, from any rabbits or small buck we knocked down driving the pick-ups at night – there was no need to go poaching or shooting on Jackson's land!

Later on in the afternoon, Jackson arrived and we sat down together with Crispin to discuss the wood issue.

He was pleasantly surprised when Crispin handed him the 'wood usage' book, and he could see that it had been regularly kept up to date.

"Yes," I remarked. "Crispin regularly *logs* in the usage!"

And Jackson started laughing at the pun.

"It's good that you're at least doing something *by the book*!" He laughed again, this time at his own intended pun!

Amicably, we hammered out an agreement:

I would supply two boys full-time to work with one of his workers, who would also supervise where to cut the hardwood we required for firewood.

Jackson's farm worker would also treat the stumps, at no cost to us.

We agreed on a reasonable price per cut cord of wood.

"But now my other concern is the timber cut for hut building – do you have a full timber permit yet?"

I handed him the **original, erroneous** permit letter, and watched for his reaction.

"What! Are they crazy? This is ridiculous!" he uttered, and I could see the veins of his neck were pumping as his face reddened with increasing annoyance; his hackles were rising.

"Yes, the mining commissioner said when he read it that your ranch would be stripped of trees as I instructed dozens of woodchoppers to swarm over your land; not even a bush would be left standing!" But I couldn't stop grinning as I handed him the new amended timber permit showing 12 huts of 3 m x 3 m metres in diameter, instead of the original typed '12 huts measuring 30 m x 30 m'.

The colour of his face returned to normal and he actually grinned back at me.

"You really enjoyed watching me boil as I rose to the bait! But I'm happy now that the timber problems have been fully resolved. However, we still have the fencing of the shafts and the mine buildings in such a way that my cattle could still use the water troughs and tanks."

"As far as I'm concerned, as the mining commissioner has said, the fencing matter deadline has been postponed indefinitely – and that to me means *stopped*! You turned down our proposed plans; they were our only offer, sorry!"

"This is not the end of it, I assure you, and I have already sent a reply to the mining commissioner that I object to his ruling – *which is only temporary, as far as I'm concerned!*"

We symbolically shook hands, and Rancher Jackson drove off.

I wrote out a cheque to Umvuma Forest, attached a note of the ordered gum poles and headed for the Fort Rixon Post Office.

There were several letters for the mine; the most important was a reply from Lightfoot of Fuel Rationing. They wanted to know why I needed an allocation of diesel fuel to run the mine day and night.

"Jesus! Why?" I said to myself, my eyes raised to the heavens. "Why doesn't anybody read what you bloody well send them? There was a whole justification I had already sent to him based on a 24-hour working day, and without enough fuel for day and night milling of the ore our gold mining operations would not be viable!"

Nothing for it but to write immediately to the Appeals Court with copies of all our previous correspondence, stressing:

No full fuel allocation = no gold production!

And send a copy to the mining commissioner and the secretary of mines, let them do some in-fighting on our behalf as well.

I left to get back to the mine so I could write such a letter whilst I was still so annoyed and in the mood, and I would make sure it was posted first thing the next day.

I was passing the police post in Fort Rixon when nature sent me a call that I had to answer urgently. Peter Ruck's house was the nearest, and I called out to him as I ran towards his veranda, "Permission to use the ablutions, sir!"

I hurried past him as he replied, "Permission denied!"

But it was too late – no, I wasn't too late; just on time, in fact.

I joined him, and the maid brought us afternoon tea and cakes.

"We had a very interesting evening last weekend at Stan and Jeanette's; it was the 95th birthday of their uncle. What a character he was! Not even 16 years old when he was involved in the Matabele massacres in the Insiza district. He told some horrendous stories of the murders on the Nelly 404 mine, and the sad background to the Cunningham Memorial situated on our gold claims."

"Yes, they were hard times for the pioneer miners and settlers; you had to be really tough in those days to survive."

"Peter, when I went to your toilet just now, I noticed some photos and pictures of old Rhodesia in the hall; ox wagons loaded to the hilt crossing swollen rivers, Bulawayo in the 1890s, soldiers on horseback, and one in particular that caught my eye; it was the framed front cover of a book: *The Matabele Campaign, 1896* by Colonel R.S.S. Baden-Powell, 13th Hussars, Fellow of the Royal Geographic Society, with nearly 100 illustrations. So Peter, besides Baden-Powell as everyone knows being the founder of the Boy Scout movement, in 1908, he had many other talents as well?"

"Yes. He was a very accomplished man indeed; a writer, an artist, providing the UK Royal Geographic Society with much material, including sketches of Rhodesian flora and fauna, the natives and their habitat, etc. As a military commander in the Matabele wars, he kept meticulous notes on his exploits and army scouting sorties, drawing dozens of sketches of enemy positions and strongholds in the surrounding hilly areas of the Matopas Mountains where the Matabele could surprise an unsuspecting column of British soldiers."

"And was he involved in the skirmishes around Fort Rixon, and on our Nelly 404 mine?"

"No. Actually, he came to Rhodesia shortly after the Cummins Store battle, assigned as Chief-of-Staff to General Carrington in June 1896."

And he began relating countless stories of B-P's escapades and some ferocious battles with the Matabele Rebels… well into the evening.

. . .

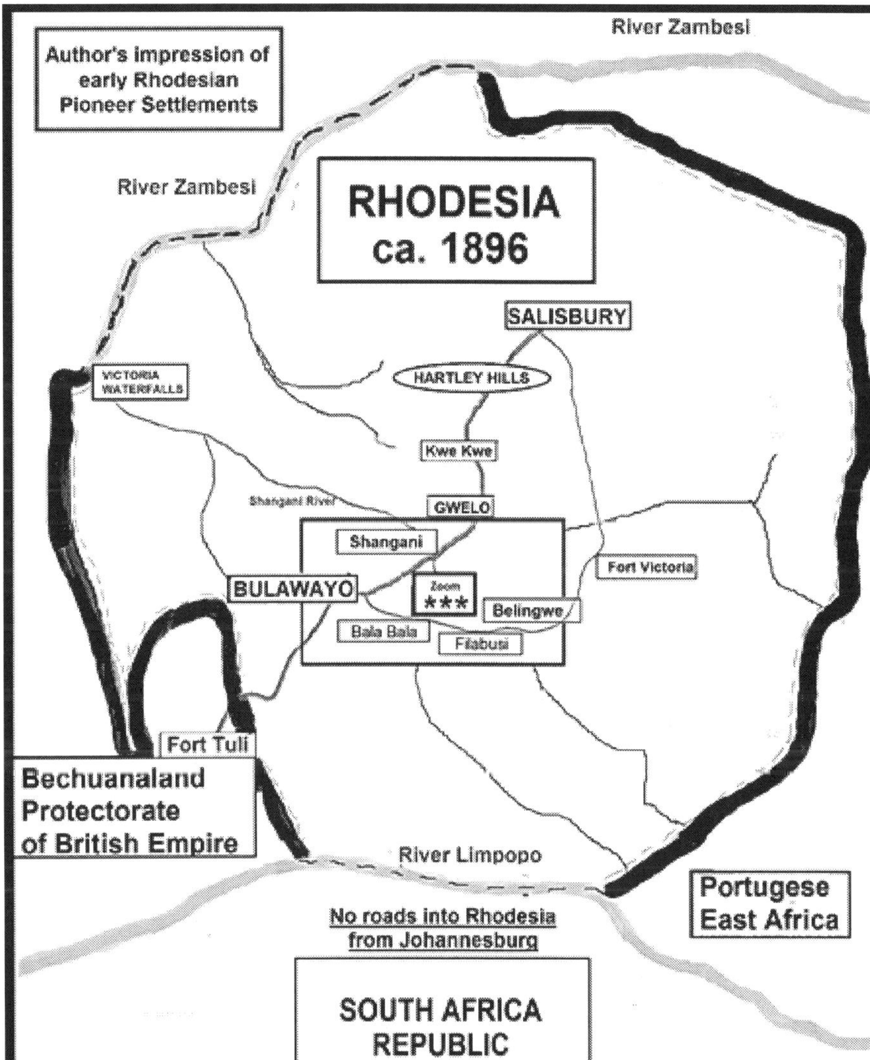
River Zambesi
Author's impression of
early Rhodesian
Pioneer Settlements
River Zambesi
RHODESIA
ca. 1896
SALISBURY
VICTORIA
WATERFALLS
HARTLEY HILLS
Kwe Kwe
Shangani River
GWELO
Shangani
Fort Victoria
BULAWAYO
Zoom
***
Belingwe
Bala Bala
Filabusi
Fort Tuli
Bechuanaland
Protectorate
of British Empire
River Limpopo
Portugese
East Africa
No roads into Rhodesia
from Johannesburg
SOUTH AFRICA
REPUBLIC

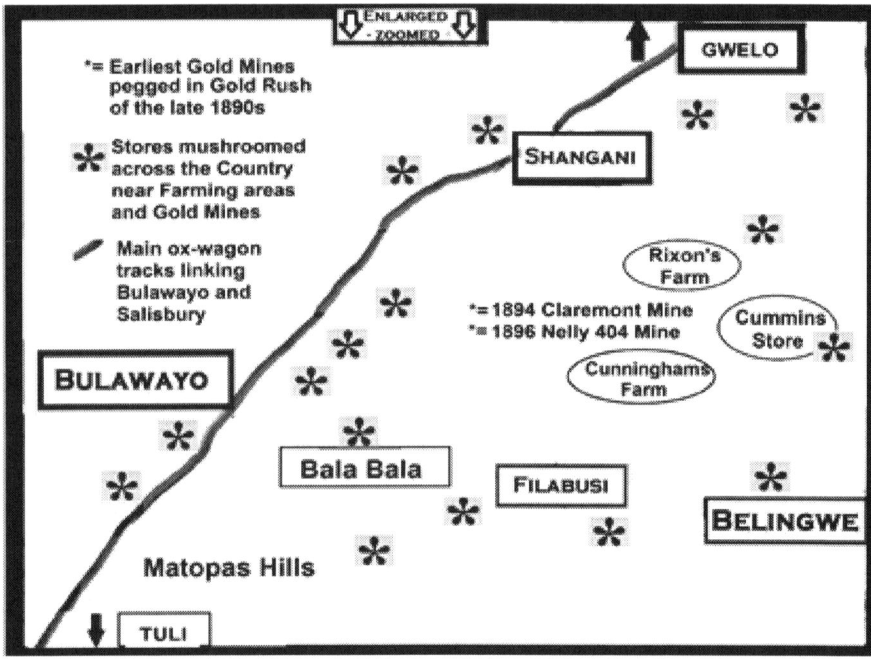

A zoomed enlarged section of the map showing the few small towns that existed then, but a proliferation of Stores that had mushroomed across the Country in close proximity to the Gold Mines of the 1890s Gold Rush and Farms of the small number of White Pioneer Settlers – 4.000 people in a Country much larger in size than Great Britain!

<u>Note:</u> Rixon's Farm, and the Cummins Store where the Settlers fled to for safety after hearing of the brutal clubbing to death of the Cunningham family near the Claremont Mine, and the murder of Mr. Maddocks, Manager of the Nelly 404 Gold Mine.

With the help of Captain Gifford's patrol of some 40 mounted Police, they barricaded the Store buildings.

As dawn broke a huge Impi of several hundred armed Matabele Warriors launched themselves fanatically at the Store – the attack was ferocious and lasted several hours before the Matabele having lost countless lives were repelled and fled, melting into the surrounding bush.

The conception of the Boy Scout Movement

Colonel Baden-Powell struck up an immediate Friendship with the American **F.R. Burnham,** who came to Africa in 1893 to Scout for Cecil Rhode's dream, **'The Cape to Cairo Railway'.**

Burnham had grown up with the Frontiersmen of the Wild West fighting the Red Indians, where scouting, woodcraft, tracking and awareness were the difference between life and death.
As Chief of Scouts for the British Army in Africa, he was known as "He-who-sees-in-the-dark", for his tracking skills at night.

The original-type of Stetson hat made famous in the old Wild West ca 1860s, similar to that worn by Burnham

When the two men met in 1896 during the Matabele Rebellions, Baden-Powell was an Army intelligence officer, an outdoorsman who had organized a small scouting section in his regiment, and had already written a booklet called *Reconnaissance and Scouting* – a Practical Course of Instruction for Soldiers, in Twenty Plain Lessons.

During their joint scouting reconnaissance missions into enemy territory in the Matopas Hills, B-P was inspired by what he learnt from Burnham, and they discussed the concept of a broad training program in scouting and self-reliance for young Soldiers.
In fact many of his later Boy Scout ideas took root here in Rhodesia.

Both men recognised that wars were changing markedly and that the British Army needed to adapt in the Bush wars. The bright red uniforms and white hard pith helmets had to go as they made such easy targets in the brown/green surroundings in the bush, and the more practical brown soft-brimmed Stetson hat and the neckerchief like Burnham wore, should be adopted by the Mounted Soldiers.

My first purchase, a Bush hat 1970s, to shield my eyes from the sun, and to stop the sun burning my neck . . .

. . . which was similar to my old Scout hat when I was with the Baden-Powell Scouts in the UK

The knowledge he gained of tracking and living off the land, his eye for detail, together with his thorough preparation for each sortie into enemy territory, germinated over the years and evolved later into his ideas of starting the Boy Scouts Movement in 1908 – an Organisation which has helped instil in millions of youngsters throughout the World, the concepts of discipline, respect, self-reliance, and above all to "Be Prepared".

Peep... peep... peep... peep... peep... The sound of a rusty bicycle approaching.

The veggie man Mzee Feet handed me two cabbages and some rape vegetables, and, with a big smile, he announced that the vegetables were growing well.

And now that he had planted more seeds he would be able to supply the mine weekly, sometimes twice weekly as the various planted patches produced periodically.

I left him chatting to Marianne and set off on the road to Bulawayo for a very serious meeting with French and Newmarch, because the deadline for the installation of the ball mill was fast approaching and we had heard no good news recently about its completion.

When I drove into the yard of K.B. Davies, what a surprise! Joseph was there on time for our meeting with Mr French.

After the preliminary niceties, fresh coffee and biscuits, I posed the question that nobody really wanted to ask, being almost certain that the reply would not only be unpalatable, but also totally unacceptable!

"What is the current state of the ball mill?"

After a few 'long' seconds, French drew a big breath and began with a brief resume of the main problems they had encountered with the production model of the Newmarch ball mill, but stressed that they were making progress.... The silence that followed only made matters worse, as four brains battled to find a productive continuation to the conversation.

"But does this progress have a definite end date?" Joseph ventured to ask.

We were then treated to a lengthy story about what still had to be done, the suppliers' that weren't delivering on time... with French and Newmarch swapping the lead in the jittery conversation... until they had exhausted all plausible arguments and relevant facts for these extreme delays.

"Thus, *no*!" Joseph and I declared in unison.

"It is only a week and a half to the agreed installation date of the end of February," I continued. "Can you give us any date at all that you plan to achieve?"

"Without being funny," French answered, "what is your timescale for all the work that needs to be completed on the mine before the installation and full production running of the ball mill?"

"A fair question," I replied. "Obviously, we both need the mill to be up and running as soon as possible, for both our sakes. Well, **the progress so far**: the largest jobs are the rail embankment from the main shaft to the mill, and the laying of the concrete slabs for the hoist and the ball mill. All are on target and will be completed by the end of this month; thus, on time! The sand pits and the slimes dams are ready, and the extraction room will be built when the ball mill is in place. The James concentrator table has been ordered; no firm delivery date yet.

"However, **the main items still outstanding are:** besides the Newmarch ball mill, of course! The mill hopper, the mill switchboard, piping and cabling to the ball mill site, all of which are ordered by Mr Newmarch and supplied by you – K.B. Davies! How long for these items to be supplied and installed again is a question you need to answer yourself!"

"Touché!" replied French with a grimace. "It's us who are holding you up, and we have to pull finger to deliver. Realistically, we couldn't be ready before the 15 March, but to help keep your costs down, and as a gesture of good will, we will double your credit limit on your mine supplies account."

"Thank you, Mr French; may I suggest then that we meet again next Friday the 1 March, when we must have firm definite dates for the installation. In the meantime, when Mr Newmarch isn't working on the production of the ball mill, we would like him to be at the mine where he can be most useful and helpful with his experience, and we can keep up to date with each other on any necessary purchases in preparation for *the big day*!"

French agreed.

You could feel that these delays were upsetting him a lot, and that he was worried about the knock-on effect it would have on the reputation of his company, K.B. Davies.

"Let's all go over to the Greys Inn for lunch, where we can unwind a bit – I don't like *not* being able to keep to an agreement!"

Indeed, there was no point in breaking our friendly relationship; it wouldn't help either party. The best was to all push on as hard as we could, and in the same direction.

Dave came over and joined us, breaking this unusually tense atmosphere.

"How's the wife and children?" he heartily enquired. "Haven't seen them for a while."

"Fine thanks, apart from Marie-Louise, who had scarlet fever, which we weren't aware of; we thought she was just running a high temperature, but she's over that now, luckily. It was a very worrying few days, though. The temperatures in our tin-roofed shack had soared, the heat inside was unbearable and Marianne had to stay outside with her under a tree swabbing her down with cold water."

"Ah!" exclaimed Mr Newmarch. "I have an old miner's tip for you that would help. When you empty the miners' carbide lamps for refilling each day, you must keep all the white-grey powder from the bottom of the lamps. This, when mixed with water, forms a thick paste, which you can paint on the corrugated iron roof sheets – you'll be quite surprised how cool it will be inside the house.

"And when I next come out to the mine I'll also show you how to make your own charcoal. I know you like braaing outside, and charcoal is also very useful for your mine workers to make a fire in a bucket, which can be used inside their huts when it's raining; much easier than trying to light a fire outside with wet wood!"

After lunch, Newmarch and French left us, and Joseph and I began to discuss other problems that we had.

"Now that Jane is better, you should be on the mine every day," I began.

"But I can't be at the mine every day; I have to stay with Jane and my son some of the time, don't I."

"Okay, stay one night on the mine, go back to Gwelo the next day in the evening, and come back the following day to the mine, alternating each day. And until we are mining full-time, the workers end their week at Saturday lunchtime, so you'll have the whole weekend to be with your family, won't you?"

Silence….

"Joseph, it's what I had to do for over two months, backwards and forwards from Gwelo until our shack was finished, when Marianne and the kids came to live permanently with me on the mine."

"I guess so, but why don't you build my house, then I'd be on the mine the whole time, wouldn't I?"

"That's right. And as you've seen we have just started producing our own cement blocks and will be making over 2,000 blocks in a month, so when the mine buildings are completed there'll be more than enough to build your house by the end of April!"

"Fabulous! Both of us will have our own families on the mine; we'll be working together, a real 50/50 partnership!" he enthused.

"Okay Joseph, so if you go back to Gwelo this afternoon, I'll see you bright and early in the morning – and don't forget to bring your pyjamas!" I joked.

On the way back home, whilst the thought of timber supplies was still on my mind, I visited my old stamping ground – the outside phone booth!

Umvuma Forest confirmed that they had received my cheque and would freight the timber on Wednesday to Shangani Rail Head Depot.

That would entail collecting almost 200 timbers of varying lengths – eight foot, 10 foot and 17 foot – sounds a lot, but, using the three pick-ups, Marianne, Joseph and I would be able to ferry all the timber to the mine in one trip!

. . .

When I updated him, Martin Curtis was so disappointed to hear of the further delays in the delivery of the Newmarch ball mill.

"We're really screwed!" I confided in him. "If we don't start producing gold by the end of March, we'll go bust and close down. We need a back-up plan, but what, and how? A 5-stamp mill is out of the question."

"Yes, we can't go down that never-ending road again; we spent over two months without any success in locating a good operational 5-stamp mill."

"It's a very serious situation for us, and we've got a make-or-break meeting with K.B. Davies on the 1st March when he has promised to give us a definite date for delivery around the 15th March. But it could be the 31st, or even later! There must be some alternatives, some temporary solutions?"

"Don't get your hopes up too high, but I visited a mine using a 5-stamp mill near Salisbury last week and I noticed that they had a small ball mill in their warehouse. They had originally used it when they started their mining operations there. Let me phone them and find out more – come back and see me in the afternoon?"

"Okay, I am having lunch with Leo de Ziel shortly, so I'll pop back around 2:30pm – it would be a great solution, if it still works and is available!"

Leo was in fine form and greeted me with some good news.

"I have the second fuel tank available for you, and if you give me a cheque for it here and now it can be delivered to your mine next Tuesday. Have you had a reply from the appeals court yet?"

"Not yet, but I sent them a very strongly worded appeal – here, read this copy."

"That's what I call straight to the point, piercing through to the heart of the matter! That should do the trick! But what about this temperamental Newmarch ball mill? No fuel = no gold! But equally so, no ball mill = no gold."

I told him of the delays, and he added, "That's the problem with a prototype new design ball mill being produced in the current economic client of Rhodesia; if a part is not available, it has to be made/produced in South Africa, which adds to the delays and, of course, the costs. But I'm pleased to see that you don't let these things get you down! You're like me, a realistic optimist – it'll come good in the end if you work hard at it! As Confucius, the Chinese's philosopher, said way back in 500BC: *It does not matter how slow you go, as long as you do not stop!*"

"Jesus, if we went much slower, we be going backwards!" I jested. "But I'll let you know the latest when you bring the fuel tank out to the mine."

Martin had heartening news for me.

He had spoken to the mine owner, who had given him a proposal:

"If we collect the small ball mill from his mine and get it fully operational, we can use it for free for two months. And then we either buy it for cash, or return it to their mine after a complete service."

"Sounds great, but… how do we afford to do that? And what is the tonnage throughput of a small ball mill?"

"It will be low, about three tons a day, but that should be enough to cover your basic costs. Now I can arrange transport to collect the mill from their mine and get it operating, even refurbishing it where necessary at the Mines Yard; that's not a problem – but it will have to go into our stock, and therein lies your problem. If you want to install it on your mine, our policy is that you have to buy it on our standard lease agreement, which means more monthly costs to you – and for a full three years! Whereas this small ball mill could become redundant after only two months, once the Newmarch ball mill is up and running."

"Hmm… perhaps there is another way. What if I take you to their mine, you give it an on-site inspection and hopefully even get it running. If you think it's a starter for us, I'll speak to French and get his K.B. Davies transport to pick it up and deliver it to the Mines Department for a full check-out. If it only needs a good service to make it fully operational, I'll cover those costs. French can fund the delivery to our mine, Newmarch can connect everything up, and we'll have two months' free usage – which should compensate us for the late delivery of the Newmarch ball mill, and bridge the two months costs-wise until we are fully operational.

"We'll only be able to re-mill the smaller waste schist from the old dumps, but if we are covering our basic costs, who cares? After that, we can return the refurbished small ball mill back to the owner in Salisbury. Martin, that's going to be our Plan B! Please let that mine owner know that we are very interested in his proposal, and to put it on hold for us until next week, the 1st March, when we'll let him know for sure, and confirm any arrangements. So Martin, would you be able to go to Salisbury on Saturday or Sunday – I'll drive us up there and back to Bulawayo. What do you say?"

"You know what, you are also a dreamer! But not like Joseph, your dreams are ideas, which, if practical, you go ahead and put the parts in place! Yes, I'm happy with that idea; it follows the Mines Department Inspection and Refurbishment of Equipment rules, and, if we go up there on Sunday outside office hours, that's even better."

"Great! Confirm that with them, Martin, and phone me at the mine tonight – this could be the last piece in the jigsaw puzzle that will complete the picture of a functioning and producing gold mine! Albeit a temporarily bridging solution."

I left Bulawayo with the feeling that we were, as they say in athletic sprinting terms, *'on your marks'*! And, if the small mill was a starter, 'get set!' Then, if French agreed, he could fire the starter pistol, and ***'go'!***

And pray we hadn't shot ourselves in the foot!

An 8pm phone call from Martin signalled that Plan B was confirmed!

He very kindly added that he would meet me at the Shangani Hotel at 10am on Sunday morning – it was silly for me to drive all the way to Bulawayo to pick him up, and later on drop him back there.

From Shangani, we'd drive in my pick-up to the mine near Salisbury – for Sunday prayers? – and hopefully immediate positive answers!

After a tiring, but exhilarating day, it was BB, BB – beer, biltong, before bed!

. . .

I told Crispin to keep all the waste carbide powder for me.

"Oh fine, but Staff had already told me not to throw away the used powder, and I have been storing it," Crispin replied. "But he didn't say why; he just remembered it was useful."

"That's great, because I've been told that if it's mixed with water it can be painted on the tin roofs and it keeps the rooms inside cool. In fact, get Langton and a helper to bring the carbide powder to the house, and they can paint my roof first. After that, we'll do the office and storeroom – Newmarch told me it really works and makes such a difference to the temperature inside."

As I was walking back to the house for breakfast, I could see clouds of dust in the distance bellowing up into the sky; a vehicle was approaching fast.

Flashing headlights and a pale blue bonnet signified the return of the prodigal son.

"Good morning," Joseph enthused. "I'm here – and I've brought my pyjamas!"

"Well, I'm pleased you remembered the way!" I ribbed him.

"That's not funny; I've had to be in Gwelo for the last two weeks, haven't I? Because Jane was unwell!"

"Yebo Joseph, I'm pleased she and your son are both well now, and that you'll be staying alternate nights on the mine. I've a feeling things are going to get very busy soon, and we'll both have to work flat-out!"

"You think French will tell us on the 1st March that the Newmarch ball mill is ready to be delivered? That would be fabulous!"

"No! I can't see that happening; French even said mid-March maybe! But let's meet him next Friday as arranged, and we can plan from there."

"Sure thing, let me go and unload the mine boys' rations, and I'll see Staff and check on the progress underground."

Langton and I experimented with the used carbide dust until we got a smooth, runny paste that was easy to apply on the tin roof, and left a whitey-grey sun-reflecting layer on the corrugated iron sheets.

"Okay Langton, you can paint the whole roof, and we'll see what difference it makes to the coolness inside the house. When Newmarch comes, he can check if the carbide coating is thick enough."

Crispin came over to the house and we sat in our outside classroom under a jacaranda tree; the teacher armed with chalks and a blackboard and easel, lecturing to the willing pupil – me.

These Ndebele lessons – two phrases relevant to mining and 10 new words each session – had boosted my knowledge of their language, and I could already express myself confidently in the basic, very basic, day-to-day running of the mine and explaining the *gwazas* each day to the workers.

Practising speaking the language was also helped by Crispin and me only talking to each other in Ndebele instead of English when we were together during our weekly administration meetings.

It was definitely helping and I could feel that my instructions and commands were getting through to the workers – less blanks faces and more instant action!

I decided that today I would jump in with both feet, and only speak in Ndebele with Crispin and two helpers, as we concentrated on the rail embankment.

The ground sloped gently from the mine shaft for about 40 metres, and then very steeply for the last 20 metres, which meant that the embankment would have to be filled up with soil to a height of possibly three metres at the mill site end, more than I had originally thought.

Time for some shoolboy elementary mathematics, to set up a series of marker poles stretching from the mine shaft to the ball mill site.

These would indicate the height that the finished embankment had to be.

The plan was to have a wooden pole sticking out of the ground every five metres and Crispin would paint a mark on each timber where I instructed him to, indicating how high the soil had to be built up to in order to have a flat, level embankment for the rail tracks leading to the hopper at the mill site.

"But how are you going to work that out?" Crispin asked with a frown.

"Elementary, as Sherlock Holmes would say, elementary, Crispin!"

And with Crispin – still looking a little puzzled – two timber boys, 12 3" x 2" timbers, a straight wooden plank and a spirit level, I began the task of the rudimentary surveying of the embankment.

At the mine shaft entrance, the wooden plank was laid flat on the ground, pointing towards the mill site, and made level using a spirit level.

Then, by squinting through one eye looking along the wooden plank at the pole Crispin was holding, I would instruct him to move his hand slowly up the pole until it came into my line of vision, when I would tell him to stop and paint a mark on the timber pole.

This was repeated, pole after pole over the next couple of hours, but, as we neared the mill site end, Crispin had to sit on Amon's shoulders to be able to reach up to paint the mark, the last one being 3.40 metres high!

When we stood way back to the side of the embankment, we could see a string of timbers sticking out of the ground, with the painted marks clearly indicating the height that the ground had to be built up to in order to make a level, flat surface for the rail tracks.

Staff came over with a big grin as he viewed our morning's work. "How did you do that? I have a good eye for building, and I can see that those marks painted on the poles indicate a pretty level embankment!"

When Crispin explained how we had done it, he was amazed and said, "When the mine surveyor comes with his theodolite apparatus, he, too, wouldn't believe that we had achieved such accurate results using a straight plank of wood and the boss' good eyesight!"

In the afternoon, Joseph told me that they had found a hive of wild bees in an old shaft when they were prospecting, and had lit some branches and thrown them down the shaft to smoke out the bees – and ran away like hell as hundreds of angry bees swarmed out of the smoking shaft.

"We'll go back later when the smoking branches have burnt out and the bees have gone. I'll get lowered down the shaft again to collect the honeycombs full of delicious wild honey!"

Crispin and I were making a list of what I should buy for our shop on my next trip to town when we heard a lot of noise outside.

Joseph and his helpers were triumphantly returning from the bush carrying the honeycombs, dipping their fingers into the holes and licking their lips.

"Crispin! Take these honeycombs to the storeroom, and scrape out all the honey into a big pot – hey, this will make my breakfast tastier in the mornings when I'm here on the mine!"

“It should last a bloody long time then!” I quipped sarcastically.

. . .

Joseph had declined to come for supper the previous evening, saying he preferred to be on his own, but he did call in for breakfast, boasting a jar of honey, which he and Crispin had extracted from the honeycombs – they filled six jars.

“There we are, kids.” He smiled as he gave them the jar of honey. “That is our natural wild bees’ honey, the best there is, and it’s all for you two, and do you know how clever bees are? Well, I’ll tell you. They build these honeycombs by making small six-sided frames, which fit together strongly to hold the weight of all the honey they deposit. Look here, I’ve brought a piece so you two kids can see that for yourselves; dip your fingers in and lick the tasty honey.”

I dipped my finger in too, and I must say it was absolutely delicious; I’d never tasted honey of such a rich texture and juicy sweetness before.

After breakfast, we decided to collect the timber railed to the Shangani depot from the Umvuma Forest. Joseph drove off with six mine boys on the back, I took Jeffrey in my pick-up and Marianne and Marie-Louise followed in the grey pick-up.

We loaded Joseph’s pick-up first so that he could drop off the timber at the mine and be on his way to Gwelo for the evening.

When our other two pick-ups were fully loaded with the remaining timber, we set off on the road to the Ridge Top Mine.

We pulled up at the Fort Rixon petrol pump store – 10 Coca Colas were quickly drained between us before we continued on our journey. I was surprised that Joseph hadn’t met us coming the other way on his way back home to Gwelo.

At the mine, we were greeted by Crispin, who told us that Joseph had phoned Belingwe to speak to his father, collected the jars of honey and sped off in the direction of Filabusi, but he had left no message for me.

The timber was unloaded on the site of our proposed second store, covered with black plastic sheeting, and we called it a day.

. . .

At 11am, I was due to see Martin and Ronnie at the Mines Yard in Bulawayo, but, being on the early side, I thought I’d pop in to see Mr French for coffee and a private chat.

It’s always easier to find a solution if there are just the two of you face-to-face; the thread of the discussion is not interrupted by irrelevant questions or the odd stupid comment.

He confided in me that, realistically, the installation and delivery date could well stretch to the end of March, because the Italian company manufacturing the Newmarch ball mill – news to me – had misread one of the specifications, which was causing other knock-on problems.

"Jesus! But we can't wait that long; we'll go under. You are telling me a possible delivery date at the end of March, but it could be mid-April, and who knows when before the installation is completed and we are producing gold!" I iterated firmly. "However, Mr French, there is perhaps another way, an interim solution for us. I have been working with Martin Curtis to have a back-up plan in place, and on Sunday he and I are visiting a mine near Salisbury, which has a small ball mill that hasn't been used for three years. The owner of the mine operated it originally for reprocessing the waste dumps whilst they were setting up the mine with a five- stamp mill.

"They have offered us a 'free usage deal' on the mill – *if* we pick it up, *refurbish* any problem parts to make it operational, and, after two months, we either *buy* the mill or give it a full service and *return* it to them. On Sunday, Martin and I will check it out and hopefully get it going, and decide if it is worth spending any money on. If the answer is positive, Martin will service the small ball mill at the Mines Department, privately, which will be at my cost.

"What we need from your side is: K.B. Davies transport to collect the mill from Salisbury. When Martin has got it running 100%, K.B. Davies can deliver it to our mine, where Mr Newmarch will set it up for processing the Nelly 404 waste dumps. Our ordered Newmarch ball mill must be operational before the two months is up, when K.B. Davies will have to transport it back to the mine near Salisbury. That's our plan, but we need you to agree to provide all the transport, and Mr Newmarch's services at your cost as well."

"Do you know, you have made my day – really, you have made my day!" French reiterated slowly, but deliberately. "Yes, yes, I've been racking my brains on how to solve our joint ball mill problem. This is a do-able plan; I'll bear the cost of Newmarch's time, and provide the transport free of charge."

The concerned look on Mr French's face at the start of our meeting – with the worry lines racking up on his forehead – had completely disappeared.

"You've lifted the monkey off my back!" he exclaimed. "Will you be around at lunchtime? I'd be pleased if we could celebrate this agreement together; it means so much to both of us. And it is Friday; the weekend can start early!"

When I told him I would definitely meet him for lunch, but only after I'd visited the mines depot to tell Martin and Ronnie that the deal was on, he enthusiastically exploded, "Bring them with you! All four of us are involved in your back-up plan, which we'll put into operation as soon as Martin gives the green light after your Sunday meeting in Salisbury!"

I hurried down to the Mines Department to tell Martin of French's agreement to fund the plan – both the costs of transport and Newmarch's time.

He was very pleased, slapped me on the shoulder with exuberance and exclaimed, "And an early Friday lunchtime session with Mr French, Ronnie and yourself will be reward enough for putting this plan together. Oh, and another thing, I haven't got the paperwork ready yet for the leasing of the rails and pipes; can we leave it for today? If you can call in on Monday, or early Tuesday to sign, we can still deliver the goods to you on the Wednesday. Come on! Let's not keep Mr French waiting!"

The glasses clinked, the beer flowed, the stories grew, some of the jokes were outrageous, but all of us were enjoying this celebration immensely, and were very relieved by this mutually satisfying and doable back-up plan.

"Here's to the four of us!" French proudly proclaimed. "What a team we make!"

"And here's to the success of *both* ball mill installations, and to Ridge Top Mine and the Nelly 404 being on the gold producers list for the Insiza District of Matabeleland, Rhodesia!

. . .

I enjoyed a very long, relaxing sleep; the last hurdle to us producing gold had been overcome by the Fabulous Four!

It was around 11am when I was awoken by Marianne.

"One of the timber boys, Joseph, is pleading with me to take his wife and their very sick child to Shangani Hospital; shall I take the kids or leave them with you?"

"No, let's all go; you can drive and I'll sit in the back with the kids; be fun together. Let the woman and her sick child sit in the front with you."

The small child had to stay in the hospital for observation, and Joseph asked for a few days off so he could take them back to his village near Shangani after treatment.

It was wonderful to just relax and enjoy being driven through the bush; you see so much more when you don't have to concentrate on the road ahead. Completely different views open up before your eyes.

Elliot the ostrich proudly strutted alongside the road for a kilometre or two, much to the amusement of the kids, who kept calling out, "Faster, faster, Elliot; you can't catch us!"

The long, open stretches of grasslands gave way to thicker bush, and many acacia trees seemed to rise before our eyes as we approached a large dry donga, which Marianne negotiated successfully and we drove on, when suddenly something caught my eye.

I banged on the roof of the cab, and Marianne stopped.

"What?" she called out through the open window.

"Just reverse slowly, 'til I bang again."

The undulating whirring sound of the reverse gear and the unintentional zigzagging of the pick-up caused the three of us to start giggling – but, when I thought about it, I remembered that she'd never driven in reverse before; even the last time we visited Shangani Hospital she had to ask an ambulance driver to reverse the pick-up out of a parking space for her.

I knocked hard on the roof, we stopped, and I pointed towards some tall trees about 30 metres away.

"Oh, look at the head of that giraffe poking out from above the trees; oh, it's so beautiful," Marie-Louise whispered.

"If we switch off the engine and wait for a few minutes, we may be lucky to see some more," I called to Marianne.

True enough. Not one, not two, not three, but four large giraffes majestically walked from one patch of acacia trees to the next, which was much closer to the road.

Now we could see them clearly, straining their long necks and eating the top leaves.

Suddenly, a much smaller giraffe appeared from behind the larger ones and started prancing and jumping about, which sent Marie-Louise into whispering a non-ending sentence of 'oohs, aahs, beautiful'.

We sat in silence for a while watching these magnificent animals, and then, unbelievably, one slowly came walking close to the vehicle with its familiar rocking gait. Towering above us, it cast a casual glance down from its full five-metre height – whilst we were only looking at the top of its legs and the underside of its belly as it passed by and crossed the road – these are close-up moments that we were so lucky to be able to enjoy. We never tired of watching the live Mother Nature shows in the bush.

It was some time before all the giraffes had wandered gracefully of out of sight, and, still talking about those beautiful animals, we headed for Fort Rixon.

We parked outside the Mine Office, and I told Crispin that Joseph would not be coming to the mine for a few days.

"But he was here an hour ago; he brought a five-ton block and tackle back from Belingwe!"

"Not Boss Joseph; Joseph, the timber boy!"

I looked over to the block-making area and could clearly see that the *gwaza*, 12 rows of 10 blocks, had not been completed, and, worse still, George and his two helpers were nowhere to be seen.

"Crispin, what's happened to George?"

"They were here only a few minutes ago!"

"But where are they now?" I enquired mockingly. "Did the Chibuku lorry come at lunchtime today?"

"Yes, sir!"

"Okay, now we know where they are! Send Amon to the village to bring George and his *gwaza* team here straight away."

I counted the blocks; there were only 90 instead of the 120 *gwaza*.

George, Peter and Miranda meandered towards me; the beer had already slowed their reactions and control of their limbs.

"Why didn't you finish the *gwaza*, George?"

"Because we ran out of cement!"

"But why didn't you ask Crispin for another bag of cement?"

"Because it was afternoon and the Chibuku lorry had arrived," George blurted out, "and it was so hot, and we were thirsty, and…"

I cut him short. "Well, the three of you must see Crispin tomorrow morning and complete the *gwaza*. I know its Sunday, but you have to make another 30 blocks before you can knock off for the day."

"Yes, Boss," George answered.

But Peter and Miranda didn't answer; they just kept looking down at the ground, and the three of them walked slowly back to the village.

"Crispin, I won't be here tomorrow morning; I'm leaving early to go to Salisbury and will only be back in the evening. So control that they finish their 30-block *gwaza*."

Crispin called me into the store. "Feet delivered vegetables again today, and the mine boys are very happy to be getting fresh greens. Here, he left two cabbages for you as well."

"Thanks Crispin. By the way, did Boss Joseph leave any message for me?"

"No sir! He only delivered the block and tackle, and drove off again, in the direction of Filabusi."

Enough said.

. . .

I met Martin at Shangani just before 10am, and we headed for the Fair Deal

Mine on the road to Salisbury.

Being a Sunday, there was little traffic and it was easy driving, until we turned off onto the dirt road to the mine – then it was shake, rattle and roll from side to side as I negotiated the badly potholed track, but luckily it was only for a few kilometres before we began to hear that magical rhythmic thumping of a 5-stamp mill.

Martin smiled and said, "There is something special about the captivating sound of a 5-stamp; it's part of a hundred-year history of gold mining in Rhodesia, and it gets me right here!" He thumped his chest a couple of times. "But you'll have to get used to a rumbling, tumbling noise as the metal balls smash the ore as the ball mill rotates at speed."

On entering the mine compound, a tall, thin figure approached us and greeted us warmly, and took us into a wooden shack.

He poured three mugs of black coffee and thumped a bottle of Johnny Walker Black Label whisky on the table next to them.

"Anyone join me for a stiffener? Gets the blood flowing again after sitting in a pick-up for several hours!" He proceeded to fill three lemonade glasses with the golden brown liquid.

"Cheers; this'll put hairs on your chest!" He chuckled as he downed the whisky in one, before refilling his glass again just as quickly.

"When in Rome, do as Romans do," I added, but it took me several large gulps before the glass was empty and I felt that I was breathing fire! Dragon breath is what some people call it, and the hot black coffee seemed to aggravate the burning sensation in my throat.

"I've moved the small ball mill out of the shed and put it near our Escom power switchboard; there's also water connections nearby, so feel free to check it all out. And if you decide to go ahead with our agreement, we can block and tackle the mill onto your transport when you send a lorry out here, anytime during this coming week."

For the next few hours, I felt like a spare fart at a wedding!

Martin was busy tinkering, removing bits, cleaning, replacing… concentrating, often nattering to himself, as he applied his trade.

Several times, Tom, the owner came past with a half-empty bottle of whisky dangling from his hand, asked Martin a few questions between *sluks* of whisky, and wandered back over to the large wooden shack and sat on the veranda.

Suddenly, with an ear-shattering noise, the small ball mill jerked to life, and I looked at Martin with a really shocked expression.

"Jesus, what a noise; it sounds like shaking a bucket of rusty nails!" I exclaimed.

But Martin was smiling triumphantly. "Don't look so worried; most of the noise is caused by the balls crashing around in the empty drum of the ball mill." He laughed. "When it's full of ore, it will run much quieter. But it's in quite good condition, and yes, it is well worth going ahead with the deal, and it shouldn't be too costly to get it running."

Handshakes all around – let's pray that they are true, honourable Rhodesian handshakes, like the ones with Pat at the tribute-signing agreement – and not like the handshake of the 'Godfather' cementing our so-called 50 /50 partnership and then extracting a 10% share from us – it still rankles when I recall his Mafioso tactics… *'I'll make you an offer you can't refuse!'*

We thanked Tom for his hospitality and set off for home.

As we turned onto the main tarmac road, I noticed a petrol station in the distance, but on the left towards Salisbury, so I did a quick U-turn in the middle of the road and zoomed off towards it.

We bought some cheese rolls and cooldrinks, and set off for Shangani.

We didn't say much as we chewed, and chewed with difficulty – they were rather stale rolls, which, even when mixed with mouthfuls of warm lemonade, were still difficult to swallow and to digest the pulp!

It was around 5pm when we pulled up in front of the Shangani Hotel; the car park was very full.

We looked at each other, swallowing with difficulty, the mixture of neat whisky and stale cheese hampering our speech.

But, two nods, and we raced up the steps of the terrace and into the bar.

"What are you two doing out here on a Sunday?" Ray, the barman, called out. "You look in desperate need of a cold beer, I reckon!" He proceeded to tap two pints and place them on the bar in front of us….

Later, as we parted ways, Martin reminded me that the paperwork for our ordered items would be ready for signing on Monday morning.

He hooted as I turned off the Bulawayo road and headed home to the mine.

. . .

Marie-Louise woke us up several times during the night complaining that the mosquito bites on her leg were itching too much and she couldn't sleep.

The kids had both been complaining for several days about itchy legs, saying they didn't like going to the long drop loo, because there were always mosquitos buzzing around and biting them.

It was a long, long night of very little sleep.

However, finally it was dawn and getting lighter.

All four of us sat outside for early morning tea, but Marie-Louise started crying again, saying it wasn't all the mosquito bites that hurt, just the two big ones that Marianne had put a plaster on two days earlier.

"Put your leg up here, Marie-Louise, and let's have a good look," I told her.

There were numerous small red marks of mosquito bites, but the plasters were covering two very red lumps, which, when I touched them, caused Marie-Louise to scream.

"Okay, hold on, I'll pull one of the plasters off quickly so it won't hurt."

Zap! I ripped off the plaster.

"Jesus!" I exclaimed. "Look at that hole in her leg; what's happened?"

"Oh no!" Marianne cried out. "Look at that thing on the plaster you're holding!"

"*Eee, yuk!*" I exclaimed, and we all looked at this fat white worm about a centimetre long that was wiggling around on the plaster, as if objecting to be awoken so rudely from its cosy bed – the hole in Marie-Louise's leg!

"Elliot! Come here, please," I called out.

"That's a maggot fly worm," he said. "You better remove the other plaster too."

Zap!

"Oooouch!" shouted Marie-Louise as we all stared at the repeat of the first plaster being pulled off a hole in her leg, and another disgusting-looking creamy coloured wiggly worm stuck to the plaster.

"Let me phone Irene straight away," Marianne said, and she went inside the house.

After a few minutes, she returned and told us, "Irene says they are maggot fly *larvae*. When clothes are hanging outside, the maggot flies lay their eggs on the clothes. They were probably on Marie-Louise's pyjamas, and, with the warmth of her body, they breed in the flesh after entering under the skin. We must always iron with a hot iron any clothes that have been hung outside; this kills the maggot fly eggs.

"When I told her we don't have electricity, so our electric iron won't work, she asked if our wood stove had been fixed yet. You know that iron-shaped plate on top of the wood stove? Well, she says that's for a hot coal iron; she's got a spare, which she'll bring over later this morning, together with some muti to put in the holes on Marie-Louise's leg – luckily, the maggot fly worms wouldn't cause any serious long-term problems for Marie-Louise."

"When Irene comes over, check if there are any other creepy-crawly flying things we should be aware of. Mosquitos are just annoying, but only cause itchy bites; there's no malaria in these parts. Snakes, we are getting used to seeing, but all except the puff adder will normally slither away on being aware of us approaching.

"The puff adder apparently remains where it is lying on the warm sand of a track in the bush and doesn't move, and bites unsuspecting people hiking on such tracks. I have a snakebite kit in the pick-up; however, I will get another one for the house when I go to Bulawayo to see Martin shortly. And what don't you do, Jeffrey, when you see large stones or rocks in the bush or on the koppies?"

"Don't move them or lift them up!" he proudly pronounced. "Because there could be scorpions, centipedes and other dangerous insects that can harm us."

I left for Bulawayo thinking that it was good that not only the children, but we adults as well were becoming more aware of the smaller dangerous creatures. They are tiny when compared to the larger wild animals – baboons, leopards, hippos and buffalo, which are dangerous, but these little armed warriors, including the inch-long black Matabele ants, can cause sickness, pain and even death if one is not careful.

When Newmarch next came to the mine, he said he would show me how to make our own charcoal – today, we learnt another use for it, filling the hot coal iron that Irene would be giving Marianne.

Martin wasn't at the Mines Yard when I called by; Ronnie told me that he had been working on the small ball mill and had gone out in search of one or two items.

He had, however, left the lease documentation to be signed for:

Twenty lengths of 20-foot rails, weighing two and a half tons and at a cost of $120 per ton.

Two hundred and sixty feet of electric cable.

Two hundred and sixty feet of both 2" and 1" water piping.

All to be added to our mounting monthly Mines Department costs.

They would liaise with B&O United Transport and co-ordinate with Mr French of K.B. Davies to collect the conveyor system from Zambesi Metals together with the second ore hopper, which would stand at the end of the rail embankment – to feed the ore onto the ball mill conveyor system.

French was also not in. Newmarch said that he had taken a long weekend break to relax after all the frustrating problems over the last month.

"He went fishing with a few friends on Lake Kariba and will only be back tomorrow. He usually comes back with quite a haul of fish, so I'm sure he'll give you a two- to three-pounder, which I can bring out to your mine when I come over tomorrow."

"And Newmarch, don't forget to show me how to make charcoal; we'll need it for use in the hot coal iron to iron our clothes properly before wearing them. Marie-Louise had two maggot fly worms growing in her legs, which we removed this morning amid her screams!"

"Oh, poor little girl; they are nasty things. Yes, I'll make a heap of charcoal together with you – you'll never be short again of hot coals for your iron."

I loaded up another 20 pockets of cement, which I would need for laying the ball mill concrete pad, a 20 x 20 foot square reinforced six-inch-thick block that would support the five-ton Newmarch ball mill.

H4H – head for home!

. . .

I woke up late, around 9am.

The house was quiet. I called out to Elliot to bring some tea.

"Where is everyone?"

"*Memsab* (boss' wife) has driven your pick-up to the store to see Crispin, so that the cement bags could be unloaded. The children are over at my hut with Judith, playing with my baby daughter."

I walked up to the mine to find not only my already unloaded pick-up, but also Mr Newmarch's rust bucket Peugeot 403.

He was chatting away happily with Marianne. That's one thing I really like about living in the bush; everyone and every caller takes the time to stop and have an unhurried friendly conversation – except Mr Worry in a Hurry, and his son, Joseph, of course!

Crispin informed me that only George had come to the office on Sunday morning to finish his brick-making *gwaza*, so it meant getting two others from the village to help him. Together, they finished the 30-block *gwaza*.

"How do I work that on their tickets?" Crispin enquired.

"The two who helped George can have an extra day put on their tickets for helping us out on a Sunday morning. But those other two lazy buggers can find another job somewhere else; I don't want them working here anymore. Work out how much we owe them up to Friday; I'm not paying them for the unfinished *gwaza* on Saturday, and send Amon to bring them here now, with all their belongings."

Peter and Maranda stood there with defiant expressions.

Crispin gave them their *stupas*, their old reference letter and the wages we owed them.

Peter shouted, "But you haven't paid us for the work we did on Saturday!"

"I haven't paid you, because you didn't finish your *gwaza*, and I've had to pay two other workers who finished off your work!"

"And where are our new reference letters from you for working on Ridge Top Mine?"

I laughed. "You expect me to give you a reference?"

"Yes; otherwise, we'll report you to the Mines Department, and to the Native Affairs Authority," Maranda eloquently informed me in very good English.

"If you worked as well as you speak English, Maranda, we wouldn't even be standing here now, would we?"

"But it's our right to have a reference letter! You have to give us one!" he shouted belligerently.

"Okay, you want one? Crispin, bring me some Ridge Top Mine notepaper and a pen."

Peter and Miranda puffed out their chests, smirking at Amon, with victorious, cocky expressions…

Until they read the reference letters I handed to them:

Name. ID No. etc.

<u>To who it may concern</u>

This man had worked on our Mine for only 2 months, until he was fired this morning for being lazy, arrogant and causing problems!

I would recommend him NEVER!

Yours faithfully,

Manager, Ridge Top Mine.

As Peter stepped towards me mouthing off loudly and waving his letter, Amon moved forward to intervene, and, with a threating expression, he told the two of them to pick up their belongings, and he escorted them off the mine.

Newmarch walked with Marianne back to the house, whilst I had a cord of cut hardwood put on the back of the pick-up, and, with George and his two helpers carrying spades and an axe, I drove off to the house for a lesson from Newmarch on how to make charcoal.

A treat of fresh milk and bread for the kids, while we drank some coffee with Newmarch, who outlined the process of making our own charcoal.

"It's quite simple; we remove spade-fulls of the grass covered earth – the sods – and lay them aside, dig a hole about two-foot deep, stack plenty of hard wood in the pit and set it on fire…"

When the wood was burning well, a layer of the grass sods were placed covering the fire and the rest of the earth was piled carefully on top, sealing the pit of still-burning embers – traces of smoke were coming out of the ground here and there.

"Now we just leave that to burn slowly. You can check it tomorrow evening, when you should have your own supply of chunks of charcoal right here in your own back garden."

We went together up to the mine to inspect how the work was progressing.

Newmarch thought I'd worked out an ingenious method for showing on the marker poles the height that the embankment had to be built up to.

Naison and Langton were busy preparing the ball mill site block area – a 20-foot by 20-foot slab of reinforced concrete, six inches thick, would have to be laid, with a run-off of one inch to facilitate drainage when it rains.

We double-checked the distance to the ball mill site for the water pipes and electric cables, and Newmarch decided that, for safety, we should increase the lengths by 10 feet of both on the Mines Department order.

He had no further news on the progress of the Newmarch ball mill, but he was still so very enthusiastic that I didn't mention our back-up plan of the small ball mill – he'd find out soon enough at the Friday meeting.

As he was leaving, a Shell lorry pulled into the mine compound with the second diesel fuel tank I'd ordered.

"It all seems to be coming together," Newmarch remarked, "and my dream will come true when I see my ball mill working and your mine producing gold."

A slight, proud grin and a confident expression appeared on his face, and he climbed into his pick-up and headed for Bulawayo.

We ate early in the evening so I could have a good sleep in preparation for a long day – the laying of the ball mill site concrete slab, which had to be laid in one go, even if we had to continue by the light of hurricane lamps to finish it off.

We would start preparing at 5am so the mixing and laying of the concrete could begin in earnest by 5:30am, 6am at the very latest, as soon as it was light.

The strength of this concrete pad was critical and it would need careful supervision.

Joseph and I would control the work being done by our three builders and a *gwaza* gang of eight to ensure that the correct cement mixture was maintained.

By 8pm, Joseph had still not arrived, and there had been no phone call from him either; I couldn't imagine him getting up at 3:30am to arrive on time so early in the morning, so I would get Crispin to help me supervise this important job instead.

. . .

It was still dark when I drove up to the office, but Crispin and I started straight away to organise the necessary wheelbarrows, shovels, drums of water and bags of cement, and instruct the *gwaza* workers on their various jobs.

Wheelbarrows-full of sand, and loose schist taken from the waste dumps would be piled up at the cement-mixing area, which was close to the proposed concrete slab.

Langton would be in charge of mixing the concrete proportions of four stones, three sand and one cement (4/3/1), which would be tipped onto the 20-foot by 20-foot area, where Naison and Goliath would spread and level the wet cement.

The area was a hive of activity as the whole team worked hard throughout the whole morning….

At 12 o'clock, Crispin brought over other workers who could stand in whilst some of the *gwaza* boys took staggered lunch breaks, so that the concrete-laying process would carry on, not stop.

And Elliot was on hand to provide hot soup and potegai for those workers having a break.

Marianne and the kids brought Crispin and me some sandwiches and a pot of coffee to keep us going.

It was around 4pm when Joseph arrived, and, before I could say anything, he blurted out a non-stop string of sentences.

"You see, the broken water pump was not ready yesterday, so I had to call in this morning to collect it, but it was still not ready, so I thought it was best that I waited around until it was fixed; that's why it took so long – but then I drove *straight here* to the mine."

I cleared my throat in a sarcastic manner, staring at him in disbelief.

"Oh, so you've been having that cough as well; it's going around in Gwelo too. I felt a bit better after a long lay-in today, I mean yesterday; I felt much better and I'm fine now. Can I do anything to help now that I'm here?"

"*Now that you're here* Joseph, there is something you can do. It'll be getting dark soon, so why don't you drive the two pick-ups down here and park them one each side of where the boys are working on laying the concrete slab, so that the headlights will illuminate the whole area. Crispin, you could also organise some hurricane lamps for the boys mixing the cement, and underground hat lamps for Naison, Goliath and his helpers; that way, we'll be able to keep going until the slab is finished – I reckon we've still got another two or three hours to go!"

It was a long, tiring session for us all, but, at 8:15pm, the last wheelbarrow-full of cement mixture was tipped into the far corner, and Naison wearily patted it down level using a wooden plank.

"Crispin, put an extra day on these workers' tickets; they have done a very good job. It seemed like it would never come to an end. And Joseph, why don't you come back to the house and have some supper with us?"

We sat inside our now-cool house, to feast on a rabbit stew that Elliot had prepared.

Joseph remarked on the coolness of the room, compared to the hot temperature in his office bedroom.

I told him the secret. We had painted the tin roof with a mixture of used carbide powder mixed with water. Newmarch had told us about this.

"Well, it makes a hell of a difference," he added. "The heat inside my place is really unbearable."

"Your place is next to get the carbide paint treatment; we'll get it done tomorrow."

Elliot brought in coffee for the three of us, and Joseph began to tell Marianne how excited Jane was getting about living on their own gold mine in their own grand house with a huge garden.

"She has been working out how to spend all the money when we strike it rich. In fact, she's already chosen some beautiful, very expensive furniture and we walked around the Meikles Furniture store this morning to look at..." – A sudden realisation that he had put his big foot in his mouth yet again, and he quickly rattled off, "Anyways, I must go; I need to sleep. See you in the morning; thanks for the supper. See you tomorrow; thanks Marianne, bye!"

"That man is like a crazy professor who forgets what he said 10 minutes earlier, and even forgets what he's supposed to do; it's unbelievable. For example, last week when he made a rare appearance at the mine and after only 10 minutes underground he told Staff to carry on with the work while he went above ground with two workers to do some prospecting on an old shaft that he'd seen back in December, which he thought could be a rich strike on the quartz gold reef.

"And what happened; the only gold he came back with was those golden honeycombs. And it's getting more and more annoying when he occasionally does turn up; he just faffs around, panning some samples here and there, whereas *his job* is to work together with me to get this Nelly 404 mine operational – then he can buy all the furniture Jane desires, and prospect in another area – preferably on the other side of the country!"

. . .

The next morning at the mine, I found Crispin in the office working away at the administration paperwork and updating the books.

In the corner on the fold-up army bed lay my snoring partner.

"Crispin, I'm very pleased we finished the slab laying; they did a really good job. Put two extra bonus days on all the workers' tickets, not one day as I told you yesterday."

The camp bed creaked and a bleary-eyed Joseph uttered, "Good morning, ask Situnda to make me some tea please, Crispin."

I continued my conversation with Crispin. "So let them all know that they have been given a double day extra bonus for their hard work – maybe that will even encourage some of the lazier workers to do better. It was late last night when we finished; have all of them turned up for work this morning?"

"All except Naison, the old builder. He came to see me late last night and said he had worked too hard; he was too old to do this anymore. He was going home to die!" Crispin announced emphatically.

Then, in my best Australian accent, I replied, "Did he go home to die, or *yesterdie?*"

Whereupon Joseph burst out laughing, leaving a confused Crispin standing there gawking at the two of us.

When Joseph had drunk his tea, he came over and asked, "Do you think French will give us a definite date for the delivery of the ball mill when we meet him today?"

I thought of telling him that a ball mill would be operational on our mine by 15 March – the small one, of course – but no, that would spoil the surprise; let him wait until French explained everything this morning.

"We'll see," I replied, "but let's leave after breakfast together; we don't want to be late for probably our most important meeting yet."

French sat down with us in his office.

He had a stern expression as he began his explanation as to why he couldn't give us a firm date. It was not under his control, he was at the mercy of the Italian mill maker who was proving to be incompetent, and his poor command of English made discussing the situation even more confusing.

"Whata mistaka tomaka!" Joseph comically interjected. "They are only good at making ice cream and pizzas!"

That broke the ice and a more relaxed atmosphere prevailed.

"To be realistic," French continued, "we have decided to pay the Italian off for the work he's done, and have invited a Salisbury company to take over the project. Newmarch and I met them yesterday and spent the whole day going through the specifications and inspecting some of the jobs they were working on. They have quoted us a firm date, which we have accepted, the 1st of May…"

"The first of bloody May!" Joseph shrieked. "The first of May; oh no, that can't be; how are we going to survive 'til then?"

"By starting gold production in two weeks' time when we deliver the small ball mill!"

"The small what?" gulped Joseph. "A small ball mill; how's that possible?"

"We call it Plan B," French continued. "We will deliver the small mill, Newmarch will get it operational and you will have two months' usage – all at no cost to the Ridge Top Mine."

"That's fabulous!" Joseph exclaimed. "It's like Christmas; what a present. How did this all come about? Hey partner, isn't this wonderful news? But where has the mill come from?"

"Why don't you ask your partner? Over the last week, Martin Curtis and he have done all the work and negotiations with a mine near Salisbury, and have convinced me to cover both the cost of transport and Newmarch's services. That gives you two months of production before the Newmarch ball mill is installed."

The euphoria was over…. A rather sad and dejected Joseph sat picking his nails. "Why didn't you tell me this?" he moped. "We could have done this together."

"Let's just be pleased that the hard work and negotiations between all parties went smoothly and were agreed quickly," I answered.

"But why wasn't I involved!" Joseph spat out, glaring at me with wild, angry eyes. "I could have helped – I wasn't busy doing anything else."

I resisted the urge to reply to his comment, and simply said, "Leave it, Joseph; we've got the answer to our prayers, which will allow us to start gold production and bring in some much-needed money to cover costs – a free stopgap solution until the Newmarch ball mill is installed."

"But, why didn't you…?"

"Joseph, it happened so quickly, just like that – one, two, three! You hadn't been at the mine or in contact with me, so how could I have involved you?"

"Yes Joseph." French took control of the conversation. "Just be pleased that your partner and Martin Curtis put the idea together and got all parties to agree. And on top of that, I have waived your account limit and repayment terms; your mine now has *unlimited credit.* The gods are on your side."

"I suppose so," Joseph grunted, and, like a tortoise, he retracted into his shell, leaving the rest of us to finalise the details of the plan and make the necessary arrangements.

"Come on, Joseph, let's go and visit Martin at the Mines Yard and check on our new small ball mill."

He followed me reluctantly and we walked over to the Mines Department.

The walk did him good, and, when he saw Martin working on the small ball mill, his face lit up again, and he enthusiastically started bubbling away, asking this and asking that – he was in his own heaven once more.

I left them together and walked back to K.B. Davies.

French looked at me knowingly, acknowledging that I wasn't in the 'perfect partnership'.

"Have a good weekend, and enjoy these fish that I caught at the Kariba Dam."

Indaba Tree

I was well pleased with what had been achieved in the last 10 days, and, if we could get the small ball mill installed and crushing ore in the next two weeks, we would be able to extract our first gold – extract our first gold! *Yebo*, that had a bloody good ring to it.

Crispin greeted me at the office and we sat down to our Saturday morning administration. It was also a time to catch up on all the local gossip, the goings-on in the mine village – good old Crispin, and he tells the stories well too.

"Oh dear," Crispin whispered. "Looks like trouble; one of Jackson's farm workers is outside."

And sure enough, the messenger was carrying a 'hot off the press' message from Rancher Jackson.

Mine Manager,

I will prosecute any of your workers who are caught poaching on my land.

I have instructed my workers to be on the lookout for any poaching traps and snares when they are walking through the bush.

And although the Rhodesian Hunting season is still over 2 months away, I also give you forewarning not to shoot any animals on my land – I will prosecute you!

Jackson

Copy: Mining Commissioner

Copy: Insiza Rural Council

"Well Crispin, I was expecting another complaint from Jackson; it had to come. It was only a matter of time, and, of course, by his copies sent to the mining commissioner, he just wants to keep stirring things up. His timber complaints have been sorted out and we have the full timber permit now. He failed in his attempt to cause us excessive costs by demanding that we fence our claims – our well-thought-out plan of fencing certain parts, which isolated the cattle-watering troughs, really upset him, and although he bitched like hell to the mining commissioner his objections were overridden and the deadline for fencing our claims has been extended indefinitely. So now he's having another go. But Crispin, this is serious. When the knock-off gong sounds, get all the mine workers together and I'll tell them that anybody caught poaching will be fired and taken to the police station."

The lunchtime poaching warning drew only the odd groan and murmuring amongst them as they went off to the village.

Crispin told me that poaching was too much trouble for most workers, but he would keep his eyes open, and ask Amon to be on the lookout too.

Back at home, a thought suddenly struck me. "Elliot, come and see me, please."

"Yes, sir?"

"Elliot, we had a delicious rabbit stew the other night; where did you get the rabbit from?"

"It was given to me, and I thought you all would enjoy a rabbit stew."

"We did, but who gave it to you, Elliot?"

"I can't remember, sir."

"Was he one of our workers?"

"Yes, sir."

"And does he have a name?"

"Yes, sir, he has a name."

"And what is his name, Elliot?"

"I can't remember, sir!"

Marianne couldn't stop sniggering; it was like listening to one of the kids' conversations.

"Okay Elliot, listen good. You weren't at the mine just now when I informed all the workers that anyone caught poaching will be fired and handed over to the police. Jackson has banned us poaching on his land. In future, don't take or buy any rabbits offered to you."

"So Marianne, yet another problem to tax the old brain – how to set a trap to catch the poacher?"

I spoke with Willias, our garden boy, who also had to be told of the no-poaching rule.

Willias had been brought up on this land and knew the area well.

He told me he had poached years ago when he didn't have a job, in order to feed his family; most of Jackson's workers still did.

"Tomorrow morning, Willias, would you take me into the bush near the mining village and show me how and where you would try to catch small animals? I want to learn."

Time for an afternoon at Fort Rixon dam.

After a jam-packed week when I had constantly, from dawn to dusk, been working on negotiations, driving and planning, it was wonderful to sit back and relax, meet a few of our rancher neighbours and just do what blokes like doing over a beer or two – chat about the latest sport results, tell a few jokes and laugh, whilst the women had their own fun, gossiping and… who knows?

Trevor and Gayle had invited us and the kids to come over in three weeks for their daughter's birthday party and stay the night – an invitation that was gratefully accepted and etched into my 'agenda' memory.

The drive back home was unusually quiet and uneventful.

It seemed that not only the rabbits, but the small antelopes too had gone into hiding to prevent us from breaking Jackson's poaching laws!

. . .

I emerged from my house at first light to find Willias sitting outside waiting for me.

We walked down the murram road and entered the bush just past the old Claremont main mine shaft.

A large granite boulder provided us with a slightly elevated view of the whole surrounding area, and we could see the mine buildings and the village, with the main tracks running between them.

One or two other well-worn tracks showed the shortcuts onto the main murram road.

"Look there," Willias pointed out. "See, from the village there is one track that is not often used, and which leads off to nowhere. Whoever is poaching uses this track. Follow me; don't talk and I'll find you what you're looking for."

As we approached that area, Willias signalled me to halt and pointed to some long grass off to the left.

"See the slight break in the tall grass over there; that is where the rabbits run. We'll follow it and you'll see where the poacher has placed his snares."

There were indeed three thin, almost invisible looped wires.

"When a rabbit runs through there, it would be snared, caught around the neck. Now over here on the flatter ground with less grass we'll look for guinea fowl traps."

A few minutes later, I was marvelling at the poacher's ingenuity.

There were two rows of sticks, like walls, supporting a heavy log about a metre long.

When the guinea fowl entered to eat some seeds at the far end which was closed off, it would trigger the fall of the heavy log, which would crash down on the unsuspecting guinea fowl, knocking it down and trapping it under the weight of the log.

"Willias, you are a genius; this is really fascinating. Now don't tell anyone what you've shown me, and I'll make a plan to catch the poacher."

I went up to the mine office and told Crispin and Amon the story of my 'PhD' course – poaching hunter diploma!

We instructed Amon to watch for anyone who took that 'track to nowhere' around dusk, and to let me know in the morning.

I told Marianne of my anti-poaching mission and how fascinating it was.

"Jackson was being so petty; what's wrong with the mineworkers living off the bush? It's natural and there are many thousand times more rabbits and guinea fowl than there are African farm and mine workers in this area – an area of hundreds of square miles of uninhabited bush. It's so ridiculous, but I have to stop it; otherwise, Jackson will try to nail us again, and we can't afford any more bad publicity – we've already had the mine workers getting drunk and pestering the local African women, the fights, the murder, and now poaching, all well documented in his letters to me, with, of course, copies to the mining commissioner!

"Those letters can only do us harm with regard to our loan application even when we have solved the problems with Jackson – like with the timber agreement and the fencing stalemate – because those copies of his complaints will still remain on file; a file that will be read by the advisory board members who will make the decision on whether we are allocated the loan or not."

. . .

"Fancy a trip to Gwelo today, all of us? I need to speak to Joseph and Jane, and try to get her to kick him out every other day so that he's at the mine most of the time, Monday through to Friday."

We pulled into Fort Rixon and I checked the post – two bits of further good news:

A letter in a brown envelop from the district advisory board, advising us that they had approved the loan, and their recommendation would be reviewed at the next ministry advisory board in Salisbury scheduled for 18 April.

Note: this approval is conditional pending further investigation by the officers of the Advisory Boards.

"Now what sort of gobblety-gook is that? Civil Servanteese or Chinese! Anyways, it's a start."

The second letter was a thick white embossed envelope with a golden crest on it: 'FINCO, Finance Corporation of Rhodesia'.

Inside was a letter with a pure golden cheque made out to Ridge Top Mine for $3,000; yes, three thousand thank-you-very-much dollars.

"When I see Joseph shortly, Marianne, if this doesn't get him out of his moods and get him to pull finger, nothing will. And this cheque has arrived just in time too; we'll deposit it today, and I can pay the mine workers this month, the smaller suppliers' overdue accounts, the Mines Department monthly leasing costs, AND… have enough over to buy milkshakes all round; let's go, go go to the Midland Hotel."

"Yebo, yebo!" shouted the kids.

And who should be there; none other than Uncle Matt with a few friends.

"Joseph phoned me this morning from Belingwe to tell me the good news that he's got the Mines Department and K.B. Davies to have a small ball mill delivered and installed at Ridge Top Mine. He was so excited too. Of course, I knew that it was you who had brokered the deal; Joseph couldn't organise a piss-up in a brewery!" Matt exclaimed. "But it really is great news, and I'm pleased for you – you've been doing the work of two men!"

His friends were just leaving, so he invited us to join him on the terrace.

He was very interested to hear all the details about the small mill, and thought it would slot in nicely to allow us to start processing the waste dumps while we awaited the installation of the Newmarch ball mill in two months' time.

His news was not so good, though.

They'd had a serious cave-in when they tried to blast open an old blocked drive tunnel.

"No one was hurt, of course, because I am always very strict on personally ensuring that all the workers are out of the mine before blasting, but it has put us back with the planned underground development. We're still reprocessing those waste dumps, which is keeping us going, but that will run out in a few months' time, so the underground sampling and development is critical to us ensuring payable ore reserves; otherwise, it's…"

No gold miner ever finishes off a sentence like that; on the contrary, it's normally *'until we hit the mother lode'!* So Matt was very down and depressed indeed.

He left us, and, as he climbed into his white Peugeot pick-up, he called out, "This 404 is a beauty; thanks for fixing up the sale. I know how much work it took to get the approval through the Reserve Bank. Go well."

"Let's quickly pop into the bank and boost our account with that $3,000, then we'll go home; there's no point in trying to see Joseph at Hudson Road. Matt said he was still in Belingwe – probably suckling on his mother's bosom!"

We arrived back at the mine just as the sun was going down, and Crispin remarked, "What good timing, sir. Amon watched on Sunday evening to see who left the village compound and used that small track. It was Mucharaveni, and he's just left again this evening. If we go over there now we can catch him red-handed."

We walked briskly and just in time to witness Amon handcuffing Mucharaveni, who was looking sadly at his catch of two rabbits lying lifeless on the ground by his feet.

"Let's go over to that fire by the huts, and Crispin, please get all the workers to gather around for a small *indaba*."

It's so effective to fire a worker in front of his co-workers, especially for this poaching violation. It will make all of them think twice before setting traps.

We frog-marched the guilty man away from the hushed crowd up to the office.

There, Crispin paid Mucharaveni his ticket wages, and I told Amon to unlock the handcuffs and escort Mucharaveni off to the main road.

"Mucharaveni, I'm letting you go free, but don't ever come here again; otherwise, you won't be so lucky and I'll call the police."

"Thanks Boss!" And he faded into the darkness.

. . .

The phone was ringing, the shrill warbling sound echoing loudly in the quiet darkness – the start gong hadn't even been struck yet.

"Hello?" I said sleepily.

An excited voice started babbling way, sending a stream of words via my ear into my slowly awakening brain.

"Jane says you were quite right, and she woke me up early so that I could leave for work on time; I'm at Matt's mine."

"Matt's mine?" I queried.

"Yes, Matt's mine, so that I can use his phone to make this phone call – you are always telling me to phone to let you know what's going on."

"And what is going on; are you on your way to our mine this morning?"

"No, I'm going to Bulawayo to the Mines Department and see if Martin Curtis needs any help with the small ball mill. It's very important that we get that working and transported to the mine as quickly as we can. And I'll pick up more rations too, and I will be staying over tonight on the mine."

And the phone went dead.

A hurricane lamp was being lit, and I could see the quizzical look on Marianne's face.

"It was Joseph, informing me of his day's agenda." I smiled wryly. "Well, at least we know where he is today, even if it is 5 o'clock in the bloody morning! Time and tide await no man, the expression says, although I'm sure Joseph is trying to amend that saying!"

Black coffee was helping to make us more alert and awake, when suddenly the phone rang again, and Marianne went to pick it up.

"If that's Joseph, tell him I've gone to the mine office!" I said quickly.

"Hello, oh hello, Peter, yes sure, he's here; just a minute."

"You're joking," I said. "You want me to come to the police station this morning, and Jackson will be there too? Why?"

"He's already made an official complaint against you for poaching and says he has the evidence too."

"Evidence? What evidence?"

"Last night he stopped one of your workers with a bag of poached animals coming out of the bush by the old Claremont mine, and he brought him to the police post where we locked him in a cell."

"Good God! Unbelievable; sometimes I think Jackson sleeps in the bush by our mine, looking for anything that can be used against us. Okay, Peter, I'll be there by 10 o'clock."

It turned out that Mucharaveni had doubled back and had collected a guinea fowl and two more rabbits from snares he had set, which I rather foolishly hadn't thought of checking before we fired him.

Jackson stormed in. "I caught one of your workers red-handed; can't you control them? Even after I warned you by letter on Saturday that I would prosecute any poaching!"

My version of what happened seemed to be accepted by Peter, even complimenting me on my anti-poaching purge and firing the guilty worker.

"But you should have brought him to the police post," Jackson stated emphatically, stabbing a finger repeatedly in my direction, "and not just fire him and letting him get off scot-free – in fact, with a bonus as well of *my* guinea fowl and two rabbits!"

"Mr Jackson, Mr Jackson, please!" Peter interrupted, trying to calm down the angry rancher.

"I want this man's African worker charged for poaching," Jackson exploded again, "and I will write a letter to the mining commissioner condemning *you* for your lax attitude in letting a criminal go free," he spat out with venom, still waving his accusing finger at me.

That said, he stormed out again, but with the ceremonial gait of a general who had just triumphed in a battle.

Peter and I looked at each other; wry smiles and raised eyebrows seemed to sum up this silly situation.

"Do you have some notepaper and a pen? I'll write a letter immediately to the mining commissioner explaining the situation, with a copy of your charge sheet, and stressing to him that we are doing everything possible to prevent poaching on any property belonging to Jackson – and I'll give a copy to you, BSA Police, and post one to Jackson as well."

I told Peter about the new small ball mill project that could be our saviour.

"If we can start producing gold in two to three weeks' time, all these copies of letters that Jackson keeps writing and are piling up on the commissioner's desk, annoying though they are, will not cause us any serious problems, because we will be a legitimate, respected, gold-for-export producer! But now, I'd better get back to the mine; let's keep each other informed of any further developments."

Newmarch's rust bucket squealed and squeaked to a gentle stop, and Newmarch carefully eased himself out of the driver's cab with a few grunts, and proceeded to stretch his legs slowly, causing the odd pained grimace on his face – probably his aged joints being in need of lubrication.

"It's these long trips sitting for hours in a pick-up; the old joints just stiffen up. But once I've walked around for a bit, all's fine again."

"Then why don't we take a walk through the bush to the Nelly 403 and the Nelly Extra mine shafts on our claims; there are a few things I'd like to ask you."

As we picked our way through the spikey thorn bushes, we came across a post with a lead registration plate attached:

<u>Nelly Extra</u>, Reg. No 3938, Gold Reef, **<u>17.6.1895</u>**, Bulawayo, J.R. Stewart & Sons Ltd.

"Ah, a bit of Rhodesiana," Newmarch remarked, "and look through there in the midst of that overgrown thicket; that's an old 5-stamp mill box. Get one of your workers to clear around it today, and I will tell you a story or two about it later on."

Behind the thicket, I showed him an area that I had already cleared, revealing some large concrete blocks with rusty bolts sticking out of them.

"Ah, yes, that's the concrete base of a 5-stamp mill when they mined here, hmm… but it's unusual for that metal stamp box that we just saw in the bush to be left behind when they closed this mine down; perhaps it was damaged. When the bush is cleared, I'll show you what to do with that old metal stamp box too."

"Mr Newmarch, over here there's a waste dump, and now that we're getting that small ball mill shortly we could re-mill it, if it's got value; should we first take samples and get the evaluations from the Mines Department?"

"No, don't waste the time; put it all through the mill. The Nelly 403 was a rich mine and the waste schist is in small enough pieces, which won't need breaking up before feeding into the small ball mill. In fact, dig out the ground all around this mill block to a metre deep, and process it through the small mill as well. I'll tell you all about recycling on a gold mine; you'll be amazed where gold hides! But first I need a cup of coffee."

Back in the office, Crispin and I listened intently, this time not to hear old mining stories about crazy characters of the past, but to learn about gold, its properties and how to find it on the surface of old mines.

Newmarch told me to start stockpiling waste schist from all the old mine dumps on our claims, for reprocessing by the small mill.

"Take from the Nelly 403 and Nelly Extra dumps, and the diggings around the stamp block as I showed you back there, and transport them to the small ball mill site. Forget using the Claremont and Nelly 404 dumps; they've almost certainly been re-milled and reprocessed already. Get Marianne and a couple of lasher boys to make trips to each of the other small mines' waste dumps as well, like the Sirius 1, Sirius 2 and Hlatin, and shovel the waste schist onto the pick-up, and make new dumps by the small mill – you'll be surprised how much gold you extract from them.

"If she does that three times each day, that will build up the stocks by about three tons per day, so when we get the small ball mill operational, we'll have weeks of stock-piled fodder for the mill; plenty to keep it running on a one-shift-per-day basis. You should extract enough gold from that process to cover your running costs – these dumps could yield you as much as 20 ounces of gold per month, which will make me feel less guilty! And help keep you going until my ball mill eventually arrives.

"And you'll be producing gold from the waste dumps of old mines, in effect from what the old miners threw away! A nice feeling! And when you're using my 30-ton-per-day capacity larger ball mill, crushing ore mined from underground in one daylight shift, even using the lower grade banded ironstone, you should be making monthly trips to the Bank Assay office with over 60 ounces of gold in your pocket! Actually, that's about two kilos of gold, so you'll need to use a strong leather bag!

"And you'll also be amazed where else you can find gold hiding in the equipment, from the stamp mill box down to the James extraction tables – as particles of gold get washed by the water down the pipes, and, being one of the heaviest metals, gold settles in any dent, nook or cranny, even in the bends and dips of pipes! In the old stamp box, the one we saw at the Nelly 403, once it's been cleaned up, who knows how much gold we'll find."

A knock on the door interrupted Newmarch's revelations.

It was Gwabuya and Agrippa, and, as if on cue, they had come to tell us that they had cleared the bush surrounding the old stamp box.

"Can I come as well?" Crispin asked. "I find this so interesting."

Crispin, myself and Newmarch hastened to examine the old stamp box. Gone were the weary, aching legs; there was a youthful bounce in his step – gold fever was pumping through his veins again.

The old stamp box had a big hole in it, and, thus, was of no use for an operating stamp mill anymore and had been discarded.

"Once you have the small ball mill running, get a worker with a chisel and a mallet and supervise him closely as he chips away at those areas and any rusty patches – gold is shy and likes to hide," he joked, and we all laughed.

"But don't leave the munt on his own; you'll be surprised that, after a day's work, the pile of rust, dust, dirt, metal shavings and bits of concrete could yield you maybe two ounces of gold; a nice little pile! Which has remained hidden in the bush for many years."

"So an ounce in the hand, is worth two in the bush stamp box!" remarked Crispin.

Newmarch laughed, and I added, "I think you make some of these sayings up as you go along, Crispin!"

And with smiles on our faces we headed back to the office, after a very informative lesson on gold – and where to find it!

Later in the afternoon when we had inspected all the *gwazas* that were on the go, Newmarch complimented me on the progress that had been made in the last two weeks, and told me that he was getting that excited feeling and couldn't wait to see gold coming off our James concentration table.

Grinning like a schoolboy who had been given a jam doughnut, Newmarch left and asked me to call in at K.B. Davies on Friday for the weekly update that he and French had agreed to give us.

Joseph arrived in a great mood and dropped off the rations in the store.

"I've had a very interesting day with Ronnie and Martin, and I watched everything they did to the ball mill from both the mechanical and the electrical point of view. They thought it was a good idea that I was involved, as I would learn the ins and outs, which could help us if we have a problem when the small ball mill is operational and running on our mine. Although the ball mill was generally in good condition, it was old, so the reliability was yet to be tested under daily working conditions, crushing three tons of rock per day. They were also pleased that we had taken on a welder, essential to any working mine, especially in these times of limited availability of new, in fact any, spare parts."

It was agreed that Joseph would stay in Gwelo for the rest of the week, and travel daily to Bulawayo to assist and learn from Martin and Ronnie, who had many years of experience that they could impart to him.

"So we'll meet up on Friday morning at K.B. Davies for a progress and an update on the Newmarch ball mill, and see Martin for the latest on the small ball mill. It's all very well having access to these two ball mills, but when? That is the big question. So it's very important, Joseph, that we sit on French and Newmarch, and if, or rather when, you are at the Mines Department every day, you should keep Martin and Ronnie concentrating on and prioritising the small ball mill."

We had just finished supper when Amon appeared at the house and beckoned me to follow him to the mine.

He jumped on the back of the pick-up and we drove to the village compound, my headlights lighting up a group of angry workers who were shouting and screaming at each other.

The light from the fire showed a visibly shaken boss boy, Staff, who was trembling and his eyes were wild.

"What's going on, Crispin? What's wrong with Staff?"

"Apparently Staff sat down on his bed to talk to his wife, when he felt something moving by his leg. They jumped off the bed and, with a long stick, removed the blanket, when a hissing cobra raised its head up in front of them. Their crazed shouting attracted Amon, who rushed in, and, with the help of others, quickly killed the cobra by hacking its head off. It's was then that Staff began to shake with fear, and his wife convinced him it was the work of the tokoloshe – a witchdoctor had put a curse on him."

"But who and why?" I prodded him for further news.

"Someone confided in me that he had seen Jeremiah earlier with a visitor to the compound and the two of them went into Jeremiah's hut and spoke for a long time. When they emerged, Jeremiah paid the man, who was recognised by another worker as an assistant to a witchdoctor. Jeremiah and Staff come from the same village, and they had a huge fight last Saturday evening, which resulted in Staff saying he would get Jeremiah fired.

"Staff is convinced that a curse was put on him, and if he had gone straight to bed the tokoloshe would have struck and froze Staff with fear so that the cobra could spit his venom into Staff's eyes. I've tried to speak to Staff – he just stares with wild eyes, his lips quivering – but I did warn him that he should always remember the English proverb before he gets into bed: *'Look before you sleep!'*"

It took a couple of 'smiling seconds' to think what to do – then I spoke to Crispin. "Take Staff and his wife to Boss Joseph's room for the night. Tell Jeremiah to stay on the mine, and don't let him have his ID *stupa* back until we sort this out. We'll meet tomorrow."

I called Amon over and instructed him to make sure Jeremiah stayed in the village; if he tried to get away, he should handcuff him to the prison tree 'til morning.

"And Crispin, come and see me tomorrow at the house at 8 o'clock."

"For your Ndebele lesson, sir?"

"No, we'll skip that. But by 8 o'clock I will have decided what to do about this cobra/tokoloshe/witchdoctor situation."

"Good night, sir. Thank you for cooling things down; thanks for pouring diesel on the troubled waters."

I smiled. "Goodnight, Crispin."

. . .

Crispin listened with interest while I told him how I would settle the Staff/Jeremiah problem.

"I want to set up a court, let both sides tell their story and we'll have a jury to give me their views in secret, and then I'll decide what I'm going to do."

"You mean an *indaba*, sir; we can hold it under the huge tree in the middle of the mine village. But how are you going to work it out?"

"We'll have five jury members; you choose them. I'll leave that up to you. You'll have to help me with translations, because it's got to be clear to all – including me! I'll start with the problem and the jurymen can ask questions, and when we've finished the session they must come up to me and drop a small stone into my hand if they think Jeremiah has paid the witchdoctor to have the curse put on Staff. I'll check the number of stones in my hand to help guide me on my verdict, which I'll announce officially. Assemble everyone by the *indaba* tree at 1pm, when they knock off."

"Put a chair on the back of your pick-up, sir, and bring it when you come. Don't worry; I'll have everything arranged."

Langton turned up with his carpentry tools and we set about fixing a wooden door to replace the heavy black plastic sheet that hung there.

I had discovered the door one day when I was walking through the village and past Willy's old house. I'd forgotten all about that door, but was surprised he had left it behind when he quit the mine.

It was solid enough, but a funny size.

That was not a problem, though, and Langton set about making a frame for it.

I began chiselling the house name 'Willy's privates' off the door; an unusual name, I thought.

When Langton screwed on the last hinge and the door opened and shut easily, we all stood back and admired the new house name that I had chiselled on the door: **1 Ridge Top Drive.**

I took Marianne and the kids and drove off to the village compound. As we approached along the bumpy track and emerged from the thick, thorny bush, we could see all the mine boys sitting near the big tree.

I parked the pick-up so that the family could see what went on, and told Marianne to take a few photos of the court in session.

My chair was put under the *indaba* tree, and I called the five to sit on the jury on my right: Maduna Joe, Juta, Boniface, Anderson and George.

Crispin stood next to me and I told him to explain to everyone what had happened, and was Jeremiah the one who had put the curse on Staff?

Was he responsible for the cobra in Staff's bed?

Crispin translated for me what was said by the witnesses, but you could feel the fear in their voices at the very mention of the tokoloshe.

Jeremiah insisted that the cobra was sent by the tokoloshe to punish Staff, who was an evil man who wanted Jeremiah fired from his job.

From the witnesses' stories, and from his own tone and actions, it was pretty obvious that Jeremiah was responsible – tokoloshe or no tokoloshe!

The five jury members were each given a small stone, and, if they thought Jeremiah was guilty, they should drop the stone in my hand; if not guilty, hang on to it.

Plop, plop, plop, plop, plop = five out of five.

I told Jeremiah that everyone thought he had tried to kill Staff, and that he was fired.

Crispin took Jeremiah to the office to pay him off, and Amon would escort him to the main Fort Rixon road.

I thanked the magnificent five for their work, and gave them each a packet of tobacco; smiles all round.

Marianne had taken several photos, and I told her all about the proceedings when we got back to the house.

"They all seem poop-scared of the tokoloshe," she remarked.

"It's unbelievable, but it seems to be deep-rooted in their culture; I've heard stories that even some of the well-educated have this fear of the tokoloshe, which, in seconds, can reduce a big, healthy, strongly built man to a weak, quivering body lying twitching on the ground, just like we saw at Cain's mine with this worker, Mobile, and the green mamba. Even Zikke is wary of the tokoloshe and the witchdoctor.

"Cain had said that I was lucky that I was 'protected' by the wooden pendent hanging around my neck – the one that the African woman had given me on the drive to Rhodesia. He said that tongue in cheek, but referring more to the fact that the workers would be scared to mess with me, knowing that I was 'protected' by the blessing of a witchdoctor."

"You are fondling that wooden pendant as you've been talking, as if it means something special to you. Are you beginning to believe in those powers?"

I laughed. "But who knows; who can be sure? I mean, it has 'protected' me twice – once from the green mamba at Cain's mine, and then again from the 40 crazed African workers threatening me when they went on strike… And the African woman told me that it would protect me as long as I wore it, so I'm not going to take it off, ever – just in case!"

. . .

The week had flown by, so much had been going on, and now the ball had begun to roll even faster.

Here I was standing next to the small ball mill in the Mines Yard with Martin, Ronnie and Joseph, and being told that this small mill would be ready to transport to our mine on the following Friday.

"Would you mind repeating that again, Martin?" I spluttered the words out in surprise, my subconscious wanting reassurance after all this time.

"*Fri-day-next-week!*" Martin responded, exaggeratingly stressing each syllable, each wonderful word. "And Joseph has been here watching/helping, so he has a reasonable knowledge now of the set-up, and should there be any problems he should be able to pinpoint it and call us at the yard; a type of early warning system. So now it is up to you two to arrange transport with K.B. Davies, and the services of Mr Newmarch. Ronnie and I will always be available, though, if any unexpected problems occur."

"Come, Joseph, let's go to our other ball mill meeting at K.B. Davies, and check if there's a planned delivery date from this Salisbury company for the big baby – the long-awaited Newmarch special."

A much more relaxed duo sat opposite Joseph and me.

French began by congratulating us on the successful servicing of the small ball mill, and confirmed that the mill would be picked up and delivered together with the conveyor system and the two-ton hopper from Zambesi Metals Company.

He would pencil in a date for B&O United Transport for Monday, 19 March, which he would confirm with all parties early the next week.

"Now that Plan B has been put in place, which will give us two months' free milling, is the original Plan A, the delivery and installation of the Newmarch ball mill, going to be completed before that two months is up?" I enquired firmly.

French leant forward and told us that they had accepted the proposal by the MMC, Mine Machinery Company of Africa, based in Salisbury.

He went through the detailed schedule with us, which included some parts being manufactured by their sister company in Johannesburg.

The Newmarch ball mill would be assembled and tested fully in their factory prior to the delivery to the Ridge Top Mine on the 1st of May.

French had built in some penalty clauses this time for any schedule breaches, and was confident that this company would meet those dates.

"That sounds great, 'cosa we donta wanta a larga ice creama maka machina this time!" quipped Joseph, to the amusement of us all.

"Mr Newmarch will be available to you full time for the preparation and successful milling of the small ball mill, as well as, of course, everything in connection with the main Newmarch ball mill installation," French added, "and I would expect milling to commence within a week of delivery, when both of us will be present, naturally."

"Fabulous, fabulous, fabulous!" Joseph rejoiced. "So we'll be producing gold before I go on my six weeks' border duty on the 15th May… which I received confirmation of… but only recently… Er, I was going to tell you that, but I didn't want to add to all your worries," he said, looking in my direction.

"Well, Joseph, nothing will spoil my day; I feel like a dog with two bones – although I will not drop the first one until I'm 100% sure the second one is working!"

Joseph was dashing back to Jane in Gwelo.

And French and Newmarch had a meeting with the bank manager; about what? I just didn't want to know.

And there I was in limbo, all on my own. Only one thing for it; it was Friday and I had to share the good news with some of my friends down at Greys Inn.

In the pub, I met Des and Brendon, both of whom were delighted with my news.

"Well, he's worked hard enough to achieve this against all the odds," Des told Brendon, "and I'm sure the mine is going to be a big success."

Dave came over and, on hearing of the latest, announced that phrase that every local regular loves to hear: "A round on the house!" It brought a huge cheer from the dozen or so of us who were sitting at the bar.

I was introduced to Dave's son, Ian, who had, that morning, returned from his spell of six weeks' border duty.

He was about my age and we instantly hit it off, and time flew by as we happily chatted away together.

Des and Brendon came over to say goodbye; Brendon was returning to his unit in Salisbury.

"Des, don't forget now, you and Irene have a date at our house on the mine on Saturday week. Marianne is preparing her speciality, a cheese fondue with her delicious home-made potent sauces; it'll be fun," I added.

As they left, another two young guys came in, and, on seeing Ian at the bar, came over and greeted him enthusiastically.

"These are two of my best mates, Paddy and Charlie; we've been mates since we were at school together, and we get together whenever we can at Charlie's ranch."

"Hey, why don't you join us there for the weekend?" Charlie said. "There'll be about 20 to 25 of us, some married, some with kids; you'll enjoy it. It's a great break from the everyday slog."

And he gave me directions to his ranch near Bala Bala.

"Come over tomorrow morning with your woman, and kids if you have; everybody is easy-going, and we try to do this once a month or so – it depends who's around, like Ian and Paddy; they're just back from service and they need to unwind after six weeks of living on the edge, doing their border duty."

"Sounds like the type of weekend we'd enjoy. What can we bring?"

"Beer is essential, but that's all; we have everything else on the farm – if you don't eat beef, you can eat *bala bala*."

"*Bala bala?*"

"Kudu, in Ndebele; there are plenty around this area."

The drive back to the mine from Bulawayo was a time to ponder life, how fast things can change. One minute, you have nothing; the next minute, all comes good.

A week ago, we had only the fading promise of an almost mythical ball mill, yet, today, **two** definite installation dates for **two** ball mills!

Marianne was delighted with my news, and the sound of an exciting weekend away on a ranch with the kids topped even that.

. . .

On checking my car map, I could see that Charlie's farm was not as far away as I had first thought.

He had told me the ranch was five kilometres on the left after Bala Bala, when you come from Bulawayo taking the Essexvale turn-off.

But for me it was easier and much shorter to bump our way from our mine down to Filabusi, and turn right on the road to Bulawayo, with Bala Bala being a mere 30 kilometres further.

We left after breakfast, and it made a real change to take this road to Fibabusi again.

We found it an exciting drive too, especially the wild game we saw – the occasional surprise as a reedbuck or a duiker bounced across the track right in front of us.

We stopped at the Filabusi petrol station for a cooldrink, and I asked the way to the Stanton ranch.

"You mean Charlie's place? Drive about 26 kilometres on this road, and look for the sign 'Stanton Ranch' on your right; you can't miss it."

At the turn-off, Marianne got out and opened the gate – and closed it again, of course – and we drove slowly along a rutted track through the bush for a few minutes before coming across open ground and a sprawling ranch house.

We pulled up alongside half a dozen or so Land Rovers and pick-ups.

Charlie appeared on the veranda, waved a welcome to us and sent the houseboy to collect our bags – and the crate of beer.

"Glad you brought sleeping bags; you can crash anywhere you like, and there are several empty rooms. Come, let me show you around the house and you can meet some of the other friends and their families."

There were long terraces on all four sides of the house, and we met several people in their twenties sitting around talking and drinking in the cool shade, and on one of the verandas there were several 'washing' lines with dozens of pieces of meat hanging there.

"This is our biltong terrace; it's perfect for drying the beef. The outside air is warm, but there's also a cool breeze along this terrace. We make great biltong here and you must take some with you when you leave. It's all beef biltong at the moment, until in the hunting season when we are treated to kudu biltong – my favourite."

During the afternoon, we gradually got to meet everyone. Marie-Louise and Jeffrey had already made friends with a few other children, who were a bit older and said they would look after our two.

As dusk closed in, a large roaring fire lit up the terraced area, and the beer and wine flowed! There was a great atmosphere; everyone was very friendly.

The cook boy offered us boerewors and biltong, whilst he prepared and braaied a banquet of roasted meats – steaks, lamb chops and chicken, which were complemented by bowls of salads, various sauces and baked potatoes with butter – *lekker*!

Charlie had told everyone that we were gold mining near Fort Rixon, and we were surprised when this teenage girl said to Marianne, "You must be the ones who are mining on the Claremont mine, on my father's ranch."

"You're Jackson's daughter?"

"Yes, that's my father, and I hear you don't get on so well with him," she chirped in, and laughingly continued. "And neither do I – a lot of the time. He's a bit of a stickler for the rules; he wouldn't allow me or my elder sister to stay overnight at Charlie's ranch until we were 18. But he's a kind man, really. I love him; he's just very old fashioned, that's all."

. . .

I have no idea how late the party finished, but it was about 10am before I opened my eyes in the warm, bright sunshine.

We all piled into several pick-ups and headed down a track until we came to a river.

It wasn't flowing fast and we camped by a series of rocks with water trickling from pool to pool; it was an ideal spot for the women and children – whilst we went hawking!

A crate of beer was placed in the pools to cool the bottles, and we also took a cool box with a few in – for when the throats get too parched in the hot sun.

Charlie spoke to me enthusiastically. "I'll introduce you to hawking. We'll go with Paddy and a few others in a Land Rover with a newly trained bird, and you can watch it hunt its prey – nature in the raw!"

We drove through the bush for a couple of kilometres, around some high ridges that encircled Charlie's ranch house, until we came to a huge open vlei meadow with long grasses about a metre high.

Charlie was standing next to me in the back of the open Land Rover with a hooded sparrow hawk perched on his 'protected' arm – the leather sleeve preventing accidental ripping from the bird's sharp claws. He said the bird weighed about a kilogram and it was quite tiring to hold out his arm with such a weight on it.

We started ploughing through the long grasses – Charlie removed the hood, and I watched excitedly as we all stared ahead of us as the Jeep drove on, kicking up lots of dust and pollen.

"Now!" shouted Charlie as he jerked his arm upwards and the hawk took off, Charlie explaining that, when the hawk had spotted something, its claws would twitch and that was the signal to go.

It was truly beautiful to follow the low flight of the hawk in front of us until suddenly it dived into the grasses.

We drove up alongside to see that the hawk had a small rodent under its claws.

Charlie took the small animal and the hawk jumped back on his arm again.

Just then, I started to sneeze uncontrollably and my eyes began watering like hell.

"Oh no, do you suffer from hayfever?" Charlie asked. "Do you have any antihistamine pills for it?"

"I haven't had hayfever since I was a schoolboy in England many years ago," I sneezed-said, and sneezed again.

"Does anyone have pills?"

"My girlfriend, Kathy, back at the ranch has some," Paddy explained, "but we're going to be out here for maybe another hour or two, and…"

Another bout of my sneezing interrupted him.

"He should get back now and start taking the antidote," Charlie remarked, "and since we've only got the one vehicle I think Paddy should walk back with you; it's not so far if you go over that ridge there. Paddy knows the way. Here, take a cold dumpy each, it's hot and dry up there on the ridge."

Paddy and I started off, accompanied by the orchestrated 'hayfever suite'; I just couldn't stop. As we climbed the ridge, I asked Paddy to slow down a bit, as I was getting short of breath – another problem-symptom hayfever sufferers have to endure.

Eventually, we reached the top, where there was a welcome gentle breeze.

After a few minutes' relaxing rest sitting in the shade of a small acacia tree, I suddenly started sneezing uncontrollably. I could not stop; sneeze after sneeze after sneeze….

"You're firing quicker than a machine gun!" Paddy joked.

"Shit!"

I sneezed so hard that I bit my lip, and felt blood trickling from my mouth.

Paddy's laughter immediately stopped, and his face became fixated with an eerie blank stare….

And he began to relate, with a pained expression, what happened on his last reconnaissance sortie across the border into Mozambique to locate and document any terrorist training camps that he came across, which he would report back to military headquarters.

When he related to me what he had witnessed on entering a Rhodesian village 15 km from the border, I went cold with disgust.

"A group of heavily armed terrorists had crossed the border and attacked the villagers, many of whom fell dead to the continuous firing by their assailants. The terrorists gathered the surviving villagers together, mainly women and children, and one old man. They hacked off his ears and cut out his tongue, symbolising that the villagers must not report anything to the Rhodesian patrols, and left the old man bleeding to death! The women were forced to eat bits of the old man's ears and tongue, and in front of the screaming children too! I almost puked on the spot, and felt the urge to go back into Mozambique to the terrorist camp I'd spotted and kick the shit out of the cowardly unfeeling bastards who had done this!"

Then silence….

I could see that Paddy was hurting emotionally, reliving the sickening event – his whole body was trembling uncontrollably.

Several minutes passed before he regained himself, when he handed me a cold Castle dumpy from his haversack.

Cure or no cure, it was bloody welcome, and I felt much easier as we descended the ridge in silence down to the homestead.

"Why are you back so early?" voices enquired.

"He's had a bout of hayfever. Where's Kathy? She's got some pills for that."

A few minutes later, I had taken a pill and sat quietly in the shade on the veranda.

My breathing had returned to normal, my eyes had stopped itching and I wasn't sneezing! What a relief.

Kathy was a nurse in a clinic that specialised in ENT – ear, nose and throat disorders, including hayfever and asthma, and she told me that I shouldn't let my throat become dry, because that would start the symptoms off again, so best to go and drink some more cold beer – and naturally, I've taken that good advice very seriously, even outside of the hayfever season!

By the time the other hawkers had returned, I felt good again.

The rest of the day, we just relaxed and sat around – the low murmuring of the conversations and the laughter contrasting with the quietness of the bush.

. . .

What a different, unusual weekend, and we thoroughly enjoyed ourselves.

Charlie told me as we were leaving that they would have another weekend bash when the hunting season started in May, and he'd leave a message at Greys Inn nearer the time.

It was dark by the time we got home, and, as we slowed to turn into our driveway, we could hear through the open windows the sounds of chanting and other weird, shrill noises coming from the village compound.

We got out of the pick-up, when the noise became even more noticeable.

The wood stove had not been lit.

Elliot didn't come when I called, and the place was deserted.

"What the hell is going on?" I uttered. "Something's wrong here!"

"It's times like this," Marianne said, "that I feel a bit scared being alone in the bush. When Elliot is here, and there are the fires and the normal sounds of the bush and the mine, that's fine, but when the house is deserted and there are strange noises and shouting coming from the distant mining village, it's scary."

"Now you know how the settlers felt in the 1896 Matabele rebellions when there were no lights and the people lived in fear, waiting for the natives to pounce, bludgeon and kill."

"Ah, you stop it! Don't try to scare me more!" Marianne said forcefully.

"But what's that?"

We heard the noise of someone coming towards us in the dark, and I flashed my torch, illuminating Amon as he stepped out of the blackness.

"Boss, come!" And he walked off.

"Hey Amon, wait; get in the back of the pick-up."

And we all drove up to the mine office, our headlights illuminating the road ahead – it gave a comforting, reassuring feeling; at least we could see where we were going, but we didn't know what to expect.

There was no grey pick-up parked outside the office, which was even more concerning.

The noise from the village compound was loud. There was shouting and people calling out loudly; sounds that rose and fell, giving occasional odd split seconds of silence.

"Amon, get Staff."

As our eyes got used to the light, we could see the flickering glows of large fires, huge flames licking the dark skies, and the noises of screaming and wailing could be distinctly heard. It sounded ominous, and I was about to say that when Staff appeared.

"Boss, there's been a terrible tragedy. Judith's young baby slipped and fell into the fire. Elliot heard the screams, rushed out of the hut and pulled the baby out, but the clothes were burning and the baby was screaming with pain. Elliot poured cold water over the baby, whilst Judith ran for help. She met Crispin at the office; he grabbed the keys to the grey pick-up and rushed the three of them to Shangani Hospital. That was about four hours ago. The women in the mine village are distraught, and you can hear their cries and wailing as they try to comfort each other, but they are scared the baby won't survive."

"That's horrible; the poor baby," Marianne gasped, and Marie-Louise burst into inconsolable crying.

"Staff, come with us back to the house; I'll phone Shangani Hospital immediately."

While I was waiting to be put through, the grey pick-up suddenly pulled up outside.

A visibly shaken Crispin came into the house and gave us some awful news. "The baby was so severely burnt that she was dead when we got to the hospital."

"Jesus, that's terrible, and what about Elliot and Judith?"

"Judith refuses to leave the hospital, saying, 'my baby won't die; my baby will be better', and Elliot told me they wouldn't come back to the mine. And now Staff and I must leave you and go to the village compound to break the tragic news."

Several minutes later, a loud crescendo of screaming filled the air – the women had been informed of the death, and the wailing, chanting and hysterical crying continued far into the night… **a dark, foreboding night.**

Part V - The Letter

"My god, I couldn't sleep for ages; that poor Judith. Your own baby burnt to death in the fire. It's horrific; that shouldn't happen to any mother," Marianne whispered, partly choking on her words. "And seeing your own child burning in front of your eyes, and not being able to do anything – how does a mother cope with that?"

"God knows, I go cold when I think about it too, and that wailing throughout the night sent shivers down my spine. Perhaps we should drive up to the hospital this morning to see if there's any help we can give them."

"No, let me go on my own with the kids; the driving will help take my mind off thinking about poor Judith, and she'll need a woman's consoling."

"Okay, do that then, and I'll go up to the mine; there's a lot of things to do, especially now we've got definite delivery dates – not on just one ball mill, but on two! Newmarch is coming this morning too, and we will be checking which items and extra equipment will be needed, so we can confirm the orders with K.B. Davies and the Mines Department.

"There'll be a lot of heavy equipment and supplies coming next week, including the small ball mill, so if we can co-ordinate with the other suppliers like Zambesi Metals, it'll help keep transport costs down. And although we're not paying for those immediately, it will be added to our K.B. Davies credit account, which we'll have to clear as quickly as we can, of course, once we're producing gold."

Newmarch was in a good mood.

He liked the professionalism of the MMC, Mine Machinery Company of Africa; they knew what they were talking about – and could talk in understandable English too!

"I'm very confident they will meet their deadline of May 1 working closely with their sister company in South Africa. And I won't have to run around in Jo'burg like a headless chicken, as I did every time the Italian had problems with his parts – steel parts!"

"Mr Newmarch, if we make that May deadline, I'll be 'Mr Happy'! In the meantime, French has agreed that you will work with us here on site, especially for the next two weeks when we'll have to run both projects at the same time – with the small ball mill installation taking preference, of course, because the sooner we start extracting some gold the better it will be for all of us."

Newmarch suggested that we should first do a 'dry run' from the main shaft to the Newmarch ball mill site, concentrating on equipment that needed to be ordered so that it could be transported the following Monday together with the small ball mill.

Items already on monthly lease agreements with the Mines Department:

– Twenty lengths of rail, each 20 foot in length;

– Two hundred and sixty feet of plastic water piping, 1" and 2";

– Two hundred and sixty feet of armoured electrical cabling.

Other equipment required from Zambesi Metals and K.B. Davies:

– The conveyor belt system with an ore hopper of two-ton capacity;

– Main switchboard, junction box;

– Newmarch ball mill site switchboard;

– A 2 hp water pump;

– Another water tank/return pipe reticulation system.

We would also need welding gear, an acetylene torch and so on, which I could borrow from Ray's mine. One of our workers, Boniface, was a welder by trade and could assist Mr Newmarch to weld the legs onto the ore hopper and conveyor system.

There was also a tremendous amount of building and digging work still to be done.

Some had been in progress for several weeks, with gangs of workers performing their *gwazas* each day, like making the embankment, or rail ramp, as Crispin calls it.

– An alternator house;

– Hoist house;

– Hoist block – concrete slab;

– Wooden headgear with pulley wheel to be constructed and erected;

– Headgear feet cemented for stability;

– Bent rails to allow the skip full of ore to be offloaded into a hopper to feed the cocopans;

– The rail embankment extended in length to 60 metres, and to a height of over 3 metres at the Newmarch ball mill site;

– The rails to be laid on the surface of the embankment for the cocopans;

– A wooden shute to collect the ore tipped out from a cocopan, the rocks being shovelled into a hopper, to be emptied onto the automatic conveyor belt system, which would feed the Newmarch ball mill;

– Already completed was the 20-foot by 20-foot, six-inch reinforced concrete mill pad.

I phoned and confirmed the orders with K.B. Davies and the Mines Department, noting which items should be delivered with the transporter the following week, while Willias, the garden boy, got the wood stove going and made us some coffee.

"Hello sir," a cheery voice called out as Feet pedalled his ancient, squeaking bicycle and trailer towards the house.

"Six fresh eggs, milk for your children, and rape and cabbage for the Madam. I've already dropped off the vegetable rations for the mine and Crispin has paid me. Thank you, sir."

He rode off ringing his bell, and, when he disappeared around the bend of our driveway, the squeaky sound gradually lessened until the quietness of the bush took over once again.

"You really have got things well organised here," Newmarch remarked. "Fresh milk, eggs and vegetables from your own vegetable farm – and delivered to your doorstep as well!"

"Yes, that Mzee Feet, he has been like a 'partner' to us from the start. He helped us sort out our water problems when Rancher Jackson was refusing to let us take water from his overflowing water tanks. Feet gave us the idea of the daily water runs in the pick-up to collect water from a local stream. Unbelievably, Jackson even tried to stop us taking water from there – it was *his* stream on *his* land!"

I recounted to Newmarch other amusing stories about Feet, the local chief who had worked for Jackson for 20 years, but had gone out of his way several times to help us when we had problems with that rancher.

The grey 404 drove quietly into our garden and parked.

Marianne told me the news from Shangani Hospital, and that Elliot had to report the death of his baby daughter to the police in Fort Rixon.

"That's why I was late getting back here. I first took him and Judith to see Peter to report the death, before driving them back to Shangani Hospital. They are leaving for their home village today, and Elliot will take a week off for the funeral proceedings. Judith does not want to come back to the mine; she's still traumatised and bursts into uncontrollable sobbing all the time, so Elliot says he will bring a cousin called Mary to help as a house girl."

"Good, and I've got Willias to do the housework until Elliot returns," I informed her. "But now Newmarch and I must go back up to the mine. He will join us for supper, though, and will sleep over in Joseph's room."

Newmarch showed me the best site for the small ball mill, close to the alternator and the water tank, and we sat outside while he sketched some diagrams and explained to me how the 'flow' should go, from the small ball mill to a 'copper plate' table to extract the gold.

"You should order the following additional items as well today so that they can be transported here with the small ball mill: a copper plate, 8'10" x 5' ('= foot, " = inches); some wire mesh fencing, two 30-foot rolls, nine-foot wide; a five-kilo flask of mercury (quick silver); a retort. When they are delivered next week, get Langton and your timber boys to build a table for the copper plate, which will be treated with mercury to capture the gold; and launder boxes, to distribute the flow of water carrying the sands, the 'crushed ore', and spreading it across the width of the copper extraction table.

"Also construct a security room using gum poles with wire mesh sides and a hessian roof. This is essential to prevent theft; nobody must be allowed inside the room. Lock it with a padlock, which only you and Joseph have the keys for. That prevents workers walking past the copper plate table and scraping their fingers across it, when some of the gold amalgam would get under their nails. If they did that every day, over time, they could easily accumulate an ounce of gold!"

"That's what Joseph's brother, Cain, warned me about too, saying the extraction room is sacred; theft is rampant on small worker gold mines, and not even the senior boss boy should be allowed to have access."

Having finalised what we required, we went to the house and I phoned K.B. Davies, the Mines Department and Zambesi Metals again to order the additional items for the small ball mill extraction room.

I wrote these items on our headed notepaper confirming my phone orders, and asked Newmarch if he could drop off copies of all the orders to French, so that he would know what was for his account and which items needed to be collected from Zambesi Metals and the Mines Department for transporting to our mine.

I would visit Zambezi Metals in the morning with the written order to confirm the delivery and the date to be collected.

. . .

The weather was changing again; gone were the clear, starry nights and bright, colourful dawns – the cold, damp guti weather was back again, with a vengeance!

I had to use the wipers to clear the windscreen of this almost-frozen slush as I made my early morning mission to the office with a flask of coffee to have a chat with Newmarch before he left for Bulawayo.

However, on entering the office and seeing the empty camp bed, I looked with quizzically raised eyebrows at Crispin, who remarked, "Mr Newmarch left last night, but said he'd be back early on Wednesday morning."

So I drove straight off to Bulawayo, and did my rounds of the Mines Department, K.B. Davies and Zambesi Metals, confirming the orders and transport arrangements.

I also popped in to see Leo de Ziel at Shell and paid for our order of 2,000 litres of diesel fuel, which would be delivered on the Friday.

A quick coffee at the Tea House shop with a large piece of black forest gateau – my favourite cake, especially when made to the traditional German recipe with the maraschino black cherries soaked in Kirsch!

Then it was literally 'happily' back on the road to Fort Rixon before midday.

Sometimes it's good to take an afternoon off; a wonderful, relaxing tonic – sticking up my feet and reading the English newspaper.

. . .

Newmarch was at the mine early, around 7:30am, and we cracked off by checking progress on the rail embankment.

The *gwaza* of six workers would be kept busy for another week still, extending it by a further 10 metres so that the rail ramp would then reach alongside the recently laid 20 x 20 foot concrete mill slab – this would allow the cocopans to be pushed up to this point where the ore could be tipped out onto the conveyor system.

When we were originally laying the mill slab, we needed easy access from all sides, so we hadn't built the embankment this far, but, now that the concrete mill slab had aired and dried hard, we could finish off the extension to the rail embankment.

We remeasured and, to our surprise, found that it needed to be three and a half metres high at the very end! A hell of a lot more wheelbarrows-full of soil!

Further visits to the slimes dams that were being dug… the siting and marking out the cyanide tank pits…. we covered a lot of work…. when suddenly, signalling the end of the day, the knock-off gong sounded: *clang yang-yang-yang-yang*….

. . .

Clang yang-yang-yang-yang, sounded again – after only what seemed like a quick blink of the eye – reverberating through the cold guti mist; the start of another chilly, shivering day.

Today, Newmarch would concentrate entirely on the small ball mill site preparation, which we had planned to be close to the alternator, water tanks and office.

He thought it would be a good idea for Marianne to start her daily trips to the waste dumps of the various old small mines on our claims – Sirius, Hlatin, and some unmarked, unknown ones.

With the help of two lashers, the grey pick-up could be filled with about one ton of waste schist, which would be dumped near the office to be shovelled into the small ball mill hopper – when it was erected.

If she did three trips a day, the dump would grow by three tons each day; more than sufficient to keep the small mill running, as, initially, the mine would only work two shifts of eight hours, processing approximately two tons per day.

With the unsampled waste dumps, it was a bit of pot luck, but even with low-grade values of some 3–4 dwts per ton, that would yield us about 12 ounces of gold in a month, helping to cover our monthly cash outlay – K.B. Davies kindly covering the rest of the costs!

Newmarch busily worked away calculating the electrical needs from the specs of the small ball mill and what provisions should be made on our main switchboard – that was what I understood in layman's terms.

We measured up for the water connections, the piping and the pump pressures required at the feed into the small mill, and also for pumping the 'waste slimes' down to the dams being dug 60 metres away at the main Newmarch ball mill site.

Although these would be only temporary solutions to milling, hopefully for two months maximum, they had to work smoothly; we couldn't afford any mishaps or downtime, which would result in a lower monthly gold output – money was tight!

Working outside in the sun all day long really does take it out of a person, and the old man Newmarch clearly showed signs of fatigue, so, although it was only mid-afternoon, I decided he should break now, take the weekend off and come back on the Monday morning – when the fun should start!

He seemed relieved and said he would love a long weekend off, the first in many months of working flat out on the design and the production of his small worker ball mill with all its problems and headaches – mostly caused by the Italians!

"I know what I'll do; I'll visit an old friend of mine near Que Que and spend some time together, as I haven't seen him for over six months. He's a keen fisherman too, so we'll spend many hours on the dams, angling the time away."

I watched his old jalopy bump its way into the distance.

. . .

What a shock; Joseph actually put in an appearance.

He had brought the rations from Gwelo, and was sitting in the reception hut, where Situnda had prepared some tea and biscuits for him.

I explained to him that, when we started blasting underground and hoisting skips of ore to the surface, we would need to keep signed and verified records on the development work we'd done, how many feet we'd extended the drive tunnels, and the tonnage of ore we hauled up from underground.

All these records were required by the Mines Department, and would actually help to back up our application for the speculative development loan.

Crispin had drawn up an 'easy to fill in' daily record sheet, which needed to be signed each day.

When I showed this to Joseph, he blew his top.

"I'm not going to sign that each day; you're just trying to keep records that you can use against me!" he shouted.

"They are necessary, Joseph, and will help us with the loan application."

"Then why don't you sign them? You're here all the time; why must I sign them?"

"You're right, Joseph, I am here all the time, but you should be too; you are responsible for all underground work, the underground supervisor, remember?"

"Underground *manager*!" he snapped. "Let the boss boys sign!"

"Joseph, don't you understand; on any back-up documentation for our loan application, your signature as underground manager carries weight, as you are also a director of the Ridge Top Mine. A thumbprint or a squiggle from a mine worker not only looks ludicrous, but is not acceptable by the Mines Department."

"Staff is the senior boss boy and his word counts. He would not fiddle the figures; everyone knows that," he petulantly added.

"So you want Staff to become a director as well?" I quipped.

"No, no, *no*!"

"You mean you don't want him as a director."

"No, no, no! Don't be stupid. I'm saying no, no, no, because I'm not signing, so there, run and tell my father if you like."

"Tell you what, Joseph, I'm fed up with your childishness; you are hardly ever here – you're still not on the mine *every day* as we agreed last month. What's your problem?"

"You! You are my bloody problem. You! And I'm not going to talk to you about this anymore; I'm not signing!"

And he pivoted on his heel, spun around and strutted to his pick-up with his head in the air, and climbed in.

Crispin had come to see what all the shouting was about, and we both awaited the customary roar and revving of the engine, the squeal of tyres and the dust clouds… but nothing; he was just sitting there.

It was Friday, late afternoon, and I had no intention of sitting and waiting for the sulky boy to get over his temper tantrums. I went back to the house to talk to my five-year-old and my three-year-old – who were both more sensible than my irritating partner.

A welcome cup of tea and some fairy cakes that Marianne had made in the wood stove were eagerly devoured in a matter of minutes.

The loud over-revving up of a pick-up broke the quietness, and we listened to it as it headed down the murram road, not past our place, but on the road to Filabusi.

"Joseph is going home to Belingwe to cry on his mother's shoulder again," I joked with Marianne. "That guy is such a tit! The sooner he goes into the army on border duty, the better; you just can't count on him to do anything!"

. . .

When I walked up to the office for my usual administration/wages session with Crispin, I was surprised to see the pale blue Peugeot pick-up of my petulant partner parked outside.

"Morning, sir, Boss Joseph came very early and went prospecting. He said he'd be back at lunchtime, before going up to Gwelo for the weekend."

I watched Crispin as he religiously entered all the goods and items that I'd bought for the shop into his store book.

Each time I purchased, he wrote pages and pages of entries, the majority being Surf washing powder, tobacco and snuff, but this trip he had also given me a list of medicines to buy: a box of 1,000 Aspirins, various different mutis and creams for bruises, coughs and stomach ache, which he noted in his store book as 'ambication, mine use'.

"What on earth does that mean?" I asked.

"For when they are sick, for ambication to their skin; you rub it in."

"Ambication! I think the word you're after is application."

Crispin laughed, but replied that all the other mine workers understood *his* word, so he would continue to use it.

I headed back to the house, smiling.

Des had phoned to say they were still coming over for a meal; however, earlier than planned, and would arrive around 3pm instead of 5pm.

I had a shave and went for a quick shower by the long drop.

"Okay Willias, is that water hot?"

"Yes Boss," he answered as he tipped it into the showerhead metal drum, and boy was it hot! That hotness that takes your breath away and leaves you gasping, but, once it's tipped, there are no hot and cold taps to adjust the temperature, just holes in the bottom of the drum through which whatever is tipped in comes spurting out – hot or cold!

When Des and Irene arrived, we walked around our two-acre garden, and they liked the way we'd arranged it.

There were some large dead tree trunks that we had found near the koppies and had dragged them behind the pick-up and laid them along the driveway.

We'd dug holes in the trunks and planted several flowering cactus plants.

Marianne and Marie Louise had their own vegetable patch, with colourful flowers around the edges.

Irene loved their playroom of a grassed roof on top of four poles, with the bright red flowering Christmas bushes growing around the poles.

While they chatted away, Des asked me to show him around the mine.

Joseph was standing outside the office next to a drum of water and was busy panning samples.

"Are you interested in gold mining too?" Joseph enquired. "Look at the gold tail in my pan? That could mean ounces of gold to the ton. Here, you have a go."

He showed Des how to hold the pan at an angle, and rotate it, swishing the water over the crushed rock, washing most of the sands out of the pan, leaving… nothing; not even a speck of gold!

"I'll stick to cattle ranching!" Des chirped. "But thanks for the lesson."

As the evening drew in, we lit the hurricane lamps in the house.

"Oh Marianne, this is so cosy. I love your beautiful wooden furniture and that dining service of black flowers and white china; it looks so lovely on the wooden Welsh dresser." (The one that Joseph had smashed and hidden in the garage in Gwelo – and Langton had repaired for us.)

"And the food looks damn good on these plain plates as well," Des remarked.

We had a cheese fondue with home-made sauces and salads, and two French loaves that Irene had brought with them.

"You are the first couple we've entertained in our mine house, and it's been a wonderful evening having you both here."

"Thanks Marianne; we've thoroughly enjoyed it too. From the outside, your house looks like an old mining shack, but inside it's a pearl; such a lovely atmosphere. Thanks again for the wonderful meal. We'd never had a fondue before; it was delicious."

. . .

On Sunday, one of Peter Ruck's daughters had her birthday party at the Fort

Rixon club and everyone was invited; the local ranchers and farmers love any excuse to get together, and it was a great day.

We met a young Dutch couple, and Marie-Louise and Jeffrey got on well with their seven, yes seven kids! And the oldest one was only 11 years old.

"Good Catholics!" remarked Marianne.

There was a log floating in the dam about 50 yards out and the big Dutch guy, Jos, and I had a bet – a swimming race to see who could get there first.

I was leading by a couple of feet as we neared the log, when… *splash!*

The bugger had pulled me under, and, as I surfaced, he was holding onto the log laughing like mad, and called out to me, "Do you keep your Rs open underwater?"

"What?" I was trying to shake the water out of my ears so I could hear a bit better.

"Do you keep your Rs open?" he repeated, and started pointing to his eyes.

"Oh, you're asking me if I keep my eyes open under water," I spluttered.

I thought even for a Dutchman that was a very rude and personal thing to ask: "Do you keep your Rs open underwater?"

We swam back and joined the main party, and downed a few beers with the men.

That story, and the phrase *'do you keep your Rs open under water'* often being repeated, caused much laughter amongst us.

. . .

I woke up early, thinking about what a busy day it would be.

The small ball mill and other equipment would be arriving later, probably after lunch, because there were a lot of items that had to be collected from the three different locations in Bulawayo; the Mines Department, K.B. Davies and Zambesi Metals.

On the mine, we continued working on the three main jobs for the Newmarch ball mill installation:

– **Extending the embankment**;

– **The headgear**.

Staff and his timber boys were constructing the side sections for the huge wooden frame of the headgear using 30-foot gum poles with criss-cross timber supports, tapering from a three-metre-wide base to one-metre-wide at the top end.

These two sides would be raised to a vertical position and fitted at the pinnacle onto a small square wooden platform, which would house a pulley wheel system.

The cable from the hoist would pass around the pulley wheel and be attached to the skip, which would be hoisted up from the shaft carrying the gold ore rocks.

– **And the hoist** itself.

We would need to lay a thick concrete block onto which the hoist machine would be bolted. This would have to be very strong and secured in the ground, as the hoist could be required to pull a skip full of ore weighing one ton from a depth of 400 feet; a huge strain, and that's why the hoist block had to be fishtailed.

Newmarch had told me a story about a mine where the foundations of the hoist block were too weak, and one day there was a thunderous noise as the hoist and the hoist block were ripped out by the weight of the heavily loaded skip and crashed and crunched into the mine shaft entrance, killing the hoist driver!

Several workers underground were badly injured too as rocks from the skip spewed out and hurtled down the shaft, showering those working below.

The clock struck 12 o'clock. I was quite surprised when the transporter and trailer pulled up on the side of the murram road; they had worked fast collecting all the items to be here so soon.

Newmarch got out of the cab and walked with the driver up to the office.

"I thought I'd come out with the transporter; save me driving, and I can always go back with either you or Joseph tomorrow, or even Wednesday. There's no rush."

Beep. Beep. An old Land Rover entered the mining area.

"O-oh!" I exclaimed. "Jackson! Surely he hasn't come to complain about the transporter blocking the main Fort Rixon-Filabusi road."

A friendly looking Jackson got out of the passenger seat, and the Land Rover did a U-turn in front of us, and his wife called out, "Good afternoon. I'm just going over to see your wife and children at your house; I've got some fruit and cakes for them."

"You looked surprised!" Jackson said. "But I thought we'd come over and call a truce since we've been neighbours for many months now, and I can see that you're serious miners, not like some of the riffraff that have mined on my land in the past. That's a lot of equipment, including a small ball mill waiting to be unloaded, so I'll only keep you a few minutes; could we inspect the wood cutters' work now with Crispin?"

Newmarch said he would gladly supervise where the transporter should park and what should be unloaded until I got back.

About one and a half cords had been cut since 10am; not bad, really, but his worker had not poisoned the stumps. Jackson was clearly disappointed and said he would put an additional worker on the job, but would want a 50/50 split of the cords cut and not the presently agreed one third.

He extended his hand, and we shook hands for the first time; it felt good.

After all the difficulties we'd had, clearly we were beginning to get on quite well.

His wife drove up and, with a cheery wave, they left.

"Well, that's a turn-up for the books, Crispin. I wonder how she and Marianne got on."

The trailer had been unhooked so the driver could easily manoeuvre his truck to the alternator site where the small ball mill would be offloaded and put in place using the five-ton block and tackle lifting equipment.

The 20 lengths of rail were taken and laid by the rail ramp embankment.

Other items were unloaded near the store; the 260-foot roll of armoured electrical cabling; massive snake-like coils of both 2' and 1' plastic piping; together with the rolls of mesh security fencing, and various sundry items.

The large copper plate, thickly wrapped for protection, was placed inside the store.

The driver drove back and hooked up the trailer loaded with the conveyor belt system, a two-ton ore hopper and a water tank, and reversed down to the Newmarch ball mill site, skilfully parking the trailer alongside the 20 x 20-foot square concrete slab, where everything was offloaded.

I signed the delivery documents and the driver left for Bulawayo, his vehicle lit up by the dying rays of the day – symbolic signs of a very tiring day for both Newmarch and I, and many of our mine boys.

While Marianne was telling me all about the visit from Jackson's wife, Susan, I placed a call to Ray in Belingwe.

Susan had apologised to Marianne for them being such unfriendly neighbours; they weren't like that at all, and it was very unfortunate that we'd all got off to such a horribly bad start.

She said the problem was that her husband had bad experiences in the past with some miners, who had no regard for his cattle, the wildlife or the upkeep of their mining claims.

The cow would not be moved to the mine from the farm near their ranch house; however, she would ensure that Feet brought fresh milk for the children two or three times a week.

The phone rang; Ray was on the line.

I asked him if we could have use of the acetylene torch and welding equipment on the coming Thursday and Friday. Joseph would collect it.

"That's fine, but where is Joseph now?"

"I haven't a bloody clue!" I retorted.

"He's not been on the mine today?"

"I haven't seen him since we had a big row last Friday."

"I know about that; he came down to see his mother. He was in a hell of a flap."

"Well, I hope he told you why we fought, because the situation with your Scarlet Pimpernel son is becoming untenable. The words 'where, when, why' sum up the questions everybody keeps asking. He is so bloody unreliable; it's best just to do all the jobs myself. At least then I know they are done, and done properly. When are you coming to Ridge Top Mine? I want the three of us to sit down and sort these things out, once and for all! *Do you understand?*" I emphasised vehemently.

"Calm down! I've never heard you talk like this before. Okay, I know it's serious and has to be worked out. We'll meet next time I'm over, towards the end of the following week on my way back from Cain's mine. Goodnight."

. . .

Perhaps he was psychic; Boss Joseph had rocked up very early at 6am – perhaps his mummy had scolded him!

"He went straight down underground with Staff to review the situation," Crispin told me. "He didn't even stop to have his usual cup of tea!"

Surprise visitors pulled up in front of the office – the dynamic duo from the Mines Department, Martin Curtis and Ronnie Cummins.

"We wanted to get away from the office today, because the big brass from Salisbury are visiting, and as you can imagine it's better not to be around – endless questions; time wasting… So we booked a visit to the Ridge Top Mine for an official check on the small ball mill installation," Ronnie said with a big smile. "For the record!"

"I'll ask Joseph and Staff to give you both a guided tour of our mining set-up."

After lunch, Newmarch took the opportunity of a lift with them back to Bulawayo, but told me he would be back early on Thursday to do all the welding jobs, like cutting and welding the legs on the big hopper, and making brackets for the small mill.

Erecting of the Headgear

This was quite an exercise.

The side sections of the headgear that the timber boys had built were lying flat on the ground near the shaft entrance.

A rope was tied to the top of one side section, and 10 boys began to pull and strain to raise it into an upright position. Joseph and I helped too; boy, what a weight, but eventually it was standing upright – definitely the biggest erection I'd ever seen.

Another span of boys similarly pulled the other headgear side section into position, so that the two sides lent against each other at the top.

Because he was thin and weighed very little, Langton was chosen to climb to the top of one of the wavering headgear sides, and, straddling it, he started pulling on a rope, slowly hauling up the square wooden hoist wheel platform.

Now the tricky bit came.

The two side sections needed to be pulled slightly apart at the top to allow Langton to fit and rope the square wooden platform in place between them.

One of the teams accidentally jerked on the rope, causing that side to wobble badly, whereupon Langton slipped and had to cling on for dear life as the side section shook and swayed.

In the vibrating chaos, Langton let go of the wooden board, which crashed down, clattering against the side of the half-built construction, whereupon he leant over to grab hold of the other side, but slipped again and almost fell, the whole structure twisting violently, leaving Langton 30 feet up, draped over the top of the two unstable sides, gasping for breath, with Staff shouting at him to hold on!

Other mine boys standing near the office immediately rushed over and joined the rope-tugging teams, helping to stabilise the towering timber headgear.

Another timber boy quickly grabbed the rope, clambered up the side and helped Langton to pull the wooden pulley wheel platform up again, and fitted it between the tops of the two side sections and roped them together.

Loud cheering rang out amongst the work force, and a relieved, but clearly shaken Langton gingerly climbed down.

Other timber boys joined to finish this major job of bolting the wooden hoist wheel platform firmly in place and cutting and fitting further criss-cross wooden struts to lock the two side sections together to form a four-sided, rigid wooden headgear.

The excitement over, the mine boys returned to carry on with their allotted *gwazas.*

Poor old Langton; he was still all of a quiver, so I told him to go back to the village, because there was no way his shaking hands could build the precision copper plate table today – it had to be made extremely carefully to the correct specifications, the angle of the slope being critical.

"Langton, take the rest of the day off, and try to relax a bit. Tomorrow, you can bring all your carpentry tools and meet me at 6am, when you can start making the copper plate table and launder boxes using these diagrams, okay."

"Yes, Boss. Thanks, I'll start making them tomorrow."

He walked off – very slowly… still looking rather dazed.

. . .

Today was Marie-Louise's birthday and we'd promised to take her to Gwelo for the day and spoil her. While she was still sleeping, Marianne got busy decorating the house with balloons and some of the other leftovers from Christmas; silver balls and crepe paper chains – it really looked quite festive.

I took advantage of the quiet of the early morning and began to write a letter to Dirk in South Africa.

Ridge Top Mine (Pvt) Ltd

P.O. Fort Rixon. Rhodesia

Dear Dirk, *2 April*

Another despatch from the North, where things are beginning to move quickly at last – No, the Big Ball Mill hasn't arrived yet, but we do have a definite delivery date with a Salisbury Company - Wait for it, 1st of May!

However we made a deal with another Mine to borrow a Small Ball Mill to bridge the gap of 2 months, and it is already being installed with all the necessary gold extraction facilities. Mr. Newmarch the inventor of the Big Ball Mill will help us set up the baby Ball Mill which has a capacity of just 3 tons per day but it will help to cover our costs which are steadily rising.

We have over 60 workers now, many with wives and children, it's like having a huge family of around 200! Marianne is making so many trips to the hospital, she should really paint a red cross on the doors of her pickup!

But let me tell you about the loves of your life – yes, about the snakes, I've seen plenty. I've run over a black mamba more than 6 feet long, a striped cobra, and seen many more shooting across the road in front of me. One of our boss boys found a large cobra in his bed, and we discovered a green mamba in a bed which we had stored at another mine. But there are many snakes, especially down the old shafts. If I come across another snake lover, I'll get him to get in contact with You Dirk.

But got any tips for me with regard to snakes. How far can a cobra spit? Is it true if a cobra goes to spit just jump over it, or does it still dose you up the jaxy!! And what if they spit, how long does the venom remain poisonous, does it penetrate easily through clothes? – I'm a real ignoramus on snakes, but it doesn't shock me anymore to see one.

Anyway Dirk, drop me a line when you can about my queries on snakes.

Directors: Ray Buffune (Managing) J.W. Bulgin Joseph Buffune

"Well Marianne, finished my letter to Dirk, so let's have a cup of coffee before the kids wake up, and then we'll go."

"No, let's go now!" The kids had woken up! And wanted to go to Gwelo. "Now, now!"

They piled into the back of the pick-up, and Willias loaded a punctured wheel from the grey 404 that needed to be fixed – we seemed to get quite a lot of punctures and this one had a two-inch-long thorn sticking in it!

We popped up to the office to see Joseph, and I asked him to keep an eye on Langton and his helpers – there were two jobs that they were working on:

Building the copper plate table, and the launder boxes, for which they had all the necessary diagrams and measurements.

Crispin was standing with Jonas, who did not look well at all; he was groaning and complaining of chest pains and wanted to be taken to Shangani Hospital.

The 'Mine 404 taxi' was filling up; the kids came into the cab with us, whilst Willias helped Jonas and his 'hospital' luggage onto the back of the pick-up – some pots, bags of mealie meal, beans and sugar; it looked like he was going away on a camping trip.

At Fort Rixon, I posted Dirk's letter and quickly opened the mail in my post box.

An airmail edition of the UK *Daily Telegraph* newspaper, and a letter from my mother saying she'd posted a parcel for Marie-Louise to the Gwelo address, because she thought it was safer there than having native runners delivering it to us in the bush – I think she watches too many old movies!

A letter from Graham saying that he'd enjoyed Christmas/New Year so much he would like to come again when the mine is running, perhaps at Easter? Optimist!

And great, our appeal had been successful. **The fuel rationing officer had finally approved the FULL 3,300 litres of diesel per month** – from the tone of their letter, I'm sure the copy of the correspondence from the Secretary of Mines had helped!

The punctured wheel was dropped off at the garage and we went to see Jane.

She was really pleased to see us all and wished Marie-Louise a happy birthday, adding that there was a card from the Gwelo post office notifying her to collect a parcel sent from England.

"Good old Gran," Marie-Louise said excitedly. "Can't wait to open it!"

After birthday milkshakes from Jane, we dashed off to the post office.

It was quite a large parcel too, and inside were some shorts and T-shirts for both of the children, and a life-like doll that cried when Marie-Louise picked it up.

The post office lady laughed and said, "You must tell your grandma to remove the batteries next time before she packs it in – we had such a shock every time someone moved the parcel and we heard this baby crying!"

Over at the Midland Hotel, the five of us, four plus the new doll, sat at a table in the dining room for a birthday lunch, which Marie-Louise chose: fish and chips with strawberry milkshakes, and fish and chips take-away for Willias.

When we collected the spare wheel, I was told that the tyre had to be replaced as well – there was a long, deep cut in the inside side wall of the tyre.

Meat rations, beans and two 60 kg sacks of meal were loaded, and we headed for home.

Back at the mine, I was well pleased when I inspected Langton's work.

The table for the copper plate had been built with thick gum pole legs, which made it rock solid.

Using the tape measure, Langton proudly showed me that the surrounding wooden rims of the table were exactly correct for the copper plate to fit on snugly, and the critical slope of the table was spot on too: a 1:8 gradient.

"A good job done, Langton. Tomorrow, you can start on the launder boxes, and building our large security room where the copper plate extraction table will stand."

The rations were unloaded and we retired to our house for the evening.

The kids had already flaked out on the journey, and, as there was no time for Willias to light a fire and prepare some food, we had only one option – biltong and a beer.

. . .

Crispin was standing outside the office admiring the table that Langton had built for the copper plate extraction process.

"How does this work?" he asked. "I've seen a ridged James concentration table, which shudders and shakes, and you see the gold tail forming in the groove on the side of the table, but the copper plate in the store has no grooves or ridges?"

"Well, in simple terms, Crispin, we smear mercury on the copper plate and, when the crushed ore comes out of the launder boxes as sands, they are washed over the table, when the gold particles get captured by the mercury and form an amalgam – you can't see the gold at all. Later, we scrape this amalgam off the table and heat it to a very high temperature, when the gold and the mercury separate again."

"So if the thieves can't see the gold, they can't steal it!" Crispin exclaimed excitedly. "*Out of sight, out of their minds!* How clever."

"Unfortunately, Crispin, it still can be stolen; that's why Langton will be building a fenced, locked security room, which only Boss Joseph and I will have the keys to."

"Good morning, did I hear someone mention my name?" a voice behind us called out, and Joseph appeared from his room.

"Please get Situnda to make me a strong black coffee; I've got to go to Belingwe this morning to collect the acetylene torch and the welding equipment. What time is Newmarch coming?"

"He said he would be here by 8am, because he's got a lot of welding jobs to do today, so it's needed like now!"

"Why don't I check things with Staff," he said as he yawned, "and then I'll leave."

Crispin said he was beginning to feel that everything was coming together at last. "The small ball mill will be working soon and I can't wait to see the gold, which hides on the copper table!"

We laughed; he really came out with some amusing remarks.

"No Ndebele lesson today, Crispin; I'll take a short break at the house for breakfast, and later help you with the stores book."

"We have so many items now, sir; I'm going to need a bigger book soon."

"Or you write smaller!" Joseph chirped in, then looked at me. "I know it's almost 8 o'clock already, but don't worry, I'm about to leave for Belingwe, and if I drive fast I'll be back before 12 with the welding gear for Newmarch."

As the dust settled on the road to Filabasi, another vehicle's dust could be seen approaching from the Fort Rixon direction.

"Eight o'clock on the dot," Newmarch bragged with a satisfied grin. "The old girl might be rusty and tatty-looking, but underneath is a heart of gold; she never lets me down. But now, let's get busy! If you get your welder, Boniface, to help me, I can start building the frames and legs for the hopper and the conveyor system."

"Unfortunately, that'll have to wait 'til Joseph gets back from Belingwe with the cutting gear, but there is plenty for you to do on the small ball mill, the switchboard and the electrical connections."

He stopped and scanned the mining area down to the slimes dams.

"I would suggest to you that the sample boys take extracts from all the excavations that are being done, as the schist is very *arsenic crystalline*, which is a good indication of *colloidal* surface gold." Three words that I'd have to look up!

I called for a gang of two timber boys and two general workers to help Newmarch, and we went down to the big ball mill site.

The block and tackle was used to get the conveyor belt system roughly into position, when they all heaved to raise one end of the conveyor slowly until Newmarch called out, "Stop, hold it there; that's the 30° angle we need. Quickly, get your boys to stack those concrete blocks to support the conveyor, so that I can measure up for the frame and the leg supports."

His words were ignored, as it began to rain hard; the workers plonked down the conveyor and ran over to get shelter in the office.

I suggested we should all have an early break for lunch, and we jumped into his old pick-up and went to the house.

"I know you get milk occasionally from the Mzee Feet, but here are two more pints and a loaf of bread for you, Marianne. It's been engraved in my mind for the last 50 years; whenever you go into the bush, first buy bread and milk."

"And I'm happy you brought them too, Mr Newmarch. Your crusty bread and some hot soup will make a good snack for this on-off rainy weather."

When the rains eased off, we chugged back to the office – no pale blue pick-up yet to be seen, so we resumed our pre-rain tasks.

Langton and three timber boys lifted the heavy extraction table into place in front of the small ball mill, and we fitted the launder boxes between the small mill outlet and the copper plate table.

It was around 3:30 pm before the son of Mr Worry in a Hurry pitched up with all the welding equipment.

He came over and said a little nervously, "Hello.... Sorry I'm late; I had problems, but I'm here now."

"What sort of problems, Joseph?"

"Er... Father had visitors, so I had to stay on a bit, didn't I?"

Ignoring Joseph, I continued discussing with Langton the day's work to be done by his *gwaza* gang.

Their next task was the security room.

We needed eight poles, but the only available gum poles left were six feet in length; not long enough.

"Crispin, get Godfrey to go and find the woodcutter boys and tell them to stop what they are doing. We need them to cut poles – say 10 to be sure – of about nine feet in length."

I gave Langton a sketch plan of the sizes for fencing the security room, and told him that the hessian roof to protect the table must be at least seven-foot high.

The rain started again, and heavier too, so I called Crispin to sound the knock-off gong – although it was only 4:15pm, there'd be no more work done today.

Joseph was helping Newmarch to set up his camp bed and belongings in the office/bedroom, and I left the two of them chatting away.

. . .

Although it was only 5:30am, it felt unusually warm; no damp guti mist hanging in the air for a change.

Joseph and Newmarch were just awakening when I entered their room.

It was quite a sight to see them struggling to get out of the camp beds, and standing there in their underwear – it was like a picture out of the Auschwitz 2nd World War camps, these two six-foot-plus, very skinny men with long white-white legs.

Because Joseph only brought the welding gear in the afternoon, which was cut short by heavy rains, we had just one day left to use it – Newmarch and Boniface would concentrate on cutting and welding the legs/frame of the conveyor and hopper on his ball mill site.

Joseph and I would make sure that both the headgear and the hoist were properly secured in the ground. Langton and his team would be needed all day helping with the laying of the concrete for the hoist block.

Looking up at the headgear, something was not quite right.

"The frame is slightly twisted, I think," Joseph remarked. "Let's get Staff over here."

Two of the timber boys climbed up the sides of the headgear, making sure all the bolts were completely tightened, but still, there was a slight skew in the tall frame of the headgear.

Staff told us that it was a common problem, and we would have to make concrete shoes for the poles at the base of the headgear to ensure that it was rock solid.

"Okay Joseph, you look after that; Langton and his gang are mixing a lot of cement for the hoist block and their other jobs, so ask them to help with concreting the feet of the headgear when you are ready."

I measured out the size of the hoist block we needed, and started two lasher boys on digging it out to eight inches deep, and fishtailing the last two inches at the bottom of the pit as Newmarch had instructed me to do.

Marianne arrived and said there was a phone call from a man called Biton, who was waiting at Fort Rixon to be picked up.

"Ah yes, that's the hoist driver who's joining us; I'll go up there straight away."

I told Langton I'd be gone about an hour and not to start concreting the hoist block until I got back.

I met Biton at Fort Rixon.

He was quite a small, thinly built man, the complete opposite of his wife, who was heavily laden at the front with huge bosoms, and, as if she was precision-made in an engineering works, she had an even larger backside for counter balance.

I pulled up outside the storeroom and left Biton and his wife with Crispin, who would sign them in and allocate one of the spare huts to them.

"She could cause us a few problems, sir," Crispin whispered to me. "Other women in our village compound probably won't like her; in our tradition, a fat, pretty woman with a huge backside is a fatal attraction for men, who will love that – but their wives won't!"

Joseph told me that the headgear feet had been concreted while I was away, and the structure seemed very firm and strong.

"I also got the builder boys to start laying the concrete slab for the hoist – they were just standing around doing nothing."

"Did you check with Langton that the dug-out pit was fishtailed at the bottom, and with a layer of rocks, before they started pouring concrete?"

"No. He mumbled something to me, but it will be strong and heavy; it's about eight bloody inches thick!"

We went over to the hoist, and, sure enough, some more concrete was being tipped from a wheelbarrow.

I told them to stop, and, on checking that the cement already in the hoist pit had not begun to set hard yet, I ordered two lasher boys to get in and shovel it all out immediately.

"But that's a waste of cement; a waste of money too!" Joseph argued.

"If that hoist block isn't fishtailed, it could be ripped out under the strain of the skip hauling one ton of ore from 400 feet down and cause a huge accident and damage to the hoist itself – just ask Newmarch about some of his horror stories."

"Well, I wasn't to know he told you that, was I?" He walked off in the direction of the mill site – hopefully to ask Newmarch about the hoist block fishtailing; he listened more to the old timer than he did to me.

After about 10 minutes, he came back with Newmarch, who looked completely knackered, and said, "I've not finished the legs for the conveyor frame yet, but I'm finished; that's it for today. I'll do the rest tomorrow in the morning."

"I'll phone your dad, then, Joseph, and, if we can keep it another day, you could take it back late tomorrow afternoon."

"But that's a Saturday, and I told Jane I'd be back tonight." He scowled.

"I'll go to the house now and check with your dad, but, if he needs it back by tomorrow afternoon, you'll just have to go! If you'd collected the welding gear yesterday morning, Newmarch could have finished by now – couldn't he?"

Four hundred metres and one phone call later sealed Joseph's fate; Ray had to have the welding and cutting gear back by 5pm on Saturday at the very latest.

The news was welcomed by Newmarch, because he had to weld a support for the small ball mill in order for it to be ready for the planned first test run.

And, if everything functioned and there were no catastrophes, we would be milling the old waste dumps in two to three days' time – and producing our first gold!

I asked Boniface if he could weld a cracked oil filter in my Peugeot pick-up, and also the broken spare wheel holder, which he could then fit back where it belonged, underneath the pick-up. Be good to have the spare wheel there again – a wheel, being round, is an awkward shape, taking up too much room in the back of my constantly-busy pick-up.

. . .

The weather was very, very cold again, and it took several cups of tea before I got rid of those cold shivers after getting out of bed on a dark early Saturday morning.

At the mine office, Staff and Crispin requested on behalf of the mine boys that we start at 6:30am, as it was too cold to work in this misty guti weather.

How could I refuse? I was finding it impossible as well.

"Okay, we'll start half an hour later each day, then, but from Monday they will have to work 'til 5pm, because we'll need everyone on the surface with both ball mill projects on the go at the same time. And this afternoon we will do our first test run of the small ball mill set-up."

I left Boniface beating my wheel carrier into shape to fit it under the vehicle again.

It's the best place for it – less chance of it being stolen, but of course it takes a hell of a bashing sometimes when you bump down a stony, rocky donga crossing, especially when the pick-up is fully loaded and the leaf springs are almost flat; a common occurrence with our never-ending ferrying of timber and supplies to the mine – 50 bags of cement already hits the car makers' recommended maximum carrying weight of one ton!

Joseph called into the office/bedroom where Newmarch was warming his hands on a large mug of hot coffee.

"I dislike this horrible guti; the cold seems to get into my bones, and look, it's not good for my arthritic fingers. I'm even having problems holding this cup of coffee." Newmarch groaned, and I could see he was in pain.

"Why don't you just supervise for the first few hours until it warms up a bit? Boniface can do the cutting and welding, and Sparky can use his huge, strong hands for any mechanical heavy work."

Staff came and asked permission for Boniface to cut and bend two 20-foot rails in order to bolt them to the rails sticking out of the shaft entrance, thus extending the rail track so that the one-ton skip could be hauled up into the headgear and tipped, the ore falling into the ore hopper.

"I'll go with them and check it out," Joseph decided, leaving Newmarch, Sparky and me to discuss what we needed to do to complete the small ball mill site for its first run.

"This first run should be to check that the crushing and flow are correct," suggested Newmarch, "and once the whole system is linked up and working, including the pumping of the slimes to the big ball mill site dams, we should be able to prepare the copper plate using mercury for our first 'crushing to gold extraction' run, hopefully on Monday."

Joseph came in to join us for some steaming-hot mealie meal porridge that Situnda had prepared. Mixed with heaps of sugar, it tastes quite nice, and certainly warms the cockles of your heart. It's like having an inbuilt heater, warming up your whole chest and body.

By 1pm, the rails had been 'bent', cut and welded in place for hauling the skip up into the headgear, where it would automatically tip out the ore into the hopper.

Newmarch and Sparky had linked up the small ball mill's electrical and water connections, and all the workforce crowded around to watch the grand opening.

Two of the lasher boys shovelled waste schist into the mill from the dump that Marianne's daily trips had created.

There were noises, real loud noisy-noises of a working crushing mill set-up, and luckily no mechanical-problem noises or overheating.

A dirty mix of crushed ore sands gurgled and spluttered into the launder boxes and spewed out through the holes across the whole width of the extraction table running over the surface – that later would house the mercury coated copper plate – into the waste removal pipes, the pump shooting out dirty water in a huge spray, soaking some of the mine boys who were standing in the wrong place. I suppose we should have warned them, really, but the roar of the laughter from the other mine boys added to the excitement of the event, and even the soaking-wet brethren found it amusing.

Most of our African workers have a sense of humour, especially slapstick humour, and I thought when we were fully operational I'd hire a film projector and some old Charlie Chaplin silent movies.

We'd erect a large white sheet screen, and, on a Saturday evening, they could be entertained while they enjoyed their pub night.

Another even louder noise took over, coupled with deafening cheering; the Chibuku beer lorry had arrived!

Now seemed the appropriate time to get Crispin to sound the stop gong, which raised an even louder cheer!

Then it was *a mass* exodus:

Joseph with the welding gear *reluctantly heading* for Belingwe.

Newmarch *happily rattling away* in the direction of Fort Rixon.

The mine boys *laughingly sampling* the creamy liquid as it spurted into the drum.

And me? *Contentedly walking back* to the house for lunch with the family.

The sun had warmed up the miserably cold morning and now it was very pleasant again.

It was a fabulous feeling after successfully completing the first small ball mill test run to sit outside the house on our veranda, having a late salad lunch served by Elliot, who had returned and brought a new nanny with him, named Mary.

Sitting there in the warm sun, gazing out across the bush towards the blue range of hills that hid Bulawayo from us, the only thing missing was a cold beer to toast this wonderful event today:

– *The start* of our gold-producing phase.

– *And the finish* of our *continual* financial battling day after day, month after month, just to make ends meet – or, rather, to keep the credit lines bridging the two ends!

All in all, this perfect panorama in my view and the feeling of elation at the day's events would remain in my mind and my heart forever.

. . .

"Morning Boss."

Elliot's cheerful voice as he brought us the tea, which tasted very good too; a marked improvement on what Willias used to brew for us.

He told us that Judith was still very sad; she had begun to relax a bit more, but even the thought of returning to the mine upset her terribly.

This Mary was a cousin, he told me – well, that's what they all say, and kissing cousins soon become live-in lovers!

Sunday morning; a gentle wakening at about 8 o'clock; tea in bed and reading the airmail edition of the *Daily Telegraph* from England. Good for news, sport and, best of all, the amusing cartoons.

Then, by about 1 o'clock, the week's work problems had been replaced by reading the even worse world's problems, but they couldn't spoil our now traditional Sunday English brunch fry-up, Ridge Top Mine style:

Feet's eggs, Newmarch's bread, our garden tomatoes and Irene's aubergines, with rolled-up bits of rabbit masquerading us bangers… unusual, but very tasty.

The noise of an approaching diesel truck drifted towards us; unusual to hear any traffic going past our place on a Sunday.

But it wasn't going past, and it presented itself, pulling up in front of our house.

A man called Darne got out, followed by a woman, and two small children who immediately started running around, happily playing with Marie-Louise and Jeffrey.

The man wanted to see the Newmarch ball mill – ooh, it hurts when people ask about that, especially when you're trying to forget about it on a relaxing Sunday.

"First of May," I told him. "Come back and see it… if we're still here," I joked.

We spent an interesting couple of hours while he related to us his personal knowledge of the string of mines in this area.

"We came up from South Africa last year to peg these mines, the Nelly 404 and the Nelly Extra, which were good gold-producing mines when I grew up here as a teenager. Unfortunately, though, we were too late; just a few weeks after Burke already had pegged them!"

"That name, Darne, does seem familiar," I ventured. "I'm sure I've seen it on a registration plate across the river, far over that way." I gestured the direction.

"Ah, that was probably my old man; he'd been small working in Rhodesia for years. But, when he died, my mother took us back down to South Africa, where for the last 12 years I had my own building business, but the lure of these gold reefs beckoned me the whole time, until… I'm back, small working on a mine called Sunace, near Bulawayo Airport, reprocessing the dumps of what was once a very rich mine, where they had mined to a depth of 3,000 feet!

"We're making a reasonable living, but there is no ways we'd be able to reopen the mine; it would cost a fortune – 3,000 feet deep! It's a real pity for us that Burke pegged all these claims before I came up from South Africa; both of the Nelly mines would have been ideal for me. Fred Stewart had written to me that there was still plenty of workable reef at the second and third levels; just the right size for a small worker. The Sunace is far too big and deep; only a wealthy mining company would have the resources to entertain such a mammoth venture!"

After they'd left, I said to Marianne, "It's reassuring to hear such a story about our mining claims by someone who knows these gold reefs well enough to come back from South Africa to peg and rework them – especially so on hearing this on the day after our successful first test run of the small ball mill set-up; *really reassuring!"*

. . .

Early Monday morning when the mist had lifted, I thought, *as a precaution*, I'd better peg the Nelly Extra claim site, which encompassed half of our garden compound. I would work out later if it was worth including it in the pegged area that I had already registered as a house site.

Godfrey was helping Langton erect the nine-foot poles that had been cut, which, with the wire mesh fencing sides, would form our security room for the copper plate extraction table.

They were also making a door. *That's Langton showing some initiative,* I thought, as I hadn't marked a door on the plan diagram I gave to him.

Later, I learnt from Crispin that Langton had come to see him, worried that there was no door on the plan, and asked him if this was a new type of extraction table that didn't need anyone ever going inside the fenced security room.

Crispin never told me the reply.

Back to the house at lunchtime and I phoned the doctor, as Jeffrey was sounding like a bull frog again, emitting foghorn-type sounds, although still running around as if nothing was wrong.

As we lived so far away, the doctor said he'd phone the chemist so that the repeat prescription could be picked up by someone else, but who?

A few minutes later, the phone rang.

It was a reverse charges call from none other than Jane, saying that Joseph had asked her to call me to say he couldn't make it to the mine early this morning, but he would be there later in the afternoon and bring the meat rations with him.

"Has he left already?"

"Er, about 30 minutes ago, when he dropped me at the Midland Hotel to phone you."

"Oh, pity; there's a prescription at the chemist for Jeffrey's bronchitis. He's coughing badly again; can you collect it? We'll work out later how to get it to the mine."

"So Jeffrey is bad again?" her concerned voice enquired… then a slight pause in the conversation, like when people put their hand over the phone mouthpiece to talk to someone.

"Yes, he needs that medicine urgently, because this damp, misty guti weather here is really down on his chest; he's wheezing and coughing like a frog!"

"Oh shame, poor boy...." Another slight pause.... "Hang on a minute; he's just walked back into the reception... Joseph, can you collect a prescription?"

An immediate response, "Hello, yes, lucky I came back.... I had forgotten to tell Jane something, but I'll pick up Jeffrey's medicine; he obviously needs it for that bullfrog-sounding cough, er... from what Jane just told me. And I'm leaving now... leaving *again* now, okay."

I replaced the phone handpiece, and, with a shaking of my head, I relayed the message to Marianne.

"And one day they will invent phones with a video screen and such deceiving charades will not be possible. But never mind, getting the medicine to Jeffrey is the important thing, not the comical antics of the participants."

It was cloudy, but certainly a warmer day for a change, and the mine boys seemed to appreciate it too and were working hard, digging, shovelling soil into wheelbarrows and tipping it out onto the rail ramp embankment as it continued to be built, getting higher and nearer to the Newmarch mill site.

The timber boys had started laying the first rails on top of the embankment by the headgear end.

Two concrete blocks were firmly rammed into the soil on the surface, and a one-metre gum pole was laid across on top of them, this action being repeated every two metres along the embankment.

With a mix of delicate adjustments using a spirit level, and sometimes thunderous hammering, the first two parallel tracks of rail were laid... and then the second set was put in place.

The timber boys stepped back, awaiting the decision of the Theodolite King – me!

There was a hushed silence as Langton and I walked along the embankment rails towards them... and, 30 seconds later, with a few swift movements of the spirit level, checking that the bubbles were between the marks, my thumb went up and the jubilant timber boys started jumping up and down, dancing and shouting with excitement and joy.

"Stop!" I ordered them. "You'll destroy the embankment!"

A short silence as they all stared at my face... which suddenly cracked into a big smile, when the joyous revelry began again. The rail track was level, and the rails could now be bolted onto the wooden gum pole cross-sleepers.

"Even without using a theodoodalite!" Crispin uttered, as the laughter continued – well, mine, in any case.

The light was fading fast as I was driving back to the house, when I saw the headlights of a vehicle that was speeding towards me – Joseph, the medicine man, was answering our emergency plea for help.

He followed my vehicle down the driveway into our garden, theatrically jumped out, ran over to the veranda and exclaimed, "I drove flat-out to get here, Jeffrey! This is your emergency medicine! Make sure you take it every night; the chemist told me. Oh Marianne, I'm so pleased that after I had already *left* Gwelo to come to the mine, I *suddenly* thought I'd forgotten something, and decided to go back there again; *luckily*, it worked out so well. Goodnight."

. . .

At 6am, the alarm gong sounded.

I peered out the window, but couldn't see a thing; that grey guti mist blankets everything and makes the hour feel like it's in the middle of the night.

It's hard to explain the feeling, but that dampness invades your body and creeps into your bones, which begin to ache.

Last month when I spent a couple of hours in the library dodging a torrential downpour in Bulawayo, I was reading about the BSAP Police in Bulawayo Town compound in the 1890s, and one article really caught my eye – about **guti**.

"…The sentries stood on guard duty in the early morning, shivering in the freezing, murky guti mist; they could hardly make out the shape of their nearest fellow sentry and couldn't feel their fingers at all. They were so numb that they wouldn't have been able to pull the trigger to fire their rifles if they had been attacked at dawn by the rebelling Matabele warriors. Tragic loss of life would have ensued…"

Whilst reading the article, I could actually feel their plight and their pain, as if I was on guard duty next to them – it's such an unbelievably excruciating, numbing pain.

The timber boys, wearing heavy coats and balaclavas, were having difficulty with handling the heavy rails in the guti mist – the only good thing about this guti weather is that it keeps the mine boys working away; if you stop, you literally freeze up!

To help them brave these cold early mornings, we had added mugs of tea to the 'nine-sies', so they now had a ten-minute break of potegai biscuits and a hot drink to help them thaw out.

The embankment had now reached full height at the mill site end.

I set a new *gwaza* to dig away some of the earth to make the banks square, so that block walls could be built as extra support for the ramp at the cocopan tipping point.

This end of the embankment was not only the highest part, almost three and a half metres, but would take the most strain and shaking as the cocopans came to a halt and tipped out their one-ton cargo of ore rocks.

Another group of boys was set the task of collecting big rocks and piling them up near the headgear hopper – they would be used later to be rammed hard into both sides of the solid embankment for the last 30 metres up to the end point.

Concrete would be poured over them to strengthen the whole tipping area.

This was critical; the rail ramp had to be strong and secure, and we couldn't afford an embankment collapse caused by the soil being washed away by heavy rains, so I would make it my priority to supervise this task, once we could use the cocopans to carry the rocks along the rails to the end of the embankment.

I gobbled down hot mealie meal porridge with the family while I awaited a call placed to K.B. Davies to order more cement.

French said he would get a further 50 pockets of Grade One cement put on RMS tomorrow for delivery to the Altyre store.

Marianne could pick up that lot when she checked the post in Fort Rixon.

Newmarch knocked at the door and stepped inside with a welcome package of goodies; two pints of milk, two loaves and a bag of currant buns.

"To celebrate the first full run of the small ball mill," he said. "And I'll be checking the final preparations today."

We walked back to the mine together; the guti had cleared and it was pleasantly warm again.

Joseph called over to us. "Can I use 10 of your workers for an hour or two? Staff and I have built this 'pump on a trolley', which will house the pump motor and the starter all on one wooden skid with rail wheels. The idea is that it could be hoisted up and down by the winch to whichever level it was needed on," he proudly announced.

"That's a smart solution for a pump being required in different parts of the mine," I complimented Joseph. "That's a winner!"

"The only problem is," Joseph began, "we should have built it closer to the main shaft! Now we've got to drag this very heavy pump-skid from outside the storeroom to the shaft, and, of course, the weighty pump is already bolted down on the wooden platform, which means that the rail wheels will cut into the ground and sink! That's why I need 10 of your group to help lift, instead of dragging it to the shaft."

This process unbelievably took the rest of the afternoon, as every now and then a heavy shower would sprint across the hills towards the mine – and the mine boys would sprint for any shelter they could find.

Eventually, it was attached to the hoist cable, and massive, muscly arms of the heavyweight class of the mine boys manoeuvred it to the collar of the shaft, where it sat nicely on the rails, and they all cheered as the hoist started and slowly lowered the pump skid down into the mine.

In the evening, the temperature dropped dramatically; the coldest we'd experienced since we were living in our shack on the mine.

We just couldn't get warm; the kids were shivering, so we all got dressed in something warm, pullovers on, kept our socks on too, and climbed into the king-size Kiaat bed, once again using the thick woolly woven Axminster carpets as blankets.

We used the pretending-to-ride-a-bicycle technique to warm up the legs and feet, and, after a while, the blood began to pump around our veins, when we became warmer, but totally puffed out, and eventually fell asleep….

. . .

However, waking up was harder still.

Even though I could see that it was light outside, being pinned down by the two heavy Axminster carpets was a good excuse for a little longer lie-in.

Newmarch had everything connected and ready to run.

We only had to prepare the copper plate, and we could make our first ever 'ore to gold' production run – I was feeling the excitement building up.

The copper plate was carefully lifted into place on the table, a perfect fit, and we followed Joseph's mother's instructions to the full:

One small cup of Surf washing powder to half a cup of water was smeared on the copper plate and washed gently to remove any dirt.

When the plate was dry, mill sand was rubbed in until the copper shone brightly.

Then a little cyanide solution was applied to the surface, immediately followed by coating the entire eight-foot by five-foot copper plate with mercury.

Then other essential ingredients to the 'gold extracting' menu were added:

One teacup of lime to every wheelbarrow of ore shovelled into the small ball mill.

And one spoon of lemon juice was added to the launder boxes.

If we had followed the recipe instructions accurately, the gold particles would combine with the mercury to form a thick amalgam from which we could later extract the gold – and sell it to the Barclays Bank Assay office for virtually instant cash!

"Five, four, three, two, one, switch on the power!"

The small ball mill began to spin. The water was sloshing around inside, the ore was being shovelled into the mill by two lashers, and the metal balls could be heard bashing around inside the ball mill as they smashed the ore to a fine sand, which came gurgling and bubbling into the launder boxes and flowed out of the holes across the mercury coated copper plate, before running into a container and being pumped down to the slimes dams.

We all hurried down to the other end of the pipes about 100 metres away, and observed the watery mixture running out of the pipes and into the dams.

Success!

I cannot describe the feeling. After five months of an uphill slog against:

The elements;

Abnormal torrential rains;

Shotgun-happy Rancher Jackson;

Water shortages, exasperated by Jackson;

Shortage of mining equipment from the Mines Department;

Unavailability of a working 5-stamp mill;

Excessive frustrating delays of the Newmarch ball mill;

Not to mention the infuriating cock-ups and the indisposition of my partner.

And now to finally see, *yes to finally see* it all in operation:

The complete A–Z of producing gold from waste dumps using the small ball mill.

Amazing, and I felt exalted and couldn't wait for our major larger project to be fully operational:

From blasting the rocks underground, to hauling them to the surface in a skip to be tipped into a waiting cocopan, which would be pushed along the rails to the big ball mill site, crushed to a powder, before the extraction of our gold using a James Table.

Hopefully, over the next two months, we would produce enough gold from the waste dumps using the small ball mill to cover our basic costs, until the Newmarch ball mill was installed and we could increase the production from a tonnage of a mere two tons milled per day, up to 30 tons per day!

This would enable us to clear all the debts, have surplus profits to live on and continue to enjoy the life on the mine in the Rhodesian bush that we'd come to love.

Dirty Washing

"Well Marianne, yesterday was a big day for us – the first gold production test run. But today is even more momentous. Ray is coming down from Hartley, when Joseph, he and I are going to have a *'crunch' meeting*. That guy, Joseph, is a right tit! He doesn't know whether he's Arthur or Martha half the time, and when he occasionally does what he says, even that seems to go wrong and unfortunately that expression 'everything he touches turns to gold' will never, ever come true. In fact, totally the opposite: 'everything he touches turns into more problems'!

"I've spoken to Ray already, and I feel the best solution is for us to sell the Nelly 404 claim, split the profit and go our separate ways. Enough is enough, and he will never change from his nutty professor-type character. If it works out well by lunchtime, we'll phone Peter, Des and some others and have a late afternoon sundowner at the Fort Rixon club to celebrate this potentially better situation, and, if we sell the mine, maybe we'll use the money to go cattle ranching in this district that we like so much."

Crispin had a surprise for me.

Apparently Jonas, whom I took to Shangani Hospital last Monday with chest pains, had 'footed' his way back to the mine last night, so he must be feeling healthy again.

He requested a rest day before starting work again.

The rail tracks had been laid from the headgear to the big ball mill site, and cocopan runs had been successful.

Even with a ton of rocks in the cocopan, two mine boys could push it reasonably easily, and, more importantly, without the cocopan running away from them and crashing over the end of the embankment!

So now, large rocks could be more easily transported to the end of the rail ramp to be cemented into the sides of the embankment – so much easier than by wheelbarrow on the bumpy, uneven terrain to get down there.

I had to wait around for Ray to turn up at the mine, so Marianne took Marie-Louise and Jeffrey with her to the Altyre store RMS depot drop-off point to collect the 50 bags of cement that French had sent to us.

Newmarch also left, going back to Bulawayo with both switchboards, which would be easier to fix up there, especially if he had to buy spare parts.

About 10 o'clock, the old man arrived with Cain, and, as Joseph was underground, I escorted them around the surface operation.

They were pleased that the temporary small ball mill was functioning and that we'd be able to extract gold over the next two months, bridging the gap until the Newmarch ball mill began to do its job – *at last!*

As we walked towards the office for a cup of tea, Ray said to me, "Do you want to see me alone or with Joseph?"

"First alone to outline the problems again, and then with Joseph to try to work out a solution to this 50/50 partnership – no, sorry, this 45/40 *partner shit!* I'd forgotten about your 10%!" I added sarcastically.

He ignored the bait and turned, and we walked to his vehicle and sat inside.

He wound down the window and shouted to Joseph, who was talking with Staff. "Stay around by the office, and we'll have a meeting in a few minutes."

I related a few instances to highlight the main problems of attendance, supervision and just wandering off in the middle of an important job.

"Basically, Joseph is unreliable, and these problems have to be sorted out today!"

"Okay, I get your drift; let's go to the office…. Now where's that son of mine got to? Joseph, Joseph!" Ray snapped.

He was over by the water tank panning some samples, quite oblivious to Ray's shouting, in a world of his own yet again.

"Joseph, we're going to the office; come on."

"Just coming," Joseph replied.

Ray was chatting to me as we entered, when he paused, turned around and looked back… Joseph had disappeared.

"Crispin!" Ray shouted. "Where did Joseph go?"

"He's gone with Cain underground; I'll get someone to fetch him."

"He always bloody disappears when there's something important to discuss; it's so infuriating!"

"I'll tell you what is *more infuriating*, Ray; I've been working bloody hard here day in, day out, yet Joseph rocks up maybe once or twice a week and rarely stays overnight on the mine."

"I know; I had a big row with him on Friday about his two- to three-day working week, and it's got to change! I told him that mining as a small worker is a seven-day week, and that's why we must build him a house for Jane and his son to live in on the mine, and then he's got no excuse."

I quoted numerous instances of his incompetence, and the things that went wrong because of lack of supervision, some of which could have caused a serious accident.

"It's just one cock-up after another!" I uttered angrily. "And if you don't watch these munts the whole time, as you told me, you won't get anything done correctly or on time. It's no good telling them to do a job and coming back when it's finished, and start moaning that it's a cock-up, because then it's too bloody late and has cost too much money and wasted time! And when it's a critical job, you must be present to supervise *the whole time*."

The conversation went on from his side and from mine, both of us agreeing on the main points.

"I know he's my son, and, therefore, I have more interest in him than in you, but I've tried everything to get him going. It worked with you, and now look what you have achieved already; a working small ball mill gold extraction set-up and the bulk of the large ball mill project completed – I congratulate you; you've become a competent small worker gold miner."

"Thanks. I've put a lot of money into this mining venture and I'm determined to make this place go, at any cost," I interjected. "And I really enjoy it, and the life out here."

"Yes, I said you would, didn't I, and it is a good life too," Ray added.

Cain knocked on the door.

"Where's Joseph?" shouted the old man.

"He's still down underground checking on the building of an ore storage hopper, and, when I asked him to come up to the office, he said he was too busy."

"Jesus Christ!" snorted the old man. He rushed outside, grabbed Situnda forcefully by the shoulder and shouted, "Go down the shaft, and bloody quickly too, and tell that *f******* Boss Joseph to come up immediately – I have to leave now!" Ray stood there fuming, with his hands on his hips in a gun duel pose, breathing heavily, but, gradually, his anger subsided. "You don't mind if Cain sits in on the meeting, do you; he won't interfere…"

Suddenly, this white-overalled figure, in fact, 'over-called' figure, streaked towards us from the shaft.

"Come on, hurry up, Joseph!" Ray shouted.

"I'm not having a meeting without figures!" shrieked Joseph as he stormed past us into the office.

Cain, Ray and I followed him, listening to his tirade.

"I'm not having a meeting with ***him***!" He pointed angrily at me. "He's always saying nasty things about me!" he screamed.

"But Joseph, we must talk about several matters," Ray pleaded.

"I don't care. I'm not having any sort of talk and that's final!" he ranted as he hurriedly tried to pull his overalls over his boots and proceeded to fall over onto his camp bed, which also decided it had had enough of this rude pig and neatly folded up, leaving a pair of lily white legs sticking out from his brightly coloured underpants – an inviting target for a big boot!

I glanced at Cain, who grinned, and was obviously thinking the same thing.

Then this ridiculous-looking character managed to disentangle himself from the collapsed camp bed, and stood there in his underpants with those wild, staring eyes glaring at me – it reminded me of a lunatic in an Alfred Hitchcock suspense film.

"I refuse to have a directors' meeting, or any other meeting; do you hear me?" he screamed loudly; enough to wake even the dead.

"Well, we'll just have an ordinary discussion, then," Ray said despairingly.

"I refuse; I refuse; I refuse!" ranted this abnormal skeleton, raving and waving his arms around. "Have it without me; you might as well, because you never listen to what I say in any case!"

And he proceeded to climb into a pair of dark blue overalls.

"And what if we decide to fire you?" Ray shouted back at him.

"Then fire me!" shrieked Joseph, and, as he tried to shake his finger at his father, he again tripped in his half-on overalls and fell forward, grabbing the chair, which slid out of the way, causing this insane human being to collapse in a heap on the floor.

Jesus, this would really make a fabulous comedy show, I thought.

"No meeting! No talking! No rude comments! Nothing! I *refuse* to talk to any of you, and that's final!"

Whereupon he stormed out of the office, knocking a tray of tea from Situnda's hands as he was entering through the open doorway – I don't know who looked more bewildered, us or old Situnda, the tea maker.

The old man grunted, snorted even, and pursued Joseph, who was heading full steam for the open bush.

Cain and I went to check on the small ball mill fenced extraction room that was under construction, but we could still hear the shouting match that was going on between Joseph and Ray, who were standing on top of a waste dump a hundred metres away.

"This is good!" Cain exalted. "I'm pleased at least someone on this mine listens to ideas from others," he added sarcastically. "And when you're producing gold, you'll be able to sleep at night knowing you've got the gold on the copper plate table fully fenced off and protected from any theft. And if I were you, I would also put an extra *askari* on your night shifts, specifically to guard this extraction area.... I'm suggesting this to you, because I know I would only receive a backlash of '*mind your own business*' from my dear brother, your partner," he uttered with an infectious lilt in his voice.

We chatted away about the long delays caused first of all by the 5-stamp mill sagas, and now the present Newmarch ball mill headache.

"But at least, and at last, you'll be producing gold from tomorrow using this bridging the gap small ball mill that you managed to secure – a very good arrangement to get this on site, and virtually at no cost too."

It was about 20 minutes before Ray returned with Joseph from the waste dump.

It looked quite funny with this short man coming towards us with Joseph following right behind him, as all we could see was Joseph's head with a bright red hat that seem to bob up and down on top of Ray's short body.

Ray said that Joseph apologised, but that in future before we have a meeting we must give everybody the proposed agenda, just like they do in the big companies!

"I agree; why not? It won't make any difference at all," I mused.

"And don't you dare do that to me again, catch me with my knickers down and arrive with a list of points, when I can't think of any good ones."

"They can't be very important if you can't think of any," mocked Cain.

"Don't you start on me as well," Joseph irritably replied. "I think that he's getting you all on his side against me; he's determined to make me look a fool."

"That's not hard to do. I mean, this ridiculous show you put on for us over the last 30 minutes; it's pathetic, and it's becoming more and more like a 90:10 partnership – I do 90% of the work, while you occasionally turn up and clown around!"

"There, see, he's running me down again. It's not fair, and why's he trying to make me look stupid?"

"Do you know, Joseph," I answered forcefully, "this whole situation reminds me of a *Mark Twain* quote, which is very appropriate in your case: *it's bad enough to stand there looking like a fool – don't open your mouth and confirm it'!*"

"You bastard!" Joseph shrieked. "I'll go on my own, and have a large gold mine, which I will run and produce much more gold than you! I'm not working with you again; never, ever with you again! That's it; *that's final!*"

"They are the first words that you've uttered today that make any sense at all. I suggest we *sell* the claims, and the entrepreneur, Joseph, can go and do his own thing. Don't you agree, Ray?"

A few seconds of silence followed before Ray spoke…. "Yes. The only way to solve this is to sell, split the proceeds and you can both pursue your own future paths. It'll probably take several months, though, to get a sale through, so in the meantime you both will have to get on and work together and get this mine producing gold! You two have laid out all *your dirty washing on the table* today – there's no turning back now! Sell! So, Joseph, do you agree to spend more time working on the mine whilst the sale proceeds and hopefully will be completed in three months, by the end of June?"

"Yes Dad, great, because I'll be on six weeks' border duty call-up from 15 May, and after that I won't have to work with *him* anymore!"

"That's the first I've heard about it; did you know?" Ray queried, turning to me.

"Yes, but only a couple of days ago when Joseph casually let it slip in a conversation, but I would have thought that he would have told his father, the MD of the Ridge Top Mine! And thinking about him being away for six weeks, it wouldn't make any real difference to the current situation – of a day here, the odd day there…"

"*That's a lie*! A bloody great lie," Joseph began to rant again. "I've been working on the mine regularly since Jane got over her illness."

"Huh! Regularly? Your definition of regularly is very different to the one in the Oxford Dictionary!" I replied sarcastically, and opened one of Crispin's admin books, which showed the days ticked off against Joseph's name.

"But Dad, you see that's not fair. He's always trying to trip me up, and it's probably all made up; it's not true. Why would there be a separate book just for me?"

"If you look, Joseph, you'll see that on the next page there is John Newmarch's name with the days ticked off when he's been on the mine. *And* if you look at the cover of the book, well that says it all!"

And I put down the book in front of them, and pointed to the cover: 'Visitors Book'.

"But you've made this especially to trap me. I'm not a visitor; I am *a director*!"

"You've got it wrong, Joseph; I told Crispin to record the times in and out when a visitor came to the mine. It was useful for security purposes, but I didn't envisage that he would put your name in it, although I do like his far-sightedness – and to cap it all you're not even our most regular visitor over the last six weeks; John Newmarch is! And Feet, our vegetable supplier, is *second!*"

When you squeeze a plastic bag so that there is no more air in it, it would resemble Joseph's face. Although his eyes were on fire and he desperately wanted to spew out a string of verbal abuse, he had no wind left; he remained speechless.

Ray jumped in and took control of the conversation. "That's enough; the only option for you two is to sell the Nelly 404 claims, which, thanks to your hard-working partner here, Joseph, is now becoming a viable gold mine proposition. I will concentrate on trying to find a buyer for the Ridge Top Nelly 404 mine; I'll spread the word around. In the meantime, you two must knuckle down; that's your jobs, whether you like each other or not. You have to work together and get the mine fully operational. You need regular gold output, verified by the Mines

Department and Barclays Bank Assay office – that will go a long way to convince any potential buyers of your mine. Come on, Cain. We've wasted enough time here; let's go."

Cain and his old man got into their truck and left. Joseph vanished too.

I gave the visitors' book back to Crispin, who remarked, "That Boss Joseph, he was shouting very loudly at you all in the office. He was so mad; I think he broke the roof!"

Well, that Crispinism put a smile back on my face and I laughingly replied, "When someone is very angry, Crispin, the expression is '*he hit the roof*'!"

"Oh, but isn't my expression even stronger, even more vivid?"

"Indeed it is, Crispin, indeed it is."

Over a late lunch, I told Marianne about what had happened in the course of the crazy morning. As I described Joseph acting like a crazy person, prancing around in his underpants like a buffoon, she cried with laughter.

"It sounds very comical, I know, but it's not funny at all really," I added calmly. "When you consider that this madman has quite an effect on our future – well, our immediate future in any case. And to have the possibility that this idiot could trip us up when we're so close to the finishing line of this very important race; first to get solvent, then to sell the mine. It is a ghost that haunts me sometimes; a monster that is lurking in the background."

But I could see why she was laughing about Joseph's comical behaviour; it cracked me up as well every time I recalled his ridiculous performance that I'd witnessed in the office.

"So tell me, Marianne, how was your trip back from the Altyre store loaded with 50 bags of cement on the pick-up, which would have made the pick-up very low to the ground? Any bad scraping noises now that my spare wheel holder is fixed under the pick-up again?"

"All went fine. I purposely drove at a snail's pace going in and out of the dongas; it went very smoothly and definitely no bashing or scraping noises! We didn't have any problems at all on the trip, and, in fact, I'm enjoying driving more and more."

. . .

A bitterly cold, damp awakening.

I was shivering as I got dressed; this guti permeated through our cement-painted hessian walls, making them wet to the touch. No wonder really that Jeffrey suffered from bronchial, chesty problems – we prayed that the hot, sunny weather would soon return.

I put on a shirt and pullover, still keeping my pyjamas on underneath, and climbed into my overalls before I braved the outside misty weather.

Up at the mine, I met a smiling, very friendly Joseph, who immediately offered me a cup of tea – he always overreacts after he's had one of his stupid blow-ups, and promises you everything under the sun, none of which he normally carries through – needless to say, I didn't get my tea!

We went underground to check the level of the water; we'd been pumping day and night now for many days and the second-level drive tunnels could now be cleaned up of rubble and rusty metal items.

One of the pumps was getting very hot and had to be switched off when running above 20 amps, but, as Joseph said, it was adding to our pumping capacity, the pump on Joseph's skid being the main player.

Good news for us was to watch the hoist fully working and winching the skip up from the second level with rocks and rubble, which were tipped into the hopper.

The timber boys were busy checking all the bolts on the rails and putting extra supports under the rails for safety at the mill site end of the embankment.

We had planned that, on Saturday, before Joseph went back to Gwelo for a day off, we would have 'dry runs' testing the rolling stock of the cocopans from the headgear hopper to the Newmarch ball mill site.

Joseph went off early to Bulawayo, we agreeing to meet at 2pm at the Mines Department.

I squeezed in a practical Ndebele lesson with Crispin in the office before leaving with the family for Fort Rixon.

Our post box was full; yes, for the first time – with creditors' bills and statements!

One letter did cheer me up, even though it wasn't the keenly awaited one from the Mining Affairs Board, but it was about some much-needed cash.

Enclosed was a $177.36 cheque, the refund of the sales tax on the green compressor that we had leased-back to ourselves almost two months previously.

On to Bulawayo on quite a bumpy road – the guti doesn't seem to have any effect or dampen the hard road surface at all.

"Let's celebrate our first real golden success so far – the small ball mill crushing the ore to sands, which flowed over the mercury covered copper plate table, capturing the gold particles! Yebo, our first gold! We'll have a mixed grill at Greys Inn, and also buy a crate of beer to take back to the mine with us – a weekend treat."

The response was enthusiastic, as was the devouring of the food.

With a full, contented feeling, I left Marianne and the kids to enjoy their bath at Greys Inn – lucky buggers; I hadn't had a real bath for a long time, and even my early morning swims in Jackson's water tank had been curtailed by this damn cold guti weather!

Joseph's pale blue Peugeot was parked in the Mines Yard and he was talking to Martin Curtis.

I went with Willias to take the 45 samples bags up to the mining engineer's office for testing and the assay results, and asked Ronnie if he could try to get them done quickly for us.

Ronnie said he'd do his best.

"By the way, you'll have to sign up for that new compressor today, because Pope, my boss, wants to allocate it to another small worker mine."

So I signed.

"Two hundred and two dollars and eighty-eight cents, please," Curtis said with a big grin.

Bummer; that nullified the tax refund!

"Okay, I'll get our bookkeeper to send you a cheque," I replied, using our first 'delaying paying' tactic, but, if the proceeds for the month from the small ball mill bore enough fruit – golden fruit – I should be able to settle that bill easily.

"The compressor will be ready for collection next week," Ronnie confirmed. "It's up to you which transport company you use."

"On Monday, I'll phone to make a definite date, Ronnie; thanks for your help."

As I neared Greys Inn, I could see the kids surrounded by ice cream men sitting on their bicycles, which had freezer boxes attached to the front.

The Eskimo ice cream factory was just around the corner, and what better prospect for them to make the last sale of the day – two little children standing on the curb sweating in the hot afternoon sun, pleading with their mother, who already had her purse out.

So, with four happy 'licking an ice cream cone' customers, both the sellers and the buyers ended their week cordially on a Friday afternoon.

. . .

I made my early morning trek to the mine with the windscreen wipers trying their best to remove the frosty guti gunge, but, in reality, only turning the windscreen into an opaque smear.

Joseph and I quickly checked that the *gwaza* gangs were busy on their tasks before ducking into the office for a mug of hot coffee, which helped reduce the shivering.

We sat down and mulled over the fact that it was the 'one month late' anniversary of the Newmarch ball mill. Thank God for the small ball mill, our saviour – hopefully.

"Our severe cash shortage is going to give us big problems too, Joseph. We must find some ways of raising cash, and we need a good $3,000, assuming the Newmarch ball mill becomes operational in early May. We must continue to order everything possible through K.B. Davies, and we will have to tread very lightly on paying debts. Also keep our own expenditure down to a minimum. For example, we should plan trips better so that we go to Bulawayo once or twice a week instead of rushing off, jumping into the pick-up and burning the rubber each time we think of something…."

"Yes, yes, we know all that," Joseph contributed irritably, "but I must pan a sample for you. Come, let's have a look at it; it's from the Claremont." He disappeared through the doorway.

I leisurely finished my coffee, pinching a few chocolate biscuits to nibble from Joseph's not-so-well-hidden stash, and went outside, only to find Joseph leaning against the wall picking his nails.

Staff came over and pleaded with me to phone Chibuku to find out what had happened, because there had been no beer delivery on Friday.

I took this very seriously, because, for the African, it seems that 'beer, women and food' is the equivalent of our 'wine, women and song'; both the key to good, enjoyable living – I went and phoned the brewery straight away.

Chibuku told me that they were trying to locate the lorry themselves; the driver had phoned in to say that he had been stuck since yesterday afternoon, but that he would be continuing with his deliveries today.

After breakfast, I was just leaving when I heard a familiar rumble – no, it wasn't the eggs! It was the Chibuku beer lorry!

I followed it into the compound, where the elated faces of the women greeted the arrival of the 'pleasant weekend' lorry.

The beer was gushing into the 25-gallon plastic drums, three of which would make up my 75-gallon weekly order, and happy women were dipping mugs into the foaming brew, all part of the Chibuku celebrations.

Then disaster; the beer began spluttering and gurgling, the flow gradually reducing to a trickle – the tanker was empty! But luckily for us our third plastic drum was just full.

Not so lucky, though, for the poor munts on the farms down the road; they would have a dry weekend.

I went into the office to check with Crispin. "Who is the lucky barman this weekend?"

"Elliot; it will help him a bit. He could really use the extra money."

It works this way; the chosen barman for the week buys the beer from me, on credit, of course, at three cents a pint, and sells it for five cents a pint, making a nice profit – equivalent to about a month's wages!

Joseph's underground workers were even luckier today; free beer!

He had brought back a 25-gallon drum full of Chibuku beer from the brewery on Friday; free beer, as he had promised to celebrate the skip working and hauling up rocks from the second level underground.

This had now been completely dewatered, and we would be able to do some trial blasting work once we had the jackhammer drills and the compressor on site.

"One thing, sir; you know you are often complaining about Situnda being drunk on Fridays and Saturday mornings. Well, I have discovered why. It's not like we thought; maybe brewing his own in the bush or buying Changaa from the farm workers. It's right here under our very noses. We store the Chibuku beer in the 25-gallon drums, which are kept here in the office after deliveries on Fridays, and I actually put tape over the lids to stop someone dipping into the brew. The tape is never broken, but I noticed a small hole in the top of one of the plastic drums, and if you tip the drum over a little bit, beer pours out from the hole. Situnda is the only one who can just walk in and out of the office without causing any suspicion, as he has to be in the office to perform some of his duties. So do we set a trap to catch him, like we did with the poacher?"

"No. I'll speak with the manager at Chibuku Brewery and ask if they'll deliver to us regularly on a Saturday morning; that would do the trick. And, as we are now one of their biggest customers in this district, we should get the right to choose our date to be on a Saturday – and then the beer theft problem would not exist anymore! But come outside now, Crispin, because today we will celebrate the first trial run from underground through to the Newmarch ball mill site; Joseph has already had rocks loaded into the skip waiting on the first level."

The workers who were not involved in this trial, together with their wives and children, were crowding around the headgear, but, to add to the fun of the occasion, I got them to hold hands to make a long chain that stretched all the way down to the Newmarch mill.

Master of Ceremonies, Joseph, wearing his bright red hat and a smile from ear to ear, shouted for everyone to be quiet…. "Power on!" he cried.

And the alternator burst into life.

"Hoist driver, start winching!"

A low, squeaking rumble of metal wheels on metal rails gradually became louder and louder, and, suddenly, the skip appeared coming out of the shaft.

Wild cheering as it was hauled up into the headgear to tip its contents of rocks, which crashed and bashed into the hopper, and from there into the waiting cocopan.

I encouraged those standing in the chain holding hands to lift and drop their arms, making a sort of wave motion as I walked along the rail embankment in front of a cocopan full of rocks being pushed slowly by two mine boys.

After a very strenuous, hard-puffing and blowing start, the cocopan rode easily along the rail tracks.

I was a little cautious as we neared the mill site, and walked slowly backwards, ready to help stop the cocopan if needed to do so.

However, schoolboy mathematics had served me well. Once the cocopan reached 'the mark', the two boys stopped pushing and the cocopan immediately came to a halt at the Newmarch ball mill site – a perfect precision performance.

Even louder cheering, like the roar of 60,000 fans at a rugby match celebrating a try, filled the air – enough noise to outdo the clatter of the rocks as they were tipped out of the cocopan down the shute and into the mill hopper.

When the noise finally died down, Staff and Crispin told the workers that today we would finish early; they could down tools now and go and celebrate in the village.

Joseph and I celebrated too, together with Marianne, Marie-Louise and Jeffrey, when we got back to the house.

We raised our bottles of beer, clinking them together.

"What a week this has been," Joseph exalted. "Firstly, gold being produced from the small ball mill, and then secondly, the successful run bringing the ore up from underground and transporting it through to the big ball mill site."

"And *thirdly,* to you being on the mine *three days running!*" I couldn't resist the jibe. "And fourthly to the buyer of the Nelly 404!"

"Yes, and the sooner the better. I can't wait to get the sale money, split it and end our partnership so that I don't have to put up with you anymore. I'll be my own boss of my own gold mine at last; my mother will be so proud of me, and…"

"To the buyer, then; may he be rich, and bloody quick!" I interjected on a lighter note, and, after a further clinking of the beer bottles, Joseph left for Gwelo.

A lovely, lazy afternoon for a change.

Marie-Louise had got Langton to paint a name on the shell of another giant tortoise that had come from the bush into our garden area.

"We've called this one Sue 2, and Jeffrey has built a small wall to stop it wandering off, and we can feed it too. We'll paint the names on the shells of others, and we'll soon have our own tortoise game park."

The chill quickly began to descend at dusk, and we moved into the house for supper before retiring for the night.

. . .

On Monday morning, a loud hooting alerted us to an early arrival… wait for it; door slammed, loud footsteps and a knock on the door, which slowly opened…

"Hellooo, it's only me." Joseph poked his head around the door. "I hope I didn't wake you; I left Gwelo at 4:30am this morning to be here on time."

"Well, Joseph, to celebrate this new partner-on-time person, come and join us for a cuppa and some toasted bread 'Elliot style' on the wood stove plate."

Later, up at the mine, I told Joseph, "Ronnie has just phoned and the new portable compressor that I signed for on Friday is ready for us."

"Oh yes, I saw it; that yellow Atlas Copco one. So it's ready for collection?" Joseph enthused. "Good; I'll go now to Bulawayo to get it. I can hitch it to the back of my pick-up. Let me get my keys."

"Wait a bit, Joseph. Ronnie said it was ready for collection, but we should liaise with Fox & Bookless Transport to arrange for delivery."

"No, no, I'll go in now and tow it back. It'll be quicker and, as you're always saying, we have to cut down on expenditure." And he dashed out the door, adding, "And don't worry; I'll drive slowly and very carefully."

And with a puff of diesel smoke out of the exhaust pipe, he disappeared.

Marianne hooted as she drove into the mine compound on her daily run of collecting mine waste dump rubble to feed the small ball mill – the heaps were getting higher.

The lasher boys quickly shovelled the waste schist out of the back of the grey pick-up, about one ton's worth, and I hopped on the back with the kids for a ride back to the house for 'elevensies' – coffee and home-made cake from the workhorse wood stove, which was turning out to be the hub of our home life.

We'd already cooked a Sunday roast in the oven, roast leg of reedbuck and roast potatoes – lekker! The plates were always piping hot for making tea and cooking vegetables, and the iron-shaped plate was proving very useful for having an always hot, instant coal iron.

"Especially for my pants and pyjamas," Marie-Louise had said. "I don't want any of those nasty painful yellow maggots in my legs ever again!"

With this miserable guti weather, the kids needed some extra clothes.

"Remember you numbered the boxes we brought up from South Africa. Where's the list of what they contain? I need to find some other pyjamas and pullovers for the kids. Some mornings, I can't get them out of bed; they shiver with this damp cold. What does guti actually mean?"

"Well, it's not gudi!" Marie-Louise chirped.

"I've no idea, but it is powerful and seems to inject itself right into the marrow of our bones. Some mornings, it is so painful; I walk carefully to the pick-up like an old man."

I found the list and started removing the large packed boxes from the dark, dingy corner of our square-shaped house.

With a lot of the boxes removed, this corner saw light for the first time, and I noticed a brown mud 'track' on one of the gum poles of our walls, then another, and… There were five poles affected by a finger-thick mud track stretching from the wall blocks up to the roof, and spreading out a few metres on the roof-supporting timbers in that corner.

As three pairs of inquisitive eyes watched, I used a stick to knock away some of the mud, and…

"Eee, look at those horrible see-through ants with light brown heads; what are they doing?" Marianne enquired.

As I poked around more, especially at the base of one of the gum poles, bits of wood fell away like rotten wood, but it was not wet; just eaten and broken up.

"Jesus, good thing we discovered this; another month or so and the whole iron sheet roof could have collapsed and fallen on us while we slept. Let's get busy knocking all this mud and ants into a bucket, and we can examine what damage they've actually caused to the timber supports. Elliot! Fetch Langton; tell him to bring his tools with him."

We ended up with two bucketfuls of this muddy, woody writhing mass of ants – they looked like white snot with a brown bogey on the end.

I took the buckets outside, poured on some diesel and set fire to the lot.

The buckets were still smouldering when Langton appeared.

I showed him the white ants' paradise, and he prodded and poked the timbers.

"You're lucky you found this; they have done little damage so far, because both the gum poles and the roof supports are made of hard wood. If we had used cheaper soft wood, the roof would have caved in long ago."

He spent the next hour or so cleaning the affected areas of the timbers, then painted all the timbers and gum poles with some timber muti to prevent this happening again.

I looked at the gum poles and could see one or two white ants scurrying, seemingly trying to get out of the light and under the cover of their ant-made tunnels.

"Hey, look at this," I called out to Marianne. "There are the same muddy lines on my luggage trunk."

Elliot helped me and we lifted the heavy wooden trunk and took it outside.

I unlocked the large brown trunk, which contained all our books that we'd brought with us on the voyage to Cape Town, that thoroughly enjoyable 10,000 kilometre sailing from Southampton on the South Coast of England.

We gasped! Inside the trunk was an unusual and amazing sight.

It was as if we were in an aeroplane looking down on New York City – the white ants had busied themselves eating into the books and, whether by artistic intention or not, our view of this 'city in a box' was quite fascinating.

Their cleansing, destructive ways had left some bits of a book standing tall like a skyscraper, whilst others were lower – there were roads between the buildings where the ants had eaten the book pages right down and you could see hundreds of ants scurrying along the pavements of this city.

"Nothing for it," I exclaimed. "New York City is about to experience severe flooding and destructive fire!"

I grabbed the jerry can of diesel quickly before the inhabitants of New York could flee the oncoming disaster, emptied it all over the trunk and sent a fire bomb into their midst – a lighted match, which ignited the diesel, the slow-burning blue flames spreading across the doomed city. I fully expected to hear the inhabitants' screaming noises, similar to those of the attacking Matabele ants, but the only noise was the crackling sound as my favourite books and the old trunk slowly burnt to ashes – I had cremated a whole city of squatters!

As the afternoon wore on, I began to have concern about the whereabouts of Joseph and the yellow compressor.

A phone call to the Mines Yard provided the answer.

"Hey Marianne, listen to his latest cock-up. Joseph arrived in Bulawayo and had actually hooked up the compressor to the tow bar on his pick-up. When he went inside to get the documents, he was told by Ronnie that he couldn't tow the compressor; it was illegal unless he had a special permit to do so. Ronnie said he became angry and demanded that he be issued a special permit straight away.

"When he was told that such a permit had to be applied for from the Ministry of Transport, he ranted and raved like a small schoolboy, shouting out obscenities, casting doubt about Ronnie's parentage, simply making an absolute arsehole of himself again. Then he stormed outside in a rage to get into his pick-up, and, when he rushed around the back of his vehicle, he crashed over the tow bar of the compressor – which he'd obviously forgotten about.

"He lay there on the ground and he was suffering a lot of pain from badly bruised shins and a dislocated finger. They had taken him to Bulawayo Hospital outpatients for a check-up and X-ray, and lucky enough there were no broken bones, just severe bruising – and a deflated ego. Joseph apparently had driven back to Gwelo Town – without the compressor. Sometimes I think he should be certified; he is without doubt the son of Mr Worry in a Hurry! But let me phone Fox & Bookless to arrange the collection and delivery of this new portable compressor."

Unfortunately, it was too short a notice for them, but a second call to B&O Transport was successful and they could collect it with the jackhammers and deliver to our mine on the Wednesday morning.

That was good to hear, because I would be collecting dynamite from the AE & CI depot for the first time on that Wednesday, so it would tie in nicely for some blasting tests and, with the help of Staff, I would select which of our numerous jackhammer boys did the best drilling work.

. . .

We'd heard nothing from Joseph since his shin-to-tow bar episode, so I put a call through to Matt's mine, but he'd heard nothing about the incident.

However, he would go and check at the Hudson Road house during the day and phone me back in the evening.

The milkman arrived at 8am. It's a good delivery service out here in the bush, probably better and earlier deliveries than people in Bulawayo can expect, and our milkman brings a loaf of bread, sometimes currant buns, together with the local Bulawayo rag to keep us up to date with the local news.

Over a cuppa, Newmarch told me that he had fixed both the main switchboard and the big ball mill site switchboard and brought them with him on his pick-up.

He would stay 'til Saturday, and return again the following week to be full-time on our mine, as we had agreed with French.

His main task would be to supervise, and also to teach me all about the small ball mill operation, together with the secrets and tips on the gold extraction processes.

He told me he had worked with many different types of ore crushing mills, from 5-stamp to ball mills, and various gold extraction systems, including copper plate/corduroy blanket/James Tables, and associated chemical processes ranging from gold amalgamation/mercury recovery retorts/zinc displacement and the cyanidation processes.

But for him, the best and most exciting gold extraction process was with a hammer and chisel cracking out visible gold – gold you could see and touch!

I laughed and told him that he was born in the wrong era; he should have lived 2,000 years ago in the times of the ancient miners who only mined visible gold, crushing the ore and separating the gold dust.

"Not only that," he replied. "They were intriguing times too, and the Phoenicians, for example, all those years ago, mined in a similar way to our current methods – it was just far more labour intensive and they didn't have electricity to drive machines, which was the main difference."

"I find it all very fascinating," I replied, "and plan to read about those eras when I have a bit more free time."

"If you're that interested, you should spend a morning in the Bulawayo library; you'd get a good background and feel for how they mined and produced gold. And there's a dear old lady called Agatha. She must be in her late 80s, much older than me, and she will be able to show you some relevant books on ancient mining."

Rather like an apprentice, I followed Newmarch's every word and action, noting down important things – well, important to me – and making various diagrams.

Whilst he was busy hooking up the switchboards, I worked with Langton and Godfrey on the gold extraction room, and, by the end of the day, it was completed.

There it stood, located at the output from the small ball mill, an eight-foot-high, wire mesh-sided room with a hessian roof and a padlocked door.

It was approximately 10 feet wide by 20 feet long, and even the smallest potential thief with the skinniest arms could not reach the gold amalgam on the copper plate table.

Newmarch came over and said all was ready with the small ball mill and we would start with two-ton-per-day operations, namely two shifts; from 6am to 2pm, and 2pm to 10pm, kicking off in the morning.

"You've done a good job on the security room, and if I were you I'd put a trusted person on duty as an evening *askari*; it all helps protect the gold you've worked so hard to produce."

"Yes, maybe I could get Crispin to do one evening from 6pm to 10pm, and Amon to do the next evening, rotating. I'd know that the gold was safe – they are the only two Africans, no, actually, the only two people on this mine who I know I can trust completely."

``Newmarch smiled and prodded me, "You're beginning to learn the two sad secrets of gold; mistrust and greed! The first lesson is never, never, ever trust your partner; he is the one who has most opportunities, and sometimes good reasons to rip you off! Remember anyone can be bought, and gold breeds greed! Gold can lure people into a trap. The longer you are gold mining, the more you realise that gold is a fever, an epidemic that can spread very fast, causing grown men to behave like wild animals as they claw and fight their way to peg claims, and even kill to protect them. It's an incurable disease. I know; I've been smitten with it for over 50 years!"

In the evening, Marianne invited Newmarch over to eat with us, and we listened with great interest to some of his experiences, some mishaps and many other very amusing incidents.

"I'm becoming an old man these days, but I wouldn't trade my life for any other; there's always been excitement, and heartbreak – but never a dull, repetitive job!"

"Then, Mr Newmarch, before you go, I'd like you to listen to this song by *Neil Young*."

And I pulled the plastic LP (long player) out of its cover, and connected the record turntable to the car battery.

Boom, boom, boom, boom…

I've been a miner for a heart of gold, and I'm getting old… boom, boom, boom, boom. It keeps me searching for a heart of gold, and I'm getting old… boom, boom, boom, boom…

There was a tear in his eye as he listened intensely to the track…

Then he stood up, paused a while, excused himself, and went out of the door and into the darkness.

. . .

Matt phoned early in the morning.

He had no idea where Joseph was, but he definitely wasn't at the Gwelo house, and neither was Jane.

I phoned the Belingwe mine and was unfortunate enough to get his mother on the line, in full flow, so to speak.

"Yes, Joseph is here. It was a shock when Jane drove him and the baby down from Gwelo yesterday. He was lucky he didn't break his leg, and he'll be staying here until his leg gets better," she burbled on. "And you must take over all his underground supervision work as well until he's fully fit again – you hear what I'm telling you?"

"Well, that won't make much difference to me at all. I'm already doing most of his work each day, except on the odd day that he comes to the mine…"

"Don't you run my son down!" she shouted. "And he's been telling me all about you too, and how you keep a log book on him, writing down every day the time he arrives and the time he leaves."

"And most pages are blank!" I replied tersely. "'Cos he's hardly ever here; that's the whole problem."

"You're so rude! I can see why Joseph gets upset with you, and when he's annoyed he can't always do his best work, so it's your fault really; you must be nicer to him!"

A slight pause in this ridiculous conversation probably prevented further warmongering, and then the phone rang…

"Hello, hello, is that you, Mabel? … Yes, I'm fine… but first I must get this rude man who works for my son, Joseph, to put his phone down."

"Done!" I replaced the receiver. "So, Popette, Mabel is playing the matron, and we can probably rule out Joseph pitching up this week. Still, with Newmarch here full-time, we won't miss him too much."

"That sounded like you got an earful from the mother." Marianne chuckled. "And is Joseph okay?"

"If we are talking about physical health, he has badly bruised shins, which I can imagine is bloody painful, so we'll have to wait and see. If his mother gets her way, he'll be off for a month, but I can't see his father, Ray, putting up with him *faffing around* their house for very long, so he'll probably pitch up in a day or two, and milk his wounded soldier act."

Newmarch was in his element. He was continually moving around the small mill site, checking, telling the lasher boys how to break larger schist pieces into smaller feed for the mill, so that it would not only increase the throughput, but also be less strain on the aged ball mill.

He took a quick break with me for coffee when we discussed progress so far.

He was so much more reasonable and easier to talk to than you-know-who, and I had no qualms about leaving him in charge while I was away on my first 'explosive' trip to the AE & CI dynamite depot.

This was located south of Bulawayo in flat bush country and it wasn't easy to find.

Eventually, I saw what looked like the built-up bank of a dam, but, driving closer, I came into a clearing and could clearly see the heavily electric-wired security gates.

On showing my ID and the official Mines Department card for Ridge Top Mine, I was allowed to drive in.

Inside, it was like a football stadium, with the embankments being the spectator stands, which housed the AE & CI offices.

When I told the supervisor that this explosives dump was hard to find, he was really pleased.

"Good; that's why we removed the red flags from the grass mounds. Under normal circumstances, it is the law to have warning flags and signs for the public's safety, but, because of the terrorist problems, we don't want to be a sitting duck for a terrorist raid; they'd love to get their hands on our babies in the underground vaults. Come to my office; there are certain procedures I have to explain to you."

It was an eerie feeling walking across this football field. It was very quiet. There was no one around, it seemed; certainly no spectators in the stands!

"You have to sign for your mine's quota, which you can collect on a Wednesday; that's the day allocated for your region. You must carry the explosives in the front of your pick-up, not in the back for obvious reasons. Lock your doors too. You must only use the route you are given, which circumnavigates Bulawayo and other towns for the public's safety, and you must stick to the lower speed limit. You are not allowed to enter a petrol station, so you must fill up with diesel before you come to this explosives dump. And you should drive straight from here to your mine, not stopping anywhere, and store the explosives immediately in your mine's underground explosives safe."

Loaded up with boxes of gelignite (600 sticks) and detonators (150), I drove out of the arena and headed for home with my potentially dangerous cargo on board.

You soon realise, however, that the boxes of gelignite sticks next to you are as harmless as a box of unopened tins of baked beans! They only become dangerous and unstable when a detonator is inserted into them.

It was a strange drive back to the mine with my explosives load.

At first, you drive over every bump slowly, you feel uncomfortable, and, when you pass another vehicle, the occupants seem to stare at you, but, by the time you get halfway home, you feel completely at ease, and, with the given slow speed restrictions, you want to get back before you doze off in the heat of the driver's cab.

And, when I eventually turned off the murram road into the mine compound,

I smiled; it was like looking at a second sun. What a lovely sight, this bright yellow Atlas Copco portable compressor parked in front of the storeroom.

Crispin came out and said that he'd booked it and two jackhammers into stores, and that Staff wanted to see me.

A brief chat with Staff, when he told me that all was ready for underground drilling in the morning, and later in the afternoon we could commence with blasting, now that I had brought the explosives from AE & CI.

Newmarch called me over and disappointedly said that the small ball mill had only crushed half a ton in the six hours that I was away, due to an intermittent electrical fault that he had been trying unsuccessfully to fix.

He wanted permission to go to Bulawayo with the faulty switchboard again where he could be sure to get any spares he needed.

I drove my pick-up down to the site of our underground safe, looked carefully all around me – why, I don't know – and then deposited the boxes of gelignite and igniters into the safe, and locked the door.

A feeling of complete knackeredness overcame me, I think due to the slow four-hour drive back in the heat from the AE & CI dump, which had seemed to take forever.

I was pleased when I fell asleep in bed.

. . .

No matter how violent the shaking became, I just couldn't, and didn't want to, wake up. My eyelashes were sealed together, and, despite several attempts to unclog them, my body automatically turned over and switched on the sleep button again.

"Lemme just snooze… another 10 minutes or so… ple-e-a-se."

Then that damn shrill ringing noise of the phone did what violent shaking hadn't achieved; I was wide awake.

"It's for you," Marianne called, and I reluctantly left my nest.

It was 6:30am. And it was Joseph!

"Hope I didn't wake you." They were probably the worst opening words he could have chosen. "But just to tell you I'm going to Shabani Hospital this morning for a double-check on the leg. It is so painful; I think it's broken. I haven't been able to sleep since Monday when that stupid towbar got in the way and smashed against my shins. Do you know how painful…?"

With a look of disgust, I put down the phone horn gently and went outside.

"Elliot, please bring me some hot, strong black coffee."

On entering the room again, I found Marie-Louise and Jeffrey giggling away to each other – they had put a cushion over the phone horn.

They looked at me with laughing eyes as I slowly lifted the cushion, whereupon we all heard: "Hello! Hello! Are you still there?"

"Of course, Joseph; why?"

More giggling from the children.

"Because I got no answer to my question!"

"I know; the line seemed to go dead, but repeat it again please."

"I wanted to know if you agreed to me taking time off to go to Shabani Hospital."

"Yes, Joseph." I sighed. "If you're not happy with what Bulawayo Hospital diagnosed, go and double-check at Shabani; it's okay."

"But I want you to write in the visitors' book that I have been badly injured while at work, and on sick leave since Monday."

"From Monday until?"

"I'll phone you again after seeing the doctor at Shabani Hospital; that's okay, isn't it?"

"Yes, Joseph."

And I replaced the receiver.

"My God, it's like having a 10-year-old as a partner. I'll be so pleased when we sell the Nelly 404. One good thing about money, contrary to the old saying, is that money *can* buy you happiness – by investing it in something hundreds of kilometres away from my irritating, whinging partner!"

And we laughed and laughed… and I quietly prayed that it would happen soon, very soon.

After my breakfast Ndebele lessons from Crispin, I walked up to the mine, and it was quite pleasant; that guti mist seemed to have gone – pity it didn't take Joseph with it.

Staff was excited, and hurried me along to the main shaft.

He and his underground boys had already connected the drilling equipment to the Atlas Copco compressor.

I climbed in the skip and went down to the second level, my hat lamp illuminating the air pipes for the jackhammer drilling machines.

Masouso, a junior boss boy in charge of the jackhammer drilling team, and Ndabazabo, junior boss boy – underground lashers – greeted me and smiled as they pointed to their teams of workers.

Masouso was in charge of Tabari, Samson, Juta and George II, and Ndabazabo's group consisted of Enoch, Misheck, Anderson, and Siyayi.

Staff joined us and suggested we go along the second-level drive tunnel to the end, where he would set the explosives in that rock face once the holes were drilled by the jackhammer boys.

He measured out and marked with chalk the position of the holes to be drilled in a pattern called a 'dras cut'.

This consisted of 21 holes, each drilled to a depth of five feet, and he explained to me as he pointed them out what function each loaded hole would do when the igniters sparked the gelignite explosions.

There were back holes, easers, shoulder holes, knee holes and lifters, and, in the centre of this maze, a concentrated grouping of eight more holes, six inches apart, with easers that would form the 'burns cut'.

Staff told Tabari and Samson to pick up the jackhammers and start drilling.

Instant, eardrum-splitting sounds, and dust clouds filling the air.

Staff and I quickly left the drilling area and climbed the ladders to the surface, 200 feet up – and fresh air.

I found climbing up the ladder much easier than the awkward climbing down, when I preferred to use the skip, if it was available.

Marianne had left a message with Crispin that Newmarch had phoned to say he was still in Bulawayo working on the switchboard problem, spare parts being the main headache.

All being well, he would be out to the mine in the morning.

So, there was little for me to do for the rest of the day until blasting time, which I was looking forward to.

When I got back to the house, Marianne was on the phone, and, covering the mouthpiece, she whispered, "It's Joseph."

A violent shaking of the head relayed my message instantly.

"I'm sorry, Joseph, but he's not here.... I'm not sure.... Do you want to leave a message for him? Okay, I'll tell him that if you're not in too much pain, you'll try to come out to the mine tomorrow.... You too!"

I laughed.

"The way you said *'you too'* made me think of '***U2***', the fingers conveying the message, instead of the voice."

Around 3 o'clock, Amon came to tell me that Staff wanted to set the explosives for the underground blasting.

I fetched 84 sticks of gelignite and 21 detonators from the explosives safe – each of the 21 holes would contain four sticks of dynamite.

At the shaft, Staff was waiting, standing in the skip, and I handed him the boxes.

"Now, Boss, if you would hold this plunger box with its reel of electrical wire, it can unwind as I go down the shaft and along the drive to the rock face that we're going to blast shortly. When I'm with the jackhammer boys, I'll give three tugs on it, and you can place the plunger box next to the main switchboard, but, for safety, don't plug it in."

Back to the house to collect the family; I'm sure the kids would enjoy the sounds and shaking of the ground when the explosion took place.

We pulled up in front of the office just as all the underground boys climbed out of the shaft, followed by Staff.

"Okay, now, little Jeffrey, I'll get the plunger box ready and when I say 'BANG' you press this red plunger down. One, two, three, BANG!"

BANG!

The loud noise echoed and reverberated in the mine, the ground vibrated and a plume of greyish smoke dust poured out of the shaft entrance and drifted above our heads up, up into the sky.

"Did I do that?" a wide-eyed, shocked boy exclaimed. "Just by pushing that red handle down! Can I do it again now?"

"Sorry Jeffrey, but you're not really allowed to touch this equipment; it was a one-off treat for you. And in any case, nothing would happen on the second time, because the explosives have all gone off!"

One or two of the mine boys laughed as they patted Jeffrey on his head when they walked past.

"Mister Master Blaster Junior!" Crispin called out, and Jeffrey walked around with a million-dollar smile on his face, which lasted well into the evening.

"So we've blasted the rock face down below underground, and we'll leave the mine overnight to allow all the smoke and dust to clear. The lasher boys will go down first thing tomorrow and get all the rocks from this explosion loaded into the skip. We'll come back then and you can see the skip bringing the rocks to the surface."

. . .

In the evening, a rather excited-sounding Ray phoned to say that he had made an appointment with a potential buyer for the mine.

He would meet me at the Holiday Inn in Bulawayo at 12pm on Friday, when the two of us would have a lunch appointment with Richard Bird, the MD of The Gold Plate Mine Company, and a personal friend of his for many years.

I didn't bother to ask if unpredictable Joseph would be there – 'when the two of us would have a lunch appointment' said it all.

When I put down the phone, Marianne's inquisitive expression had to be answered.

"A potential buyer for the mine," I announced, my fingers making a drum roll noise on the table. "This could be a good start, and if the meeting is successful it could signal the beginning of the end, so to speak. Ray said that a company would normally sign a three-month option sale agreement, subject to a full survey conducted by their geologist, and if it works out well we could be celebrating the sale early in July!"

"In Paris or Monte Carlo?"

A night of fanciful dreaming, just lying there side by side; no words were spoken, but thousands of pictures were flashing through our minds, until we eventually surrendered to the inevitable power of sleep.

. . .

Up early, and on the road to Bulawayo before 7am, on the way to the Mines Department to buy or to borrow a copy for the day of the geological survey of the Nelly 404 mine, which would augment my notes' 'reasons to buy', together with the highlighted paragraphs of a previous survey report that Pat Burke had given me at the tribute signing.

A knock on the stenograph office door, and I was politely asked to come in.

"Good morning to you," I began. "I'm from Ridge Top Mine, and I know it's very short notice, but is it possible to borrow a geological survey of the Nelly 404 mine this morning for a meeting and return it later this afternoon, or better still if you could run me off a copy, which I would pay for?"

"I can only release it to Ronnie, who might let you study it, but only in the office, of course!" she added with a wink and a knowing smile.

Minutes later, Ronnie handed it to me and wished me good luck.

So, armed with my sales presentation portfolio, including the copy of the Nelly 404 geological map with more than 300 sampling points indicating gold values, I just made it by 11:59am to the Holiday Inn foyer.

Ray met me and we went to the pub to have a beer while we waited for this Mr Bird.

"Now, he's an old friend of mine; we were actually partners together in a chrome mine when we were in our thirties, before we fell out – a bit like you and Joseph, and he blamed me, would you believe.... Let me do the initial talking, and outline our proposal... mmm, it's a pity I didn't ask you to bring some back-up information and documentation, but he's an old mate, so I'm sure we'll battle through successfully."

"Hello Ray," a man called from the open doorway. "You haven't changed at all, still short and ugly!" And he roared with laughter, his flabby chins wobbling away, as did the rest of his rather over-plump body.

Ray looked a bit embarrassed, but soon they were merrily chatting away about old mutual friends they had or had not seen for ages.

Then, over lunch, Ray told him of the claims that we had tributed from Pat Burke….

"Oh yes, Ray, and he was a right Burke too, I seem to remember."

"To continue, we have recently started milling the waste dumps using a small three-ton capacity ball mill, and the whole mine is set up ready for blasting on the second level, the ore being railed to a large ball mill with an automatic conveyor feed system. We are presently awaiting the final piece, a 30-ton capacity ball mill, which is due to be delivered in three weeks' time."

"And do you have any back-up documentation, sampling and geological survey plans?"

"Now Dick, you know I can't read or understand those things; I just go with my nose and gut feel."

"Well, it would have helped…"

"Would you be meaning these?" And I opened a folding leather binder that Ronnie had lent me containing on one side the geological survey underground plan with sample values, and on the other a plastic sheaf of back-up documents.

"Well, yes, but I won't study them now, but it looks comprehensive. Can I take them with me and study them fully with my geologist?"

"Yes, that was the idea, but would you make copies for yourselves and return the originals to me?"

"Will do, and I suggest we meet here again on Monday to discuss a potential agreement, okay?"

Three heads nodded tacitly and three hands were shaken – deal on.

As we went outside to the vehicles, Ray said to me, "That was good thinking; a nice touch. So have a good weekend and we'll meet again on Monday at 12pm, here at the Holiday Inn."

Many thoughts filled my head on the drive back to the mine.

It was great news having a potential buyer, and one who wanted to formalise a possible sale agreement in three days' time on the coming Monday, when he would bring his geologist along to verify the potential of the mine – well, the potential paper viability to start with.

But it would be good to have a signed contract document at an agreed sales price; I'd frame it and hang it in the house as a reminder that the increasingly untenable partnership with Joseph actually had an end date – a potentially profitable one too.

Then, whenever Joseph had one of his pathetic blow-ups or cock-ups, it would be reassuring to look at it, even though the completion date was three months away still and subject to their geologist's favourable viability report.

However, whatever the final outcome, we were well on our way to producing gold on a daily basis, on which we could live handsomely.

As I approached the mine, I saw a pale blue Peugeot 404 pick-up turning into the mining compound, and I pulled up behind it.

Joseph cautiously got out of his vehicle and limped slowly towards me.

"So Joseph, how's the leg doing?"

"Well, Shabani Hospital said it was severe bruising too, and that luckily nothing was broken. I'll just have to hobble around for a week or two."

"Are you back at work and staying the night?"

"No! I'll be going to Gwelo shortly, but hopefully I can make it back to the mine after the weekend."

"After the weekend, meaning Monday?"

"Yes, don't worry, my father has spoken to me, and I've assured him I'd be working on the mine again from Monday."

I thought to ask 'this Monday or next', but quelled the desire in the name of peace.

"Let me update you on the many happenings during the week. The first one being your fruitless journey to collect and tow the Atlas Copco compressor…"

"You don't have to rub it in," Joseph interrupted. "My shins are painful enough without your sarcastic comments about that compressor."

"If you'd let me finish, Joseph, I was going to say that the compressor has been delivered and is over there, see, by the Nelly 404 shaft?"

"Fabulous, so when I come back on Monday I'll be able to go underground – in the skip, of course, because of my bad leg, and instruct Staff where to drill."

"Too late, Joseph; the jackhammer boys drilled the holes for a 'dras cut' yesterday, and we loaded the explosives that I'd collected from AE & CI, and our first blast took place late yesterday afternoon."

"What! Who gave you permission? I'm the underground manager, not you; that's my job!" he blurted angrily.

"Actually, your mother did; she told me that you'd be off work for a while and that I should take over and do your underground jobs until you were better again."

"But you should have told me that you were going to drill and blast, and I could have come back to the mine to help underground."

"Joseph, you called me early yesterday morning saying you were going to Shabani Hospital for a second check-up on your injuries, and didn't know when you'd be back at work." A short silence and then I continued. "We are trying to run a producing gold mine, and can't wait for you to do your job 'as and when', or, rather, 'if and when' you decide to pitch up."

"That's not fair!" he snarled, and walked off towards the headgear.

Just then, a motor started and the hoist began winching up the skip. The loud screeching noise of metal wheels on metal rails seemed particularly loud, as if making a statement to Joseph – 'we are working, even when you're not here'!

There ore was tipped and emptied into the hopper, the clattering sound continuing when the hopper opened its slide and the rocks noisily filled the waiting cocopan.

Two boys began to push this loaded cocopan along the rails towards the Newmarch mill site.

"Stop! Stop! Stop!" shouted Joseph.

I ran over to the hopper. "What's the matter, Joseph; why are you shouting at them to stop?"

"Because there's no Newmarch mill there yet to crush the ore, stupid! I want the ore stockpiled here for the small ball mill."

"Look here, Joseph, you keep harping on about how you are the underground manager and that I shouldn't interfere with your work. Well, mate, this is surface work; I'm the mine manger and my surface gangs and the mill set-up is this – so listen, and listen good. The small ball mill is being used to re-mill the schist waste from the smaller mine dumps like the Sirius and the Hlatin. Marianne and a gang of lashers do three trips a day to collect the waste and stockpile it here next to the small ball mill, for processing through to the copper plate extraction table. Those rocks from underground are being loaded into the cocopan and wheeled along the rail ramp 'til the end, where they are being tipped out to be used for strengthening the embankment by ramming them into the soil, and later concreted."

"What, are you crazy? You're using rocks containing gold to strengthen your railway; we're losing money! You fool!"

"Joseph, cool it! When the rains come, if that embankment isn't strengthened and rock-solid so to speak – ha ha – the whole lot could be washed away and we'd have no way of feeding the Newmarch ball mill – now *that* would cost money, big money! We are only pulling out some ore of very low grade from a worked-out area in order not only to strengthen the embankment, but primarily to test all the equipment, rolling stock and operations thoroughly before next month when the Newmarch ball mill arrives, when hopefully we can start full production – 30 tons per day of ore, which could yield several ounces of gold each day, and every day!"

I signalled to the workers to carry on with their *gwazas* of pushing the cocopan, tipping the rocks, and pressing the rocks hard into the soil sides of the rail embankment.

On hearing the thud of a door closing, I turned around to witness Joseph trying out his infamous Formula 1 racing start – off to Gwelo!

In all the commotion, I'd failed to notice that Newmarch was back.

When he has his head inside a problem and he's quietly working away, he's like a mouse; you don't hear him or see him.

He's a good, dedicated man who gets on with his work, and you only notice him when there's a problem.

"Drat! It's blown again!" he said loudly. "Sorry, but there'll be no more milling this weekend! I'll fix this once and for all in Bulawayo over the weekend. I'll be off now and come back here on Monday."

As Newmarch left in his old banger, the knock-off gong sounded loud and clear, and I obeyed, immediately! Why should I be the only boss still working on the mine? I drove back to the house.

. . .

Situnda gave me a cup of coffee, and I sat down with Crispin for our usual Saturday morning when we update each other, and I also get to know what's been happening in the mine village as well.

"Yes, Crispin, it's vitally important to know all of that news and to quell any potential domestic problems before they do a *'Joseph'*! – that's a new word in our mine dictionary, and it means *'blow up'*."

"And another meaning of *'he broke the roof'*!" Crispin added.

He has a good sense of humour; an invaluable member of our mine.

I walked over to the mine shaft, where Staff spoke to me. "Thanks for taking over and organising the blasts and hauling the rocks to the surface. I don't know what's got into the Boss Joseph these days; he always used to be so friendly when I knew him on his father's mine. I wish you were one of the brothers in the family instead of him."

"That's a strange thing to say, Staff."

"I shouldn't have said it, really," he continued in an embarrassed tone, "but you'll understand one day."

It was perhaps, in hindsight, something I should have taken more seriously, but the conversation abruptly stopped on hearing…

"Chibuku, Chibuku!" shouted a group of the workers' wives as the beer delivery lorry arrived at midday, and Staff hurried with the rest of the crowd down to the village.

I told Crispin to put Amon on duty 24 hours per day over the weekend and base him next to the new extraction room, which had some gold amalgam on the copper plate table already, albeit a small amount – but gold is gold, and to us at the present time every speck helped towards paying the bills.

From Monday onwards, the small ball mill should be operating seven days a week, but no one would be working this weekend.

I left early and took Marianne, Marie-Louise and Jeffrey over to Gayle and Trevor's ranch for their daughter's birthday party.

The kids enjoyed it immensely and, for us, it made a lovely two-day break away from the mine, meeting and mixing with some newfound friends.

I Am Your Ears and Your Eyes

Things were beginning to move at last; still a few hiccups with the small ball mill set-up, but it had produced our first gold on the extraction test runs, and I had every confidence that Newmarch would be back, and if his repairs held out we should be able to get a complete week's run in.

Even more exciting. Today was a day of huge importance and I was busy writing the draft sale agreement letter to The Gold Plate Mine Company for our meeting with their managing director in Bulawayo at lunchtime.

After discussions, this draft agreement with any amendments would be formalised by their lawyer for our signatures the coming Friday. And, once this had been signed, a three-month process would begin, with their geologist being a frequent visitor, performing sampling and other tests to confirm the long-term viability of the mine.

I had also included for discussion two interim loan payments to be made to us of $5,000 each, on 30 April and 30 May.

Ray and I had agreed to push for these as an essential part of any sale agreement – these would help us wipe out our escalating debts.

This would be yet another iron in the fire, augmenting the helpful gold output from the small mill and the potential healthy gold production from the large Newmarch ball mill, due to be installed in less than three weeks.

I was feeling in a much lighter and happier mood than I was a few dark and sombre weeks ago, and I climbed into my pick-up and happily headed for

Bulawayo.

A I approached Fort Rixon, what did I see pulling into the petrol station; the rusty old Peugeot belonging to Mr Newmarch.

"Morning, you run out of gas?" I chirped.

"No, cigarettes!"

"Oh yes, I can believe that. I don't think I've ever seen you without a cigarette in your mouth when you're working."

"But it helps me concentrate when I'm busy, and now I've located and fixed the problem I'll be with you all week, so I'll need to buy a few packets of baccy."

"Tell you what, why don't you call in to see Marianne and ask her for a page of the *Daily Telegraph* airmail edition? She says it's thin, and it rolls much better cigarettes than any of the cigarette papers she's used. And ask Crispin to put three packets of tobacco on my bill; I'll sort it when I'm back, okay?"

"I'll try Marianne's airmail papers to roll the cigarettes, thanks, but I prefer to pay for my own tobacco, if you don't mind," Newmarch stated proudly.

Point taken.

"Okay, I'll be back from Bulawayo this afternoon, but since Joseph's not around yet I'd be pleased if you would take over all operations."

That said, on my way I sped!

At the Holiday Inn, we were introduced to Ernest Roksplitzer, the geologist.

"If you don't mind, we can't stay for lunch, I'm afraid, so it'll have to be a brief meeting out here in the Foyer," Richard Bird announced.

Ray looked quizzically at me with a touch of apprehension; apprehension that gave me a cold shiver down my back.

"Is there something wrong, Dickie…?"

"No, no!" he cut Ray short. "In fact, everything looks dead right! It's just that we have to drive back earlier than expected – internal company matters. Ernest and I have studied the very comprehensive documentation and underground plans, and have decided to go ahead with the three-month option we spoke about last Friday. If you would put that in a letter to me, I can put it in the agenda for our next board meeting."

"Well…" I climbed straight in. "I've taken the liberty to draft a sales agreement letter, which I'd be pleased if you would peruse now and we can discuss basic terms."

"Hey Ray, your right-hand man is on the ball; I like that." And he began to read the letter.

"Yes, that covers everything we discussed based on a sale for $100,000, but the two interim payments of $5,000 each will have to come off the purchase price if we go ahead, and it will have to be on the basis of a loan repayment with 8% interest should we decide not to finalise the purchase in three months from now."

"Agreed!" Ray and I simultaneously and smilingly replied.

"Here are your originals, young sir; we've taken copies for our records, thanks, and we'll get our lawyer to formalise the agreement in contractual form. How about we meet here on Friday for the signing ceremony, and then I promise we'll have lunch and a few 'wetners' to celebrate."

We shook hands, they left together quite quickly, and 'Mr Worry in a Hurry' also rushed off, leaving me standing there alone.

"Do you still want that table for lunch, sir? And perhaps a beer?" enquired a waiter.

"Is the pope a Catholic?" I replied, whereupon the waiter, chuckling to himself, led me to Table 13 – my lucky number! And I proceeded to munch my way through the full five-course celebration menu quite happily on my own.

And, a few hours later, I was enjoying a sundowner with Marianne as I related the day's exhilarating events, which, if the gods were with us, could turn into something phenomenal. It was a lovely feeling, and we were letting our imaginations run wild, when, all of a sudden…

There was a light tapping on the door.

"Crispin? What are you doing out late? It's almost midnight!"

"Sir, take this note," he whispered nervously. "Read it carefully and keep it to yourself. I must go now."

And he rushed off, vanishing into the darkness.

"That's very strange behaviour from Crispin. Pass me the hurricane lamp; I had better read it straight away."

Ridge Top Mine
8th April
Dear Sir,

I am your ears and your eyes, now try to talk to Tachibona privately as though you are giving supervision or advice to him about the Gold Tables, he'll have to tell you something of very private. Take this for granted and don't utter even a word to anybody, even to your partner Joseph but, what you have to do is just inform some of the Boys and not Staff, because he's a private friend and informer of Boss Joseph, so he might let him know about this private story Sir.

We dislike to break your friendship, but the thing is this, you will phone for police having missed something, yet it's stolen by one of your two partners, and it'll be unfair to blame the boys instead.

So have this in your mind, be as though you know nothing, it'll come out for itself, Sir.

Thank you Sir
Crispin

"That's a strange message from Crispin; he also doesn't trust Staff and has suspicions about Joseph as well. I'll have to talk with him in the morning; it sounds very dramatic – 'I am your ears and your eyes'!"

. . .

Six o'clock, I was up like a shot, this sale deal burning holes in my brain.

I sat outside in the early morning sun and dashed off a letter confirming the main points of our second brief discussions the day before at the Holiday Inn, and that we would meet again this coming Friday the 12th, to sign the sales contract, with the three-month option.

'Dashed off the letter' was rather optimistic; it, in fact, took me five hours!

But it had to be factual and accurate.

And if it was in contractual-like wording, I thought Mr Bird would probably use it as **the base of the sales contract** – and also by backdating the letter to **5 April**, which was the day of our first discussions and tacit agreement, I hoped that would be **the official start date on the contract** that we all would sign!

With the red-hot handwritten letter in my sticky paw, I headed for the police compound to see Pete.

"Can the desk constable type out this very important letter for me? It's to the company that is interested in buying our mine."

"Buying your mine! Of course you can get it typed here, but it'll cost you 10%!"

Now where had I heard that before?

With the sound of 'click, click', a slight pause, then 'click, click, click' in the background as the constable on duty bravely hit the keys of an old upright 'sit and beg' typewriter, Peter and I sat outside on the veranda discussing the implications of the letter being typed.

"What would you do, assuming the sale goes through in three months' time; start up another gold mine in the area? We'd be sad to lose you and your family from our small Fort Rixon community; you fit in so well, and you've turned out to be a real good mate!"

"I'd be loath to leave this part of the country too; that's one of the downsides of the possible sale of the mine – but the huge upside, besides the money, would be to get away from that whinging, unreliable so-called partner of mine – he behaves like a four-year-old in a man's body…."

"If you can call that spindly white frame a body!" Peter quipped. "But I know about him; you've recounted some pathetic stories of his weird antics and crazy behaviour. The one I like best is when he goes berserk, shouting out 'I'm not going to stay and have the meeting, because I can't think of anything to say; it's not fair; I'm not staying and that's that', and then proceeds to trip over as he hurriedly tried to get out of his overalls, falling onto the camp bed, which collapsed and folded up with just his legs sticking out! That one just cracks me up when I think of it, 'cos I can just see the scene unfolding in front of me."

"Yeah, but the bed didn't unfold!" I chuckled. "We had to prise him out! But it's been very hard work with him, such a lot to put up with, but dotted with many comical events like the one you've just described, and even with all his bullshit I really love the gold mining work and the life out here in the bush."

"You know what?" Peter suggested. "Perhaps you should write a book about your mining adventure. From what I know and have heard, it would make a very interesting and often highly amusing novel, and, if they made it into a film, you could let me play myself – Peter the particularly perfect policeman of the Fort Rixon Police Post!"

And so Peter continued with the banter – we had become great friends and enjoyed each other's company.

It was almost 1 o'clock by the time the 'two-fingered' typist had a reasonably clean draft of the letter.

I scribbled a note to go with the letter apologising for the typing, saying that we didn't have a secretarial pool to call on for such an important letter; just the constable from the nearest police post!

But the main points were quite clear and would be put into a more legal framework of a contract agreement, which The Gold Plate Mine Company would have drawn up to be signed on the coming Friday.

I gave the letter to Peter to read.

Ridge Top Mine (Pvt) Ltd

P.O. Fort Rixon. Rhodesia

THE GOLD PLATE MINE COMPANY
P.O.BOX.3327. BULAWAYO

5 April

Dear Mr. Bird, Ridge Top Mine, Fort Rixon.

I have been able to discuss the proposal with the third member of the Company, who is preparing to go on active service on the Border. He would also have preferred participation to an outright sale but in the circumstances, he is agreeable to the negotiations being carried on between our two Companies.

I therefore set down the proposals that were made on 5 April.

1. That this Company grants a 3-month option until the 5th July, to purchase the entire shareholding of the Ridge Top Mine (Pvt) Limited for the sum of $100,000 (one hundred thousand dollars). During this period you will be entitled to carry out a detailed survey of the claims, but it is agreed that this investigation will not interfere with the normal working of the Mine.

2. That in consideration of this option being granted, you would advance the Company the sum of $10,000, in two instalments of $5,000 each, at the end of April and the end of May this year, which loan would carry interest at the rate of 8%. Should the option be taken up on the 5th July, then the loan would be treated as a portion of the purchase price, otherwise this loan would be repayable in full within one year from that date, interim payments being acceptable to you.

3. That at the end of the 3-month option, subject to mutual agreement by both parties, the Sale would be concluded.

4. And during the period that the full purchase price has not been paid, we would require some form of security, and would suggest a General Notarial Bond on the assets of the Company.

5. You are only interested in the Claremont and Nelly 404 Mines, and the other claims held by our Company may be removed from the Company before the sale.

We look forward to meeting you again on Friday 12th April.

Yours sincerely, Manager.

Directors: Ray Buffune (Managing) J.W. Bulgin Joseph Buffune

"Man, those dollar amounts! Hey, ***they are huge!*** Lottery type numbers, which are about 40 years of my salary! If this comes off, you'd be able to start up a ranch in this area and we wouldn't lose you after all. And you'd have plenty of ranchers and farmers around you who would like to help you and Marianne get started – no lack of friendly advice there," Peter concluded.

"Now that is a fantastic idea, Peter, because I love the life out here, and to trade the mine and 60 workers and their families, for a ranch with 60 head of cattle that can't ask me to take them to a hospital in the middle of the night would suit me right down to the ground – but not underground!"

"Until the good Lord decrees that it is your time!" Peter uttered in a distinctly dull vicar-type tone, causing us both to laugh yet again.

And so the banter continued; oh, that aching feeling from laughing too much – as one stopped, the other would start; it was hilarious.

"Tell you what, I'm done for the day and all this laughter has made my mouth dry too! Let's post this letter and have a break at the Fort Rixon club; can you get off for the afternoon?"

"Just watch me!" he replied, and, moments later, we drove off!

I purchased stamps for the letter, which was in a brown envelope that Pete had given me from the police stationery cupboard.

As I stuck on the stamps, old Davison croaked, "Oh that is a government envelope? Here, take this thick black marker pen and scrub out any trace of the police address; otherwise, I should really report you for theft/misuse of government property!" he mused, looked at it slowly, and popped it into the post bag. "Next collection is due this afternoon, so it should be delivered in Bulawayo tomorrow or Thursday at the latest – I assume this is important?" he probed, and waited for some more news behind the contents of the envelope addressed to The Gold Plate Mine Company… but the sealed lips of both Peter and myself eventually exhausted his patience, and he broke the silence and wished us all the best and, "Good day."

We got back in my pick-up and drove down to the dam.

Although there was no one at the club, it mattered not; Peter had brought a cool box of ice-cold beers with him.

As he opened the box and handed me a cold Castle dumpy bottle, he said, "And here, to go with the beer, from my limited stock is a traditional Yorkshire pork pie – enjoy every mouthful."

Which I did, and we idled away the afternoon sitting on the grass by the water, storytelling, helped on by a platoon of Castle soldiers!

. . .

The next morning, just after hearing the start gong sounding in the distant misty corners of my hungover mind, I was rudely awakened by a loud knocking.

I stumbled out of bed and opened the door, revealing a hazy blue-clad figure – Joseph, with his red hat, mumbling something that my mind could not translate, but the noise of the words caused me to squint and hold my head in pain. This was the last thing I needed to remind me of the late-night session at the police post.

The louder Joseph's questions became, the more annoyed I got, until ignition time.

"Joseph!" I exploded and bellowed, "Go away. Go away *now*! I'll see you up at the mine at 8 o'clock. Goodbye!"

And I slammed the door shut and climbed back into bed, hearing only the faint sounds of giggling, whispering children in the background, with Marianne's soft, calm voice whispering in my ear, "Sleep on. I'll wake you at a quarter to eight, don't worry."

Black coffee following two hours' sleep helped to chase away the cobwebs and the aftertaste of the night before, and I strode off down the road to visit my partner. The brisk walk performed a major curing ingredient, helped even more by sticking my head in the cold water of Jackson's water tank.

Dutifully refreshed and in a wonderful frame of mind thinking about the sale of the Nelly 404, I walked into the office.

Joseph looked at me apprehensively for a few seconds, trying to gauge if I had calmed down or not, and then, with a loud sigh, he braved the situation. "I shouldn't have woken you up like that," he began slowly, "but!"

His face changed drastically, colouration was increasing, the eyes were beginning to flame and bulge, he seemed to be building up a head of steam, and finally he blurted, "But where were you yesterday? I waited the whole afternoon for you, and even when I locked the gold extraction room late at 10pm you were still not back home, and I had something very important to discuss with you! And it's so important that I'm going to tell you now, tell you that it's not fair what you're doing, going behind my back and selling the mine without me being there. It's just not good enough; I won't stand for it anymore, do you hear!" he shouted.

"Hear? I should have thought everyone in Fort Rixon would have heard you. Now what's your problem, Joseph?"

"My father told me that he and you had held talks on Friday with a company interested in buying our mine for $100,000. Well, I'm telling you *now*, without my signature, you *cannot* sell the mine!"

"Perfectly true, Joseph, and I wouldn't try. But I'm sure your father told you of the sudden impromptu situation and that he and I had to meet them the next day to discuss a possible sale, and then again on Monday to agree on terms for a three-month option to buy our mine."

"Yes, he told me that," Joseph concurred irritably, "but that's not the point; you shouldn't have had those meetings without first discussing everything with me!"

"With your elusive nature and unknown whereabouts? Even though we have a phone at the house, you have only called once in the six weeks since it's been installed! You're just totally insane – we'd still be waiting for the first meeting to take place!" I forcibly stated. "Obviously we need all three signatures of the directors on the sales option contract that will be drawn up for the Friday confirmation meeting."

"Yes, I know, but my father said it's only going to be you and him again at that coming meeting – I told him we'd see about that! So, partner, if you and I vote together against him, then I'll be able to attend the meeting as well, won't I?"

"Joseph, to introduce another face and a frequently unguarded tongue at the final crucial signing of the sales agreement could only jeopardise the sale of the mine, and I'm certainly not going to risk that."

"That's what my father said as well," Joseph let slip. "In fact, he told me to give you this letter if you decided to prevent me from attending the meeting."

"I'll read it later, Joseph; I've got other things to do."

"No, no! My father insisted that I must give it to you straight away, yesterday! But you weren't here, were you, so how could I have given it to you? But you must read it now, please!"

I opened the envelope, in which there were two pieces of paper.

The one had a few notations of the main points that we'd agreed with Dickie Bird on the Monday, to which he'd added: *Probably best if you write them a letter reiterating these points, so that they can be confirmed in the legal sales agreement on Friday the 12th April.*

"You see, that's why you should have been here yesterday!" Joseph remarked, having also read it looking over my shoulder. "And now there's no time left. My father is going to be so mad with me; he told me it was very important. Oh why do these things always happen to me? It's just not fair!"

I calmly handed Joseph a copy of the typed letter I'd posted to The Gold Plate Mine Company the day before.

He read it slowly and exclaimed, "Oh wonderful! So you'd already sent the letter. Oh, what a relief; what a relief! So now everything is set up properly for the Friday meeting that you both don't want me to attend."

I glanced at the other piece of paper Ray had sent; it was a proxy form for the 12th April meeting between Ridge Top Mine and The Gold Plate Mine Company directors to approve a sale agreement of the Nelly 404 mine – and it was *signed* by Joseph!

"So you're happy; you signed the proxy form for Friday, which means that you don't have to be there."

"Not happy, but I know you and my father will get the sale agreed, but I wanted to be there as well. Jane said it was unfair that all the major decisions were made by my father and you, and I should put my foot down and make sure I could attend such important meetings…"

"And probably put your foot in your mouth too!" I interjected, which started off another whinging stream of verbal diarrhoea, which slowly became less and less loud… the further I walked away in the direction of my house.

Strong black coffee and a fried breakfast was first on the essential agenda for the rest of the day, and I felt much better when that tasty intake began its job of quelling the hungry stomach.

Marianne listened intently to me as I related the latest stupid outburst.

"God, he's got a screw or two loose, I reckon," she observed. "Perhaps he's escaped from the Funny Farm! And all those days that he's not here on the mine are compulsory days when he has to attend for monitoring and assessment!"

"Yeah, well, we'll know soon enough; next month he's in the army reservists for six weeks' border duty. Surely they'll find out that he's as nutty as a fruit cake, lock him up and leave us in peace. But let's forget about him, and since it's my turn to lock up the extraction room later tonight, let's go for a drive for a couple of hours. We still haven't visited the Regina ruins or the Dhlo Dhlo ruins – some of the smaller *zimbabwes*, so they obviously won't be as impressive as the Great Zimbabwe ruins, but they're less than half an hour away."

We only spent about 20 minutes viewing the overgrown Dhlo Dhlo ruins, which weren't very big – but were very ruined! It was rather disappointing after our amazing two-day visit to the Great Zimbabwe ruins, which were spread over hundreds of acres, when we just didn't have the time or the energy to explore them properly.

"Tell you what Marianne, I look forward to another visit to the Great Zimbabwe ruins when we have a weekend free, and this time we'll go without the kids so we can really take it all in. They were so fascinating, and we could climb the hundreds of steps to the upper ruins, which were thought to be a temple for rituals and human sacrifices. Originally, the huge soapstone sculptures of the Zimbabwe birds stood there on a high balcony overlooking the whole site."

Newmarch was pleased with the small ball mill set-up, which had been chugging along nicely for several days now without any problems.

He told us that, from the look and feel of the amalgam building up on the copper plate, we should be in for 15 ounces of gold come the end of the month.

"That'll cheer us all up, won't it?"

Contented grins on Joseph's and my face said it all, and he continued. "This two-shift system is allowing us to put two tons of ore through each day, but I don't think we should risk running a three-shift day; it's a solid little mill, but best we give it a few hours' break each night." He turned to me. "And what's this I hear from Joseph; you're selling the mine?"

"Yes, we're in negotiations with a company, and hopefully on Friday we'll sign them up for a three-month option to buy."

"Sounds good, but be careful; there are plenty of miners who have been legally cheated out of their gold claims. Which company is it, if I may ask?"

"They own The Gold Plate Mine 20 kilometres south of Bulawayo; have you come across them before?"

"Listen, I've known literally hundreds of names of gold mining companies and consortiums; they change the names all the time due to one reason or another – quite often to 'hide' some massive gold theft or financial swindling. It's been like that since the original gold rush of the 1890s in Rhodesia – but there are only a limited number of good gold mines and still fewer good, solid, honest companies run by people with a sound track record. Who have you been dealing with?"

"Mr Bird, the managing director of the group."

"But is he a dove… or a hawk?"

Joseph and I both started laughing at his amusing remark.

"I'm not being funny; you should check into his background. You never know when it comes to gold; there are plenty of wolves in sheeps' clothing around."

"All we know is that he's an old friend of Joseph's father, and…"

"Stop, say no more, but check him out! Ray has been known to be involved with one or two shady characters in the…"

"What are you accusing my father of? He's a good man and a successful gold miner, and he's gone out of his way to set up this possible sale. I'll hear no more of this talk, and since I'm not allowed to be present tomorrow at the contract agreement signing, I'm leaving now and will go back to Jane and my son in Gwelo!" he petulantly whined. "And I'm going to make it a long weekend too, so, goodbye to you both!"

. . .

Friday morning didn't come around quick enough for me.

It was still dark when I went and sat outside under the porch. I could see Elliot lit up by his open fire, and he waved on hearing me clattering about.

Minutes later, he brought over a mug of tea, which was most welcome.

Sipping away as the horizon began to glow was such a peaceful beginning to the day and it allowed my thoughts plenty of time to be very active as they flitted in and out – sale, money, Joseph, another gold mine or a ranch… yes, a cattle ranch would be preferable….

Then the gong sounded; 'bleary-eyed, but becoming noisier' children appeared; a morning hug, even a double hug, was always welcome.

After checking with Crispin, Staff and Newmarch that all was in order for the day, I left early for Bulawayo.

I thought it would be prudent and correct to first call in to see Mr French.

Despite all the delays of the Newmarch ball mill, he had bent over backwards to help us through this difficult period.

He was pleased to see me and very enthusiastic about our potential sale.

"If it goes through and they take the three-month option, they will loan us $10,000, available in two lots of $5,000, one this month and $5,000 at the end of May. My plan is, and I hope you'll be agreeable to it, that the $5,000 available in two weeks' time will be used first to clear any Mines Department outstanding monthly payments, and also clear several of the other suppliers' accounts, which are at the limit of the 60 days' or 90 days' credit. We're hoping that the gold output from the small ball mill will be enough to cover most of the current bills at this month-end. Then next month we should be able to reduce your account drastically when the second $5,000 loan payment is made to us. Is that acceptable to you?"

"That would certainly allow me to get back on speaking terms with both my partner, and the joint owner of the company – the wife!"

I left the K.B. Davies parking area with a lighter feeling.

French, although the culprit of our dilemma, was an upright and honest businessman of high regard and reputation, and he had done everything possible to rectify the Newmarch ball mill disaster with its extended delay in delivery and installation.

I'm not a religious man, but I can see why people pray for good to be rewarded with good, and if this sales deal went through at lunchtime it would not only be 'our saviour', but would also mean that the 'good Samaritan' French would be rewarded – here on Earth!

As I pulled into the Holiday Inn hotel complex, I could see Ray pacing up and down by the hotel entrance.

I quickly parked my pick-up and went over to join him.

"Good you got here on time, because there are problems! I've had a phone call this morning that Dickie Bird was in hospital; he was rushed by ambulance on Wednesday when he collapsed with acute appendicitis. He's been operated on successfully and is now recuperating, but the meeting has been postponed until a later date."

"Shit! We couldn't have seen that coming. Out of all the possible scenarios I thought about during the wee hours of the night *that* was definitely not among them."

"Look here, it's been postponed, not cancelled! And since I've cleared my whole day's agenda for this event, and unusually for me I have a few hours free, let's go inside and have some lunch – we can discuss the situation and any other options we have."

It felt strange sitting in the dining room with Ray, who, just like his son, Joseph, was fidgeting around uneasily, and the conversation – if it could be called that – went in short fits and starts, and I was pleased when the T-bone steak I'd ordered was placed in front of me, Ray having a plate of spicy chicken legs.

Both of us ate our way through our meals – the only thing breaking this strange silence was the occasional sound of a stripped chicken bone landing on a side plate.

He ordered a coffee, I ordered a beer and this weird scene continued to be enacted in a most awkward manner.

I was beginning to wish that Ray hadn't taken a few hours off; if he'd left straight away after telling me the bad news at least I could have enjoyed my meal, even though I would have been seated on my own.

My two favourite sayings are the Boy Scouts' *'be prepared'* and *'always expect the unexpected'*, yet I'd been caught completely off guard – *twice* today!

The one thing, though, that gave me hope was that small word 'postponed'. At least it hadn't been 'cancelled', as Ray emphasised, so a delay for sure, but the deal was still on the table – but not on this bloody table we were sitting at!

The agony of this over-an-hour-long, uncomfortable lunch break thankfully ended when Ray signalled to the waiter to bring the bill.

As we passed in silence through the reception area, a voice called out, "Hello, are you Ray?"

We both spun around to see that it was the desk clerk who was calling him.

"Yes, I'm Ray, why?" he snarled.

"Were you here to have lunch with a Mr Bird? Because I have a message for you."

"It had better not be that the deal is cancelled, or I'll break his bloody neck!" Ray spat, and went over to collect the message.

He angrily ripped open the envelope and scowled at the contents of the message; he was not in a very good mood.

"What!" he shouted, and suddenly his whole appearance altered from a snarling bulldog into a glowing, grinning 'I've just won the jackpot' look.

"Well bugger me!" he continued. "Old Dickie is progressing well, and he wants to meet the two of us at the hospital at 3pm to sign the sales contracts!"

"Magic news," I iterated. "Magic!"

"Well, don't just stand there; come on, come on. Let's quickly get to the hospital before he changes his mind…"

"Or his appendix erupts again!" I added, but Ray's hard 'glare-stare' told me that it was not an appreciated comment at this moment.

We walked through the long, cold, clinical corridors reeking of disinfectant – I hate visiting people in hospital; it gives me the shivers – until we came to his room.

On entering, we saw a cheerful Mr Bird siting up and beckoning us to come over. Ernest Roksplitzer was also there with a briefcase, which he opened.

"Now if you two sign – or put your mark! – right here on both copies," he joked as he gave Ray the contracts, which had already been signed by himself and another director, a Mr Rommel.

We both appended our signatures. I gave him Joseph's proxy letter and signed on his behalf.

Dickie extended a hand, which Ray spontaneously grabbed and shook warmly.

"So it's agreed then," Dickie continued. "When I'm out of this hospital I'll phone you and we can agree a date for Roksplitzer and me to visit your mine at Fort Rixon. We can make a plan for the future – starting with the next three months' evaluation."

A very different Ray and I walked out of the hospital, both smiling and a little bewildered by the strange sequence of the events, but happily events that did a complete U-turn from disastrous delays to smiling signings.

"I'll make copies for you and Joseph, and one to hang on the office wall," I called out as we parted ways.

French was even more over the moon than I was on reading the contract agreements, probably a huge relief for the major creditor who was holding a big, worrying 'loss', as opposed to me, who had a large debt, but one that was agreed by French and not one that I would lose any sleep over.

French ran off three copies, we smiled at each other as we clasped hands firmly, and French added very appropriately, in a deep, gruff Churchillian tone of voice, "A day to remember, and, as Churchill would have said, today is not the end of the struggle, but it is the beginning of the end!"

I popped into Greys Inn, bought a crate of Castle beers and zoomed off to the mine – to celebrate the day's events with Marianne – well into the evening.

. . .

Joseph arrived around midday, with some lame excuse for coming late, which went in one ear and out the other. I had no interest in listening, and told him I'd taken the rest of the day off and I'd see him in the morning.

"By the way, Joseph, ask Crispin to show you the new picture I've hung in the office." It was the signed contract with The Gold Plate Mine Company – but he'd probably not even notice it.

For a change, we drove to Shangani for a late lunch at the Shangani Hotel.

We passed through Fort Rixon on the way, where I picked up the post.

No bills this time; only one letter – from South Africa.

However, it was a letter that I was looking forward to from my good friend, Dirk, and I was not disappointed either; it was jam-packed with information about poisonous snakes in Rhodesia and how to handle them without being scared – or bitten!

Hi, it was good to hear from you again.

We all hope that your Large Ball Mill arrives on 1st May, but glad that you're all milling like mad on the small Ball Mill – that's great news.

Boy! It sure sounds like heaven up there with all those snakes. The green and black Mambas are to be watched – especially the black mamba cos he's twice as dangerous as the green mamba which is bloody dangerous itself.

My advice to you is that if you come across any Mambas – run in the opposite direction – a cobra is easily caught if held by the tip of the tail.

The cobra that's spits is the M'Fesin black-hooded Spitter – he can spit anything up to 6 foot – if he gets your eyes or an open wound, then just wash it out immediately – if the poison is on your face or clothes no problem because it disintegrates very rapidly and becomes harmless.

The bit about jumping over a spitting snake is Bull, it will still zap you.

Any way let me know how things are going,

and give my best regards to all.

Good digging!!

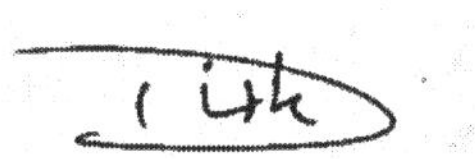

Lunch was served on the terrace, where we met Al Schwarz, who was back from border duty and enjoying an afternoon with his friends.

"Hi, it's great to be back to normality; six weeks up there is more than enough! I heard my boss fixed the house phone line for you; you must be pleased after all these delays – but don't worry, I've made a note to come out and visit you to install the mine phone line."

"*In three weeks!*" we uttered simultaneously!

Darkness descended as we arrived back at the mine.

We were just finishing a glass of wine when I whispered, "Quiet; what's that noise?"

I went outside, flashing the torch as I walked around the house slowly, but I couldn't see anything and, after a few minutes, I went back inside.

"I didn't see a thing out there."

"Maybe your ears and your eyes aren't as sharp as Crispin's!" Marianne teased me.

"Well, Marianne, you're probably right, but I must say that his clandestine message, 'I am your ears and your eyes', certainly caught my attention. It was so strange for Crispin to act that way, and to accuse Joseph outright of stealing gold from the extraction table... although he's only passed on to me what Tachibona thinks he has seen – but I'll keep it in the back of my mind for now. However, there are two things that I must act on.

"One, increase the security of the extraction table by protecting it at night with a wooden cover when we lock up at 10pm. And also increase the number of lights to illuminate the extraction area, and we'll leave it lit up throughout the whole night. The second point is of more concern; Staff's loyalty – Crispin refers to him as a spy, and there have been one or two incidents over the last month, when I got the feeling that his loyalty was divided between Ray and us.

"Just the other day, he said spontaneously 'I wish you were one of the brothers in the family, instead of Boss Joseph'. And when I said to him that it was a strange thing to say, he bit his tongue and quickly replied that he shouldn't have said that really, and continued in a rather embarrassed tone 'but you'll understand one day'! Now if Crispin can pick that up as well, I'll have to be more careful not only what I confide in Staff, but watch him more closely too. Joseph is too stupid and not crafty enough to use anyone as a spy, a source of information, but we know another director who is, don't we?"

. . .

The following morning when I went up to the mine, I saw Tachibona by the extraction room and casually remarked to him, as Crispin had suggested, that we needed to be more vigilant and that I was going to get Langton to build a wooden cover to put on the copper plate table when we locked up at night. That was the catalyst and spontaneously Tachibona remarked to me, "That would stop your partner from scraping the table when you're not around."

Well, I couldn't actually follow his logic, because the table would only be covered when the room was locked and there was nobody inside the extraction area – but it showed that he must have seen Joseph pawing over the table, trying to gauge how much gold amalgam had built up in his eagerness; something that both Newmarch and I did frequently.

However, Tachibona, Crispin and the note, 'I am your ears and your eyes', had served as both a warning and the need for increased security and extra lighting of the extraction area at night.

Newmarch thought a table cover and extra lighting were a good idea.

"The harder you make it for a potential thief, the better. I've been on so many mines over the years where it's been a bit slap-dash, and the theft of gold by the mine workers, and sometimes even by the miner's partners, has been considerable. And after all, why go to all the back-breaking and costly work to get the gold out of the ground, just to put it on a plate for some greedy person?"

"On a copper plate, you mean!" I added wryly, which caused the old miner to smile and pat me knowingly on the shoulder.

The reaction from Joseph was totally the opposite.

"That's bloody ridiculous. The extraction room is secure enough as it is; why go to all that trouble and extra expense for nothing?"

'Overruled, Joseph! As mine manager, I feel the extra few dollars that the improvements will cost would be far less than half an ounce being stolen; think about it."

"Well, it's up to you. Do what you like; you normally do – like the meetings with The Gold Plate Mine Company when you went behind my back to sell the mine, and wouldn't even allow me to be there for the contract agreement signing!"

"Did I sign a proxy form, Joseph? Was it my father who prevented you from going? Get real, Joseph. Just think of it this way; no matter how the sale has been arranged, if it goes through in three months' time, we'll be shot of each other! If the situation stayed as it was, we probably would have actually *shot each other!*"

Joseph half-laughed, shrugged and went inside his room.

"I couldn't help but overhear that conversation," Newmarch remarked, "but what you said to him actually hit the nail right on the head..."

"I tell you, it wouldn't take much for me to hit him on his head; it might knock some sense into him."

"Partners are always problems; that's why I prefer to work on my own. Oh, I've seen several shootings in the past, and one or two miners being killed – not always by a bullet either; being pushed down a 100-foot shaft also does the job!"

"Don't put ideas into my head, please," I retorted.

. . .

Funnily enough, that night, I had a dream where Joseph and I were arguing by the headgear. He was shouting, raving mad, when suddenly he lunged forward to push me down the shaft.

Luckily, my reactions were quick enough, and with my rugby playing skills I neatly sidestepped him and he plunged into the dark chasm, his loud screaming gradually fading as he hurtled downwards, until… with a faint, sickening thud – it stopped!

Early in the morning, sitting outside having a cup of tea, I told Marianne of my dream, to which she reacted unexpectedly alarmed.

"Just make sure you never stand near the shaft when that nutcase is around; in one of his freak outbursts where he loses complete control, he's quite capable of doing something like that!"

I met up with Langton and drew a diagram as to how I wanted the wooden cover to fit on top of the copper plate table, but without any screws; just the pure weight of it and some small retaining wooden blocks would be enough to prevent one person attempting to lift it or slide it off on his own.

Another diagram was given to Sparky, who set about erecting more powerful lights; one at each corner of the extraction area would illuminate the whole place totally.

Meanwhile, the small ball mill chugged away, the lashers breaking any bigger rocks from the daily drop-offs by Marianne before feeding them into the small mill.

I was really pleased with myself for doing the deal to get this two months free loan of the small mill; it certainly was a lifesaver at the time, and fits in beautifully to the time frame of the Newmarch ball mill installation, which was now only two weeks away – yes, unbelievably a mere two weeks!

The gold output from the small mill would go a long way to covering our running costs, but, when the Newmarch mill was up and running, the output should provide us with a healthy monthly surplus.

And the icing on the cake was definitely the sale option contract, which removed the dark cloud of our burgeoning debt to our suppliers hanging over us by giving the loan cash injections of $5,000 shortly, and another $5,000 at the end of May.

Even if the sale didn't eventually go through, we would be making a decent profit each month to live on comfortably, although, of course, we'd have to put up with the new 'neighbours from Hell'!

And the flexibility of the 'Dickie Bird Deal' too, because not only did they have the option to pull out, but, if we decided not to sell, we had a year to pay back the loan.

But God help us if it didn't materialise; the fragile partnership would crumble and our mining compound would become a war zone!

. . .

On Friday, Newmarch came over to see us and we had breakfast together.

He had enjoyed the past two weeks running his own mine again, but was looking forward even more to the next two weeks when he would be in Salisbury, working together with the engineers from MMC, the Mine Machinery Company, to finalise and perform stringent test runs on his invention that he would personally supervise!

He wanted his ball mill, the Newmarch ball mill, to be perfect, and promised that both he and the ball mill would not let us down.

It was sad to see him go; he was a good man and he certainly had taught me a lot. However, he would be back on May Day, the first of May, with a transporter.

"To bring you the mill that will make all your dreams come true."

He'd hardly driven out of sight when another visitor popped into the house – Joseph.

"Well, since Newmarch has knocked off early, I'm going to do the same," he stated emphatically. "It's my weekend off to be with Jane and my son, and I'll be very happy when I get back to Gwelo."

'Won't we all!' sang a choir of angels – in the back of my subconscious. *'Won't we all!'*

. . .

The weekend shifts went smoothly; up at 5:30am until locking the extraction room in the evening at 10pm, with the odd break or two back to the house when I was hungry or needed to use the phone.

Staff and his underground team worked hard, as did Marianne on her daily *gwaza* of three daily trips of one-ton loads of waste schist, which the mill lashers fed into the small ball mill.

And there were no electrical or mechanical problems… and no partner problems either; a truly harmonious few days.

. . .

Six in the morning changed all that – Joseph arriving at the house full of beans, and with some cakes for the children.

"I left Gwelo at 4 o'clock this morning to get here on time. Jane told me I had to be punctual and work my shifts, just like you do, and get used to the daily routines, because when we sell the Nelly 404, and I run my own gold mine I'll have to do everything on my own."

"That sounds like a good, but rather late New Year's resolution. Keep it up, though, Joseph; you'll find you get more satisfaction and the time goes quicker too."

"Oh dear!" Joseph whispered. "The only thing I forgot to do today was to bring the mine boys' ration meat! I mean, I couldn't have really, could I, because the butcher isn't open at 4 o'clock in the morning, is he? But I can always go back this afternoon and collect the rations…"

"Better idea, Joseph; you stay here running the mine, both underground and surface operations on your own; good practice, as Jane told you! I'll go later for them and to collect the post as well."

A slight nod, and he got back in his pick-up to drive to the mine office – I hoped… but, on listening to the sound of the engine, it was confirmed; he was heading for the mine, and not Gwelo.

"Boss Joseph said you are going to Gwelo later; here's a list of goods we need for the shop, and can you take Gwabuya with you? His grandmother has died and he wants to take a few days off for the funeral preparations. And if you could post these letters for some of the workers – I've already put the stamps on and deducted the cost from their pay. We also need some more postage stamps, by the way; I'm amazed, but we've posted over 20 letters since the rains stopped."

I thought 20 did seem a lot to him, but it was actually only about 10, as I have a rule about posting letters.

Any private mail I post, no problem, but any letter addressed to the mine manager, XXX Mine, etc., I open, and if it's about asking for a job with that mine, I don't post it. Sorry for them, but the difficulty in getting and keeping mine workers out here in the bush far from any towns needs such drastic censorship action to be taken.

Armed with the shopping lists, I set off for Gwelo using the grey Peugeot 404 pick-up for a change. Marianne said she was having trouble getting into first gear, so I left her with my beige one for her daily *gwaza* runs of three tons of schist.

Old Davidson was bending over the desk, busy sorting the post; he didn't even see me come in, or did he? He seems to have eyes in the back of his head.

"These three are for you," he called out, without looking around, but holding them in the air over his shoulder. "There's one from the district advisory board, Mines Department; hope it's the loan you're after!"

There are no secrets out here in the bush.

I hastily opened the letter to see if it had been approved.

Absolute disappointment.

Due to a backlog of applications, the MAB Board couldn't review our loan, but would hold another meeting on 6 June. And, we had to resubmit our application! Otherwise, quote: *We will presume you are no longer interested.*

Sometimes you wonder why you bother to put up with all this bureaucratic crap; they like to play the role of God and watch you squirm and beg for a few dollars more, but if you need this capital injection you have no choice.

But, the good thing was our *sudden* recently improved situation.

We were producing gold using the small ball mill, while we awaited the installation shortly of the Newmarch ball mill, and The Gold Plate Mine Company was loaning us $10,000.

These three significant things caused me to shrug, look at Davidson and say, "What is to be, is to be!" And I left for Gwelo to collect the rations for the workers.

Pink Turns Red

On my way back from town, I was still a few kilometres away from Fort Rixon when I saw a flash emanating from a group of trees in the distance, and as I rounded the next corner I could see that it was the flashing light of an ambulance, which started clanging its bells as it sped towards me.

When the dust settled, I pulled back onto the murram road and continued towards Fort Rixon.

Near a dry donga, partially hidden by large trees, there was a police Jeep, which I pulled up next to.

"Afternoon Pete. What's going on; who was in that ambulance?"

He pointed to the mangled wreck of a black car with a large tree protruding from the passenger side.

"Oh oh, not our Lady in Pink?"

"Afraid so; she's been rushed off to hospital – with the body of George in that ambulance as well. A passing rancher radioed us a call, and when we arrived a few minutes later we saw the Ford Popular rammed into the tree! I think George was killed instantly; his face was badly bruised and cut where he'd cracked his face against the windscreen with the impact. But I don't think he felt a thing; he was dead drunk and reeked of booze. She was still conscious and drunk as a skunk, but she must have crushed her chest against the steering wheel, which was bent at a strange angle.

"She looked at me and pitifully enquired, 'And how's George? He always falls asleep when I drive; I think he gets scared. George, George, wake up; open your eyes, darling; no need to keep your eyes closed. I've parked the car now amongst these shady trees, so just pass me the gin bottle and we can have a relaxing drink here'. Even when the ambulance came, she couldn't understand why they were carrying George on a stretcher.

"Suddenly, she started violently coughing, and blood spewed out of her mouth, pouring down the front of her pink dress, turning it dark red! 'Oh', she exclaimed indignantly, 'I don't remember putting tomato juice in my gin; I always take tonic! George must have thought I was drinking Vodka – he knows his drink mixes so well'! And then, with a huge, loud retching noise, she puked a bloody mixture all over herself and collapsed across the bent steering wheel.

"As she was lifted from the wreck, you could clearly see a rib poking out of her dress, and although the movement woke her up she didn't seem to feel a thing; God knows how many bottles of spirits they'd consumed. That's the most horrific accident scene I've ever been called out to – so macabre; a real sick comedy. But, now I'd better get on with my investigations and the report; why don't you pop in at the weekend. Catch up with you later."

I checked the post again at the administration office – you never know – but old Davidson looked very down; news travels fast in the bush.

"It's so sad. I've known George since we were schoolboys. And I've always said the drink would be the death of him… but I didn't envisage it happening this way!"

And he went over to the window and stood there, quietly staring into the distance.

I observed one minute's silence, leaving him to mourn, and headed for home.

When I arrived back at the mine, I showed Joseph the letter from the mining commissioner informing us that our loan application had been postponed and we had to reapply.

He read it, and, with a show of bravado, he tore it in pieces.

"We're not going to crawl to them; we don't need them. We're getting the $10,000 from the company buying the mine, and tomorrow we retort the gold amalgam, which could yield 15 ounces of gold; that's another $1,500, so we are okay – we don't need them, and that's that!"

"Yes, Joseph, I feel the same way too, but we will resubmit. It's only going to cost us a photocopy, which we resign, and a postage stamp – that's no effort at all, and, of course, the more capital we have in the pot, the better. I know $10,000 sounds a lot, but in reality it only covers the overdue accounts with our suppliers, so let's not be silly; the bigger the buffer we have, the easier it will be to run the mine, and have a back-up for any short-term problems that may occur."

"I guess so. I got carried away a bit. Here, have the pieces of that letter back," he said with a big grin. "Crispin can stick them together again." And he walked away a few steps before turning around and saying, "You can knock off now if you like. I'll supervise and lock up the extraction room tonight; leave it to me."

Well, I thought, hopefully this is the 'new' Joseph – although I reckon he's more scared of Jane than he is of his father, and that's saying something.

. . .

I left after breakfast in the grey pick-up to go to collect the explosives from the AE & CI depot, but took a small detour to go to a garage in Bulawayo that Dave had told me about, which was run by a friend of his called Simon.

"What do you know about gearboxes and gear shifts?" he asked.

"Probably about the same as you know about gold mining – absolutely zilch!"

"You're right there!" He laughed. "But it is a common problem with the Peugeot 404 diesel pick-ups; it seems to be their Achilles heel. It's the slots that the gear stick slides in – if you treat them like a woman, they'll never give you a problem…"

"Are there such women?" I jibbed.

"Yeah, good one, but do you drive this 404 all the time?"

"No, the wife does mostly, and our mine clerk occasionally. I drive a new beige diesel Peugeot 404 pick-up."

"Give me an hour to sort this, and in future I would advise you to be the only one who drives it, nobody else, and let your wife drive the newer vehicle. And one other thing. I notice that you have a lot of rust in the floor, especially by the pedals; in fact, by the clutch pedal there's quite a big hole a couple of centimetres long. I'm sure you must have got wet feet driving through the dongas in those heavy rains we experienced.

"When you've got a day that you can spare this 404 workhorse, bring it in and I'll repair it – that'll save you getting wet feet again, although now that it's hot and dusty, dusty feet; otherwise, you might find a mouse makes use of the vehicle as a nice warm guest house at night, and, where there are mice, there are hungry snakes. Imagine climbing into the pick-up one morning and finding a snake coiled up on the floor!" He laughed and added, "Only joking, but seriously, it's better to have all the gaps closed."

"Yes, Simon, that makes good sense and I'll definitely do it next time, but now I've got a few errands to do; I'll collect it in an hour or so, thanks."

I walked over to Greys Inn and had coffee with Dave.

"Oh, so you're giving Simon a try to fix your gear problem. He will too; he's the best. Now tell me all your latest news; we haven't seen each other for a few weeks."

Over the next hour or so, I updated Dave, who seemed very pleased that good progress was being made.

"And your first gold will be retorted this afternoon and brought to the Assay office here at Barclays in Bulawayo tomorrow? Tell you what, bring it in the morning, with the wife as well, and we can have a celebration lunch together with my wife – she'll be so happy that things are improving for you both."

The gear lever moved easily into first, as well as second as I drove off to the explosives depot – that Simon had done a good job.

I collected my usual Wednesday order of gelignite and detonators and drove out of the explosives bunker area.

I'd only gone a short distance when I saw this black mamba, about three metres long, slithering across the baked mud track in front of me.

I don't know why I did it, but something inside urged me to run over this renowned killer snake.

There was a slight bump as I scored, and I slowed down, looking in my rear-view mirror expecting to see a flattened snake, but no, there was nothing to be seen.

That's odd, I thought. *I definitely felt the bump as I drove over the black mamba.*

Then a thought flashed into my mind. I'd heard on several occasions ranchers relating stories about a snake being flipped up onto the chassis as they drove over it – then a cold chill ran down my back; what if…?

I looked down at the hole by the clutch pedal. What if…? Yes, there was certainly space enough for a snake to slide through and into the driver's cab.

I opened the cubbyhole looking for a rag, but couldn't find anything, so I took a handkerchief from my pocket and stuffed it into the hole.

The clutch pedal was a bit stiffer than before, but I drove off feeling a little less concerned – until I drove over a bumpy stretch of road, when the handkerchief disappeared, leaving the hole gaping open. The more I looked down at it, the larger it seemed to become, and the more I began to imagine the worst – the head of the snake appearing through the hole and zapping me in the foot!

I stopped to think; well, the quicker I got back to the mine the better, but, when carrying dynamite explosives, one had to obey the speed restrictions or face losing the explosives licence.

Becoming scared of the possibility of the snake coming into the cab, I took off my shirt and wrapped it around the clutch pedal, so that when I wasn't changing gear I could put my boot down on it to hold it in place….

This felt like one of the longest journeys I had ever made, the incessant heat of the midday sun causing me to sweat like hell, and the road seemingly had been 'stretched'. It took oh so long to cover the distance at this slower regulatory speed – perhaps the excessive sweating was in part due to my fear of the black mamba snake. Imagination plays a powerful part in our minds, and countless possible scenarios of being attacked by the black enemy below the floor of the cab continued to invade my thoughts….

At last, drained of bodily sweat caused by both heat and fear of the unknown, I drove slowly into the mine compound, and, as Crispin advanced towards me, in a fit of panic of him being bitten by the snake, I shouted out the window, "Danger; there's a black mamba under my pick-up!"

And I drove further away from the office, where I parked, opened the window fully, levered myself through the window and heaved myself up onto the roof of the cab.

"Quickly Crispin, get a long stick and poke away under the pick-up. I don't want to get bitten by a black mamba!"

Joseph and a few worker onlookers just couldn't stop laughing at this comical scene, and, whilst Crispin poked away under the pick-up, I jumped from the cab roof; one huge leap to land well away from the vehicle!

"Oh, this is the funniest sight I've seen for a long time," Joseph shouted loudly, and, when Crispin said there was no snake hanging underneath on the chassis, I also joined in the laughter.

"Jesus, I've been sweating and shit-scared all the way here, ever since I ran over the black mamba, on purpose mind you, outside the explosives dump. You see, Joseph, I've got a hole in the floor of the cab, one big enough for a slippery snake to slither through…" Then, realising what a right tit I must have looked, I kept it shut and sat down with Joseph in the visitors' open hut, dying for a cup of strong black coffee.

"That'll teach you not to mess around with snakes again," Joseph stated knowingly. "My father always told us to let them live, leave them alone, and they will go home…"

This caused me to join Joseph in singing that well-known nursery rhyme – with Crispin standing there, staring at us, bemused.

Back at the house, I was given a similar lecture… Leave well enough alone; give them a wide berth; their bite can be fatal!

Snakes or no snakes, today would be very special – extracting our first gold from the amalgam that had built up on the copper plate over the past few weeks.

After the first shift finished at 2pm, Joseph unlocked the extraction area door and, with special scrapers, we pushed and worked this thick silvery porridge into the bottom corner of the copper plate.

The next stage was to use a retort – a bulbous metal ball-shaped flask with a long neck, from which protruded a glass pipe connected to a mercury recovery unit.

I opened the clamps and packed the amalgam solidly into the flask.

A roaring fire had been built, and now the retort on its stand was placed firmly in the red-hot coals and it gradually began to heat up, turning into a yellowy-white hot unit, when, out of the top glass pipe of the retort, gases could be seen swirling through a glass tube into a glass bulb standing in a cold water container.

We watched with excitement as the vapour turned back into the shiny silver-coloured liquid mercury, which could be used again to recoat the copper plate – recycling the expensive mercury.

When no more mercury vapours were emitted, I removed the retort from the fire and it was allowed to cool down.

Joseph and I stood there waiting. It seemed to take forever before it was cold enough to open the clamps, and… four human eyes stared at one dirty gold 'sponge' the size of a tennis ball.

"It's taken four weeks of sweat, labour, cracking rocks and crushing the ore in the small ball mill to achieve this dirty looking gold sponge tennis ball!" I exclaimed.

"And one that would certainly never grace the tennis courts of Wimbledon!" shouted Joseph excitedly. "Now, where are we going to keep it until we take it to the Bank Assay office tomorrow? In the safe?"

"No. Best I keep it under my pillow tonight!" I joked.

"That sounds just like the miners of old," Joseph declared. "They dared not let it out of their sight, fearful of thieves and even their own partners – they couldn't trust anyone, and were only able to relax once they had taken it to the Assay office for weighing and receiving cash money for it."

"Well, tonight I will take it to the house for safety, and about 10 o'clock we can all go into Bulawayo to the Assay office – our first gold run!"

The excitement over, we retired to our places of sleep.

It only took one cup of coffee before I crashed out, after having placed the gold sponge in a leather pouch under the bed.

. . .

I awoke suddenly as I was being violently shaken. Strong, rough hands clasped my neck firmly, choking me.

"Where is the gold sponge?" Joseph whispered. "You give it to us now, or Staff here will strangle you and squeeze the life out of your miserable body!"

"No, never, never!" I shouted as I fought off my attackers, kicking and lashing out wildly at them.

"What's the noise; what going on?" Marianne shrieked. "You're shouting your head off, and look, you're sweating like hell; that must have been some nightmare!"

My anger and my breathing slowly subsided until the reality of the situation had taken over from the events in a very *'real'* bad dream.

"My God, I really thought those two bastards were trying to *murder* me for the gold!"

"Yes, you acted as if they were too, as you fought them off you, and almost punched me in the face."

After a few seconds, I spoke more calmly. "I really had the fever, *the gold fever, didn't I?* I can easily imagine partners killing each other in the old days, the suspicion and the mistrust all helped to cause them to suffer from that incurable disease – gold fever! But now let's try to get some sleep. Tomorrow, we will all go to town to weigh the gold and get paid. It'll be a day we've worked hard for, and to cap it all Dave and his wife have invited us afterwards to Greys Inn for lunch together."

"That sounds wonderful, and, while you and Joseph are weighing the gold, the children and I will spend a relaxing half hour in a bathroom at Greys Inn – it will feel so good."

. . .

Morning came – and so did a wicked idea.

"Marianne, I want you to drive up to the mine, now quickly while it's still a bit dark; act panicky and blurt out that I've been attacked and the gold has been stolen. Go now; act really panicky, and don't give anything away. Let's see how Joseph reacts."

Not many minutes had passed before I heard the noise of an over-revving diesel pick-up in the distance, the gunning of the engine as a pick-up was being driven flat-out, the squealing of brakes before it turned onto the track leading to our house with the full-beam headlights bouncing up and down as they came towards me, probably mimicking Joseph's wide-open eyes as he raced in panic to the crime scene.

His door opened as he skidded to a halt, and he leapt out, shouting, "Our gold has been stolen?" He bounded onto our veranda, making for the door.

His bulbous eyes, his panic-stricken face and his trembling voice made me think I'd gone a little too far with this joke, especially when, with tears in his eyes, he wailed, "No, no, no! Why me; why did they steal my gold? What are we going to do now?" And then, looking at my calm posture, he realised, and shouted, "*You bastard!* You really had me going there…. I was in shock, but… you tricked me completely!" And he started to laugh, me too, and Marianne.

Marianne said, "I think all of us should drive together to the bank; we don't want to be hijacked on the way, do we?"

Laughter really is the best medicine and a now a relaxed Joseph, still smiling, joined us for breakfast and we had the first non-confrontational hour that we'd had in ages.

The phone rang – it still makes me jump when that shrill warbling noise breaks the silence in our house, and Joseph jumped too and looked at me a little apprehensively as I picked up the horn. It was Ernest Roksplitzer.

"Ah, good morning to you too…. Tomorrow afternoon, on Friday; yes, that's no problem." And speaking louder so that Joseph could hear, I said, "I won't be here myself, but my other partner, Joseph, will be."

Joseph nodded in accord as the conversation continued.

"He's the third member; yes, the one who wasn't at the directors' signing meetings…. That's right; okay…. He'll be able to show you around and organise any help you need with taking samples…. Yes, he's sitting here with me right now having breakfast before we leave for Bulawayo with our first gold sponge from the small ball mill production…. Too true, Ernest; we are both very excited. It's a great feeling…. Okay, Joseph will look after you…. Thanks."

At 10am: "Wagons ho!"

And the convoy started the trek to the Assay office in Bulawayo, our three vehicles making a lot quicker progress than those miners in the 1890s on their donkeys or in their ox wagons.

Marianne stopped at Greys Inn – Joseph and I proceeded on to Barclays Bank.

With great excitement, we both nervously waited outside the Assay office door; my hands, holding the pouch of gold sponge, were wet with sweat.

"Let's knock again," Joseph whispered. "Maybe they didn't hear us."

Three loud strikes on the door. One! Two! Three! Like in the films of the old Tower of London prisons – and we waited….

We could hear approaching footsteps, and, suddenly, the flap of the peep hole was slid open and piercing eyes glared at us through the opening.

"Which mine are you from and what is your accredited number?"

"The Ridge Top Mine, Fort Rixon, and my agent's licence number to carry gold..." These were the keywords for the door to be unlocked, and we proudly followed the official down the corridor of the Assay office and into the weighing room.

Weights were added to the old-fashioned scientific scales… 10 ounces, two ounces, one ounce, half an ounce… Both Joseph and I were willing even the smallest extra weights to be added… a quarter of an ounce, an eighth of an ounce – the scale quivered slightly before achieving equilibrium.

"Thirteen and seven eighths ounces of gold sponge," announced the clerk through the (probably bullet-proof) glass.

Several minutes passed while the official made all the various calculations.

He was reviewing the previous assay results from the claims that were last mined in the early 1960s to determine the average percentages of pure gold, pure silver, lead and other impurities, before he wrote on a form, which he handed to us.

The silver, lead and other impurities had reduced the content of gold in the sponge to 12½ fine ounces of gold, which, at $100 per ounce, was a cool $1,250 – 75% of which would be credited to our account in 24 hours – a very tasty amount for us of $937.50 – and the balance of $312.50 would be added to our account within one to two weeks.

Joseph and I looked at each other.

Both of us had a satisfied grin on our faces as we shook hands – for the first time since our gentleman's handshakes sealing the 50/50 partnership in that café in Shangani some nine months earlier – nine months! – the last five of which had been an increasingly untenable and virtually unworkable period, which had seen constant disagreements, outrageous time-keeping by Joseph, and **all the dirty washing being thrown onto the table** with spite and hatred, resulting in the only conclusion possible:

Sell the mine!

End the partnership!

With both of us praying for the speedy conclusion of the three-month sales contract option, the dividing of the money and the parting of our ways!

Before we left each other, it was agreed that Joseph would go back to Gwelo for the night, returning with Jane and his son to the mine on Friday morning, and work the whole long weekend.

He would first re-mercury the copper plate and run the 2pm to 10pm shift that evening, then, on both the Saturday and the Sunday, double shifts, 6am to 2pm and 2pm to 10pm, and the Monday morning shift from 6am to 2pm.

This would give us a good start to the next period of one month's gold production using the small ball mill.

"And don't forget that Ernest Roksplitzer is coming tomorrow afternoon; it's very important that he gets a good feeling about the mine. After all, it's a Shakespearian-type question – *'to buy or not to buy'* – which rests entirely on **his positive report**!"

"Don't worry, partner; I know how important this geologist is to us. I will personally make sure his visit is a success. I want the mine to be sold just as much as you do!"

"Good. Marianne, the kids and I will leave early in the morning to spend the long weekend up at my cousin, Michael's, place outside Salisbury, and return to the mine around lunchtime on Monday to relieve you and Jane as agreed."

"*Thirteen ounces of gold! That's great news!*" bubbled Dave. "Really great news!"

And we joined the wives and children in the back room of the hotel for a private lunchtime together.

It was late in the afternoon when our celebrations finished, and we thanked them for their fabulous hospitality.

"If you can produce 13 ounces by milling on a small scale of 60 tons over the last month, God, just think what you could earn working three shifts a day on the big ball mill milling 900 tons a month! *You'll need several garages for your 'his and hers' Rolls Royces!*"

Dreams Come True

On the drive back to the mine, we joked about what Dave had said, and began to fantasise and daydream – out loud.

"Would you like a dark maroon Rolls Royce?" Marianne asked in a polite upper-class British accent!

"Oh, definitely not, my dear; we'd look like those damn Dunhill cigarette salesmen! The ones who have a chauffeur-driven maroon Rolls Royce with a boot full of boxes of free cigarettes.... I met one once, a bloody nice bloke called Gordon, who told me it was the cushiest and most fun job he'd ever had, and the ladies used to flock to see him and go for a ride in the Rolls – or was it a backseat roll in the Rolls! However, he stopped when he found that he was smoking three packets a day; that's 60 cigarettes per day! No, I'd like an Aston Martin. British racing green – that would suit me just fine!"

"And what about an aeroplane? You could continue your flying lessons that you started when we lived in Cape Town. With a pilot's licence, you could fly us all over Southern Africa. I love that feeling flying in a small plane."

"And a six-berth launch on Lake Kariba would also give us a weekend retreat..."

But, we were quickly brought back down to earth when we drove our second-hand diesel pick-up and parked next to our tin-roofed shack in the African bush!

. . .

A leisurely mid-morning start saw us off on the road to Salisbury for a four-day break from the mine.

It made a nice change too, sitting in the back of the pick-up with Jeffrey.

Marianne was looking forward to driving on a long trip after the past few weeks of doing the short 'schist' runs – from the old mine dumps to the small ball mill site about a kilometre away; a lot of sitting and waiting, but very little time actually driving.

At Gwelo, we took a break to have a drink and some sandwiches.

I took over the driving and, four hours later, we were at Michael's in Borrowdale on the outskirts of Salisbury, where we would be spending the long weekend with them before heading back to the Ridge Top Mine early on the Monday morning.

It was great to see him again, and we were treated to the customary braai, plenty of food and drink, as we chatted the evening hours away.

Before retiring for the night, I enjoyed another real treat – an evening bath; my first in a hot tub for many, many months. My normal daily cleaning routine had been either standing under the 'holes in a bucket shower' whilst Elliot tipped the hot water, or in Jackson's swimming pool.

The conveniences of modern living in our duplex house in Windsor Park, Johannesburg had been long forgotten, and I didn't miss that life at all – however, in the middle of the night, I opened the bedroom door, walked to the toilet, switched on the lights… pulled the chain to flush the toilet, switched off the light again and climbed back into the bed – it took less than one comfortable minute.

As I lay there, I contemplated how long a similar relieving expedition would take at our house in the bush. First finding the matches in the dark, lighting a hurricane lamp – with difficulty when the matches were damp – peering out of the door to make sure there were no lurking unfriendly humans or animals, rushing to the long drop, hopefully not in the middle of a thunder storm with the rain pelting down, doing the business and trekking back to the tin-roofed shack – at least five minutes, minimum!

. . .

Being with Michael and his family over the long weekend made a wonderful break for us, which we all thoroughly enjoyed, but it just flashed by, and it seemed like in two blinks of an eye it was Monday morning and we were back on the road again, driving to our home on the mine in Fort Rixon.

. . .

Elliot was pleased to see us, and he prepared hot coffee and some food – we were very hungry after that six-hour non-stop drive.

After he cleared away the plates, Elliot uncharacteristically quickly excused himself, and went over to his hut.

"Well, Marianne, that was a good break at Michael's, but let me get up to the office to see how Joseph has been getting on; hopefully completing six lucrative sessions of gold extraction! He can update me on all the action over the last three days, and I'll relieve him so that he can take Jane and the baby boy back to Gwelo. And I'll walk up; it'll be nice to be in the bush again – the tranquillity of nature."

Tranquillity – that was odd… and then it struck me; there was no crushing and clattering noises coming from the direction of the mine.

Oh shit, I hope they didn't have any disastrous breakdowns or accidents while I was away, came into my thoughts. *I don't want to see or have to listen to a dejected or disquieted Joseph.*

On coming out of the bush and into the compound of the mine buildings, I had that cold feeling that something was very wrong – the small ball mill was not working, the door to the extraction room was wide open, there was no one around and Joseph's pale blue pick-up was not parked next to the grey pick-up in front of the office.

Immediately, bad thoughts began to flow into my head; *maybe another strike! Perhaps a violent one, worse than the one that I had managed to quell; had Joseph done something stupid to cause a riot!*

I sighed a deep breath and walked up to the office door, knocking as I entered.

"Good afternoon, sir!" a cheerful Crispin greeted me as he stood up. "Did you have a pleasant weekend in Salisbury?"

"Thanks, yes, Crispin, but where are Joseph and all the mine workers?"

"The workers are in the mine village, sir, awaiting your arrival…"

"Awaiting my arrival, Crispin? *Jesus,* what's been going on while I've been away? Where's Joseph? Didn't he come on Friday?"

"Yes, sir; he arrived at lunchtime with his wife and son. But, when the wife saw his 'bedroom' with two camp beds, she screamed at him, 'I'm not sleeping here; do you think this is any place for a small baby; look at it; cold cement floors; walls not plastered, and there's no bathroom, not even a toilet'! When he answered that there was a toilet, a long drop, she burst into tears and shouted at him again. 'Joseph, are you mad! You told me you were building a house for us; you even showed me the plans and said it was going well. Now you bring me here to this hovel! My son and I are not going to stay here…' Then she shrieked 'did you see that? I thought I saw a rat dash under the bed! Joseph, we must get back into the pick-up and leave immediately for Gwelo. Come on, hurry up; we're going *now*', she screamed at him. 'er… er… okay, darling, we…'; 'don't *you* darling me. We are going NOW! MOVE'! 'I will! But I have to quickly write out a short note about what has happened; otherwise, my partner will go crazy and blame me for everything, and tell my father'!"

Crispin continued, "Then it was pure chaos. Joseph's hand shaking as he tried to write the note to you, and, the more she screamed at him to hurry up, the more the writing squiggled. They were still squabbling like two small children as they drove off – when, finally, peace returned to the mine. Here's the note, sir; see if you can read it?" He chuckled.

I scanned the scrawl, and exploded. "That man is an out and out *arsehole!*

Unbelievable!"

In the note, Joseph explained why he had to take Jane back to Gwelo, and blamed me for not having his house ready; it was all my fault!

He had given Staff the keys to the extraction room and told him to coat the copper plate with mercury, but had said that surface operations were closed until I arrived back on the Monday!

"It's just unbelievable; he must have been in a panic – *but*, that's *six lost shifts*, or, in money terms, Crispin, maybe *two ounces of gold*! Does he think we've got money to burn? The guy's an imbecile! Well, Crispin, clang the start gong. Let's get the workers back to work after their four-day holiday – I should really charge their wages to Joseph's account."

"And sir, Mr Roksplitzer left a note for you as well."

"Oh shit, yes! And Boss Joseph wasn't here when he arrived?" I cringed.

"No, sir, he'd already left for Gwelo, but don't worry; Staff and I looked after him. I explained to Mr Roksplitzer that Boss Joseph had to rush home on a family emergency and had asked me to give his apologies for not being here for the visit."

"Crispin, you're a gem! Thanks; otherwise, that could have given Roksplitzer a very damaging first impression, *and possibly killed the sale!*"

I left Crispin and Staff to organise the gangs and the *gwazas*, but couldn't help thinking to myself that, in hindsight, Joseph's absence was probably a blessing in disguise – although nothing was done, at least there were no riots, or strikes!

It could have turned into an absolute disaster!

I took the grey pick-up and three lasher boys and drove back to the house, where I briefly told Marianne what Joseph had done, or rather NOT done, and asked her to get at least one load of schist from the waste dumps so we could start milling.

By 5 o'clock in the afternoon:

The copper plate had been coated with mercury again.

Marianne had dropped off a one-ton load at the mill site.

The small ball mill was in operation, with the lashers feeding it with schist.

And the familiar sounds and noises of a working gold mine broke the quiet of the early evening – we were producing gold again.

I locked the extraction room door and went back to the house for some supper.

Marianne was busy cooking on the wood stove, and her raised quizzical eyebrows were answered by a slow shaking of my head.

"Let's not mention the *J-word!*"

By 10pm, still no sign of Joseph; not even a phone call.

I closed down the mill, Tachibona and I put the heavy wooden cover on top of the copper plate table, and I locked up for the night.

"Tachi, be back at 6am sharp please."

"Yes Boss."

. . .

Morning came; still no word from Joseph.

The whole mine, both underground and on the surface, carried on without him – as per usual!

After Marianne dropped off her first *gwaza* one-ton of the day, we went back to the house for a 10-minute coffee break.

Elliot had heated up the steak and kidney pie that Michael had given us, and we all munched away, clearing the plates in no time at all – delicious.

The shrill sound of our phone ringing broke the stillness – it was the Scarlet Pimpernel.

"And, Joseph?"

"I'm in Bulawayo. I came to see Mr French to ask him, *face-to-face* if the Newmarch ball mill was completely ready, *and it is!* It's being delivered on Wednesday!" he emphatically blurted. Then he continued in rapid-fire mode. "And I'm bringing Mr Newmarch out to the mine this afternoon; his pick-up has broken down. So all of us can prepare for the delivery and installation of the big ball mill; isn't that wonderful? We won't have to play around with that silly little mill anymore, and we'll soon catch up on the weekend production we lost because I couldn't stay on as planned. I had to take Jane back to Gwelo, didn't I, and I've got the plans for my new house with me, which I'll give to you when I get there, and then you can start straight away building it, can't you, and then Jane and my son can move in for good, and then…"

"Jesus! Joseph! Say no more! My ears are aching from your over-acting and loud tirades of jumbled-up, incoherent mumblings. *Just stop!* I'll see Newmarch and you when you both arrive, and we'll sit down together and plan the new installation – *properly*! Goodbye!"

The sun was just beginning to set when the pale blue pick-up pitched up at the office.

Newmarch climbed out of the passenger side, smiled and said, "At last, my ball mill invention is 100%; it has passed all the stringent testing at the Salisbury factory, and tomorrow will be one of the happiest days of my life," he enthused, with a proud look on his face that said it all.

Joseph, in the meantime, had walked around the vehicle and was standing right behind Newmarch, as if using him as a shield against what he was expecting me to unleash on him, and uttered, "Wonderful; we'll be in full production soon, won't we?"

I looked at him. He had that guilty look on his face, and then he suddenly plucked up courage and said, "Here, take these; they are the plans for my house, which you will be building. Let me show you my designs…"

"Joseph, in the morning will be fine."

Newmarch could feel the frustration in my voice, and had undoubtedly had to listen to the same story of the last few days' events over and over again on the drive from Bulawayo.

He took centre stage and said, "Why don't you knock off. Joseph and I will see the shift through, and we'll meet at 6am in the morning."

"Thanks Mr Newmarch."

. . .

Early in the morning, fresh minds eagerly checked on what had to be done in preparation for the arrival of the Newmarch ball mill.

"We have a major problem, and it is a big one; the transporter truck delivering the mill from Salisbury doesn't have an unloader system," Newmarch informed us.

"Even with the five-ton-lifting block and tackle we have over there next to the store, the shear legs are not long enough to give sufficient clearance room to swing the huge drum of the ball mill over the side of the transporter. So how on earth do we get the heavy five-foot-diameter ball mill drum installed at the ball mill site at the end of the rail embankment?"

Various alternatives didn't get us anywhere, until I suggested, "If we could back the transporter close against the waste dump at the Nelly 404, we could roll the drum, using restraining ropes, off the back of the lorry and onto the top of the piled-up waste dump…"

"That's stupid!" remarked Joseph. "How are we going to get the drum off the waste dump and down to the ball mill site?"

"Easy! Well, easy-ish! Once the mill drum is off the lorry, we can secure it with the ropes and get some lasher boys to shovel some schist away in order to make a gentle slope, down which we could slowly allow the drum to roll until it is on flat ground."

"Yes." Newmarch perked up and smiled. "That would get it off the lorry safely; that's a great idea." He smiled again. "And then… what?"

"If we get all 60 of the mine boys using shovels, spades and picks, they can make a special smooth-surfaced path, down which the mill drum could slowly be rolled over to the ball mill site, taking the strain with ropes attached to two of the pick-ups. The speed of the 'the roll' could easily be controlled by our two slowly reversing vehicles."

"Wonderful; wonderful!" Joseph shouted. "And with those two large, thick reinforced rubber mats that are in the store, we could lay them down 'one by one' in front of the rolling drum so that it wouldn't suffer any damage at all! Yes, Mr Newmarch, your ball mill will be a roll mill!"

Smiles all around.

"And once the ball mill drum is down there, the five-ton block and tackle can hoist it into position when we've erected the frame," Newmarch concluded.

"Well, that gives us about six hours or so to build this new 100-metre long 'motorway' before the transporter lorry gets here from Salisbury – I wonder if we need to get permission from the Insiza Council Roads Department!"

"And from Jackson too!"

The atmosphere was vibrant.

Newmarch was in seventh heaven and chain smoking continuously, cigarette after cigarette – each one could be a nail in his coffin, bringing him closer to his Maker, in the real Heaven.

It was quite a sight to watch 60 African workers beavering away under the supervision of three 'boss' boss boys – Newmarch, Joseph and I – ensuring that there were no rocks, nasty bumps or dips, and, gradually, a smooth earth track began to appear leading from next to the office down towards the big ball mill site at the end of the embankment.

At 1 o'clock, the task was completed and Crispin rang the gong.

The mine boys gathered around our reception hut, where Elliot and Situnda had prepared pots full of steaming soup and trays of potagai biscuits.

The women had collected all the cups and mugs they could find in the huts in the village, and were happily handing out soup and potagai to their hard-working men.

This was the first time the whole workforce had been working together on the same job, and they seemed to have enjoyed Part One of the Newmarch ball mill installation saga.

Joseph, Newmarch and I went to my house, where Marianne had prepared lunch.

The 2 o'clock gong sounded and everyone assembled, waiting around the office area for the arrival of the long-awaited – hopefully the saviour of our mining venture – Newmarch-designed small workers big ball mill crusher!

Three o'clock passed. Most of the Africans were sitting or lying on the ground in the sun.

We sat in the shade under the thatched roof of the open reception hut....

Four o'clock.... Still nothing....

"I'd better go and phone the Salisbury MMC office to find out what's going on."

Back at the house, I tried and tried to get through to their office in vain – the joint party line was busy with 'hot' gossiping traffic, and my pleas to interrupt their afternoon rumour-mongering sessions were to no avail.

I went back to the mine; it was now getting on for 5 o'clock.

"Everybody, knock off!" I shouted, and told Staff and Crispin to make sure that all the workers were outside the office at 6am sharp! But would the transporter be?

. . .

At 6am, our phone rang – it was Shangani Police Station.

"Is that Ridge Top Mine?"

"Yes?"

"The driver of a transporter carrying mining equipment wants to speak to you."

"Put him on, please!"

The driver explained that his brother and family were celebrating the birth of their first son, and he was obligated by tradition to join in the celebrations.

Once it became dark, the party really went wild, and there was no way he was in a fit state to drive.

He couldn't contact us, because there were no phones in the village.

Luckily, the driver didn't use that Josephism... 'So I couldn't phone, could I' – yes, really lucky for him!

"What time will you get here? I've had 60 men sitting around since yesterday lunchtime waiting for you; your company will have to pay us a late delivery charge!"

Up at the mine, I explained the whole situation to the others, and that we could expect the ball mill to arrive by 10 o'clock.

"Well, four letters, TCOD – transport cash on delivery – is at least in our favour, and we will negotiate an amount with the Salisbury transport company.

However, it doesn't really help or compensate for a full lost day for 60 workers, not to mention the non-running of the small ball mill – the gold extracted would have covered all the transport costs. But let's await the delivery; at least our 'gang of 60' are ready, and the road to the Newmarch mill site is smoother than the Fort Rixon-Filabusi main murram road!"

Around 9:30, a distant noise caught our attention – it was like a slow drum roll, steadily getting louder and louder, and finally bursting into a thunderous crescendo as the transporter arrived and the driver pulled up in front of the office, revving the engine like mad!

Sixty African voices cheered and shouted; it was like a crowd applauding a drum solo at an open-air music festival!

The mine workers were in fine form, laughing and smiling as they gathered around the huge transporter, waiting expectantly for us to give them instructions.

When we told the driver of our plan to unload the five-foot-diameter mill drum from his transporter, he smiled dubiously, but did as he was asked and slowly backed up his vehicle, nudging it into the mine dump and coming to a halt.

Half a dozen lashers set to work to smooth the loose schist near the tailgate of the transporter until the gate could be lowered flat against the rubble.

Ropes were attached to the ball mill and it was slowly rolled off the transporter and onto the waste dump.

The transporter drove away and parked, whilst the lashers made an off-ramp from the waste dump, and, with ropes acting as brakes, the large ball mill was gently eased down the slope and onto flat ground.

The Africans cheered and cheered, and I whispered to Newmarch, "Well, that went easily; I didn't expect it to go as faultlessly as that!"

"Nor me," he replied, chuckling away, "and now I think we'll only need one pick-up with ropes to help control the roll to the mill site, don't you?"

"Control the roll! I like that," Joseph enthused. "Let me get my pick-up; let me finish the job, okay!"

He reversed into place, ropes were hooked onto the towbar, he took up the strain, started slowly reversing, and the ball mill moved slowly forward.

With Newmarch guiding the ball mill down the slope and two boys laying the mats in front of the rolling drum, we didn't need any other muscle power, and, within 15 minutes, the Newmarch ball mill drum was proudly standing next to the conveyor system at the end of the rail embankment.

The three of us smilingly congratulated each other on a job well done – and much quicker than we could ever have imagined.

"It's almost 2 o'clock; I'll get Crispin to bang the gong and your underground mine workers can knock off for the day, Joseph. I'll get the 2pm to 10pm shift on the go at the small ball mill operation, and the rest can work with you this afternoon to help Mr Newmarch to unload the other parts of the ball mill and take them down to the Newmarch site. Do you both want to come for some lunch at the house?"

"Not today, thanks; Joseph and I will get Situnda to fix us a sandwich. We'll get together later." And the two of them went up to the office.

Marianne was chuffed that the Newmarch ball mill had arrived at last and had been safely unloaded.

"So when will it be operational?"

"Newmarch estimates about 10 days for trial runs, and another week or so to get the gold extraction rooms ready and functioning… so the 25th! Which would fit in nicely, because we can run the small mill and keep producing gold up until that date, which is when our two months' free trial will be over and the mill will be returned to the Mines Department for a service check-up, before K.B. Davies transport it back to the Fair Deal mine near Salisbury.

"Our mine will be fully operational by then, and with Joseph being in the army on border duty for six weeks, I'll be doing the underground work and supervision with Staff, whilst Newmarch has kindly agreed to stay on over that period to control the milling and gold extraction processes. I feel really happy about that too, because not only from an experience point of view, but I know I can count on Newmarch. If he says he'll be there, he'll be there, every day. He is a true Rhodesian; his word *is* his bond. I don't have to rely on the somewhat dubious 'gentleman's handshakes' that some like to hide behind – and even flout!"

The phone rang; it was Charlie.

"Hey, that's fabulous. This weekend? Definitely; we'll be there… and okay, we'll come late Friday afternoon for the weekend…. Thanks mate; see you tomorrow."

"Another weekend at Charlie's; ooh, the kids will love that too!"

"Yes, I'm sure they will. He wants us to be there on Friday evening, so that I can go early Saturday morning with him and a few others to his brother, Bob's, ranch, where we will go hunting. He says Bob wants to bag a kudu for a large wedding feast that he's laid on for one of his worker's families, and I could shoot an impala for roasting on the Sunday for our whole group."

"*Lucky you!* I'd also love to go tracking the kudu; to me, they are the most beautiful animals in the bush – such graceful antelopes with majestic, twisted horns, and for such a large animal it's so amazing to watch them running, almost gliding over the rocky ground of the hillsides."

"Well, not this time, Marianne, but we'll arrange a day's tracking next time we visit Charlie, but let me go up to the mine and arrange things with Joseph and Newmarch, so we can leave about lunchtime tomorrow."

"That's no problem at all," Joseph graciously stated. "Mr Newmarch and I will cover for you while you're away. Can you bring back some biltong; you said it's the best – I'll pay for it, of course."

"Yes, Joseph, for sure and I'll knock it off your monthly cash travel allowance, and by the way you haven't submitted any receipts to Crispin for last month, have you?"

"No!" Joseph cut me short. "All those silly bits of paper get lost so easily, but I'll ask Jane to sort it out for you. And I'll do the evening lock-up tonight for the small mill extraction room, so you can go home and prepare now if you like. Newmarch and I are quite capable of running things when you're away," he added, a little sarcastically.

Back at the house, I told Marianne and the kids to get in the pick-up.

"Let's go to see Peter and Pete at the weekly police evening braai, and, if we pick up the post as well today, then tomorrow, instead of having to come through Fort Rixon to go on the Bulawayo route to Charlie's ranch, we can go in the other direction from the mine, taking the scenic drive through the bush to Filabusi – it's much shorter, and you always see plenty of game when driving through that virgin bush."

"I think that's probably the letter you're dying to open," Ian Davidson chirped. "It's from The Gold Plate Mine Company! And if things are as good as I hear on the grapevine you could be eating off *solid gold plates* soon, like King Solomon in biblical times!" And he chuckled away to himself as he pursued the more mundane matters of his job.

I hurried out to the pick-up and slit open the letter with my Swiss Army knife.

"A big fat cheque for 5,000 delightful dollars!" I shouted loudly in jubilation! "That's what I call a fantastic start to our weekend. Come, we can celebrate at the braai this evening with the two Peters; they'll be chuffed at the news!"

. . .

An unexpected early morning visit; Joseph called in to see me just after 8am.

"I forgot to give you the plans for my new house. There's not a great rush now, of course, because Jane won't come and live on the mine until I'm back from border duty at the beginning of July. But you can get the builders digging the foundations so I can see what it looks like before I go."

I glanced at the house plan, which was for a three-bedroomed bungalow.

"But Joseph, you're not serious? These corridors are almost as big and as wide as the bedrooms?"

"Don't exaggerate. We like wide, roomy corridors; helps keep the place cool. I grew up in such a house."

"That's true, but you should increase the size of the bedrooms as well. I know your parents' house is much bigger than your plan, and we've got plenty of concrete blocks to build you a good-sized house."

"No thanks; this is the plan. I've shown Jane; it's what she wants too, so don't muck around with it and change it. We want it built *exactly* to those specifications in the plan!"

"If I build it to these sizes, Joseph, you'll be mad at me when it's finished – the eight-foot-high inner walls will make the rooms look so pissy small."

"Stop arguing with me; just build it! You agreed with my father that you would build me a house, so do it!"

"Joseph, I'll build it exactly to this plan of yours, *if*, and I repeat *if*, you sign it, so you can't change your mind later and blame me!"

"I will not sign it! No, no, no!"

"Then I won't, I won't, I won't build it!" I replied, mimicking his childishness. "The rooms are far too small – unless it's for a house full of pygmies! And until you sign it, I won't start building it."

A huff and a puff… end of conversation.

Bala Bala

"It's a bit early to leave, but if we take those rolls and drumsticks take-away from last evening's braai, together with a six-pack of dumpies Peter gave me, we could take a track off the Filabusi road and spend lunchtime by a small lake tucked away in isolated bush."

The kids counted more than 30 animals that came to drink, including a mean-looking old male buffalo, which luckily was on the opposite side of the water – those beasts give me a bad feeling. They're so ornery; they are the one animal I really distrust, so, when it started ambling along the water's edge towards our corner, I got into the driver's cab and slowly drove off, back onto the Filabusi murram road.

"That was a very enjoyable treat," Marianne said, "We must come here again; it's only half an hour away from the mine, and it's beautiful, quiet, and you feel part of the surrounding nature."

Before long, we turned onto the tarmac road to Bala Bala and drove on until we saw Charlie's sign board, took the track off to the right and bounced and bumped along for a few hundred metres until we came into the clearing of Charlie's ranch house and several out-buildings.

Although it was only around four in the afternoon, we certainly weren't the earliest; eight other vehicles were parked in the shade of some acacia trees.

Charlie introduced us to two other families, those of Dave and Sam, who had recently returned from border duty – that said, no more mention was made of the T-word, or Terrs, as they were commonly referred to.

As the evening stretched on into the night, both the people and the roaring flames of a wood fire slowly faded, and I slipped into a sublime sleep.

. . .

Up early at first light, Charlie and I took two 308 Winchester rifles and went down to the stream for some target practice before heading into the bush to bag an impala for Sunday's spit braai.

After two or three shots, I was regularly hitting the tin can targets nailed to a tree.

"Fine, I can see you've got used to that rifle; let's go on foot and see who can get tomorrow's supper," Charlie remarked.

It was still a little cool, but the sun was getting brighter as we followed the two African trackers silently through the bush downwind of a group of impala in the distance.

About 150 yards away, we stopped and watched the impala grazing contentedly.

"You shoot first; that young male on the left of the group. Remember, go for the 'BLAD' shot like I told you. The target area is large and you have three spots that are vital from the point of view of the survival, or the escape, of the animal – the heart, the lungs and the shoulders. If you don't drop him, I'll be covering you and will fire a second shot."

I steadied the rife by resting it on a low branch, and, keeping my eye on that BLAD area of the impala, I steadily increased the pressure on the trigger… and…

CRACK.

To my amazement, and Charlie's as well, I think, the impala dropped on the spot.

His two African workers raced up to the animal – stone dead – and bled it.

We sat in the shade for a smoke and a breakfast chew of some biltong.

"That was a crack shot; you're either very good – or a little lucky!"

We grinned at each other, neither of us giving a hint one way or the other.

His workers had racked the impala on two poles, the body and head hanging downwards and they carried it off back to the ranch house.

A few cheers as we approached the veranda, where mouths were being filled with bacon sandwiches.

Charlie and I grabbed a couple and went off for a nosh – and a wash!

"That impala will be delicious tomorrow when we spit roast braai it. You did well."

"I enjoyed it too; it must be in my genes to hunt for food to feed the family!"

Charlie's ranch must be what Heaven is like – the people are so genuine, everybody gets on with each other, both big and small, the surroundings are idyllic, and Mother Nature's wild game larder is always full.

In the afternoon, four of us drove off to Bob's ranch, where we saw some of his hunting dogs, including two large beautiful Rhodesian ridgebacks named Hannibal and Genghis.

I was amazed when Bob told us that they were still just puppies, only 10 months old!

"And today is a bit of an experiment; I have never taken these young dogs on a hunt before, so it will be interesting to see how they get on. But the main aim of today is for us to cull a large kudu, which I have promised for a wedding ceremony for one of my workers on the ranch. Here Charlie, you take this other rifle as second shot; the rest of you can just enjoy the game walk in the bush."

We had walked for several minutes along game paths when Genghis must have picked up a scent and rushed off into the bush, with his brother, Hannibal, racing after him.

Five minutes later, we could hear one of the dogs barking in the distance.

Gradually, the barking became closer and louder, and suddenly, right in front of us, a big kudu bull burst through the bushes, escorted by Genghis alongside on its flank. He was barking, taking evasive actions from the horns of the bull and snapping at its flank, but not biting. Hannibal was close behind the kudu to prevent it from running off to its left.

So, remarkably, these two novice puppies had brought the kudu bull directly to their master, but Bob – the professional hunter – was so flabbergasted at this *totally unexpected* incident that he wasn't ready to shoot.

"That's incredible! But let's wait and see how good my young Rhodesian ridgeback hunters are," Bob mused. "If they chase the kudu back into our line of fire again, I'll take the shot this time, for sure!"

A few minutes passed before we heard the sounds of animals crashing through the bush, and the kudu bull appeared, with Genghis set on baying this big antelope – he jumped high in front of the kudu's head to stop the bull in its tracks.

CRACK!

Bob had shot, and the large kudu bull fell.

The dogs approached slowly, gave it a sniff and wandered back to Bob's side.

"I just can't believe this," Bob uttered in amazement. "This is the first contact those young dogs have had with a big antelope, and without any training or experience too – which shows beyond doubt that it is instinctive genetic behaviour. These two young Rhodesian ridgeback puppies have shown the complete repertoire of good hunting hounds; tracking down the kudu, skilfully guiding it to me and then baying it so that I had a good clean shot! And all of this without any training; unbelievable! AND would you believe it, neither Genghis nor Hannibal has a scratch on them; their quick movements and reactions prevented the kudu's horns from ripping open their flanks and badly injuring them."

We left the African trackers – who were probably bewildered by the young dogs taking over their tracking jobs – to prepare the kudu bull ready to be transported back to the compound in a Jeep. This large 600-pound antelope was far too heavy to be carried back on poles like we had done with the impala in the morning.

What an afternoon!

And back sitting together on Bob's veranda;

five frosties were downed;

by five thirsty hunters;

in five seconds flat!

And we achieved our plans of filling the food larder with:

a KUDU – weighing more than 600 pounds; enough to feed the wedding party of 100 guests;

and an IMPALA – weight 160 pounds; sufficient on a roasting-spit braai for 20 people.

We heard other fascinating stories and reasons for using dogs to help the hunter.

"Sometimes a shot is not as accurate as I would want; perhaps a thin twig affects the flight of the bullet, but if I have only wounded the animal the ridgebacks will quickly locate the wounded prey, and I can put it out of its misery. I was told of an incident by a friend of mine who was out hunting with his dogs, when a kudu that he shot was not fatally wounded, and that kudu ran for over a kilometre before falling dead, but his ridgebacks tracked it down and alerted him by making small barking noises so he was able to locate it – before any other wild predators did!"

The day's hunting stories were recounted many times during the evening.

Truly amazing experiences for me:

Shooting tomorrow's impala supper.

And to witness that amazing sight of the untrained, inexperienced young Rhodesian ridgebacks bringing and baying a large kudu bull to their master, Bob, who finished off the job – a wonderful wedding present that would feed the expected 100 guests.

After a weekend packed full of:

Comradery and conversation;

Food and fun;

Beer and biltong;

Rounded off with the roasting of the impala buck over hot coals;

We left at dawn on the Monday, and headed back home to our mine.

Elliot helped unload the pick-up. "Boss Joseph called by last night and again at 8 o'clock this morning and left this envelope for you."

It was his house plan, and he had signed it at the bottom, with the comment: *Agreed, and now you must start building this house! Joseph.*

While we were at Charlie's over the weekend, Jeffrey had fallen asleep several times during the day, and one of the wives had told Marianne that we should have him tested for bilharzia at the hospital; a type of sleeping sickness caused by minute bilharzia snails entering the body. They are commonly found in still, non-running water, quiet pools – just the places young kids like to splash around in!

I waved goodbye to Marianne as she drove off with Jeffrey to Gwelo for a bilharzia check-up, and reminded her not to forget to deposit the cheque for five grand – the first of those two agreed payments from The Gold Plate Mine Company.

With Joseph's signed house plan rolled up and stuffed into my shirt, I walked towards the mine.

The noise of the small ball mill and the shovelling of the lashers grew in intensity as I neared the action – what a lovely sound, and hopefully the two shifts per day had continued without mishap while I was in Bala Bala hunting impala.

Newmarch and Joseph were sitting in the reception open hut having a tea break, which I gratefully joined in with – tea can be so refreshing.

Joseph was happy to report that there were no problems over the weekend.

"In fact, we didn't miss not having you around at all; everything had run smoothly without you!" he proudly boasted.

"Pleased that Newmarch and you had run the mine so well, Joseph – pity there aren't any more days available before you go to the border next week."

I told Joseph that I would get Langton and his helper to start work on his house in the afternoon.

"Now don't forget," Joseph stated seriously, "I don't want it built on the ruined house site near your house. Jane says it would be much better to be further away, on our own, on the other side of the road, and we want new foundations built as well."

"Fine, Joseph, so why don't you go with Langton, show him where you want it built, and help him measure out exactly where the foundations are to be dug. I'll go with Newmarch and catch up on the progress of his ball mill installation."

Newmarch and I walked along the rail embankment, and he pointed out the water pipes and the heavy gauge cabling that had been neatly laid alongside the rails.

"It is better than burying them or having them lay across open ground; there's enough problems on a mine without exposing the pipes and electric cables to accidental damage. And if there is a water leakage or an electrical problem, just by walking along the rails that can be easily checked and fixed."

At the mill site end, we stopped where the cocopan pulls up and the ore is tipped out onto a shute – the complete conveyor belt system was already in place.

However, none of the electrical cabling would be connected until the whole structure that housed the ball mill was completed.

Good progress had already been made, Newmarch and Boniface assembling the huge steel frame and welding it together.

It had been firmly bolted down onto the large concrete slab base that had been laid a month or so earlier. At the top of the frame was a gallery that could be accessed by a metal ladder to allow inspection and easy maintenance of the two electric motors that were installed there.

These would drive the ball mill, which hung on thick, linked metal chains rotating around cogs each side of the ball mill – a similar concept to the spinning of the back wheel of a bicycle.

"If everything continues to progress well," Newmarch continued, "come the weekend, we should have completed the ball mill installation ready for a FULL test run – the cocopan tipping the ore onto the electric conveyor system feeding the rocks into the ball mill for crushing. Next step is to start adjusting and calibrating so that the ball mill runs smoothly and effectively, and crushes the ore to fine sands for the extraction of the gold particles.

"We should be able to do this trial run on Monday for Joseph to see before he goes on border duty. He is so excited about seeing the mill in operation, knowing that we are just a few steps away from a fully running and producing gold mine. Of course, we still have to build the concentration/extraction rooms, but we'll be ready to completely take over the milling from the small ball mill before the end of the month."

I left Newmarch, Boniface, Sparky and four other workers to continue with the big ball mill installation and popped in to visit Crispin to get an update of the weekend's village activities.

"On Saturday night, we did have a few incidents, arguing and fighting between several of the workers, but Amon soon put a stop to that. They weren't really serious fights – more pushing and shoving and shouting abuse at each other – but the disagreements are real, and as usual it's about money – who owes, who cheats and who steals!

"So I got them all together on Sunday morning and told them that I would ask you to hold another *indaba* court under the big tree, when all their complaints can be heard and judgements can be made – just like we did last time. That was a good system you introduced, sir; their fellow workers being on the jury and giving their decisions secretly, so that the problems were sorted once and for all, for everybody to see, and nobody could point fingers or blame any individual."

"That'll be a good idea, Crispin; let everyone know the court will be in session after work on Saturday afternoon. It's more interesting after a few Chibuku beers; they certainly lubricate the tongue to make the truth – and the lies – flow freely!"

Walking along the murram road towards my house, I could hear the sound of several voices arguing, and, as I turned off into my driveway, I recognised one, that of Langton, and another voice louder than the rest, that of Joseph….

Even when I sat down on my veranda, I could hear him shouting and screaming from the vicinity of his proposed house.

I thought it best to stay out of the way; let them sort it out. No doubt, Joseph would give me a verbose description of any problems.

It was after dusk when I heard a Peugeot pick-up approaching, and, minutes later, Marianne pulled up next to the house.

"Jeffrey is all right!" Marie-Louise shouted out the window. "The doctor said he's just a lazy boy who falls asleep when he gets bored!"

"Yes, thankfully the tests proved negative," Marianne added, "so another worry less."

"And another crate of beer for Daddy," shouted Jeffrey. "Elliot! Elliot!"

Elliot came running over, smiling broadly. "What's up, little Boss, what's up?" He proceeded to put Jeffrey down at the table with a bottle of beer in front of him.

"Elliot! Elliot! They are not cold!" Jeffrey bellowed – and laughter filled the night air.

Cold or not cold, the beer was welcome – and its twin even more so.

After the two beers and some biltong, I felt 'bilharzia-ish' myself, and soon followed the rest of the family into the Land of Nod.

. . .

Over the next few days, Joseph was like a man possessed, working hard helping Newmarch from early morning until late in the evening – he wouldn't even let me do the nightly lock-up of the small ball mill extraction room at 10pm.

"You've worked solidly for several months," he said to me. "Soon, I'll be away on border duty and for six weeks you'll have to work day and night again running the mine on your own. So, relax a bit; take it easy this week."

Was this a genuine resurrection of my partner starting to participate? Or just another showboating performance aimed at trying to please his mama and papa?

Even Staff and Newmarch remarked on this 'new' Joseph.

"And long may it last!" Newmarch wryly commented.

Joseph didn't even leave as planned on Friday afternoon to spend his last weekend with Jane and their son, insisting on locking the extraction room at 10pm and sleeping overnight on the mine.

. . .

Early Saturday morning, we heard him hooting as he drove past the house towards Fort Rixon to be with his family in Gwelo.

"I wonder what the next six weeks will have in store for us," I remarked to Marianne. "Will Joseph safely complete his army duties and return to a fully operational gold mine? Will the Newmarch ball mill, after a three-month-late installation, be successfully milling three shifts a day? Only time will tell; we will have to wait and see."

Staff, Newmarch and I sat in the office to agree on a basic timetable for our daily operations and the allocation of workers to the various *gwazas* starting on Monday:

Underground operations beginning at 6am:

The underground lashers would start clearing the rocks from the previous afternoon's blasting,

breaking the larger rocks down in size using sledgehammers,

shovelling the rocks into wheelbarrows,

and pushing them along the drive tunnels to the main shaft,

where they would be shovelled into the skip for later hoisting to the surface.

The jackhammer boys would then take over, drilling the planned holes in the rock face that Staff had chalk-marked, ready for loading the sticks of gelignite and igniters, followed by blasting again later in the afternoon.

Surface operations: The most important tasks:

The small ball mill operation:

Crispin would control the daily shifts, one starting at 6am and the second at 2pm.

Marianne would make two collections of waste schist to feed the small ball mill.

I would supervise the gold extraction and lock up the security room at 10pm after the second shift.

The Newmarch ball mill site:

The electrician/welder and a gang of four workers would help Newmarch from 6am until 5pm to get the larger ball mill in operation.

Goliath, the builder, and two helpers would build the extra retaining walls of the rail embankment, and the extraction/concentration room.

Concrete block making:

George and his helpers would produce 120 concrete blocks per day, to be used at the big ball mill site, and also for Joseph's new house, which Langton and his *gwaza* boys would build.

Crispin would have his work cut out, with all the administration and stores as well.

I would supervise the whole mining operation:

Weekly AE & CI trips for gelignite and detonators.

Collect rations three times a week, and the post – if Marianne hadn't already.

Attending only essential – to us – meetings with the Mines Department and the banks.

That was the plan, man…

And until the Newmarch ball mill was fully operational on a three-shift system seven days a week, Sundays would be a day of rest/prayer/finishing the leftover Saturday Chibuku beer!

Today at 2 o'clock work would stop, and the *indaba* court sessions would take place in the village after the full quota of 80 gallons of celebration beer was delivered.

You could feel an expectancy in the air; workers were keeping one ear open for the first sound of the approaching Chibuku lorry, when the stop-work gong would sound and the workers would be treated to a free pint each at the *indaba* court.

I find that a pint of beer relaxes them, puts them in the right mood for the often most entertaining sessions of the *indaba* – it also loosens tongues, which speak more freely; sometimes the truth, sometimes huge lies, but that would be for the jury to decide – and the judge to give sentence.

As in the first *indaba*, five men were chosen for jury service; they would judge someone guilty by dropping a stone into my hands – three or more stones equalled guilty as charged!

Crispin was the clerk in charge of the court proceedings, and I was the judge!

All rise for the judge!

The first case:

Crispin stated that Cleinke wanted to leave the Ridge Top Mine, but he had to clear any disputed debts before leaving.

"Cleinke, do you owe Tauchira $2.30?"

"Yes, but he owes me $2."

"Tauchira, do you owe Cleinke $2?"

"No!"

Cleinke began his story, and he told of some card gambling sessions on the local farms a while ago.

He had won, and had given 50 cents to Tauchira to keep for him.

They went drinking on another farm, where he won again, and gave Tauchira another 20 cents… until they went back to the mine, with Tauchira holding the winnings totalling $2.

"What do you have to say to that, Tauchira?"

Tauchira was obviously a good orator, an amusing speaker who had the others howling with laughter, but all to no avail; the jury had dropped all five stones into my hand.

"My judgement is," I proceeded, "Tauchira owes Cleinke $2, so in total Clienke only owes Tauchira 30 cents."

"And there's another case against you, Cleinke," Crispin announced.

A small, wiry, bow-legged wizen old man called Masauso stood up and shouted, "Cleinke owes me $1.75."

Clienke replied that the old man had given him $1.75 to get him a woman – loud laughing cut him short… but he continued to say that he had gone out and spent some of the money drinking beer with the woman to get her ready and wanting, but, on the way back with her, he thought about Masauso's wife and started feeling sorry for her, and, not wanting to cause any trouble, he spent the rest of the money on beer, and Masauso had never asked for the money back.

Masauso replied that he would forget about the $1.75 if Cleinke would get him another woman before he left the mine! Raucous laughter stopped the proceedings for several minutes – even the wives who were sitting nearby and listening began rocking and shaking with amusement – all except maybe for Masauso's wife!

The jury verdict was not guilty; Cleinke was let off the $1.75.

Crispin announced another case where the hoist driver, Biton's, wife had been stripped and beaten by two of the other wives.

One woman stood up and explained, "She is a devil; she has no children and her body is firm, especially the large bottom, which she wiggles around to entice our men. So we taught her a lesson; we tore her clothes off and beat her!"

I interrupted and said, since this woman had admitted to the crime, I as the judge would set the penalty – the two women would each have to pay Biton's wife $3 to replace her ripped-up clothes, and if there was any more trouble from them they would have to leave the mine.

Crispin told me that Nelson was leaving Ridge Top Mine as well, and he wanted to be paid his wages.

I had never liked Nelson. I had already placed him on a warning; 'any more trouble and you are fired'.

Crispin had told me stories about his rudeness, how he would con people in the village, but they were all too scared of his vicious temper to bring the matter to the *indaba* court, but, now that he was leaving the mine…

Crispin stated, "The next case is against Nelson – Juta claims he had sold his wife to Nelson for $5 and had not been paid!"

Murmuring and sniggering broke out amongst the workers, but I burst into uncontrollable laughter, which caused Crispin to look at me, bemused.

"Oh Crispin, it's not really that funny, but when I was at school I had to read an English literature book by Thomas Hardy, a famous English author of the 1880s, in which the Mayor of Casterbridge sold his wife for five shillings! I always thought that was ridiculous – who would sell their wife, and for so little! – until today, that is!"

Juta stood up and declared, "Nelson owes me. I sold him my wife for $5, and he still hasn't paid me!"

Nelson glared at Juta menacingly as the two of them stood in front of me; a look that prompted Amon to move closer to the two of them, anticipating trouble.

Nelson suddenly pushed Juta hard so that he fell backwards over my chair, knocking me to the ground as well.

As I stood up, the necklace hanging from my neck caught around the arm of the chair, causing me to stumble just as a rock whizzed past my head, knocking off my bush hat!

Amon sprang like a leopard and pounced on Nelson, pinning him to the ground.

"Are you okay, sir?" Crispin asked with concern in his voice.

"Yes! I'm okay! But Amon, lock this dog, Nelson, to the prison tree! I'll go and phone the police to come and pick him up; let him rot in the cells for a few days until the next visit of a magistrate to Fort Rixon."

As I was walking back to the office with Crispin, Amon came running up to us, and kept pointing to my necklace with the wooden pendant and uttering some strange and, for me, unintelligible words – it was weird and eerie!

Crispin eventually grasped what Amon was trying to say.

"He's saying that the witchdoctor's pendant protected you from that madman, Nelson. If the necklace hadn't got caught up in the arm of the chair, that rock would have crushed your head, splitting it open. It has saved your life again sir!"

The *indaba* over, the barrels of Chibuku were muscled onto the pick-up and we drove them down to the village.

Spontaneous cheering and clapping greeted us as the beer was unloaded; everyone was in a good mood.

Juta called out, "Thanks Boss; we are glad Nelson is going to prison. We can all celebrate now and we don't have to fear him anymore!"

Back at the house, I phoned Fort Rixon Police and told them of the incident, and they arranged to come and collect Nelson.

I was pleased to see the back of him, as he was sneaky, underhand and always stirring up trouble. In fact, on reflection, he would have fitted easily into the 'gang of five' that had given us so many problems early on, causing friction between Rancher Jackson and us, culminating in the drunken fighting when Paniche had stabbed Phillemon to death.

The police constable arrived to collect Nelson.

Amon handed him over, shoving him forcibly into the back of the police Jeep, and insisted on accompanying him to the police compound. He told Crispin that he didn't trust Nelson at all and would make sure he was locked up – only then would he come back to the mine.

The constable told me that Nelson would remain in the cells for two weeks until the magistrate made his monthly visit, and would I file a complaint against him when I next came to Fort Rixon.

. . .

Newmarch called in for breakfast with us, and to give me an update on the progress of his ball mill installation.

He looked a little nervous, not his normal calm self, which prompted me to ask, "Is there a problem at the mill site?"

"No, I'll finish off the final connections and calibrations today, so we'll be able to let Joseph see the mill in full operation tomorrow before he leaves for the border."

"So why the frown?"

"Well, I don't like to ask, but, as I don't have my vehicle here, I can't drive to Fort Rixon – and I'm completely out of cigarettes!"

"Oh no, we can't have that!" Marianne exclaimed, handing him a cigarette, which he hastily lit, and, with a deep sigh, slowly exhaled the cigarette smoke.

He relaxed immediately and the frown disappeared; the sudden transformation was amazing – and, with the promise of more tobacco, which Marianne would fetch shortly from Fort Rixon, Newmarch donned his hat and walked off slowly to the mine to carry on monitoring the love of his life – an invention that, if successful, could prove to be a Rhodesian-manufactured crushing mill alternative to the ageing stamp mills.

It would be 'his dream come true', after more than 50 years mining for gold as a small worker – and obviously it would help to make our dreams come true as well!

. . .

Talking of dreamers and their dreams, Monday morning found another dreamer knocking on our door – Joseph.

"I've come early," he began, "so I can witness Mr Newmarch's ball mill in action, fully operational, before I dash back again to Gwelo to spend my last evening with Jane. Tomorrow, I join my army unit, and then that's it; no more sex for six weeks. Six bloody weeks!"

Marianne looked quite shocked to hear these very out-of-character remarks from Joseph, but politely asked if he would care for a cup of tea.

Joseph declined, went quickly back to his pick-up and set off for the mine.

An hour or so passed before a loud 'clang yang yang, clang yang yang, clang yang yang' announced that the full test of the Newmarch ball mill would shortly begin.

I climbed onto the back of the pick-up with the kids, and Marianne drove us up to the mine for the 'grand opening'.

We parked outside the office and scanned the view before us.

"It's quite unbelievable what you've all done," Marianne said proudly. "I mean, look at the high railway embankment stretching from the tall wooden headgear down to Mr Newmarch's dark green ball mill installation – what a lovely picture it makes."

"And by the end of the month there will be cocopans being pushed up and down, feeding ore into that big round monster, which hopefully will be digesting it and passing *golden excrement!* They say 'where there's muck, there's money'!"

We walked down to the mill, where a contented-looking Newmarch was sitting in the sun puffing away as usual, cigarette butts scattered around by his feet – this was obviously his favourite spot where he had relaxed and smoked, virtually chain smoked over the last two weeks.

Marianne took a picture of Newmarch standing on the rail tracks, looking down at the conveyor system and his finally-installed Newmarch ball mill.

"Would you take one of me by the headgear?" Joseph asked. "I want to carry a photo of my gold mine around with me all the time, so that when people don't believe me, I can show them a photo of my own gold mine, can't I?"

"While you're up there, Joseph, signal to the hoist driver to bring up a skip full of ore so we can start the test run."

As they walked off, we could hear Joseph asking Marianne, "What would look best; should I put on a yellow miner's helmet, or keep this on, my favourite red hat?"

Luckily, they were soon out of earshot. Newmarch raised his eyebrows, smiled to himself and started explaining to me that the object of today's run, besides putting on a show for Joseph, was to successfully crush the ore to the correct size. He would check the output from the mill to see if it was fine enough to be washed over a James concentrator table.

He would add more metal balls as required into the ball mill each run until the emerging sands met his criteria.

"I've told the hoist driver to start the winch up!" shouted Joseph, and we heard a slight rumble, which became louder and louder until we saw the skip emerging from the shaft, continuing on up the steep rails into the headgear, where its contents were tipped into the large hopper.

Followed by even louder crashing noises from the hopper as a cocopan was filled with rocks and pushed along the metal rails to the tipping shute, where once again the noise level was thunderous as rocks from the cocopan emptied out and rattled onto the shute.

A lasher shovelled the rocks onto the conveyor belt, which carried its load up and into the mouth of the ball mill when the sound of intense crashing and bashing filled the air as the heavy metal balls in the mill mixed and spun around with the rocks, gradually pounding them to a powder.

Joseph and I watched as Newmarch scrutinised the emerging watery surry, feeling it with his fingers as he stretched across the Launder boxes.

"*Oh balls!*" he uttered and stepped back quickly.

"My balls are giving me a problem!" he uttered. Then, looking rather embarrassed, realising that his comment had been misconstrued by the laughing trio of Joseph, Marianne and me, he added, "I meant, I need to put several more metal balls in the mill; these sands are too thick to be processed over the James Table. But Joseph, I think you've seen what you came to see; it's now just a question of trial after trial until we get it exactly right, and also of course the extraction of the gold when the sands are washed over the James Table – when it's delivered."

"Well, I'm going to the Mines Department in Bulawayo tomorrow," I responded, "so I'll check on the date it can be picked up by Fox & Bookless for delivery to our mine."

"And I can't wait to get back from border duty; it's so exciting, even watching these initial tests," Joseph exuded. "Six weeks is a long time, though, but at least I've got this picture in my mind – as well as in my wallet – and I know that all is going to be well, whether we sell the mine or not, eh partner!"

He kissed Marianne Dutch-style, 'peck, peck, peck', patted the kids on their heads – Jeffrey backing away with a *'get off of me'* look on his face, and shook hands with Newmarch so vigorously that Newmarch's Trilby hat tipped forwards, covering his eyes!"

Smiles all around, and Joseph and I walked to his pick-up.

"I know you'll get along fine without me, but I will be back. I'll be back to work harder now that I've seen the whole mine operating. Over the last few months, I've been so worried that we wouldn't get it all completed, and my father would be mad at me! With all the delays caused by the rains, not being able to find a 5-stamp mill, and the Newmarch ball mill being nearly three months late, I was at the end of my tether. I don't like to be laughed at by my brothers, who think I'm a failure; even at school they used to…"

"Well Joseph," I butted in, "if you work like you have done the whole of last week, the mine will run properly and you'll have the last laugh on them."

"But that was easy; I was at the mine the whole day and sleeping overnight. My house will be ready when I return, and Jane, my son and I will be living on the mine full time; no more driving backwards and forwards to Gwelo, which was so boring and very tiring. Come with me now, and I'll show you where Langton is making the foundations for my new house; come, let's go in my truck."

We pulled up 100 metres past my driveway on the Fort Rixon murram road where he had selected to build on the opposite side to our place, near the Claremont mine.

As we emerged from the bush some 200 metres from the road, we saw Langton and his gang digging trenches for the concrete foundations.

"See, the rooms are big enough," he exclaimed, standing on the ground between the trenches. "Plenty big enough, so please, build as agreed; stick to my plan, okay!"

I swallowed hard, controlling the urge to tell him that, when the eight-foot-high walls were built, the rooms would look smaller and dark, but thought, *it is Joseph's last day; he's in a happy mood; let him go off to war that way.*

And he'll see for himself when he gets back that it really is a house for midgets, when he can curse and argue with me again.

"Don't worry, Joseph; I'll make sure that Langton builds your concrete-block house with a corrugated iron roof *exactly* to your specifications on that signed plan."

We shook hands. He looked very apprehensive, but who wouldn't if one knew that for six long weeks they'd be exposed to the very real danger of being injured, or worse still, killed, traversing unknown areas, fighting a virtually invisible enemy who used hit and run killing tactics.

I wished him well and walked back to my house on the other side of the road, knowing that at the end of the following month our nearest neighbours would no longer be eight miles away, but a mere 400 metres away!

After a week of having the luxury of two partners working with me, Joseph had gone, leaving me to run the whole mine again, whilst Newmarch concentrated on the ball mill site and the extraction processes.

I drove up to the mine to supervise the 2pm change of shifts working on the small ball mill. The workers had got into a good routine, knew their own jobs, and this part of our mining was running like clockwork.

I spoke with Crispin and told him to supervise the small ball mill operation on Tuesday, as I had an important meeting in Bulawayo, but would pick up the meat rations, two 60 kg bags of maize and beans, and anything else of his shopping list for the mine store.

"I'll do the 10pm lock-up tonight in the extraction room with the spare key you entrusted me with," Crispin said. "And thank you, sir, for not letting anybody know my suspicions that I wrote to you in that note."

"I am your ears and your eyes – yes, I'll never forget that, Crispin! And that's why I told Staff that only you would have a key to the extraction room, because it was surface work, not underground work!"

"Yes, sir, that was good, because it sounded quite the normal thing to do, and didn't alert him to the fact that we had our suspicions about his loyalty, and him being a spy for Boss Joseph and for Big Boss Ray."

The conversation caused me to think back to several occasions when both their actions could be construed as underhand, devious.

Newmarch was so right; the worst thing when you are a 'small worker' mining for gold is to have *partners*, and gold seems to bring out the worst in their characters – ***mistrust*, *greed*** *and* ***lust for gold!***

. . .

At the meeting in Bulawayo with Ryan, the mining engineer, he began to tell me more about his time working for R.J. Stewart on the Claremont and Nelly mines.

His last six months with them before they closed down in the early 1960s was concerned with the future development and assaying of the Nelly 404 mine.

He laid out on the table a large stenographed geological diagram, titled 'NELLY 404 MINE, proposed development under a 50% speculative development loan, dated 14.10.1963'.

"And was it approved?" I enquired briskly.

"Yes, by the MAB in Salisbury, but we didn't take it up, because we were closing operations to concentrate on another mine owned by R.J. Stewart & Sons."

"Shit! So what's all this civil service hoo-ha, and all the plans and assay results they've demanded from us since late January – *when*, all the time, they have had this underground geological survey chart, with all the test assay results approved for the Nelly 404 by their own Mines Department head office in Salisbury for a *50% speculative loan* – Jesus! The mine hasn't been in operation since that date, the assay results would be exactly the same; nothing has happened to change that – what a bunch of stiff, paper-mad f-f-fools they must be."

"I know; I actually showed this same geological survey to the mining commissioner three months ago when you applied for a 50% speculative loan. He said it was an old, out-of-date survey, and your mine would have to follow the full laid-down procedures on applying for a loan – that's the rules! It drives me mad as well; 'common sense' are two words that don't exist in the Mines Department administration vocabulary. It's only the good practical men like Ronnie and Martin who I get on with here."

We spent the rest of the afternoon pawing over the underground diagram of the shafts, the drive tunnels, the stoped-out sections, and the various areas where he felt good gold values could be mined.

We arranged that he would come out to the mine on Thursday and we'd review, together with Staff, the potentially good areas we should start mining for gold.

"I'm sorry to ask; I know it has gone 5 o'clock and you've got a two-hour drive back to the mine, but could you do me a small favour and take me to a mine 15 kilometres south of Bulawayo where I have to drop off the results of a big survey I completed for them recently? They're waiting for it, before they can proceed with their new mining development."

It was gone 7pm when we finally arrived back in Bulawayo and I dropped off Ryan at his house, when he thanked me for going out of my way to help him.

I drove off feeling rather tired, heading for home on the smooth tarmac road with my headlights lighting up the long, straight road ahead of me.

I took the dirt road at the Insiza turn-off, where the darkness seemed even denser.

As I drove along, my head was full of thoughts about a few dickheads who worked in the Mines Department administration; rather dull people who didn't have the gumption or the will to put a rubber stamp on a loan application that they had already approved before and sent to the MAB, who had also approved it!

What nonsense is that! I just couldn't get it out of my head, their ineptitude and the waste of everybody's time and duplication of effort – I was really getting annoyed with these people.

I was deep in thought, wondering what the best thing to do would be… when…

"*Wooh!*" I shouted loudly as a large zebra was lit up by my headlights, galloping towards the dirt road about 15 metres in front of me.

I eased off the accelerator to slow down, when, suddenly, another zebra appeared just to my right, only metres away, but, realising that it didn't have time to cross, it tried to turn and swerved into the front side of my pick-up with an enormous '**BANG**', its head smashing against my windscreen, causing its body to swing around and swipe against the side of my pick-up, knocking me across the murram road and skidding sideways down an embankment!

I battled, hitting the accelerator and turning the wheels into the slide, snaking left and right trying to regain control of the vehicle… and, after what seemed like minutes, I managed to bring the pick-up to a halt, leaning at an angle, but thankfully partly back on the murram road – at least the pick-up hadn't rolled!

I looked back, but it was too dark to see anything.

Judging by the blood all over my smashed windscreen, and the fact that I couldn't open the driver's door, I reckoned the zebra was either dead, or very badly injured.

Any injured animal can be dangerous if approached, so I got the powerful torch out of my B-P kitbag and slowly opened the passenger door, which was not damaged.

I flashed the light down the road and could see a zebra lying there, probably a large male, but I wasn't going to go near it to check!

I could hear it suffering, coughing, choking, gasping for breath, but I didn't have a gun to put it out of its misery.

Flashing the light around the bodywork of my pick-up revealed a totally smashed-in right bonnet and driver's door, and a badly dented right-side body – a big panel beating job for sure; hopefully no damage to the chassis.

The front right wheel was punctured and virtually hidden by smashed, bent metal from the impact; there was no way that I'd be able to drive this again tonight.

I went around to the left-hand side, where the passage door opened reasonably easily.

I listened… but could no longer hear any noise coming from the zebra lying on the road. A flash of the torch revealed no movement, and, although I was sure it was dead from where I stood 30 metres away, I wasn't going to risk approaching it, and resigned myself to sitting in the vehicle waiting for a Good Samaritan to come along.

It was one of those moonless nights, pitch-black, which added to my apprehensive feeling as I sat there in the dark in the small space of the pick-up cab – like hiding in a wardrobe with the door shut!

A few hours passed; it was now around midnight.

I locked the side door and made myself as comfortable as I could lying on the front bench seat, and sleep began to take over….

I suddenly awoke to a loud ear-piercing noise; that weird sort of blood-curdling barking-laughter of a group of hyena.

I wound down the window a little and shone the torch in the direction of the noise, illuminating a scene of vicious fighting amongst a group of hyenas, some more intent on fighting each other than ripping chunks off the dead zebra's abdomen.

My stomach turned at the sight and noises of the destructive scavengers, but I tried to get some sleep, and gradually switched off….

WHAM!

The pick-up rocked. I sat up; what on earth was that?

THUMP, THUMP!

And my vehicle started rocking from side to side.

I shone my torch through the back window of the cab and almost jumped out of my skin! The torch lit up the head of a hyena staring at me, with blood dripping from the teeth of its open mouth.

Jesus that gave me such a fright!

I banged on the glass, but it just looked at me for a split second, before it joined another hyena ripping open the meat rations in the back of the pick-up.

Even hooting didn't distract them from the ferocious feeding, and I sat there and had to listen to their ghastly eating noises, barking and fighting…

For how long? I didn't know; I must have finally dozed off and gone to sleep.

The bright light of the sun was shining in my eyes as I awoke; it must have been about 5:30am.

I looked around to make sure I was on my own – and only then ventured out.

The back of my pick-up was a bloody mess; bits of meat lying amongst burst-open bags of maize and beans. Hardly a welcome sight for a man with an empty stomach.

I looked down the road to witness another ongoing party.

The remains of the zebra, its hide and bone structure was the backdrop to another frenzy – fighting between various predators that had taken over from the hyenas when they had eaten their full share and left.

Jackals, wild dogs, groups of those horrific-looking vultures and large back ravens were taking it in turns to strip the remains from the zebra's carcass, and… the rest of Mother Nature's scavengers would get their turn to clear up the untidy mess of a dead zebra – smaller animals, ants and bugs we can't even see, down to the smallest of nature's workers… until the bush clear-up job is done.

All I could do was to wait inside the pick-up for a tractor or a Jeep to come along and end my night-long ordeal – and hopefully take me somewhere for some strong black coffee and something to eat!

Such a someone who could do all of that for me and arrange for my crashed pick-up to be towed away was my mate, Policeman Peter, who pulled up in a Land Rover and ferried me to the police compound, with the words, "Well, I must say, each time I find you stranded in the bush, you always have an unusual and surprising story to tell!"

During breakfast, I told Peter what had happened.

"Man. You had a very lucky escape last night. That was a large zebra that smashed into your pick-up; you did well not to roll it when that powerful sideways swipe from its body smacked into you – a zebra like that one weighs easily 800 to 900 pounds!"

"Yeah, thankfully I was lucky, but as we've spoken about before, Peter, driving on dirt roads with soft sand edges is similar to driving on snow, and I had plenty of practice as a student in Hull, North Yorkshire during those severe winters in England in the 1960s. That taught me how to react quickly and calmly, zigzagging, turning the steering wheel and accelerating into the slide to get your way out of rolling the vehicle, but, as you say, I was indeed extremely lucky not to be hurt at all."

"But not so lucky with the state of the pick-up; that's going to need a costly panel beating job. I hope you're insured?"

"Yebo! All our vehicles are fully insured, and I'm pleased that I wasn't driving my new beige Peugeot pick-up, just a second-hand one – we'd had problems with the first and second gears on this old grey one, and, when they were fixed, Simon from the Bulawayo garage suggested that I should be the only one to drive this vehicle, because the selection of gears would always be a bit awkward and stiff."

"He'll have a bloody shock now when he sees the rest of it!" Peter mused.

"Too true, and could I phone Simon and ask him to come out with a trailer and take this crashed pick-up for repairing at his garage workshop? I'll leave the keys with you, if that's okay?"

"No problem, and I'll get a constable to drive you back to the mine; the family must be wondering where you are!"

Marianne said she hadn't slept well; she'd only gone to bed around midnight after waiting for a call from me that I was staying over in Bulawayo and she'd been really worried and annoyed that I hadn't phoned her.

But now she realised why, and was so pleased I wasn't hurt in the crash.

When I related the incident to Newmarch, he wryly commented, "And the police say zebra crossings *are safe!*"

The old man has a keen, dry sense of humour, which I do like.

"So *your unfortunate* trip was to visit the Mines Department. I don't know this man, Ryan, who you tell me about, but if he used to work for Stewart on the Nelly 404 he'll have all the knowledge about the quartz and the banded ironstone reefs they were working on – that's great news. And yes, I'd like to join the two of you on Thursday and spend it reviewing and looking at the options you have for development and mining at the Nelly 404.

"Together with the geological survey charts he gave you, and our three heads, we should be able to determine the best areas for you to start your underground blasting and mining operations. And for me, to take a whole day off from the ball mill installation will make a nice welcome break; it'll bring back many memories too from the last 50 years when I'm down there underground in your mine."

Crispin was shocked to hear about the zebra crash, but relieved to see me in one piece, although he reminded me: "Now we really are short on food rations for the mine boys, after feeding the hyenas."

"Not only that, Crispin, but we're also short on vehicles! We had four pick-ups a few months ago – I sold one to Matt, Joseph's is with Jane in Gwelo, and I've just crashed the grey one, which leaves us with only one working pick-up now! So do we have enough schist piled up ready for the small ball mill?"

"Yes sir, Madam had been doing her two runs a day, so we've got enough for maybe five or six shifts."

"Okay, that's good, now here's what we'll do. You keep supervising the small ball mill set-up, and I'll go to town to collect some more meat rations, meal and beans – I just hope the hyenas won't be lying in wait to ambush me! I'll also have to make a plan to be able to use Joseph's blue Peugeot; hopefully Jane will be agreeable, because we simply can't operate with only one pick-up."

At the house, I took a quick coffee break and phoned Matt at his mine and told of my recent mishap, and that we were now in desperate need of another pick-up.

"Would you go around and see Jane at Hudson Road, explain our position and the problems we now face, and try to convince her to loan us Joseph's vehicle until the grey one is repaired?"

"Well, I'm pleased someone is looking out for you and protecting you; perhaps it's the witchdoctor's pendant you wear around your neck!" Matt joked. "But seriously, that you are not badly injured is a blessing; we can do without one vehicle, but we can't do without you, mate! I'll phone you back this evening to let you know about Joseph's pick-up."

"Okay Matt, let me get off to Bulawayo now to collect some more food rations and also check at the garage to get an idea of when we could expect to have the grey pick-up back in action again."

Marianne and the kids sat in the front and we headed for Bulawayo.

The grey pick-up had already been removed, but I slowed down to point out the remains of the once large, strong zebra, which was now an unrecognisable heap of bones and hide – the last remnants of its flesh being pecked at by ravens.

"It's so sad," remarked Marie-Louise. "I love those striped horses, but you can only see a bit of the stripes; where's the rest of the body gone so quickly?"

"It's Mother Nature's way of cleaning up; all the animals helping, and having a meal at the same time. If they didn't do this, there'd be heaps of rotting, mouldy flesh lying around all over the bush, which would bring bad diseases for both the animals and us humans."

Marie-Louise and Jeffrey looked sad, and sat quietly between Marianne and myself – not another word was spoken.

As we pulled up in front of Greys Inn, the two little quiet ones instantly became the noise makers. "Sausages and chips, please!" Jeffrey shouted.

"Me too; me too!"

"And I'll have a ploughman's lunch," Marianne added.

"Tell you what, why don't you and the kids have a bath while I go to see French and update him on Newmarch's progress with the ball mill installation, and we'll have lunch when I've finished."

Doug French was so pleased that we'd already had a full test run, and that within the next two weeks the rest of the concentration and extraction areas would be completed to give us a fully operational small worker gold mine.

He asked if he could join us for lunch; he hadn't seen the family in weeks.

On the way to the hotel, I was telling French about the zebra crash that had happened the day before. He was shocked, but pleased I'd escaped from a smashed-up vehicle without being hurt at all.

"That's my pick-up over there in the corner of the yard." I pointed as we entered Simon's garage area.

"But there's hardly a scratch on it!" French exclaimed. "Are you having me on?"

We got out and approached the grey pick-up; indeed, looking at the passenger left-hand side of the vehicle, everything looked completely normal.

However, when we walked around to the driver's side…

"My God, it's crunched up like a bit of paper!" French exclaimed. "You are a lucky man – and not to have even a scratch; it's amazing."

Dave greeted us as we entered the foyer of Greys Inn.

"Good afternoon, you lucky man! I hope you don't mind repeating the zebra story again, but I'd love to hear it, and I've arranged that Marianne and your children can lunch with my wife so that we can go into the bar, because the news of the crash is all around town, and besides me, the bar is full of regulars who would love to hear all the gory details. You won't get away without being repeatedly toasted to 'your good luck and your continued health' during the afternoon, but don't worry, though; Marianne knows, and will drive you home, picking up the mine boys' rations on the way. So, let's join the boys at the bar; the first round is on me!"

Sometime around 4pm or 4:30pm, I was eased into the passenger seat of the pick-up, and, after a few farewells, I closed the door… and closed my eyes for the day.

. . .

A slow, dull start to the day was suddenly brightened up when Marianne told me that she was pregnant! Another piece of Rhodesian gold!

This was great news indeed, and Marie-Louise was already suggesting names, as she was so sure it would be a pretty little sister!

"I like the name '*Markita*'; it will be nice to play with a sister with such a lovely name."

"And if it's a boy?"

"I hope not; I've got enough problems with the brother I've already got. Jeffrey can be so rude sometimes! But, if it is a baby boy… then we should call it ***Mark!***"

"Matt phoned early last night and wanted to talk to you, but, on hearing about your long afternoon session yesterday at Greys Inn, he just passed the message on that Jane had no problems with us using Joseph's vehicle until the grey one was repaired, and she would drive it down to the mine on Saturday. She would like to stay overnight with us – however, in a real bed, not a camp bed!

And on Sunday morning we could take her and her son back to Gwelo."

"That's a relief. Yebo, and she can sleep in the big bed with you; I'll use one of the long settees, no problems."

Ryan drove into the mine compound.

"This is weird, being on the Nelly 404 mine again," Ryan admitted. "It's 10 years since I last was involved here."

"A blast from the past?" quipped Newmarch.

"Yes, you could say that, and I've arranged with the mining commissioner that I can work out here for three days next week, from Monday if you agree."

"We'd like that very much. This will get us off to a great start and I can use all the help and advice working with you, which will also allow Newmarch to concentrate fully on his ball mill site extraction complex."

Coffee was arranged – with the last of Joseph's 'secret hidden' stash of biscuits – and we sat in the reception hut, Ryan excitedly pointing out known areas of 'good' gold as all three of us keenly studied the geological survey charts of the Nelly 404 mine.

I learnt a hell of a lot about the underground reefs and structures, which became even more real when the three of us went down below into the mine.

The water had been pumped out of the second-level drives, which were now clear, and we were now busy pumping to get down to the third level (300 feet).

On one side of the main inclined shaft was **the quartz reef** that had originally been worked by the ancient miners thousands of years ago.

They followed the **narrow visible gold reef** and mined, virtually burrowed, down to the current second level.

The chart showed where R.J. Stewart had continued mining on this irregular lenticular reef down to the fourth level – which was still underwater.

On the other side of the main shaft was the **wide, banded ironstone reef** with lower gold values, and the **gold was not visible to the eye**.

However, although the values were less, all the ore rock blasted out from this five-foot-wide reef and hoisted to the surface contained some gold, which meant that the actual gold extracted was quite profitable – this reef would be our bread and butter once the mine was fully operational, running the around-the-clock three shifts per day.

Ryan pointed out an area of quartz reef at the far end of the second-level drive tunnel, which he and Stewart had planned to 'stope out' further, but that had not taken place, because Stewart decided to close the Nelly 404 and concentrate on another mine they were developing, which was only down to the first level and the extraction costs were much less.

Ryan suggested that, as the gold values of the quartz reef in that stope area were richer than the banded ironstone reef, and the estimated ore reserves would last for three, possibly four months, it would be a good idea to start 'stoping' mining there – blasting the rocks out of the 'side wall' above the drive, instead of blasting and extending the drive tunnels. This would give a good return, and a boost to start us off.

And, once the mine had been pumped dry to the fourth level, there was another potential quartz reef for 'stoping' out.

This had been part of the valuation that had led to the granting of R.J. Stewart's original 50% speculative loan by the MAB advisory board; the loan that they didn't action before the mine closed – and the *same one* that we were still relentlessly pursuing!

I agreed with him that the quartz reef on the second level would be the area that we would stope first, and, as Newmarch had stipulated that we should only run his ball mill for one shift a day for the first month, it would be this quartz reef that could help us to achieve a monthly gold output of more than 50 ounces – *lekker*!

Staff slowly nodded, and so the plans were set.

As we travelled back along the tunnel towards the hoist skip, my headlamp lit up some thin mud 'tubes' on the smooth rock face.

I stopped for a closer look and could see they were very similar to the ones we had discovered on the gum poles in our house.

I knocked a bit away and, yes indeed, there were the translucent white ants with the light brown heads.

"That's amazing," I uttered.

"And they'll go down to wherever the water table level is," Ryan informed me. "In parts of the Claremont mine, they were there on the rock walls even 700 feet down!"

That was the most informative day I'd spent on the mine, and I was now really looking forward to seeing the large ball mill in action and watching the 'gold tail' coming down the side gully of the James Table – bringing to mind those exciting images on that trip to Cain's gold mine; images that germinated into this 50/50 partnership, working our own gold mine, the Ridge Top Mine!

. . .

On Friday, I spent more time underground with Staff, revisiting the quartz reef stope area. He showed me where they would place the gelignite for the first blast, and chalked the marks showing where the holes should be drilled.

"On Monday morning, then, Staff, we'll get the jackhammer boys to start drilling at this spot, but, when Ryan arrives later that day, we'll ask him to go around underground with us and highlight and explain why they mined or stoped these different reefs. It'll be good to learn the history of the mine and get a feeling for Stewart's reasoning. The more we know, the better our instincts will be, and should lead us to a more profitable gold mine. I'm going up to Fort Rixon now to collect the post, and I'll buy you a tin of that snuff you like so much; you'll need it to sneeze out all the dust from your nose once the drilling starts in earnest."

. . .

After lunch on Saturday, we were sitting outside singing nursery rhythms with Marie-Louise and Jeffrey to pass the time while we waited for Jane to come in Joseph's pick-up.

It began to get late.

"Are you sure she was to bring the pick-up this afternoon?" I asked Marianne.

"That's what Matt told me. We'll just have to wait patiently for her; there's no rush."

As the light began to fade, we heard a vehicle and could see the approaching headlights through the trees, but it was not a blue Peugeot 404 diesel that pulled up – it was a Land Rover.

Out climbed Jane, holding her son in her arms.

"Are you okay? What happened? Where's the blue pick-up?" Marianne nervously enquired.

The tall, rangy Rancher Ashburner appeared from behind his Land Rover. "That blue pick-up is about 10 miles down the road – with *double* punctures! This lady waved me down, but there was nothing I do could, really, as there was only one spare wheel. I suggest you let one of your *askaris* go with me and I'll drop him off by the punctured pick-up, which is on the side of the road, and he can sleep the night in it. It's best and safest that way, and you can bring an extra spare wheel with you tomorrow morning and sort it all out in the daylight."

I drove with Ashburner to the mine to collect Askari Amon.

"Thanks for helping our stranded lady friend; what actually happened?"

"One of those freak accidents. A small piece of farming machinery must have fallen off a tractor near the bends by that donga crossing, and she drove straight over it, causing both left-side tyres to be punctured, but there's no other damage."

"That's good to hear. Thanks again, Jack, and we'll see you at the Fort Rixon club sometime for a drink."

"I'll still be around, but I don't know about you!"

We laughed, as he repeated his quote of several months ago.

Jane had told Marianne the same unfortunate story, but she was okay, and, after supper, she took my half of the bed and I lay down on the long settee.

. . .

The next morning, the six of us set off in my pick-up and drove to where the blue pick-up was parked in the soft sands on the side of the murram road.

I fixed the tow rope to it and slowly began to pull the vehicle out of the sands, with the kids standing there watching and cheering excitedly.

"Stop!" shouted Amon as he grabbed Marie-Louise and quickly moved backwards a few steps, then put her down and, with his knobkerrie, beat around ferociously under the pick-up. "Okay Boss!" he uttered. "Go!" And, as the blue pick-up was slowly pulled out of the sands and onto the road, Amon bent down and then proudly stood there displaying a dead snake draped over his knobkerrie.

"That's a puff adder!" I remarked, recalling the information that Dirk had written in his letters to me. "That's one of the most dangerous snakes, because it doesn't slither away when anything approaches or moves. It likes to just lie on the warm sand, and, when you get too near, it strikes and bites quickly, and their venom can kill if the snake serum antidote is not immediately injected that's why we carry a 'snakebite' kit in the pick-ups. Thanks Amon, your quick reactions probably saved Marie-Louise's life!"

With the two spare wheels bolted in place, we headed for Gwelo, the girls in Joseph's vehicle while I drove the beige one, with Jeffrey and Amon in the back.

The two punctured wheels were taken to a garage, where I was told to come back in two hours to collect them.

"Come on everybody, as a treat let's all have ice cream at the Midland Hotel."

"And Daddy can have a beer-flavoured milkshake!" Marie-Louise quipped.

As we sat and drank our beers, Jane told us that she was very worried about Joseph leaving for the border.

"He wouldn't tell me where he was being sent; he's not allowed to, but he said they would be in an area near the border where there was increased terrorist activity. Recently in a fierce skirmish, a friend of his had been killed as they mopped up a group of terrorists trying to flee across the border back into Mozambique after raiding a village – 10 of them were shot dead, but two eluded them in the dense bush.

"So I really am worried, and I'm not sleeping well at night, but my mother-in-law is coming for a few days, which will help, and then she'll take my son and me down to stay with her at the Belingwe mine. So that works out quite nicely for you, because I won't be needing Joseph's pick-up."

We dropped off Jane at the Hudson Road house, collected the spare wheels from the garage and headed back to the mine in the two pick-ups, not stopping at the Fort Rixon dam club – although the noises coming from that place were very enticing, but enough is enough, and we could all do with an early night.

. . .

Now that the mine was almost ready for full production, I had initiated a 6am Monday morning meeting to plan the week's main events.

Staff, Crispin, Newmarch and I gathered together in the reception hut.

The major task for the week was to complete the Newmarch ball mill installation, which would replace the small ball mill set-up, hopefully by the weekend.

"Is this feasible, Mr Newmarch?"

"Yes, we are only waiting for the James Table to be delivered and tested."

"Good. Well, Fox & Bookless will be bringing that to the mine later this morning, so that you can install it in the concentration/extraction room, which is complete except for a roof. But Goliath can fix that using the corrugated iron sheets that will also come with the transporter today. Crispin, the stockpile of schist to feed the small mill; how many days will that last?"

"Plenty to complete the shifts up to Thursday, sir."

"Okay. So Crispin, you will be in charge of the small ball mill site. And on Friday we can dismantle the small mill, which will be collected by B&O Transport on Saturday and taken to the Mines Yard for a service and check-up. Then French will use K.B. Davies transport to return it to the Fair Deal mine by the end of the month as agreed – a fully serviced, operational mill. Now, as we have enough waste schist to keep the small ball mill running up 'til then, that frees up one of the pick-ups to deliver concrete blocks to Joseph's house site.

"Good news too that Ryan, the engineer from the Mines Department who was here last week, comes back this morning to assist us underground for three days. So Staff, you will look after him please, and I'll join you when I can, especially to help identify the rock face areas where we will be blasting in the quartz reefs. We are very fortunate to have him on loan from the Mines Department, and can really benefit from his knowledge and 10 years' experience working for R.J. Stewart on the Nelly 404.

"And Mr Newmarch, Ryan can have Joseph's camp bed in your room. I'm sure you'll have long, long interesting conversations together about the Nelly 404 and other mining stories from the Fort Rixon, Insiza area. If we get through this week successfully, the mine boys will be able to enjoy an extra free barrel of Chibuku, and have Sunday off as well – Crispin, please pass the word around; all the mine boys deserve it, especially if we can complete all these tasks by Saturday morning.

"Then on Monday we can start full production, from underground blasting to gold extraction using the Newmarch ball mill – initially for only one shift per day during the first month. Newmarch feels this will allow him to do any tinkering and necessary adjustments – hopefully no breakdowns, so that we can confidently start two shifts a day the following month."

I went over to the block-making area and checked with George, who told me that we had a stock of 1,250 concrete blocks, and were producing 120 blocks a day.

That would be more than enough to build Joseph's new house by the end of June, and to extend and rebuild our present shack-house by the end of July.

I estimated that we would need 1,500 for Joseph's midget house, and 2,500 for our extension/rebuild.

The idea behind enlarging our house, which would be three times bigger, was that we first build the outside walls encircling the present hessian-walled shack, leaving it in the middle.

This would allow us to continue to live in it, while the outside walls and the majority of the new planned inside walls were being built using concrete blocks.

Then we would demolish the shack and erect the timbers to support a corrugated iron sheet roof that would encompass the whole building.

In the former shack area, we would build new concrete-block walls for a kitchen, a scullery and storage room.

That would complete our new three-bedroomed bungalow, with a sunken lounge, a dining room leading out onto a covered veranda, a kitchen, scullery and storerooms, and, most importantly, for the girls, a bathroom with a toilet – although I would still use the 'loo with a view' long drop – when the sun was shining!

However, the views from the veranda would be even more spectacular, looking across vast areas of bush to the distant hills some 30 kilometres away – an intoxicating panorama of the landscape to enjoy after a hard day's work on the mine, relaxing with a sundowner.

What more could a man want?

Our new house should be completed by late July – it was almost as exciting a project as the almost-gold-producing Newmarch ball mill installation.

Ryan arrived by motorbike, much to my astonishment – it was the first one I'd seen in Rhodesia, where traffic on the roads was mainly pick-ups, Land Rovers and tractors.

He was happy to double up with Mr Newmarch in that one room, and cheerfully went off with Staff for a morning underground exploratory session.

The James Table arrived around midday, and the Fox & Bookless driver reversed down our 'new' road – the one we made specifically for 'rolling' the Newmarch mill.

The solid James Table was soon offloaded, together with 20 corrugated iron sheets that I'd managed to buy from the Zoom Mine in Fibabusi that had recently closed down.

After a mug of soup from Situnda, the driver and his mate were ready to leave for Bulawayo.

"It makes quite a change to have such a short visit," the driver remarked. "Last time, we were here for two days!"

Blasts on the hooter and the transporter went on its way.

I went back to the house for an afternoon phone session; there were a lot items I had to order for building Joseph's house.

I placed orders for timber for the roof framework, five C2H windows and a metal door. Joseph had insisted on a metal door, which he had underlined on his house building plan. It was for security; nobody can break through a metal door, he had told me, and I was pleased that he was becoming a bit more security conscious.

We hadn't had any problems so far with break-in or theft, but you cannot be too careful out here in the vast area of uninhabited bush, especially nowadays when you hear about the odd terrorist attack that had penetrated well into Rhodesia – not just close to the Mozambique border anymore. A Rancher had been *murdered* near Shangani, but it was not clear yet if it was terrorists, or an unfortunate domestic ranch dispute!

I, too, was becoming more wary.

That night I had spent in the bush with the frenzied hyenas after the zebra crash had *triggered off* – if that's the right word to use! – thoughts about my vulnerability in such circumstances, stuck all night without any serious weapon to fend off potential thieves or criminals, not to mention a possible prowling predator that was in search of an evening meal!

Peter and I had spoken about this after he rescued me that morning, and we discussed getting a firearm permit for me, but for which type of weapon?

"There is only one that I'd feel completely okay with, no matter what attacked me, whether human or animal, and that is a double-barrel sawn-off shotgun!" Peter had said. "And I'll put some feelers out for you. Even if you never have to use it, it will give you a comforting feeling of protection. I'll call you as soon as I have managed to locate a suitable one."

The necessary orders were placed for the building materials, which I could collect when I was in Bulawayo the following week.

While it was still on my mind, I tried to get through to Peter at the police compound.

Unfortunately, he was out on patrol, but I spoke with Pete Ruck, who said he'd pass on the message, and also keep an eye open for a sawn-off shotgun – perhaps a gunsmith he knew might be able to 'adapt' one for me.

I'd just finished my phoning session when there was a knock at the door, and I was greeted by Ryan and Staff.

"We were wondering when to start blasting and where, and if you want to stockpile any ore for the large ball mill."

"The way I see it, Ryan, is this: you are here for three days, trying to locate the best areas for us to mine, so we must blast today and again on Tuesday and Wednesday, in three different areas for test purposes. Although we will not be in full production and feeding ore into the Newmarch mill until next Monday, we could keep the ore temporarily in three different piles from the three test days. We would be able to gauge the potential value of the gold in each of these three chosen areas by watching the size of the 'gold tail' coming off the James Table."

"That's a clever idea," Ryan replied, "but you don't want awkward and unnecessary double handling of the ore rocks that would be hoisted to the surface. Each blast will be in a different area, and just big enough to dislodge two or three tons, but only one ton of which we will hoist up to the surface for testing gold values.

"And we can avoid double handling of the ore by planning it so: the first day's test ton of rocks would be railed by cocopan and tipped into the shute by the conveyor system, ready for feeding into the Newmarch ball mill. One ton of ore from the second day would remain in the cocopan by the shute ready for the second test. And the final ton of ore from the third area would be hoisted and tipped from the skip into the headgear hopper, ready for railing to the mill site for test number three.

"Then on Monday you gentlemen can start the tests, the large ball mill can crush ore from each of these test areas, and with Newmarch's keen eye you should be able to gauge the values coming off the James Table from the three sampled areas. If one of the areas is significantly richer than the others then that would give you a good indication that you should start full daily blasting at that particular section in the mine."

"That makes good sense, Ryan. Okay, that's settled then, and I'll leave it all up to you and Staff to supervise our blasting plans over the next three days."

"Actually, that would entail me being here for the Thursday morning as well, which is fine by me, but it's best if I phone the mining commissioner and request that it is important for me to stay a further day to complete my assessment of the Nelly 404 mine. He's bound to say yes, as I'll convince him that without a full three-day trial the Bulawayo Mines Department wouldn't have enough data if the advisory boards requested more information regarding the application for your loan – that should do it; he is dead scared of blotting his copybook and damaging his career path!"

Eventually, the telephone bird started its shrill warbling, and Ryan was able to confirm that he would be with us until Thursday.

. . .

The mining complex was running smoothly; everybody knew their job and the junior boss boys kept them at their daily *gwazas*.

Underground, the jackhammer boys were drilling the holes in the first section of the quartz reef; the drilling was going much slower than when we test-drilled in the banded ironstone reef the week before, due to the hardness of the quartz.

Staff had organised two teams of jackhammer boys, and was rotating them every hour in order for them to finish so that we could blast by late afternoon.

Crispin was helping Marianne to lay the thick wire-reinforced rubber mats in the back of Joseph's blue pick-up. He was very particular about keeping his vehicle in mint condition, so we didn't want any unwelcome denting damage done when loading the concrete blocks to be carried to his house site for building.

On my way to collect the boys' rations in Gwelo, I called into see Peter at the police compound.

He took down a statement from me concerning Nelson, who had attacked me at the *indaba* court.

"He'll be held here for another two weeks before the magistrate conducts his monthly session, on the charge of attacking you with intent to cause bodily harm."

"And if he had hit me with that rock, I would have laid a charge against him for attempted murder!"

"Or, I would have had to charge him – for your actual murder!" quipped Pete.

I felt like a lazy day, and took my time continuing on to Gwelo to collect rations, supplies and goods for the mine shop – not forgetting that special tin of snuff for Staff that I'd promised him.

I drove down to Matt's mine to see how he was getting on and to tell him of our progress on the Nelly 404.

He was not in a very good mood, and told me that the three-month funding from his father ran out a few days before, and he was still none the wiser whether to continue mining or not – the values were so patchy and his enthusiasm was waning.

"If I had a proven mine like Cain's or an exciting development like you have on the Nelly 404, I'd be as happy as a pig in shit, but that's life, I guess. You have a great set-up at the moment; you've swapped Dreamer Joseph for an experienced gold miner, Mr Newmarch, while Joseph is away for six weeks on border duty. And now you tell me you've got an ex-Nelly 404 miner called Ryan from the Mines Department assisting you with underground development.

"Following your disastrous first five months, you've had two months of gold production from the small ball mill and are on the verge of running the Newmarch big mill full-time, three shifts a day. And on top of that, you've had a $10,000 cash injection from The Gold Plate Mine Company, who have an option to buy the Nelly 404 for $100,000! That's what I call an amazing turn around, and you've deserved it too, mate.

"Come on, buy me a beer to cheer me up. Pity we can't make a swap whereby I replace Joseph on the Nelly 404 and he takes over my mine here in Gwelo – you and I would make a much better team; you're almost like a brother!"

Well, the beers certainly cheered him up, and, when he met a few friends who were lunching at the Midland Hotel, I could see they were settling in nicely for a long afternoon session, so I took my leave and visited the supply stores with Crispin's shopping list on my way home.

. . .

Staff reported to me the next morning that the first blast was successful and the lashers were underground shovelling the rocks to fill the skip.

As I was handing him the tin of snuff, which put a smile on his face, the hoist started up and we saw the skip emerging from the shaft, followed by loud crashing noises as the rocks were emptied into the hopper and down into the waiting cocopan, which was pushed along the rail embankment, where, at the Newmarch ball mill site, the cocopan tipped the rocks onto the shute by the conveyor system.

"Quartz Reef Test No. 1 – for milling on Monday," he uttered contentedly.

It was a good feeling too, watching and knowing that the cocopan had offloaded ore that could contain an ounce or more of gold – very satisfying.

Ryan, Staff and I were discussing the day's *gwazas* when a Land Rover pulled up – a brand-new one too – and, as the door opened, I read the door logo:

The Gold Plate Mine
Bulawayo, Rhodesia

"Good morning, Ernest; let me introduce you to Ryan from the Bulawayo Mines Department."

Ryan shook hands with Roksplitzer as I explained why he had come this morning.

"As you know, Ryan, The Gold Plate Mine Company has a three-month option to buy the Nelly 404, and Ernest has been surveying our mine in order to produce a report for his company on the long-term viability of the 404. His first sampling results on the banded ironstone reef a couple of weeks ago averaged 5–6 dwt."

"Yes, that's what we averaged month in, month out from the mine," said Ryan. "Consistency personified, giving a good monthly cash flow."

"So I thought it would be a good idea, Ryan, if Ernest came out and spent the day with you and Staff underground. He should be able to get a thorough insight and first-hand knowledge of the different reefs in the mine, their compositions and potential ore reserves, especially the quartz reefs that we are working on at present."

As Ernest was walking back to his Land Rover to get his overalls and mining hat, Ryan whispered to me, "Certainly looks as if they've got money. A brand new out-of-the-box Land Rover, which they must have imported from South Africa."

"Well Ryan, let me know later what you think of him. He seems very competent and has recently joined The Gold Plate Mine Company from working for Anglo American Gold Mines down south."

I joined Marianne, who was having the pick-up loaded with concrete blocks.

"It's amazing, you know, but those blocks only cost us five cents each in materials. Our new bungalow, when it's ready, will use about 3,000 blocks maximum, so excluding the cost of the roof, timber and windows, that's a spacious three-bedroomed bungalow for a mere $150!"

"Well, let's have two then, one each!" she joked. "His and hers, each with their own garage for their own Rolls Royces – Dave would like that!"

When offloading the blocks at Joseph's site, Langton called me over to where he was finishing the last corner of the new foundations.

"Are you sure, Boss, that these are the right measurements? The rooms are smaller than the huts in the village!"

"Langton, Boss Joseph gave you that house plan; just get on with it so that it's complete before he returns."

"Okay Boss."

"Marianne, tell you what, with Crispin running the small ball mill, Newmarch working away on his own, and Staff, Ryan and Ernest underground in the Nelly 404, I've been made completely redundant for the day. Fabulous. Let's take the kids up to the dam. It's Fish Wednesday; there'll be quite a crowd there. It'll be fun. Come on, let's go!

"I've also arranged with the geologist, Ernest, from The Gold Plate Mine Company to meet me there on his way from our mine when he heads back to Bulawayo. We'll have a beer together and discuss his findings and views on mining the quartz reef at the Nelly 404 – that could be the icing on the cake, as they had initially planned to mine only the lower grade banded ironstone reef. So, fingers crossed!"

Des and Irene were there, and, as always, Irene updated Marianne on all the local gossip, which gave Des and me a chance to talk about cattle ranching.

He thought it was a great idea if we managed to sell the mine, and was really enthusiastic.

"Just make sure, though, if you do take over a cattle ranch, that there are no bloody gold miners on the property!" he quipped.

Around 4 o'clock, Ernest drove up, his brand new Land Rover causing quite a stir.

Parked amongst the dusty, and some rusty old Jeeps and pick-ups, it shone and sparkled like a diamond.

A couple of the ranchers immediately engaged in conversation with him. The bonnet was lifted up and, for half an hour or more, there was a constant exchange of information, facts and figures about engines, performance and horse power, etc., etc.

It turned out that Ernest was a Land Rover fanatic as well.

When I eventually managed to prise him away from the other motor enthusiasts, he said to me, "You've got a good set-up out here, and to have a local club by the dam where all the ranchers and the miners drink and socialise is an extra bonus. I can't put that in the final report, of course, but I will certainly mention it to Dickie Bird when we are discussing the pros and cons of buying your mine. After what I've seen today, and heard from Ryan of the Mines Department, together with the initial assay results of the samples that I took last time on the banded ironstone reef, I can tell you, *off the record, of course*, that my findings are quite positive. Well, let me get off now, but I'll be out again in two to three weeks to take some further quartz reef samples, to be included in my final survey report to my company at the end of June."

"That sounds promising, Ernest, and I look forward to that visit. Just phone me the day before you want to come so that I can arrange a few quiet hours underground for you to complete your assaying tasks."

One last beer with Des and Irene before we bought some bream for a good old traditional English fish and chips supper, and some fish rations for the boys as well, so that they could eat the fish while it was still fresh, cooking it in their own particular traditional ways.

. . .

I got up early, even before the start gong was struck, as I was keen to hear from Ryan how the day had gone.

Were there any problem areas?

Did Ernest make any negative remarks?

Did Ryan feel that Ernest would recommend that the sale went through?

All of these questions were buzzing through my mind as I walked through the bush up to the mine.

Ryan was sitting with Newmarch in the reception hut drinking tea.

"Good morning to you both."

But, before I could pose any of the questions, he jumped up and eagerly told me that Ernest thought the Nelly 404 had good potential, and his report would recommend that the option to buy the mine be taken up at the end of June – which was just the news I was hoping to hear!

"I've really had a great four days out here working on my old Nelly 404. It brought back some good memories too. I'd like to come again, perhaps on a Saturday morning next month, and catch up on your latest developments."

"Any time, Ryan, any time at all. Would you like some breakfast before you leave?"

"Next time; now, all I want to do is to get back home and climb into a nice hot bath."

"Okay, have a safe trip, and we'll meet again in a month's time."

We shook hands and he drove off towards Fort Rixon.

"He is a good miner," Newmarch remarked, "and I enjoyed his company too. With yesterday's blast, we now have ore from the three test areas of the quartz reef, and on Monday we can start milling them through my ball mill, and check the visible gold from each test coming off the James Table. Then it's for you to choose which quartz reef area you want to start mining to provide 10 tons of ore per day to be put through my mill, starting next Tuesday."

All of a sudden, there was instant quietness – the small mill had stopped abruptly.

Newmarch and I looked at each other, surprised, and walked over to the mill.

"*Bugger it!* That temperamental switchboard has blown again; that's the end of its use on this mine, and a day earlier than we had planned, but we can't waste time trying to fix it now."

"No, there's no point, but it was lucky that it only happened today and not weeks ago! Mr Newmarch, would you be able to start dismantling it now? Then I'll phone the transport company; maybe they can pick it up tomorrow instead of Saturday. And don't let's forget that it's been a major help to us over the past two months while you've been busy getting the Newmarch mill site ready for full operation – we've had two months' gold production from it, and in reality it has saved our mining venture! Last month was 12½ ounces; that's $1,250 into our bank account, and, when I clean up the copper plate shortly and retort the gold amalgam, hopefully it'll register 15 ounces of pure gold when I take it tomorrow to the Assay office in Bulawayo."

"Yes, luck seems to be on your side now; that's the way small worker gold mining goes – you can never be completely sure of what's going to happen tomorrow."

"Yes, and I'm learning all the time how fragile a mine's production can be, like today, for example, and that's why I employed another electrician/welder last week, because most of the problems we've experienced over April and May have been electrical faults, and when you're not here, Mr Newmarch, I couldn't rely on one sole electrician."

Newmarch spent the afternoon dismantling the small ball mill set-up, whilst I scraped the gold amalgam from the copper plate in the extraction room.

"Hey, Mr Newmarch, it feels bigger than last time!"

"You're getting that incurable eye disease!" He laughed.

"And what is that?"

"It's like the fishermen, always imagining that the fish is bigger than it really is, especially the one that got away! Same as the gold miners, dreaming of the mother lode… the one that…!"

Imagination or not, it felt heavier and I was very happy as I took the leather pouch with its golden contents back to the house – the end to an unusual and very varied day; a mix of bad luck and good luck!

. . .

It was sad to see the small ball mill leave our mine to be transported to the Mines Department yard, but it had bridged a two-month gap, helping us to stay afloat while we waited, seemingly forever, for the delivery of the large Newmarch ball mill.

I just hoped that the service and extra costs of repairs to the switchboard would be reasonable; we didn't want any more nasty surprises when Ronnie started work on it before it could be returned to the Fair Deal mine as agreed.

However, in its place, ready and waiting, was Big Brother – the Newmarch ball mill, which could mill 30 tons of ore per day, 10 times more than the small ball mill; the difference between good profit… and loss, with the closure of our mine!

I watched Newmarch standing quietly on the rail embankment, with the inevitable cigarette between his fingers, staring at his invention, but not hoping and dreaming anymore – **his dreams had come true!**

. . .

Do you know what it's like to carry a lump of raw gold in your pocket?

I do; it's an amazing feeling, and, as I climbed the wooden steps and entered the Bank Assay office, I could literally feel the excitement and commotion caused by miners of the past when they came into town on their donkeys to convert their hard-earned gold to cash.

For many of them, that yellow metal was quickly swapped for other enjoyable colours of entertainment as they indulged themselves – the golden browns of malt whisky, and the blonde, brunette and redhead women they desired in the saloons.

The Assay results made it an even better day – more than last month's output!

The gold sponge was weighed and recorded as 15¼ ounces, our account being credited with 14 ounces of pure gold.

No whisky or women for me, though; that $1,400 would go straight to our creditors to pay off outstanding accounts – but it was also a good feeling knowing that our debts would be completely cancelled shortly, when the second cheque of $5,000 from The Gold Plate Mine Company contract settled in our post box.

Then at the end of next month… three best guesses – from Newmarch, Ryan and myself – pointed to around 60 to 70 ounces of gold being produced by the Newmarch ball mill milling ore from the quartz reef.

After monthly mining costs and wages, more than half of that would be profit, at least $3,000 – three thousand dollars; looks even more when written in words, and sounds even better when pronounced very, very slowly: "Three… thousand… dollars!"

With a golden hue in my eyes and a smile on my face, just like those miners of the past I'm sure, I headed straight for the saloon – the Greys Inn pub.

I love the buzz, the hum of conversation and the laughter that fills the air, especially on a Friday lunchtime when the bar is packed solid by ranchers, miners and office workers.

Dave announced loudly, "As the men's toilets are being renovated, you'll have to use the women's instead." This raised some audacious comments!

"But please, please behave yourselves; knock politely, and shut the door of the cubicle you use. There shouldn't be any problems at all; there's only two old ladies staying in the hotel, so it's mainly for you blokes in the bar."

Dave could see from my smile that I'd had a good day at the Bank Assay office.

"Good for you, mate; so this month's gold was even more than your first month's. Fabulous. So you better start building the garage for the Rolls Royce!"

"Well Dave, I've got hundreds of cement blocks and I'm producing more by the day, because the garage will have to be big enough for the wife's as well!"

"And for a house for the chauffeurs!" ….

And so the friendly joking continued as one or two of the locals joined in.

The noise level in the bar was steadily rising as more and more men poured into the pub – one of them, I'd only met half an hour before at the Bank Assay office; he was mining for gold near West Nicholson.

"Hello Inaki," Dave called out to him. "Come over here; have a drink with me and a fellow gold miner who has just come from the Assay office with a smile on his face."

"Drinks are on me, for the whole bar!" Inaki called out. "We've hit a rich vein and our output of gold this month has almost doubled!"

"You must have been buying illegal gold and adding it to your output figures!"

"But double very little, is *very, very little!"* ….

And other such comments caused laughter all around.

"Let them laugh," Inaki said to me. "I was laughing all the way to the Assay office today, and I'll be laughing even more when I next check my bank balance! But excuse me for a minute, mate; I'm bursting – got to go and 'splash me takkies'. Where's the 'Gents'?"

"The 'Gents' are being renovated, Inaki!" Dave shouted above the noise. "You'll have to use the women's toilets in the foyer."

A few minutes later, we heard a loud, piercing scream. The pub went silent as everyone looked towards the doorway into the foyer….

Suddenly, Inaki came rushing into the bar!

The bar hushed as he tried to regain control of himself; he was crying with laughter.

"I went to the women's toilet," he gasped, "and was standing there pointing Percy at the porcelain pot when the door opened. Suddenly, this woman screamed and shouted, *'This is for ladies only'!* I spun around with Percy still in hand and replied, *'And so is* ***this****, madam'!*"

The uproar as the bar exploded with noise, cheering and laughter; it was pure madness, and probably the funniest thing anybody had heard for ages.

Needless to say, Inaki became more inebriated as the afternoon wore on. Beer after beer was bought for him, men still laughing at what had happened; it was such an amusing story, with an incredibly funny punchline – *'And so is* ***this****, madam'!*

It was hard to drag myself away from such a convivial crowd, but I had to get back to the mine.

As I pulled into my driveway, I had a nice surprise.

Des and Irene were sitting on the terrace with Marianne enjoying a sundowner.

A cold beer for me was also very welcome. I had such a dry throat after the hot, dusty two-hour drive from Bulawayo.

I told them the story of the old lady and the gold miner in Greys Inn.

Des shook with laughter, gasping for breath; he just couldn't stop – until Irene put an ice cube down the back of his shirt!

That story started off a whole chain of amusing incidents, as they often do, and, as one finished, another would start, and then spark off yet another… and so on.

A wonderful evening and a pub story to remember – *forever!*

. . .

The Saturday morning session with Crispin was as informative as ever – he was a similar source of gossip to the joint party line, but limited only to the happenings on our mine and in our village compound.

There was an unusual quietness on the mine after so much activity had been going on during the past week.

Visits by Ryan and Roksplitzer, both enhancing our chances of selling the mine.

The small ball mill breakdown on the very last day of the two-month free loan period.

Followed by dismantling and transporting it to the Mines Yard in Bulawayo.

Underground blasting of the quartz reefs for sampling the potential ore reserves.

And this coming week I had plenty to look forward to:

The Newmarch ball mill test runs this Monday.

The new ball mill complex and concentration/extraction rooms being completed ready for full-scale gold production operations starting on the Tuesday.

These promised to be landmark events for the mine – and our futures!

And now on this Saturday afternoon there was nothing going on; two free days for our workers. It was strange indeed – they could be seen either in the village or lying around near the office chatting to each other; everyone seemed to be enjoying the unexpected break.

The appearance of several women brandishing metal mugs signalled the start of the weekend's frolicking – it was as if they could smell the beer from miles away, and, gradually, we heard a faint noise getting louder; the distant diesel rumble of the Chibuku lorry approaching.

That was the sound they'd all been waiting for, and they gathered expectantly around the office area knowing that the weekend partying would soon start.

Crispin had arranged it so that today there would be three drums of Chibuku beer available using our *'barman for the day/selling the beer system'*, and at Sunday lunchtime the extra free drum of 25 gallons would be served by Crispin himself.

"It's best that I am the barman on Sunday; otherwise, there would be chaos. The thought of free Chibuku always causes lots of pushing and shoving to be first in line – before the beer runs out!"

I left them all to get on with it. I was intending to enjoy these two days off as well, just pottering around the house and in the garden with the family.

Marianne's vegetable garden was beginning to bear fruits – well, vegetables, actually, of course!

And the herb garden, which was Marie-Louise's hobby, was flourishing nicely.

It made a welcome change to have fresh carrots, potatoes and tomatoes to add to our culinary dishes, together with the cabbage and rape that Feet provided.

Elliot and Marianne between them were cooking up some very tasty dishes, both on and in the wood stove.

We currently had quite a long list of items available on our menu.

Reedbuck and duiker when available, providing us with fillet and legs to roast; bream fish; the odd guinea fowl, which, combined with all the different types of vegetables and potatoes, led to a proliferation of different dishes.

Stews, roasts, meat pies and shepherds pies; all good, tasty meals, which were enjoyed, as well as keeping us healthy.

I helped Jeffrey build a compound enclosure on the grass for his giant leopard tortoises to prevent them crawling back into the bush. It was about five metres by five metres using concrete blocks, with a small shelter in the corner.

He had three of these half-metre-long tortoises now; Sue 1, Sue 2 and Thomas 1, which he watched with pride as they slowly roamed around in his tortoise enclosure.

I think he got the name 'Thomas' wrong, though, because Thomas had laid an egg! And Jeffrey built a special area for mother Thomas and the yet-to-be-hatched egg.

This weekend was the quiet before the storm, and I took every opportunity to relax on the veranda, reading the *Daily Telegraph* airmail editions that my mother sent me regularly from England.

Some of the stories and articles printed *were very disturbing.*

The English press blasted our prime minister, Ian Smith, for his illegal white racial government, which had to be toppled, no matter what, and as quickly as possible!

They praised Mugabe for his efforts for freeing his people using his Liberation Army.

The stories about his terrorists' brutal rapings and killings hardly filled one paragraph – and even then they were described as the odd unfortunate result arising from the conflict. And if there was a detailed incident, it was not about acts of terrorism, but about how Mugabe had to use force for the sake of future democracy in Rhodesia – ***'What a load of bollocks!'***

And yet, further down the same page, British reports slammed the Irish for their murderous acts of terrorism carried out in London, UK using the Irish Liberation Army IRA!

What's in a name; just buzzwords to suit their own political stances – crazy world!

. . .

The start of a critical week and the start of an exciting month ahead that would seal my destiny.

Would I be stuck in a partnership with Joseph if the sale didn't go through?

Or would I become a cattle rancher or start another gold mining venture if the sale was concluded successfully?

The start gong sounded even louder this Monday morning, and, judging by some of the mine boys' reactions to this loud noise, there were a few sore heads from the weekend revelry.

Newmarch looked spritely and couldn't wait to get on with the morning's test trial runs of the ore from different parts of the quartz reefs.

The motors started up and the lashers began to shovel the ore of Quartz Reef Test No. 1 from the shute onto the conveyer belt, which took the ore and fed it into the awaiting Newmarch ball mill, when the thunderous clattering noises took over.

Staff, Newmarch and I gathered around the James Table in the extraction room.

The 'tail' of the gold particles as they merged together to form a golden snake could be seen edging down the side of the vibrating table and into a collection pot.

"About an ounce to the ton of pure quartz ore, I reckon," stated Newmarch, and a nodding head from Staff concurred.

The ore from the second quartz reef area was tipped from the waiting cocopan onto the shute and fed via the conveyor system into the mill.

The two wise men looked a little disappointedly at the gold tail from this test area; it was definitely less than on the first run.

Meanwhile, the cocopan had been pushed back along the rails to the headgear to be filled with ore from the hopper – Test No. 3.

Newmarch lit up his first cigarette of the day; it was gone 9 o'clock, and he couldn't believe in all the excitement that he hadn't had a cigarette hanging from his lips whilst he worked – which was the norm.

Squeaking wheels announced the return of the cocopan, which emptied its contents of ore from the third test area to be fed into the ball mill.

Smiles all around again as we watched the gold tail, all agreeing that it was about the same as the Quartz Reef Test No. 1.

"Of course," Newmarch began, "to clarify the situation, these one-ton tests of quartz ore have been selective. The lashers having time to sort out the quartz ore from the other rocks, so they are actually giving a false expectation, because when we're blasting day in day out the lashers won't have the time to sort out the ore. They will just shovel any rock that is dislodged by the blasting into the wheel barrows.

"Depending on the width of the quartz reef lens, the values will be diluted by the mass of the accompanying non-gold-bearing rocks that are blasted out. But having said that, it should yield us maybe three ounces per single day shift, and if we hit a wider lens pocket it could yield four to five ounces – and if we hit a rich vein of gold… so let's keep our fingers crossed!"

I smiled as I saw Newmarch's eyes twinkle, growing wider and wider as he watched, captivated by the visible gold tail, perhaps envisaging the miners' dream – of hitting the mother lode!

"Staff, get your jackhammer boys to start drilling in the first quartz area to enable us to blast late this afternoon, so that the lashers can start shovelling tomorrow, when we can run our first eight-hour milling shift using the big ball mill."

Newmarch wanted only one shift a day during this start-up month, so that it would be easy to monitor both machinery and gold production.

Also, we'd make Sunday a day off for the workers, giving Newmarch a day each week to check, clean up and make any necessary adjustments to his mill.

We'd monitor the quartz reef mining, and, if the quartz lenses began to peter out, we'd switch to mining the banded ironstone reef instead, which was closer to the main shaft as well.

So either way, we'd be mining enough payable ore to keep all of us happy.

The following month, we'd run two shifts, or possibly three shifts – we'd play it by ear.

After lunch, I phoned French and told him that we would begin milling with the Newmarch ball mill in the morning.

He sounded very pleased, and I could imagine his relief to know that at last his 'baby' – the Newmarch ball mill invention – which had been in labour for many months, had finally been born, and would be crushing ore for many years to come.

The heavy financial burden that French had been carrying on his shoulders for so long would also be removed – costs were covered.

My invitation to him to come out to the mine on Wednesday was gratefully accepted.

"If you arrive about 10 o'clock, we can spend a couple of hours seeing the Ridge Top Mine in full operation, with your star attraction, the Newmarch ball mill, crushing ore from the second level underground. Later, we can go and have lunch at the Fort Rixon dam club with Marianne; it'll make a nice and informative day out for you, and from there it's an easy hour's drive back to Bulawayo."

"I'll be there, and I'll bring my wife as well; it'll be good for her to see the Newmarch ball mill in action, and working on an operating gold mine. It will also allay some of her concerns for the never-ending, money-consuming, Newmarch protégé project, and give her faith in K.B. Davies' plans for further sales of the Newmarch ball mill to other mines to replace some of the ageing 5-stamps."

"And we will be a good endorsement for it too, so you're welcome to bring any prospective customers out to see the Newmarch ball mill in action – anytime."

Staff came to the house and reported that the day's drilling was complete and they were ready to blast.

"This would be a major one, dislodging around 10 to 12 tons. Everybody will feel this explosion through their feet, and, as it's a special 'first' so to speak, why not bring little Jeffrey over and he can push the plunger down again."

Small kids have ears as large as elephants, and, from inside the house, we heard: "I'm coming, I'm coming now. Thanks, I can blow up the mine again!"

And he was lifted by Staff onto the pick-up and we drove up to the mine.

Minutes later, the plunger of the control box was plunged down hard, with all the force that a three-year-old boy could muster.

BOOM!

"I feel the earth move under my feet; I see the stars come a tumbling down…"

I instinctively started singing this *Carole King* hit song on feeling the strong vibrations reverberating through my body.

A successful blast would provide enough ore for the Tuesday shift.

The lashers would shovel and wheelbarrow the rocks to the skip tomorrow, when the dust had cleared.

. . .

Have you ever had that feeling of butterflies in your stomach, that nervous excitement before a big event that is about to happen, whether it be a school exam, an important football or rugby match – or, for some, a wedding day?

Well, today was such a day.

THE FIRST FULL DAY'S RUNNING OF THE NEWMARCH SMALL WORKER BALL MILL CRUSHER!

Much, and many people, depended on its success, and today could well see the making or breaking of:

+ Mr Newmarch;

+ Mr French;

+ The sale to The Gold Plate Mine Company;

+ And also for the Ridge Top Mine! A possible looming massive setback for both Joseph and myself – a financial disaster!

However, for us, we were still young and in our early 30s, with years of computer experience, and there were plenty of jobs in the IT industry down south.

Mr French had once said to me: "You're lucky; if the gold mining doesn't work out, you have a back-up in the computer industry. For most small worker gold miners, it's a case of shit or bust!"

But fortunately the back-up plan was not necessary. The Newmarch mill purred away; the metal balls smashed the ore to dust to allow the gold particles to be washed across the vibrating James Table, producing a thin gold tail sliding down the left-hand side of the table and into the collection pot – our mini bank!

The day was a complete success, and happy, contented smiles creased the faces of the main hard-working protagonists: Newmarch, Staff, Crispin and me.

We had no way of getting the news to the fifth protagonist, my partner, Joseph, who in reality had, for several months, been little more than a sleeping partner – in all senses of the word! And now, on such a successful day for our mine, he was somewhere on the border helping to protect all Rhodesians against the Mugabe madness and his cowardly comrades with their hit and run inhumane killings, torture and intimidation.

I hoped Joseph would use his Scarlet Pimpernel skills of '*they seek him here, they seek him there'* – to avoid being shot at by terrorist insurgents, and that we'd see him back safely at Ridge Top Mine in a few weeks' time, when we could all celebrate together… the month of June's gold output… and…?

. . .

A bottle of milk, a loaf of bread and a newspaper were handed to me by Doug French as he alighted from his vehicle. And, putting a smile on the younger generation's faces, a large bag of sweets, Liquorish Allsorts, and some chocolate cupcakes were given to them by Mrs French.

Over the next two hours, we made a tour of the surface mining operations, the highlight being the dark green Newmarch ball mill – the noisy beast that had caused so many sleepless nights for us all.

"In my dreams, or rather nightmares," Mrs French began, "it wasn't green, but bright red with horns, and flames were coming out of it, not gold!"

We swapped other nightmares and relevant stories that had frequently occurred over the long, drawn-out three-month period, when every day it was the same questions, which were never fully answered.

However, watching the Newmarch mill rumbling away, all that was in the past and we could witness, like the alchemist's dream – *rocks being turned into gold!*

A lunch on the lawns of the Fort Rixon club cemented our relationship completely, and Mrs French was now even more enthusiastic than her husband.

She envisaged booming sales of the Newmarch ball mill as more old mines opened up, there being very few 5-stamp mills available in Rhodesia.

We raised our glasses to the success of the ball mill, and to Ridge Top Mine, and then, having purchased some fresh fish, two three-pounder bream, they set off home to Bulawayo.

. . .

Simon phoned early in the morning; the grey pick-up that was involved in the zebra crash was ready for collection.

Although it was a hefty bill, I would only have to pay $100 excess to the insurance company – it's always essential to have fully comprehensive insurance cover, and a friendly car repairer!

I drove up to the mine to discuss with Newmarch and Staff the planned day's operations, and to let them know that I'd be away in Bulawayo to collect the repaired grey Peugeot pick-up.

And, to my surprise, I saw a dusty old pick-up parked in front of the office, and, as I opened the door, there was an even greater surprise – Mr 10%!

"Well, well, I haven't seen you for almost two months, not since the signing of The Gold Plate Mine Company sale contract!"

"You don't have to be so sarcastic!" Ray barked. "I too have a mine to run! But what pleases me is to see that you've got the whole mining operation on the go; you've done a really good job," he said in his smarmy manner. "I've been looking at the production logbook that Crispin keeps, and in both April and May you managed to produce around 15 ounces of gold from the small ball mill. That's good, and goes a long way to covering our monthly costs."

Our costs, I thought. *Now it's* ***our mine*** *again; he's done bugger all to earn the 10% that he stole from us!*

A cold stare from Ray focussed on me – did I just say that out loud? It was as if he could read my mind.

"I know what you're thinking, and like it or not, a deal is a deal – *and* it's recorded in the minutes of our first directors' board meeting. Tough! So get used to it."

Then, instant transformation; the icy glare vanished, the eyes sparkled and lit up again, and the familiar devious look took over – that look I'd seen several times before, and under several different circumstances:

"I'm going to convince you…"

"I'm going to screw you…"

"I've just thought of a new opportunity to rip you off…"

"I'll make you an offer…" That is the one I hated to hear the most!

But I wondered which one of these he was going to use.

"Listen, Staff tells me that Newmarch and the Mines Department engineer, Ryan, reckon the output for June could be as much as 60 to 70 ounces!" he exclaimed. "Which would be fantastic; more than half of that will be *our first profits*!"

Here we go again; ***our profits***, I thought.

And he was now in full sales mode flow.

"So if it turns out to be a 70 ounce month while you are running just the one shift per day, just think of our profit when we run three shifts, 24 hours a day around-the-clock!"

A smile creased his lips; his thin black Clark Gable moustache adjusted accordingly, and I swear I saw 'dollar signs' in his eyes.

"Yes! Yes, wonderful!" he reiterated – it was almost like listening to his son, Joseph.

He was now bubbling with enthusiasm, and fidgeting around as he blurted out, "Okay! I'm going to leave you now; got plenty of things to do. Life is just one long contest, rearranging this, swapping that, and I have to sort out some pressing family business, and quickly too! I must go now to see Matt, who has cost me a lot of money. You probably don't know, but I funded him for three months and it looks like we'll have to close one of the family mines down; a big loss of *my money,* which I must find ways of recuperating!"

He spun on his heel, climbed into his pick-up, shouted at the two of his workers who were chatting to Crispin, and drove off with one of them running alongside the pick-up whilst his friend was trying to pull him up into the back… but he lost a shoe.

They banged hard on the driver's cab, and we saw the brake lights come on as the vehicle slid to a halt.

"Hurry up!" Ray shouted as the mine boy legged it back to where his shoe was lying on the road, but, when he sat down to put it on, that irritated Mr Worry in a Hurry to such an extent that he hooted loudly again… and again – and then drove off.

The bemused African just sat there, staring in disbelief that Ray had left him behind sitting in the road.

"I've seen that happen before," Staff pronounced. "He'll have to stay with us until he can get a lift back to Belingwe, but he can work here until then; these are all family mines."

As I drove back to the house to collect Marianne and the kids, odd, disturbing words that had been said today kept recurring and flashing through my mind: "*Our mine; our profits*; recuperating *my money*; these are all *family mines…*"

Marianne drove me to Bulawayo, with Elliot, Willias and the kids in the back.

First stop was to see Simon.

The old grey pick-up looked well repaired; there was no trace that it had been in a bad crash. But the only weird thing was – it was black!

On seeing my reaction, Simon said, "Black was the nearest colour to grey that I had in my storeroom; hope you don't mind, but it allowed me to make a bit of profit. The insurance companies are very tight on costs for car accident repairs. The black paint was left over from a previous insurance claim – the Bulawayo Crematorium hearse! Are you happy with that?"

I had to smile, and climbed into the pick-up.

"When I'm sitting inside, I can't see the black sides or the black body, but I want you to put another colour on the bonnet, beige or white; I can't drive for hundreds of kilometres looking at a black bonnet in front of me, sorry – it's a bit morbid looking."

"I've got some dark beige paint I can respray the bonnet with, so next time you come into Bulawayo, drop it off early and I'll do it right away. Oh, and I also fixed the floorboards, and blocked the dangerous 'snake hole'!"

"That bloody snake hole! Let me tell you, Simon, I had a harrowing journey from the explosives dump after running over a black mamba snake, on purpose, but when I looked in my rear-view mirror I couldn't see the flattened snake on the road. Instantly, your story about snakes coming through that bloody hole came into my mind, and panic set in. I stuffed a handkerchief into that gap by the clutch pedal to prevent the snake slipping inside, but for the whole journey I kept glancing down at the clutch pedal, and I sweated all the way back to the mine, and arrived feeling totally knackered!"

Simon laughed. "And I was only joking!"

At the builders' yard, we loaded both pick-ups with the ordered timber for Joseph's house, the windows and the doors.

After shopping – meat rations, beans and meal and a list of items for Crispin's mine store – we set off for Fort Rixon, 'the hearse' Peugeot 404 leading the way.

The stop-off at Fort Rixon Post Office provided a very welcome piece of news – well, piece of paper, actually; a $5,000 cheque, part two of our loan from the sale contract with The Gold Plate Mine Company.

Although it was a large amount, it didn't really put that much of a smile on my face – the FIVE ZERO ZERO ZERO would virtually instantly become a BIG FAT ZERO after the suppliers' overdue accounts had been cleared.

However, the anticipated gold output for the month of June should provide us with a good $3,000 profit.

And when we stepped up from one shift to two shifts a day… and later around-the-clock milling 24 hours a day, seven days a week, even healthier monthly profits would follow – and that would definitely make a huge teeth-flashing smile spread from ear to ear!

Both Ryan from the Mines Department and Ernest Roksplitzer from The Gold Plate Mine Company had endorsed the projected ore reserves, which should provide a future gold output from the Nelly 404 that would reward us handsomely for all our hard work – whether it be a regular profitable monthly income or a $100,000 windfall if the sale was concluded.

So that was the current status; we had the two very attractive situations, and it was now heading towards a question of the proverbial *'to be or not to be'* – the balancing of the scales:

'Gold output' versus *'sale money input'*.

Both parties having the option to choose – either confirming or pulling out of the sale by 5 July.

After months and months of battling against the odds, the latest throwing of the Newmarch dice had given us **two great options to bank on**! To bank on in both senses of the word! And life was getting really exciting.

. . .

Elliot made us some tea and we sat outside on the veranda as the sun came up, the rays first illuminating the tree tops, then gradually moving down the trees to the bushes, and, finally, creeping across the grass towards us – always an enthralling, uplifting early morning treat to watch.

The one thing it didn't light up, though, was the black 404; it looked menacing.

"We're going to have to change that colour," I irritably iterated. "It spooks me; it's hearse graveyard black!"

"Or," quipped Marianne, "we just never wash it, and in a few days it will be a sandy dirt road dust colour!"

She had a point, but I'd just have to park it around the other side of the house for now – so it didn't spoil these early morning sun-ups, until Simon repainted the bonnet a beige colour.

I climbed inside, started the engine and drove out of our compound following Marianne on the way to Gwelo, but I couldn't get used to the black bonnet constantly in my view, so I made sure that I drove very closely behind the blue pick-up for a while, so that the dust she kicked up had a better chance of toning down the hearse-black colour of the bonnet.

Jane was not at home, so I locked the blue Peugeot in the garage.

She had spare keys, and when she came back from Popette's place in Belingwe she would have wheels again.

Mr Crow, the bank manager, was all smiles as I handed him the $5,000 cheque to be deposited into our account, although, with his lazy eye problem, he extended his hand gingerly, until one of his eyes confirmed that the cheque could be grasped firmly!

He then leant across the table and congratulated me on the recent deposits that had been made from our gold output, and the two cheques from The Gold Plate Mine Company.

"I had a gut feeling that you were going to make a success of the mine, and now my faith in you has been justified. Your overdraft facility will be increased from today to a higher limit of $3,000 – it's always good to have a pot to dip into; cash flow is never constant in any business."

Over a leisurely lunch at La Chat restaurant, Marianne and I spoke about our sudden change of fortune.

"When you're battling, nobody really wants to know; money and credit are hard to come by. You literally have to beg for it – or die! But just look at it now; a little gold output, two fat cheques deposited, and now even the bank manager is chucking money at us – and long may it rain! Mr Crow might have a feeling of positive justification when he looks at our fat bank balance of today, but, after I've written out these cheques to our suppliers and dropped them off, he'll have a shock, as the large plus balance will have turned into an equally large minus in the red overdraft!"

We both felt good, however, when we walked into the Farm Aid store.

Instead of our usual rush, rush, pick, pick, sign the card and exit as bloody quickly as possible, today we took our time, slowly selecting what we required, and, when we came to the counter and the cashier gave me that 'your account is over the limit' stare, I handed her a cheque for the total outstanding balance.

This evoked a curious look on her face, and she double-checked the cheque I'd given her, suspiciously looking for anything that would make it invalid, because we had been regularly in the 120 days credit zone.

With a pencil, she lightly ticked the boxes, one by one:

Date: √ Amount: √ Amount in words: √ Payable to Farm Aid store: √

Signed: √

Then, with a big smile, she spoke. "Thank you, and are you going to pay for today's goods in cash?"

A burst of laughter simultaneously from both of us signified 'no', and she took our store card to update our just 'zeroed-out' business credit account.

Similar occurrences at the Midlands Bakery, Paramount Butchers and Miekels stores gave us a pleasant shopping outing for a change, and we left Gwelo with a pick-up full of mine rations and supplies, two monster candles about a foot high and four inches thick – they'd give such a soft, cosy light compared to the harsh flickering light of the hurricane lamps – together with other personal articles that we really needed.

When we were in the Miekels store, we looked at their range of refrigerators.

Once we had power at the new house when it was rebuilt, a fridge would be the first essential item we would buy.

A fridge is commonplace in every household in the towns and cities, and is taken for granted – it's a convenience, really, because you could actually go and buy fresh food each day.

But out in the bush we had neither of those options – so it would be a godsend.

. . .

Saturday's Ndebele session with Crispin at the house concentrated on words and sentences to be used when *'telling someone off'*, or *'you are fired, and will not get a reference letter from Ridge Top Mine'* – that would have been the most overused Ndebele phrase in the last few months, as I had already had to dismiss eight workers for various reasons, and firing them through an interpreter not only didn't feel right, but could also be misunderstood – this 'number of workers fired' didn't include of course the remnants of the 'gang of five' who were in jail and didn't get reference letters from us, nor the murdered Phillemon, who *definitely didn't need one!*

Suddenly, Jeffrey shouted, "Where's the egg; who stole my egg!"

We rushed over to the tortoise enclosure; the egg was not there and Jeffrey was very upset.

"Unfortunately," Crispin began, "the eggs of a tortoise are highly prized by the African, being a real delicacy, and are very easy to conceal, so we'll never be able to find out who stole it. If your giant tortoises weren't so big and heavy, they'd be stolen too; their flesh tastes like chicken."

"That's not fair; nobody is going to eat my Sue! Or Sue 2 or Thomas; we need an *askari* to look after my tortoises. I'll talk to Amon right now!" And he and Marie-Louise stormed off down the driveway, heading for the mine.

Beep, beep!

Then the kids came running back, shouting 'it's Uncle Matt', followed by our old white Peugeot 404.

"Thought I'd come out and see you. My father told me that the Newmarch ball mill was fully operational now; let's go over and see it."

A bottle of lemonade took Jeffrey's mind off the missing egg, and he climbed up into the back of Matt's pick-up.

"Your set-up here is good, and it's quite impressive as you drive out of the bush and in towards the offices to see that high railway embankment stretching from the headgear down to the ball mill site; it's very picturesque too."

We spent about an hour talking with Newmarch, who was keen to explain every nut and bolt of his invention. He was in seventh heaven, and said to Matt, "Happily it's all working well, and we're anticipating a good month of gold production, even running just the one daylight shift."

As we walked back up to the office, he confided in me. "Can you and I go off somewhere privately to talk? My father is confusing me and I'm not happy. I've got a cool box with some beers and some fishing rods; is there a dam nearby, nearer than Fort Rixon?"

"Yebo, it's about 10 minutes' drive down the Filabusi road, and it's very peaceful there. We won't be disturbed at all, except for the occasional splashing sound as you reel a fish in! Let's go!"

It was indeed peaceful; what a tranquil place for Matt to unload his troubled mind.

"As I told you before, my father funded me for three months so that I could determine the viability of my mine. A week ago, he stopped the free cash flow, and I told him that the mine was not worth carrying on with, and I was thinking of going to South Africa to look for a job. He told me that was that, he'd had enough of pouring money down the drain."

"A bloody big drain too!" I joked, breaking his tension, and he grinned.

"But now, just two days ago, he visits me again and tells me he's going to fund me for another month, and I should start up the mine again! It doesn't make sense. When I asked my father why, he said he was working on a new master plan that should come to fruition shortly, and then we'd all be mining and making money. More, he would not say; he just gave me a wad of cash to pay the workers to carry on again, and said in one month all would become clear.

"But I don't like it when he treats us all like puppets, pulling our strings at a whim, but it gives me another free month, but I won't be concentrating on the mine, though. I'll be busy phoning and writing letters to solicit a good job down south. Do you know of any good job agencies that I could contact in Johannesburg? I need to get away from my father; he's a control freak! He's never open about what he is doing either, and he had that *devious sparkle* in his eyes – which *always* spells danger!"

We fished away, pretty much in silence – is there any other way to fish?

Occasionally, he would come out with a comment or a question that didn't really make sense to me, but then again, he had to clear his mind, and the tranquillity and the cold beers certainly helped to do that.

A couple of hours later, a more relaxed and refreshed Matt dropped me off at the mine on his way back to Gwelo.

The shifts had finished, the Chibuku Brewery lorry had been and gone, and there was a happy buzz coming from the mine village.

I could see a wisp of smoke coming from the ball mill, which was strangely silent.

On investigating, I found Newmarch with a fag hanging from his lips, puffing away and flicking the cigarette up and down between his lips as he mumbled to himself – he looked very annoyed.

"Do we have a problem?" I posed the question.

Silence, apart from the odd puffing sound.

I looked at him quizzically, but got no response at all; it was as if he was on a faraway planet.

"We need bigger balls!" he suddenly erupted. "That's it; *bigger balls!* Don't you agree we need bigger balls?"

He ignored my laughter and then continued in his normal, calm manner, "Can we go to your house? I need to phone Salisbury urgently. We must have bigger balls – that's why the mill throughput is lower than expected; we need bigger, heavier balls to crush the ore quicker in order to achieve my stipulated output flow to the James Table."

A lengthy conversation ensued between Newmarch and the engineer of the MMC Company in Salisbury, with Newmarch scratching his head incessantly and scribbling down formulae and notes.

Eventually, his tense expression relaxed a little and he turned to me and asked, "Would you be kind enough to drive me to Salisbury tomorrow? I know it's a Sunday, but I need to collect some heavier balls from the Salisbury factory."

"Well, Newmarch, it's only about 3 o'clock now; why don't we leave immediately? We can stay overnight at Cain's mine and collect the balls from the factory early on Sunday morning. Ask them if 8 o'clock is possible, then after your meeting we've got an easy ride back to the mine, and you'll still have time to tinker with your ball mill in the afternoon, to ensure that the problem has been corrected before starting the Monday morning milling session."

The appointment was confirmed, and, 10 minutes later, Newmarch and I set off in the beige 404 – direction Salisbury.

Four hours later, we pulled up in front of Cain's house.

There were no lights on; that was strange, as the whole mine itself was ablaze with light, and the 5-stamp mill could be heard thundering away.

As we alighted from the vehicle, the house door opened and Zikki came out holding a hurricane lamp.

He was excited to see me and asked if this man with me was my grandfather.

A chuckling Newmarch proudly replied, "No, I am the inventor of the Newmarch ball mill."

Zikki showed us into the kitchen and lit another hurricane lamp.

"Problems, problems, problems! No power to the house, Mdevu! And Boss Cain has gone to Belingwe again. But I'll heat up some guinea fowl stew on the wood stove for you two, and the beers in the fridge should still be cold."

Such a super little man; Cain was lucky to have such an amazing cook/houseboy.

It wasn't long before the hurricane lamps were doused, allowing both darkness and sleep to consume us.

. . .

We got a little lost in the industrial area of Salisbury. Newmarch's recollection of where the factory was situated was poor, but we eventually found it, and apologised for being half an hour late.

Roger, the technical director of the company, met us, and was so pleased to hear first-hand from Newmarch that the mill was functioning well, and enquired, "No real teething problems then, Mr Newmarch?"

"I need bigger balls!"

"Don't we all?" mused Roger thoughtfully.

They sat for 30 minutes or so with an engineer, scribbling away and making further calculations to check 100% that the new, heavier balls would correct the ore milling throughput problem.

Then, with 'bigger balls' – mining terminology – Newmarch and I headed down the Bulawayo road on the way back to the mine.

Newmarch slept the whole way, only waking up when we arrived at the house.

He asked me to drop him off at the office, where he would get Staff and

Crispin to allocate some workers to help him put his heavier balls into action!

It was still early in the afternoon, so I invited the family to join me and we headed for the Fort Rixon dam for the Sunday braai and some liquid refreshment.

Hours of comradery and enjoyment quickly past, until it was time to head back home.

It took a while to get to sleep – as people who drive long distances know, when you close your eyes, you still see the road in front of you. It takes a long time before that image of the long road ahead disappears from the eye retina.

My sleep was further delayed by the strange situation Matt had told me about. What was his old man up to now?

. . .

An early morning phone call from Pat Burke started off my day.

He had received my letter and would like to come over and see the Newmarch ball mill in action.

"Can you make it on Wednesday, Pat? Newmarch has closed the mill down for the day to do some more tests to increase the ore throughput rate using some heavier metal balls."

"Judging from the little tribute money I have received for the months of April and May that ball mill must have huge throughput problems – it's even bloody slower than a ***1-stamp mill!***"

"Not so, Pat; due to the delays of the delivery and installation of the Newmarch mill, we had been using a small ball mill recycling waste schist dumps and were milling only two tons per day. That's why the gold output was as low as you just remarked. The Newmarch ball mill has performed well in all the test runs, and, once Newmarch sorts out the ore throughput rate, we'll start milling again, working daylight shifts for the next month processing about 10 tons of ore per day, so that should be reflected in your tribute royalty payments in your bank account for the month of June. But when you come over on Wednesday, Newmarch can explain everything to you and you'll be able to see the new ball mill in action, and *our* gold coming off the James Table."

I walked over to Joseph's house site to check on progress.

The walls were built up to a height of four feet already, eight blocks, and the concrete floor had been laid, but, even in this partially built house without a roof, the rooms already looked so small and dingy.

Langton saw my reaction. "Boss, when Boss Joseph comes back and sees his house, he'll go mad, blame it all on me, and probably kill me!"

"Maybe you deserve it!" I joked.

"No Boss, I'm only building to his plan; it won't be my fault."

I pondered for a few seconds and could picture six-foot-plus Joseph glaring down at a mere five-foot-tall Langton – what a mismatch that would be!

Then the penny dropped.

"Ah, what we'll do is this, Langton. You stop working on it, and I'll get Goliath to carry on with building Boss Joseph's house."

His face lit up. "Goliath, yes, Goliath the giant builder; he's much bigger than Boss Joseph!"

"And then you can start building my extended house instead."

"Yes, thanks, Boss." And he started packing up his tools.

"Not yet, Langton! You work here today, and tomorrow Goliath will take over. Now back to work."

It would actually made more sense for Langton to work on extending my house, as he had done a lot of the work building our original hessian-walled shack.

When the ball mill was not running, it was so quiet. The block makers producing the concrete blocks noiselessly like little mice; Newmarch and his team silently beavering away in the distance – whilst the sound of the jackhammer boys drilling 200 feet below the surface of the mine couldn't be heard; only the purring of the Atlas Copco compressor near the shaft.

However, all that would change later in the day when the mine was cleared for blasting.

And then, the following day, the whole noisy process would kick off again.

Hoist winching, the cocopan's wheels squeaking, and the ball mill bashing the balls around crushing the ore. And those are good noises to hear; they are the noises that help transform the blasted rock faces into pure gold – I found myself slowly repeating those two words, *'pure gold'*; they induce an intoxicating feeling – perhaps I was beginning to suffer from a mild dose of *'gold fever'* already!

I went down to the mill site and told Newmarch about Pat Burke coming to see his ball mill in action.

"You mean that crazy man with the huge rottweilers. I worked for him once on a small mine near Que Que. He knows what he's doing, but he lives like an animal, and his house was like a long drop – the awful smell and the flies and mosquitoes. He must have elephant-hide skin not to catch any diseases from bites and stings – and he just couldn't understand why I preferred to live in my small tent and cook my own food on a paraffin burner, rather than have a room in his hovel and eat with him.

"Now tomorrow I'm going to give the mine machinery a full service, including all the motors; on the conveyor, the pumps and the James Table. I want my ball mill to work 100% and be the pride of the small worker gold miner. The mill will be ready, though, for Burke's visit."

I went and phoned Simon to see if he could do the respray job on the black 404.

"Simon, how long will it take if I bring the pick-up in tomorrow, Tuesday morning?"

"I'll give it priority, but after it's been spraypainted you'd have to leave it overnight."

"If I stay at Greys Inn, would I be able to drive it by 8am on the Wednesday? I've got a visitor coming to the mine around midmorning."

That was settled then; Tuesday it was.

. . .

Marianne arranged with Elliot and Mary to look after the children, and by 7am we were on our way to the garage paint shop.

We met Simon there, who said he'd start straight away preparing for the respray, so that the pick-up would definitely be ready to collect the following morning.

It felt strange to have so much free time in Bulawayo, nothing really to do for the rest of the day, nothing to collect and nowhere that I had to be – really strange.

We ambled in and out of various shops and stores, checking which sold what and which was where…. Normally, they were all just part of one big blur as I sped through Bulawayo on one hurried errand after another.

But today I could walk leisurely around with Marianne, chat over a coffee and smoke a relaxing cigarette, or two.

We walked past the public library, an old colonial building of character built of formidable granite blocks and standing grandly on its own plot, dominating and eye-catching in a street of bland look-alike modern concrete multi-storey buildings.

"Hey Marianne, I'd like to spend an hour or two in here reading up about the ancient gold miners of 2,000 years ago, which I've become very interested in. Newmarch told me to speak to an old lady, the librarian, who would help me locate the references and books that would be relevant."

"Okay, you do that then, and I'll go and windowshop in Miekles and the other big stores, get some ideas for our new house. Where shall we meet up?"

"One o'clock on Greys Inn terrace, and book us in for the night. We'll have a quiet dinner there as well – if we can keep away from the locals in the pub!"

Agatha; she was a dear old lady.

"I'll be 89 next birthday," she stated coyly, but proudly. "I was a child growing up in those awful times of the Matabele rebellions in the 1890s. Sad, sad times, and today the killing madness has started all over again with that Robert Mugabe – how can he slaughter innocent women and children? He was a headmaster once, teaching to improve children's minds, not killing them; now he's nothing but a cold-blooded, unfeeling butcher!" she ended angrily, with a tear forming in the corner of her eye.

Agatha paused and cleared her throat. "Well, young man, sit here at this table. What types of books have you come to read? What subjects are you interested in, dear?"

"I'm a small worker out at Fort Rixon, working on the Nelly 404 gold mine, and a Mr Newmarch who is installing his ball mill invention…"

"Ah, Mr Newmarch; I've known him for many years. Such a quiet, unassuming gentleman. He's always been busy inventing this, inventing that – is his thingamajig and balls working alright?"

"Well, we've just finished all the test runs, and coincidently his ball mill will be running full-time starting tomorrow."

"Oh, that's so fine to hear; give him my best wishes. Oh, I am pleased for him."

And she walked off towards the reception desk.

I sat there, a little embarrassed, as she had not waited for me to tell her what I was interested in before she went back to her desk.

A few moments passed, then she suddenly looked over at me and gasped.

"Oh, how silly of me," she whispered in a loud voice. "I left you in the middle of our conversation, sorry. Oh, sometimes I get really annoyed with myself, and if I don't finish doing something straight away, it slips my memory and I become obliviously involved with something else. So sorry, dear, but what can I get you?"

"Your old friend, Mr Newmarch, suggested…"

"Oh yes, he's such a dear man, and how is he?"

"He's fine… and, and he told me that you would be the ideal person to contact. I'm interested in information on the ancient miners of 2000 BC to 1000 BC, who mined for gold in this region of Rhodesia, especially the Nelly 404 mine and some of our other gold claims that were first mined way back in time by the ancients."

A few minutes later, Agatha placed some books in front of me, including the Bible!

My surprised look sparked her off. "Yes, the Holy Bible; there are dozens of references to the ancient miners, gold, King Solomon and the Queen of Sheba, mainly in the *Book of Kings*."

And she opened the Bible and read from the *Book of Kings*:

"Now the weight of gold that came to Solomon in one year was six hundred threescore and six talents of gold. And he made three hundred shields of beaten gold; three pound of gold went to one shield: and the king put them in the house of the forest of Lebanon. Moreover, the king made a great throne of ivory, and overlaid it with the best gold. And all King Solomon's drinking vessels were of gold, and all the vessels of the house of the forest of Lebanon were of pure gold; none were of silver: it was nothing accounted of in the days of Solomon. For the king had at sea… the navy of Hiram: once in three years came the navy bringing gold, and silver, ivory, and apes, and peacocks. So King Solomon exceeded all the kings of the Earth for riches and for wisdom."

She cleared her throat and turned to another section, then added, "And also here in the *Book of Chronicles*… 'I have given,' says Kind David, the father of Solomon, 'even *three thousand talents of gold, of the gold of Ophir*, and seven thousand talents of refined silver, *to overlay the walls of the houses* withal'."

After a few seconds, she put down the Bible, and, looking at me curiously, said, "Good luck with becoming a priest, dear." And she went back to her desk.

I was now even more intrigued.

The first thing I did was to look up what **one talent** was.

One talent of gold = 1,128 troy ounces of pure gold = approx. 35 kg of pure gold

King David gave 3,000 talents of gold just to cover the walls of his palace, which is an enormous amount of gold; that's more than ***3 million ounces of pure gold*** – (over 4 billion US dollars) – *just to paint his walls!*

Then I checked where the **Land of Ophir** was, reading from several different articles.

There were many fascinating biblical verses from 1000 BC that point to **Ophir** being located in Monomotopa, the present-day **Rhodesia**, and give insight to the wealth of King Solomon and his temples of gold, the Queen of Sheba, and King Hiram, the son-in-law of King Solomon, who undertook voyages to the South East African coast to collect gold – 'King Solomon's Mines', which inspired the book and the film.

The presence in Rhodesia of ancient gold workings covering areas of many hundreds of square miles with the most extensive alluvial and shed-gold workings by the ancients provided enormous quantities of gold to the likes of King Solomon, as seen in the biblical verses of the *Book of Kings*.

The intrigue over the gold mining by the ancients is further heightened by the vast numbers of ruined settlements linked across the country.

The exploration in Rhodesia of these ancient ruins have shown that the principal industry of the ancient occupiers was that of gold mining, and the settlements were always found in close proximity to ancient gold workings/ mines – such monster buildings as the famed Zimbabwe ruins were not erected for a 'non-payable industry', someone quipped! They were built by a civilised occupation of Rhodesia hundreds of years before, for the sole purpose of mining for gold. These fortified stone-built settlements were for the occupying people to live in and worship, whilst giving protection and guarding their trade routes for handling gold and ivory.

In a local article, I read about the gold mining of the ancients in the Insiza District of Matabeleland, Rhodesia:

"Stretching along the gold belts from Fort Rixon to Filabusi are countless ancient gold mine workings and the accompanying settlement ruins such as the Dhlo Dhlo ruins (near Fort Rixon) and the Regina ruins close to the Claremont and Nelly mines. Both mines were extensively worked by the ancients down to depths of 250 feet – amazing depths for those times – and many of the African workers had to live below ground in these deeper mines, some of them never, ever seeing the light of day…"

With copious notes and a head full of information and facts, I strolled over to Greys Inn feeling even more inquisitive now about the way the ancients mined, and the trade routes to transport the gold through East Africa on foot, before being taken by ships via the Red Sea to the Mediterranean countries of Phoenicia (Lebanon) and Israel.

. . .

Marianne signalled to 'half pint', the friendly midget waiter, to bring me a cold beer, and I sat down next to her.

"I've seen some beautiful furniture today, but nothing that compares to our Kiaat wood settees and tables – what I saw would be completely out of place in our new house in the bush. I think we should keep the whole of our new place, wood, wood and more wood, rough, locally made beds – with good comfortable mattresses, of course. And perhaps we could get the smashed Kiaat wood double bed that got badly broken in the green mamba incident, together with the Kiaat armchair and table that Joseph wrecked, mended by a professional carpenter. But what we do need, as essentials, are a large fridge for fresh produce, eggs, milk, and a chest freezer for game meat. Irene told me that Des would carve up any reedbuck or impala into oven joints and fillets for us – we'd have 'meat for Africa'!"

"And a small beer fridge!" I stated. "That's is most essential, most essential!"

"Apart from those, we could later buy a larger wood stove/aga. But we don't need a washing machine."

"True, we already have a black automatic! Housegirl Mary."

We managed to steer clear of the bar, and spent a delightful evening meal on our own, talking and chatting about many things that we never seemed to find time for during the busy mining '5:30am to 10pm' day.

. . .

Oh, the pleasure of having tea brought to the bedroom at 7am, not 5:30am, and to let its healing powers slowly and soothingly work their wonders.

Then a leisurely egg and bacon full English breakfast and two strong cups of coffee, and we were ready to head to Simon's garage.

"Wow, that's smart!" exclaimed Marianne as we stared at our pick-up in disbelief.

It was indeed very smart. The bonnet was a dark beige/brown, but with a black edging, and the driver cab roof was similarly painted – class, and unusual too.

"So you're happy with my creativity," Simon joined in. "It turned out better than I expected, but it'll now be in my colour combination options for future clients. It not only looks smart, but I don't need to use so much paint either; just use up leftover paint from previous insurance claims – it all adds to my profit, and is an unusual advert – 'where did you have that done? At Simon's garage in Bulawayo'! Pleased you like it, there's no extra charge; it was my mistake not to ask you before I went ahead and blackened the grey, so to speak. Drive carefully, and get back to the mine on time for your meeting out there."

As we approached the Fort Rixon petrol pump/shop, I pointed out to Marianne a pick-up parked outside with two giant rottweilers standing in the back.

A group of Africans who were heading for the shop saw them and quickly turned around and went back the other way.

"And they are scary too!" Marianne remarked. "I wouldn't go near that vehicle, which I assume is Pat's."

I got out to go to the shop, walking close to the side of Pat's pick-up.

As I looked up – and you have to look up to them standing in the back – I saw one of them staring at me, and I think it winked, but certainly gave a low, welcoming growl, and not an *'oh shit, run for it'* snarl.

Pat greeted me, and I swear he was wearing the same dark blue chequered shirt I'd seen him wearing on *every occasion* that we had met – although maybe there were more yellows and browns located around the neck, cuffs and armpits!

He came over to where Marianne was standing stretching her legs, and vigorously shook her hand, causing her head to nod up and down.

She couldn't stop laughing, which made Pat smile and laugh too.

"I'll follow you." And he drove behind us as we headed for the mine.

At the house, I updated Pat on our progress and the potential sale of the mine – that put a smile on his face!

"That's $5,000 in my pocket if the sale goes through; you're making my day already! And can we see the Newmarch ball mill now?"

We drove down to the mill site and I left him to grill Newmarch for an hour or two, while I checked with Crispin various records and who was due to be paid on Saturday – no one! That's odd; with more than 60 workers on the mine, it was an unusual computation of the date started and the days worked that gave the answer = not one to pay today; amazing.

Crispin was impressed with my new black and dark beige/brown 404; quite an improvement on the hearse black respray job to our original grey pick-up – the one we'd bought last year at the mine auctions at East Geduld in Johannesburg

Pat looked very happy and content after his session with Newmarch.

"I can feel now that to tribute the claims out to you two youngsters was a good idea, but where is your partner, that son of Mr Worry in a Hurry?"

"He's probably got more *worry* than you or me. He's on border duty and won't be back for another three weeks or so."

"So you're lucky to have Newmarch on the mine then, a senior partner as it were, probably helping far more than Ray does, I bet – and I heard through the grapevine that he conned you two youngsters into ceding 10% to him! I should probably have warned you to be careful, but the opportunity was not there, and how could I address such a situation concerning an old mate of mine to a complete stranger like you? He's a crafty old sod; a weasel, some people call him – he spent maybe only five minutes conning you out of 10% of your gold mine, whereas it took me many months with different possible tribute options, for a mere 5%!

"But be careful with Ray, already he knows that he's bagged $10,000 if the sale goes through, *$10,000 for doing bugger all!* He'll be happy with that neat con, but, if the sale doesn't happen, keep a wary eye open, as he is known to be the most devious scoundrel in Rhodeaia."

. . .

Now that the Newmarch ball mall was operating smoothly, all the familiar sounds returned to the mine, and the workers went about the daily *gwazas* that were allocated to them and supervised by the respective junior boss boys each day.

With Newmarch controlling the mill site area, Staff, the underground jackhammer boys and the daily blasting, and Crispin, the administration, the mine was running effortlessly, allowing me to float around in an overseer manner.

Newmarch was doing a great job, and I wondered when he left us on Joseph's return in a few weeks' time what effect that would have – was this the calm before the tempestuous storm?

Would that spell in the army make him more used to routine, more reliable, more responsible? Maybe yes, maybe no, maybe rain, maybe snow!

Nothing is predictable when he's around.

However, until that day when the pale blue Peugeot 404 pick-up came skidding to a halt with the hooter blaring, a good harmonious hardworking atmosphere was prevailing on the mine.

I could see now how Cain could take so much time off away from his 'model' mine. He was regularly going down south to purchase personal goodies and to have a few days' break from his mine – i.e. he was enjoying his gold mining life to the full.

I remembered his words on that initial trip with Joseph to his mine in Hartley: "You organise the mine to run like clockwork, with a senior boss boy, junior boss boys, an electrician, a welder/mechanic and a competent storeman-administrator. All of them, together with an excellent houseboy/cook to look after you and feed you well, would ensure you stay healthy, wealthy and wise enough to enjoy your life."

And, unbelievably, thinking about it, we had employed mine workers in all of those jobs, and they had proved themselves to be very competent – and, dare I say it, it was turning out to be a 'model' gold mine as well, giving me much more freedom compared to the initial few months.

The driving load in particular had been reduced considerably – no longer daily commuting from No. 7 Hudson Road to Fort Rixon to work on the mine – which had made life so much easier. I rarely went to Gwelo anymore; in fact, only really to see our friendly bank manager, or to have lunch with Matt at the

Midland Hotel.

By opening some new additional credit accounts with suppliers' stores, a butcher and a miller, Bulawayo had replaced Gwelo as the hub for everything associated with our mining activities.

Food rations could be conveniently collected each time I visited K.B. Davies, the Mines Department, the AE & CI explosives depot, or Greys Inn – staying there overnight occasionally also cut down on the mileage and the hours spent behind the wheel. I was indeed becoming the *antonym* of 'Mr Worry in a Hurry'!

But there is no doubt that the phone at the house had made the biggest impact on my working time, and also on our social life with our local rancher friends.

Life was becoming very agreeable.

However, another instant, unavoidable Bulawayo journey was caused by a telephone call from the mining commissioner's secretary, this time to attend a meeting with him at 12 midday.

I stopped to check the post box on the way; the decision from the Mines Board was due any day now – but no such letter from them; perhaps the mining commissioner would have more news, and maybe that was the reason for his out-of-character instant meeting that he had just arranged by phone.

It's funny; a couple of months ago, I'd be hyped up waiting, worrying constantly. Was the loan going through or not? What would we do if it wasn't granted? Would we survive without the speculative loan money?

But:

* The monthly $1,500 of gold output for the last two months;

* The potential sale of the mine for $100,000; and

* A sweet $10,000 loan from The Gold Plate Mine Company had completely swung the pendulum right to other side – from worrying, frustration and desperation to mild expectation and consolidation;

*Together with the cherry on the cake – an extra $3,000 kitty overdraught for a rainy day, thanks to our generous bank manager, Mr R.E.S. Crow!

And, I soon learnt the truth about the loan.

"Unfortunately," the mining commissioner began, "very unfortunately, I'm afraid I've got bad news for you. The MAB have had such a workload that yours is one of the cases they can only review at the next meeting…"

"Jesus that was the same as last time. How many are there on these advisory boards, just two? Two white-haired old men with hearing aids; it's ridiculous!"

"If you would let me finish," he continued dispassionately. "They have called an extraordinary MAB meeting, especially to review the three outstanding loan applications. It will take place on the 21st June…"

The phone started ringing, interrupting the tense atmosphere.

"Yes, he's here. Okay, I'll send him down to the yard office." Then, turning to me, he said, "You must understand, we are talking about large sums of money, and everyone involved has to consider these situations very, very carefully. You'll hear from us by the 25th June. Good day."

I was pleased to leave the 'stuffed shirts' department and talk to real hard-working, helpful men like Ronnie and Martin in the Mines Yard.

"Judging from your face, it's a good thing you weren't packing a gun!" joked Ronnie. "In the old days, last century, miners had to unbuckle their gun holsters not only when they entered the Bank Assay office, but also when visiting the Mines Department – there were frequent disputes and gun fights. But by the sounds of it, though, you don't really need that speculative loan anymore; that small ball mill really did help you out."

"Yes, it turned out to be a real lifesaver, and now, with the Newmarch ball mill running day shifts, that should provide us with our first month in profit."

"That's good to hear – so there'll be more than enough to pay the bill of $350 for the service and repairs to the small ball mill!" He laughed.

"You caught me there, Ronnie, but yes, we'll settle that."

"Okay, and if you would post a cheque to me, I will make the transport arrangements with Mr French for the return of the mill to the Fair Deal mine near Salisbury. Three hundred and fifty dollars sounds a lot, but put in perspective it's only a small amount compared with the two months' gold output that it delivered for you. And Ryan told us that his survey confirmed the potential ore reserves of the Nelly 404, so the future looks very bright for you.

"It was also very timely for the geologist from The Gold Plate Mine to meet with Ryan and spend the day together underground in the Nelly 404; that can only have helped to cement the sale of your mine. By the way, are you going in for stock car racing on the Bulawayo dirt track? Your 'rottweiler-looking' black and tan pick-up has an aggressive look about it – but mind you, you'd have to have it re-panelbeaten after every event; the way those cars side swipe each other, it would feel like a zebra is trying to bash you off the road again!"

And that name stuck; even the kids started to call the pick-up *'the rottweiler'*.

. . .

The block makers and the builders between them were racing through our cement supplies and I had to drive up to the Altyre store to collect another load.

"You must be building a lot," Chris remarked. "You're my biggest user of cement. What about sand; where do you get that from? If you like, you can borrow my tractor and trailer on Sunday morning and I'll show you a place on my brother's ranch – a dry river bed where it's very easy to park and shovel the sand onto the trailer.

"Oh! Wasn't that a terrible tragedy, though, Lilly and George being killed like that, but the way they drank, day and night, it was bound to happen sometime. I heard she drove straight into a tree, smashing their Ford Popular car, instantly killing George and leaving the lady looking like a porcupine with smashed ribs poking out the front of her blood-stained dress. Apparently she was so drunk that she didn't feel a thing, joking with the ambulance nurse as she was rushed to hospital – but she was DOA – dead on arrival. So sad."

I resisted the urge to pop into the police post – Peter's famous instructions, 'take the left turn, right', caused me to laugh, but I obeyed them and headed on home to the mine.

As the cement bags were being unloaded from my pick-up, I heard, and felt the 5 o'clock explosion underground.

Staff came over and reported, "The underground teams of jackhammer boys and lashers were working well, and will be supplying 10 to 11 tons of ore per day to Mr Newmarch's ball mill."

And, as if on a theatrical cue, a creaking sound from the door 'stage left', and Newmarch appeared wearily from his room – the vibrations from the blasting had awoken him from an after-shift nap, but he still managed a grin as he told us, "The quartz we're mining currently is giving us very healthy gold on the tables. If it stays like this, we should hit 70 ounces this month."

"That's great! But come back to the house with me now, relax a bit and have supper with us; tomorrow is another day."

. . .

Now that we were well into the hunting season, invitations came thick and fast to spend the day at a game meat braai on one of the ranches, and this weekend it would be the turn of a rancher called Hector.

So this Sunday we had two choices, but chose to go to the dam, as it was more of a family outing than at Hector's, a bachelor, who I'd heard preferred a totally liquid braai, and often got so smashed that his dogs ended up eating all the meat.

Loneliness, boredom and living on your own in the bush seem to be a recipe for such an unfortunate life, and so many people turn to the bottle for solace.

We'd seen that for ourselves first-hand with the Lady in Pink and her husband, George, who were tragically killed – there was more alcohol than blood in their veins!

. . .

We were awoken by a shrill ringing noise.

I shone the torch at the clock by the phone; it was 1:30am.

"Who on earth can that be?" Marianne called out as I picked up the receiver.

"Just listen, and listen well! My dear son, Joseph, has been shot by terrorists! His father, Jane and I have just arrived at Cain's place, where we'll stay the night before visiting poor Joseph in the military hospital early in the morning, when I'll expect to see you there as well. Good night!"

"Shit, that was Popette barking instructions down the phone, commanding me to leave immediately to visit Joseph in a military hospital in Salisbury."

"Has he been shot by terrorists?" Marianne asked in a panicky voice.

"That's what his mother said and very disturbing news too, but there's no way I'm going to rush up there now as she demanded – she didn't even give me the directions to the hospital. I'll phone Cain in the morning and find out how Joseph is; hopefully not too badly wounded by those renegade insurgent killers!"

. . .

After a restless night, with the mind sometimes running wild with horrific images of Joseph being shot and badly bleeding, being carried on a stretcher in the bush back to base camp, dawn finally arrived.

"They've all gone to the hospital in Salisbury to visit Boss Joseph," Zikke updated me. "They should be back for lunch."

"When they come back, get Cain to ring me at the mine, not the mother, okay Zikke?"

"Yes, Mdevu, only Cain. I'll tell him quietly so that Madam doesn't hear, because she has got a violent temper when she gets upset. When they arrived in the middle of the night, she was very angry and so rude to me!"

I told Marianne the latest. "Looks like this morning we'll stay around the house until Cain phones us; there's nothing else we can do but wait. I'd better call Chris at Altyre store and check if it's okay with him if Crispin can use the tractor and trailer today to collect five tons of river sand."

The morning dragged on slowly, very slowly.

"Did she say how bad he was, where he was shot?" Marianne enquired.

"No, only that he was shot by terrorists. I hope he wasn't wearing his silly little red hat! That would have made an easy target for even the blindest of shooters."

Lunchtime came and went, and it was well into the afternoon when the phone finally rang – it was Cain.

"What's the latest; have you seen Joseph at the hospital?"

"He's okay, doing well, but let me phone you later; my mother is fussing around like a mother hen, so it's not really the time to talk. It'll be late, though, after 10pm when they've gone to bed. They are very upset and moody, so let me get back to you and talk when they are not hovering around."

There was no point us hanging around the house any longer either, so I suggested that we go and see if we could find Crispin and the tractor.

Good timing too; the rasping blast of a tractor horn announced Crispin was back.

The sand was offloaded near the block makers' site and Crispin chugged off to the Altyre store with the tractor – with Marie-Louise, Jeffrey and Elliot on the trailer – and would drive back later in the 'rottweiler' pick-up with some more bags of cement.

Newmarch was very upset to hear the news. "Bastards! What happened? Was anyone else shot or hurt?"

"We'll know nothing more until Cain phones me back this evening. Then I'll let you know straight away."

It's a bit like waiting at the doctor.

You know you are next, but the patient in with him is taking an abnormally long time.

You can't go anywhere – just sit and wait.

Playing Snakes and Ladders helped pass the time; cups of black coffee helped keep us awake. Eventually, the kids flaked out and were put to bed; the clock struck 10! But still no call.

It was gone 11 when the phone finally rang.

"Sorry I'm late, but my parents were still up faffing around, so I thought it best to go down to the pub and phone, which I'm doing now by the way from behind the bar – and with a pint in the other hand! Get this; this is the latest news about Joseph. I couldn't talk to you freely while my parents were still around; they didn't want me to tell anyone about the incident. I think they are very embarrassed."

"About what?"

"You heard from my mother that Joseph had been shot by terrorists, right? Well, to start with, the nearest terrorist was probably 100 kilometres away at the time, and sleeping in his bed."

"What?"

"Joseph shot himself in the calf as he jumped off a lorry whilst at the training camp. His weapon wasn't on the safety catch, and he slipped as he was about to jump, catching one foot in the tailgate chain, and spun around. The rifle went off, discharging one bullet, which went through his calf muscle, clean through; it didn't touch the leg bones at all luckily, and another bullet glanced off a colleague's backside, giving him a painful flesh wound. Joseph was very fortunate he didn't kill someone!"

"Oh… I can see now why you couldn't talk to me when your mother was around; that's the last thing she'd want me to hear."

"And my father too; he was so embarrassed when we visited Joseph in the military hospital. Other soldiers in his ward had head wounds and serious body damage from landmines, but our Joseph had to go and shoot himself in the leg!"

"Well, he's had a lot of practice over the years; he's always shooting himself in the foot, isn't he!"

And we both broke out in laughter.

"Pity you're not up here at the pub. Henk would love to buy you a beer, and I could do with some lively company too, after spending most of the day at home listening to my mother saying what a terrible accident to happen to her Joseph, and my father blurting out *'don't be so damn stupid, woman!* That idiot son of yours *shot himself in the leg*, a colleague in the bum and is lucky not to be court-martialled; he could easily have killed a fellow soldier!' My father was fuming, and asked me, no, rather, ordered me not to tell a living soul how it had really happened. We should just say that he'd been shot whilst on border duty fighting the terrorists!"

"And how long will he be laid up for? When will he be walking again?"

"The doctors said he'd have to stay at the hospital for approximately two weeks whilst the wounds healed, and build up the muscles in his leg before he could walk without crutches. So you'll have the pleasure soon of watching him hobbling around on your mine, telling some outrageous story about this patrol he was on that was ambushed by terrorist insurgents, who eventually fled, being no match for Joseph and his brave soldiers – he's a corporal, you know! On the catering side."

By the time I'd retold the whole sad story to Marianne, we were both ready for sleep, a hanging-around-waiting day is always far more tiring than a busy-on-the-go day.

. . .

I sent Elliot to tell Staff and Crispin to come to the house – they had to be told of Joseph's injury, but **not how** it happened.

"Boss Joseph is in a military hospital in Salisbury recuperating after being shot whilst on border duty," I stated semi-officially. "Luckily it's not too serious, and he should be back on the mine good as new in the next two weeks, when undoubtedly he'll explain what happened. No point in telling the workers; it doesn't affect them all, and shortly they'll see him for themselves."

"How was he shot?" Staff asked anxiously.

"Well, I don't know the full details yet," I lied through my bloody teeth, "but we will hear soon enough from his own mouth, I'm sure."

Crispin and Staff walked off, upset to hear the official a-la-Ray news, and I hoped they'd never get to hear the real unfortunate story.

By now, Joseph must have been embarrassed and humiliated many times over as the news of his freak accident spread through the military camp, and probably the soldier he'd shot in the bum would have got a few laughs and a few drinks each time he recounted, "That guy, Joseph, is a pain in the bum!"

Jokes aside, it was a painful injury and he needed to recover, from both the medical point of view as well as the mental point of view, I think.

Crispin delivered my message to Newmarch, who came straight to the house for breakfast, when I told him the true story about the shooting.

Newmarch listened intently to how the patient was progressing in the hospital and the details of the injury.

"What! He was shot in the calf by a terrorist bullet? What was he doing, handstands? I don't believe that. It sounds more like someone's gun went off accidently and a bullet struck him in the leg – that happens occasionally with our part-time soldiers."

He looked at me quizzically, and read from my face that was exactly how it had happened, and, as much as I tried to hold back a grin from forming, he spotted it and then he exploded, "Oh God, Joseph ***shot himself*** in the leg! That could only happen to Joseph!"

He shook his head with a wry grin as we looked at each other, bemused.

"But my ball mill isn't having any accidents, though! It's proving its worth; it remains robust and so far we've not experienced any downtime since Burke's visit last week. If we get through this month in a similar fashion, I recommend that we increase the milling next month from the one daily shift and start milling on two shifts per day, 6am to 2pm and 2pm to 10pm, rather like we did using the small ball mill.

"And obviously your goal is to run 24 hours a day – three shifts, seven days a week. But let me get back to my work; I'm really enjoying being a small worker again. It's like reliving part of my life, except that the gold mines I worked on were of low quality, not like your Nelly 404, which already will give you a nice profit this month, and Ryan says it's got ore reserves to last you many years!"

. . .

For the next few days, the mine ran like a precision Swiss clock – a gold-plated one.

Joseph's house was nearing completion; Goliath and his *gwaza* team were timbering the roof support frame together.

Already, the rooms looked so dark and dingy, and, when the iron roof sheets were nailed into place, even during the day you would need to use a torch.

But what Joseph wanted Joseph would get, even though I felt bad to waste so much time, labour and materials just to prove a point – as I knew as soon as he saw it he would want it pulled down and a house with larger rooms built, and still on the other side of the Fort Rixon murram road, of course – thank God!

My enlarged house would look like a mansion compared to Joseph's doll house.

Langton had put a damp-course row of blocks on the old concrete foundations floor for both the outer walls and the inner walls.

I was taking no chances; we'd already experienced the clinging dampness in the air during the misty guti weather and we didn't want a repeat of Jeffrey's bronchitis problems.

I walked around the inside floor area; the rooms were of a good size and large windows would ensure that the house was light and airy.

It was quite strange to walk across the floor and into the one large 20-foot by 20-foot room – our hessian-built house, which we were still living in even though it was being encircled by the new outer concrete-block walls.

Once all the outer and inner walls were built to roof height, large timber frames would straddle the whole area and support an all-enveloping corrugated iron-sheet roof.

The last stage would be to demolish the old hessian walls and finish off the interior by building some walls in that area to make a large kitchen, with a scullery and a storeroom.

. . .

"Ernest Roksplitzer is coming today to review the whole mining complex, both on the surface and underground, where he will take some more assay samples of the quartz reefs," I told Marianne before I went up to the mine. "Make him a coffee if he comes directly to the house; otherwise, I'll bring him back here for some lunch."

When he hadn't arrived by midday, I went to the house and phoned The Gold Plate Mine Company and was told that he'd left long ago, at 9am, but perhaps he'd visited someone on the way out to the mine.

Not long after that call, his Land Rover pulled into the garden and Ernest parked in front of the veranda.

"I hope you didn't have any teething problems with your new 'Landy'?" I jibed.

"No, she's running beautifully. The Land Rover is a true faultless British mechanical wonder for the African bush – but I did suffer from a faulty Dunlop tyre, which, unknown to me, was a remould, and a whole sheaf of the rubber tread on the tyre must have peeled off when I was driving on the tarmac road, only to be punctured when I hit a bad pothole on the murram road. I had to use one of the *two* spare wheels, which I always carry, because I have to drive on some atrociously bad roads to outlying mines in the bush. And being an ex-Scout, I cater for even a double puncture incident – be prepared!

"But please could we sit down for 10 minutes and over a cup of coffee I can outline to you what I want to do and see this afternoon, and the information I need in order to complete my survey report of the Nelly 404. However, don't worry; I'm already convinced that my company should go ahead and buy the Nelly mine, and that'll be my recommendation. I just need to add photos and details of the surface operation from the headgear to the ball mill site and the extraction room area, listing all the pieces of equipment that we would be taking over. I was planning also to do some more assaying sampling on the quartz reef, but Ryan from the Mines Department has already sent his assay results to me, and they prove to be more than adequate."

We walked around the mine together, Ernest clicking away at different areas, before discussing with Newmarch his views on the performance of the ball mill.

Newmarch told him that the mill was running well and he could provide him with the full specifications, as he had the details with him in his room.

On collecting a copy of the ball mill specifications from Newmarch, Ernest shook hands with us.

"My survey report will be presented to Mr Bird by the end of the month, when I'm in no doubt that you will receive a letter confirming the sale contract of the Nelly 404 to The Gold Plate Mine Company."

As he drove off, Newmarch patted me on the shoulder, grinned and then went back down to the love of his life – the Newmarch ball mill.

"What a promising way to end the week; I like Fridays," I commented, after telling Marianne of the positive news from Ernest Roksplitzer's very own lips.

. . .

Not only do I like Fridays, I like Saturdays too, especially this Saturday – the yearly police braai day for all the families in the Insiza-Fort Rixon area.

We drove up to the police compound, where there were already dozens of vehicles parked outside lined up along the murram road; the parking inside was full.

The kids were whisked away by a clown dressed up as a British policeman to join their fellow age-mates in a huge tent, decorated with brightly coloured flags and multicoloured balloons.

Entertainment and refreshments would ensure they had a magic afternoon – and evening, as there was no way anyone would leave early from this bush party.

There must have been at least 100 guests, and the bubbling conversations rippled across the mingling crowd on a warm Saturday afternoon.

As dusk fell, two huge fires were lit, which added to the party atmosphere.

A kudu had been roasted on a spit over hot coals, and there were four other large braais where boerewors, chops, kebabs and hamburgers for the kids were constantly being served to awaiting expectant empty mouths and empty plates.

The evening flowed; a very appropriate word, as there must have been dozens of crates of beer, countless bottles of wines and cooldrinks that literally evaporated – full one minute, empty the next. The place hummed.

One unusual incident was when Rancher Jackson came over and stood next to me in the braai queue.

"I hear the mine is operating successfully. Congratulations to you; you've worked hard." And he extended his hand towards me. "I think we're going to be good neighbours from now on. We didn't get off to a good start, and it wasn't really your fault either. When I heard who was going to reopen the Claremont mine, a man known for his disregard for all the rancher-miner rules laid down in the mining regulations of Rhodesia, I went out of my way to try to stop the mining here on my property. And I've heard that you've also had trouble with this man and his son, but I hardly ever see either of them."

"Nor me!" I quipped. "Luckily!"

"By the way, are you still enjoying your early morning swims in my large water tank?" he added with a slight grin.

We both laughed.

"Out here in the bush," he continued, "sound carries, especially at dawn when it's so very quiet – your splashing in the water tank could be heard for miles around! I even once could distinguish some words that sounded like *'up yours, Jacko!'*, but I could be wrong!"

My smiling face acknowledged that he might well have been right!

We now stood at the head of the spit braai queue, and the smell of roasting venison filled the air – and my nostrils! I was getting very hungry.

"Some fillet, Mr Jackson?" Peter asked, and laid two large pieces on his plate.

I had the same. We added some salads and French bread, and sat down together and cleared our plates in silence.

"That was absolutely delicious, Peter," Jackson remarked as he left to go and join his wife and two daughters.

That comment brought the other Peter, Peter Ruck, over to where we stood.

Naughty grins spread across their faces – the Peters were sharing a little secret.

"Come on, what's the joke?" I asked.

"Well, if Jackson knew that the kudu fillet that he found so delicious actually came from one of *his* kudus, on *his* land, he would have freaked out. You see, we were hunting for some game meat for this police party on an adjacent ranch when we spotted a large young male kudu. I was just beginning to squeeze the trigger, the kudu was smack in the middle of my sights, when something spooked the animal and we watched it gracefully bound away up and over the slope of a small hill… but when we rounded the hill, there it was grazing away, not a care in the world…"

"Well, not a care in this world!" Peter Ruck jumped in. "Because we shot it, clean through the heart, dead! And it was then that we realised that we were on Jackson's property; we'd shot one of Jackson's kudus! We were in a quandary what to do, because we couldn't drive a police Jeep onto his property and load a poached kudu into the back in broad daylight, could we? It took an anxious half hour before we had four boys organised to carry the kudu on two poles around the hill to an awaiting pick-up that we had radioed for. There, safely hidden under a tarpaulin in an unmarked public pick-up, the dastardly deed was done, Your Honour!"

And we all rocked with laughter.

"That was a close one that could have sparked a major incident; the visiting magistrate would have had a field day!"

"Policemen poachers!" I teased.

"No, our clandestine undercover operation would have to be known as KKK – not Klu Klux Klan, but *Krazy Kudu Killers!*" Peter joked.

As the fires began to burn down, the light began to dwindle, as did the number of guests, and, when midnight came, the last stragglers headed for home, amongst them Marianne and me, plus our snoozing little ones.

Golden Balls

A loud knocking on the door.

"Quickly, come with me; we have to talk to Staff before the jackhammer boys start drilling today," Newmarch urged. "The quartz ore from Saturday's milling shift was incredible. I watched a thick yellow tail of gold coming off the James Table! We must have hit a richer pocket. Let's get Staff immediately and go underground to the spot where he last blasted – this is exciting, so exciting!"

And we rushed up to the mine.

The three of us moved quickly, eager to go underground to see this rich lens of gold.

Newmarch manoeuvred himself into the skip, and Staff and I clambered down the ladders to the second level, then, carrying carbide lamps, we hurried along the drive tunnel. Staff placed the lamps near the rock face to light it up.

Then, with our powerful mine-helmet lights, we scanned the surface of the quartz reef in front of us.

"*Look!*" shouted Newmarch enthusiastically. "***Visible gold!*** See those golden speckles in the quartz – that means possibly four ounces per ton, maybe even more; that's why the gold tail on the James Table was so much thicker than before. Forget the other quartz rock faces and get Staff to blast here again today; it might just be a small lens, but with gold mining you never know."

And laughing to himself he literally pranced along the drive tunnel like a teenager as he headed for the skip.

Back on the surface, the compressor was started up for the jackhammer boys and Newmarch and I hastened down to start up the big ball mill, which would run on the ore the lashers cleared out early on the Sunday morning.

"Keep your fingers crossed that today's milling produces the same richness, and that the ore Staff blasts out this afternoon will reveal the same gold values too."

Newmarch was like a small boy who had opened his Christmas present early and found it to contain his favourite toy. He nervously paced up and down by the James Table while we waited for the first sands to come from the ball mill and be washed across the vibrating concentrator James Table.

"*Jesus!*" I exclaimed. "I can see why you were so excited this morning – that is what I call a fat tail of gold."

I left Newmarch, his wide-open eyes locked on the slow-moving golden snake – compared to the previous thin snakes, this was a thick black mamba!

Marianne was also elated at the news, and I think she could visualise the long-awaited refrigerator being loaded onto the pick-up!

"Joseph's mother phoned while you were away to let us know that he was doing well, already hobbling around on crutches; he's so courageous! And the doctor had told her that he was making very good progress and in another week he'd be walking normally again, although maybe with a slight pronounced limp initially. 'And tell your husband that there's no need for him to visit Joseph in hospital; he'll soon be out and back working on his gold mine – I just wanted to tell you the latest news about my beloved son, Joseph, straight from the horse's mouth as it were', the mother had stated emphatically."

"More like straight from the horse's ***arse!***" I wisecracked. "But it was good that I wasn't here for that phone call. It would have been difficult not to tell Ray about our latest coup, which would have led to them all descending on the mine like bees around a honey pot – Ruthless Ray, Pompous Popette and the Jester, Joseph! But they will know soon enough."

Too true.

A few hours later, Mr Worry in a Hurry roared into the mining compound.

He leapt out of the pick-up, shouting, "Newmarch, come here, come! Tell me all about this rich strike we've just hit."

I'd noticed that Newmarch was a little deaf sometimes, but could feel that he was pretending not to hear Ray's loud, bossy commands; he didn't want to be summoned like a dog! And in any case, it was not his mine.

Ray, getting annoyed by Newmarch's disinterested stance, quickly came over to me. "The gold you're mining now *must be very rich*; *rich enough to make Staff go to Fort Rixon to phone us in Hartley* at Cain's place with the good news. You took a chance on the quartz and it looks like it's paid off; that's what small worker gold mining is all about. But I can't stop and talk. I've got to get back to Belingwe; I've been away far too long. And the thieves that work for me would have had a free hand to rob me blind."

Abracadabra! And the magician disappeared.

I am your ears and your eyes. Staff *sneakily* going all the way to Fort Rixon to phone – he ***was*** the spy for Boss Ray, just as Crispin had suspected, and warned me!

. . .

Monday's output from the quartz ore held firm, good values coming off the table.

And on the Tuesday when milling the ore from the quartz lens with visible gold that we had inspected on the second level, Newmarch was exuberant.

"A few more days like this, young man, and you'll have produced 100 ounces of gold this month; that would be fantastic!"

That was decidedly food for thought, and it was hard to keep the mind from dwelling on the gold miners' dream of '**hitting the mother lode**'!

And it definitely eats away at you; it really is a kind of cancerous fever, an incurable disease of the mind, which recalls that intoxicating vision from the subconscious *instantly* when you see that fat tail of gold on the James Table – either when you are physically looking at it, or at night when you start dreaming about a rich seam of visible gold, as I had been experiencing recently myself as soon as I closed my eyes!

I can imagine how some of the early miners went crazy, especially those living on their own in the bush far from any town, as they poured their gold dust from one hand to the other before returning it to a leather pouch, anxiously looking this way and that before they went to sleep, the pouch gripped tightly as if rigor mortis had set in – until they woke up in the morning and headed for the Bank Assay office in town.

Many were robbed of their gold on the way. Some found on their return to their mine that other ruthless miners had taken over their gold claims.

Many were shot dead during such disputes.

There is no doubt at all that **gold breeds greed**, and **mistrust**, and the **gold fever**, which brings about an even worse state of mind – **the insatiable lust for gold!**

. . .

With Joseph due any day now, I spent time on ensuring that his house would be ready for his arrival.

But my misgivings about the dingy rooms were emphasised even more when the final corrugated iron sheets were nailed onto the timber A-frame to complete the roof. It reminded me of those dark, dank medieval prison cells you see in films like *'The two young princes locked up in the Tower of London'.*

An administration afternoon of paperwork, checking which mining claim protection notices were due so that we could pay them in good time; we certainly didn't want to forfeit our mine through lack of payment, when we were now producing gold and on the verge of the sale of the mine.

. . .

The excitement was building up; everyone on the mine knew that the quartz ore would provide good benefits to the mine, and, of course, for their jobs and futures.

The news spread fast too.

Cain phoned in the evening to add his congratulations on the amazing gold output we were producing. "Just hold on a minute. My mother is standing next to me trying to grab the phone!"

"My son, Joseph, will be out of hospital on Tuesday!" she boomed. "After his terrible ordeal, being shot whilst on his six-week border duty protecting Rhodesia!"

I noticed how unusually slowly she spoke, carefully choosing her words so that she gave no hint that Joseph had actually shot himself.

"Terrorists are nothing but cold-blooded murderers! We need our brave young men like my son, Joseph, fighting these cowards to prevent them destroying our country," she added, deliberately trying to convey to me a picture of her brave son being under fire from terrorist insurgents – totally unware that Cain had told me the real story.

"And another thing; I find it in bad taste that you didn't come to the military hospital in Salisbury like we did as soon as we heard the news of the shooting. Poor Joseph…"

"Okay Mother…" Cain took over again. "That's all the news for now. I'll call you from the pub over the weekend when we can talk more about *the rich quartz ore* you're mining, okay. It sounds like you've got a potential big-producing mine, with a gold output that will exceed my mine's production – that's fabulous news!"

. . .

When I went up to the mine after my Monday morning Ndebele lessons, I was met by a super-hyped-up Newmarch.

"I hope you don't mind, but I spent yesterday morning preparing the gold so that you could take it into the Assay office in Bulawayo today." And he handed me a hefty leather satchel.

"Could I come with you to Bulawayo? I want to pop into see Mr French and report the progress of the prototype ball mill. I think we've got a winner; he'll be very pleased! But most of all, I'd like to go into the Bank Assay office with you and share the excitement of watching the gold being weighed – it's something that I haven't experienced for many years now."

And so we left together.

Although I wasn't really expecting any trouble, we took Amon with us – those stories of the miners in the past still fresh and very vivid in my mind.

Inside the Assay office, big weights were being added to the weighing scales, but the officer weighing the gold had his back to us, so it was not possible to check the actual weights being added.

"I reckon 85 ounces, maybe more," Newmarch whispered in a quiet, trembling voice.

We waited nervously, our thoughts running wild – this is what gold does to you!

The officer turned around, and, as if adding to the drama, he very slowly approached the counter and looked me straight in the eye. "I've checked the records; this gold must have come from the quartz reef that hasn't been mined for the last 12 years." He spoke in an almost accusing manner.

"That's right; it's from the second level stoping of the 'hanging wall' of the quartz reef – but please tell us how much it is?"

"I've recorded; the quartz reef; one hundred and three point two-seven ounces of fine gold."

A complete hush swathed my mind. I wanted to shout out happily, but my throat had become so dry, I couldn't even mouth the words.

I looked at Newmarch expectantly.

"One hun-dred and three oun-ces!" He spoke the words very slowly, exaggerating with bold lip movements syllable by syllable, and then burst out, "*We've hit the mother lode!* Oh, it's so good to have this feeling of elation again – once a gold miner, always a gold miner! It's a life sentence!" And he started thumping me on the back!

"We'll credit your account with $7,745 immediately," the Assay officer said dispassionately, "and the balance of $2,582 within two weeks."

I'm not sure how I got from the Assay office to the Mines Department; perhaps I flew, or even floated – I just don't know.

"*A hundred and three ounces!*" exclaimed Ronnie. "That's great news; hey, you are well on your way now. Let's go upstairs and tell the commissioner."

He was even more surprised, but soon brought us all down to earth again as he began to speak in a disinterested civil servant tone.

"The ministry advisory board have sent you a letter regarding your loan application. Shall I read to you from my copy?" And, without stopping for breath, he continued with those nasty sounding words, 'regret' and 'rejected'.

"But don't get disheartened, because your gold production figures from the Nelly 404 this month are outstanding, and with the back-up of Ryan's survey report on the ore reserves of the Nelly 404, I would like to offer you a discretionary loan of $4,000. As the name implies, this loan is at my discretion; we don't have to go through another lengthy DAB-MAB process, and if you sign this form now I'll initiate it immediately and the money should be available in three working days! And even with your healthy gold output figures, it's reassuring to know that your monthly lease costs for the Mines Department equipment are covered for nearly three months."

With these overwhelming figures being thrown at me; *$10,000-plus by the Assay Bank*, and now *$4,000 by the mining commissioner*, I just had to celebrate, and took Newmarch and Ronnie to Greys Inn.

Dave was so happy for us, and suggested that I phone Marianne straight away and get her to drive to Bulawayo for an evening of celebrations – and stay overnight at the hotel – *'on the house'!*

'I'll make you an offer you can't refuse' sounds totally different coming from Hospitality Dave's mouth, as opposed to Ray's threatening Mafioso snarling lips.

Newmarch stayed on with us until Marianne arrived, to toast to us both and to the success of the Nelly 404 gold mine.

Before leaving for home, he asked what time he should come to Greys Inn in the morning to get a lift back to the mine.

"Join us for breakfast about 8am and we'll take it from there, but if you want to spend tomorrow morning with Mr French at K.B. Davies take the beige 404 pick-up now, and we'll see you back at the mine in the afternoon."

With all the excitement, and a good few swift beers in the pub, I only just managed to keep my eyes open long enough to finish supper, before shutdown!

All bodily and mental functions closed down for the night!

. . .

What a wonderful uninterrupted sleep at Greys Inn, complemented by a sumptuous breakfast and a leisurely drive back to Fort Rixon still smiling at that magic number – ***103***.

On arrival back at the mine, I went straight to the office to see Crispin and gave him copies of the weighing results from the Assay office, and the official Barclays Bank receipts for the gold we had deposited.

"A hundred and three point two-seven ounces of fine gold! That is incredible, sir; what a good month we've had."

I went outside and saw Staff, who had taken over responsibility at the ball mill site, which was running nicely – and noisily!

I told him to stay with it until Newmarch arrived from Bulawayo later in the day.

An old Land Rover pulled up and out stepped a smiling Rancher Jackson.

“Hello, what a good evening that was at the police braai party; it’s always a successful affair, and the food was so delicious – I must ask Peter which butcher he buys from; it was top quality! When my wife was chatting to Marianne, it became apparent that you didn’t have a fridge. That’s not good with young kids; milk and eggs soon go off in this heat.

“If you like, we have a spare paraffin fridge in good working condition that you can have. Drive down to the ranch house; Feet can organise it for you. I’m on my way to Insiza for a meeting of the Insiza Rural Council. Don’t worry though, *you’re not on the agenda anymore!* There’ll be no more complaints from me about conservation or mining issues.”

When my three, Marianne, Marie-Louise and Jeffrey, saw Feet and me unloading a paraffin fridge, they all groaned, and Marie-Louise shouted out, “Oh no! Not again. Not another stinking fridge; it was bad enough over Christmas!”

However, a few minutes later when it was inside the house working, and Feet gave us a container of fresh milk, six eggs and some cheese, all the ‘oh nos’ turned into ‘yes pleases’ – we really needed this fridge.

Then Feet opened the drawer for vegetables at the bottom of the fridge, but there were no vegetables in it; there was no room! It was packed with Castle dumpies and a note from Jackson: *A beer fridge for you! Enjoy them.* Could things get any better?

I went back up to the mine, where I was surprised to see the pale blue Peugeot 404 pick-up of my partner.

Joseph appeared in the doorway of the office and brushed aside my greetings and questions on how he was getting on following the accident.

“Don’t you talk to *me*!” he shouted. “Staff was just telling me how you overruled him, and refused to mine the banded ironstone reef as I had instructed him to do. And worse still, you’ve been mining the quartz reef! I’m the underground manager, not you!”

“Joseph, you weren’t here, so naturally I took control of the underground operation.”

“Yes, yes, there you go again; you want to take control of the whole mine and be in charge of everything. Well, that’s not going to happen. And Jane agrees with me too! And how ridiculous of you to mine the patchy quartz reef; we probably won’t even cover costs this month!”

He suddenly went quiet as Staff was staring directly at him gesticulating with his eyes, pleading for Joseph to keep his mouth shut and not to say anything more.

But all to no avail; Joseph ignored him and blissfully continued his tirade.

"Running that big ball mill costs much more than using the small mill; the gold output this month won't be enough to even cover part of our costs! Crispin! Let me see the gold production register!" he demanded.

His mouth dropped open with a grunt.

"Huh! That can't be right; 103 ounces of gold. No, Crispin, you've made a mistake, and you can't fool me. Neither of you can!"

Then, like a puppet whose mouth strings had broken, his lower jaw just hung quivering, but no words came out as he read the Barclays Bank Assay slip, duly officially stamped, stating 103.27 ounces of pure gold.

"You bastard!" he shouted. "You're trying to make me look bad, and it's not fair. I've been shot by terrorists, which hurt, but now this hurts me even more! You think that you're better than me just because the mine is operating fully and you produced over 100 ounces of gold this month! You're trying to turn my father against me!" he screamed, as he rushed off to get into his pick-up.

"But I'll get my own back on you, just you wait! You were just lucky gambling on the quartz reef – you think you've got ***golden balls*!**"

The Letter

An hour or so later, Newmarch arrived in the beige Peugeot pick-up and parked in front of the office.

"What's up with Joseph?" Newmarch asked me. "I saw this cloud of dust being kicked up in the distance by someone driving very fast, and, as the vehicle hurtled towards me with dust clouds billowing out behind it, the bonnet of a blue Peugeot pick-up was clearly visible. It belted past, but before I became completely enveloped in the dust I could see that Joseph was the driver, and my fleeting glimpse showed a bright crimson face about to burst! What's happened?"

I explained to him about Joseph's outburst, which was directed at me for running the mine too well, producing too much gold, and get this, he said I was only doing all this just to show him up in front of his father while he was in the army being shot at and badly injured by terrorist attackers.

"Phe-e-ew." Newmarch exhaled slowly. "That Joseph has got a huge chip on his shoulder, and behaviour like that often leads to a complete nervous breakdown. But, what can one do to help him?"

"Nothing; it's been building up for months, fuelled by his father always running him down, treating him as an imbecilic child – together with the fact that the mine has been running sweetly without him whilst he's been away in the army – being shot at by terrorists! God, if he knew we'd heard the full true details of how he shot himself in the leg, that would be it; he'd be mentally finished. But worse is that in his mind he knows that Ray was told the facts at the military hospital, and that will be a dark cloud always hovering above him; he'll live in dread that his father will one day blurt it out in a fit of anger. Poor sod!"

"Yes, it's sad indeed. But now with all that's been said by you both, all the wild accusations and the hatred, it will be virtually impossible for you two to work together in the future. It'll be the best thing that could happen when the sale of the mine goes through, and you two can go your own separate ways. But let me go and relieve Staff at the mill site, check the output and I'll lock up today. Are you going to collect explosives tomorrow? We are down to our last box."

. . .

I fancied driving along different roads for a change, and left early for the AE & CI explosive dump via the scenic route through bushland rich in wildlife, down the dirt tracks to Filabusi and onto the murram road towards Bala Bala.

I resisted the temptation to call in and see Charlie, and drove straight through to the AE & CI depot south of Bulawayo.

After loading up with my regular order of gelignite and detonators, I turned left out of their compound only to see – déjà vu – a black mamba slithering across the baked earth.

It was easily two metres long, perhaps a relative of the one I'd tried to flatten; however, this time I only watched it gracefully zigzagging off into the bush.

Dirk was right; I was beginning to get quite fascinated by them, but did not ever intend to try to catch one – 'it's easily done by just holding it by the tail', Dirk had written.

Jesus, but first you have to get near enough without being zapped by the snake to be able to do that – not for me; I'd leave that to the collectors such as Dirk.

The journey back to the mine went by slowly, as if I was floating in a wonderful dream. I seemed to have so much time to enjoy driving through the bush; I hadn't been so relaxed for months – and I could think of 103 reasons why!

I called in at the Fort Rixon Post Office; only one letter, though, from Frost & Co. stating that the board meeting of 5 July had been brought forward one week to this coming Friday, because of Joseph's earlier release from army duty.

The main items on the agenda were:

* Inviting Marianne to be a director;

* Gold production for April, May and June;

* The sale of the mine.

Any day now, we should hear from The Gold Plate Mine Company, and I felt the growing excitement and was eager to read the letter that would change our lives.

Back at the house, I phoned Ryan.

I would call in to see him early in the morning when I was in Bulawayo to collect rations and told him I was particularly interested in hearing again, in detail, his last conversations with Ernest, and that I would appreciate a copy of the sampling survey assay results he had given to Ernest – this would be good back-up factual information for our coming board meeting.

The thought of the sale was *constantly* on my mind whenever I wasn't busy concentrating on a particular *gwaza* or project, especially so when driving alone on the seemingly endless dirt roads.

Also at night when the light went out and it was quiet and pitch-black, those thoughts went crazy, throwing up all sorts of different computations.

. . .

I arrived in town earlier than expected and went to see Doug French at K.B. Davies.

He looked his happy old self again, the worry of the possible white elephant ball mill a thing of the past.

Newmarch had told him of the reliability of the mill, and they would travel together to Salisbury next month to meet with the directors of the Mine Machinery Company of Africa that had produced his prototype – **our golden guinea pig**!

French already had received two enquiries, and would be bringing the prospective miners out to the Ridge Top Mine in the course of the following week.

"I'll phone you the day before to warn you, because I'd like you to be present and help me with my sales spiel – a satisfied customer, and on a working gold mine showing our Newmarch ball mill in full production; what an advert! I'm convinced many small workers will consider this modern ball mill a better alternative to the ageing 5-stamp mill."

"Well, it was a long time coming," I reminded him. "We could call it a 10-month pregnancy, but your baby eventually came into the world, and now I'm completely happy with the role it plays in our gold production business."

"Any more news on the sale of your mine? The Gold Plate Mine Company should be well pleased with the gold production figures last month, and I hear from Newmarch that their geologist made several trips to the mine to conduct his own assays for his survey report – and seemed pleased with what he saw. It was also a clever idea to have Ryan from the Mines Department to meet with him and take him underground – he would have made an excellent silent salesman for you too."

"Yes, that worked out bloody well, especially since Ryan had worked for years on the Nelly 404, and could show this Roksplitzer guy the actual development plans that R.J. Stewart & Sons had for the future of the mine. Actually, I'm on my way to see him after I finish this mug of coffee, thanks."

"Pity I have nothing to toast to the success of the sale; the days must be getting nearer… a countdown to the successful conclusion – we are all with you! And I bet you'll be so pleased when you're shot of that despicable little man Ray, not to mention his rather pathetic son, Joseph!"

Ryan was also in a buoyant mood, and told me of the real enjoyment he'd derived from working on the Nelly 404 again; it was like visiting an old relative in a home that he'd grown up in.

"These are copies of the reports that I gave to Ernest Roksplitzer to augment his detailed findings for his presentation to the board of The Gold Plate Mine Company."

He handed me, in addition to the Mines Department charts, copies of all his personal charts and assay results from his last six months working on the Nelly 404 – each of them full of golden words that would further support our cause – the sale!

"Roksplitzer was very happy with all this additional information, which he would incorporate into his survey report, and he told me that he would recommend the sale to go through, which he thought was a formality. I imagine this is the best news you could hear, and I bet you can't wait to have the contracts finalised – and $100,000 in the bank!"

"Too true, Ryan, and thanks for those four days spent with us at the Nelly 404. Let's have lunch together before I head back to the mine to prepare for the board meeting tomorrow in Gwelo."

"Next time please; I have to finish off an internal report by this afternoon – the mining commissioner is breathing down my neck!"

"Okay. But probably just as well; once you get into the Greys Inn pub it's very hard to get out again; you meet so many friends, which generates a kind of magnetism that roots your boots to the floor!"

I went instead to Lloyds Tea House and had a coffee and a ham and tomato omelette to sustain me for the journey home, collecting the ration meat, sacks of mealie meal and beans en route.

We spent a quiet evening together, playing cards and listening to music.

Crib is an interesting game for two people to play, and not too taxing either, allowing us to chat about this and that….

. . .

Ray came strutting outside to meet us, and with the usual smarmy self-important look on his face he welcomed Marianne and me to the board meeting being held in Frost's accounting office.

We were joined by Frost himself – and a frosty looking Joseph, who was looking very uncomfortable.

Ray started the proceedings, and unexpectedly announced, "*We are pleased to have Joseph back from border duty*, and delighted that he has fully recovered from being shot." A slight pause whilst he removed something that was irritating him in the corner of his eye, causing Joseph some concern, as if he was dreading that the following remarks would reveal how it had actually happened… but luckily Ray continued with the words: "I think we should applaud my son, Joseph, and all the fellow Rhodesians who put their lives at risk to protect us from Mugabe's murderous terrorists. Well done, Joseph; I'm proud of you."

If Joseph had been a peacock, he would have puffed up his tail feathers – instantly, his expression changed, a smile travelling from his lips to light up his eyes; Joseph, the prodigal son, had returned and was being welcomed back.

He veritably glowed with satisfaction.

Ray formally continued. "Now, *the first item is to welcome Marianne to be a full director of Ridge Top Mine* – Marianne, well done; it's been a long time since we agreed that, but believe it or not this is only our second board meeting ever.

"*The next matter gives me really great pleasure – the marvellous start to our gold production* from the mine for the last three months. Whilst you've been away, Joseph, there have been some impressive results on the mine. It's fully operational, the Newmarch ball mill is performing well, and the production was 103 ounces of fine gold last month – *103 ounces of pure gold!*"

Then, turning towards me, he added, "Congratulations, you've been doing a good job; you are fast becoming a real small worker miner with a nose to find gold!"

"But he disobeyed my orders that I left with Staff to mine only the banded ironstone!" Joseph reacted aggressively.

"Joseph, I took the joint advice from Ryan, the mining engineer, Newmarch, and Roksplitzer, the geologist from The Gold Plate Mine Company, and decided to mine the richer quartz reef."

"But you had no right to do that!" he stated forcefully. "You are not the underground manager of this mine, I am!"

"Joseph, when you were away, everything, including underground operations, falls under me, as mine manager."

"You did it to undermine my authority, and in front of the African workers too, and in any case you were just lucky that the quartz gave 103 ounces; it could have been only three ounces!" he shouted, a reddish tint colouration working steadily up his neck and into his cheeks.

"Stop bickering, you two! What your partner has done, Joseph, was exactly what we needed; a real financial boost – 103 ounces of gold, which has netted us *over $10,000!*

"That's so encouraging, and now leads me on to *the third item on the agenda*: *the sale of the Nelly 404 mine.* Following their three-month evaluation, we have received the much-awaited letter from The Gold Plate Mine Company. Here," he said to me, "you're the man of the moment; you read it to us, please."

"But the letter has already been opened?"

"Yes, of course; it was addressed to me, the managing director of Ridge Top Mine, but opened or not, come on, just read it out loud – we're all waiting to hear the news!"

I silently perused the contents of the letter.

"Come on, read it out loud!" Ray insisted enthusiastically, with an excited expression spreading across his face.

"Yes, read it out loud!" Joseph added. "This is so electrifying!"

But I continued in silence to reread words, which made no sense at all:

...Our geologist... unhappy with the ore reserves... and we cancel our option to buy...

"That's ridiculous!" I stated as I handed the letter to Joseph.

"Both the geologist and Ryan of the Mines Department agreed that the gold values and ore reserves were good, and even above their benchmark!"

"What! What's going on!" shrieked Joseph.

"This is wrong. I was with them both. I even saw some of the report; the ore reserves are good – there's something not right here..."

"But come on, you just read it yourself," Ray reiterated. "And why would the MD of a company write such a letter to cancel the sales agreement if the underground ore reserves were that good?"

"Yes, Dad's right; you've just been getting our hopes up. You think you know everything, always trying to show to my father that you are better than me. But I'm bitterly disappointed too. I wished that company had bought the mine, then we could split the money and I could have opened up another gold mine – I would have showed all of you, including my brothers, that I would be the boss and owner of my very own successful gold mine. Now that the sale has fallen through, I will still have to work with ***you***! And you'll try to be the boss over me as mine manager all the time; I'm not looking forward to that at all."

"Joseph! We are not going over that again! We went through the problems three months ago when all the dirty washing was laid out on the table, and the three of us agreed that the only way forward so that you two didn't have to work together anymore was to sell the Nelly 404. And now today we've learnt that the sale is not going to happen, and we have to make some decisions together about the future of Ridge Top Mine, and some hard choices regarding your 50/50 partnership. So its crunch time; I have to back one of you."

Ray turned to me and continued, "Either you or Joseph. Over many months, you have really worked hard developing the mine, and Joseph was often nowhere to be seen. And for the last six weeks while Joseph was on border duty, you have run the entire mine, both surface and underground, without any help from him."

"But that's not fair, Dad. I couldn't help, could I; I was on border duty. You've never liked me, I know. You don't want me to have my own gold mine. You're always running me down, and why don't you treat me the same as my other brothers? Cain has always been your favourite, and Matt…"

He stopped in midstream. Ray's ice-cold stare made the words freeze in Joseph's mouth; he reddened drastically and looked as if he was about to explode into an epileptic fit!

"Joseph, ***be quiet!*** As I was saying, for the last six weeks, the whole mine has been functioning without you, run entirely by your partner – and producing good gold too, which has cleared all the outstanding supplier debts except for K.B. Davies. Now that the sale has fallen through, I have to back one of you. The logical choice, Joseph, is your partner; he has…"

"Shit! There you go again!" Joseph screamed. "Can't you see, he's always had it in for me, going behind my back, trying to make himself look good *in your eyes!* Are you blind? This is not fair, not bloody well fair! You're supposed to be my father and help…"

Ray was now getting really mad; he was literally breathing fire and his flaming eyes glared at Joseph, delivering the necessary telepathic blow that stopped Joseph's incessant ranting.

"Let me finish! Don't you *dare* interrupt me again, Joseph, or I'll have you thrown out of this board meeting. I'm the senior director and the MD here!"

Then he paused, to regain his composure. "As I was saying, Joseph, the logical choice is your partner… but, blood is thicker than water, so, Joseph, I'm backing you!"

Joseph could not believe what his father had just said, and sat there with a silly grin on his face.

Ray continued, "So, directors, let's vote on it…"

Ray checked all our reactions to his question.

"Okay, as I thought, it's Joseph and me against you and Marianne. Two-two! Stalemate! But if you look on the director's agenda that you all have received, there is an addendum on Page 2 stating that a shareholders' meeting will be held immediately after the board meeting."

"What!" I exclaimed. "I've not received anything like that; just the one-page board meeting agenda. I even checked the post in Fort Rixon on the way here. That's absolute *bullshit!*"

"Calm down; I have my copy here!" And, handing a sheet of paper to Joseph, he said, "This is your copy, which we had posted to the family home in Belingwe in case something like this happened. And Frost, you received it as well; I can see your copy in front of you on the table."

"Yes, Ray, the two-page notice was posted to all directors and shareholders."

"So…" Turning to me, he forcefully carried on, "It looks like you are trying to scupper a legitimate shareholder's meeting. Frost, the copies were sent out to every shareholder, so is it all right, in legal terms, to continue now with the shareholders' meeting?"

"Yes, Ray, it is."

"Well…" He looked straight at me. "I propose that Marianne and you are *dismissed* as directors, and that *you lose* the positions of mine manager and accredited gold agent for the Ridge Top Mine."

"Let's vote!" Joseph shouted with a grin. I vote *'yes'* with you, Dad."

"So that's a majority 'yes vote', against your 45%, with Marianne having no shares in the company!"

And that was that, as if I was in a bad dream. I couldn't believe what I was hearing – end of the road for me; outvoted!

Joseph stood up and glared at me in childish triumph. "I am *the boss* of my own gold mine at last!" he boasted. Then he proceeded to walk around and around the table in an exaggerated, almost ape-like manner, repeating, "My own gold mine; my own gold mine. Thanks Dad; at last, my very own gold mine. Yippee, my own…"

"Sit down, Joseph! For Christ's sake, *sit down!*" Ray bellowed.

This had been like a sucker punch to the gut. I was left speechless, and my mind couldn't focus on this sudden out-of-the-blue horrific situation that had developed – and like clockwork too… as if it had been well rehearsed.

I could hear them all continuing talking in the background.

"And the second vote is to issue more shares to raise money for our increased mining activities at the Nelly 404. All vote."

"Carried," said Frost. "Only you and Joseph have voted, but that's sufficient for a majority vote."

With this devastating news, I was still swimming in a quagmire of indecision. I just couldn't pull myself out of this morass. I just couldn't concentrate – no longer managing the mine, nor a director, and my shareholding not counting for anything…

"Well then, we agree, and I propose that 2,000 more shares be issued forthwith. Let's vote again!"

"Yes, yes!" Joseph blurted out. "I agree; more money coming in, and I won't have to work with *him* anymore." He wagged his index finger at me arrogantly.

"Carried," said Frost.

"Then, Joseph, meet our new shareholder… and mine manager…"

Frost got up and opened the door, and there stood none other than Cain.

"Your brother, Cain, now majority shareholder and the new mine manager."

Joseph gasped, and started shrieking as his brother, Cain, calmly strode in.

"*It's not fair!* It's not bloody well fair! You always favour my brothers!" he whinged and started abusing everyone.

"And that stupid mother of mine gave me the wrong biblical name; she should have called me Abel! And…" He ranted on and on….

It took several minutes before his rage began to wane, and, looking very embarrassed, he eventually shut up.

Then quietness, all three of them standing there staring at each other, exchanging angry glances, but no one uttering a word….

It was this quietness that eventually allowed me to get out of being bogged down by the crippling events of the last few minutes.

"Hey Ray! Just a minute! I've been looking at the letter from The Gold Plate Mine Company; there's something wrong here…. It's not on The Gold Plate Mine Company letterhead, and it's typed with an old-fashioned upright 'sit and beg' typewriter; the letter shapes are exactly the same as on this copy of the minutes of our last board meeting – which your wife typed!"

"*But it's legal!* And anyways all the voting has been done now, and duly recorded by Frost. Even if you were right and the letter is a fake, you can't do anything about it *now!* The Nelly 404 is *mine!*" And he laughed in my face.

THUD!

A hard right fist landed square on Ray's nose, and blood splattered across his face as he staggered backwards, shouting, "*Stop him! Stop him; he's a madman!*"

But they were all too slow.

"*OUCH!*" Ray gasped as I punched him hard in his stomach, causing him to double up, leaning forward, when…

CRUNCH!

A ferocious left hook sent Ray crashing backwards against the table and falling on the ground clutching his mouth, which was oozing a mixture of blood and teeth!

Hands and arms gripped me tight, as Joseph, Cain and Frost struggled to keep me from destroying my prey.

Staff had rushed into the room on hearing the noise, and, with his added strength, I was eventually held, my arms clamped by my sides – but my legs were still free agents and I lashed out at Staff, hitting him in his private parts, whereupon he sank to the floor, wheezing, but still managing to hang onto my legs – this time restraining me completely.

"*Don't just stand there gawking, Joseph; get me up!*" Ray squealed.

Joseph bent down to assist his father to stand up, whereupon Marianne shouted, "*Jullie klotzakken!*"

She charged like a wounded buffalo and crashed into the back of Joseph, sending him flying and sprawling on top of his father on the floor, both of them snivelling like pathetic wimps!

Marianne then stormed out of the room, pushing past Cain, spat at him and called out, "And *you,* posing the whole time as a friend; you're worse than Judas!"

So now it was just the men left, all shouting – Joseph and Ray struggling to get up, and Cain, Frost and Staff hanging onto me to prevent me launching another few feisty missiles at that rat Ray's messy, bleeding face.

"*Now let's all calm down!*" he uttered with difficulty – unusually for him – the mix of blood, snot and tears slowing down the exit of the words from his damaged mouth.

He glared at me with wild, fiery eyes, but still with a very apprehensive expression. "*Hold onto him tight!* He's hooked me with vicious punches, and I don't want to be hit anymore!"

Joseph went to help the other three to contain me, as I continued to struggle to free my arms so that I could have another swing at that little bastard.

Then Ray looked at me and laughed again, revealing two gaps in his teeth and blood trickling from the corner of his lips – that would spoil his *smarmy* Clark Gable smile!

"It was worth it though to take those hard punches, because I have now, legally, *taken half of a producing gold mine from you!*" And he laughed and laughed. "A good trade, don't you think? And as I said it's all legal and above board, and it will be documented in the minutes of the meeting by Frost, exactly as I dictate it to him shortly. Won't it, Phil?"

"Yes, Ray, exactly as you tell me."

"Now back to you; there will be a police charge against you for an unprovoked attack on me with the intent to kill or severely maim me. I have my witnesses here, Joseph, Cain, Frost and Staff, against your word and that of your wife, unless…" He paused to wipe away an irritating trickle of blood from the corner of his mouth, and continued, "Unless… you leave this room quietly, and agree not to pursue the matter of the *'fake'* letter, which, of course, is just a figment of your imagination, right chaps?"

"Yes Ray!" concurred his three cronies.

"If you do this now, and promise no more violent attacks on me, I will drop the charges and we will all forget that it ever happened, okay!" he said, with difficulty in pronouncing the words. If only he could see how he looked, with his Clark 'Garbled' moustache dishevelled and coated in drying blood, and the missing teeth spoiling his smarmy smile – yebo, it was worth it! *The bastard had stolen my mine!*

Images of déjà vu began flashing through my mind, of miners in the gold rush days fighting each other, even killing for that intoxicating yellow metal – **gold!**

Have you ever had that feeling, perhaps in a bad dream or more probably a nightmare, where your arms won't function, you are pinned down, your heart wants to fight on, but your mind gradually begins to win the battle, and slowly convinces you that you are done for, you've lost, you've been completely and entirely duped… by a truly professional conman – worthy of the title *'The Godfather'*?

Once again, Ray was making me an offer I couldn't refuse – in hindsight, I should have fought harder against him the first time at the initial set-up of the company, where he ***'stole' 10%*** of the mine. But reality is reality, and now I had no choice but to agree – *to lose my half* of a producing gold mine, a mine that I had virtually single-handedly got up and running against all odds – shotgun Jackson, the abnormal rains, delays in delivery and installation of the Newmarch ball mill – *but,* the dice on this throw were weighted, cunningly weighted by Ray against me.

And the more I thought about it, I just *had* to retrieve *something* out of this now catastrophic mining venture; *all the hard work* month after month that I'd put into the mine, together with *all the money* I'd injected and invested in pick-ups and mining equipment – *I had to insist and fight for the immediate payback of my Director Loans!*

"I hit you, Ray, with good, solid punches that got through and really hurt you and sent you staggering backwards to the floor, but you, Ray, you have KOd me with a simple 'didn't see it coming' sucker punch. However, I'll go along with that, if we also make an agreement for me to *receive my directors' loans back in full over the next two months*, so I can at least get on with my life."

"Agreed," Ray calmly replied. "We have cleared our main pressing outstanding suppliers' debts – mainly thanks to you!" He laughed again. "And now that the Newmarch ball mill has proven its reliability for a month running only a day shift, we'll be able to mill three shifts a day, which should easily exceed the June output.

"That would give us, even at a mere 100 ounces a month, an inflow of $10,000 a month – with well over 50% profit. So that won't be a problem for us to repay your directors' loans, *but it will have to be over the next four months*.

"The plan now is to proceed like this; Cain will not be taking over as mine manager for a month, not until Matthew works himself in at the Hartley mine…"

"***Shit!*** You've had it all planned for bloody months, right down to a tee!" I interrupted.

"So until then," Ray continued haughtily, "Joseph, you can be mine manager…"

"*Yippee, yippee!* Manager of my own gold mine at last, even though you tried everything to steal my mine from me," he shouted at me, wagging his finger. "See, I am Joseph, the mine manager! And you are *nobody – and with nothing!*"

"Joseph, keep it shut for a bit, please!" Ray continued, addressing to me, "And because you and Joseph are now even fiercer foes – more antagonistic enemies – this is how it's going to work. Tomorrow is Saturday, so over the weekend you must clear all your personal effects and furniture from the mine house; Cain is generously allowing you to store your furniture at his mine until you need it.

"You can also make use of the company 404 pick-up as well, but it must be returned to Joseph at the mine on Monday morning before 12. Frost and I will be there by lunchtime and we'll draw up a legal agreement to repay your directors' loans completely, split over the months of July, August, September and October. Agreed?"

"Do I have a choice?"

"Yes, Hobson's choice!" Joseph laughed. "No bloody choice at all, *sucker!*"

Ray could see that Joseph's taunting was causing my blood-stained fists to firm up, and, at the slightest provocation, even if it meant losing my loan money, he knew I would decimate them all if necessary; he could feel that I was about to launch a killer strike – so he quickly intervened.

"Joseph and Cain, do you agree too?"

"Yes, Dad," they replied automatically, as if this *'Yes, Dad'* was in their genes and had been repeated unthinkingly, many, many times before.

"Okay, let's shake on it, then," Ray said, extending his hand to me.

"Oh, don't tempt me, Ray; that hand is a provocative weapon to me. I remember the last time we shook on a Rhodesian gentleman's handshake. *Put your hand back in your pocket, Ray*, or I'll unleash the rest of my building-up fury, ***and bury you!*** " I menacingly stated, causing both him and Joseph to back away. "I agree with what you've proposed; I'll move out over the weekend, and meet you at Ridge Top Mine for the last time on Monday, when Frost, Joseph, you and I will all sign the repayment of my directors' loan agreement."

And with that said, I turned and headed for the open door.

Staff – still holding his jewels, and breathing erratically – and Joseph, Cain and Frost all stepping aside slightly to let me through, as if forming a guard of honour at a wedding – I think I should have carried on fighting and made it a funeral – *Ray's bloody funeral*!

I strode to the pick-up, where Marianne was waiting, and, as I was getting in, I could hear laughing and shouting coming from Frost's office, Joseph's enthusiastic comments out-booming the rest of those cheating crooks.

"Yippee, thanks Dad, my own gold mine at last. *And* I'll show him *who's the boss* when he comes to *my gold mine* on Monday!"

I slammed the door to cut out the rantings of that lunatic and we drove off in silence. Both Marianne and I had heard more than enough for today and just wanted to get home as quickly as possible. The night would be a sleepless one, and we'd have plenty of time then to vent our thoughts – and anger!

I was in a trance, thoughts flashing through my mind as the kilometres ticked on… Suddenly, a red warning light on the dashboard started flashing.

O-oh, I thought. *It's just one of those bloody days!*

My diesel fuel indicator was nudging on '*empty*'!

In all the anticipation of the board meeting and the sale of the mine, I had forgotten to fill up in the morning before we left for the meeting in Gwelo.

But luckily for us we were approaching Fort Rixon.

"Damn, almost out of diesel! We'll have to pull in at the store pump ahead; not enough fuel to get us home! Bugger it, I didn't want to stop; I just wanted to get to the house and relax."

I went into the store to pay, and heard a familiar voice – Policeman Pete.

Perhaps this was fate, because we were taught as kids 'if you're in trouble, always talk to a policeman'!

"Hello," Pete said. "I was just out for a refreshing evening stroll to get some tobacco for Peter Ruck and sweets for his kids. Hey, you look mad about something – I've never seen you without a smile on your face; what's happened?"

He followed me outside and we walked over to the pick-up, where he greeted Marianne.

"Evening, ma'am," he stated in an official policeman's stern voice. "I was just asking your husband here what… Oh, okay… so you have had really bad news. Why don't you give me a lift back to the police compound; you can tell me all about it – it might just help."

Peter listened in silence as the unbelievable day's events were unveiled to him.

As I told the bit about punching Ray and knocking out some teeth, I felt my hands clench again and secretly wished that Peter sitting there in front of me was actually Ray, so I could finish off those good punches that I landed with the final knockout blow – it would have made no difference to the outcome. We would have lost the mine in any case, but at least I would have had the satisfaction of watching his sons and cronies trying to revive *that lying, cheating bastard as he lay there in a pool of his own blood.*

"At least those two solid punches to his head dislodged a couple of his teeth, and put an end to his smarmy smile – it will be a constant reminder to him every time he looks in the mirror when he's shaving each morning."

"*Jesus Christ!*" gasped Pete. "It's like the plot of a movie – such things don't happen in real life. So what are you going to do now?"

"They've given us the weekend to move out, and we meet Monday morning at the mine to sign an agreement to repay my directors' loan account – that's the capital from South Africa I put in; a mix of cash, second-hand vehicles and mining equipment. That's how we financed the mine initially."

"But where will you store all the stuff, and where will you live? Let me get you a strong drink; you both look as if you need one."

"Beers would be just fine thanks, Pete."

He left Marianne and me sitting in unusual silence, staring out across the bush.

Pete returned with the drinks and said, "Now listen, you two, I've just spoken to Des and he's coming over straight away so we can talk about any help we can give. We can't leave you stranded, homeless; we'll sort something out – these ranchers are good, caring people."

It wasn't long before Des and Irene arrived, and the whole sad story was retold.

"*The bastards!*" Des spat. "To cheat you like that, after all the hard work you two have put in to make the mine running and producing gold, and not just a few ounces either; it is now a fully productive gold mine, 103 ounces of gold last month running only one shift per day, you told me. *That smarmy little crook!*"

"And let me tell you, Des, that little crook, Ray, has been plotting this for many months. The way it unfolded at the meeting, it had been worked out in detail; a plan that has been systematically followed week in, week out, and, as one phase had been completed methodically, the next one came into operation. And one of his sons, Cain, and our senior boss boy, Staff, have been integral co-conspirators from day one.

"Another brother, Matt, Joseph and I are the three who have been duped. Joseph thought when he sided with his father and voted me out of the mine that it would then all be his, and he was as happy as a pig in shit! Well, for about two minutes, until he rather stupidly voted for more shares to be allocated, when '*bang*', the door flew open and in came co-conspirator, his own brother, Cain.

"Joseph went absolutely berserk, swearing and cursing like a man possessed as he realised that he'd also been thrown out. But with his naive loyalty to his father, he became happy enough to accept being temporary mine manager for a month or two until Cain could take over, during which time *he'd be the boss of his own gold mine*, and he could lord it over me for three days and then kick me off ***his mine***. Sucker; as soon as Cain takes over, Joseph will be out as well.

"The only family member who is still probably completely unaware of what's happened this afternoon is brother Matt, who will be made to take over Cain's mine, like it or not – to start the chain reaction off – but only when father, Ray decrees. The family will have taken over a good producing gold mine from me, and shed the non-viable mine that Matt had been running. And what *pisses me off* even more, was Ray's last throw-away phrase, 'and Cain has generously invited you to store your belongings on his mine'. *Bollocks!* I'd rather set fire to it all than take it up there, and have to be subservient to him, the smarmy son of smarmy Ray, any time I wanted to collect some of our things. *No bloody way!*"

The phone rang.

Peter came back, saying, "That was fast. Your latest news is all over the joint party lines. Rancher Jackson has a three-bedroomed bungalow in Bulawayo where you can stay, and store your goods in a large garage. He said he'd call by the mine early tomorrow morning to explain the whole set-up in Bulawayo."

"Well Marianne, that's good news for you," Irene said, consoling her, "and you can count on us as frequent visitors until you get back on your feet – and don't forget, you are always welcome to come and stay a weekend with us, any time."

In times of trouble, you really do find out who your true friends are – within a few hours, our homelessness and desperate situation had been overcome, and, led by our former arch-enemy, Rancher Jackson!

"Thanks Pete, Des and Irene for helping to resolve the solutions to our unexpected devastating problems – and so quickly too! Now we must really go; the kids are being looked after by Elliot and Mary."

. . .

Neither of us slept well, constantly tossing and turning, the events of the day provoking thoughts of revenge…

At about 3am, it was too much.

I got up to make us some hot coffee on the wood stove, and we sat on the veranda.

It was a beautiful moonlit night, and the silvery grey shadows blanketed the bush and the trees, which took on the appearance of a huge concrete-sculptured mural.

We sat in complete silence, except for the occasional slurp, bewitched by the enchanting scene stretching across to the distant hills, lit up by Mother Nature's night sun.

The dogs came out too and lay across our feet, looking up with sad eyes. Animals have that instinct; they know when something is wrong and could sense, I think, that we'd all be moving from the bush to a new home.

"We are not going to be able to enjoy such wonderful sights when we move into Bulawayo, so let's just sit here quietly; the sun will be up shortly."

We were still sitting there on the veranda as the day began to get brighter.

Elliot, looking a little surprised, came over and made us some fresh tea, before I sent him up to the mine to tell Newmarch to drive to the house to see me; it was important!

A little later, his old rusty pick-up appeared and Newmarch slowly got out, walked wearily towards us and plonked himself down on a chair.

He looked exhausted. He had worked very hard for the last month to get his pride and joy successfully milling gold ore – enjoyable, but heavy going; long hours for an old man in his 70s.

But, hot black coffee quickly revived him though.

"What's so urgent to ask me to come and see you so early in the morning?"

I related to him the stormy boardroom meeting:

The fake letter.

Being outvoted.

Being cheated.

The punch-up.

Loss of the mine.

Newmarch listened intently, sitting there in silence, slowly shaking his head.

"I've witnessed this so many times before in my life," he began. "Partners cheating partners, sometimes with fatal results. Gold really is a disease, and *it is incurable*! ***Gold breeds greed***, *mistrust and an insatiable desire to have more – the lust for gold* … But, where are you going to live now?"

"Believe it or not, Rancher Jackson has offered us to stay in a furnished three-bedroomed bungalow in Bulawayo that he uses as a town retreat. There's a large garage there where we can store all our furniture and belongings. Today and tomorrow, we'll use the two pick-ups to transport everything to Bulawayo, then that's it; our gold mining days on the Nelly 404 are over! Joseph comes on Monday to take over as mine manager, temporarily, until Cain moves down from his Hartley gold mine."

"Well, if that is the case, I want to leave this mine *today*!" Newmarch stated angrily. "Will you give me a lift into Bulawayo with you this morning? I've had enough. What I'd heard about that cheating fox, Ray, has been re-enacted again here. Such things make me sick to the pit of my stomach! I will *not* be here to help either *him*, or *his whinging, unreliable son, Joseph.*

"The ball mill is up and running, and it has proved itself to be reliable over the last month, so my involvement here is at an end, and I'll be getting back to work with Mr French to market and install this Newmarch ball mill on other small worker gold mines; *I'm very proud of my invention.*"

"And so you should be, Mr Newmarch, and I'm sure there'll be many more that you will install on small worker mines across Rhodesia. *Elliot!* Go and ask Crispin to come and see me please, straight away."

Newmarch and I continued to make a plan for the day.

He would not start up the mill today; we would leave the extraction room locked and give my key to Crispin.

Crispin would inform the miners after we'd left for Bulawayo that there would be no work on Saturday or Sunday, and Boss Joseph would take over as mine manager on the Monday.

As Crispin approached, I observed that he knew something was wrong, but he politely asked, "And how are you today, madam? And you, sir?"

And then he stood there quietly, looking a little embarrassed.

I asked him to sit down, and, when Elliot was out of earshot, I began…

"Serious news, Crispin. I'll tell you what has happened, but I want you to keep it to yourself until I decide when it is a good time to tell the rest of the mine boys, okay?"

Crispin could see that Marianne had sad, wet eyes, and knew straight away that today would be a day that changed all of our lives.

"Yesterday, Ray and Cain outvoted me; the culmination of a cleverly planned and orchestrated series of events over the last few months. They had waited until the Nelly 404 was fully operational and producing high-value gold, and then they pounced like a leopard to kill their prey! We are to leave the mine with all our belongings over the weekend, and Boss Joseph will come on Monday to take over as acting mine manager."

Crispin gasped, and stared at me in total disbelief.

"Yes, Crispin. They've screwed me, but legally too; there's nothing I can do. '*Your ears and your eyes'* saw correctly that Staff was *the spy*, and it's him who has been keeping Ray up to date with all the progress as it happened, so, although we hadn't really seen Ray for almost three months, he didn't need to come, because his trusted silent spy, Staff, was here – *listening and watching!*

"Staff was also at Frost's office, and he, Cain, Frost and Joseph had to forcibly hold me back after I exploded and landed two big punches directly into Ray's face, knocking out some teeth! Hopefully I broke his nose as well – he won't look so pretty anymore; his smarmy smile will look silly with a couple of gaps! That will remind him of my left hook! Now Crispin, this is what we are going to do.

"We are going to start packing, and you and Elliot will help us load furniture and boxes onto the two pick-ups – Newmarch is coming with us as well; he's had enough of them too, and does not want to work or help them on this mine anymore. After we've left for Bulawayo, I want you to call all the workers together and tell them the news. We'll be back tomorrow to load up the rest of our belongings, when I'll address all the mine workers myself."

"But where will you stay in Bulawayo?"

"You won't believe it, Crispin, but…"

I was cut short as Rancher Jackson drove up in his Jeep and his wife got out and came over to Marianne and gave her a hug.

"… But we'll be staying at Jackson's bungalow in Bulawayo. But now, leave us for a while please; Jackson is going to explain to us where the place is and give us directions, etc. I'll send Elliot to get you when we are ready to load, okay – but not a word yet, please. We'll be taking Elliot with us as well to Bulawayo to help unload."

Jackson and his wife were very sympathetic to us and said we could stay in the bungalow in Bulawayo as long as we liked.

"The houseboy's name is James, and the larder is fully stocked, so you won't have to worry about shopping immediately, at least for several days."

Jackson gave me the keys, shook my hand warmly and wished us a safe trip with all our belongings; adding that they'd call by in a few days' time when we were settled in.

Out of the frying pan, and… into a furnished bungalow in Bulawayo!

This would give us plenty of time to think about our options, and decide whether to stay in Rhodesia or go back down to South Africa. Marianne was already talking about wanting to live in Cape Town again, or possibly Durban; either way, it would be by the ocean.

Our dreams of our life on a gold mine in the Rhodesian bush were abruptly over.

And even if we got the director's loan capital money back, it would not be nearly enough to buy a cattle ranch in Rhodesia.

Shakespeare's famous quote was being modified: *"To be,* ***was*** *not to be!"*

By early afternoon, all the boxes were packed and loaded onto the two pick-ups, together with our personal effects; the dogs lying down in the drivers' cabs.

We would return very early on Sunday morning, when we'd only have the big furniture and beds to load up from the mine house, and could then easily get back to Bulawayo by lunchtime and spend a quiet, relaxing afternoon in the large garden – far away from *my conniving, sneaky, cheating ex-partners!*

"Well, Crispin, keep this extraction room key and give it to Boss Joseph on Monday. Let me know tomorrow the reaction from the mine workers when you tell them that we have been forced to leave the mine. Put Amon on guard of our house straight away. And we'll see you early tomorrow morning."

A quiet evening at Jackson's bungalow in Bulawayo was very welcome, and an early night for us all. At least we were all safe and soundly sleeping in comfortable beds, thanks to the ranchers rallying around so quickly.

. . .

"Come and look! What a wonderful surprise!" I called out as I opened the fridge door. "Bacon, mushrooms and eggs."

That was enough to make Marie-Louise and Jeffrey eject themselves from their beds and literally fly into the kitchen.

Marianne quickly made a fry-up, followed by some buttered toast and marmalade, and, when I had drained my second cup of coffee... we were all on the road to Fort Rixon in the two pick-ups, nice and early, at 7am.

As if in a dream, or perhaps a silent movie, I seemed to drift along the roads, the bush on either side being a hazy browny blur.

I stopped at Fort Rixon to get a bit of fresh air and a cooldrink, which instantly kicked me out of this dreaminess and into the reality of a Sunday morning in Fort Rixon – dead quiet; not a soul in sight!

The sweets and drinks started the little chatting machines off – back to normal again.

We drove on past the mauve jacarandas of the Schur ranch, past the turn-off to the Ashburner ranch, and then I could see the Ridge Top Mine headgear poking proudly out of the bush a few kilometres ahead – a view I'd enjoyed hundreds of times, but this was the first time it had brought a lump to my throat.

As I approached the house, I slowed down on seeing a group of African women sitting at the entrance to our driveway.

Immediately, they stood up, waving their arms, and began an eerie chant – almost a wailing dirge, which sent shivers down my spine, causing my shoulders and back to twitch and shudder involuntarily.

They stood aside to let the pick-ups through – their sad expressions and large, weepy eyes were distinctly disturbing, and they continued with a low moaning sound – a heart-wrenching scene.

Elliot jumped off the back of my pick-up and came up to the open window.

"The women are wailing for the loss of you and the madam. No one wants you to leave the mine; they are all so sad and will be sitting here chanting until you leave again today."

"Elliot, what can I say, we're all very touched by this support. We don't want to go either, but it has been decreed; it cannot be changed. Now please go and get Crispin down here."

Amon greeted us as he stood up. "'Ello Boss. 'Ello Madam. How you?" Spoken very slowly, word by word in his best English.

To see this giant of a man trying to convey to us in his best few words of English was even more touching to me than the wailing women. I turned to Marianne.

"Jesus, it's going to be even harder today to drive away from the mine. We won't forget these people for a long time. They have been part of our huge family of over 200 men, women and children for a chunk of our lives."

We sat outside, and Elliot made us some coffee – then I began to hear the sound of wailing again, very faintly at first, but then slowly getting louder, a growing noise; the wailing sound of the women who, together with a group of workers, 30 or more, came walking down the driveway, headed by Crispin.

He signalled to them to be quiet.

"Good morning, sir; what a sad day. These men have come to help load your furniture onto the pick-ups. None of them want you to leave, and they are not happy about working for Boss Joseph – these men all want a reference letter signed by you, but first show them how you want the goods to be loaded."

Within an hour, I had orchestrated the loading and securing of our furniture onto the two pick-ups, utilising the carrying and lifting power of a dozen of my workers; actually, *sadly,* ex-workers.

The previous year at our Letaba house in Johannesburg, it had taken almost a whole day to load the furniture onto the pick-ups with just a few friends helping, before we left for Rhodesia.

The workers all sat around quietly listening while I told them officially that I was no longer the mine manger, and that from Monday they would be working for Boss Joseph….

An instant outburst of loud shouting and fist waving erupted.

I couldn't understand much of what they were shouting, but I could feel their anger. It was so similar to what I felt as my fist smashed into Ray's face, knocking his head backwards, blood and teeth spurting out from the split lips of his mouth – *yes! The same wrath* that I had felt on being told that I could no longer work on the mine!

Crispin eventually quietened them down, and then asked me if I would sign a reference letter for each of them.

"I've already written the reference letters, copying your words used on previous references. All you have to do is to write their names at the top and sign."

So there I was, sitting at a table, with Crispin standing next to me at the head of a line of more than 30 of my mine workers.

I felt like a school headmaster, writing an end-of-year report for each student.

First in line was Crispin.

I wrote his name, and signed it and dated it for the previous Thursday, when I was still officially mine manager.

"Thank you, sir, and now if you would do the same for the rest of them."

I called them by name, and one by one they came forward, and I addressed each one of them in my best Ndebele.

"Godfrey, you're a good worker, but don't wear Boss Joseph's old school blazer on the mine again."

Raucous laughter broke out, as not only Crispin, but also the ones who had witnessed that buffoon Boss Joseph's crazy outburst, began to visualise a replay of that *ridiculous* 'Charlie Chaplin' scene.

"Langton, I'm sorry we won't be able to finish off building my new house."

"Sir, if Boss Joseph tells me in one of his angry moods to knock down that silly little house of his, I'll leave and take my reference letter and look for another job!"

"George, you've been with me the longest; the first worker I employed. Say goodbye to Feet for me, and thank him for all his help. And Tachibona, you were also one of the first who worked at the Ridge Top Mine, and you were a big help as boss boy of the gold extraction process…"

And it went on, Biton, Boniface, Gwabuya… until the last worker in the queue came up to the table and stood in front of me – causing a large shadow to move across the papers.

"Amon, my pet gorilla. I owe my life to you; you stopped that thief, Nelson, from smashing that large rock into my face. Thank you."

As I wrote his name and signed the reference letter, Crispin translated to him what was written, whereupon a huge smile, revealing yellow tobacco-stained teeth, spread across his dark black face, and he shook my hand gently.

"Tell him, Crispin, that when he smiles his face looks like the 'rottweiler' pick-up – black and tan – and dangerous!"

More laughter; there was much merriment now amongst the workers, although it was gradually subdued by this sad, last leaving session.

"Amon says, sir that he will not work for Boss Joseph. If he did, he would have to beat Boss Joseph for the trouble he's caused to you, sir. He would like you to take him to Bulawayo, where he could be your *askari* at the new house."

"Great; I would like that too."

"And don't worry, sir! You'll be all right. Remember, *'every dark cloud has a silver Limousine'*!"

It took a while before I had stopped laughing at yet another Crispinism, probably the last one that I would hear – and I felt even sadder; I would miss working with him. He had been a true African gentleman.

The furniture was rearranged, and an armchair strapped down on top of the other furniture so that Amon could sit there.

Ring, ring. Another true African gentleman, Feet, came towards us on a bicycle, and, between panting hard, said, "Madam, we will never forget you; here are eggs and bags of vegetables for you all."

He stood there ringing his bell, adding to the concocted symphony: the hooting, waving, shouting and wailing as a crowd of men and women saw us off, and we drove on the murram road towards Fort Rixon, Amon looking like a king siting on his throne in the back of the 'rottweiler' pick-up – very appropriate too; *a matching pair of formidable foes!*

Amon, Elliot and I unloaded the furniture from the pick-ups and, with the help of James, Jackson's houseboy, it was carefully stored in the garage next to the mountain of our packing boxes that we'd dropped off on the Saturday.

When James took Amon and Elliot over to his quarters at the end of the garden amongst some tall trees, I realised what a large garden Jackson had.

With the help of the workers on the mine, Amon and Elliot, we had completed the collection of our furniture, including the journey there and back, unbelievably in just five hours – as the 12 o'clock chimes of a nearby church clock verified.

James appeared with a tray of drinks for us as we sat outside on the veranda; beers for the big ones, 'kuul-drinks' for the kids.

"I'm so pleased we can relax at last." Marianne sighed. "To be away from the mine and that wimp, Joseph. I was actually smiling, a smile of relief as we drove away for the last time, away from our mine that the cheats, Ray and Cain, had stolen from us."

"Almost the last time, Marianne; don't forget we have to drive the 'rottweiler' pick-up and Elliot back to the mine tomorrow to drop off the pick-up, and then meet briefly with Ray and Frost to finalise the repayment of my directors' loans."

"Do you think they will honour that?"

"I've no idea. That was what we agreed on Friday, but we are talking now of a *fait accompli*; whether we can get their words transformed into the large cash sum they owe us is another matter. There is no one's word that we can trust 100%, is there? Mafioso Ray, Conniving Cain, Yes-sir-three-bags-full-sir Frost, and that imbecile, Joseph, who can't tell fact from fiction. I mean, he's as happy as hell now that he is the acting mine manager of his own gold mine, whereas in reality he's been kicked out of the Ridge Top Mine as well. But let him dream on as the big all-powerful mine manger… until, as history repeats itself yet again, in the story of the biblical brothers' tragedy, Cain killed Abel! And although Joseph would dream of a revenge killing, he wouldn't be ***able*** to do a thing about it – he '***cain*** *'t*'!

"Instead, he will probably have a nervous breakdown, as Newmarch prophesied. But after tomorrow we'll have a week off; give us time to talk and decide our future, maybe down south again, or, even as I had almost finalised a year ago, that computer consultancy job in Rio de Jeniero, Brazil. There are plenty of options, and if we sell our duplex house, 8 Letaba, and those two plots of land in Vereeniging, south Johannesburg, that would fund any move we decide on. However, for now, we'll enjoy a couple of frosties, some biltong and maybe this evening James and I can organise a braai."

"Fine; there's lots to look forward to still. We'll just take it one step at a time."

And so our quiet Sunday proceeded… until later in the afternoon.

Suddenly, a hell of a noise erupted! The dogs started barking, and we jumped up and ran around to the front of the house to witness James opening the gate for a veritable fleet of dusty bush vehicles, headed by a police Jeep.

"Jesus, the Fort Rixon Cavalry has arrived!" I exclaimed, and an exited Marianne ran and almost pulled Irene out of her Land Rover as she hugged and hugged her.

What an unbelievable sight; vehicle after vehicle filled with our friends from Fort Rixon slowly drove inside the compound.

Policeman Pete, Peter Ruck and his family in a BSAP police Land Rover, Des and Irene, Stan and Jeanette, Jack and Mary, Gayle and Trevor, and last, but certainly not least, our foe-turned-saviour, Jackson and his wife, Susan.

They parked, and then started carrying items into the house; bags of potatoes, vegetables, fruits, a leg of venison… together with boerewors and other meats; enough for a braai for 20-plus people!

Instead of the three wise men bringing their gifts of gold, frankincense and mire, we were lucky to have half a dozen surprise 'Fort Rixon-ers' bringing vegetables, fruit and gamemeat – manna from Heaven.

"So you two, we have come over today to celebrate two wonderful people following the tragic theft of their gold mine, to lift your spirits and to show you that you still have good friends in Fort Rixon – ranchers, *not bloody miners!"* Des exclaimed, to the amusement of us all.

"And I now understand," I replied, "*why the cowboys can't be friends with miners'* – certainly not with ones such as my two ex-partners!"

"James!" Jackson ordered. "Bring the large half-drum braai over to the veranda and start a full charcoal fire; there's plenty of meat to roast before the evening is over."

"Now where's that Dave got to? He's supposed to be here by now with all the booze." Des sighed. "Jacko, can I use your phone to check if Dave has left the Greys Inn already and is on his way?"

A loud blast on a hooter provided the answer – there was no need to phone him.

Eager male helpers opened the gate and then lightened Dave's load of liquids.

Crates of beers, flagons of wine and cool drinks were rushed to the fridge at true *emergency speed* to avoid a terrible *crisis.*

"There's nothing as bad as a braai without beer!"

The hours spent in revelry, chatting, eating, drinking and the occasional serious discussion quickly sped the clock's hands around, and about 10pm, two very grateful people waved goodbye to their Rancher friends, the BSAP Fort Rixon Police and the Greys Inn landlord, Dave.

"You really do get to know who your true friends are in a time of crisis, and what wonderful, spontaneous people they are too."

. . .

During our early breakfast break, we discussed what should happen when we arrived at the mine to meet with Ray and Frost.

"I know we talked briefly about it yesterday," Marianne began hesitantly, "but

I've got this ominous feeling that something will go wrong. Perhaps they won't pay you the money they owe."

"I'm pretty sure about that too. They can sign any bit of paper, but whether those crooks honour it, that's pretty doubtful. But no matter what happens, Marianne, this has been the richest experience of my life. Let's face it, when you have had a family of 60 African workers, many being illiterate, who are totally dependent on you for everything, *and I mean everything*, then your attitude, tolerance and understanding of people changes dramatically. And as my command of the Ndebele language grew, so did the realisation that African village and family life and respect for their elders were actually far more caring and compassionate than in our Western culture.

"Crispin and I often discussed the folly of the Africans to abandon their culture and values in their rush to go to live and work in the city so that they can have the materialistic Western way of life – and, in fact, the Europeans should try to move in the other direction, and get back to some of the basic and selfless values, and the respect they'd had for the elderly. But come; let's get going. I want to make *an early morning start*."

How ironic that I should use that phrase, which had been repeatedly spoken by that imbecile, Joseph, echoing many incidents from the past year, beginning with my first journey to a gold mine in Rhodesia – and now symbolically the start of my very last trip to my ex-gold mine in the Rhodesian bush!

Elliot asked us if he could stay in Bulawayo at the Jackson house for the day looking after the children.

He said he sensed trouble; there was too much anger hovering over the mine and he didn't want to witness the bosses fighting each other, but then told me: "Amon wants to go back, because he feels the same tension in the air as well – but to help protect you should there be any further flare-ups."

So Amon climbed on the back of Marianne's pick-up and we drove off to Fort Rixon to deliver the 'rottweiler' pick-up, and to act out the final scene before the curtain was brought down on our gold mining adventure in the Rhodesian bush.

. . .

Joseph was pacing up and down outside the office as we drove up.

"Where the hell have you been!" he demanded. "And how *dare* you send Newmarch off the mine? The ball mill hasn't been milling the whole weekend; that's two days of full gold production lost!"

"Get real, Joseph; that's all your responsibility now. You should have come on Saturday to be the big boss of the gold mine, just as you've always wanted," I added in a strongly sarcastic tone.

"But the arrangement was that we'd all meet here on Monday morning, wasn't it? How was I to know that Newmarch wouldn't be working over the weekend? Do you think I'm psychic?"

"Don't know about that, Joseph, but you're definitely *psychotic!*"

"You can't speak to me like that; otherwise, I'll have you thrown off my mine!"

"And what about our meeting on the mine with your father shortly?"

"There you go again, trying to trick me with words, to make me look ridiculous."

"Joseph, let me repeat yet again that 'oh so applicable to you' quote: Mark Twain said *'it's bad enough to stand there looking like a fool, don't open your mouth and prove that you are one'!*"

"*That's it*! I should get Amon to lock you up to the prison tree at as a trespasser until my father gets here for the meeting!"

Amon felt the animosity towards me and moved towards Joseph menacingly, causing Joseph to back off a few steps.

Joseph now looked even more frustrated, and shouted to Staff and Crispin to come out of the office – where they'd probably sought refuge away from this buffoon.

"*Staff!* Why isn't the mine working? The ball mill can't operate without ore! Get the lashers to start filling the skip and start the ball rolling."

"It's actually plural, Joseph; 'balls' rolling. There are many in a ball mill!" I quipped.

"I know, of course I know. I meant get the skip bringing the ore to the surface. I'm not stupid, you know."

I gave him the keys to the black and tan Peugeot pick-up, then manoeuvred my beige 404 pick-up next to the diesel tanks and asked Crispin to fill it up.

"But you *can't* fill it up without my permission; I'm the manager now!" Joseph barked. "And you don't need a full tank to reach Bulawayo. Crispin, make it half full!" he stated with an 'I am the boss' smirk.

As Joseph turned back towards me, Crispin smiled and mouthed 'I'll fill it FULL'!

"Do I have to wait around for the meeting with Ray?" Marianne asked. "You could be here for hours. I think I'll drive over to see Des and Irene; you can phone me later when you want to be picked up."

"Only if I let him use it!" Joseph forcefully interjected. "It's mine property, you know!"

"Just come back at 2 o'clock, Marianne; that'll give us plenty of time to get to Bulawayo before dark – we can't rely on this silly bugger, Joseph, and his weird behaviour!"

Crispin and I were chatting away together, much to Joseph's annoyance, judging by the fierce glances directed at us as he paced up and down, looking very uncomfortable and seemingly not really sure of what he should be doing as 'the mine manager'!

Then his mood changed as Staff announced that the first skip of the day had been loaded, and Joseph could shout out his first official order as the new mine manager to Biton, the hoist driver.

"Start winching up the skip!" he bellowed.

As the rumble of the wheels grew louder, he puffed out his chest, glaring at me with satisfaction, when, suddenly… *CLUNK!*

And the skip stopped abruptly!

I went quickly over to the shaft where Staff was standing.

He told me that there was a knot twisted loop in the steel strands of the cable, and he had signalled to Biton to stop the hoist immediately, which had caused the skip to 'hang' about 30 feet down below the surface.

Although I now harboured an intense dislike for Staff, I instinctively called out, "Staff, bolt the skip down on the rail and get the welder here; we're going to have to cut the cable and…"

"Who the hell do you think you are!" Joseph shrieked as he stormed towards me. "You can't tell *my* workers what to do!"

"It's a dangerous emergency, Joseph. It can't wait until you decide to wander over – some of the lashers working down below at the bottom of the shaft could have been killed!"

I turned to Staff with raised eyebrows, and could read from his eyes that he wished I was still the mine manager – and then I remembered the strange thing he had said to me previously: *'I wish you were one of the brothers instead of Joseph; one day, you'll understand'.*

"Get out of my way!" Joseph screamed, and, as I looked over my shoulder, I felt an enormous shove in the back, causing me to fall head-first into the mine shaft.

"***Shi-i-i-i-i-i-t!***" I yelled as I disappeared and plummeted down the shaft, crashing into the stationery skip, which broke my fall, but also broke my nose as I bounced off it with blood streaming down my face, only to get my leg caught in the rungs of the ladder, twisting me completely so my face scraped across the timbers, the bolts tearing away my flesh.

I heard a crack and experienced excruciating pain as my leg snapped and I hung there upside down, helpless, blood filling my eye sockets.

I tried to wipe the blood from my face and neck. I felt… but shit, my necklace had gone, ripped off in the fall…. *Oh shit! What about the witchdoctor's protection!* I must find it… but I couldn't see or feel a thing… only severe pain, everywhere… I became woozy. I was slowly losing consciousness, but I had to fight it, to stay awake! I felt myself getting weaker… then, strangely, I began singing. "*So long, Marianne; it's time for us to go, to laugh and cry, and cry and laugh about it all again…*" This Leonard Cohen song gave me a sudden adrenaline boost, and I shouted out, ***"Help! Someone help!"*** Instantly, I felt the ladder vibrating violently. Someone was coming to rescue me…

. . .

Hold on… The shaking became stronger and stronger, and then I felt powerful arms trying to lift my head. "Boss, Boss, Boss!" I could hear Amon's voice, but I could see nothing, only feel the pain and blood pouring down my face…. *Got to hang on; Amon will save me… Crack!* "***Shit!***" The pain shot through my body as I was being slowly lifted…. Think of good things…. Must stay conscious…. I focussed on Marianne's face; oh, that helped a bit…. Must focus…. Her face flashed again in my thoughts… but I was getting so weak… concentrating on her face, which was fading fast…

"You were…always on my mind… yeah, you were always…always on… on **my**…my…I feel like I'm going…**No! Ple**assee……………………

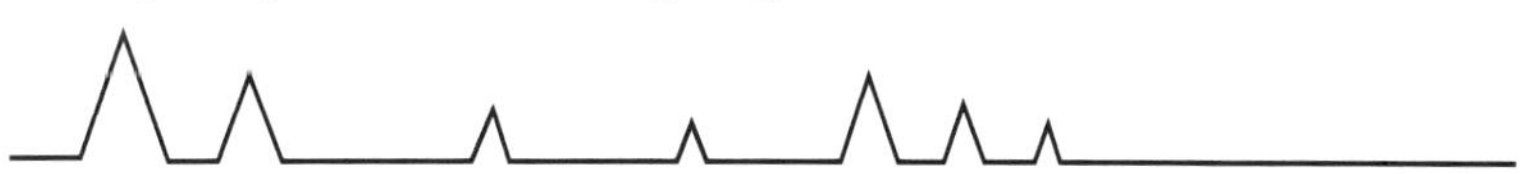

……. and darkness consumed me.

The Epilogue

A hand grasped the rung of the ladder…then Amon's head appeared…and he heaved himself up onto another rung, when the badly-broken bleeding body could be seen, draped over his massive shoulders in a fireman's lift position.

Crispin and Staff rushed to help Amon out of the shaft, as he struggled to climb the last few rungs… then, snorting like an over-worked horse, he stood for a few seconds, glaring at Joseph with fierce burning eyes, before he gently laid the body on the ground.

Joseph hastily backed off, shouting, "It was an accident, he slipped, you all saw that…"

But his voice was drowned by the sudden utterance from Crispin, who was wiping the blood off the disfigured face, "*He's breathing, he's still alive!* Amon, *quickly*, carry him and lay him in the back of the pick-up, he has to get to the Shangani hospital right away! *Quickly, every second is critical for our Boss, every second*!

"We must phone the hospital and ask for an ambulance to meet us on the road past Fort Rixon, then phone Memsab to tell her that her husband is badly injured, and she must go *immediately* to Shangani hospital."

And as he climbed into the driver's seat he shouted, "And I'll call into the Police post on my way back, to report that ***you***, Boss Joseph, deliberately pushed him down the shaft, ***you tried to murder him!***"

Two drivers, driving flat out roared past each other in clouds of dust, each oblivious to who the other driver was:

Crispin, with Amon in the back cradling the broken body in his arms, rushing to the hospital to try to save their Boss – before reporting ***the attempted murder*** to the police; and

Ray, and Frost, probably plotting how to avoid repaying the Directors loan as agreed – but shortly no doubt, huddling together with a sniffling, whimpering Joseph, to build an alibi for the ***'accident'***… *who would believe Crispin's story, against* ***the word of the four eye-witnesses;***

Ray, Frost, Staff and Joseph…

Author's note:

The sequel, *"GOLD Breeds GREED – Relentless Pursuit!"*

Due early 2018

JeffwBulgin.Author@gmail.com

PS: I hope you enjoyed reading my Book - as much as I did writing it, and would love to know, how do you rate it? – on a scale of 1 to 10.

21950320R00383

Printed in Poland
by Amazon Fulfillment
Poland Sp. z o.o., Wrocław